DOING BUSINESS
WITH
GOVERNMENT

DOING BUSINESS WITH GOVERNMENT

Federal, State, Local & Foreign
Government Purchasing Practices
for Every Business and
Public Institution

SUSAN A. MACMANUS

University of South Florida, Tampa

with the assistance of
Steven A. Watson and Donna Camp Blair

Foreword by Thomas R. Dye

PARAGON HOUSE

New York, New York

First edition, 1992
Published in the United States by
Paragon House
90 Fifth Avenue
New York, N.Y. 10011
Copyright © 1992 by Paragon House Publishers

This research was funded through a grant from the Lynde and Harry Bradley Foundation,
Milwaukee, Wisconsin, with additional support from the Hillsborough County (Florida)
Purchasing and Contracts Department. The interpretations are solely those of the author.

10   9   8   7   6   5   4   3   2   1

Library of Congress Cataloging-in-Publication Data

MacManus, Susan A.
Doing business with government : federal, state, local & foreign government
purchasing practices for every business and public institution / Susan A. MacManus ;
with the assistance of Steven A. Watson and Donna Camp Blair ; with a preface by Thomas
R. Dye. — 1st ed.
p.   cm.
Includes bibliographical references and index.
ISBN 1-55778-515-5
1. Government purchasing—United States.   I. Watson, Steven A.   II. Blair, Donna Camp.
III. Title.
JK1673.M33   1992
353.0071'2—dc20   91-28969
                                                                                         CIP

Manufactured in the United States of America

This book is dedicated with love to my nephew and nieces
Cameron and Allison MacManus
Susan and Genelle Harrison

Contents

Figures

Tables

Abbreviations

ABA	American Bar Association
AID	Agency for International Development
ASTM	American Society for Testing and Materials
BSC	Business Service Center (GSA)
BXA	Bureau of Export Administration
CBD	*Commerce Business Daily*
CPPO	Certified Public Purchasing Officer
DCAS	Defense Contract Administration Services
DLA	Defense Logistics Agency
DOD	Department of Defense
Eximbank	U.S. Export-Import Bank
FAR	Federal Acquisition Regulation
FAS	Foreign Agricultural Services
FIRMR	Federal Information Resources Management Regulations
FPMR	Federal Property Management Regulations
FRPS	Federal Property Resources Service
FSS	Federal Supply Service
GAO	General Accounting Office
GSA	General Services Administration
IFB	Invitation for Bid
IRMS	Information Resources Management Service
ITA	International Trade Association
MBDA	Minority Business Development Agency
MBE	Minority Business Enterprise
NAPM	National Association of Purchasing Managers
NASA	National Aeronautics and Space Administration
NASPO	National Association of State Purchasing Officials
NCMA	National Contract Management Association
NIGP	National Institute of Governmental Purchasing
NIMLO	National Institute of Municipal Law Officers
NIST	National Institute of Standards and Technology
NMFS	National Marine Fisheries Service
NOAA	National Oceanic and Atmospheric Administration
NTDB	National Trade Data Bank
OETCA	Office of Export Trading Company Affairs
OMB	Office of Management and Budget
OSDBU	Office of Small and Disadvantaged Business Utilization
OUSTR	Office of the U.S. Trade Representative

PBS	Public Buildings Service
PO	Purchase Order
PPB	Professional Public Buyer
RFP	Request for Proposal
RFQ	Request for Quote
SBA	Small Business Administration
SBE	Small Business Enterprise
USTTA	U.S. Travel and Tourism Administration
WBE	Women Business Enterprise

Acknowledgments

IT IS IMPOSSIBLE to conceive of undertaking any large-scale project such as this book without the help of many professional colleagues, students, friends, family, and—in this case—thousands of businesses.

I deeply appreciate the grant from the Lynde and Harry Bradley Foundation. Without the Foundation's financial support, this project simply would not have been possible. I especially appreciate the assistance and patience given to me by Hillel Fradkin, Vice President for Program, and the other members of the Foundation.

I am also greatly indebted to the Hillsborough County (Florida) Purchasing and Contracts Department, especially to its Director, Theodore Grable, and to Michael Maffeo and Paula Arnold. Their assistance in designing the survey instrument, their willingness to educate me and a class of graduate students about the world of purchasing from the perspective of the professional procurement officer, their help in compiling names and addresses of businesses on the county's vendor registration list, and the Department's financial assistance made the project a much better one. I am extremely grateful to Dr. Nikki R. Van Hightower, County Treasurer, and Jack McGown, County Purchasing Director, of Harris County, Texas, for their assistance in designing the survey instrument and obtaining business names and addresses. I thank Richard A. Hardesty of the Small Business Development Center, University of South Florida, for his assistance in helping design the survey instrument. The willingness of each of these public servants to investigate ways to improve the public sector reinvigorates my faith in government.

Certainly no project of this magnitude could be completed without input from professional colleagues and students. I am indebted to the National Institute for Governmental Purchasing (NIGP) for making the large volume of NIGP's excellent publications available to me and my students at the University of South Florida. The students in my graduate public administration Seminar on Financial Management were invaluable in combing through the purchasing codes of a large number of governments. Thanks to each of them: Nancy J. Bradley, Gerald E. Carrigan, Bernard J. Coryer, Ruben A. Matox-Ortiz, J. Stephen Odem, Karen F. Piscetelli, Mary A. Poritz, Steven A. Watson, and Mark S. Woodard.

The contributions of two students have been outstanding and invaluable: my graduate assistants, Steven A. Watson and Donna Camp Blair. Both are bright, highly energetic, and a real tribute to the public administration profession; and both are friends. Steve assisted on this project from start to finish. He spent countless hours doing everything from reading detailed purchasing manuals to developing survey questions, to coordinating the mailing of more than ten thousand questionnaires and follow-ups, to library searches and proofreading. Donna is responsible for the book's outstanding graphics and for the comprehensive bibliography. Special thanks must also go to my professional colleagues who reviewed this book in its infancy: Professor Irene Rubin, Northern Illinois University; Professor

Robert D. Lee, Jr., Pennsylvania State University; and Professor Maurice Woodward, Howard University. Their comments and recommendations were invaluable.

I am extremely grateful to my executive assistant and close friend, Marilyn Byram. She was wonderful at helping with each phase of the project and making sure that everything was finished in a timely and correct fashion. Without her fine work and daily moral support, the manuscript would never have made it to press in the superb condition it did. Special thanks to Barbara Langham, a professional writer and editor in Austin, Texas, for editing the manuscript.

I am thankful to the Rice Institute for Policy Analysis, Rice University, Houston, Texas, and Dr. Joseph Cooper, who as Dean of the College of Social Sciences approved my affiliation with RIPA to conduct the Houston portion of this research. Of course, I am much indebted to the University of South Florida for its support of faculty research activities. I must also single out Delores Bryant, assistant to the USF Public Administration Program, for handling the grant paperwork and the mailout of the questionnaires in such a superb fashion. Thanks are in order, too, for Michael Suarez, an aide in Senator Bob Graham's office, who helped me gather government publications in a timely fashion.

I also am greatly indebted to a number of other close friends who helped with various aspects of the project. Ann Martin coordinated each phase of the Houston survey of businesses. My mentor, Professor Thomas R. Dye, of Florida State University, encouraged me to undertake the project and wrote the excellent foreword to the book. Kim Strunz offered me a place to which I could escape to write the book and encouraged me to finish it.

I extend profuse thanks to my family, especially my mother and father, but also my sister and brother and their families, and various aunts, uncles, cousins, and children for their support and understanding throughout the project.

Finally, to the thousands of businesses across the United States who willingly shared their assessments of government purchasing practices, I thank you and hope that the findings reported herein will make it easier and better for you to sell to the public sector, should you so choose.

SUSAN A. MACMANUS
Tampa, Florida

Foreword

IF PRIVATIZATION IS ever to be more than merely a fashionable label, we must undertake serious studies of troubled relationships between business and government.

We know that even when there is a legitimate need for government to *provide* collective goods and services, government does not need to *produce* them and can better serve the interests of society by contracting with private enterprise to do so. The values of privatization extend well beyond efficiency; individual freedom, the market economy, limited government, and democratic accountability are all enhanced when the government is small in size and reliant upon the private sector.

But if privatization is to become a practical alternative to expansive government, we must develop a better understanding of exactly how private enterprise can serve public purposes.

Virtually all of the commentary to date on privatization, including the literature in support of the idea, proceeds from the viewpoint of government itself. Little has been said from the viewpoint of private enterprise. And however important it may be to understand the problems confronting government in contracting out for goods and services, it is equally important that we understand the formidable obstacles confronting private enterprise when it seeks to do business with government.

Doing Business with Government is a major contribution to the serious study of privatization because it describes the challenges, frustrations, and attractions of government contracting *from the perspective of private enterprise*. This is not an exercise in theory-building or argumentation, but rather an inquiry into the attitudes and opinions and reported experiences of private entrepreneurs who have attempted to do business with government.

Susan MacManus reports on the hard realities confronting businesses that would undertake to contract with government. Her reporting is informed by the most extensive survey to date of business opinion of government contracting—3,282 business respondents representing all sizes and industrial classifications of firms, newly formed and established firms, all ownership types, minority-owned firms, and even a control group of firms that have never won a government contract.

The results are alarming, especially for those who wish well for privatization. Private business is generally frustrated with government contracting, convinced that it is inefficient, ineffective, burdensome, wasteful, expensive, and unfair. Perhaps part of this frustration arises from the very nature of public business: the need to insure honesty, openness, impartiality, and competition. Certainly this is the oft-stated bureaucratic rationale for complex advertising and bidding procedures, burdensome applications, detailed specifications, legal entanglements, performance bonds, delayed payments, mandated employment policies, and excessive paperwork.

We generally know what government thinks about business. This book gives us the other side of the story—what business thinks about government bureaucracy. Susan MacManus is critical of private business for failing to appreciate the "fishbowl" environment of public administration. But she concludes her study with common-sense recommendations to governments, derived from her systematic survey of business, to improve competition, efficiency, and equity in government contracting.

THOMAS R. DYE
McKenzie Professor of
Government and Public Policy
Florida State University

Preface

IN TEACHING GRADUATE courses in public budgeting and financial management at the University of South Florida in Tampa, I was well aware of the extensive literature on government procurement from the perspective of the public sector. It occurred to me that my students—most of whom worked in government—had no idea of the private sector's perspective.

Furthermore, having been a contractor myself, I had developed some definite opinions about dealing with government purchasers. I wondered whether other private contractors had similar views or whether my experiences were somehow isolated or peculiar to my own professional services field.

At the same time, I sensed that governments wanted to broaden their vendor pools but were always running into trouble attracting more and better vendors. I wanted to know more about why specific businesses shied away from bidding on government contracts.

To find some answers, I conducted a large-scale survey of businesses, funded with a research grant from the Lynde and Harry Bradley Foundation. I wrote this book to share those findings and encourage dialogue about how to improve the system.

Chapter 1 sets the stage by identifying the reasons governments have increased their reliance on the private sector in recent years. One section reviews the advantages and disadvantages of privatization from the perspectives of both business and government.

Chapter 2 presents an overview of the purchasing and contracting practices of federal, state, and local governments, along with the rationale for these practices. The overview is intended to promote a better understanding of the environment in which business must operate if it wishes to sell to public sector customers.

Chapter 3 begins the report of findings from the survey. Essentially, it presents what businesses think of the overall effectiveness of government purchasing practices in promoting competition, efficiency, and equity.

Chapter 4 examines the major reasons businesses sell to government. The reasons include confidence about being paid, previous experience in selling to government, and contracts as a predictable revenue source.

Chapter 5 looks at the negatives—the problems businesses encounter in contracting with governments. Not the least of these problems are slow payment cycles, lack of information, and excessive paperwork.

Chapter 6 compares the performance of different levels of government as judged by businesses. They report how long it takes them to get paid, the overall quality of the government's purchasing policies and procedures, and the governments to which they prefer not to sell.

Chapter 7 identifies future challenges and suggests strategies for revamping purchasing practices. One section focuses attention specifically on the roles of small, minority-owned (black, Hispanic, Asian, and American Indian), and women-owned businesses in light of the nation's changing demographic and socioeconomic profile. Another section discusses the role of government procurement policies in promoting U.S. businesses abroad and the urgency of such business expansion as a consequence of heightened global competition. The book concludes with a summary of the persisting dilemmas in public purchasing.

The book's Appendices provide "how to" information of interest to purchasing professionals, elected officials, scholars, and business owners. The survey instruments used to solicit the opinions of the business community toward public procurement practices comprise Appendix A. A contrast of the firm characteristics of respondents selected from the Harris County, Texas, and Hillsborough County, Florida, vendor lists appears in Appendix B. Appendix C shows the contents of various model procurement codes. Appendix D contains model prompt pay regulations (federal, state, local). Appendix E provides the names and addresses of government agencies to contact about selling to the federal government. Application forms for selling to the federal government are included in Appendix F. Appendix G contains a detailed list of various federal and state agencies that help U.S. firms sell to foreign governments and industries, along with their addresses and phone numbers. Appendix G also includes an Export Guide that outlines the steps a firm should take to sell abroad.

I have included an extensive bibliography, amassed through three years of research, for the benefit of business and government leaders interested in becoming more informed about the issues and learning what they can do to make the system better for everyone.

June 1991

CHAPTER 1

Government as Buyer;
Business as Seller

"Bidding on government contracts is like rolling dice," says the general manager of a printing company. "You don't know who will be bidding or how it will turn out. You just have to cross your fingers and wait."

"Contracting with government is a game," says the executive director of a nonprofit rehabilitation program for adolescent drug addicts. "The main rule is, the rules change every year."

"When I hire new employees to work on a federal building," says the owner of a construction company, "I tell them there's a right way, a wrong way, and a government way."

"It's been a totally friendly and rewarding relationship," says a businessman who produces a radio program for a state university. "It's like doing business with another business."

DOING BUSINESS WITH government can be a curse, a blessing, or anything in between, depending on whom you ask in the business community. Unfortunately, most of what we know about business's assessments of government purchasing practices has come from isolated comments in business periodicals. Until now, no one had made a large-scale, comprehensive examination of privatization from the private sector's perspective. This book takes a first step in filling that gap.

Do a significant number of businesses regard government a desirable customer? To find out, we obtained the views of 3,282 businesses of all sizes and shapes across the United States regarding the purchasing and contracting practices of federal, state, and local governments. We asked for their opinions of the competitiveness, efficiency, and equitability of procurement policies and procedures. We asked businesses why they do business with government and what problems they encounter.

Knowing what businesses think is important if we expect to have a first-rate procurement system. Actually, business and government both have much to gain from understanding each other's perspective with regard to the good and bad of purchasing policies and procedures. Both business and government see costs and benefits in doing business with each other. Officials in both camps believe that government purchasing can be more efficient and equitable, but they do not agree on how to accomplish that goal. In this book we emphasize the need to expand the vendor pool—not merely increasing its size but also attracting businesses that are more competent and more representative of the gender, racial, and ethnic composition of U.S. businesses.

Even within the business community, assessments of purchasing practices frequently differ. We find, for example, that the views of firms that have won government contracts differ considerably from those of firms that have competed but lost and from those of businesses that have chosen not to compete at all. We also find that *specific* likes and dislikes about certain elements of the public purchasing system vary by ownership pattern, firm size, and experience. This means that we cannot improve the public purchasing process by treating all businesses the same.

WHAT IS PURCHASING?

We use the terms *purchasing, contracting,* and *procurement* interchangeably. Technically, *procurement* is a broader term, encompassing the other two. According to the *Dictionary of Purchasing Terms* of the National Institute of Governmental Purchasing, procurement consists of "the combined functions of purchasing, inventory control, traffic and transportation, receiving and receiving inspection, storekeeping, and salvage and disposal operations." The same text defines purchasing as:

> the act and the function of responsibility for the acquisition of equipment, materials, supplies, and services. In a narrow sense, the term describes the process of buying. In a broader sense, the term describes determining the need, selecting the supplier, ar-

riving at a fair and reasonable price and terms, preparing the contract or purchase order, and following up to ensure timely delivery.

A wider definition of purchasing comes from the Council of State Governments and the National Association of State Purchasing Officials: "a comprehensive program that includes the acquisition process, general oversight inventory management, and the ultimate transfer or disposition of excess and surplus property . . . [and] contracting for many kinds of services, in addition to equipment, material, and supplies."

With these broad definitions in mind, we can turn to the scope of government purchasing activity and the opportunities it presents for business.

GOVERNMENT: AN AVID SHOPPER

The private sector can truly regard the public sector as one of its biggest customers. In 1988, the federal government alone spent an estimated $195 billion on goods, services, and research and development—a conserva-

tive estimate, according to the General Services Administration. To put the purchasing power of the federal government in perspective, Mark Goldstein, in an article in *Government Executive*, describes it this way:

Nobody shops like Uncle Sam. . . . The U.S. government is the non-communist world's largest purchaser of nearly everything. Private sector firms pale in comparison. General Motors Co., for instance, spent a paltry $30 billion on procurement in 1988, or less than a sixth of the government's reported procurement outlays.

In 1988, 150,000 procurement officials in 5,000 contracting offices approved or modified 22 million federal contracts. Nearly 500,000 federal employees were actively involved in some phase of the acquisition process.

The magnitude of government purchasing staggers the mind even more when one takes into account the other governments that are active buyers: fifty state governments and 83,186 local governments (3,042 counties; 19,200 municipalities; 16,691 townships and towns; 14,721 school districts; and 29,532 special districts). Each of these types of government processes a heavy volume of purchase orders and contracts each year (see Table 1.1). According to a 1989 survey by the National Institute of Government Purchasing, nearly 40 percent of all municipalities issue more than 5,000 purchase orders or contracts annually. This same volume of purchasing is conducted annually by more than 60 percent of all counties, 79 percent of the school systems, 49 percent of special authorities, and 58 percent of all health districts. The same 1989 survey showed that 20 percent of all municipalities have purchases totaling more than $30 million annually. Similar figures for counties are 40 percent; school systems, 22 percent; special authorities, 33 percent; and health districts, 42 percent (see Table 1.2).

While few estimates of the total dollar volume of state and local government procurement exist, the sheer number of governmental units indicates a significant market for private sector goods and services.

INCREASED RELIANCE ON THE PRIVATE SECTOR

The decade of the 1980s will long be remembered as a major period of growth in governmental reliance on the private sector for a wide array of goods and services. In the language of the business world, it was the decade of divestiture and restructuring. Governments, like their business counterparts, focused long and hard on the bottom line in an effort to make their balance sheets more palatable to their stockholders—the taxpayers. Frequently the easiest solution to a widening revenue-expenditure gap was to turn to the private sector. In some cases governments sought complete takeovers by the business community; more often, partial takeovers were the preferred route to fiscal solvency.

Degrees of Reliance on the Private Sector

Governments have traditionally relied on the private sector to supply equipment and materials ranging from "brooms to missiles, from paper clips to computers, and from hand tools to vehicles," as Herman Holtz's book *The $100 Billion Market: How to Do Business with the U.S. Government* notes. Governments have never been equipped to manufacture these items and have always purchased them from the private sector. Through the years, in response to changing societal needs and new products, governments have changed the sorts of things they

Table 1.1
Number of Purchase Orders/Contracts Issued Annually by Type of Government

Number of Purchase Orders/ Contracts Issued Annually	Federal/State Provincial Central	City Municipality Town/Village	County Region Parish	School System University College	State Provincial Special Authority	City County Health	Total
	(n = 65)	(n = 267)	(n = 118)	(n = 85)	(n = 57)	(n = 19)	(n = 611)
Over 20,000	21.5%	5.2%	4.2%	12.9%	15.8%	31.6%	9.7%
10,000 - 20,000	26.2	15.4	22.9	32.9	8.8	21.1	20.0
5,000 - 9,999	18.5	19.1	33.9	32.9	24.6	5.3	23.9
2,500 - 4,999	13.8	31.1	22.0	16.5	24.6	42.1	25.2
Under 2,500	20.0	29.2	16.9	4.7	26.3	0.0	21.3
Totals[1]	100.0%	100.0%	99.9%	99.9%	100.1%	100.1%	100.1%

[1] Totals may not equal 100.0% due to rounding.

Source: National Institute of Government Purchasing, *Results of the 1989 Procurement Research Survey*. Falls Church, VA: NIGP, P. 6

4

Table 1.2
Annual Dollar Value of All Purchases and Contracts
Awarded by Type of Government

The Approximate Total Dollar Value of All Purchases and Con- tracts Awarded Annually	Federal/ State Provincial Central	City Municipality Town/ Village	County Region Parish	School System University College	State Provincial Special Authority	City County Health	Total
	(n=63)	(n=272)	(n=118)	(n=85)	(n=57)	(n=19)	(n=611)
Over$ 300 million	33.3%	1.1%	0.8%	0.0%	8.8%	5.3%	5.0%
$70 - $300 million	25.4	5.9	12.7	11.8	14.0	15.8	11.1
$30 - $69 million	12.7	12.9	26.3	10.6	10.5	21.1	15.1
$2 - $29 million	19.0	67.6	51.7	75.3	54.4	42.1	58.6
Under $2 million	9.5	12.5	8.5	2.4	12.3	15.8	10.1
Totals[1]	99.9%	100.0%	100.0%	100.1%	100.0%	100.1%	99.9

[1] Totals may not equal 100.0% due to rounding.

Source: National Institute of Government Purchasing, *Results of the 1989 Procurement Research Survey.* Falls Church, VA: NIGP, P. 3

buy. Even so, they continue to depend on the private sector for most commodities.

Services are another matter. This is the area in which the most significant changes in public procurement patterns have occurred. In the 1980s, private sector delivery of a number of services previously delivered by government became commonplace. According to a survey reported by Irwin David in *The Municipal Year Book 1988*, nearly 80 percent of all cities and counties use some form of private sector service delivery. By the 1990s the contracting of a wide array of services has become so common that one analyst, Jeffrey Katz, concludes "somewhere, sometime, virtually every government service has been contracted out."

The term *privatization* actually encom-passes a wide range of activities, from discontinuing a service entirely (total divestiture) to simply contracting with a private firm to provide a specific service (partial divestiture). In the 1980s a small percentage of local governments chose to totally divest themselves of certain services, a practice often called "load shedding" (see Table 1.3). The most commonly divested services were the most easily priceable, making them the most attractive to the private sector (e.g., solid waste disposal, meter maintenance, collection, ambulance service, tax assessing, delinquent tax collection, animal shelter operation).

A much higher percentage of governments chose partial privatization—particularly contracting with the private sector for a spe-

Table 1.3
Local Government Service Discontinuation in the 1980s

	Service has been discontinued[1]			
	Cities (%)		Counties (%)	
Service	1982	1988	1982	1988
Public works/transportation				
Residential solid-waste collection	2	5	1	2
Commerical solid-waste collection	5	0	1	3
Solid-waste disposal	8	22	3	7
Street repair	0	0	1	1
Street parking lot cleaning	1	2	1	1
Snow plowing/sanding	0	0	1	2
Traffic signal installation/maintenance	2	2	1	1
Meter maintenance collection	10	22	1	1
Tree trimming/planting	2	3	1	1
Cemetery adminstration/maintenance	1	2	2	2
Inspection/code enforcement	1	1	1	1
Parking lot garage operation	1	2	1	1
Bus system operation/maintenance	4	5	1	2
Paratransit sytem operation/maintenance	3	3	1	2
Airport operation	3	4	2	4
Public utilities				
Utility meter reading	1	1	1	1
Utility billing	1	1	1	2
Street light operation	1	2	0	2
Public Safety				
Crime prevention patrol	0	0	2	1
Police/fire communication	2	3	1	2
Fire prevention/suppression	1	2	1	1
Emergency medical service	3	6	2	4
Ambulance service	4	8	2	7
Traffic control/parking enforcement	0	1	1	1
Vehicle towing and storage	2	3	1	2

Table 1.3 (*continued*)

| Service | Service has been discontinued[1] | | | |
| | Cities (%) | | Counties (%) | |
	1982	1988	1982	1988
Health and human services				
Sanitary inspection	5	6	2	3
Insect/rodent control	3	5	2	3
Animal control	3	5	1	2
Animal shelter operation	3	8	3	4
Day care facility operation	1	2	3	3
Child welfare programs	2	1	2	2
Programs for elderly	3	2	2	3
Operation/management of public/elderly housing	2	2	2	2
Operation/management of hospitals	2	3	5	11
Public health programs	2	2	3	2
Drug/alcohol treatment programs	2	1	4	3
Operation of mental health/retardation programs/facilities	1	1	4	3
Prisons and jails	–	2	–	0
Parole programs	–	1	–	3
Operation of homeless shelters	–	0	–	1
Food programs for the homeless	–	1	–	2
Parks and recreation				
Recreation services	3	4	1	2
Operation/maintenance of recreation facilities	2	2	1	2
Parks landscaping/maintenance	1	1	1	2
Operation of convention centers/auditoriums	1	2	1	1
Cultural and arts programs				
Operation of cultural/arts programs	1	2	1	1
Operation of libraries	4	4	1	1
Operation of museums	2	1	2	1
Support functions				
Building/grounds maintenance	7	1	1	0
Building security	5	2	0	0
Fleet management/vehicle maintenance				
Heavy equipment	1	1	0	1
Emergency vehicles	0	1	1	2
All other vehicles	0	1	0	1
Payroll	1	1	0	0
Tax bill processing	7	6	1	0
Tax assessing	6	10	1	2
Data processing	1	1	1	0
Delinquent tax collection	5	8	1	1
Title record/plat map maintenance	–	3	–	0
Legal services	1	1	1	0
Secretarial services	0	0	0	0
Personnel services	0	0	0	0
Labor relations	0	0	1	1
Public relations/information	0	1	1	1

[1] When a local government discontinues a service, one of three results may occur. First, another local government may begin to provide the service. Second, individuals and/or organizations in the private sector may begin to provide the service, or third, the service may no longer be provided.

Note: dashes (–) indicate that data were not included in 1982 survey.

Source: Elaine Morley, "Patterns in the Use of Alternative Service Delivery Approaches," in International City Management Association, *The Municipal Year Book 1989*. Washington, D.C.: ICMA, Page 36.

Table 1.4
Service Delivery Approaches of Cities and Counties

Service	Number of cities and counties reporting	Local government employees		Inter-govern-mental (%)	Con-tract with private firm (%)	Partial privatization approaches					
		In part (%)	Ex-clusively (%)			Fran-chises (%)	Sub-sidies (%)	Vou-chers (%)	Volun-teers (%)	Self-help (%)	Regu-latory & tax incen-tives (%)
Public works/transportation											
Residential solid-waste collection	1,049	9	52	0	36	13	0	0	0	1	0
Commerical solid-waste collection	685	22	40	1	38	20	0	0	0	1	1
Solid-waste disposal	732	16	51	18	25	5	1	0	0	0	1
Street repair	1,541	42	51	6	36	0	0	0	0	0	0
Street parking lot cleaning	1,310	13	77	2	15	0	0	0	0	0	0
Snow plowing/sanding	1,210	19	74	4	15	0	0	0	0	0	0
Traffic signal installation/maintenance	1,406	39	50	17	27	0	0	0	0	0	0
Meter maintenance collection	427	9	85	2	7	0	0	0	0	0	0
Tree trimming/planting	1,308	44	47	3	36	1	0	0	0	3	1
Cemetery adminstration/maintenance	584	13	76	4	11	0	1	0	3	1	0
Inspection/code enforcement	1,482	19	76	10	9	0	0	0	0	0	0
Parking lot garage operation	639	15	74	5	14	2	0	0	0	0	0
Bus system operation/maintenance	306	20	37	31	26	3	10	1	1	0	1
Paratransit sytem operation/maintenance	408	28	27	28	30	4	14	7	7	1	0
Airport operation	474	31	38	18	30	15	3	0	1	0	1
Public utilites operation/management											
Electricity	274	11	51	9	11	31	0	0	0	0	1
Gas	162	7	35	4	12	51	0	0	0	0	1
Water distribution	1,084	8	82	9	4	1	0	0	0	0	0
Water treatment	924	8	79	12	3	1	0	0	0	0	0
Sewage collection and treatment	1,093	19	68	21	6	1	0	0	0	0	0
Sludge disposal	847	17	62	12	19	1	0	0	0	0	0
Hazardous materials disposal	304	35	31	24	44	2	0	0	1	1	2

Service	Number of cities and counties reporting	Local government employees		Inter-govern-mental (%)	Con-tract with private firm (%)	Partial privatization approaches					
		In part (%)	Ex-clusively (%)			Fran-chises (%)	Sub-sidies (%)	Vou-chers (%)	Volun-teers (%)	Self-help (%)	Regu-latory & tax incen-tives (%)
Public utilities											
Utility meter reading	1,011	11	79	5	7	3	0	0	0	0	0
Utility billing	703	30	56	6	32	2	0	0	0	0	1
Street light operation	975	25	30	9	46	13	0	0	0	1	1
Public Safety											
Crime prevention patrol	1,544	26	68	6	4	0	0	1	16	8	0
Police/fire communication	1,534	15	74	16	1	0	0	0	3	0	0
Fire prevention/suppression	1,316	17	67	7	1	0	1	2	19	0	0
Emergency medical service	998	29	47	14	18	2	4	2	18	0	0
Ambulance service	757	21	42	12	24	4	6	2	17	0	0
Traffic control/parking enforcement	1,387	7	86	5	1	0	0	0	2	0	0
Vehicle towing and storage	712	24	6	2	80	8	0	1	0	0	0
Health and human services											
Sanitary inspection	699	13	62	30	3	0	0	0	0	0	1
Insect/rodent control	704	26	50	29	15	0	1	0	1	1	0
Animal control	1,307	15	64	15	11	0	1	0	2	1	0
Animal shelter operation	788	15	50	20	17	1	4	1	6	1	0
Day care facility operation	181	27	25	15	34	3	19	7	8	4	4
Child welfare programs	368	44	33	36	17	1	10	3	11	2	1
Programs for elderly	970	57	22	38	19	1	13	4	25	7	1
Operation/management of public/elderly housing	447	28	22	54	14	1	7	4	4	2	1
Operation/management of hospitals	144	19	36	32	24	3	5	0	6	0	2
Public health programs	571	37	32	41	19	1	8	1	8	3	1
Drug/alcohol treatment programs	383	41	14	43	34	2	14	1	10	4	1
Operation of mental health/retardation programs/facilities	315	40	14	46	35	1	15	1	9	4	1
Prisons and jails	825	23	64	26	1	0	0	1	0	0	0
Parole programs	228	22	47	38	3	1	1	0	1	0	1
Operation of homeless shelters	184	32	4	29	43	2	36	9	26	5	2
Food programs for the homeless	252	43	5	42	26	1	25	9	37	6	1

Table 1.4 (continued)

Service	Number of cities and counties reporting	Local government employees		Partial privatization approaches							
		In part (%)	Exclusively (%)	Intergovernmental (%)	Contract with private firm (%)	Franchises (%)	Subsidies (%)	Vouchers (%)	Volunteers (%)	Self-help (%)	Regulatory & tax incentives (%)
Parks and recreation											
Recreation services	1,256	20	53	12	8	2	4	1	26	6	0
Operation/maintenance of recreation facilities	1,368	35	58	10	12	10	2	1	14	3	0
Parks landscaping/maintenance	1,401	20	73	5	13	0	1	0	7	1	0
Operation of convention centers/auditoriums	365	21	66	8	11	5	4	1	5	1	0
Cultural and arts programs											
Operation of cultural/arts programs	476	52	14	19	23	3	24	2	41	7	0
Operation of libraries	970	22	54	25	1	1	6	1	13	1	1
Operation of museums	357	35	25	16	8	1	19	3	34	3	0
Support functions											
Building/grounds maintenance	1,572	31	63	2	27	1	0	0	1	0	0
Building security	1,158	14	77	2	13	0	0	0	0	0	0
Fleet management/vehicle maintenance											
Heavy equipment	1,497	44	50	1	41	0	0	0	0	0	0
Emergency vehicles	1,366	44	47	2	41	0	0	0	1	0	0
All other vehicles	1,496	41	52	1	38	0	0	0	0	0	0
Payroll	1,621	8	85	1	7	0	0	0	0	0	0
Tax bill processing	1,072	18	65	20	9	0	0	0	0	0	0
Tax assessing	863	20	58	25	10	0	0	0	0	0	0
Data processing	1,463	22	70	6	17	0	0	0	0	0	0
Delinquent tax collection	1,020	20	61	18	14	0	0	0	0	0	0
Title record/plat map maintenance	872	25	58	22	14	0	0	0	0	0	0
Legal services	1,297	34	34	3	55	1	0	0	0	0	0
Secretarial services	1,457	8	86	1	7	0	0	0	1	0	0
Personnel services	1,485	10	83	2	8	0	0	0	0	0	0
Labor relations	1,286	34	57	2	33	0	0	0	0	0	0
Public relations/information	1,415	14	79	2	10	0	0	0	1	0	0

Source: Elaine Morley, "Patterns in the Use of Alternative Service Delivery Approaches," in International City Management Association, *The Municipal Year Book 1989.* Washington, D.C.: ICMA, Pages 42–43.

cific service (see Table 1.4). The services most likely to be contracted were those for which user fees could be assessed, those already provided by private or nonprofit firms, or specialized services too costly for government to staff or equip.

Contracting is only one form of partial divestiture (see Table 1.4). Others common in the 1980s were franchises and concessions, subsidies, vouchers, volunteers, self-help, and regulatory and tax incentives.[1] In each of these cases government continues some direct involvement in the design, choice, level, and financing of a service, but the private sector actually delivers the service.

Forecast: Continued Reliance on the Private Sector

Most government officials expect the privatization trend to continue well into the 1990s. In a 1987 survey by Touche Ross, the International City Management Association, and the Privatization Council, nearly 80 percent of the governments predicted that "privatization [would] represent a primary tool to provide local government services and facilities in the next decade."

The primary reason for a governmental entity to increase its reliance on the private sector is to save money. According to a 1988 survey of 1,681 U.S. cities and counties by the International City Management Association, the leading stimulant is "internal fiscal pressures to decrease cost" (83 percent of cities, 74 percent of counties), followed by "external fiscal pressure including tax restrictions" (45 percent of cities, 41 percent of counties). In descending order, the other stimulants are "concerns about liability" (also a fiscal issue); "unsolicited proposals from providers" (aggressiveness by the private sector); "intergovernmental mandates"; "altered political climate regarding role of government"; and "active citizen groups favoring privatization" (see Table 1.5).

Local fiscal stress also emerged as the prime reason in a 1987 ICMA survey of 1,086 cities and counties (Table 1.5). More than 60 percent of the respondents said they turned to the private sector because of constituents' demands for more services without tax increases. Cutbacks in federal aid to local governments, a consequence of the federal government's efforts to reduce its own deficit, also motivated local officials to seek alternative service delivery methods.

Likewise, state governments are feeling the fiscal pinch. A 1989 survey of the states by Deloitte & Touche shows that state governments increasingly have turned to the private sector because of high demand for services (69 percent), budget cutbacks (58 percent), bond credit limits (32 percent), bond issue failures (16 percent), and taxpayer revolts (11 percent) (see Figure 1.1).

Similar comprehensive surveys of privatization are not available at the federal level, but numerous incidences of service shedding and contracting have occurred (see *Privatization: Toward More Effective Government: Report of the President's Commission on Privatization* by David F. Linowes and other sources in the bibliography). As John A. Rehfuss observed in *Contracting out in Government: A Guide to Working with Outside Contractors to Supply Public Services*, federal contracts "are usually designed to meet staff shortfalls, which are often caused by personnel ceilings, shortages of time to complete tasks, shortages of expertise among current staff, and the need for an 'outside' viewpoint."

In *Privatizing Federal Spending* Stuart Butler notes that functions typically contracted by the federal government range from "data processing, catering, health services, maintenance, cleaning, printing, security, research, and transportation to the development and production of major weapons systems." In the 1980s the federal government increased its reliance on the private sector for information technology equipment and services, government building leases, equipment lease-to-purchase plans, and other

Table 1.5
Major Stimulants to Greater Local Government Reliance on the Private Sector

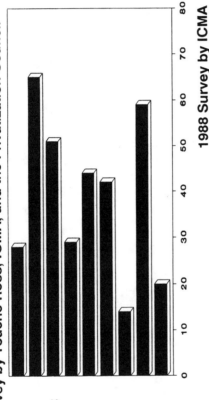

1987 Survey by Touche Ross, ICMA, and the Privatization Council

Changes in the tax-exempt bond
Demand for services
Elimination of federal revenue sharing
Federal deficit-reduction program
Infrastructure decay
Programs to downsize government
Specific initiatives in your state
Taxpayer resistance to tax increases
Tax Reform Act of 1986

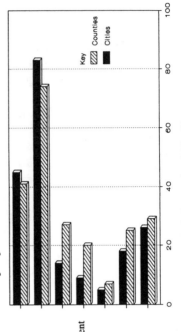

1988 Survey by ICMA

Key
Counties
Cities

External fiscal pressure including tax restrictions
Internal fiscal pressure to decrease cost
Intergovernmental mandates
Altered political climate regarding role of government
Active citizen groups favoring privatization
Unsolicited proposals from providers
Concerns about liability

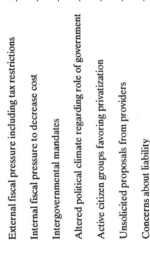

Source: 1987 data are from Irwin T. David, "Privatization in America," *The Municipal Year Book 1988*. Washington, D.C. International City Management Association, P. 44 (data base: U.S. cities with population over 5,000 and U.S. counties with population over 25,000); 1988 data are from Elaine Morley, "Patterns in the Use of Alternative Service Delivery Approaches," *The Municipal Year Book 1989*. Washington, D.C.: International City Management Association, P. 44 (data base: U.S. cities with population over 10,000 and U.S. counties with population of 25,000 and over).

Figure 1.1
Factors that Could Push States Toward Privatization

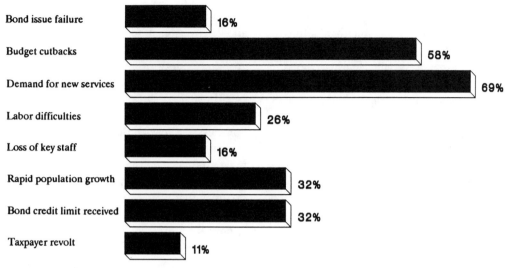

Source: 1989 survey of states by Deloitte & Touche, New York. Reported in Mary Colby, "Jurisdictions Catch Privatization Wave," *City & State 7* (June 4, 1990): 14.

private service contracting. Butler and other observers have recommended that the federal government shed or contract numerous services, including the postal service, Social Security, air traffic control, Amtrak, and public housing.[2]

Among state governments, contracting is the dominant form of privatization. The states are most likely to contract for social services, health care, highways and transportation, police and corrections, and education.[3] In addition, a number of states contract for energy services, economic development, employment training, facility maintenance and management, parks and recreation services, and professional and administrative services. According to Keon Chi in *Privatization and Contracting for State Services: A Guide*, reasons for privatizing state services vary greatly but fall under four headings: cost savings, administrative expediency, management improvement, and ideology.

Regardless of the form of privatization (service shedding or contracting) or the level of government, the major beneficiary, at least in the short term, has been the private sector. In *Contracting out in Government*, Rehfuss concludes that "the privatization movement is an effort (1) to reduce public expenditures, (2) to reform public expenditures by making them more efficient and effective, and (3) to turn more public services over to private operation." Government's decision to divest and business' decision to invest has not always been an easy one for either party.

THE PROS AND CONS OF GREATER RELIANCE ON THE PRIVATE SECTOR

Staunch advocates of greater privatization assume that such efforts unequivocally benefit *both* public and private sectors: government saves money and business earns money (but less than it would cost for government to provide the good or service). However, the distinction is often not quite that clear-cut.

Government's Perspective

The major advantages of greater reliance on the private sector from the government's vantage point are more economic than political.

Saving money As noted earlier, the primary motive for all types of privatization efforts is cost saving. Seventy-four percent of the 1,086 cities and counties responding to a 1987 ICMA survey claimed that cost saving is a major advantage of contracting; 47 percent also saw cost saving advantages from privatizing facilities (a private sector firm builds or acquires a facility, then owns and operates it for the government); and 46 percent realized a cost saving advantage from selling assets (total divestiture).

The perception that privatization saves money is true. Numerous studies have verified that private provision of certain services can be more cost-effective than public provision.[4] One of the most widely cited studies, reported in *National Productivity Review*, is Barbara Stevens' examination of eight services in twenty California cities in 1984. She found that for seven of the eight (street paving, refuse collection, tree maintenance, ground maintenance, signal maintenance, janitorial services, and street cleaning), private provision is cheaper; for the eighth service (payroll preparation) the costs are about the same.

The reasons for the private sector's more cost-effective service delivery range from greater competition among suppliers, benefits from economies of scale, and the effectiveness of the profit motive to more efficient and effective use of labor and new technology. Stevens' analysis shows that private employers use less labor, have 5 percent lower absenteeism rates, hire younger and more part-time workers, terminate more employees, and give managers more responsibility for labor and equipment than governments. It is not surprising, then, that 50 percent of all local government officials see privatization as a solution to their labor problems and as a way to control or reduce the size of government.[5]

In addition to saving money, privatization allows government to avoid start-up costs in providing a new service. A 1988 survey of city and county officials conducted by the International City Management Association (see Table 1.4) shows that 43 percent used the private sector to operate shelters for the homeless—a service that emerged as a high priority in the late 1980s. In some cases, greater reliance on the private sector has enabled governments to provide services and facilities that would otherwise not be available because of monetary or legal constraints.[6]

Flexibility Relying on the private sector permits more rapid reactions to changing service needs and constituent demands. It also avoids the negative fallout from angry public employees when changes necessitate reductions in the level of service because of fiscal crises. The private sector's labor use patterns promote this flexibility. As Rehfuss notes,

> Private contractors are more flexible. They are not bound to follow civil service rules and regulations in hiring, promoting, or disciplining employees. This reduces costs as well as increasing flexibility, since private employees can be more easily transferred and reassigned to more effective roles. Private employees can also be rewarded more quickly for good performance—a "plus" for morale in these organizations.

Risk avoidance The skyrocketing costs of insurance and legal services have prompted governments to search for ways of reducing liability by avoiding provision of high-risk services. However, a case law is emerging that links liability for subcontractor failure to government and increases government responsibility for service specifications, monitoring, and evaluation.[7]

Promotion of social and economic objectives This aspect of government procurement is frequently ignored in the standard public administration literature on privatization but emphasized in the purchasing literature. According to *Alijan's Purchasing Handbook*, edited by Paul Farrell, procurement officials readily acknowledge:

> [Government] procurement involves much more than buying. The process is used extensively to promote such social and economic objectives as interests of small businesses, use of minority business, fair employment practices, payment of fair wages, safe and healthful working conditions, employment of the handicapped, rehabilitation of prisoners, and use of recycled materials.

In a number of jurisdictions, purchasing policies also promote American, in-state, or locally produced goods and services.[8]

Government reliance on the private sector makes the most sense, according to Rehfuss, "when the intent is to reduce costs, when the contract can be well monitored, when technical or complex services are required, when benchmark job costs must be set, and when it is important to avoid management or policy constraints." To this list another key condition must be added: the availability of a number of willing, capable, and competing private sector suppliers.[9]

Since the above conditions are not always prevalent or guaranteed, government officials sometimes hesitate to step up privatization efforts. The situation was described best in an article published in *The Economist* in 1985: "At its best, 'privatisation' creates competition, efficiency, and wealth. At its worst, it substitutes insensitive privately owned monopolies for insensitive publicly owned ones and feeds corruption."

Government Hesitancy

The major obstacles to greater reliance on the private sector are often more political than economic.

Political opposition A 1988 ICMA survey of cities and counties revealed considerable opposition from public employees and elected officials, an insufficient supply of competent private deliverers, lack of evidence on the effectiveness of private alternatives, and bureaucratic and legal constraints (see Table 1.6).

In a 1987 ICMA survey of local governments, half (51 percent) of the respondents identify loss of control as the major impediment to greater privatization efforts (see Table 1-6). Other major barriers are government union and employee resistance (47 percent), politics (42 percent), lack of belief in the benefits of privatization (38 percent), lack of awareness of the benefits of privatization (24 percent), bureaucratic inertia (26 percent), and hostile public opinion (24 percent).

Questions about cost savings and competition Although a number of studies have shown that privatization can save money, other studies come to the opposite conclusion or to no conclusion at all.[10] As reported in one study, "it is probably fair to say that for every successful contract, there is an unsuccessful one." For example, studies in 1983 and 1987 by the American Federation of State, County, and Municipal Employees (AFSCME) have challenged most of the assertions of privatization proponents. The federation has found that costs actually escalate when certain services are privatized, often as a consequence of corruption and collusion. These studies also claim that privatization can reduce accountability to the taxpayers and reduce services to the poor.[11]

Other studies have questioned whether privatization actually increases competi-

Table 1.6
Barriers to Greater Local Government Reliance on the Private Sector

1987 Survey by Touche Ross, ICMA, and the Privatization Council

Barrier	% (n = 838)
Bureaucratic inertia	25.5%
Lack of awareness	24.1
Lack of belief	37.5
Loss of control	51.2
No confidence in private sector	13.2
No interest in private sector	16.1
Politics	42.1
Public opinion	23.9
Need for legislation	8.2
Union/employee resistance	46.5

1988 Survey by ICMA

Obstacles (Multiple Responses)	Obstacles in adopting private alternative service delivery	
	Cities (n = 898)	Counties (n = 251)
Opposition from citizens	29%	21%
Opposition from elected officials	37	39
Opposition from line employees	40	38
Opposition from department heads	26	29
Restrictive labor contracts and agreements	28	27
Insufficient supply of competent private deliverers	35	35
Lack of contract management expertise among staff	18	21
Lack of evidence on effectiveness of private alternatives	33	29
Institutional rigidities or lack of precedent	25	29
Legal constraints	21	37

Source: 1987 data are from Irwin T. David, "Privatization in America," *The Municipal Year Book 1988.* Washington, D.C. International City Management Association, P. 44 (data base: U.S. cities with population over 5,000 and U.S. counties with population over 25,000); 1988 data are from Elaine Morley, "Patterns in the Use of Alternative Service Delivery Approaches," *The Municipal Year Book 1989.* Washington, D.C.: International City Management Association, P. 44 (data base: U.S. cities with population over 10,000 and U.S. counties with population of 25,000 and over).

tion.[12] One author, Lyle Fitch, summarizes these concerns well:

1. Intergovernmental competition may be equally effective.
2. Competition may diminish the advantages of economies of scale (economies of scale require large-scale operations which, in turn, are usually associated with a degree of monopoly).
3. Competition is not always synonymous with integrity or honest workmanship.
4. Competition increases lobbying efforts on the part of contractors to secure future contracts and may drive up the costs of service delivery so that no cost savings are generated in the long term by privatization efforts.

The unreliability of some contractors and the difficulty, legal necessity, and costs of monitoring and evaluating contracts have made privatization less desirable for other governments.[13] Cost overruns, price gouging, and bribery historically have been problems in the defense, construction, and health care arenas but are not limited to these functional areas. At any rate, the costs of contract monitoring and auditing have escalated tremendously in recent years in reaction to negative publicity regarding private sector bilking of government agencies. One study by John Rehfuss in *State and Local Government Review* estimates that the true cost of monitoring "may well exceed 10 percent."

Failures of privatization are not limited to those involving scandals and corruption. They can include businesses that go bankrupt or businesses that simply cannot deliver the product or service in a quality, timely fashion. Regardless of the cause, liability for the failures of privatization falls back on government. Consequently government must consider potential costs of failure (new start-up costs, transitional costs, legal costs, and the loss of service) in any decision involving privatization.[14]

Reduced citizen participation Some studies have suggested that greater privatization can reduce citizen participation in government and threaten the foundations of democracy.[15] Paul Starr, in an article in *Prospects for Privatization*, claims that privatization of public schools through vouchers can diminish the participation of parents in local elections and threaten the vitality of local government. Other scholars have suggested that privatization erodes constitutional rights.[16]

Questionable quality Studies showing cost savings from privatization frequently have failed to determine whether those savings came at the expense of service quality.[17] Starr criticizes the general "lack of evidence about the quality of services, thereby making it difficult to judge whether lower costs result from greater efficiency or deteriorating quality." Relatedly, some government officials fear that low bid requirements do not always attract a large pool of high-quality bidders.

Little progress toward social and economic objectives Critics of privatization point to scant evidence that social and economic objectives of government procurement policies have been met to any great degree through privatization, particularly the so-called set-aside programs, which are aimed at certain groups. Economic development efforts designed to stimulate creation and expansion of small and minority-owned businesses have not been overwhelmingly successful.[18] According to an article by Joe Schwartz in *American Demographics*, women still make up only 27 percent of all business owners, blacks 3 percent. The President's 1990 report on *The State of Small Business* shows that small businesses receive only 15 percent of federal prime contracts (amounts larger than $25,000); small minority-owned businesses 3 percent, and women-owned businesses 0.9 percent.

Tax obstacles   Federal tax reforms of the 1980s dampened state and local government enthusiasm for stepped-up privatization efforts, particularly those involving sale of assets and privatization of facilities.[19] The 1986 Federal Tax Reform Act limited the use of tax-exempt revenue bonds, repealed the investment tax credit, and increased depreciation periods. One study estimates that the federal tax reform acts of the 1980s created a 30 percent penalty on state and local governments choosing to privatize.

Deciding When to Privatize

The long list of concerns about privatization has made governments more cautious in increasing reliance on the private sector, but fiscal realities have made such calculations more urgent. In deciding whether to rely on the private sector for a good or service, Lydia Manchester in an article in *Public Sector Privatization* advises governments to consider five factors: (1) cost; (2) service quality, level, and effectiveness; (3) impact on other local services; (4) potential for service interruption; and (5) responsiveness to citizens' needs and expectations. Another authority[20] recommends privatization only under the following conditions: (1) relatively narrow objectives, readily defined and easily measured; (2) specifiable tasks and familiar production processes, monitorable at a modest costs; (3) a number of willing and able competing private sector suppliers; and (4) a competent, honest government to enforce the rules of a fair market.

The Business Perspective

Until now, no one has conducted a comprehensive survey of business officials' attitudes toward selling to government. One exception is a 1986 survey by David Lamm of 427 firms in the defense industry. Unlike the large-scale surveys of government officials delineating their likes and dislikes for buying from the private sector, our knowledge of what the business community finds attractive and unattractive about selling to government has come largely from journalistic accounts in the nation's leading business periodicals. Those accounts form the basis of the discussion below as well as the design for the survey that prompted this book.

Profit   The profit motive is the major stimulant to the private sector's decision to sell goods and service to government. Since profit is integral to a capitalistic economy, it should not unilaterally be regarded as an unethical or undesirable motive.

Special needs   In some instances, businesses have been created specifically to meet the unique product and service needs of the public sector. One example is tanks for the military. Many of the hundred firms selling the most to the federal government (see Table 1.7) supply defense-related goods and services, according to an article in the May 1989 issue of *Government Executive.* In fact, several of the federal government's largest suppliers sell more than half of their products and services to the federal government: Lockheed Corporation, 86 percent; General Dynamics Corporation, 85 percent; Martin Marietta Corporation, 85 percent; McDonnell Douglas Corporation, 65 percent; and the Raytheon Company, 55 percent. However, in *The $100 Billion Market,* Holtz maintains that the vast majority of government contracts (measured in numbers, not total dollars) go to medium-sized and small firms.

Predictable revenue   For many businesses, government is just another customer, not their primary one. These businesses find government a desirable buyer for a number of reasons. The preeminent reason, according to an article by David Gumpert and Jeffry Timmons in the *Harvard Business Review,* may be that government *will* pay its bills— eventually. Unlike private sector customers, governments rarely refuse to pay their bills, although they may not pay as promptly as businesses would like.

Businesses that have sold to government for quite some time may find that government contracts are a fairly predictable revenue source, far less elastic than the private sector. More established businesses may also have less difficulty winding through the government procurement maze and may be less intimidated by it than newly established firms. More established firms most likely have less difficulty in meeting government surety requirements such as bid and performance bonds.

Established firms also most likely benefit from reputations for delivering goods and services of high quality in a prompt fashion. (As Chapter 2 shows, there is a movement toward awarding contracts not just on the basis of cost but also on quality.)

Opportunities to get established For the new firm, according to Gumpert and Timmons, the advantages of contracting with government may be the opportunity to become established and expand their business—and make a profit. Many of these firms may initially venture into selling to government as a consequence of aggressive recruitment campaigns by governments. Government programs designed to stimulate the growth and development of small businesses, women-owned businesses, minority-owned businesses, businesses owned by the handicapped, and locally owned businesses may require government purchasing officials to offer incentives to these firms.

In other instances, businesses sell to government because, as John Hanrahan says in *Government by Contract*, they genuinely believe that "private sector know-how and private sector efficiency [can] save the government and taxpayers a lot of money." Business owners are taxpayers, too!

Request For some firms the incentive to sell to government comes from their interac-

tions with elected officials and their perceptions about the liabilities of refusing to sell to government. For example, a firm may place itself on the vendor list and apply for contracts at the request of an elected official out of fear that failure to do so may have negative consequences in the regulatory arena (e.g., loss of tax incentives).

Technical assistance In some cases, businesses can receive detailed yet easy-to-follow guides or help sessions describing how to complete the necessary forms to get certified (if necessary), how to compete for government business, and who makes the decisions. Without such help, many small firms often are not willing to invest the time and energy it takes to sell to government. And if a particular unit of government has a reputation in the business community for being helpful, efficient, and equitable in its procurement practices, the chances of a business being interested in selling to it are much greater.

The bottom line is that selling to government can be profitable even for small businesses selling to the federal government. Jane Bahls summarizes the situation well in an article in the March 1990 *Nation's Business*:

> Doing business with government agencies can be profitable for those familiar with the rules and processes. Red tape may delay your payment for months, but you are sure of payment. And while the government's general insistence on accepting the lowest bid means the profit per item may be marginal, the sheer volume of business can make up for it.

Business Hesitancy About Selling to Government

Only a small proportion of American businesses, either majority- or minority-owned, sell to government. Holtz estimates that less

Table 1.7
The Top 100 Federal Contractors

(Total Purchases: $177,645,770,000)

Rank	Parent Company	Fiscal 1990 Contract Awards ($000s)								
		Total	DoD	Civilian	DoD Rank	Civilian Rank	R&D	Products	Services	Market Share
1	McDonnell Douglas[1]	9,791,433	$8,923,457	$ 867,976	1	11	$3,112,554	$6,092,134	$ 586,745	5.5%
2	General Electric[2]	6,692,079	5,823,497	868,582	3	10	1,174,092	4,291,879	1,226,108	3.7
3	General Dynamics[3]	6,613,547	6,569,018	44,529	2	94	920,839	4,895,706	797,002	3.7
4	Martin Marietta[4]	6,451,475	4,246,032	2,205,443	5	3	2,895,270	1,633,416	1,922,789	3.6
5	Westinghouse Electric[5]	5,762,783	2,274,377	3,488,406	12	1	729,810	1,691,428	3,341,545	3.2
6	Lockheed[6]	5,036,152	3,854,622	1,181,530	7	7	1,601,611	2,270,145	1,164,396	2.8
7	General Motors[7]	4,532,880	4,305,974	226,906	4	29	407,203	3,433,281	707,921	2.5
8	Rockwell International	4,387,972	2,230,389	2,157,583	13	4	1,130,395	2,468,818	788,759	2.5
9	Raytheon[8]	4,369,484	4,166,633	202,851	6	34	789,563	2,853,776	726,145	2.4
10	United Technologies[9]	3,336,201	2,950,932	385,269	8	19	439,214	2,483,554	413,433	1.9
11	Boeing[10]	3,130,836	2,423,547	707,289	10	13	1,073,237	1,170,928	886,671	1.8
12	Grumman	2,840,651	2,725,294	115,357	9	44	515,300	1,830,045	495,306	1.6
13	AT&T	2,409,497	944,756	1,464,741	23	5	188,094	381,436	1,839,967	1.3
14	Tenneco	2,371,865	2,370,675	1,190	11	2002	22,574	886,940	1,462,351	1.3
15	University of Calif. System	2,364,417	40,145	2,324,272	280	2	291,490	144	2,072,783	1.3
16	Unisys	1,674,552	1,457,445	217,107	15	30	76,810	1,137,894	459,848	0.9
17	IBM	1,636,124	1,235,234	400,890	18	17	184,203	1,159,269	292,652	0.9
18	Litton Industries	1,568,734	1,562,349	6,385	14	538	288,540	1,122,645	157,549	0.9
19	Allied-Signal[11]	1,501,846	783,379	718,467	28	12	187,945	528,365	785,536	0.8
20	EG&G	1,457,350	99,421	1,357,929	112	6	31,242	13,964	1,412,144	0.8
21	TRW	1,377,946	1,097,223	280,723	19	24	639,969	466,156	271,821	0.8
22	GTE	1,313,537	1,304,641	8,896	16	397	118,954	1,010,847	183,736	0.7
23	Textron[12]	1,249,636	1,245,562	4,074	17	770	167,356	993,197	89,083	0.7
24	Gencorp	1,122,953	1,094,966	27,987	20	137	277,540	163,727	681,686	0.6
25	California Inst. of Technology	1,119,649	4,845	1,114,804	1679	8	12,828	0	1,106,821	0.6
26	Ford Motor Co.[13]	1,071,869	799,874	271,995	26	25	400,093	225,131	446,645	0.6
27	LTV[14]	1,070,646	1,054,864	15,782	21	233	222,006	723,775	124,865	0.6
28	ITT[14]	1,004,816	947,110	57,706	22	79	72,668	617,279	314,869	0.6
29	Foundation Health Corp.	865,272	865,272	0	24	0	515,206	0	350,066	0.5
30	Alliant Techsystems[15]	856,858	855,841	1,017	25	2241	292,971	537,910	25,977	0.5

#									
31	MIT	852,308	787,850	64,458	27	72	844,592	155	7,561	0.5
32	Northrop	798,734	748,478	50,256	29	86	425,490	184,415	188,829	0.4
33	Gibbons, Green & Van Amerongen	790,317	737,312	53,005	31	83	0	775,380	14,937	0.4
34	Thiokol	789,490	290,554	498,936	58	15	510,190	156,878	122,422	0.4
35	Teledyne	757,090	629,311	127,779	33	40	274,838	382,007	100,245	0.4
36	Texas Instruments[16]	749,837	745,631	4,206	30	755	151,923	551,517	46,397	0.4
37	Computer Sciences Corp.[17]	719,754	377,650	342,104	49	20	180,386	137,543	401,825	0.4
38	McDermott	673,662	19,094	654,568	541	14	14,463	655,970	3,229	0.4
39	Science Applications Intl.	655,036	503,556	151,480	38	38	198,420	53,865	402,751	0.4
40	FMC[18]	650,071	649,632	439	32	3985	59,385	555,194	35,492	0.4
41	Royal Dutch Petroleum	625,205	625,205	0	34	0	0	618,018	7,187	0.4
42	Honeywell[19]	580,775	546,179	34,596	36	114	111,761	358,192	110,822	0.3
43	Loral[20]	557,921	556,846	1,075	35	2157	59,654	451,397	46,870	0.3
44	Avondale Industries	546,162	546,162	0	37	0	0	519,441	26,721	0.3
45	Olin	539,025	495,557	43,468	40	97	37,921	332,863	168,241	0.3
46	Dyncorp	509,090	500,873	8,217	39	430	7,573	23,207	478,310	0.3
47	Mitre	500,924	412,354	88,570	46	57	416,295	0	84,629	0.3
48	Hercules	483,203	476,047	7,156	41	485	87,017	175,037	221,149	0.3
49	E-Systems	468,847	434,446	34,401	43	115	41,339	72,957	354,551	0.3
50	Morrison-Knudsen	467,434	331,335	136,099	53	39	1,297	265,927	200,210	0.3
51	Johnson Controls	461,017	384,041	76,976	48	62	170,512	5,511	284,994	0.3
52	Motorola	460,531	357,701	102,830	51	47	37,507	388,582	34,442	0.3
53	Exxon	453,468	453,084	384	42	4373	275	452,468	725	0.3
54	Penn Central	444,078	433,323	10,755	44	334	16,535	26,058	401,485	0.2
55	Aerospace Corp.	417,921	416,217	1,704	45	1554	417,905	0	16	0.2
56	University of Chicago System	416,902	1,404	415,498	4229	16	2,614	0	414,288	0.2
57	Universities Space Res. Assn.	392,989	1,027	391,962	5311	18	188,444	0	204,545	0.2
58	Atlantic Richfield	390,559	390,312	247	47	5804	756	389,720	83	0.2
59	Johns Hopkins University	388,451	374,239	14,212	50	256	382,911	68	5,472	0.2
60	Battelle Memorial Institute	385,159	63,108	322,051	185	21	63,435	2,242	319,482	0.2

Table 1.7 (continued)

(Total Purchases: $177,645,770,000)

Rank	Parent Company	Total	DoD	Civilian	DoD Rank	Civilian Rank	R&D	Products	Services	Market Share
							Fiscal 1990 Contract Awards ($000s)			
61	Defense Facilities Admin.[21]	354,752	354,752	0	52	0	0	0	354,752	0.2
62	CAE Industries	344,065	227,359	116,706	65	42	77,697	174,715	91,653	0.2
63	Chrysler	343,459	227,480	115,979	64	43	23,991	230,549	88,919	0.2
64	Black & Decker[22]	334,928	209,721	125,207	69	41	42,426	2,685	289,817	0.2
65	Coastal Corp.	331,930	331,117	813	54	2611	0	328,514	3,416	0.2
66	Eaton	316,886	304,804	12,082	56	300	47,110	222,422	47,354	0.2
67	Diversified Energy	316,819	0	316,819	0	22	0	316,819	0	0.2
68	Philips Gloeilampenfabrieken	313,423	296,703	16,720	57	216	61,890	231,484	20,049	0.2
69	European Utilities Co.[23]	313,300	313,300	0	55	0	0	0	313,300	0.2
70	Mason Hanger-Silas Mason	292,998	82,529	210,469	141	31	0	10,028	282,970	0.2
71	Canadian Commercial Corp.[24]	287,123	259,722	27,401	60	142	15,942	231,265	39,916	0.2
72	Associated Universities	286,587	50	286,537	23631	23	50	0	286,537	0.2
73	Harris	283,034	183,637	99,397	77	50	55,745	168,268	59,021	0.2
74	Astronautics Corp. of America	275,346	274,721	625	59	3152	108,494	142,992	23,860	0.2
75	Control Data Corp.	270,786	243,907	26,879	62	148	51,609	181,254	37,923	0.2
76	Oshkosh Truck Corp.	259,183	259,183	0	61	0	31,047	228,136	0	0.1
77	Mobil	241,205	237,694	3,511	63	888	0	240,924	281	0.1
78	Ohio Valley Electric	240,748	0	240,748	0	26	0	0	240,748	0.1
79	Tom Coal Company	233,450	0	233,450	0	27	0	233,450	0	0.1
80	Arch Minerals	233,166	0	233,166	0	28	0	233,166	0	0.1
81	Bechtel Group	231,982	59,571	172,411	194	36	8,486	0	223,496	0.1
82	Stanford University	230,768	25,052	205,716	424	33	80,407	0	150,361	0.1
83	CSX	226,375	225,601	774	66	2705	0	0	226,375	0.1
84	Enserch	218,975	117,341	101,634	96	48	5,164	0	213,811	0.1
85	Kaman	215,228	213,623	1,605	67	1619	88,045	79,663	47,520	0.1
86	SRI International	213,604	53,718	159,886	218	37	194,007	2,018	17,579	0.1
87	Contel	212,172	117,268	94,904	97	53	84,975	37,323	89,874	0.1
88	Peterson Builders	211,643	211,643	0	68	0	0	211,140	503	0.1
89	Electric Energy Inc.	208,685	0	208,685	0	32	0	0	208,685	0.1
90	Forstmann, Little & Co.	202,706	199,171	3,535	70	883	0	40,289	162,417	0.1

Rankings are based on prime contracts of $25,000 or more for all federal agencies.

1. Includes $277.5 million from a joint venture with General Dynamics for development of the A-12 advanced tactical aircraft and $51.8 million from a joint venture with Textron for the development of the light helicopter.

2. Includes $159.3 million from CFM International, a joint venture with SNECMA of France for the CFM56 engine, and $12.4 million from a joint venture with Lockheed for the integrated electronic warfare system.

3. Includes $277.5 million from a joint venture with General Dynamics for development of the A-12 advanced tactical aircraft, $13.3 million for a joint venture with Westinghouse for development of the advanced air-to-air missile and $5.8 million from Armored Vehicles Technologies Association, a joint venture with FMC for the heavy forces modernization program.

4. Includes $24.8 million from a joint venture with Texas Instruments for the advanced antitank weapons system-medium, $22.4 million from MDTT, a joint venture with Diehl of West Germany, Thomson-CSF of France and Thorn EMI of Great Britain for development of the terminal guidance warhead, and $7.7 million from a joint venture with ITT for development of microwave/millimeter monolithic wave integrated circuits.

5. Includes $43.2 million from a joint venture with ITT for the development of the airborne self-protection jammer, $13.3 million from a joint venture with General Dynamics for development of the advanced air-to-air missile, and $2.1 million from a joint venture with Texas Instruments for development of the advanced tactical fighter radar system.

6. Includes $12.4 million from a joint venture with General Electric for the integrated electronic warfare system and $10.4 million from a joint venture with AEL for the TACJAM-A ground-based jamming system.

7. Includes $40.8 million from LHTEC, a joint venture with Allied-Signal's Garrett Corp. for development of the T800 engine, $15.8 million for a joint venture with Raytheon for development of the advanced air-to-air missile and $853,000 from Tactical Truck Corp., a joint venture with Harsco's BMY for the family of medium tactical vehicles program. Additionally, GM acquired Perkin Elmer Corp.'s Electro-Optics Technology division in October 1989.

8. Includes $45.2 million from a joint venture with Computer Sciences Corp. for administration of the Eastern Test Range, $15.8 million from a joint venture with General Motors for development of the advanced air-to-air missile and $10.2 million from a joint venture with Texas Instruments for development of microwave/millimeter monolithic wave integrated circuits.

9. Includes $51.9 million from a joint venture with Boeing for the development of the light helicopter.

10. Includes $51.9 million from a joint venture with United Technologies for the development of the light helicopter and $875,000 from a joint venture with Textron for the V-22 aircraft.

11. Includes $40.8 million from LHTEC, a joint venture with General Motor's Allison Gas Turbine for development of the T800 engine.

12. Includes $51.8 million from a joint venture with McDonnell Douglas for the development of the light helicopter and $875,000 from joint venture with Boeing for the V-22 aircraft.

13. Ford's Aerospace division was sold to Loral in December 1990.

14. Includes $43.2 million from a joint venture witn Westinghouse for the development of the airborne self-protection jammer, $7.7 million from a joint venture with Martin Marietta for development of microwave/millimeter monolithic wave integrated circuits and $782,000 from a joint venture with Varo for night-vision equipment.

15. Alliant Techsystems was formed in September 1990 when Honeywell spun off its Defense and Marine Systems Business, Test Instruments division and Signal Analysis Center.

16. Includes $24.8 million from a joint venture with Martin Marietta for the advanced antitank weapons system-medium, $10.2 million from a joint venture with Raytheon for development of microwave/millimeter monolithic wave integrated circuits, and $2.1 million from a joint venture with Westinghouse for development of the advanced tactical fighter radar system.

17. Includes $45.2 million from a joint venture with Raytheon for administration of the Eastern Test Range.

18. Includes $5.8 million from Armored Vehicles Technologies Association, a joint venture with General Dynamics for the heavy forces modernization program.

19. Honeywell spun off its Defense and Marine Systems Business, Test Instruments division and Signal Analysis Center in September 1990 into an independent company called Alliant Techsystems.

20. Loral acquired Ford Motor Co.'s Aerospace division in December 1990, including BDM International, which it subsequently sold to the Carlysle Group.

21. Defense Facilities Administration handles contracts for work done on U.S. bases in Japan.

22. Includes $15.3 million from a joint venture with VSE & Assoc. for engineering, technical and operations service at the Naval Weapon Station, Seal Beach, Calif.

23. European Utilities Companies represents the aggregate of utilities contracts for U.S. bases in Europe.

24. Canadian Commercial Corp. is a Canadian government agency that processes DoD contracts for Canadian companies.

25. Includes $80.1 million for joint venture with Research Cottrell's Metcalf & Eddy for the Saudi Arabian "Peace Shield" program.

23

Table 1.7 (continued)

(Total Purchases: $177,645,770,000)

Fiscal 1990 Contract Awards ($000s)

Rank	Parent Company	Total	DoD	Civilian	DoD Rank	Civilian Rank	R&D	Products	Services	Market Share
91	Digital Equipment Corp.	199,909	135,905	64,004	88	73	5,596	149,221	45,092	0.1
92	CRSS[25]	194,794	192,302	2,492	71	1154	476	0	194,318	0.1
93	International Marine Carriers	190,924	190,924	0	72	0	0	0	190,924	0.1
94	Federal Express	190,531	190,511	20	73	20460	0	0	190,531	0.1
95	Chevron	187,724	187,751	-27	74	29481	0	187,588	136	0.1
96	Amoco	187,270	186,949	321	75	4925	2,705	184,565	0	0.1
97	Westmark Systems	187,043	185,573	1,470	76	1737	29,819	41,999	115,225	0.1
98	Harsco[26]	179,520	179,382	138	78	8227	71,315	107,532	673	0.1
99	Bell County Coal	172,693		172,693	0	35	0	172,693	0	0.1
100	Sverdrup	171,409	90,655	80,754	130	60	55,609	0	115,800	0.1
101	Hewlett-Packard	169,856	131,939	37,917	89	103	1,739	161,787	6,330	0.1
102	Bollinger Mch. Sp. & Shipyard	166,818	166,791	27	79	18772	0	166,818	0	0.1
103	Snecma[27]	159,317	159,291	26	80	19176	0	159,291	26	0.1
104	Rolls Royce PLC	158,153	157,831	322	81	4906	249	149,629	8,275	0.1
105	Plessey Co. PLC	155,943	155,943	0	82	0	117,112	34,954	3,877	0.1
106	Varian Associates	155,692	151,562	4,130	84	764	6,301	128,127	21,264	0.1
107	Eastman Kodak	154,829	125,588	29,241	90	133	5,450	41,482	107,897	0.1
108	Logicon	152,900	152,688	212	83	6363	70,059	10,844	71,997	0.1
109	World Airways	144,891	144,891	0	85	0	0	0	144,891	0.1
110	Day & Zimmermann	142,388	141,703	685	86	2957	323	7,153	134,912	0.1
111	Halliburton	140,926	70,218	70,708	163	68	5,580	0	135,346	0.1
112	MIP Instandsetzungsbetric	138,857	138,857	0	87	0	0	0	138,857	0.1
113	United Industrial Corp.	130,256	123,784	6,472	94	532	19,216	57,372	53,668	0.1
114	Brand Name Contractor[28]	129,322	0	0	0	0	0	129,322	0	0.1
115	Nichols Research	124,896	124,046	850	93	2536	115,926	2,525	6,445	0.1
116	Amerada Hess	124,708	124,708	0	91	0	0	124,582	126	0.1
117	Esco Electronics[29]	124,171	124,171	0	92	0	14,072	109,991	108	0.1
118	Air Products & Chemicals	123,753	93,218	30,535	126	130	1,608	35,943	86,202	0.1
119	Todd Shipyards	123,627	27,255	96,372	391	52	641	93,792	29,194	0.1
120	Schneider Group	123,424	110,819	12,605	102	286	0	0	123,424	0.1

121	Booz Allen & Hamilton	122,251	96,291	25,960	118	151	37,519	1,095	83,637	0.1
122	Goodyear	120,646	120,387	259	95	5638	0	120,493	153	0.1
123	Arinc	120,545	104,393	16,152	106	227	16,459	11,166	92,920	0.1
124	Xerox	115,858	83,966	31,892	139	125	8,296	46,465	61,097	0.1
125	Charles Stark Draper Lab	114,728	101,107	13,621	110	268	83,865	523	30,340	0.1
126	Kopper Glo Fuels	114,131	0	114,131	0	45	0	114,131	0	0.1
127	Norfolk Shipbuilding Dry Dock	113,639	111,266	2,373	99	1195	0	937	112,702	0.1
128	General Electric PLC	113,150	93,354	19,796	125	185	93	108,392	4,665	0.1
129	Duchossois Industries	112,206	112,206	0	98	0	15,315	38,668	58,223	0.1
130	Mitek Systems	111,285	111,224	61	100	12791	0	111,090	195	0.1
131	Delta Dental Plan of Calif.	110,957	110,957	0	101	0	0	0	110,957	0.1
132	Fairchild Industries	109,982	65,613	44,369	177	95	41,598	28,530	39,854	0.1
133	Bolt, Beranek & Newman	108,668	104,690	3,978	105	788	66,419	3,607	38,642	0.1
134	Pacific Resources	108,240	108,240	0	103	0	0	108,240	0	0.1
135	Bahrain National Oil	107,898	107,898	0	104	0	0	107,898	0	0.1
136	Arvin Industries	107,666	91,497	16,169	128	226	90,630	340	16,696	0.1
137	Princeton University	104,729	5,821	98,908	1444	51	103,530	0	1,199	0.1
138	B&L Utility Contractors	104,002	0	104,002	0	46	0	0	104,002	0.1
139	Sun Company	103,942	103,327	615	107	3186	0	103,327	615	0.1
140	Israel Aircraft Industries	102,923	102,923	0	108	0	70,011	31,984	928	0.1
141	Billfish	102,689	2,360	100,329	2927	49	0	0	102,689	0.1
142	Amelco	102,138	99,322	2,816	113	1047	0	2,811	99,327	0.1
143	Harnischfeger Industries	102,129	83,910	18,219	140	203	28,847	8,453	64,829	0.1
144	Alcoa	101,950	101,272	678	109	2979	846	101,104	615	0.1
145	CTA	101,829	86,028	15,801	136	232	6,908	35,801	59,120	0.1

26. Includes $853,000 from Tactical Truck Corp., a joint venture with General Motors for the family of medium tactical vehicles program.

27. Includes $159.3 million from CFM International, a joint venture with General Electric for the CFM56 engine.

28. Brand Name Contractor represents the aggregate awards of off-the-shelf goods purchased for the Army under various procurements.

29. Esco Electronics was formed in Sept. 1990 when Emerson Electric spun off its Electronics & Space, Hazeltine, Rantec Microwave & Electronics, Southwest Mobile Systems, Vecco Industries and Distribution Control Systems.

30. Emerson Electric spun off Electronics & Space Corp., Hazeltine Corp., Rantec Microwave & Electronics Inc., Southwest Mobile Systems Corp., Vecco Industries, and Distribution Control Systems

Table 1.7 (continued)

(Total Purchases: $177,645,770,000)

Fiscal 1990 Contract Awards ($000s)

Rank	Parent Company	Total	DoD	Civilian	DoD Rank	Civilian Rank	R&D	Products	Services	Market Share
146	Mapco	100,805	97,219	3,586	116	871	0	100,805	0	0.1
147	Cubic Corp.	100,078	99,076	1,002	114	2257	3,245	69,578	27,255	0.1
148	Perkin-Elmer	99,483	68,329	31,154	167	127	47,730	49,271	2,482	0.1
149	RAND	98,841	98,004	837	115	2565	98,004	0	837	0.1
150	Sequa	98,701	93,400	5,301	124	622	22,299	50,133	26,269	0.1
151	Analytic Sciences Corp.	97,431	93,854	3,577	122	874	69,738	4,576	23,117	0.1
152	Young & Rubicam	97,190	97,190	0	117	0	0	0	97,190	0.1
153	Sundstrand	95,905	95,032	873	120	2477	11,459	76,189	8,257	0.1
154	RJO Enterprises	95,842	86,618	9,224	133	384	14,829	11,764	69,249	0.1
155	Maersk Line Ltd.	95,506	95,506	0	119	0	0	0	95,506	0.1
156	Roy F. Weston Co.	94,850	33,532	61,318	322	77	19,316	0	75,534	0.1
157	Emerson Electric[30]	94,327	93,739	588	123	3280	12,128	76,502	5,697	0.1
158	Bay Tankers	93,870	93,870	0	121	0	0	0	93,870	0.1
159	Wackenhut	93,231	0	93,231	0	54	0	708	92,523	0.1
160	Smiths Industries	92,809	92,779	30	127	18091	10,258	76,040	6,511	0.1
161	Karastan Bigelow Carpet Mills	91,154	91,116	38	129	16108	0	0	91,091	0.1
162	Ashland Oil	90,776	27,135	63,641	393	74	0	1,281	89,495	0.1
163	Research-Cottrell[31]	90,234	86,085	4,149	135	762	349	0	89,885	0.1
164	British Petroleum PLC	90,042	0	90,042	0	55	0	90,042	0	0.1
165	Management & Training Corp.	90,017	0	90,017	0	56	0	0	90,017	0.1
166	Wang Laboratories	89,808	56,556	33,252	204	118	0	58,248	31,560	0.1
167	Metro Machine Corp.	87,351	87,351	0	131	0	0	0	87,351	0.0
168	AEL Industries[32]	87,219	86,931	288	132	5269	15,858	47,514	23,847	0.0
169	Imperial Chemical Industries	87,066	84,941	2,125	138	1303	223	4,551	82,292	0.0
170	Harbert International	87,054	35,654	51,400	306	85	0	0	87,054	0.0
171	Translant	86,486	86,486	0	134	0	0	86,486	0	0.0
172	UNC[33]	85,573	99,683	-14,110	111	29627	6,510	-76,302	161,875	0.0
173	Brunswick	85,281	85,079	202	137	6564	0	78,355	416	0.0
174	Supra Products	84,024	0	84,024	0	58	0	84,024	0	0.0
175	Fluor	83,847	34,579	49,268	317	88	0	85	83,762	0.0

	Company									
176	NJ Vardinoyannis Group	82,427	82,427	0	142	0	0	82,427	0	0.0
177	Conagra	81,845	12,791	69,054	763	71	0	81,845	0	0.0
178	General Atomics	81,817	26,232	55,585	400	81	63,341	4,325	14,151	0.0
179	Phoenix Petroleum	81,642	81,642	0	143	0	0	81,642	0	0.0
180	Southeastern Univ. Res. Assn.	81,475	0	81,475	0	59	81,475	0	0	0.0
181	Scientific Atlanta	81,317	77,248	4,069	147	771	727	76,122	4,468	0.0
182	Southern Packaging & Storage	80,477	80,477	0	144	0	0	80,477	0	0.0
183	Figgie International	79,813	78,783	1,030	146	2220	22,741	16,222	40,850	0.0
184	VSE	79,267	79,262	5	145	25647	5,670	0	73,597	0.0
185	Archer Daniels Midland	79,053	3,382	75,671	2248	63	0	79,053	0	0.0
186	IIT	78,444	74,131	4,313	154	740	61,559	1,786	15,099	0.0
187	PMI Commercio Internacional	77,001	0	77,001	0	61	0	77,001	0	0.0
188	AIC International	76,820	76,820	0	148	0	0	0	76,820	0.0
189	Waterman Steamship	76,682	76,682	0	149	0	0	0	76,682	0.0
190	Enimont Supply	76,436	76,436	0	150	0	0	76,436	0	0.0
191	Andalex Resources	75,656	0	75,656	0	64	0	75,656	0	0.0
192	Flightsafety International	75,514	57,260	18,254	203	201	0	34,469	41,045	0.0
193	Philip Morris	75,437	75,437	0	151	0	0	75,437	0	0.0
194	Cummins Engine	75,118	72,338	2,780	158	1067	17,862	57,256	0	0.0
195	Midwest Research Institute	75,105	956	74,149	5588	65	71,374	0	3,731	0.0
196	Maxus Energy	74,980	74,980	0	152	0	0	74,980	0	0.0
197	Sparton	74,661	73,383	1,278	156	1905	13,026	61,635	0	0.0
198	Morton International	74,505	73,997	508	155	3617	113	11,633	62,759	0.0
199	Facilities Systems Engineering	74,175	74,175	0	153	0	0	74,134	41	0.0
200	Barrett Refining	72,428	72,428	0	157	0	0	72,428	0	0.0

Inc. into an independent company called Esco Electronics in Sept. 1990.

31. Includes $80.1 million for joint venture with CRSS for the Saudi Arabian "Peace Shield" program.

32. Includes $10.4 million from a joint venture with Lockheed for the TACJAM-A ground-based jamming system.

33. Negative numbers denote de-obligations of previously committed funds.

than 2 percent of U.S. businesses sell to the federal government. The proportion of businesses selling to state and local governments is probably somewhat higher, although we found no estimate in our research. Why, in this era of privatization, are businesses reluctant to sell to government?

Different and difficult   The most common explanation is that businesses see public sector purchasing and contracting practices as different, more difficult, and potentially riskier from a liability perspective than private sector practices. One attorney specializing in public contract law, quoted in *Nation's Business*, argues that "government contracts differ markedly from customary business contracts for three reasons—the laws, the specifications, and the performance standards."

The laws require businesses selling to government to make various certifications and representations about the way they do business. Edward Meyers, in an article in *Public Administration Review*, lists such certifications as the firm's level of compliance with federal equal opportunity laws, environmental protection acts, and drug-free workplace laws; federal wage, health, and safety standards; and federal goals for subcontracting with small or minority-owned firms. The result, says Alan Yuspeh in an article in *Government Executive*, is "substantial costs to contractors: extraordinary amounts of time, energy and effort involved in preparing such certifications."

Unquestionably, government procurement has become more time-consuming in reaction to "painful headlines decrying criminal indictments over contractors' possession of confidential bid information, allegations of bribery and influence peddling, and charges of poor contractor technical performance, mischarging, or the like," says William Gregory in *Internal Auditor*. But should a firm fail to accurately comply with the necessary federal certification requirements, it

now faces both civil and criminal sanctions.[21]

The possibility of criminal sanctions has become a big deterrent to doing business with the public sector. Changes in federal cost, pricing, accounting, and profit calculations lie at the heart of the conflict between businesses and the federal government.[22] An attorney dealing with public contract law, cited in Yuspeh's article, describes the problem:

> For years, concerns about deceptive pricing under the Truth in Negotiations Act were resolved by adjusting the contract price to represent any errors in cost and pricing data that were submitted with a proposal. Now the Inspector General has published an entire booklet about various defective pricing anomalies as indicators of fraud. Auditors may believe they will be highly evaluated or even tangibly rewarded if they move audit concerns into a criminal investigative mode. When one considers the incredible disruption that a criminal investigation causes in a large business organization, and the huge distraction of corporate resources and management energy, the cost of this highly questionable trend as a means of resolving business disagreements is clear.

Businesses are frequently disenchanted with the seeming inflexibility and inefficiency created by government's rigid adherence to (and interpretation of) standard specifications. According to one attorney, quoted in *Nation's Business*:

> The law holds that the government is entitled to receive exactly what's in the specifications. In some instances, contract specifications are outmoded, leading contractors to assume they can substitute more up-to-date parts and techniques. Not so. In federal contracts, no changes are permitted unless the contract is specifically modified.

The sheer volume of specifications is sometimes enough to deter a business from selling to government. One example comes from an article by Leon Hoshower in *Financial Executive*:

> Defense firms typically face an array of 44,000 specifications when selling a product to the government. In fact, the instruction book on procurement runs 32 volumes and takes up six feet of shelf space. Some 50 percent of small high-technology defense contractors drop out of competition for government contracts or go out of business completely due largely to bureaucratic regulations.

Businesses also are often baffled by the government's failure to abide by the legal principle of substantial performance that governs ordinary private commercial transactions. Instead of allowing a contractor to substitute a cheaper part upon certification that the product complies with the specifications, the federal government adheres to a standard of strict compliance. The federal standard "means that if the product or service differs in any way from the specifications, the government has a right to terminate the contract or reduce the price considerably," and the company may be open to criminal prosecution, according to Bahls.

Slow payment   Some businesses avoid selling to government because of government's bad reputation for paying its bills in a timely fashion in spite of federal, state, and local prompt-payment laws.[23] According to Larry Reynolds in a 1988 article in *Management Review*, "Winning [a government] contract may turn out to be only half of the battle. When it comes to getting paid on time, companies selling goods and services to the government have faced lousy odds."

For many businesses—especially small, newly established ones—slow reimbursements can put a severe cash flow strain on their operations and even cause bankruptcy. A 1980 study by the General Accounting Office, cited by Reynolds, estimates that federal contractors had to borrow between $150 and $375 million just to cover operating costs over and above normal borrowing needs because of government payment delays. The study does not report how many businesses failures were caused by these delays.

Small and newly established firms, particularly those operating on the margin (as is commonly the case), often perceive surety bonds as unaffordable. These firms may also avoid selling to a government that has a paper-heavy procurement process particularly if no detailed, easy-to-understand manuals or training sessions are available.

Paperwork   Large and small firms alike find the paperwork associated with government procurement (pre- and postbid) as overly burdensome. Lamm's survey of defense-related firms found that almost 70 percent identified burdensome paperwork at both ends of the process as a major problem in dealing with the government. One company he studied claimed it was "too much paperwork for 3 to 5 percent profit," and another lamented that a "recent quote on a government job required three weeks and 100 pages of paperwork, in contrast to a similar commercial job that required three hours and 10 pages of paperwork." Nearly a third of the businesses surveyed by Lamm identified "low profitability" as a deterrent to contracting with the Department of Defense.

Problems with the procurement process.   Not knowing which government agency official has the major responsibility for a specific purchasing decision or not knowing precisely which agency or official will actually use the service or product can deter businesses from trying to sell to government. They would rather sell in the private sector, where they can identify their potential market more easily. According to John McClenahen, in *Government Executive*, many firms "have become convinced that squandering money on the purchasing process results in reduced profits" and is just not worth it.

A number of firms that have never done business with government before (and many that have) frequently perceive the government procurement process to be highly political and noncompetitive, wrought with sole source contracts. Even in competitive bidding situations, some feel that bid specifications are written so specifically as to produce limited competition among potential suppliers. Others feel just the opposite—that specifications are written too generally and imprecisely, effectively giving too much latitude to government officials to choose the supplier.

In Lamm's study of defense-related firms, 57 percent of those surveyed said government bidding methods are a problem. Their reasons ranged from excessive bid package documentation requirements to "solicitation drafters' lack of knowledge of the product." More than 28 percent of the firms identified government delays in making contract awards once the bids were in. Another 6 percent objected to set-asides for small businesses.

Extensive media coverage of dishonest business deals between government and certain private sector firms has given all procurement a bad reputation. Some firms perceive that government rarely cleans house and gets rid of incompetent or corrupt business suppliers. They also doubt the utility and objectivity of government protest or appeals procedures for unsuccessful bidders.

Poor proprietary protection   Firms specializing in high-tech goods and services criticize the Office of Federal Procurement Policy for being "slow to introduce guidelines to protect them from losing proprietary information to the government and the commercial market." Mark Goldstein says in an article in *Government Executive*: "The gov-

ernment often gives information supplied by one company to other companies during the course of [system or product] development; when such data is proprietary and developed through private financing, 'its release usually destroys its commercial value." Rather than risk the loss of investment, some high tech firms have simply decided not to sell to government until the problem is resolved.[24] In Lamm's study, 13 percent of the defense firms surveyed identified technical data rights problems as a reason for not doing business with the Defense Department.

Government's resistance to new products Firms selling new products or services are frequently frustrated by the reluctance of public sector purchasers to consider something new or different. An article by Mark Lewyn in a 1989 issue of *Business Week* refers to this phenomenon as "bureaucrats' fear of high tech." The article describes the frustration that American Telephone & Telegraph and U.S. Sprint Communications Company experienced in trying to sell electronic mail, videoconferencing, and high-speed facsimile transmission to federal officials. "While such services are commonplace to business customers, they're space age technology to risk-averse bureaucrats who worry about glitches and start-up snafus."

Perception of animosity   Some business leaders perceive a growing animosity toward them from government personnel, particularly at the federal level. In Lamm's study, almost one-third of the businesses surveyed indicated that "the uncooperative attitude of government personnel was a principal factor in their dealings with DOD buying offices." Yuspeh notes that "the apparent skepticism of numerous government personnel and Congress about contractor conduct, motives, integrity, and business practices makes the entire business environment for government contractors much more unpleasant on a day-to-day basis than it ought to be."

Ironically, at the very time governments are most aggressively seeking more opportunities to rely on the private sector, the business community is more cautious about selling to government. According to Goldstein:

> The consensus in private industry is that the last decade [the 1980s] enormously increased the burden of costs and regulations necessary to do business with the federal government. Officials in both private and public sector procurement are concerned that the current environment is fraught with more restrictions, confusion, and mistrust than at any time in recent memory.

What is less clear is the degree to which the business community's assessment of federal contracting practices extends to other levels of government: cities, counties, school systems, hospital districts, and transit authorities. Unfortunately, most examinations of business perspectives to date have centered on the federal government as a business partner. *One major purpose of this book is to contrast business assessments of the purchasing policies and procedures of all levels of government: state and local, as well as federal.*

BUSINESSES IN THE STUDY

The results in this book are based on the responses of 3,282 businesses replying to a mail survey conducted in the spring and summer of 1989. We obtained business names and addresses from the vendor mailing lists of two counties: (1) the Hillsborough County (Tampa), Florida, Purchasing and Contracts Department and (2) the Harris County (Houston), Texas, Purchasing Department. We selected these two counties for several reasons. First, both are among the fifty largest U.S. counties. Second, both are located in highly fragmented governmental arenas, thereby enhancing the likelihood that businesses surveyed would be able to assess the purchasing and contracting practices of a wide range of governments. Third, the heads of the purchasing departments in these two counties were willing to share their vendor mailing lists.

A *vendor mailing list* is not necessarily the same as a *bidders list*. While the general purpose of a mailing list is to disseminate information, a bidders list is for eliciting competition, according to the Council of State Governments and the National Association of State Purchasing Officials. Purchasing offices add new suppliers to these

lists to enhance competition and make sure that newly established businesses are not ignored. Importantly, businesses frequently do not place themselves on the vendor mailing list; we received a number of calls from businesses wanting to know how to get on the official bidding lists.

The overall survey response rate was 36 percent (3,282 of 9,040 surveyed).[25] This response rate is well within the typical response rate range of 20–40 percent for mail surveys.[26] Our response rate exceeds the response rates of the International City Management Association surveys of local government officials' assessments of privatization (19 percent response rate in 1987 and a 35 percent response rate in 1988).

We designed the survey instrument (see Appendix A) with help and advice from the chief executives of the two purchasing departments, an administrator of the Small Business Development Center of the University of South Florida, and the author's graduate seminar in public financial management at the University of South Florida.

Businesses responding to the survey (Table 1.8) are quite diverse in firm structures, years in business, number of employees, firm

Table 1.8
Characteristics of Businesses in the Study

Firm Characteristic	Number	% of Survey Respondents
Firm Structure		
Individual owner	417	12.8%
Partnership	99	3.0
Nonprofit organization	66	2.0
Corporation	2655	81.7
Other	13	0.4
Years in Business		
Less than 1 year	55	1.7
1-2 years	205	6.3
3-5 years	474	14.5
6-10 years	511	15.6
Over 10 years	2027	61.9
Number of Employees		
1-25	1944	59.5
26-50	418	12.8
51-100	270	8.3
101-500	340	10.4
501-1000	79	2.4
1001-5000	121	3.7
Over 5000	93	2.8
Firm Gross Revenues ('88)		
Below $200,000	546	17.3
$200,000-499,999	468	14.9
$500,000-999,999	440	14.0
$1-$10 Million	1062	33.7
$11-$25 Million	221	7.0
$26-$50 Million	108	3.4
Over $50 Million	302	9.6

Table 1.8 (*continued*)

Firm Characteristic	Number	% of Survey Respondents
Industry Classification		
Retail trade	482	17.2%
Wholesale trade	462	16.5
Finance	17	0.6
Insurance	7	0.3
Utility	8	0.3
Construction	462	16.5
Manufacturing-durable	250	8.9
Manufacturing-nondurable	89	3.2
Real estate	36	1.3
Communications	95	3.4
Service	552	19.7
Agriculture	30	1.1
Mining	7	0.3
Transportation	49	1.8
Professional Service	250	8.9
Other	1	0.0
Owner		
Minority-owned	679	21.2
Not minority-owned	2529	78.8
Minority Owner-Gender[1]		
Female	369	55.4
Male	133	19.9
Minority Owner-Race[1]		
Black	128	19.2
Hispanic	143	21.4
Puerto Rican	8	1.2
Asian	39	5.8
American Indian	15	2.2
Other	15	2.2

[1] Question was answered only by the subset of the respondents meeting the definitional criterion (minority-owned).

Table 1.8 (*continued*)

Firm Characteristic	Number	% of Survey Respondents
Size-Economic Classification		
Small, economically disadvantaged	712	22.5%
Not small, economically disadvantaged	2453	77.5
Current Contract Status		
Has contract with government	2301	72.7
No contract with government	866	27.3
No Government Contracts at Present[2]		
Have had one in past	422	54.5
Have not had one in past	352	45.5
Level of Government Firm Does Business With (Multiple Responses)		
Federal	1555	49.2
State	2038	64.5
City	2256	71.3
County	2387	75.5
Transit Authority	758	24.0
School district	1679	53.1
Hospital district	820	25.9
Other special district	206	6.5
Other	264	8.3
% of Gross Revenues From Government Contracts		
Less than 10%	1718	56.0
10-25%	615	20.0
26-50%	303	9.9
51-75%	187	6.1
76-90%	117	3.8
Over 90%	128	4.2

[2] Question was answered only by the subset of the respondents meeting the definitional criterion (firm does not have a government contract at the present).

Table 1.8 (*continued*)

Firm Characteristic	Number	% of Survey Respondents
Procedures for Getting Government Contract (Multiple Responses)		
Formal competitive bid (with negotiation)	908	30.9%
Formal competitive bid (sealed)	2135	72.7
Local vendor preference	659	22.4
Request for Proposal (competitive negotiation)	857	29.2
Government solicitation of written quote	1194	40.7
Government solicitation of telephone quote	846	25.8
Participation in Minority Business Enterprise program	148	28.8
Participation in Small Business program	134	5.0
Other procedure	173	4.6
Type of Product Delivered to Government (Multiple Responses)		
Service	1586	51.2
Commodity/good	1693	54.8
Construction	619	20.0
Geographical Location		
In-State	2802	86.7
Out-of-State	428	13.3

Source: Random sample survey of businesses listed on the Harris County (Houston), Texas vendor mailing list (conducted May–June, 1989) and mail survey of all businesses listed on the Hillsborough County (Tampa), Florida vendor registration list (conducted June–July, 1989).

gross revenue, reliance on governmental contracts, industry classifications, ownership characteristics, size and economic classifications, history of contracting with government, types of government they do business with (or would like to do business with), procedures used to solicit government business, type of product or service sold to government, and geographic location. More than 13 percent of the firms responding to the survey are located outside either Florida or Texas, in thirty-six states and the District of Columbia.

Profile The typical firm in our study:

- Is a corporation
- Has been in business longer than 10 years
- Has fewer than 25 employees
- Has assets below $1 million
- Is in the retail or wholesale trade
- Is owned by a white male (but by a female, black or Hispanic if a minority-owned firm)
- Is not classified as a small, economically disadvantaged firm

- Currently holds a contract with one or more governments (most likely the state and several local governments)
- Has secured government business through a formal competitive (sealed) bid
- Relies on government contracts for less than 10 percent of its sales.

When compared with business firm characteristics nationwide, our sample contains a higher proportion of corporations, large firms (measured in terms of dollars and employees), and women-owned and minority-owned firms.[27] Importantly, as the figures in Table 1.8 show, enough variation exists among the firms in our sample to permit a careful empirical contrast of the relationship between firm characteristics and firm assessments of government purchasing practices.

NOTES

1. Elaine Morley in *The Municipal Year Book 1989* defines these other forms of privatization as follows: (1) franchises and concessions—the local government awards a right to provide service within a specified geographic area to one or more firms and may also impose price controls, service standards, and requirements to serve all customers within the area; payment for the service is made directly to the firm by the citizen; (2) subsidies—financial or in-kind contributions by local governments to private organizations or individuals to encourage them to deliver a public service at a reduced cost to consumers; (3) vouchers—coupons or tickets with a monetary value that the local government distributes to citizens needing a service; the citizen can generally choose a provider from competing public or private organizations that have been designated as eligible to receive the vouchers; the voucher obligates the government to reimburse the service provider, usually at an agreed-upon rate per unit of service provided, which can cover up to the full cost of the service; (4) volunteers—volunteers can be used in a variety of capacities, ranging from direct service delivery to provision of support services; (5) self-help—local government encourages citizens to undertake or participate in providing some portion (or all) of a service for their own benefit (e.g., neighborhood crime watch programs); and (6) regulatory and tax incentives—government uses its regulatory and taxing authority to provide incentives for service provision by the private sector or to reduce the need for a service.

   Studies describing or reporting the incidence of various forms of partial privatization (alternative service delivery) include Savas, 1982, 1987; Shulman, 1982; Hatry and Valente, 1983; Ferris and Graddy, 1986; Seader, 1986; Mercer/Slavin, Inc., 1987; Touche Ross & Co., 1987b; David, 1988; Morgan and England, 1988; Morley, 1989; Rehfuss, 1989.

2. See Bellante, 1983; Poole, 1983a, 1986; Fixler and Poole, 1986; Marshall, 1984; Fixler, 1985b, f; Wood, 1986; Ferrara, 1987; Hanke, 1987; Blake, 1988; Crutcher, 1988; Frank, 1988; Miller, 1988; O'Connor and Olson, 1990.

3. See Chi, 1986a, b,; 1988; Feldman, 1986; Clarkson and Fixler, 1987; Hatry, 1989; Wedel, Katz, and Wieck, 1979; Wedel, 1980; DeHoog, 1984; Hatry and Durman, 1985; Chi, Devlin and Masterman, 1989; Shonick and Roemer, 1982; Bromberg and Brand, 1984; LBJ School, 1986, 1987; Schlessinger, Dowart and Pulice, 1986–7; Bovbjerg, Held and Pauly, 1987; Demone and Gibelman, 1987; Higgins, 1989; Mennemeyer and Olinger, 1989; McQuire and Van Cott, 1984; Baker, 1985; Guskind, 1987; Allen, 1989b, c; Teal et al., 1988, 1989; Spitzer and Scull, 1977; Kassenbaum et al., 1978; Lindquist, 1980; Hutto and Vick, 1984; Krajick, 1984; Levinson, 1984; Logan, 1985a, b; Mullen 1984a,b; Mullen,

Chaboter and Carrow, 1985; National Institute of Justice, 1985; Woolley, 1985; Palumbo, 1986; Hackett et al., 1987; Matthews, 1988; Robbins, 1988; Zalud and Lydon, 1990; Fixler, 1986a; Lieberman, 1986a,b, 1987, 1988.

4. Cf. Robert Poole, 1980; Borcherding et al., 1982; Savas, 1982, 1987; Bennett and DiLorenzo, 1983a,b; Armington and Ellis, 1984; Brooks, Liebman and Schelling, 1984; Stevens, 1984; Butler, 1985; Kolderie, 1986; Clarkson and Fixler, 1987; Hanke, 1987; Kent, 1987; Berenyi and Stevens, 1988; David, 1988; Morgan and England, 1988; Donahue, 1989; Finley, 1989c; and Rehfuss, 1989 for summaries of a wide range of studies. See also Carver, 1989.

5. Cf. Spann, 1977; Robert Poole, 1980; Savas, 1982, 1987; Moore, 1987; Carver, 1989.

6. Cf. articles by David, 1988; Renner, 1989.

7. See American Bar Association, 1984; Del Duca, Falvey and Adler, 1986a; Lee, 1987; Flener, 1989; Kinosky, 1989; Napoleon, 1989. See also Muzychenko, 1987.

8. See Zee, 1988; National Institute of Governmental Purchasing, 1989.

9. Cf. Farrell, 1982; Bendic, 1984; Hatry and Durman, 1985; Chi, 1988; Carver, 1989.

10. See Hatry, 1988; Donahue, 1989; Valente and Manchester, 1984.

11. See summary in Fixler and Poole, 1987.

12. Cf. Starr, 1987; Bailey, 1987; Fitch, 1988; Carver, 1989.

13. See Pack, 1987; Sappington and Stiglitz, 1987; Fitch, 1988; Rehfuss, 1990; Starr, 1987.

14. See Bailey, 1987; Flener, 1989; Manchester, 1989.

15. Cf. Starr, 1987; Morgan and England, 1988; Donahue, 1989.

16. See Moe, 1987; Sullivan, 1987.

17. An exception is Berenyi and Stevens, 1988.

18. See *Government Executive*, November 1978; *Business Week*, Aug. 31, 1979; Ross, 1979; Hanrahan, 1983; Magnotti, 1986; Blake, 1987; Owens, 1987; Andrews, 1988; Branch, 1988; Black, 1989; Cantor, 1989; MacManus, 1990b.

19. See Fixler and Poole, 1987; Holcombe, n.d.

20. See Bendic, cited in Fitch, 1988.

21. See Graham, 1988; Alston, 1989; Bahls, 1990.

22. Cf. Holter, 1987; Lovitky, 1987; Feldman, 1988; Fishner, 1989; Worthington, 1989.

23. See Donnally and Stone, 1987; Coalition for State Prompt Pay, 1987, 1989.

24. See Duberstein, 1988; Gabig and McAvoy, 1988; Lamm, 1988.

25. The response rate was higher (44 percent) for the survey mailed to businesses on the Hillsborough County, Florida, mailing list than for the survey mailed to businesses on the Harris County, Texas, list (31 percent). The lower response rate for Harris County was primarily a product of an older mailing list that included a large number of public officials and agencies and a number of businesses whose addresses had changed.

In spite of the differential response rates, few significant differences exist in the profiles of the two business respondent groups (see Table B-1, Appendix B). The profiles are nearly identical with regard to breakdowns for type of firm, number of employees, gross revenue in FY 1988, percent of small and economically disadvantaged firms, current contract status, type of governments firms do business with, percent of gross revenue from government contracts, and the procedures utilized by businesses to secure government contracts.

The respondent groups differ somewhat in the percentage of minority-owned firms (higher in Hillsborough County), of female-owned firms (higher in Harris County), and of firms owned by Hispanics (higher in Hillsborough County) and Asians (higher in Harris County). Firms responding to the Hillsborough County survey are also relatively newer than those responding to the Harris County survey. Finally, there are some differences in the industry classification breakdown. Hillsborough County's list contains a higher percentage of construction and service firms, whereas the Harris County list has a higher percentage of firms in the communications industry.

26. See Nachmias and Nachmias, 1987.

27. Our sample differs most sharply from all U.S. businesses in ownership breakdowns. Na-

tionally, 71 percent of all business enterprises are sole proprietorships, 20 percent are corporations, and 10 percent are partnerships (U.S. Bureau of the Census, 1990:521). Of the firms in our sample, 13 percent are sole proprietorships, 82 percent are corporations, and 3 percent are partnerships (the other 2 percent are nonprofits). This basic difference explains why the firms in our sample are somewhat larger both in terms of number of employees and revenue generated than U.S. businesses at large (U.S. Bureau of the Census, 1990:529). The differences confirm that small individually owned businesses are the least likely to do business with government. They also suggest that vendor lists are not updated as frequently as they should be.

CHAPTER 2

An Overview of Government Purchasing and Contracting Policies and Procedures: Federal, State, Local

"I went to San Antonio for a bidders conference put on by the federal government," says the head of a nonprofit drug-abuse facility. "The hotel ballroom was packed. There must have been a thousand people there. Everybody wanted a contract, but we all knew that only three or four of us would get one."

GOVERNMENT PURCHASING TAKES place in a highly public environment. The strong likelihood that public purchasing activities will come under intense scrutiny by taxpayer advocacy groups, candidates for public office (especially those challenging incumbents), the media, and unsuccessful businesses competing for public business has promoted a purchasing system much more complex than that of the normal privately owned firm. The Council of State Governments and the National Association of State Purchasing Officials state in the widely cited *State and Local Government Purchasing* that public purchasing, by necessity, is governed by a complex, even overwhelming, system of "statutory law, operating rules and regulations, court decisions, administrative rulings, recommended practices, designated procedures, specific conflict of interest provisions, and the overall proprieties that attach to public service."[1]

Businesses frequently do not fully understand or appreciate the basic distinctions between public and private sector purchasing, especially the necessity and difficulty of operating in a fishbowl environment day in and day out. Harry Roberts Page, in *Public Purchasing and Materials Management*, has identified seven attributes of public purchasing that distinguish it from private sector purchasing:

1. The funds being expended are public funds, not those of a business proprietor or a corporation, and thus they may be expended only as prescribed by law; rigid budgetary restrictions and public auditing procedures apply.
2. The objects being acquired and distributed are for the use of several requisitioning bureaus or departments; they are generally not for resale or for use in manufacturing.
3. The personnel performing and managing the function are merit-system employees; they are not motivated by the need to show a profit, as are employees in the private sector.
4. The process is, or should be, conducted in full public view; everything done is a matter of public record; in the private sector, management is not required to divulge requirements, specifications, sources, bid provisions, or prices paid.
5. The process is much more closely prescribed; with few exceptions, public purchasing managers must operate within rigid legal and administrative restraints; they have relatively little flexibility compared to that of their peers in the private sector; as a result, innovations in the public sector take place rather slowly.
6. As public officials, managers are subject to censure by the public and the press; instances of malfeasance, misfeasance, and nonfeasance are news; in private business only the most flagrant instances of incompetence or fraud are reported by the press; the rest are settled internally.
7. Government, particularly the federal government, can and does act in a sovereign capacity; government can dominate a market; these conditions place a public-purchasing official in a position of considerable leverage, which can be unfairly used; few businesses hold such leverage.

While these differences do not justify public purchasing practices that may effectively impede competition, efficiency, or equity (principles of good purchasing), they help to account for government's seemingly overly bureaucratic procurement practices. In this chapter we describe the basic principles and processes of public purchasing, present the rationale for these practices, and contrast the complexity of government purchasing practices at the federal, state, and local levels.

BASIC PRINCIPLES OF PUBLIC PURCHASING

As stated in *State and Local Government Purchasing*, the fundamentals of public purchasing and contracting are competition, impartiality, efficiency, and openness: "Public business is to be offered for competition; bidders are to be treated alike and contracts administered alike, without favoritism; economy and value are basic aims; and the documents used and actions taken are public information."

Purchasing involves the acquisition of equipment, materials, supplies, and services. But it is more than the simple act of buying: The purchasing process also encompasses the determination of need, selection of a supplier, arrival at a fair and reasonable price and terms, preparation of the contract or purchase order, and an evaluation of whether the good or service was delivered and met the conditions of the contractual agreement between buyer and seller. Government purchasing policies and procedures cover each of these activities, some in much more detail than others.

In designing, implementing, and evaluating their purchasing policies, most governments endorse the general policy guidelines outlined in the Federal Acquisition Regulation (FAR):[2]

1. Promotion of procurement from private enterprise to the maximum extent feasible.
2. Adherence to fairness and equity and generally accepted business principles.
3. Reliance upon and promotion of effective competition, to ensure the availability of alternative offers that provide a range of concept, design, performance, price, total cost, service, and delivery.
4. Facilitation of new vendors into the system.
5. Provision of the opportunity to vendors to earn a profit commensurate with the contribution made to meeting public needs and comparable to the profit made in commercial endeavors requiring similar investment, technical and financial risk, and skills.
6. Recognition and acceptance of all ordinary and customary costs accepted in commercial practice to meet public needs at the lowest total cost in the calculation of price to be paid.
7. Prompt payment of vendors selling to government and payment of interest where payment is unduly delayed.
8. Government surveillance of vendor operations and performance at the minimum level necessary to ensure satisfactory performance.
9. Encouragement of innovation and application of new technology by stating needs so that prospective suppliers will have maximum latitude to exercise independent business and technical judgment.
10. Recognition of the role of government contracts in counteracting unemployment and poverty.
11. Promotion of opportunities to new and small businesses and minority firms.
12. Requirement of vendor compliance with laws and rules pertaining to equal employment opportunity, air and water cleanliness, occupational health and safety, and other cross-cutting statutory requirements.

Many of these principles are also reflected in the American Bar Association's *Model Procurement Code for State and Local Governments*, the ABA *Model Procurement Ordinance for Local Government*, and the *Model Purchasing Ordinance* developed by the National Institute of Municipal Law Officers. (See Appendix C for summaries.) All public procurement codes address the four principles of purchasing: competition, efficiency, impartiality, and openness.

PROMOTING PUBLIC PURCHASING PRINCIPLES: TECHNIQUES, RATIONALE, AND DIFFICULTIES

Sometimes it is difficult for government to meet all four objectives of purchasing simultaneously. A decision to structure the purchasing process to promote competition may actually result in some businesses perceiving that the system is not impartial. A procedure designed to enhance impartiality may be regarded by some types of businesses as extremely inefficient. But few in either government or the private sector would deny the importance of competition in the design and evaluation of a public purchasing system.

Without competition, the public purchasing process is likely to be criticized for violating the most basic and sacred of the purchasing tenets: "In principle, competition is the centerpiece around which the public contracting process turns." As stated in *State and Local Government Purchasing*, "The importance of competition demands that acquisitions be made under conditions which foster competition among a sufficient number of potential vendors representing a wide spectrum of producers or services or marketplaces."

Governments utilize a wide range of techniques to attract private sector vendors. Variations are necessary because of unevenness in the supplier market and government commitments to social and economic policies (preferred-customer policies such as those promoting purchases from local, small, or minority-owned businesses).

Formal Methods for Awarding Contracts

Competitive sealed bids The vendor's perception that the selection, or contract award, process is impartial weighs heavily in its decision to enter the competition for a government contract. The method generally perceived as the most impartial for obtaining competitive bids on the great majority of needs, according to *State and Local Government Purchasing*, is the competitive sealed bid. The National Institute of Governmental Purchasing has defined *competitive sealed bidding* as "the process of publicizing government needs [public notice], inviting bids, conducting public bid openings, and awarding a contract to the lowest responsive and responsible bidder." A number of governments require that this process be utilized when the proposed purchase exceeds a certain dollar amount (see Table 2.1). This method's effectiveness, says Stanley Zemansky in *Contracting Professional Ser-*

vices, depends on "clarity of the specified requirements; the timely availability to prospective bidders of the data required to prepare an appropriate response; and the availability of more than one organization capable of performing the required work."

While not all governments require consideration of contractor responsiveness and responsibleness in their formal competitive bidding process, the trend in recent years has been in this direction. A 1987 survey of 288 cities larger than 50,000 in population found that 58 percent selected contractors on the basis of the lowest bid among *qualified* companies; only 12 percent were selected exclusively on the basis of lowest bid (see Table 2.2).

The rationale behind competitive sealed bidding is that it best meets the four principles of purchasing. The formal policy of requiring public notice and public opening of bids demonstrates the principle of openness; the awarding of contracts to the lowest and most responsible bidder demonstrates the principles of efficiency and fairness; and the openness, impartiality, and efficiency of this method promote competition by increasing the number of high-quality businesses willing to sell to government.

From the perspective of business, the government's assumptions regarding the effectiveness of the competitive sealed-bidding process are not always correct. For example, if the Invitation for Bid (IFB) is voluminous and overly detailed, it may deter businesses—especially small, new firms—from entering the competition. (IFBs typically delineate work specifications, bidding procedures, contract terms and conditions, and evaluative criteria. See the American Bar Association's *Identifying and Prosecuting Fraud and Abuse in State and Local Contracting*.)

Relatedly, specifications in the IFB written too precisely or narrowly may deter firms from competing. But government justifies detailed, precise specifications on the ground

Table 2.1
Dollar Threshold for Formal Competitive Sealed Bids

Formal Competitive Sealed Bids/Sealed Proposals – Requirements, Dollar Threshold	Type of Government						
	Federal/State Provincial Central	City Municipality Town/Village	County Region Parish	School System University College	State Provincial Special Authority	City County Health	Total
	(n=64)	(n=269)	(n=113)	(n=82)	(n=55)	(n=16)	(n=559)
Less than $500	1.6%	0.4%	0.9%	0.0%	1.8%	0.0%	0.7%
$500 - $1,000	1.6	3.7	1.8	4.9	7.3	6.3	3.7
$1,001 - $5,000	29.7	25.7	21.2	28.0	32.7	31.3	26.4
$5,001 - $10,000	35.9	39.4	35.4	35.4	21.8	25.0	35.7
$10,001 - $20,000	14.1	22.3	32.7	19.5	21.8	31.3	23.2
Over $20,000	17.2	8.6	8.0	12.2	14.5	6.3	10.4
Totals[1]	100.1	100.1	100.0	100.0	99.9	100.2	100.1

[1] Totals may not equal 100.0% due to rounding.

Source: National Institute of Governmental Purchasing, *Results of the 1989 Procurement Research Survey.* Falls Church, VA: NIGP, P. 18.

Table 2.2
Method Used to Select the Contractor

Method	Refuse Collection	Vehicle Towing	Animal Control	Street Maintenance	Transportation	Health Care	Park Landscaping	Tax Collection	Other	All Services
Lowest bid	11.9%	12.0%	0.0%	16.7%	15.4%	9.5%	25.0%	0.0%	0.0%	12.3%
Best reputation	7.5	4.3	0.0	0.0	7.7	23.8	8.3	0.0	8.3	6.3
Lowest bid among qualified	61.2	54.7	37.5	83.3	61.5	33.3	66.7	66.7	50.0	57.5
Other	19.4	29.1	62.5	0.0	15.4	33.3	0.0	33.3	41.7	23.9
Totals[1]	100.0	100.1	100.0	100.0	100.0	99.9	100.0	100.0	100.0	100.0

[1] Totals may not equal 100.0% due to rounding.

Source: Harper A. Roehm, Joseph F. Castellano, and David A. Karns, "Contracting Services to the Private Sector: A Survey of Management Practices," *Government Finance Review*. (February, 1989): 22.

that standardized specifications permit true price comparisons; thus they promote efficiency. The American Society for Testing and Materials, in the foreword to its *Selected ASTM Standards for the Purchasing Community*, which covers more than 200 standards, states that its primary mission "is to develop voluntary full *consensus* standards for materials, products, systems, and services" for use by the professional purchasing community.

Conversely, specifications that are too broad and imprecise may deter firms from competing because they may perceive that purchasing or political officials have too much latitude in the award process. In other words, businesses encountering these types of "specs" may perceive that the purchasing process violates the principle of impartiality. But governments occasionally write specs broadly to promote innovation. As these examples indicate, one of the biggest challenges facing governments is to design a purchasing system that promotes impartiality and openness without limiting competition.

Awarding a contract to the lowest bidder without some calculation of the vendor's capacities to deliver a quality product or service in a timely fashion also contributes to a government's bad reputation among potential suppliers. This is especially the case if a firm engages in *low-balling*, which occurs when a firm intentionally bids excessively low just to get the contract and then cannot deliver the goods or services in the manner prescribed in the contract. Requiring that awards be made to the "lowest responsive bidder" is designed to prevent this problem. A *responsive bidder* "conforms in all material respects to the IFB, that is, delivery, terms and conditions, and items requested," according to the ABA's *Identifying and Prosecuting Fraud and Abuse in State and Local Contracting*.

The rationale from the government's perspective for responsive bidder clauses, according to the ABA book, is to "ensure equality among bidders by prohibiting an award to a bidder that has offered something different from that requested and to promote competition free from corruption, favoritism, and fraud." From the viewpoint of business, however, "strict adherence to this concept would require rejection of any bid deviating from the IFB, with the result being the loss of a significant number of bids from responsible contractors" then and in the future. Some businesses may therefore see this type of requirement as reducing competition and as being inefficient. Others may see it as an excellent way to weed out unethical or incompetent competitors. Like government, the business community is not monolithic.

Businesses also may have different perspectives when it comes to requiring awards to the "lowest responsible bidder." A *responsible bidder*, according to the ABA book, is "one whose integrity, past performances, and business and financial capabilities are such that he/she is judged to be capable of satisfying the government's requirements." Government's rationale for this qualification is that it helps "curb waste and inefficiency in the awarding of public contracts by requiring contractors to meet minimum standards of competency and integrity." But strict adherence to such definitions may be perceived by some businesses, especially newly established firms, as unfairly giving the advantage to larger, more established firms that have already been successful in securing government contracts. However, the larger firms may see it as a way to promote efficiency.

Competitive sealed negotiations When competitive sealed bidding is not practical, competitive sealed negotiations (also referred to as competitive sealed proposals) are used by government to attract vendors and award contracts. The National Institute of Governmental Purchasing defines *competitive sealed negotiations* as "the process of publicizing government needs, requesting proposals, evaluating proposals received (evaluation criteria must be included in the Request for Proposal, or RFP), negotiating (discussing) proposals with acceptable or potentially acceptable offerors, and awarding the contract after consideration of evaluation factors in the RFP and the price offered." This technique is most frequently used to obtain competition when the number of potential vendors may be so small that reliance on public notices and mailouts to all firms on a vendor mailing list may be extremely cost-ineffective or when the good or service is new and the number of suppliers is limited.

A potential drawback of competitive sealed negotiations from the vendor's perspective is government decision makers will be more likely to use subjective, judgmental criteria to award the contract—threatening the principles of impartiality and openness. To be judged fair and impartial by business, and in order for the government to have "the maximum flexibility of determining which proposal actually represents the best value, price, and other factors considered [e.g., technical excellence, past history of performance], the solicitation must include a statement regarding the relative importance of these factors," says Zemansky.

Two-step formal advertising and bidding The two-step (or *multistep*) formal advertising and bidding process originated with, and is most often used by, the Department of Defense in making purchases of a highly technical nature in which existing performance specifications cannot suffice, as in the purchase of aircraft, missiles, weapons. This technique, as stated by *Alijan's Purchasing Handbook*, is used under the following conditions:

(1) available specifications are inadequate or are not sufficiently definite to permit full and free competition without technical evaluation or technical discussion to ensure mutual understanding between the government and the prospective contractors;

(2) definite criteria exist for evaluating technical proposals;

(3) two or more technically qualified sources are expected to compete;

(4) sufficient time is available to permit use of the two-step method; and

(5) a firm fixed-price contract or a fixed-price contract with escalation will be used.

In the first step of the formal two-step process, the government issues a request for a technical proposal based on performance or requirement specifications laid out in the IFB. Upon receipt of the vendors' proposals, according to the handbook mentioned above, government "makes the determination as to the technical acceptability of the supplies, service, or materials offered [frequently after discussions with the interested vendors] and may summarily reject unacceptable proposals or make provisions for modification of technical proposals that are marginal in order to raise them to a level of acceptability." Price is not discussed during the first step.

The second step is conducted in the normal manner associated with formal competitive bidding except that only those vendors who submitted technically acceptable proposals during the first phase are permitted to enter the bidding pool. "These offerors then bid on the basis of meeting the performance specifications and providing the exact supply or service as proposed or as modified in discussions with the [government] and approved by the [government] at the initial step." Awards are made on the basis of price alone at this stage.

The advantages to government of the formal two-step process, as outlined by the handbook, are that it provides government with the opportunity to explore, explain, and clarify the bidder's understanding and proposed means of providing government's requirements; encourages innovation and initiative on the part of competing firms to develop new approaches, techniques, and methods in the production of an item by not tying firms to existing processes or rigid specifications; and lets government receive the benefit of an industry's best technical efforts.

However, from a business perspective, the two-step method may be viewed as costly (in both time and money) and not necessarily impartial, unless the government has developed clear statements of performance requirements and precise criteria for evaluating proposals. In that case, government may lose the benefits of innovation and be back in the situation in which specification development may cost it more than it would save.

Informal Methods for Awarding Contracts

Unlike formal methods, informal methods of awarding contracts do not necessarily require public advertising, public opening, or awarding of the contract to the lowest, most responsible bidder. Informal methods are most likely to be used in coping with emergencies, contracting for professional services, contracting for goods and services for which there is only one source (sole-source contracts), contracting for goods and services falling under certain dollar threshold amounts, and fulfilling policy goals such as promoting local vendors, small businesses, or businesses owned by women, minorities, or the handicapped, among others.

The major advantage to government of using informal techniques in these situations is efficiency—measured in both money and time. Furthermore, government sees these methods as a way to make the procurement process more flexible, less bureaucratic, more innovative, and more attractive to vendors. The major drawback is that informal methods may lead some potential private sector suppliers to doubt the impartiality, openness, and competitiveness of the system.

Request for proposal An RFP, as defined in the National Institute of Governmental

Purchasing's *Dictionary of Purchasing Terms*, is "a request for an offer, by one party to another, of terms and conditions with reference to some work or undertaking." (The request may also be called Request for Application, or RFA.) RFPs are increasingly being used to secure professional services, according to Zemansky and others, and are intended to increase competition and reduce the cost of professional services—one of the fastest-growing budgetary items.

Request for quote An RFQ is "a form of informal solicitation, including oral (telephone) or written quotes from vendors, without formal advertising and receipt of sealed bids." Like the RFP, it is considered a good business practice by government in that the RFQ promotes price competition, flexibility, and adaptability to rapidly changing times and conditions.

Set-aside A set-aside is "a procedure whereby an established percentage of expenditures is designated for exclusive bidding, or purchase from a specified [class] of businesses." The Department of Commerce defines these businesses in specific terms. A *small business* is "one that, including its affiliates, is independently owned and operated, and not dominant in the field in which it is bidding on government contracts." A *woman-owned business* "is at least 51 percent owned, controlled, and operated by a woman or women." A *minority-owned business* "is at least 51 percent owned, controlled, and operated by a member of an economically or socially disadvantaged minority group, including blacks, Hispanics, Native Americans, Asian-Pacific Americans, and Asian-Indian Americans."

Proponents see set-asides as a way of promoting competition by expanding the vendor pool to include small and minority businesses, for example, and demonstrating the impartiality of the public purchasing process. Opponents see set-asides as violating the principles of competition, impartiality, and efficiency.

Governments differ considerably in their definition of what constitutes an emergency condition, a small purchase, a special service to be exempted from formal competitive bidding or negotiating requirements, and a class preference policy. They also differ considerably in who has the statutory or legal authority to make such determinations (a point discussed later in this chapter).

Emergencies Typically, an emergency condition is "a situation that creates a threat to public health, welfare, or safety, such as may arise by reason of floods, epidemics, riots, equipment failures," or other means defined by a government, according to the American Bar Association. The rationale for a government's reliance on informal methods of contracting under these conditions is speed—ability to respond quickly to urgent, unexpected, and unusual situations. From business' perspective, quick decisions may not necessarily be the most efficient or impartial ones. But, as noted in *State and Local Government Purchasing*, governments believe this method can be fair, efficient, and competitive through maintenance of current, comprehensive lists of eligible vendors.

Small purchases Time and money savings are the primary justifications for using informal purchasing techniques to make small purchases. (Competitive bidding and negotiating methods require much more time and expense than the informal methods.) Historically, a small purchase has meant one lower than $100, $500, or $1,000, depending on the level and size of a government, but in recent years this dollar threshold has risen in response to inflation and the rising cost of goods and services (see Table 2.1).

In recent years the trend has also been toward allowing governmental agencies to make small purchases on their own, partic-

ularly among larger governments (see Table 2.3). The rationale for this decentralization is that it creates greater efficiency and that the "users" of the commodity or service (the agencies) know best which purchases are needed—and when. Some observers also argue that this technique expands the vendor pool overall, thereby promoting competition and efficiency gains. From the perspective of business, however, this technique may be responsible for some of the complaints referred to in Chapter 1—not knowing who is responsible for a purchasing decision regarding their product or service.

Exempted services Services typically exempted from formal competitive award criteria, according to the ABA, are "those provided by medical, legal, or performing arts professionals or on an infrequent, technical, or unique basis." In the past the primary rationale for awarding these contracts through informal procedures was that the provider was the "sole source" of a highly specialized, highly technical service. But with the growth of the service sector in the U.S. (and world) economy this argument began to erode.[3] A number of lawsuits have successfully challenged these informal methods of purchasing professional services, mostly on the grounds that they violate federal and state antitrust laws.

Ironically, the rationale of some government officials, and some long-time service providers, for maintaining seemingly less-competitive methodologies of securing professional services is precisely that they do not promote competition. As indicated in Zemansky's book, price competition among professional service providers "causes waste, delay, inefficiency, and unnecessary expense; that specification development required for such actions may cost more in government time and money than the product being delivered." These same individuals make the case that competition does not nec-

Table 2.3
Agency Authority to Make Small Purchases

Small Purchases—User Agency May Purchase:	Type of Government						
	Federal/State Provincial Central	City Municipality Town/Village	County Region Parish	School System University College	State Provincial Special Authority	City County Health	Total
	(n=51)	(n=214)	(n=88)	(n=65)	(n=43)	(n=13)	(n=472)
Less than $100	3.9%	41.1%	39.8%	44.4%	34.9%	30.8%	36.4%
Up to $300	9.8	18.7	28.4	25.4	16.3	23.1	20.3
Up to $500	39.2	30.4	22.7	23.8	34.9	30.8	29.4
Up to $2,500	19.6	4.7	5.7	3.2	9.3	15.4	7.0
$2,501 - $5,000	21.6	4.7	1.1	1.6	4.7	0.0	5.3
Over $5,000	5.9	0.5	2.3	1.6	0.0	0.0	1.5
Totals[1]	100.0	100.1	100.0	100.0	100.1	100.1	99.9

[1] Totals may not equal 100.0% due to rounding.

Source: National Institute of Governmental Purchasing, *Results of the 1989 Procurement Research Survey*. Falls Church, VA: NIGP, P. 20.

essarily guarantee either efficiency or impartiality:

> Government personnel still can use suppliers to participate behind the scenes in writing the specifications or wiring the award. Sealed prices submitted by offerors still can be made available to favored contractors. Awards can be made to other than the "right" offerors, based on subjective valuation of responsibility or ability to perform. Contracts may be awarded as sole source by breaking the total task into smaller parts, each costing less than the bidding ceiling. Bid rigging is still possible.

These concerns about exclusive reliance on price for award of contracts have some legitimacy and explain why the trend is toward procurement decision making techniques (formal and informal) that emphasize both cost and quality. The new conventional wisdom is that any system that disregards either cost or quality violates the principles of sound public purchasing.

Preference policies The controversy about what stimulates competition is nowhere more obvious than in the purchasing policies designed to promote social and economic goals. "Most favored customer" policies, according to *State and Local Government Purchasing*, are generally regarded as "anticompetitive and self-defeating" by professional purchasing groups, primarily because they "have the effect of setting artificial floors on prices and of fixing prices at one level." Many observers believe these policies violate most of the public purchasing principles, most notably competition, efficiency, and impartiality.

Opponents of set-asides lauded the U.S. Supreme Court's *Richmond* v. *Croson* ruling (January 23, 1989) against the City of Richmond (Virginia) minority set-aside program, although the ruling did not declare all set-asides unconstitutional. The Richmond policy required white prime contractors who

were awarded city construction contracts to subcontract at least 30 percent of the dollar value of the prime contract to one or more minority business enterprises. The Court rejected the policy primarily on the grounds that the 30 percent figure was not based on data reflecting the eligible pool of minority suppliers.[4]

Proponents of vendor preference policies vehemently maintain that they promote both competition and impartiality. Without such policies, they argue, little change will occur in the current vendor pool, the development of new business firms will be stunted, and in the long term competition will suffer and government will pay more for goods and services than it might otherwise.[5]

The proportion of governments legally requiring vendor preferences policies is actually quite small. A 1989 survey by the National Institute of Governmental Purchasing reported that vendor preferences for locally based businesses are legally required in only 13 percent of all governmental jurisdictions (see Table 2.4). The proportion requiring vendor preferences for small or disadvantaged businesses is slightly higher, nearly 18 percent. "Buy American" preferences are required in 22 percent of the jurisdictions responding to the NIGP survey.[6] Surprisingly, set-asides for Minority Business Enterprise (MBE) and Women Business Enterprise (WBE) programs are required in only 13 percent of the jurisdictions surveyed by NIGP. When asked about the effects of the *Richmond* v. *Croson* decision, 61 percent of the jurisdictions with these set-aside requirements claimed the decision had no impact on their program; only 9 percent said the *Richmond* decision caused their MBE program to be suspended. But a number of critics of this ruling say these figures are far too conservative.[7]

Most vendor preference policies provide for the vendor preference rule to go into effect only in the case of tie bids (see Table 2.5). This policy does not violate the princi-

Table 2.4
Status of Vendor Preference Policies by Type of Government

			Type of Government				
Type of Preference/Status	Federal/State Provincial Central (n = 65)	City Municipality Town/Village (n = 272)	County Region Parish (n = 120)	School System University College (n = 85)	State Provincial Special Authority (n = 57)	City County Health (n = 18)	Total (n = 617)
Locally-based Businesses							
Not legally required & not practiced	55.4%	52.6%	57.5%	48.2%	52.6%	50.0%	53.2%
Not legally required, but practiced	23.1	37.5	33.3	31.8	31.6	33.3	33.7
Legally required	21.5	9.9	9.2	20.0	15.8	16.7	13.1
Totals[1]	100.0	100.0	100.0	100.0	100.0	100.0	100.0
Small or Disadvantaged Businesses							
Not legally required & not practiced	46.2	65.1	66.7	65.9	49.1	50.0	61.6
Not legally required, but practiced	16.9	20.6	20.8	20.0	26.3	16.7	20.6
Legally required	36.9	14.3	12.5	14.1	24.6	33.3	17.8
Totals[1]	100.0	100.0	100.0	100.0	100.0	100.0	100.0
Buy American							
Not legally required & not practiced	47.7	58.1	57.5	61.2	63.2	44.4	57.4
Not legally required, but practiced	9.2	25.7	24.2	11.8	14.0	27.8	20.7
Legally required	43.1	16.2	18.3	27.1	22.8	27.8	21.9
Totals[1]	100.0	100.0	100.0	100.1	100.0	100.0	100.0

[1] Totals may not equal 100.0% due to rounding.

Source: National Institute of Governmental Purchasing, *Results of the 1989 Procurement Research Survey*. Falls Church, VA: NIGP, P. 13–15.

Table 2.5
Procedure for Granting Vendor Preferences by Type of Government

Preference Given	Federal/State Provincial Central	City Municipality Town/Village	County Region Parish	School System University College	State Provincial Special Authority	City County Health	Total
Locally-based Businesses	(n=39)	(n=161)	(n=67)	(n=46)	(n=35)	(n=14)	(n=360)
Less than 5%	17.9%	27.3%	23.9%	26.1%	28.6%	8.3%	25.0%
5 - 10%	20.5	21.1	6.0	19.6	14.3	25.0	17.5
Over 10%	0.0	7.5	11.9	2.2	5.7	8.3	6.7
0% but limited competition	15.4	6.2	10.4	13.0	17.1	16.7	10.3
Tie bids or reciprocal	46.2	37.9	47.8	39.1	34.3	41.7	40.6
Totals[1]	100.0	100.0	100.0	100.0	100.0	100.0	100.1
Small or Disadvantaged Busines	(n=36)	(n=103)	(n=43)	(n=23)	(n=28)	(n=11)	(n=244)
Less than 5%	16.7	38.8	27.9	30.4	28.6	0.0	29.9
5 - 10%	11.1	17.5	16.3	13.1	35.7	45.4	19.3
Over 10%	5.5	4.9	11.6	0.0	3.6	18.2	6.1
0% but limited competition	25.0	17.5	23.3	26.1	21.4	18.2	20.9
Tie bids or reciprocal	41.7	21.3	20.9	30.4	10.7	18.2	23.8
Totals[1]	100.0	100.0	100.0	100.0	100.0	100.0	100.0
Buy American	(n=28)	(n=80)	(n=33)	(n=17)	(n=16)	(n=6)	(n=180)
Less than 5%	14.3	20.0	27.3	29.4	25.0	0.0	21.1
5 - 10%	21.4	12.5	9.0	5.9	12.5	16.7	12.8
Over 10%	10.7	18.8	18.2	5.9	12.5	16.7	15.6
0% but limited competition	28.6	26.2	27.3	17.6	12.5	50.0	25.5
Tie bids or reciprocal	25.0	22.5	18.2	41.2	37.5	16.7	25.0
Totals[1]	100.0	100.0	100.0	100.0	100.0	100.1	100.0

[1] Totals may not equal 100.0% due to rounding.

Source: National Institute of Governmental Purchasing, *Results of the 1989 Procurement Research Survey*. Falls Church, VA: NIGP, P. 3–15.

ple of competition, only of impartiality, although it may ultimately reduce the size of the vendor pool. The most controversial policies are those that set aside a certain percentage of government business for a class of vendors or limit bids for a certain percentage of products or services to a specific vendor group. But the NIGP reports that less than 5 percent of all jurisdictions use these "offensive" vendor techniques.

Type of Contract

Government choice of contract type, like its choice of contract award, can greatly affect business perceptions of the overall quality of government purchasing practices. From the government's perspective, the type of contract issued for a specific good or service may vary according to external market conditions, its own fiscal condition, and other economic and political realities.

The National Institute of Governmental Purchasing defines a contract as "a solemn agreement between parties, usually written, with binding legal and moral force; usually exchanging goods or services for money or other considerations." While contracts may be oral, the Uniform Commercial Code requires that contracts for amounts larger than $500 be written to be enforceable in a court of law.[8]

Definite- versus indefinite-quantity contracts Governments use two basic types of formal contracts.

As stated in *Alijan's Purchasing Handbook*, *definite-quantity contracts* (also known as open-market purchase contracts) "provide for specific quantities of items to be delivered at one time or for specific quantities to be delivered on a schedule over a stated time period." Governments use this type of contract less often than indefinite-quantity contracts primarily because it is difficult to estimate exact quantities in advance.

This contract can cause inefficiencies by under- or overpurchasing. Its major advantage is that it can lock in a specific price for a specific amount of time, which can be extremely efficient in an inflationary economy. These types of contracts are most often associated with fixed-price requirements (discussed later).

Indefinite-quantity contracts, more commonly known as term contracts, blanket orders, open-end contracts, or requirements contracts, "establish a source or sources of supply for a specified period of time and are usually characterized by an estimated or definite minimum quantity, with the possibility of additional requirements beyond the minimum, all at a predetermined unit price," according to the National Institute of Governmental Purchasing. This type of contract has some major advantages, from government's perspective. *State and Local Government Purchasing* says it can "reduce administrative costs by avoiding the highly repetitive activities involved in preparing and issuing IFBs on the same or similar items and receiving, handling, and evaluating the responses. Widespread use of term contracting permits handling larger volumes of purchases with fewer personnel."

Term contracting also has some benefits for vendors: "It represents business in volume and an opportunity to secure an increase in volume and an opportunity to secure an increase in sales that will be spread over a period of time, permitting the successful bidder to plan ahead. It also spares the supplier the administrative time and expense of repeatedly preparing and submitting quotations and bids." On the other hand, many governments have found that unless term contracts contain price adjustment criteria, they may not be attractive to business, especially in tight markets.

Fixed-price versus cost-reimbursement contracts Contracts are also classified by their treatment of price. *Fixed-price* *contracts* are based on an agreed-upon unit cost for a selected unit of a good or service (such as labor, pound, gallon, or mile). The National Institute of Governmental Purchasing's *Dictionary of Purchasing Terms* defines the different types of fixed-price contracts as follows:

1. *Firm fixed-price contract*: provides a firm price that is not subject to adjustment because of circumstances arising during the performance of the contract; maximum risk is borne by a contractor who has full responsibility for his/her costs and any resultant profit or loss.

2. *Firm fixed-price, level of effort contract*: provides a fixed dollar amount for a specified level of effort for a specified period of time for work which can only be described in general terms; usually suitable for research and development; payment is based on the level of effort expended rather than the results achieved.

3. *Fixed-price with economic adjustment contract*: provides a fixed price that can be adjusted upward or downward upon the occurrence of certain contingencies specified in the contract; e.g., materials costs, labor costs, etc.

4. *Fixed-price incentive contract*: provides for adjusting profit and the final contract price by a formula based on the relationship of final negotiated cost to total target cost; intended to encourage the contractor to effectively manage contract costs to the mutual benefit of both parties to the contract.

5. *Fixed-price price redetermination contract*: provides for a firm fixed-price for a stated period of time, after which the price may be redetermined for a subsequent period of time; provides for an equitable adjustment based on experience.

According to the Council of State Governments and the National Association of State Purchasing Officials, most state and local governments use fixed-price contracts for definite-quantity purchases, with construction and public works contracts (usually larger, longer-term contracts) having special provisions for modification and price changes. Likewise, most indefinite (term) contracts are fixed-price contracts with some provisions for price adjustments downward or upward.

Cost-reimbursement contracts are less common. According to the NIGP's *Dictionary of Purchasing Terms*, these contracts "provide for payment of incurred costs which are allowed under the contract; total cost is estimated for the purpose of obligating funds; a ceiling is established that the contractor may not exceed." NIGP recommends use of cost-reimbursement contracts "only when performance uncertainties do not permit accurate estimation of costs required by fixed-price contracts." The types of cost-reimbursement contracts are:

1. *Cost-reimbursement, cost contract*: provides for no fee for the contractor; particularly appropriate for research and development contracts with nonprofit educational institutions or other nonprofit organizations.

2. *Cost-reimbursement, cost-plus-award-fee contract*: provides for a base amount fee fixed at inception of a contract and an additional fee at the time of award which is based on a judgmental evaluation as to the amount necessary to motivate the contractor toward excellence.

3. *Cost-reimbursement, cost-plus-fixed-fee contract*: provides for payment of a negotiated fee that is fixed at the inception of the contract; the fee does not vary with the actual cost, but may be adjusted when there are changes in work to be performed; these contracts

permit contracting for work which otherwise presents too great a risk to contractors.

4. *Cost-reimbursement, cost-plus-incentive-fee contract*: provides for an initially negotiated fee to be adjusted later on the basis of a formula based on the relationship of total allowable costs to total target costs.

5. *Cost-reimbursement, cost sharing contract*: provides that the costs of performing the contract will be shared between the parties to the contract on agreed-upon portion of allowable costs, no fee is paid the contractor; generally used when the contractor may expect substantial compensating benefits.

Groups such as the National Association of State Purchasing Officials (NASPO) and the Council of State Governments advocate greater use of cost principles. They recommend that cost principles "should be used more extensively in connection with contracts for research and development, sole source requirements, professional services arrived at by negotiations and for determining contract price adjustments, and cancellation charges." They contend such practices would generate cost savings to both government and the vendor.

From government's perspective, the establishment of fair prices and cost-reimbursement schedules is often difficult and expensive. Such determinations require extensive surveys of catalogs, markets, and prices paid by other governments and private sector buyers, adding to the government's true cost of purchasing from the private sector. If the government's purchasing or finance personnel do not have the expertise to make these calculations, competition may suffer as the pool of interested vendors evaporates. As noted in Chapter 1, one of the major controversies in public purchasing today is the conflict between public and private sector

methods of applying cost-accounting principles.

Provisions for Protest and Appeal

The National Institute of Governmental Purchasing defines a *protest* as "a complaint about a governmental administrative action or decision brought about by a bidder or vendor to the appropriate administrative section, with the intention of receiving a remedial result." Not surprisingly, most vendor protests and appeals center on methods of awarding contracts and on price and cost calculations. Most commonly, vendors allege violation of two principles of purchasing: competition and impartiality.

Vendor violations Protests may involve improper vendor practices such as collusive bidding, bid rigging, and price fixing—all of which violate federal or state antitrust laws. The American Bar Association defines *collusive bidding* as "the response to bid invitation by two or more vendors who have secretly agreed to circumvent laws and rules regarding independent and competitive bidding." *Price fixing* is an "agreement between competitors to sell at the same price, to adopt formulas for the computation of selling prices, to maintain specified discounts, to maintain predetermined price differentials between different quantities, types, or sizes of products, or to set prices charged to purchasers by other means."

Public purchasing breaches Protests and appeals can also identify practices by public purchasing officials that violate ethics laws and codes. (See Table 2.6 for the Code of Ethics of the National Institute of Governmental Purchasing.) Unethical behavior can range from the most blatant forms of corruption such as bribery, kickbacks, and conflict-of-interest violations to practices such as "ordering an item from a vendor without

Table 2.6
Code of Ethics of the National Institute of Governmental Purchasing

The Institute believes and it is a condition of membership that the following ethical principles should govern the conduct of every person employed by any public sector procurement or materials management organization.

(1)   Seeks or accepts a position as head or employee only when fully in accord with the professional principles applicable thereto, and when confident of possessing the qualifications to serve under those principles to the advantage of the employing organization.

(2)   Believes in the dignity and worth of the services rendered by the organization and the social responsibilities assumed as a trusted public servant.

(3)   Is governed by the highest ideals of honor and integrity in all public and personal relationships in order to merit the respect and inspire the confidence of the organization and the public being served.

(4)   Believes that personal aggrandizement or personal profit obtained through misuse of public or personal relationships is dishonest and not tolerable.

(5)   Identifies and eliminates participation of any individual in operational situations where a conflict of interest may be involved.

(6)   Believes that members of the Institute and its staff should at no time or under any circumstances, accept directly or indirectly, gifts, gratuities or other things of value from suppliers.

(7)   Keeps the governmental organization informed, through appropriate channels, or problems and progress of applicable operations, but personally remains in the background by emphasizing the importance of the facts.

(8)   Resists encroachment on control of personnel in order to preserve integrity as a professional manager. Handles all personnel matters on a merit basis. Political, religious, racial, gender and age considerations carry no weight in personnel administration in the agency being directed or served.

(9)   Seeks or dispenses no personal favors. Handles each administrative problem objectively and emphatically without discrimination.

(10)   Subscribes to and supports the professional aims and objectives of the National Institute of Governmental Purchasing, Inc.

Source: National Institute of Government Purchasing, Falls Church, VA, 1991. Reprinted by permission of the National Institute of Government Purchasing.

requisitioning in the prescribed manner, creating emergency purchases in situations that are not, in fact, emergencies, or dividing requirements into smaller amounts to bring them below the dollar limit for which competition quotations or sealed competitive bidding is required," as stated in *State and Local Government Purchasing*.

In its *Identifying and Prosecuting Fraud and Abuse in State and Local Contracting*, the American Bar Association states that where effective bid protest and appeals procedures are in place, "there should be increased competition, decreased competition for collusion, and more effective identification of improprieties in the system."

Timing The National Association of State Purchasing Officials and the Council of State Governments recommend that "vendors need to be given the opportunity to appeal both at the point specifications are issued, and shortly after the award decision is made."

Protests and appeals at the *pre-bid* or *pre-award stage* usually involve challenges to the government's determination of a potential vendor's financial capacity, work (and supply) capacity, experience and past performance, ownership or control (for determination of preferred-customer status where required or permitted), and access to necessary equipment where relevant. Some legal experts, cited in the ABA book, recommend: "The governmental entity should have a structured appeals procedure that allows an applicant who is dissatisfied with the decision affecting his/her classification, the performance rating, or similar measures to bring the matter before the agency in an administrative process" in a timely fashion.

The vendor may also challenge the accuracy and comprehensiveness of government vendor mailing lists and official bidding lists, especially if his or her firm has been omitted, suspended, or removed from the list without cause. *State and Local Government Purchasing* says: "Rules should provide guidelines for suspension, debarment, and reinstatement, and should allow flexibility where the need for competition is a factor."

In the *immediate post-contract award period*, firms should have the right to protest or appeal any aspect of the contract decision, whether it be contract specifications, the contract award method, or the final choice of contractors.

In addition, vendors should be able to issue protests for disagreements arising *in the course of the contractual period*. These disagreements may involve differences in the interpretation of various contract clauses and conditions, most commonly changed clauses and clauses dealing with suspension of work,

termination, or default. As noted by Page in *Public Purchasing and Materials Management*, "there are a limitless number of occasions in which the contractor may believe she/he has a claim against the government. The contractor has a right, an obligation, to come forward with her/his claims whenever she/he feels one exists. . . . [But] government [also has the right] to make a claim against a contractor."

The proper forum for appeals and protests differs by type of government and type of complaint. Optimally, protest and appeals procedures should be clearly described in the jurisdiction's vendor manual.

Contract Compliance

As a measure of security, government proposals and contracts sometimes require bidders to obtain surety bonds. These bonds, as defined in *State and Local Government Purchasing*, are:

- *Bid bond* or bid security. This type "affords protection against a bid being withdrawn after bids have been opened. The amount of the bond required is either a proportion of the amount of the bid, usually 5 to 10 percent, or it may be a specific dollar amount. The security is retained until award of a contract, or if no award is made, until the bids may be withdrawn."
- *Performance bond*. These bonds "are invariably required for public works contracts and not infrequently on contracts for equipment and services. The bonds are furnished by a properly licensed surety company and provide for fulfillment of the contract obligations by others in the event of default by the successful bidder. The amount of a performance bond is usually 100 percent of the amount of the contract and may be reduced proportionately as performance under the contract moves forward successfully."

• *Payment bond.* These bonds are "used almost exclusively for construction contracts. They guarantee payments by the successful bidder to material suppliers and subcontractors. As a rule, the bond is equal to 100 percent of the amount of the contract, with provision for reduction as work progresses, and the contractor makes payments to his/her suppliers and subcontractors."

Apart from requiring bonds, governments monitor and evaluate products and performance periodically. Such contract-compliance efforts safeguard both government and competent, ethical vendors because they help promote the quality of the product or service delivered and the integrity of the vendor delivering it. As stated in *State and Local Government Purchasing*: "The public purchasing system, which has the duty to see that awards are made to suppliers capable of providing the items specified, is incomplete if it does not take measures to see that the items delivered conform to the purchase specifications."

Inspections Inspections by purchasing personnel and audits by appropriate agencies reduce the likelihood of collusion between suppliers and receiving personnel. They also make sure the public is getting what it is paying for. Inspection can take place at the point of delivery, but increasingly government quality-assurance programs call for inspection of the product and the vendor's quality-control program at the vendor's facility.

Testing Testing is essential at various stages of the procurement process and can either be done in-house or contracted out. The Council of State Governments estimates that 70 percent of the states have testing resources available to check on the compliance of products received. Testing programs can also aid in the development of specifications

or purchase descriptions before IFBs or RFPs are issued. Once bids or proposals are submitted, bidders' samples are tested to determine whether their products meet the specifications and to make comparisons of competing products.

Lack of inspection and testing procedures may promote inefficiencies in purchasing and ultimately limit competition. Legitimate, ethical contractors may become discouraged if they see no efforts by government to eliminate unethical, incompetent contractors from the vendor pool. However, inspection and testing programs will have a negative impact on competition and efficiency if they are excessively bureaucratic and untimely or delay prompt payment of legitimate vendors.

Timely Payments "Slow-paying jurisdictions adversely affect competition by reducing the number of vendors who are interested in bidding, or causing bidders to increase prices to cover the cost of doing business."[9] From a purchasing perspective, it is in government's best interest to pay promptly to promote competition. Model prompt payment laws have been developed for both the federal and state governments (see Appendix D for abstracts.) However, from a cash-management strategy, paying promptly may be viewed as inefficient if it necessitates actions that reduce interest earnings.

Audits Governments are responsible for evaluating whether the purchasing process meets the four principles of public procurement. Internal and external audits should examine whether the government's purchasing system is open. With the exception of unopened bids, bids awaiting award, and technical proprietary data, purchasing records should be available on request to any vendor or citizen. Detailed records documenting each step of a purchasing decision should be open for public inspection: establishment of specifications, solicitation of bidders, identification of bidders who responded, proposals of bidders who responded, name of the vendor who was awarded the contract, terms of the contract, and data about whether the vendor satisfactorily met the conditions of the contract. Such openness is important, according to the Council of State Governments, because it "keeps prospective bidders informed and more competitive and shows the public that the purchasing process is being carved out honestly [and impartially]."

Governments have become more aware of the critical role contractor-performance evaluations play in maintaining the integrity of the purchasing process. Increasingly, statutes delineate intricate systems for conducting fiscal and performance audits. Without a clearly specified process, government efforts to withhold payment to suppliers or to suspend, disbar, or prosecute vendors are less likely to be sustained by appeals boards or the courts. As part of the documentation process, many governments now rigorously and methodically maintain complaint records. These records help identify instances of nonconformance with specifications, noncompliance with contractual terms and conditions, and other types of complaints regarding suppliers' performance. The responsibility for recording and analyzing vendor-complaint records usually lies with the central purchasing office.

Authority for Purchasing Decisions

At all levels of government, the trend is toward centralized purchasing.[10] From the government's perspective, the major advantage of centralized purchasing is greater efficiency, but governments realize that centralization also promotes competition, impartiality, and openness. The National Association of State Purchasing Officials outlines the advantages of centralized purchasing as follows:

> An effective central purchasing program reduces the cost of government. It inspires

public confidence in government. It directly improves the quality and timeliness of services rendered by program departments and agencies. It is the government's meaningful link to the business community. It promotes honesty and integrity throughout governmental operations. It is an everwidening channel of intergovernmental cooperation.

The same group contends that centralized purchasing can help a government accomplish a number of management objectives. These objectives are:

- Unification of policy
- Consistency of purpose and decision-making
- Adherence to the spirit of rules and principles of public contracting
- Policy-sensitive planning and scheduling
- Timing to advantageous markets
- Management of assets through interagency transfer
- Unified cost-containment management of all aspects of the procurement spectrum
- Emphasis on the interest of the jurisdiction and its taxpayers with that interest vested in a single office

Purchasing officials maintain that, to be effective, the centralized purchasing function should be positioned high enough in the governmental organizational hierarchy to effectively carry out its legal responsibilities in a professional manner. As stated in *Alijan's Purchasing Handbook*, the public purchasing function should be structured so that:

- The purchasing director occupies a management level high enough to deal authoritatively with the requisitioning departments being served and the suppliers with whom the government contracts.
- Suppliers selling to government know the purchasing director has the authority

to make purchasing decisions and to award contracts.

- The central purchasing unit's authority is broad enough to permit delegation of certain purchases to the using department to capture the benefits of efficiency and economy.
- The purchasing unit is isolated from improper political pressures and influences.

Governments differ in where they place the purchasing function on the organizational chart. Usually, the larger the government the more likely purchasing is to be a separate department or organizational unit, with a larger and more professionally trained purchasing staff on board.

The degree to which the purchasing function is intertwined and coordinated with other financial management functions, including budgeting, risk management, cash management and investment, debt management, and accounting, can be critical to the overall success of the procurement process.

John L. Mikesell notes in *Fiscal Administration: Analysis and Applications for the Public Sector* that a good public budgeting system "will provide citizens with the quantity and quality of desired public services, at the desired times and locations, and at the least cost to society." Without a well-functioning procurement system in place, these budgetary goals cannot be met.

Budgetary cycle   A strong relationship exists between a government's budgetary cycle and its purchasing timetable. For example, if the government has a quarterly allocation system (meaning that there are expenditure limits for each quarter of the fiscal year), purchases must be scheduled as much as possible to coincide with that timetable. If purchasing cycles and business cycles are out of sync, both government and business can incur extra costs.

Purchasing decisions and schedules are critical to the success of the capital budgeting process. Capital expenditures are those that "purchase assets that are expected to provide services for several years." Purchasers must use special care when making capital expenditure decisions, says Mikesell, especially since the "price tag on most of these items tends to be high and purchases typically occur at irregular intervals." Capital expenditures frequently necessitate borrowing, which "alters the cash receipts and disbursements patterns of the spending unit for an extended period," according to Richard F. Wacht in *A New Approach to Capital Budgeting for City and County Governments*. Thus "the decision to acquire fixed assets or create new programs influences the patterns of cash flow into and through a [governmental entity] both immediately and for longer periods than almost any other kind of spending decision."

Cash management   Cash-management strategies must take into account certain public procurement laws, namely prompt payment statutes and regulations. These two activities often appear to work at crosspurposes, with cash management prevailing. Because "the cash manager seeks to control the largest fund pool for as long as possible by speeding collections and slowing outflows,"[11] prompt payment to businesses selling goods or services to government may not occur. The long-term danger of such a policy may be to shrink the vendor pool and reduce competition. It may cost government more in the long term than the revenue gained from delaying payment to a vendor. But if coordinated well, both purchasing and cash-management goals can be achieved.

Risk management   "The objective of risk management for any governmental entity is the conservation of its resources from accidental loss," according to Lauren Cragg and H. Felix Kloman in *Risk Management Today: A How-to Guide for Local Government*. Today "the most serious loss exposures in terms of both frequency and severity potentials are third party liabilities. These losses can arise out of intentional or unintentional torts, statutory liabilities, and contractual liabilities." The continuing erosion of governmental immunity and the increase in contracting out have made the linkage between purchasing and risk management imperative.[12]

Accounting Purchasing and accounting are intertwined in a number of ways. First, accounting rules and procedures can dictate whether a good or service has to be put out for bid. Relatedly, they can determine whether a purchase is classified as an operating expense or a capital expense, an important budgetary consideration.

Third, accounting and auditing activities play an integral role in determining whether government received the good or service it paid for and whether it was in the quantity and quality called for in the purchase order.

Fourth, accounting principles can affect the timing of purchases, which in turn affects cash management and investment strategies and debt administration. With the mandate to achieve a balanced budget at the end of the fiscal year, state and local governments may speed or delay purchases in order to achieve this goal.

Finally, the accounting and auditing function can play a key role in demonstrating to businesses that government can and will get rid of unsatisfactory and unethical contractors.[13]

The degree to which purchasing is well integrated into a government's overall financial management system is heavily contingent on the breadth of financial management training received by the individuals overseeing each component and the attitudes of a government's elected officials. Until recently, purchasing has not been as strongly emphasized in financial management curricula as the other elements.[14]

Furthermore, in many governments, purchasing personnel typically have not been included in the decision loop of financial management activities as much as one would expect in light of the integral role purchasing plays in each.

An increase in purchasing-related litigation has made elected officials reluctant to extend more authority to purchasing personnel. Even so, however, the long-term benefits of completely integrating purchasing into the government's financial management system may far outweigh any short-term liabilities.

Reluctance to extend authority Governments vary considerably in the award authority they vest in purchasing personnel (see Table 2.7). But contrary to purchasing professionals' prescriptions, the trend has been to restrict the award authority of purchasing personnel. A 1989 study by the National Institute of Governmental Purchasing found that fewer beginning-level buyers now have approval authority for purchases exceeding $5,000 than in 1985 (23 percent versus 29 percent). The award authority of chief procurement officers has also declined. In 1985, 52 percent of the CPOs had approval authority of $25,000 or more; by 1989 the percentage had declined to 48.

As the figures in Table 2.7 show, federal and state governments are more likely to delegate more authority to their purchasing personnel than are local governments. Among the local governments, counties and cities are more likely to delegate than school boards or special districts.

The National Institute of Governmental Purchasing attributes the restrictive trend to "a more conservative management philosophy and greater control." A quite plausible explanation for this pattern, again, may be the sharp rise in purchasing-related litigation. Elected officials, knowing they are ultimately accountable for purchasing decisions, are less likely to delegate authority for contract awards to staff.

Table 2.7
Dollar Approval Authority of Government Purchasing Officials by Type of Government

Employee Class/Authority Level	Federal/State Provincial Central	City Municipality Town/Village	County Region Parish	School System University College	State Provincial Special Authority	City County Health	Total
Chief Procurement Officer	(n=61)	(n=229)	(n=105)	(n=78)	(n=53)	(n=16)	(n=542)
Under $5,000	8.2%	38.9%	21.9%	12.8%	17.0%	37.5%	26.2%
$5,000 - $10,000	6.6	20.5	15.2	14.1	18.9	18.8	16.8
$10,001 - $15,000	3.3	3.1	6.7	5.1	1.9	6.3	4.1
$15,001 - $25,000	1.6	3.9	5.7	7.7	5.7	0.0	4.6
Over $25,000	21.3	6.1	5.7	9.0	15.1	18.8	9.4
Unlimited	59.0	27.5	44.8	51.3	41.5	18.8	38.9
Totals[1]	100.0	100.0	100.0	100.0	100.1	100.2	100.0
Procurement Officer/Supervisory Buyer	(n=61)	(n=128)	(n=76)	(n=54)	(n=46)	(n=15)	(n=380)
Under $5,000	13.1	48.4	36.8	37.0	30.4	46.7	36.6
$5,000 - $10,000	21.3	17.2	19.7	3.7	13.0	6.7	15.5
$10,001 - $15,000	3.3	6.3	5.3	7.4	4.3	13.3	5.8
$15,001 - $25,000	8.2	1.6	5.3	11.1	6.5	0.0	5.3
Over $25,000	54.1	26.6	32.9	40.7	45.7	33.3	36.8
Totals[1]	100.0	100.1	100.0	99.9	99.9	100.0	100.0
Buyer–Fully Qualified–Non-Supervisory	(n=57)	(n=162)	(n=95)	(n=58)	(n=40)	(n=13)	(n=425)
Under $3,000	21.1	46.3	31.6	31.0	35.0	61.5	36.9
$3,000 - $5,000	8.8	22.8	20.0	29.3	12.5	7.7	19.8
$5,001 - $10,000	22.8	13.6	12.6	19.0	17.5	7.7	15.5
$10,001 - $15,000	8.8	3.7	6.3	5.2	2.5	0.0	4.9
Over $15,000	38.6	13.6	29.5	15.5	32.5	23.1	22.8
Totals[1]	100.1	100.0	100.0	100.0	100.0	100.0	99.9

Type of Government

[1] Totals may not equal 100.0% due to rounding.

Table 2.7 (continued)

Employee Class/Authority Level	Type of Government						
	Federal/State Provincial Central	City Municipality Town/Village	County Region Parish	School System University College	State Provincial Special Authority	City County Health	Total
Beginning Level Buyer	(n = 58)	(n = 155)	(n = 88)	(n = 61)	(n = 47)	(n = 14)	(n = 423)
Under $1,000	32.8	48.4	36.4	45.9	53.2	42.9	43.7
$1,000 - $3,000	13.8	13.5	17.0	19.7	12.8	21.4	15.4
$3,001 - $5,000	19.0	18.7	17.0	19.7	14.9	21.4	18.2
$5,001 - $10,000	19.0	9.0	11.4	4.9	10.6	7.1	10.4
Over $10,000	15.5	10.3	18.2	9.8	8.5	7.1	12.3
Totals[1]	100.1	99.9	100.0	100.0	100.0	99.9	100.0

[1] Totals may not equal 100.0% due to rounding.

Source: National Institute of Governmental Purchasing, *Results of the 1989 Procurement Research Survey*. Falls Church, VA: NIGP, P. 9–12.

The same restrictive trend appears in emergency and protest and appeal situations. While some businesses see this trend as making the purchasing process more political and inefficient, elected officials see it as the fulfillment of their legal mandate to represent and protect the public at large. The whole purchasing process has become more complex for both vendors and governments, largely because of differences in purchasing policies and procedures at the federal, state, and local levels.

AN OVERVIEW OF THE FEDERAL PROCUREMENT SYSTEM

The federal procurement system is extremely complex; it is much more confusing to potential vendors than state or local procurement systems (see Figure 2.1).[15] Authority is splintered, and the number of statutes, rules, and regulations governing different aspects of purchasing is overwhelming even to experienced vendors and public purchasing professionals.[16] Breaking into this intricate maze requires knowledge, skill, and no small amount of persistence.

How to Sell to the Federal Government

In *Doing Business with the Federal Government* the U.S. General Services Administration (GSA) advises businesses of the complexity of the federal procurement system: "In general, a firm must know where in the Federal structure to market its products, how to make itself and its products known, how and where to obtain the necessary forms and papers, and how to bid for the opportunity to sell specific goods or services." Some federal agencies are bigger buyers than others (see Figure 2.2).

Federal regulations When selling to the federal government one must know that three sets of regulations issued by GSA apply to all procurement and supply programs: (1) The Federal Acquisition Regulation (FAR), maintained jointly by GSA, the Department of Defense (DOD), and the National Aeronautics and Space Administration (NASA); (2) the Federal Information Resources Management Regulations (FIRMR); and (3) the Federal Property Management Regulations (FPMR).

FAR is the primary regulation followed by all federal executive agencies when acquiring supplies and services with appropriated funds. This regulation contains uniform policies and procedures governing acquisitions (including construction) through purchase or lease, regardless of whether the supplies or services already exist or must be created, developed, demonstrated, and evaluated. It is published as Chapter 1 of Title 48 of the *Code of Federal Regulations.* Regulations affecting individual agencies appear in subsequent chapters of Title 48.

FIRMR outlines the system for administering government-wide regulations on the management, acquisition, and use of automated data processing, telecommunications resources, and records management. The regulations are published in the *Federal Register* and consolidated in the *Code of Federal Regulations* in Title 41, Chapter 201.

GSA's Federal Property Management Regulations dictate policies and procedures for management of government property, travel by federal employees, defense materials, public buildings and space, supply and procurement, public utilities, transportation utilization and disposal of property, and other programs and activities of GSA. These regulations are published in the *Federal Register* and in the *Code of Federal Regulations*, Title 41, Chapter 101. The *Code of Federal Regulations* can be purchased from the U.S. Government Printing Office, Washington, D.C. 20402.

Figure 2.1
The Federal Acquisition Process

* Lists all military procurement invitations of $10,000 or more; all NASA invitations over $25,000; and all other procurement invitations of $5,000 or more.

Source: Abstracted from William Thybony, *Government Contracting Based on the Federal Acquisition Regulation (FAR) and the Competition in contracting Act of 1984*. Reston, VA: Thybony, Inc., 1987.

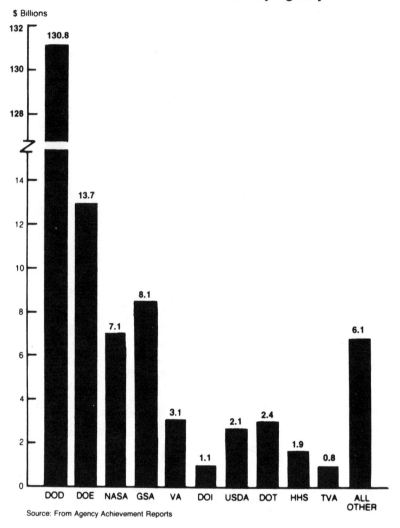

Figure 2.2
Federal Procurement Totals by Agency

$ Billions

Source: From Agency Achievement Reports

DOD—Department of Defense
DOE—Department of Energy
NASA—National Aeronautics and Space Administration
GSA—General Services Administration
VA—Veterans Administration
DOI—Department of Interior
USDA—U.S. Department of Agriculture
DOT—Department of Transportation
HHS—Department of Health and Human Services
TVA—Tennessee Valley Authority

Source: U.S. Small Business Administration, *Women Business Owners: Selling to the Federal Government,* Washington, D.C.: U.S. Small Business Administration, Office of Women's Business Ownership, June 1990, p. 1.

Two classifications of purchases   Federal purchases fall into two broad classifications: (1) Those for general use (e.g., office equipment and space, transportation and janitorial services, computers, telephones) and (2) those for special, mission-oriented applications (e.g., special ink for printing U.S. currency, weapons systems for the armed services).

All agencies need general-use items. The General Services Administration and the Defense Logistics Agency (DLA) serve as the primary purchasing agents for these goods. Specialized items, on the other hand, are purchased by the agencies needing them.

Guides and information   Each federal agency making specialized purchases publishes its own how-to guide for vendors outlining the items the agency purchases, describing bidding practices, delineating how to get on its vendor mailing list, giving addresses and phone numbers of procurement offices, and identifying special programs for small and disadvantaged, women-owned, and minority-owned businesses.

Any firm wishing to sell to the federal government should consult the *Commerce Business Daily* (CBD), published Monday through Saturday by the U.S. Department of Commerce. This publication tells which federal government agencies are planning to buy products or services and identifies persons to contact for more information (see Figure 2.3). Specifically, the CBD contains requests for bids and proposals for planned civilian and military purchases of $10,000 or more; procurements reserved for small businesses; contractors seeking subcontractors; research and development leads; and opportunities to sell to foreign governments.

The CBD does not list procurements that are classified for reasons of national security, perishable items, certain utility services, items required within fifteen days, items placed under existing contracts, personal professional services, services from educational institutions, items made only from foreign sources, or items not to be given advance publicity as determined by the Small Business Administration.

The *Commerce Business Daily* is available on a subscription basis from the Superintendent of Documents, U.S. Government Printing Office, Washington, D.C. 20402-9371, phone number (202) 783-3238. It is also available for review at International Trade Administration Offices, GSA Business Service Centers (BSCs), Small Business Administration field offices, Department of Commerce field offices, and at local public libraries. (See Appendix E for addresses and phone numbers of these offices; the ITA offices are listed in Appendix G.)

The Department of Commerce also publishes the biweekly *Business America*. This magazine provides helpful interpretations of government policies and programs that may affect international business decisions, tells of export opportunities, and announces trade conferences. It is also available by subscription through the U.S. Government Printing Office.

Three Categories of Federal Procurement Programs

Federal buying programs fall into three broad categories: GSA procurement, military procurement, and procurement by other civilian agencies.

1. GSA Procurement   GSA buys, warehouses, and distributes common-use items throughout the federal government. DOD is GSA's largest customer. GSA has four major subdivisions:

a). Information Resources Management Services (IRMS), which is responsible for procurement, management, and use of automated data processing and

Figure 2.3
How to Read *Commerce Business Daily* Announcements of Purchasing Opportunities

---

Commerce Business

Daily is a unique Federal procurement publication charged by law with publicizing:

● All proposed procurements of $25,000 or more by **Federal Agencies**

• All Federal Contract Awards of $25,000 or more for the benefit of potential subcontractors

• **Foreign Government Procurements**

Most **Commerce Business Daily** synopses are somewhat compressed to save space. However, they're easy to read once you get used to the format and abbreviations.

This sample entry, taken from the **Supplies and Equipment** section, is typical of the format—though, of course, the contents are much too wide-ranging to be typified by a single example:

All symbols used are explained in each issue. For example:

⬤ The Procurement item is 100 percent set aside for small business concerns.

★ This synopsis is published for informational purposes to alert potential subcontractors and/or suppliers of the proposed procurement. Additional proposals are not solicited.

NUMBERED NOTES are published only on the first working day of each week. The pages containing the "notes" should be retained for reference.

There are 96 subject codes used in Commerce Business Daily.

The number in parenthesis is the Julian Date indicating when this item was edited. It is not part of the synopsis.

★ 10--SWITCH ASSY: NSN 1R01095-00-560-0806 DA—Part Nos. 61A107D66 & 3554173-605—175 ea—Issuing Order N00383-77-A-7501-0650 on 17 May 78 with McDonnell Douglas Corp., Douglas Acft. Co., Long Beach, CA. See note 46.
⬤ 10--FIRING LANYARD—Used on the Multiple Bomb Rack of the Various Acft.—NSN 1RM1095-00-151-4385 BX—Navair Drawing No. 292AS110—8611 ea—East & West Coast Destinations—S8SA IFB N00383-B-0417—Bid opening 12 Jun 78. See note 42. (129)
Navy Aviation Supply Office, 700 Robbins Ave., Philadelphia, PA 19111

Common abbreviations used

IFB	Invitation for Bid
RFP	Request for Proposal
RFTP	Request for Technical Proposals
RFQ	Request for Quotation
P/R	Purchase Request
P/N	Part Number
Sol	Solicitation
PIN	Pre-Invitation Notice
NSN	National Stock Number
ASPR	Armed Services Procurement Regulations
FPR	Federal Procurement Regulations
NSNA	No Stock Number Assigned
FSN	Federal Stock Number
o/a	On or About
BOD	Bid Opening Date
BOA	Basic Ordering Agreement
IAW	In Accordance With
NLT	No later than
PED	Project Engineering Development
SBSA	Small Business Set Aside

AGENCY TO CONTACT for bid documents and information.

Note: In cases where several synopses from the same agency are grouped together (as in sample), the address is only run once after the last item and separated from other entries by horizontal "spacer" lines.

Source: U.S. Small Business Administration, *Women Business Owners: Selling to the Federal Government*, Washington, D.C.: U.S. Small Business Administration, Office of Women's Business Ownership, June 1990, p. 5.

telecommunications equipment, software, and services.

b). Public Buildings Service (PBS), whose activities include the design and construction of buildings, the planning of space, interior design, leasing of offices, and maintenance and security of buildings, among others.

c). Federal Supply Service (FSS), which is responsible for supplying thousands of common-use items ranging from paper and paper clips to office and photographic supplies, laboratory equipment, furniture, appliances and cars, vans, trucks, and buses.

d). Federal Property Resources Service (FPRS), which is responsible for disposal of federal real property determined to be surplus to the needs of the federal government.

A firm interested in selling to a GSA program can obtain more information by contacting any of the twelve GSA Business Service Centers (see list in Appendix E). BSCs provide information on current bidding opportunities and have business counselors available to assist entrepreneurs in their search for federal contracts. These centers issue solicitation forms and bidder mailing list application forms, furnish invitations for bids and federal standards and specifications to prospective bidders, maintain a current display of bidding opportunities, receive and safeguard bids, provide bid-opening facilities, and furnish copies of publications designed to assist business representatives in selling to the federal government. BSCs also play key roles in promoting GSA's small business set-aside program and its small and disadvantaged business subcontracting programs, and in identifying and recruiting minority and women-owned firms.

2. Military Procurement Firms interested in selling to the military should obtain the *Selling to the Military* guide for sale by the Superintendent of Documents, U.S. Government Printing Office, Washington, D.C. 20402. General-use military procurement is handled by the Defense Logistics Agency. Typical items DLA buys include food, clothing, textiles, fuel and petroleum products and services, medical and dental equipment, construction equipment, and automotive equipment (see Appendix E for addresses of the six DLA supply centers). DLA publishes its own guides for vendors: *How to Do Business with DLA, An Introduction to DLA*, and *An Identification of Commodities Purchased by the DLA*, among others. These are available from the Public Affairs Office, DLA, Cameron Station, 5010 Duke St., Alexandria, VA 22314.

Specialized military purchases are coordinated by the Department of Defense. The Assistant Secretary of Defense for Acquisition and Logistics is responsible for the purchase of weapons systems as well as procurement policy and production planning. While each of the three military services (Air Force, Army, Navy) is authorized to purchase certain specialized items, purchases are coordinated by the Assistant Secretary's office. Defense contracts are managed by the Defense Contract Administration Services. DCAS has eleven regional offices. DOD acquisition policies and procedures are spelled out in the FAR and the DOD supplement (DFAR) to the FAR. DOD also publishes a *Guide to the Defense Acquisition Regulation*. All these documents are available from the U.S. Government Printing Office. An excellent guide for businesses on how to compete for and manage defense contracts is Sammet and Green's *Defense Acquisition Management*.

3. Civilian agency procurement This third category is highly decentralized. Regional and field offices often purchase their own supplies; however, GSA procures common-use supplies. Federal agencies that make substantial open-market purchases are the departments of Agriculture, Commerce, Health and Human Services, Housing and Urban Development, Justice, Labor, State, Transportation, Treasury, and Veterans Affairs. Independent or quasi-independent agencies that buy a sizable amount from the private sector are the Agency for International Development, Environmental Protection Agency, NASA, National Archives and Records Administration, Tennessee Valley Authority, and United States Postal Service. The addresses of procurement divisions within each of these agencies can be found in GSA's *Doing Business with the Federal Government*, available from the U.S. Government Printing Office. Each of these agencies also has an Office of Small and Disadvantaged Business Utilization (see Appendix E for a list).

The U.S. Small Business Administration and the Department of Commerce's Minority Development Agency have special missions to help small, women- and minority-owned firms. Minority Business Development Centers promote the participation of federal, state, and local governments in programs designed to develop strong minority businesses (see Appendix E for a list). These centers also offer management and technical assistance to minority firms upon request. The SBA frequently publishes guides to assist firms in selling to the federal government. An excellent example is the SBA Office of Women Business Ownership's *Women Business Owners: Selling to the Federal Government* guide. These guides generally contain standard federal bidder mailing list application forms along with a number of other forms (see Appendix F for these sample forms).

Entities Involved in Federal Contracting

No single identifiable unit bears responsibility for all dimensions of procurement; purchasing is not highly centralized. The purchasing-related office located highest in the federal organizational hierarchy is the Office of Federal Procurement Policy (OFPP) within the Office of Management and Budget. OFPP is charged with establishing a system of uniform procurement policies and regulations throughout the executive branch (but not for the legislative or judicial branches).

A large number of other federal agencies and offices also have major responsibility for various aspects of the purchasing process. Page, in *Public Purchasing and Materials Management*, identifies these other actors as:

1. The agency comptroller and budget officer, who controls the availability of operating and acquisition funds and who monitors in detail the spending out of the program.

2. The agency inspector general, who conducts audits and investigations relating to the programs and operations of the agency and recommends actions to promote economy and efficiency and to prevent and detect fraud.

3. Authorizing, appropriating, and oversight committees of the Congress, who expect to be kept informed of problems and who reserve the right to approve reprogramming.

4. The General Accounting Office, an arm of Congress, which conducts external audits, prepares cost-effectiveness studies, critiques procedures and monitors cost overruns.

5. The Defense Contract Audit Agency, which conducts internal audits of purchasing, enforces the truth-in-negotiations concept, and adjudicates price reduction, among other things (for activities in the Department of Defense).

6. The Office of Management and Budget (OMB), which approves the budget, controls the apportionment of funds for acquisition, monitors obligation rates, and examines purchase requirements.

7. The Small Business Administration, which may actually contract, and then subcontract, work it sees suited to small

business; it can refer firms and arrange set-asides of contracting opportunities.

8. The Cost Accounting Standards Board, which promulgates accounting standards to be followed by contractors and subcontractors and requires disclosure of accounting practices.

9. The Board of Contract Appeals, which resolves contract disputes and breaches of contract.

10. The U.S. Court of Claims and the district courts, which render judgment upon claims against the United States founded upon any express or implied contract with the government.

In addition to the splintered authority at the federal level, the number of statutes, rules, and regulations governing different aspects of purchasing is overwhelming, even to experienced vendors and public purchasing professionals.

Principles of Federal Contracting

In reviewing statutes, regulations, and court rulings, William Thybony in a 1987 book for the National Institute of Governmental Purchasing, has identified thirty principles that form the backbone of federal government contracting policies and procedures:

1. The power of the United States to contract is based on the general and implied powers contained in the Constitution of the United States.

2. The President of the United States, as the nation's Chief Executive Officer, is responsible for government purchasing functions.

3. Upon entering a contract, the government becomes subject to the rule of federal law as a private individual.

4. The U.S. government as a contractor is not liable for its sovereign acts.

5. No contract or purchase on behalf of the United States can be made unless it is authorized by law or is under an appropriation adequate to its fulfillment; a contract

liability expires when the appropriation is exhausted.

6. Expenditures or contract obligations in excess of funds appropriated are prohibited.

7. Federal agencies may make use of funds only for the purpose appropriated, in the absence of specific authority for another purpose.

8. No contractor can be required to perform a government contract in a manner prohibited by law or in response to coercion or promised reward by a government official or employee.

9. No official or employee of the government may give away any vested right of the government.

10. The government contracting officer is the agent of the government under any government contract. His or her authority is limited; a government contracting officer may bind the government only to the extent of his or her actual authority, whether it be expressed or implied; authority may be implied from a duty imposed upon the government agent or from some express authority given to him or her.

11. The risk of dealing with a government agent not authorized to act is on the contractor; unlike a private contractor, when a government agent does not have actual authority to act, the government is not bound by his or her acts.

12. Full and open competition is required, except within seven limited statutory exceptions.

13. Competitive procedures consist of sealed bidding and competitive proposals.

14. Property and services are to be acquired of the requisite quality, within the time needed, and at the lowest reasonable cost.

15. Fraud and waste are not condoned.

16. Redundant administrative requirements placed on contractor and federal procurement officials are to be eliminated.

17. The government relies upon the private enterprise system to supply its needs, except where it is in the national interest for the government to provide directly the products or services it uses.

18. Generally, in contracting by negotiation, written or oral discussion are conducted with responsible offerors within a competitive range, price, and other factors considered.

19. Contract awards are made to responsible sources whose offers are most advantageous to the United States considering (a) only price and price-related factors in sealed bidding and (b) only price and the other factors included in the solicitation in contracting by negotiation.

20. Supplies and services are purchased from responsible sources at prices fair and reasonable to both the government and the contractor.

21. Normally, reasonableness of price is based on adequate price competition (forces of competition in the marketplace) and is determined by price analysis.

22. Generally, in negotiated procurements exceeding $100,000 where price has not been based on the competitive forces of the market place, offerors are required to submit cost or pricing data to assure reasonableness of price or cost estimates and to form a basis for cost analysis.

23. Contracts are priced separately and independently, and no consideration is given to losses or profits realized or anticipated in the performance of other contracts.

24. Contracts are awarded only to those (a) responsive to the government's requirements, and (b) technically and financially able to perform.

25. Government contracts promote equal employment opportunities for all persons, regardless of race, color, religion, sex, or national origin.

26. Government contracting promotes small business and small disadvantaged firms; it also promotes women-owned and minority-owned business.

27. U.S. domestic source products are preferred over foreign products; products produced by the blind, severely handicapped, native Americans, and prisoners are promoted.

28. Fair dealing and equitable relationships with the private sector are fostered.

29. Payments in a timely manner, and only for value received, are to be ensured [see Appendix D for a Summary of Federal Prompt Pay Regulations.]

30. Legal and administrative remedies provide for fair and equitable treatment of the contracting parties.

Shortcomings of the Federal System

In spite of numerous attempts to improve the federal procurement process, it remains complex. As Thybony suggests, this complexity has resulted in fewer prospective sources of supply, decreased competition, and higher costs to the taxpayer. Private contractors are often intimidated by the size of solicitations and contracts, bewildered by the variety and perplexities of contractual requirements, and frustrated with excessive and duplicative reporting requirements. Contracts often create needless and costly paperwork and documentation; they frequently contain unnecessary, disparate, and confusing restrictions in addition to ambiguous descriptions of government technical and quality requirements. Long, unclear, and tortuous contract clauses lead to acceptance without risk analysis as well as inconsistent interpretations. The process holds the potential for misunderstanding between the contracting parties and invites protests, disputes, and contract claims, all of which results in adverse public opinion.

AN OVERVIEW OF STATE PROCUREMENT SYSTEMS

State purchasing systems are much more centralized than the federal government's. A survey by the National Association of State Purchasing Officials shows that all but one state (Mississippi) has some form of centralized purchasing. However, in forty-six states certain departments or agencies may be exempted from centralized purchasing requirements. Most commonly exempted are agencies in the legislative and judicial branches, state colleges and universities, and state highway and transportation departments.

The Structure of State Purchasing Systems

The NASPO survey, reported in detail on a state-by-state basis in *State and Local Government Purchasing*, shows that statutes, rules or regulations, or administrative procedures affirm a management role for central purchasing in forty-three states. The specific responsibilities of central purchasing differ from state to state. In forty-nine states, for example, central purchasing has the final responsibility for the Invitation for Bids. In thirty-three states central purchasing has the authority for acquiring, or approving contracts for, professional services required by other state agencies. In thirty-four states the central purchasing unit has the authority to send back purchase requisitions on the basis of need or quality. In forty-six states central purchasing can void a contract that is entered into contrary to statutes, rules, or regulations.

States vary in the delegation authority they give their central purchasing units. All set dollar thresholds allowing agencies to obtain their own quotes locally. In thirty-two states central purchasing can refer bids to the using agency for its review and recommendations. Central purchasing staffs can also be assigned to interact with local governments. In forty-five states central purchasing offices have the authority to assist local governments, formally or informally, with specifications, mailing lists, and other relevant activities.

Central purchasing units are frequently assigned responsibility for keeping records of the overall dollar volume of purchases issued by them and delegated agencies (twenty-eight states). Many state central purchasing agencies are just getting around to automation. In 1987, when the survey was taken, only sixteen states had automated systems tracking dollars spent by units produced; twenty could track dollars spent by type of contract. The figure is probably much higher for each today.

Bidding procedures Most states have specific written criteria outlining bidding requirements and procedures and other forms of contracting. For example:

- 46 states publicly open sealed bids
- 21 have written procedures for holding pre-bid conferences
- 30 have provisions authorizing confidentiality of certain types of information
- 40 specify criteria for including applicants on bidder lists
- 44 have written criteria for suspending or debarring bidders from the list
- 42 spell out criteria for deleting inactive bidders from their bid lists
- 47 have written procedures for handling sole source providers
- 49 have written procedures for handling emergency purchases
- 49 have written criteria outlining the conditions under which competitive bidding may be waived

All fifty states set specific dollar amounts above which sealed bids must be used. All have criteria for determining bidder responsibility and bid responsiveness; all can reject any or all bids in whole or in part. Furthermore, all list legal requirements for handling mistakes in bids.

The trend is for states to take into account more than just price in determining the low bidder; forty-four report they more frequently take into account the cost of supplies, energy, parts, warranties, and other costs of owning and operating the product than five years ago. Almost all (forty-eight) consider whether sales and service of a manufacturer's product can be rendered locally when choosing between bidders. Thirty-eight states permit use of two-step or multistep bidding, a process that builds in consideration of more than price.

States have split in the detail of their bid specifications: thirteen increased and sixteen decreased use of detailed design specs. Only fourteen increased use of brand name or equal specifications; twenty-two increased reliance on qualified products lists. A much higher number now use performance functional specifications of some type (forty-one states).

Contracts   More states use indefinite-rather than definite-quantity contracts. In their IFBs all include specific, approximate, or estimated quantities expected to be purchased. Forty-three have provisions in their indefinite-quantity contracts that allow for renewal without rebidding at the end of the designated time period, but of these fewer than half (twenty) report that these extensions occur "often." Forty-three states permit economic price adjustments in indefinite-quantity contracts; thirty-eight of those states allow price adjustments both upward and downward. The usual period for an indefinite-quantity contract is one year (forty-eight states).

Monitoring vendors   States generally have fairly rigorous authority and procedures for monitoring vendors and their products and services. Nearly all (forty-seven) have a product testing program or use product testing; forty-one have materials inspection manuals or published guidelines. In twenty states the central purchasing office has its own inspectors to assist or supplement inspection of the products delivered to agencies. In forty-one states central purchasing maintains a record of vendor performance. Thirty-five states have a wide range of rem-

edies available by statute or regulation in the event of default or fraud by suppliers (replacement of item, suspension from bidding, recovery of payments, debarment as a supplier, or collection against the supplier's bond). Twenty-four states have an established format for reporting noncompetitive bidding or purchasing practices to the state attorney general.

Monitoring purchasing personnel   States are likely to have fairly explicit policies for monitoring and correcting inadequacies of government purchasing personnel. In thirty-one states statutes or regulations require that the purchasing program be subject to an independent audit. Fourteen states have a statutory board or commission whose primary responsibility is to oversee or enforce state purchasing procedures. Thirty states have conflict-of-interest statutes or regulations that apply specifically to the purchasing process; forty-two prohibit the central purchasing department and line agencies from making purchases on behalf of state employees.

Policy manuals   The need to develop clearly spelled-out policies and procedures has led a number of state central purchasing units to prepare written policy manuals (forty-eight), internal agency procedures manuals (forty-three), and vendor or how-to manuals (forty-three).

The design and implementation of state purchasing systems have been heavily influenced by the American Bar Association's Model Procurement Code for State and Local Governments. The ABA has reported that, as of July 1987, twelve states had adopted the code: Kentucky, Arkansas, Louisiana, Utah, Maryland, South Carolina, Colorado, Indiana, Virginia, New Mexico, Arizona, and Alaska.

An even greater number of states have been influenced by the statutory, regulatory, and purchasing practice recommendations presented in *State and Local Government Purchasing*. Almost all have also incorporated prompt pay recommendations or adopted the model statute developed by the Coalition for Prompt Payment (see Table 2.8).

How to Sell to State Governments

The National Association of State Purchasing Officials and The Council of State Governments' *How to Do Business with the States: A Guide for Vendors* (1990) is an excellent source for firms interested in selling to states. For each state government the publication reports whether a vendor's guide is available, the state's criteria for getting on its bidder mailing list, the address and phone number of the centralized procurement office, and whether the state has any set-aside programs. The publication identifies state agencies that are exempt by law from purchasing through the centralized purchasing office. For each state the publication also lists standards required for defining commodities, the type of procurement handled by the centralized procurement office (e.g., commodities, services, construction), other primary state agencies with centralized procurement authority, and the type of procurement handled by them (e.g., commodities, services, or construction).

In most states, all that is required to get on a state bidder mailing list is to complete a bidder-list application. A few states (Alaska, Idaho, Louisiana) also require a registration fee. Others (Arizona, Florida, Michigan, New Mexico, Ohio, Tennessee, Virginia, Washington) require registration with the state purchasing office. Firms wishing to sell to the state of Hawaii must watch the newspaper for announcements of state purchases in excess of $8,000.

Most states' bidder-list application forms are designed to determine the firm's legal status and its ability to fulfill contracts for an item, service, or project. Information on the form also helps officials determine whether a firm meets special definitions (woman-owned, minority-owned, handicapped-owned, small business, disadvantaged business, in-state firm).

Getting on a state's bidder (or vendor) list is just one step in the procurement process. Of equal importance is how long a firm stays on the list once it gets there. Firms should ask how a state updates and reconfigures its bidder list and how often the updating occurs. A firm should ask whether it needs to reapply annually or each time a new bid category is announced, or whether it remains on the list indefinitely. In some states a firm is removed from the vendor list if it fails to bid within a specified period of time or if its performance has been judged unsatisfactory. Firms should also inquire whether separate bidder mailing lists are maintained for different types of commodities, services, or equipment.

Detailed vendor guides delineating how to go about selling to state government are available in all states except Arkansas, Connecticut, Hawaii, Idaho, Indiana, Minnesota, Mississippi, Nevada, New Hampshire, North Dakota, Pennsylvania, Rhode Island, and Virginia. In those states, inquiries should be made to the central procurement office.

States with formal set-aside programs usually have an agency or division responsible for their administration. State set-aside programs often parallel those of the federal government and target small, disadvantaged, women-owned, minority-owned, and handicapped-owned businesses. Some also target vocational or prison-owned industries, firms in depressed areas of the state, or in-state firms (local preference regulations). The set-asides and vendor preference policies of each state appear in Tables 17 and 18 of the third edition of *State and Local Government Purchasing*.

For vendors doing business with a wide range of governments, the state purchasing system may be easier to deal with than the

Table 2.8
Summary of Key State Prompt Pay Provisions

State	Interest Penalty	Automatic Interest	Local Government	Subcontractors	Pending Legislation
Alabama	Legal amount currently charged by the state	No	No	No	No
Alaska	1.5% per month	No	No	No	No
Arizona	10% per year	No	Yes	Yes	No
Arkansas	8% per year	No	No	No	No
California	0.25% per day—small businesses and nonprofits. 8.874% per year for fiscal year 1988-89 — other businesses.	No	No	No	No
Colorado	1% per month	No	No	Yes	No
Connecticut	1% per month	No	No	Yes	No
Delaware	Not to exceed 12% per year	No	No	No	No
District of Columbia	1% per month	Yes	N/A	No	No
Florida	1% per month	Yes	No	Yes	Yes
Georgia	No law				Yes
Hawaii	12% per year	No	Yes	Yes	No
Idaho	12% per year (As of May 1989)	No	Yes	No	No
Illinois	2% per month — State 1% per month — Local	No	Yes	No	No
Indiana	1% per month	No	Yes	Yes	No
Iowa	1% per month	No	No	Yes	No
Kansas	1.5% per month	No	Unified school districts, libraries and community colleges	No	Yes
Kentucky	1% per month	Yes	No	No	No
Louisiana	Pursuant to Civil Code Article 2924(B)(3) (0.05% per day as of May 1989)	No	No	Yes	Yes
Maine	Normal late charge levied by vendor	Yes	No	No	No
Maryland	As specified in 11-107 of the Courts Article (10% per year thru June 30, 1989; 12% per year after July 1, 1989)	No	No	No	No
Massachusetts	Equal to discount rate charged by Federal Reserve Bank of Boston. As of May 1989 6% per year	No	No	Yes	Yes
Michigan	0.75% + 0.75% per month	Yes	No	No	
Minnesota	1.5% per month	No	Yes	No	No
Mississippi	1.5% per month	Yes	Yes	Yes	No

State	Interest Penalty	Automatic Interest	Local Government	Subcontractors	Pending Legislation
Missouri	3 percentage points above the Federal Reserve Prime Rate (14.5% per year as of May 1989)	No	No	No	No
Montana	0.05% per day	No	Yes	No	No
Nebraska	Rate specified in Sec. 45-104.01 (14% per year as of May 1989)	No	No	No	No
Nevada	Rate quoted by 3 financial institutions for 90-day certificate of deposit (7.25% per year as of May 1989)	No	Yes	Yes	No
New Hampshire	No law				Yes
New Jersey	Specified by State Treasurer (11% per year as of May 1989)	No	No	No	Yes
New Mexico	1.5% per month	No	No	Yes	No
New York	10.2% per year until Sept. 1989	Yes	No	Yes	Yes
North Carolina	1% per month	No	Yes	Yes	No
North Dakota	1.75% per month	No	Yes	Yes	No
Ohio	11% per year thru 1989	Yes	No	No	No
Oklahoma	5.95% per year thru July 1, 1989	No	No	No	No
Oregon	No more than 2/3 of 1% per month or 8% per year	No	No	No	No
Pennsylvania	11% thru 1989	Yes — for qualified small businesses	No	Yes	Yes
Rhode Island	Equal to prime rate	Yes	No	Yes	No
South Carolina	15% per year	No	No	No	No
South Dakota	1.5% per month	No	Yes	Yes	No
Tennessee	1.5% per month	No	No	Yes	Yes
Texas	1% per month	Yes — political subdivisions No — state agencies	Yes	Yes	No
Utah	Equal to IRS rate on refunds + 2%	No	No	Yes	No
Vermont	No law				Yes
Virginia	Equal to prime rate	No	Yes	No	No
Washington	1% per month	No	Yes	No	No
West Virginia	6% per year	No	No	No	No
Wisconsin	12% per year as of May 1989	No	No	No	No
Wyoming	1.5% per month	No	Yes	No	No

Source: Coalition for Prompt Pay, *Guide to Getting Paid Promptly by State and Local Agencies,* 3150 Spring Street, Fairfax, VA 22031, 703/273-7200: Coalition for Prompt Pay, 1989, pp. 8–9. Reprinted by permission of Coalition for Prompt Pay.

1. *Applies to payments for most goods and services.*
2. *Limited statutes.*
3. *May be covered under separate statutes.*
4. *In draft stage; not yet introduced.*

federal procurement system but more complex than local government procurement systems, depending on their size and the degree of intergovernmental contracting.

AN OVERVIEW OF THE LOCAL PROCUREMENT SYSTEM

The purchasing policies and procedures of local governments vary greatly within the same state and metropolitan area. Each local government's purchasing practices depend heavily upon:

1. Its legal relationship to the state, specifically the degree of autonomy it is granted by the state government.
2. Its reliance on federal and state funds, thereby putting it under federal or state regulations for purchases made with these externally generated revenues.
3. The degree to which it participates in cooperative purchasing programs.
4. Its size—as a rule, smaller jurisdictions have less complex purchasing systems.

While it is extremely difficult to generalize about all local procurement systems, studies have identified some common practices.

Counties

A 1988 survey of forty-six of the fifty largest U.S. counties showed that a significant percent (78 percent) revised their purchasing policies in the latter part of the 1980s.[17] Some of the revisions incorporated the changes in purchasing practices and codes that were taking place at the federal and state levels. However, 79 percent of the counties reported that their purchasing policies do not closely parallel state statutes. Some counties also revised their purchasing practices to conform, at least partially, to the model codes developed by the American Bar Association, the National Institute of Municipal Law Officers, and other professional groups. Fifty percent of the counties reported model-

ing their practices after these professional purchasing codes: ABA, 19 percent; NIMLO, 3 percent; other, 28 percent.

Centralized purchasing   All large U.S. counties have centralized purchasing systems. The most common chain of command is for the purchasing director to report to a Director of General Services (45 percent), with a County Administrator (18 percent) or the Budget/Finance Director (18 percent) following far behind.

Cooperative purchasing   A significant percentage of counties participate in intergovernmental cooperative purchasing arrangements, strongly encouraged by professional purchasing groups like the National Institute of Governmental Purchasing and the National Association of State Purchasing Officials. Counties most commonly cooperate with their state government (31 percent) or other local—but not county—governments (31 percent).

Furthermore, cooperative purchasing policies tend to focus externally on other governments rather than internally on agencies within the county. However, when counties do delineate internal cooperation, they often spell out requirements for standardization across departments (50 percent). They also cover in some detail the technique of pooling purchases (33 percent). What is most lacking is a detailed description of the procedural steps for entering into intergovernmental purchasing agreements.

Bid solicitation and award   County purchasing policies are the most detailed in their outlines of award authority, emergency authority, and the method of soliciting bids.

The most common award practices are for a governing (elective) board to reserve the right to make all awards from $10,000 to $24,999 (24 percent) or more than $25,000 (24 percent) or for the board to have unilateral award authority for only certain kinds of contracts (29 percent). The 1989 NIGP survey showed that only 45 percent gave unlimited approval authority to their chief procurement officer; 38 percent restricted it to amounts lower than $5,000 or under $10,000 (see Table 2.7).

Counties define emergency purchases in a similar way. Most commonly, an emergency occurs when a situation threatens the health, safety, or welfare of the public (43 percent). Purchasing directors generally bear the primary responsibility to make emergency purchases (67 percent). One quarter of the counties give department heads authority to make emergency purchases during nonworking hours.

By far the most commonly used method to solicit bids is the competitive sealed bid (88 percent). Fifty percent require sealed bids when the contract amount exceeds $10,000; 45 percent set the threshold much lower, somewhere between $1,000 and $9,999. The most commonly exempted items are sole source goods or services (14 percent), professional services (59 percent), or emergency purchases (14 percent). A number of counties also use other methods to solicit bids: competitive negotiations, requests for proposals, multistep sealed bids, or open-market purchases.

Small purchase authority, which is often less well spelled out than policies mentioned above, focuses on two dimensions: who has the authority and the dollar threshold that dictates delegation of authority. For those counties delegating authority downward from the central purchasing office, most (80 percent) delegate small purchase authority to the department head. The most common dollar threshold for labeling a purchase "small" is between $50 and $399 (75 percent).

Professional services most commonly exempt from the county competitive bid process are architectural (100 percent), engineering (91 percent), and surveying (45 percent). However, reflecting the national trend toward making professional service acquisition more competitive, most counties now include RFP elements in their processes for acquiring services in noncompetitive bid situations.

Minority and local vendor preferences   A little over half of the county policies examined discuss minority business enterprise programs (52 percent). Common structural elements, where they appear, include definitions of minority business (25 percent), targets (38 percent), and affirmative action (EEO) procedural requirements (38 percent). Definitions are more clearly spelled out than the actual steps involved in contracting with minority businesses.

Local-vendor preference policy statements appear in only 40 percent of the large county purchasing policies. Where such policies exist, tie bids are the normal way of granting local vendors an edge (60 percent).

Monitoring and protests   Contract monitoring elements are found in only 44 percent of the policies examined. Authority for monitoring is evenly distributed among three options: (1) Those that give responsibility to the line department first, then the purchasing department (27 percent); (2) those in which the line department has total responsibility (27 percent); and (3) those in which the purchasing department has total responsibility (27 percent). No counties mention external (on-site) monitoring of contractors in any of the policies examined.

Surprisingly, only 8 percent of the purchasing policies examined include any discussion of a protest and appeals process. Even in these counties, the steps and actors, dollar thresholds for appeals, and the statute of limitations are not well covered.

In summary, county purchasing practices are the most comprehensive with regard to award authority, definitions, and delineation of bidding procedures. They are the least comprehensive in their coverage of precise procedures to be followed at each stage of the purchasing process: solicitation, acquisition, and monitoring of contract compliance.

Municipalities

In *Management Policies in Local Government Finance* (published by the International City Management Association) David S. Arnold reports that city government purchasing has become more "professional, intergovernmental, diversified, and procedural (in the legal sense)." The need to respond to information technology, antitrust laws, and public–private ventures has prompted municipalities of all sizes to restructure their purchasing systems. Many have been greatly influenced by the ABA and NIMLO model codes and by recommendations from the NIGP and NASPO (see Appendix C for the elements of each code).

A survey conducted by the ICMA in 1979 (before the model codes were formalized) showed that at the beginning of the 1980s purchasing was rarely a separate city department. According to Dan H. Davidson and Solon A. Bennett, who reported the survey findings, the municipal purchasing function was most likely to be placed in either a finance (31.7 percent) or administration (25 percent) department. Only 10 percent reported having a separate purchasing department. The same survey reported that 64 percent of all cities larger than 10,000 had a centralized purchasing system. If a similar survey were conducted today it would undoubtedly show that a much higher percentage of U.S. cities now have separate purchasing departments and centralized purchasing systems.

Municipal purchasing practices closely parallel county practices with regard to their coverage of bid solicitation and award methods, cooperative purchasing arrangements, and affirmative action programs. But cities tend to be more explicit than most counties in spelling out the steps involved in various purchasing activities and in identifying conflict-of-interest situations.

Bid solicitation and award According to a 1989 NIGP survey, the most common dollar threshold above which competitive sealed bids or proposals are required ranges between $5,001 and $10,000 (39 percent). Davidson and Bennett found in their 1979 ICMA survey that 97 percent of all cities require competitive sealed bids under certain conditions; 90.2 percent require legal notices for formal sealed bids. Eighty-seven percent waive competitive bidding under certain conditions: emergencies (86 percent), professional services (75 percent), and sole source purchases (54 percent). Reflecting the trend toward considering more than just price in awarding the contract, 81 percent can consider factors other than price if the factors are spelled out in the IFB or RFP. (This figure is consistent with the one reported in Table 2.2.)

Cities most commonly limit the approval authority of chief purchasing officials to amounts less than $5,000; $1,000 for beginning-level buyers (see Table 2.4). Cities are also most likely to grant departments the authority to make small purchases of less than $100 (41 percent) (see Table 2.3).

Nearly 40 percent of the cities surveyed in 1979 had written purchasing manuals (the percentage would undoubtedly be higher today). Of these 90 percent spelled out acquisition policies and procedures; 68 percent included all laws related to purchasing; 59 percent addressed ethics and conduct issues; 39 percent included quality assurance guidelines; and 24 percent contained affirmative action guidelines.

Conflict-of-interest regulations Most cities have fairly extensive conflict-of-interest regulations: 89 percent prohibit government employees from making any public purchasing decisions in which they or their relatives have a financial interest; 84 percent prohibit government employees from being a partner, board member, or employee of a corporation that sells to the city; 10 percent prohibit former employees from selling services or supplies to the city for a specific time period following their departure from city employment; and 7 percent prohibit former employees from accepting employment with any contractor they dealt with professionally while employed by the city. Cities may be more sensitive than other local governments to these conflict-of-interest issues because of their higher visibility.

Affirmative action Cities include affirmative action statements in their purchasing policies more than other local governments because they depend more upon external funds, particularly federal funds, and have higher percentages of minority constituents than counties. However, consistent with information generated in more recent surveys such as the 1989 NIGP study, the 1979 ICMA survey found the proportion of cities requiring formal set-asides (5 percent) or guaranteeing that minority contractors be given a percentage preference (4 percent) to be fairly low. The more common practices are for cities to have stringent requirements for making sure minority-owned businesses are on their vendor mailing and vendor bidder lists (50 percent) or requiring that prime contractors award a portion of their contract to minority subcontractors (27 percent). The larger the minority population, the more likely the city is to maintain minority preference policies even after the *Richmond* v. *Croson* ruling.

Cooperative purchasing Cities of all sizes are more likely to participate in cooperative purchasing than are counties (65 percent in 1979). Their most common pur-

chasing partners are the state (72 percent), other cities (45 percent), counties (37 percent), school districts (24 percent), and regional councils and districts (11 percent). While one might expect smaller cities to be more actively engaged in cooperative purchasing ventures, the ICMA survey showed little variation by size.

School Districts/Other Special Districts

There are unfortunately few in-depth surveys of the practices of school districts or other special districts except the NIGP surveys (Tables 2.1 through 2.5).

The 1989 NIGP survey shows that more than half of the school systems set the dollar threshold for requiring formal competitive sealed bids on proposals at $1,001 to $5,000 (28 percent) or $5,001 to $10,000 (35 percent). The same pattern appears among special authority and city/county health districts (see Table 2.1).

School systems tend to grant more unlimited approval authority to their chief procurement officials (51 percent) than either special authorities (42 percent) or city-county health districts (19 percent). But all types of these other local governments generally restrict purchase authority to amounts less than $500: 94 percent of the school systems, 86 percent of the special authorities, 85 percent of the city/county health districts (see Table 2.3).

Special districts and authorities are more likely to have legally mandated vendor preferences, especially for small businesses and preferences for U.S.-produced goods than other local governments (see Table 2.4).

The more specialized nature of the products and services utilized by these special-purpose local governments undoubtedly restricts the potential supplier pool and makes it even more difficult, although imperative, for them to have purchasing practices that stimulate competition and involve minority contractors.

How to Sell to Local Governments

Selling to local governments requires a great deal of research by businesses, especially in localities with many local governmental units (counties, cities, school districts, special districts). Seldom are the procurement policies and practices similar, even within the same metropolitan area or state. A business must contact each local government individually to determine how to get on its vendor list, which items it purchases, how it purchases them (competitive bidding, RFPs, telephone quotes), its requirements for certification or bonding (bid, payment, performance), and all other features of its purchasing process.

Many local governments publish vendor guides similar to those published by the federal and state governments. When contacting a local government, it is best to ask for the office or agency in charge of purchasing, procurement, or contracts (the nomenclature varies across governmental entities).

SUMMARY

Government purchasing practices are generally adopted for "the public good," not to be intentionally onerous or burdensome. The unique requirements of public sector purchasing—openness, impartiality, and competitiveness—make government policies and procedures more complex, and frequently more confusing, than private sector practices.

The purchasing systems of the federal, state, and various local governments resemble each other in many ways, especially with regard to the principles that guide them. However, they differ in their complexity and in the types of goods and services they buy from the private sector. These differences contribute to the frustrations businesses experience in selling to government. Chapter 3 takes an in-depth look at how the business community assesses the competitiveness, efficiency, and impartiality of government purchasing practices.

NOTES

1. Cf. Farrell, 1982; Page, 1987.
2. See Page, 1987.
3. See Short, 1987; Zemansky, 1987. Cf. Page, 1987.
4. For reviews of the specifics of the *Croson* ruling see Bell, 1989; Benjamin, 1989; Cohen, 1989; Fried, 1989; Anthony Lewis, 1989; Mackie, 1989; Rasnic, 1989; Reuben, 1989a,b; Sandoval, 1990; Scherer, 1990; Rice, 1991.
5. Cf. Cohen, 1989; Norton and Norton, 1989; *Yale Law Journal*, 1989a.
6. See also Zee, 1988.
7. Cf. Bell, 1989; Cohen, 1989; Dobrovier, 1989; *Yale Law Journal*, 1989a; Scherer, 1990.
8. See the American Law Institute National Conference of Commissioners on Uniform State Laws, 1987; Page, 1987.
9. See the Council of State Governments, 1988; Coalition for State Prompt Pay, 1989.
10. See Farrell, 1982; Page, 1987; the Council of State Governments, 1988.
11. See Mikesell, 1991. See also Berne and Schramm, 1986; Miller, 1986; Steiss, 1989.
12. See Johnson and Ross, 1989.

13. For good discussions of the role of governmental accounting in financial management see Herbert, Killough, and Steiss, 1984; Chaney, 1989; Steiss, 1989.
14. See Kull, 1989–90; MacManus and Watson, 1990.
15. For excellent detailed descriptions see Thybony, 1987; Page, 1987; Farrell, 1982.
16. The most significant federal laws affecting contracting are Office of Federal Procurement Policy Act, 1974; Small Business Act, 1953; Competition in Contracting Act of 1984; Defense Procurement Reform Act of 1984; Small Business and Federal Procurement Competition Enhancement Act of 1984; Antideficiency Act of 1905, 1982; Buy American Act, 1933; Assignment of Claims Act, 1940; Contract Disputes Act of 1978; Prompt Payment Act, 1982, amended 1988; Davis–Bacon Act, 1931; Contract Work Hours and Safety Standards Act, 1962; McNamara–O'Hara Service Contract Act, 1965; Anti-Kickback Act, 1946, rev. 1986; Budget and Accounting Act of 1921; Walsh–Healey Public Contracts Act, 1936; Service Contract Act of 1965; Fair Labor Standards Act, 1938; Occupational Safety and Health Act, 1970; Convict Labor Prohibition Act, 1948; Wagner–O'Day Act, 1938; Miller Act, 1935; Clean Air Act, 1963; Federal Water Pollution Control Act, 1972; Clean Water Act, 1977; Trade Agreements Act of 1979; Noise Control Act, 1972; Resource Conservation and Recovery Act, 1976; Energy Policy and Conservation Act, 1976; Patent and Trademark Law amendments, 1980; Defense Production Act, 1950, including the Cost Accounting Standards Act; along with numerous congressional authorization and appropriation acts. For details of these acts, see Thybony, 1987; Page, 1987.
17. MacManus and Watson, 1990.

CHAPTER 3

Government's Reputation as a Buyer Among the Business Community

"Yes, you can make money on government contracts," says the owner of a construction company, "as long as you build in the cost of dealing with their red tape."

"The state has to buy at the lowest price, and if they're not careful about their specs, they get an inferior product," says the general manager of a printing company. "I'd say they get what they want about 40 percent of the time."

IF A GOVERNMENT is to attract a large and representative pool of potential vendors to participate in its procurement process, it must have a reputation among a wide range of businesses for being a desirable customer. Government's procurement practices must be perceived as competitive, effective, and equitable. But is this the case?

The focus of this chapter is on the business community's perceptions of government as a buyer. Do businesses generally see government purchasing practices as attracting high-quality vendors to compete for government business? Do they believe that government procurement practices result in government buying high-quality goods and services at the lowest price? And do businesses regard government purchasing policies and procedures as fair and impartial? Finally, do some types of business firms rate government purchasing practices more favorably than do other types of firms?

In an effort to determine the general reputation of government as a buyer, we asked businesses to respond to three questions:

Businesses like yours believe that government purchasing policies and procedures are effective in attracting first-rate vendors to compete for contracts.

____Yes ____ No ____ No opinion

Businesses like yours believe that government purchasing policies and procedures result in government purchases of quality goods and services at the lowest cost.

____Yes ____ No ____ No opinion

Businesses like yours believe that government purchasing policies and procedures are fair and impartial.

____Yes ____ No ____ No opinion

GOVERNMENT PRACTICES SEEN AS NONCOMPETITIVE, INEFFICIENT, AND UNFAIR

The results indicate that *businesses do not think too highly of government purchasing practices* (see Figure 3.1). Only one-third (35 percent) believe that government has a reputation for attracting first-rate vendors to compete for contracts; more than half (52 percent) do not; the remainder have no opinion.

Business assessments are even harsher with regard to government's effectiveness and efficiency. Only 30 percent perceive that government purchasing practices result in government purchases of quality goods and services at the lowest cost; 60 percent do not believe so (see Figure 3.1).

Businesses also criticize the government's fairness and impartiality (see Figure 3.1), although slightly less so than its competitiveness or efficiency. Nonetheless, only one-third (34 percent) of the businesses regard government purchasing practices as fair and impartial; nearly half (49 percent) do not. A high proportion (17 percent) have no opinion.

The proportion of businesses having no opinion about the fairness or impartiality of government purchasing practices suggests that businesses tend to have somewhat more negative perceptions of the outcomes of the process (attracting large, competent vendor pools and securing high-quality goods and services at the best price) than of the equity of the process (fairness and impartiality). Nonetheless, none of these figures can provide much comfort to government procurement officials. A closer look at variations in these assessments among different types of firms may offer some insights in helping government develop strategies to improve its reputation in the business community.

DO GOVERNMENT POLICIES ATTRACT HIGH-QUALITY VENDORS TO COMPETE FOR CONTRACTS?

Although businesses generally do not believe government purchasing practices attract high-quality vendors to compete for government contracts (Figure 3.1), some types of businesses judge government purchasing practices more favorably than others. As the figures in Table 3.1 show, firms more likely to believe that government procurement policies promote competition among high-quality vendors are:

- Nonprofits and partnerships
- Firms that have been in business a relatively short time
- moderate to large firms (100 to 5,000 employees)
- Firms having gross annual revenue of $26 to $50 million
- Firms in finance, insurance, mining, manufacturing, and retail trade

- Minority-owned firms (particularly those owned by males, blacks, and American Indians)
- Small, economically disadvantaged firms
- Firms currently holding a government contract
- Firms generating a high percentage of their gross revenue from government contracts

Firms that have obtained a government contract through participation in a Minority Business Enterprise (MBE) or Small Business Enterprise (SBE) program or through a Request for Proposal (RFP) see the process as more competitive than vendors securing contracts through other means. Construction firms are slightly more positive in their assessment of competitiveness than firms

Figure 3.1
Government Purchasing Practices Judged Noncompetitive,
Inefficient, and Unfair By Business

"Businesses Like Mine Generally Believe Government Purchasing Practices Attract First-Rate Vendors to Compete for Contracts."

"Businesses Like Mine Believe Government Purchasing Practices Result in Government Purchase of Quality Goods and Services at the Lowest Cost."

"Businesses Like Mine Believe Government Purchasing Practices are Fair and Impartial."

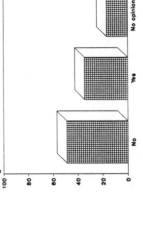

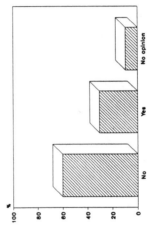

Source: Mail survey of businesses on the Harris County (Houston), Texas vendor mailing list and the Hillsborough County (Tampa), Florida vendor registration list, May–July, 1989.

Table 3.1
Business General Assessments of the Effectiveness
of Government Purchasing Practices by Firm Characteristic

Firm Characteristic	% Rating Practice		
	Attract First Rate Vendors to Compete for Contracts	Ensure Government Purchase of Quality Goods & Services at Lowest Cost	Practices are Fair & Impartial
All Firms (n = 3217)	34.7%	30.3%	34.4%
Firm Structure			
Individual owner (n = 411)	30.4	33.5	31.3
Partnership (n = 99)	36.4	31.3	29.3
Nonprofit organization (n = 64)	39.1	20.3	38.1
Corporation (n = 2607)	35.1	29.9	35.0
Other (n = 13)	30.8	30.8	30.8
Years in Business			
Less than 1 year (n = 54)	46.3	34.0	37.3
1-2 years (n = 201)	40.8	34.0	29.4
3-5 years (n = 467)	35.5	32.8	30.7
6-10 years (n = 505)	35.0	33.0	34.2
Over 10 years (n = 1984)	33.5	28.6	35.7
Number of Employees			
1-25 (n = 1919)	33.3	30.9	30.8
26-50 (n = 404)	34.4	28.3	34.7
51-100 (n = 266)	34.6	28.6	38.0
101-500 (n = 322)	38.0	27.4	40.5
501-1000 (n = 76)	47.4	42.3	45.5
1001-5000 (n = 120)	44.2	39.5	50.8
Over 5000 (n = 91)	29.7	20.9	44.0
Firm Gross Revenues ('88)			
Below $200,000 (n = 536)	32.3	34.3	27.4
$200,000-499,999 (n = 461)	36.4	31.8	30.7
$500,000-999,999 (n = 433)	33.3	30.4	30.6
$1-$10 Million (n = 1040)	33.3	27.2	35.9
$11-$25 Million (n = 216)	38.4	29.0	37.9
$26-$50 Million (n = 104)	44.2	30.1	38.5
Over $50 Million (n = 297)	36.0	30.1	45.8

Table 3.1 (*continued*)

Firm Characteristic	% Rating Practice		
	Attract First Rate Vendors to Compete for Contracts	Ensure Government Purchase of Quality Goods & Services at Lowest Cost	Practices are Fair & Im-partial
Industry Classification			
Retail trade (n = 475)	39.4%	39.6%	35.0%
Wholesale trade (n = 455)	34.1	31.9	35.8
Finance (n = 17)	47.1	35.3	29.4
Insurance (n = 7)	42.9	28.6	42.9
Utility (n = 7)	28.6	12.5	42.9
Construction (n = 454)	35.9	28.9	37.6
Manufacturing-durable (n = 246)	29.3	24.5	35.2
Manufacturing-nondurable (n = 88)	27.3	27.6	41.6
Real estate (n = 31)	29.0	40.0	40.0
Communications (n = 92)	31.5	25.5	28.3
Service (n = 548)	33.4	32.0	34.0
Agriculture (n = 30)	30.0	36.7	36.7
Mining (n = 7)	42.9	28.6	42.9
Transportation (n = 47)	27.7	25.5	37.5
Professional Service (n = 246)	32.9	16.5	26.1
Other (n = 1)	0.0	0.0	0.0
Owner			
Minority-owned (n = 668)	38.0	37.0	31.1
Not minority-owned (n = 2480)	33.6	28.2	35.3
Minority Owner-Gender[1]			
Female (n = 364)	34.9	35.8	51.5
Male (n = 133)	45.9	42.0	31.8
Minority Owner-Race[1]			
Black (n = 127)	50.4	50.0	31.1
Hispanic (n = 139)	38.8	35.7	23.8
Puerto Rican (n = 8)	37.5	37.5	62.5
Asian (n = 39)	38.5	30.8	31.6
American Indian (n = 15)	46.7	13.3	33.3
Other (n = 15)	26.7	33.3	14.3
Size-Economic Classification			
Small, economically disadvantaged (n = 692)	39.1	38.5	33.3
Not small, economically disadvantaged (n = 2387)	33.3	27.9	34.8

[1] Question was answered only by the subset of the respondents meeting the definitional criterion (minority-owned).

Table 3.1 (continued)

Firm Characteristic	% Rating Practice		
	Attract First Rate Vendors to Compete for Contracts	**Ensure Government Purchase of Quality Goods & Services at Lowest Cost**	**Practices are Fair & Impartial**
Current Contract Status			
Has contract with government (n = 2256)	38.0%	31.8%	38.3%
No contract with government (n = 853)	25.6	26.4	23.3
No Government Contracts Presently[2]			
Have had one in past (n = 417)	25.9	25.2	25.1
Have not had one in past (n = 377)	24.4	28.1	21.0
Level of Government Firm Does Business With (Multiple Responses)			
Federal (n = 1523)	37.4	30.8	39.2
State (n = 1998)	37.5	31.9	37.2
City (n = 2210)	37.9	31.7	37.8
County (n = 2340)	37.1	31.3	37.4
Transit Authority (n = 742)	40.6	35.2	40.2
School district (n = 1642)	37.4	32.0	37.4
Hospital district (n = 798)	39.6	33.6	43.4
Other special district (n = 197)	38.1	30.8	34.4
Other (n = 259)	18.1	25.7	16.2
% of Gross Revenues From Government Contracts			
Less than 10% (n = 1689)	30.0	26.8	31.6
10-25% (n = 603)	39.5	33.9	40.5
26-50% (n = 298)	40.6	38.0	39.2
51-75% (n = 185)	40.0	29.8	31.3
76-90% (n = 115)	48.7	35.3	43.1
Over 90% (n = 123)	51.2	37.1	39.5
Procedures for Getting Government Contract (Multiple Responses)			
Formal competitive bid (with negotiation) (n = 1995)	34.5	33.3	39.9
Formal competitive bid (sealed) (n = 2097)	37.8	32.8	38.5
Local vendor preference (n = 645)	34.4	30.1	36.0
Request for Proposal (competitive negotiation) (n = 843)	40.2	30.7	35.7
Government solicitation of written quote (n = 1170)	35.9	31.5	39.2
Government solicitation of telephone quote (n = 830)	38.0	32.2	40.4
Participation in Minority Business Enterprise program	48.3	45.6	42.5
Participation in Small Business program (n = 132)	43.2	38.3	45.0
Other procedure (n = 168)	24.4	18.6	23.1

[2] Question was answered only by the subset of the respondents meeting the definitional criterion (firm does not have a government contract at the present).

Table 3.1

	% Rating Practice		
Firm Characteristic	Attract First Rate Vendors to Compete for Contracts	Ensure Government Purchase of Quality Goods & Services at Lowest Cost	Practices are Fair & Impartial
Type of Product Delivered to Government (Multiple Responses)			
Service (n = 1557)	35.9%	30.4%	34.1%
Commodity/good (n = 1661)	35.2	31.7	36.3
Construction (n = 607)	36.8	31.5	39.6
Geographical Location			
In-State (n = 2749)	35.0	30.0	33.4
Out-of-State (n = 417)	32.9	31.0	39.9

Source: Random sample survey of businesses listed on the Harris County (Houston), Texas vendor mailing list (conducted May–June, 1989) and mail survey of all businesses listed on the Hillsborough County (Tampa), Florida vendor registration list (conducted June–July, 1989)

delivering commodities or services, although little variation occurs by type of product delivered.

Firms more critical of the effectiveness of government purchasing policies in promoting competition among high-quality vendors are:

- Individually owned firms
- Firms in business longer than ten years
- Small firms (as measured by number of employees and gross revenue)
- Firms in the utility, transportation, communications, manufacturing (durable and nondurable), agriculture, and service sectors
- Firms not owned by minorities—and, among minority firms, those owned by women, Hispanics, and Asians
- Firms not classified as small, economically disadvantaged
- Firms currently without a government contract or that have never received a government contract

- Firms receiving less than 10 percent of their gross revenues from government contracts
- Firms having received contracts through the formal competitive bid or local-vendor preference methods

Positive Findings

Although a relatively small percentage of businesses of any type see government procurement policies as effectively promoting competition among high-quality vendors, several significant and positive points emerge from the findings:

1. *Minority-owned firms, especially those owned by racial or ethnic minorities, view government procurement as more competitive than nonminority-owned firms* (38 percent versus 34 percent). Still, less than 40 percent of minority-owned firms see government purchas-

ing as promoting competition among high-quality vendors.

2. *Firms classified as small, economically disadvantaged view the effectiveness of government policies in promoting competition more positively than firms not so classified* (39 percent versus 33 percent).

3. *Firms that have participated in MBE or SBE programs assess the competitiveness of government procurement more positively than nonminority firms.* Nearly half (48 percent) of the MBE and 43 percent of the SBE firms see government purchasing practices as attracting first-rate vendors to the procurement process.

4. *Newly established firms (in business less than two years) rate the competitiveness of government procurement more positively than older, more established firms.* Nearly half (46 percent) of those in operation less than one year see government purchasing practices as competitive, compared to 41 percent of those in operation one to two years and only 34 percent for firms in business longer than ten years. This finding could mean that companies become more cynical with age and experience.

These positive findings are encouraging in light of the nation's changing demographics. They suggest that strategies aimed at broadening the pool of vendors through social targeting can be effective in improving government's reputation among minority-owned businesses, destined to be the largest pool of vendors in the next century. The findings also show that new businesses are not automatically discouraged from doing business with government. However, other statistics suggest that if government procurement practices do not effectively encourage these new firms to enter and successfully compete in the vendor pool, they soon will be discouraged.

Negative Findings

A more negative assessment of purchasing competitiveness comes from the following types of businesses:

1. *Individually owned businesses.* Only 30 percent rate government procurement practices as competitive, compared to 39 percent of the nonprofits and 36 percent of the partnerships. While the differences may not seem so great, the significance for the future is that 71 percent of all U.S. businesses are sole proprietorships (note 27, Chapter 1).

2. *Small businesses, particularly those in business for quite some time.* Only 33 percent of the firms with 1–25 employees see government practices as promoting competition among high-quality vendors, 32 percent of those with gross revenues below $200,000, and 34 percent of those in business longer than ten years—compared to 47 percent of the firms with 501–1,000 employees, 44 percent of those with 1,001–5,000 employees, and 44 percent of those with revenues of $26–$50 million. Again, the major significance of this pattern is that 60 percent of the U.S. labor force is employed in small firms, according to *The State of Small Business.*

3. *Women-owned businesses*, the fastest-growing segment of the small business sector according to the U.S. Department of Commerce. Only 35 percent of female-owned minority businesses see government procurement as competitive, compared to 46 percent of their male counterparts.

4. *Hispanic and Asian minority-owned firms.* These two groups are far less positive in their assessments than black-owned or American Indian-owned firms. Only 39 percent of

Asian-owned firms and the same proportion of Hispanic-owned firms see purchasing practices as promoting competition among high-quality vendors, compared to half (50 percent) of black-owned firms and 47 percent of American Indian-owned firms. If a group's success in contracting parallels its political clout, then perhaps Hispanics and Asians, as they increase their political clout, may generate more contracts and change their assessments for the better. But in the short term, racial and ethnic tensions are frequently heightened by government contracting patterns. Minority contractors often judge the fairness of the system by comparing their success to that of other minority groups.[1]

5. *Vendors that have had no success in securing government contracts.* Only one-fourth (26 percent) of those that have no government contracts see government procurement as promoting competition, compared to 38 percent of those with contracts. Firms that have had a contract in the past as well as those that have never had one give government procurement low ratings: only about one-fourth of each (26 percent and 24 percent) see it as competitive. These two types of firms appear to be the most alienated from the government procurement process. Government officials should carefully analyze these firms' assessments of specific problems with the procurement process to attract them back into the pool of vendors.

6. *Firms that have secured government contracts through the more competitive methods* (formal competitive bid, with negotiation; formal competitive bid, sealed). These firms are more cynical about the competitiveness of government purchasing than firms that have secured contracts through less com-

petitive means such as government solicitation of telephone quotes and participation in MBE or SBE programs (vendor preference policies). This finding supports some claims that competitive bidding policies and procedures designed to promote competition may actually alienate high-quality vendors from participating if they perceive that government contracts are awarded in a less competitive fashion.

7. *Firms doing business with general purpose governments* (federal, state, city, and county) as opposed to smaller, special purpose governments (transit authority, hospital district). The belief that procurement practices promote competition among high-quality vendors is less likely to occur among firms doing business with general purpose governments (federal government, 37 percent; county government, 37 percent) than among firms doing business with special purpose governments (transit authorities, 41 percent; hospital districts, 40 percent).

This finding may reflect the specialized nature of goods and services that special purpose governments buy (school desks and textbooks purchased by school districts, for example) and thus the closer relationship that vendors have to these governments. This finding should cause concern for general purpose governments, which, according to the National Institute of Governmental Purchasing, typically have larger, more professionally trained procurement staffs and more detailed procurement policies and procedures.

Significance of the Findings

Governments generally have not been effective in promoting the notion that their procurement practices attract high-quality vendors to compete for government business. This finding holds true across all types of firms. If governments attract only second-rate vendors to the public procurement arena, all the competitive bid requirements in the world will not result in government purchases of high-quality goods and services at the lowest prices. Ultimately, the ones who will suffer are the American taxpayers. Governments need to reexamine the simultaneous, cumulative effects of *all* their purchasing policies and procedures to see what is alienating potential vendors. Surveys of the business community, like this one, can help governments develop strategies to strengthen competition, but not at the expense of high-quality vendors.

DOES GOVERNMENT PURCHASE QUALITY GOODS AND SERVICES AT THE LOWEST COST?

In spite of government efforts to adopt policies and procedures designed to inject quality into the purchasing decision (see Chapter 2), businesses generally remain unconvinced. As shown in Figure 3.1, nearly two-thirds (60 percent) of businesses do not believe that government purchasing practices result in government buying quality goods and services at the lowest cost. Among businesses, it appears that government has failed to achieve one of its prime functions. Zemansky points out in *Ethics and Quality Public Purchasing*: "It is the prime function of purchasing to secure [materials, supplies, tools, equipment, systems, facilities, and services] *at the lowest ultimate cost consistent with prevailing economic conditions and appropriate standards of quality* and continuity of service while establishing and maintaining a reputation for openness, fairness, and integrity" (author's emphasis).

Negative Findings

The most negative assessments of the efficiency outcomes of government purchasing come from:

- Nonprofit organizations and corporations
- Firms in business longer than ten years
- Extremely large firms (more than 5,000 employees)

- Firms with gross revenues higher than $1 million
- Firms in the utility and professional service sectors
- Firms not classified as minority-owned or small and economically disadvantaged—although among minority-owned firms, those owned by women, American Indians, and Asians
- Those currently without a government contract
- Firms with less than 10 percent of their gross revenue from government contracts
- Firms not securing contracts through MBE or SBE set-asides (see Table 3.1)

Positive Findings

Firms somewhat more favorable in their assessments of the success of government purchasing in securing quality goods and services at the lowest cost are:

- Individually owned firms
- Those in business less than two years
- Moderate-sized firms (500–1,000 employees)
- Firms with gross revenues below $500,000
- Those receiving a moderate to large percentage of their gross revenue from government contracts

- Those securing government contracts through MBE or SBE programs
- Businesses selling to special purpose governments
- Minority-owned firms, especially black-male-owned firms
- Small and economically disadvantaged firms
- Firms in the real estate, retail trade, agriculture, and finance sectors (see Table 3.1)

Most Significant Finding

The harshest criticism of government purchasing outcomes comes from the professional service sector. Only 17 percent of the firms classified as professional service establishments believe that government purchases high quality goods and services at the lowest cost. This assessment no doubt stems from the belief among many in the professional service sector that high-quality services cannot be purchased at the lowest cost. They see the two principles as incompatible.[2] As Rehfuss observes in *Contracting out in Government*: "Many professional individuals and their firms do not like to compete on the basis of money. They wish to be selected for their professional qualifications and until fairly recently, professional organizations frowned on competitive pricing competition as 'unprofessional'."

Another explanation for the professional service sector's negative assessments may be that a large portion has never received a government contract and thereby views the system as closed. Other survey results support this notion—only 26 percent of professional service firms see purchasing practices as fair and impartial (Table 3.1). In general, though, few businesses see government getting a good deal through its purchasing policies and procedures.

ARE GOVERNMENT PURCHASING PRACTICES FAIR AND IMPARTIAL?

All model public procurement codes (see Chapter 2) stress the importance of fairness and impartiality. According to the Council of State Governments and the National Association of State Purchasing Officials in *State and Local Government Purchasing*, governments should design their purchasing practices to "guard against favoritism and profiteering at public expense, and to promote the interest of private enterprise by providing equal opportunities to compete for government business."

However, many in the private sector believe the fairness and impartiality principle, which is unique to public sector purchasing, quashes the government's achievement of another procurement goal—quality buying at the best price. Government purchasers acknowledge that "*prices are not as critical as fairness and impartiality* in obtaining them."

Our survey results affirm that businesses are more critical of government's failure to acquire high-quality goods and services at the best prices than of government's failure to be fair and impartial (see Figure 3.1). Predictably, the firms most critical of government procurement's effort to ensure fairness and impartiality are among those least critical of its competitiveness and efficiency. For example, a much higher proportion of black-owned firms believe that government purchasing practices attract first-rate vendors to compete for contracts (50 percent) and secure quality goods and services at the lowest cost (50 percent) than believe that government procurement is fair and impartial (31 percent). The same pattern appears among Hispanic-owned businesses and businesses classified as small and economically disadvantaged.

One explanation for this seeming aberration can be found in other survey results. As noted in Table 3.1, minority and small businesses that secured government contracts through participation in MBE and SBE programs judge government procurement practices as fairer and more impartial (43 percent, MBE; 45 percent, SBE) than minority-owned businesses in general (only 31 percent). However, only 23 percent of the minority-owned businesses responding to our survey indicate they had secured a government contract through participation in an MBE program; for small businesses the comparable proportion is a low 8 percent. Furthermore, more than a third (37 percent) of the minority firms surveyed do not currently have a government contract; of those, 55 percent have never had one. Thus the differentials in minority-firm fairness and impartiality ratings may reflect their relative success in winning government business.

Positive Findings

The most positive assessments of the fairness and impartiality of government purchasing practices come from:

- Nonprofit organizations and corporations (38 percent and 35 percent respectively)
- Firms currently holding a government contract (38 percent)
- Newly established businesses or those in operation longer than ten years
- Large firms (more than 500 employees and more than $10 million in gross revenues)
- Those in the insurance, utility, real estate, nondurable manufacturing, and mining sectors
- Women-owned businesses (women-owned businesses have benefited more from government contracts than racial and ethnic minority-owned firms)

- Firms selling to special purpose governments
- Out-of-state contractors
- Those securing contracts through less competitive means (minority preference policies, telephone quotes)

Negative Findings

Firms less likely to perceive fairness in government purchasing practices are sole proprietorships (only 31 percent) and partnerships (29 percent). As our results show, individually owned firms are among the most critical of both the competitiveness and impartiality of government procurement policies. They are also among the most numerous firms. Consequently, government procurement officials face a big challenge in developing strategies to encourage these types of firms to do business with government.

Other Findings

Years in business bears little relationship to a firm's judgment regarding fairness and impartiality. The newest firms (in business less than a year) and the oldest firms (in business longer than five years) are more likely to consider purchasing practices fair and impartial, while those in operation one to two years are less likely to do so. These figures suggest that new businesses anticipate they will be able to compete successfully for government contracts but quickly find out differently once they try.[3]

Small firms are less likely to regard government purchasing practices as fair and impartial than large firms. (The same pattern characterizes their assessments of competitiveness.) For example, only 31 percent of the firms with fewer than 26 employees see government purchasing practices as unbiased compared to half (51 percent) of those with 1,001 to 5,000 employees. Likewise, only 27 percent of the firms with revenues below $200,000 rate government procurement as fair and impartial, compared to nearly half (46 percent) of the firms generating more than $50 million in gross revenue. But as is true among minority-owned firms, small firms that have secured government contracts through their participation in SBE programs see government purchasing practices as more objective than small businesses in general.

A firm's government contract status definitely affects its judgment regarding fairness and impartiality: 38 percent of the firms with government contracts rate procurement practices as impartial compared to only 23 percent of the firms without such contracts. However, the proportion of a business' revenue generated from government contracts bears little relationship to fairness ratings (see Table 3.1). Apparently, businesses judge fairness less on the magnitude of contracts generated and more on their success in securing some government business.

Firms that have secured contracts through more competitive means (formal competitive sealed bids, competitive RFPs) see government procurement practices as more biased than firms that have obtained government business through less competitive means (minority preference policies, telephone quotes). This finding highlights one of the biggest dilemmas facing those responsible for designing and implementing government procurement policies today. *Government policies designed to broaden and increase the representativeness of the vendor pool are effective in improving government's reputation for fairness and impartiality among the group(s) of vendors who had previously been excluded for one reason or another. But these same policies are perceived as biased by vendors not benefiting from them.* The Council of State Governments and the National Association of State Purchasing Officials has stated the problem well:

> Preference, accorded one class of vendors over all others, strikes at the basic principles of public purchasing: equity, impartiality, open competition, and the least cost to the taxpayer. The genesis of preference laws and administrative fiat is political, and the trade-off of anticipated socioeconomic goals must be weighed against the demonstrable adverse effect upon other public policies and goals, not the least of which is excellence in public purchasing.

THE LINKAGE BETWEEN COMPETITION AND IMPARTIALITY

The nation's changing demographics have made government policies aimed at broadening the pool of vendors an integral step toward improving competition for government business. Government's immediate challenge is to demonstrate to the private sector that such policies can effectively promote greater and fairer competition in the long run.

Competition stands at the heart of the American economic system. As Zemansky observed in *Contracting Professional Services*:

> Over the centuries, the concept of competition has evolved as a basic fundamental of

economic life. The United States has had an ideological commitment to such competition over the 200 plus years of its existence. As such, competition has been found and held, by as high a tribunal as the people and the Supreme Court of the United States, to be as fundamental in the economic sense as are the freedoms guaranteed by the Constitution in the sense of our social aspirations.

A public sector procurement system that promotes competition can also promote efficiency and equity. As noted by Harry P. Hatry and Eugene Durman in *Issues in Competitive Contracting for Social Services*:

A carefully implemented competitive contracting process can achieve cost savings or, at least, a slowing of cost increases; competition motivates contractors to become more efficient, more innovative and to provide better service; emphasis on cost competition has the greatest impact on dollars saving; competition based on results-oriented criteria can result in higher service quality; [and] competition encourages a decision-making process that is open, fair, and rational.

SUMMARY

As shown by the data presented here, businesses of all sizes and shapes think poorly of public sector purchasing practices. Only one-third (35 percent) believe government attracts first-rate vendors to compete for contracts; 30 percent perceive that government purchases high-quality goods and services at the lowest cost; and 34 percent judge government purchasing practices as fair and impartial. Government's reputation as a desirable customer is, in a word, bad. If the situation worsens, it could threaten the U.S. economy, especially if the size of the public sector expands.

Some types of firms rate government purchasing practices more favorably than others, but the differences are slight, for the most part. Firms that have been successful in securing government contracts generally tend to view government purchasing more favorably than those that have not. Another finding that may bode well for the future in light of the nation's changing demographics is that newly established firms, minority-owned firms, and small, disadvantaged firms are less critical of government procurement policies than older, more established firms.

Importantly, the firms most critical of procurement practices form the largest proportion of American businesses. These are young, small, individually owned firms. These same firms are the least likely to do business with government. Firms that have never secured a government contract, when compared to firms that currently have a contract, tend to have been in business less than five years (39 percent versus 19 percent); have 1–25 employees (80 percent versus 53 percent) and take in gross revenues less than $200,000 (40 percent versus 12 percent); and be individually owned (22 percent versus 11 percent).

Many valid reasons exist for government's procurement practices being different, and often more burdensome, than those of the private sector (see Chapter 2). Government simply has not done a good job of educating the taxpayers or the business community about why it is in their best interests for government purchasing to be unique. As it stands, businesses give government procurement practices low marks, whether warranted or not. Consequently, the process far too often results in government doing business with incompetent, unethical contractors. Many first-rate vendors are repelled by government's bad reputation and regard selling to government as risky business. What government needs most is a marketing campaign that will establish its reputation as a desirable business partner. A good beginning point would be an analysis of what the business community already sees as the major advantages of doing business with government. This analysis forms the focus of Chapter 4.

Notes

1. Cf. MacManus, 1990b; Arellano, 1984; Cain and Kiewiet, 1986.
2. See Zemansky, 1987; Rehfuss, 1989.
3. For comparison, we conducted a mail survey in July 1989 of 500 businesses not on a government vendor mailing or bidder list. Rather, the businesses were randomly selected from the *Contact Influential Marketing Information Directory* (Tampa, Fla.: Contact Influential Marketing Information Services, 1989), a directory of local businesses in Hillsborough and Pinellas (Florida) counties.

We found that nearly one-third (32 percent) of these firms had bid on government contracts but lost. Nearly one-fifth (19 percent) said "bidding process was not genuinely competitive" was one of the reasons they lost the contract. Another 11 percent laid the blame on government procurement officials: "We received no help or guidelines from the purchasing office in preparation of the bid." Half of these businesses had been in operation less than ten years.

CHAPTER 4

Why Businesses Do
Business With Government

*"One thing about federal contracts—you know you'll get paid," says the owner of
a construction company.*

*"There are probably some misconceptions about how hard it is to get contracts,"
says the executive director of a drug abuse rehabilitation center. "Once you
establish a track record, it's not hard to get contracts—or even to increase your
budget if you do a good job."*

*"A lot of people bad-mouth government contracts—maybe it's the fashionable
thing to do," says a self-employed training consultant. "But I've had contracts
with large corporations, too, and some of them are just as bureaucratic as any
government agency."*

WHAT ATTRACTS BUSINESS to sell to government? In light of the generally poor reputation government has as a customer, what makes businesses sell to it anyway? Is it money, civic duty, aggressive recruitment of the firm by government officials, or what? Are some firms drawn by certain factors more than other types of firms?

In this chapter we look at the major reasons businesses sell to government in spite of the complexities of government procurement practices. The results should be useful to government purchasing officials charged with developing strategies to encourage a broader, more representative pool of vendors to sell to the public sector. As noted earlier, only a small percentage of U.S. firms do business with government at any level.

Our survey asked respondents this question:

Which of the following are major reasons your firm does business with government? (Check all applicable)
Confident that payment will be received
Predictable revenue source
Firm produces service/commodity primarily used by government
As a new business firm, government contracts offer an opportunity to get established
Actively recruited by government purchasing staff
Participation in Minority Business Enterprise program
Participation in Small Business Enterprise program

99

Have been doing business with same governments for years

Good relations with government purchasing office

Good relations with elected officials

Purchasing procedures are efficient and
easy to follow

Purchasing policies are administered
fairly

Other (Specify)

Even with the option of checking more
than one of these reasons, if applicable,

three-fourths (76 percent) identify no more
than three reasons; 57 percent identify two or
fewer reasons. But less than 1 percent (0.8)
identify no reason.

An interesting pattern appears: older,
larger, more experienced firms (in terms of
doing business with government) identify
more reasons than the less experienced
firms. The less experienced firms tend to
identify only a few factors, mostly those related to the profit motive and the chance to
get established.

MAJOR REASON: GOVERNMENT PAYS ITS BILLS

*The vast majority (61 percent) of businesses
sell to government because they are confident
they will be paid* (see Table 4.1). With few
exceptions, all types of firms rank this item
as the most important reason they do (or
would like to do) business with government.
Even among the exceptions (nonprofit
organizations, large firms, out-of-state contractors, and firms participating in SBE programs), sure payment ranks among the three
most important reasons (see Fig. 4.1).

Firms most likely to identify this bill-
paying factor are the smaller, relatively
young, in-state firms, and firms in the construction, agricultural, mining, and utility
sectors (some of the most cyclical industries). The specific proportions of firms cit-

ing this reason are 65 percent of the firms
with fewer than 26 employees, 71 percent of
those that have been in business one to two
years, 62 percent of the in-state firms, 70
percent of the construction firms, 80 percent
of the mining firms, 71 percent of the firms
in the utility business, and 73 percent of the
firms in agriculture.

These findings should come as no surprise
to entrepreneurs: payment is critical to
smaller, newer firms that usually operate on
margins and to firms in sectors most heavily
impacted by fluctuations in the economy. But
as the results here show, government's reputation for paying its bills (eventually) is its
biggest asset in attracting vendors of all
types.

SECOND REASON: EXPERIENCE IN SELLING TO GOVERNMENT

The second most frequently cited reason for
selling to government is that the firm "has
been doing business with the same governments for years." *Forty-one percent of the
firms surveyed identified this item as a major
reason for continuing to do business with
government.* This factor is actually the most
frequently cited reason among large firms
(more than 500 employees and more than
$50 million in gross revenues) and out-of-

state firms (most likely to be large firms).[1]
Large firms, according to Gumpert and
Timmons in their widely cited article in the
Harvard Business Review, have an inherent
advantage in securing government contracts
over small firms: "Whereas large corporations have staffs to learn in advance where
the red tape lies, small businesses do not.
Learning the government's procedures and
making initial sales is difficult, and certainly

Figure 4.1
Reasons Businesses Do Business With Government

Reason	Percentage
Confident payment will be received	61.3%
Long-term experience in doing business with government	41.4%
Predictable revenue source (inelastic)	32.8%
Firm produces service/commodity primarily used by government	23.5%
Good relations with government purchasing office	22.2%
Purchasing policies are administered fairly.	14.7%
Recruited by government purchasing staff	12.2%
Purchasing procedures are efficient and easy to follow	11.1%
Other	10.4%
Offers new businesses chance to get established	9.2%
Participation in Minority Business Enterprise program	7.5%
Participation in Small Business Enterprise program	7.1%
Good relations with elected officials	4.6%

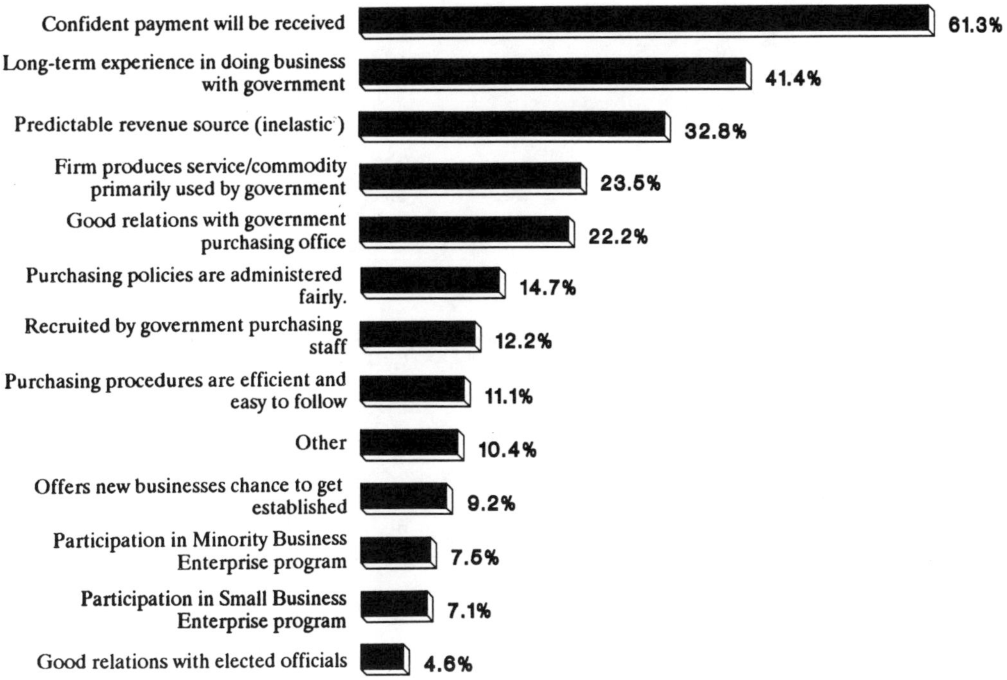

few [new] businesses should attempt to rely solely on . . . government procurement." "Start-ups in particular should wait until their businesses are well established before attempting government sales," they caution.

Furthermore, older firms (in business longer than five years) more frequently cite experience as a reason for doing business with government: 52 percent of firms in operation longer than ten years and 34 percent of those in operation six to ten years, compared to 11 percent of those in operation one to two years.

Newcomers to the government contracting arena are less likely to identify experience. The same is true of minority-owned firms (with the exception of woman-owned firms[2]) and small, economically disadvantaged firms. A larger percentage of these firms identify participation in MBE programs or the predictability of government-contract revenue as a major reason for selling to government than cite experience.

These findings suggest that a business' willingness to contract with government depends heavily upon its success in maneuvering through the procurement maze. Therefore more vendors must succeed in securing government business to expand the vendor pool. The system must be opened to ensure broader and greater competition.

Table 4.1

Reasons Businesses Do Business With Government by Firm Characteristics

Firm Characteristic	% Citing Reason					
	Confident Payment will be Received	Predictable Revenue Source	Firm Produces Service/Commodity Primarily Used by Government	Offers New Business Opportunity to Get Established	Recruited by Government Purchasing Staff	Participation in Minority Business Enterprise Program
All Firms	61.3%	32.8%	23.5%	9.2%	12.2%	7.5%
Firm Structure						
Individual owner	61.1	26.8	19.9	15.3	10.4	11.5
Partnership	58.0	27.2	32.1	9.9	12.3	1.2
Nonprofit organization	35.1	38.6	28.1	1.8	17.5	1.8
Corporation	61.9	33.7	23.7	8.3	12.4	7.2
Other	81.8	63.6	18.2	9.1	9.1	18.2
Years in Business						
Less than 1 year	61.7	36.2	25.5	48.9	10.6	12.8
1-2 years	71.3	32.3	18.9	41.5	7.9	17.1
3-5 years	64.0	35.7	21.1	26.1	8.9	16.1
6-10 years	65.6	32.1	21.3	6.6	11.5	10.9
Over 10 years	58.8	32.2	25.1	2.1	13.5	3.8
Number of Employees						
1-25	64.6	30.2	21.0	13.3	11.2	10.6
26-50	61.3	36.1	21.1	6.1	11.6	5.8
51-100	61.2	37.3	23.9	3.9	13.3	2.4
101-500	54.9	37.3	31.7	2.5	13.2	3.1
501-1000	58.9	30.1	31.5	2.7	11.0	0.0
1001-5000	50.9	36.2	35.3	0.8	12.9	1.7
Over 5000	38.6	37.5	31.8	1.1	26.1	1.1

		% Citing Reason					
Firm Characteristic	Participation in Small Business Enterprise Program	Been doing Business with Same Government for Years	Good Relations with Government Purchasing Office	Good Relations with Elected Officials	Purchasing Procedures are Efficient & Easy to Follow	Purchasing Policies are Administered Fairly	Other [1]
All Firms	7.1	41.4	22.2	4.6	11.1	14.7	10.4
Firm Structure							
Individual owner	8.9	33.7	20.2	3.7	14.1	14.4	10.9
Partnership	1.2	43.2	14.8	8.6	9.9	9.9	3.7
Nonprofit organization	0.0	36.8	10.5	14.0	1.8	7.0	26.3
Corporation	7.2	42.8	23.1	4.3	10.9	15.0	10.2
Other	9.1	18.2	27.3	9.1	9.1	9.1	0.0
Years in Business							
Less than 1 year	10.6	14.9	10.6	0.0	4.3	17.0	2.1
1-2 years	8.5	11.0	9.8	3.0	12.2	8.5	7.9
3-5 years	10.9	18.9	20.3	3.7	9.7	14.1	12.4
6-10 years	9.0	33.9	19.9	4.3	9.0	11.8	10.9
Over 10 years	5.5	51.6	24.5	5.1	12.0	16.0	10.3
Number of Employees							
1-25	8.7	35.1	21.3	3.8	11.1	14.6	9.6
26-50	6.8	46.8	21.1	4.7	9.2	10.8	11.1
51-100	6.3	49.8	21.6	4.7	14.5	18.8	9.4
101-500	5.0	48.0	21.3	6.3	10.0	11.9	11.9
501-1000	1.4	61.6	31.5	1.4	12.3	24.7	15.1
1001-5000	1.7	52.6	26.7	9.5	10.3	13.8	9.5
Over 5000	1.1	55.7	35.2	9.1	12.5	22.7	17.0

[1] Nearly three-fourths (70%) of these respondents identify the profit motive as a major reason to sell to government; 25% identify a public service motive; and 5% identify personal benefits to their firm's reputation.

Table 4.1 (continued)

Firm Characteristic	% Citing Reason						
	Participation in Small Business Enterprise Program	Been doing Business with Same Government for Years	Good Relations with Government Purchasing Office	Good Relations with Elected Officials	Purchasing Procedures are Efficient & Easy to Follow	Purchasing Policies are Administered Fairly	Other
Firm Gross Revenues ('88)							
Below $200,000	11.5%	18.7%	15.5%	3.0%	11.2%	11.0%	10.1%
$200,000-499,999	8.3	32.4	20.4	4.3	11.8	14.0	9.8
$500,000-999,999	7.6	43.2	25.0	5.0	11.1	15.5	9.2
$1-$10 Million	6.7	47.8	21.5	4.8	10.2	14.6	10.5
$11-$25 Million	5.4	51.0	23.3	3.5	11.4	17.3	8.4
$26-$50 Million	6.6	47.2	23.6	5.7	12.3	10.4	11.3
Over $50 Million	1.4	54.2	31.1	7.0	10.5	17.1	14.0
Industry Classification							
Retail trade	8.2	43.3	42.9	3.5	16.2	16.9	8.0
Wholesale trade	6.0	48.1	15.8	19.7	14.9	14.9	7.7
Finance	5.9	23.5	19.5	11.8	23.5	17.6	23.5
Insurance	0.0	42.9	20.8	14.3	14.3	28.6	14.3
Utility	14.3	57.1	14.6	28.6	14.3	14.3	14.3
Construction	8.7	31.8	33.3	2.9	7.3	16.0	10.0
Manufacturing-durable	6.3	51.6	17.1	3.6	5.0	13.6	13.6
Manufacturing-nondurable	3.7	43.9	11.5	3.7	11.0	15.9	18.3
Real estate	0.0	36.7	20.0	6.7	6.7	13.3	20.0
Communications	5.1	30.8	17.8	5.1	9.0	10.3	14.1
Service	7.9	35.3	17.8	3.7	9.6	11.2	10.7
Agriculture	0.0	23.1	0.0	0.0	0.0	7.7	3.8
Mining	0.0	60.0	20.0	0.0	0.0	20.0	20.0
Transportation	0.0	44.4	17.8	4.4	8.9	13.3	15.6
Professional Service	2.7	44.0	17.8	16.9	6.7	10.2	10.2
Owner							
Minority-owned	18.1	27.6	18.8	3.7	10.3	13.3	7.2
Not minority-owned	4.3	44.8	23.1	4.8	11.2	14.9	11.2

104

Firm Characteristic	Confident Payment will be Received	Predictable Revenue Source	% Citing Reason Firm Produces Service/Commodity Primarily Used by Government	Offers New Business Opportunity to Get Established	Recruited by Government Purchasing Staff	Participation in Minority Business Enterprise Program
Minority Owner-Gender[2]						
Female	61.3%	30.5%	20.3%	17.1%	8.9%	27.0%
Male	64.1	29.1	12.6	32.0	6.8	41.7
Minority Owner-Race[2]						
Black	63.7	27.5	14.7	42.2	3.9	55.9
Hispanic	70.2	38.0	14.9	19.0	4.1	46.3
Asian	62.1	34.5	10.3	17.2	6.9	34.5
American Indian	46.2	38.5	15.4	0.0	7.7	38.5
Other	41.7	25.0	8.3	33.3	0.0	16.7
Size-Economic Classification						
Small, economically disadvantaged	67.6	32.4	20.2	18.9	7.7	23.5
Not small, economically disadvantaged	59.7	33.2	24.7	6.7	13.4	2.8
Current Contract Status						
Has contract with government	61.7	34.3	26.6	8.4	13.6	6.8
No contract with government	60.4	26.7	12.3	12.5	7.5	10.2
No Government Contract Presently[3]						
Have had one in past	64.0	30.2	13.2	10.4	11.8	7.7
Have not had one in past	52.8	25.6	9.4	14.4	6.7	13.9

[2] Question was answered only by the subset of the respondents meeting the definitional criterion (minority-owned).

[3] Question was answered only by the subset of the respondents meeting the definitional criterion (firm does not have a government contract at the present).

Table 4.1 (continued)

Firm Characteristic	Participation in Small Business Enterprise Program	Been doing Business with Same Government for Years	Good Relations with Government Purchasing Office	Good Relations with Elected Officials	Purchasing Procedures are Efficient & Easy to Follow	Purchasing Policies are Administered Fairly	Other
				% Citing Reason			
Minority Owner-Gender[2]							
Female	13.7%	32.4%	21.0%	4.1%	11.4%	10.8%	6.0%
Male	17.5	23.3	16.5	1.9	8.7	15.5	10.7
Minority Owner-Race[2]							
Black	30.4	15.7	10.8	1.0	12.7	12.7	7.8
Hispanic	22.3	27.3	14.9	2.5	6.6	15.6	7.4
Asian	6.9	17.2	13.8	10.3	6.9	13.8	10.3
American Indian	30.8	38.5	30.8	7.7	23.1	23.1	15.4
Other	25.0	33.3	8.3	0.0	0.0	8.3	8.3
Size-Economic Classification							
Small, economically disadvantaged	17.4	32.2	19.1	3.3	11.0	12.8	9.5
Not small, economically disadvantaged	4.2	44.1	23.0	5.0	11.1	15.1	10.6
Current Contract Status							
Has contract with government	6.9	46.1	25.0	5.2	11.9	15.9	10.0
No contract with government	7.8	24.2	11.2	1.8	8.4	10.1	11.7
No Government Contract Presently[3]							
Have had one in past	5.5	28.3	16.8	3.6	8.0	10.4	11.3
Have not had one in past	10.6	21.7	8.9	1.7	11.1	9.4	16.6

[2] Question was answered only by the subset of the respondents meeting the definitional criterion (minority-owned).

[3] Question was answered only by the subset of the respondents meeting the definitional criterion (firm does not have a government contract at the present).

			% Citing Reason			
Firm Characteristic	Confident Payment will be Received	Predictable Revenue Source	Firm Produces Service/ Commodity Primarily Used by Government	Offers New Business Opportunity to Get Established	Recruited by Government Purchasing Staff	Participation in Minority Business Enterprise Program
Level of Government Firm Does Business With (Multiple Responses)						
Federal	60.1%	34.9%	27.9%	6.0%	15.5%	4.7%
State	61.4	34.2	27.3	7.0	13.4	5.2
City	61.0	33.4	26.1	8.0	13.3	6.4
County	62.0	34.0	26.0	8.2	13.4	5.9
Transit Authority	62.4	36.3	28.4	7.3	16.7	6.1
School district	63.1	35.1	24.0	6.8	14.4	4.6
Hospital district	58.8	32.7	26.1	5.8	16.3	3.5
Other special district	62.1	35.9	43.4	6.6	16.7	5.1
Other	66.3	36.0	9.3	23.3	1.2	22.1
% of Gross Revenues From Government Contracts						
Less than 10%	58.6	26.6	14.7	9.2	10.9	5.8
10-25%	64.5	36.8	18.5	7.9	14.5	5.7
26-50%	67.2	45.3	36.8	7.4	16.6	11.5
51-75%	65.1	43.0	54.3	14.0	9.1	8.1
76-90%	68.7	39.1	48.7	13.0	13.9	18.3
Over 90%	60.6	37.0	55.1	8.7	7.9	11.0

Table 4.1 (continued)

Firm Characteristic	% Citing Reason						
	Participation in Small Business Enterprise Program	Been doing Business with Same Government for Years	Good Relations with Government Purchasing Office	Good Relations with Elected Officials	Purchasing Procedures are Efficient & Easy to Follow	Purchasing Policies are Administered Fairly	Other
Level of Government Firm Does Business With (Multiple Responses)							
Federal	7.5%	50.8%	25.3%	5.0%	11.5%	16.6%	11.0%
State	7.2	49.3	24.4	5.0	12.2	16.2	10.5
City	7.0	47.1	24.9	5.4	12.1	16.6	9.7
County	6.5	45.8	24.7	5.4	11.8	15.8	9.9
Transit Authority	8.4	54.4	30.6	7.5	13.6	19.9	8.9
School district	6.4	48.9	27.4	5.5	13.1	14.5	10.1
Hospital district	6.8	54.3	30.4	4.9	15.1	19.7	9.9
Other special district	7.6	53.5	29.8	11.6	10.1	16.6	13.1
Other	16.3	9.3	5.8	1.2	4.7	3.5	5.8
% of Gross Revenues From Government Contracts							
Less than 10%	5.6	32.3	17.8	2.4	9.6	12.3	12.6
10-25%	8.6	50.6	28.2	3.5	13.3	19.3	8.9
26-50%	7.8	50.7	27.7	8.1	11.8	16.2	8.4
51-75%	5.4	54.8	28.5	12.4	8.6	13.4	2.2
76-90%	7.0	55.7	16.5	9.6	10.4	16.5	6.1
Over 90%	11.8	47.2	26.8	11.8	15.0	16.5	12.6

Firm Characteristic	% Citing Reason					
	Confident Payment will be Received	Predictable Revenue Source	Firm Produces Service/Commodity Primarily Used by Government	Offers New Business Opportunity to Get Established	Recruited by Government Purchasing Staff	Participation in Minority Business Enterprise Program
Procedures for Getting Government Contract (Multiple Responses)						
Formal competitive bid (with negotiation)	62.1%	39.2%	34.4%	7.5%	15.0%	5.7%
Formal competitive bid (sealed)	63.1	34.0	25.3	8.3	13.4	6.5
Local vendor preference	65.9	34.5	28.7	6.5	17.8	4.3
Request for Proposal (competitive negotiation)	60.5	39.3	35.8	8.2	17.8	5.9
Government solicitation of written quote	62.5	32.3	29.7	7.6	19.7	4.9
Government solicitation of telephone quote	67.9	32.7	31.1	7.5	20.9	4.7
Participation in Minority Business Enterprise Program	65.7	34.3	23.1	26.6	11.2	79.7
Participation in Small Business program	61.4	36.4	34.1	12.1	13.6	26.5
Other procedure	46.4	28.5	22.5	7.3	8.6	6.6
Type of Product Delivered to Government (Multiple Responses)						
Service	59.5	34.7	25.4	9.8	13.4	7.4
Commodity/good	61.1	29.8	24.6	8.1	13.6	4.3
Construction	69.0	34.3	18.6	10.2	9.8	13.8
Geographical Location						
In-State	62.4	32.7	21.3	9.8	11.6	8.1
Out-of-State	53.3	32.1	36.4	5.8	14.9	4.0

Source: Random sample survey of businesses listed on the Harris County (Houston), Texas vendor mailing list (conducted May–June, 1989) and mail survey of all businesses listed on the Hillsborough County (Tampa), Florida vendor registration list (conducted June–July, 1989)

Table 4.1 (continued)

Firm Characteristic	% Citing Reason						
	Participation in Small Business Enterprise Program	Been doing Business with Same Government for Years	Good Relations with Government Purchasing Office	Good Relations with Elected Officials	Purchasing Procedures are Efficient & Easy to Follow	Purchasing Policies are Administered Fairly	Other
Procedures for Getting Government Contract (Multiple Responses)							
Formal competitive bid (with negotiation)	7.4%	51.8%	29.7%	7.1%	13.3%	19.5%	8.9%
Formal competitive bid (sealed)	7.4	45.8	24.8	4.3	12.5	17.0	9.1
Local vendor preference	7.3	54.4	34.1	6.6	15.5	17.2	8.5
Request for Proposal (competitive negotiation)	7.4	53.1	29.4	8.8	13.0	17.6	9.6
Government solicitation of written quote	8.1	54.8	32.5	4.8	13.9	19.9	7.9
Government solicitation of telephone quote	8.4	57.0	35.8	4.3	15.3	20.7	6.9
Participation in Minority Business Enterprise Program	34.3	35.7	27.3	9.1	16.1	25.2	6.3
Participation in Small Business program	59.8	64.4	40.9	9.8	17.4	28.0	8.3
Other procedure	5.3	33.1	14.6	6.0	8.6	7.3	35.8
Type of Product Delivered to Government (Multiple Responses)							
Service	6.3	42.1	24.1	6.7	11.4	14.2	10.0
Commodity/good	6.7	46.7	26.1	3.0	12.1	16.0	10.7
Construction	9.3	33.5	17.9	4.0	8.2	16.3	10.3
Geographical Location							
In-State	6.6	39.4	22.3	4.8	11.2	14.7	9.9
Out-of-State	10.4	53.8	21.7	3.5	10.6	14.6	12.9

Source: Random sample survey of businesses listed on the Harris County (Houston), Texas vendor mailing list (conducted May–June, 1989) and mail survey of all businesses listed on the Hillsborough County (Tampa), Florida vendor registration list (conducted June–July, 1989)

THIRD REASON: PREDICTABLE REVENUE SOURCE

More than one-third (33 percent) of the firms cite the predictability of government contracts as a revenue source as a major reason for selling to government (see Figure 4.1). In line with earlier findings, firms most likely to rank this reason even higher than third are small firms (generating less than $200,000 in gross revenue), newer firms (in operation three to five years), nonprofit organizations, small and economically disadvantaged firms, Asian-owned firms, and firms in construction, real estate, communications, and professional service industries (some of the more cyclical industries).

One construction firm responding to our survey wrote "Governments must spend even when the private economy is slow." A professional service contractor says that government work "helps us cover gaps in private work." These comments confirm what Gumpert and Timmons note in their article advising small firms to sell to the public sector: Government "doesn't usually subject suppliers to the same kind of abrupt cancellations that, in industry, are a feature of recessions." Of course, government revenue is more predictable when the business has a fixed or multiyear contract.

Among the firms in our survey, the highest percentages identifying the predictability of government revenue as a major reason are:

- Nonprofits (39 percent)
- Businesses in operation less than a year (36 percent) or three to five years (36 percent)
- Firms with more than 5,000 employees (38 percent)
- Firms with more than $50 million in gross revenues (37 percent)
- Those that have been successful in winning government contracts (34 percent)
- Those receiving 25 to 75 percent of their gross revenues from government contracts (43–45 percent)
- Firms in professional services (45 percent), mining (60 percent), real estate (43 percent), and construction (36 percent)

These findings suggest that once a firm secures government business, it is fairly confident that it will continue to get it. (This is certainly true among nonprofit organizations, according to Rehfuss in *Contracting out in Government*.) In spite of cutbacks in government spending, many private sector firms in the more cyclical industrial sectors still see government revenue as more predictable (less elastic) than revenue generated from the private sector.

FOURTH REASON: GOVERNMENT IS A FIRM'S MAJOR MARKET

Nearly one-fourth (24 percent) of the firms responding to our survey do business with government because they "produce a service/commodity primarily used by government" (see Figure 4.1). In other words, these firms originated primarily to provide goods or services to government; they range from weapons manufacturers to nonprofit domestic violence shelters. Predictably, firms more likely to rank this reason higher than fourth are those receiving more than 90 percent of their gross revenue from government contracts. (This is the second most commonly cited reason, behind confidence in receiving payment, among firms earning the bulk of their money from the government.)

A higher than average (above 25 percent) of nonprofit organizations, partnerships, businesses in operation less than one year, businesses with more than 100 employees, businesses generating more than $11 million in gross revenues, and firms in the finance, utility, manufacturing (all types), communications, and professional services sectors (see Table 4.1) see government as a major market for their goods or services. Some sample comments from respondents:

"Government is the biggest market for our service and is a very easy market to identify" (professional services firm).

"The government's priorities coincide with our mission so it is easy to get money from government for the mission" (nonprofit firm).

"We are in the business of serving a population generally funded by government" (nonprofit firm in health care).

"We sell a product that government needs" (durable goods manufacturer); these products are usually concentrated in the military, space, and nuclear energy industries.

One of the most significant findings here may be that a fourth of the newest firms (in operation less than a year) see their primary market as the public sector. For many of these firms, their success depends upon their competitiveness in the public sector vendor pool—and in the openness of the competitive arena. Yet, as Gumpert and Timmons note, newer and smaller firms often have the most difficulty in realistically assessing government as a market: "The best way to learn the needs of each government market is to look at what it has bought in the past and what it is ordering for the future. Unfortunately, no one source lists all this information." Thus purchasing offices could assist new, small, and minority businesses by making such a master list available.

CHARACTERISTICS OF THE PROCUREMENT PROCESS AND STAFF

A fairly small proportion of the businesses surveyed identify characteristics of the government procurement process and purchasing staff as reasons for doing business with government. As shown in Figure 4.1, 22 percent say they are influenced by their firm's "good relations with the government purchasing office"; 15 percent cite the fair administration of purchasing policies as a factor; 11 percent cite the efficiency and clarity of purchasing procedures; and 12 percent identify recruitment efforts of the government's procurement staff.

Larger, more established firms that have successfully competed in the government contracts arena are most likely to cite characteristics of the government procurement process and staff among their major reasons for doing business with government (see Table 4.1.) For example, the firms most likely to identify "good relations with the purchasing staff" as a major reason are corporations (23 percent), firms in operation longer than 10 years (25 percent), firms with more than 5,000 employees (35 percent), firms with gross revenues more than $50 million (31 percent), firms currently holding a government contract (25 percent), and firms receiving more than 10 percent of their revenue from government contracts. This finding affirms what Gumpert and Timmons noted: that large firms have the advantage in "establishing trusting relationships with government procurement officials" because they have the resources to have "a special sales force or a Washington representative akin to a manufacturer's representative to keep abreast of the government market."

Our survey results suggest that *government procurement officials need to be more aggressive in their outreach programs to new, small, and minority-owned businesses to expand the vendor pool and improve their image of helpfulness.* This need comes across clearly in the statistics showing which firms said they were "recruited by the government purchasing staff" as a major reason for doing business. While relatively few firms in general cite this factor, the highest percentages occur in large, established firms, with histories of securing government contracts, in sectors characterized by relatively few young or minority firms (insurance, utility, communications, professional services).

Similar patterns appear in business citations of procurement processes. It is the larger, more established, nonminority-owned, successful government-contractor businesses that identify the administrative fairness of government purchasing policies or the efficiency and clarity of purchasing procedures as a major reason for doing business with government (see Table 4.1).

A Chance for New Businesses to Get Established

Less than one-tenth (9 percent) of the firms surveyed cite the chance to get established as one of the major benefits of doing business with government. Predictably, this reason stands as more important among young, small, minority-owned firms without much experience in government contracting. In fact, it is the second most commonly cited reason among firms in business two years or less. It is the third most commonly cited reason among firms generating less than $200,000 annually in gross revenues and black-owned firms.

The highest percentages of firms reporting they do business with government to get established are:

- Individually owned firms (15 percent)
- Firms in business less than one year (49 percent) or between one and two years (42 percent)
- Firms with 1 to 25 employees (13 percent)
- Firms with gross revenue less than $200,000 (26 percent)
- Minority-owned firms (21 percent)

- Black-owned firms (42 percent)
- Hispanic-owned firms (19 percent)
- Asian-owned firms (17 percent)
- Small, economically disadvantaged firms (19 percent)
- Those currently without government contracts (13 percent)
- Those that have never had a government contract (14 percent)

Business organizations and publications apparently have been somewhat successful in promoting the notion that government contracts can be a good starting point in business expansion. Gumpert and Timmons report that government contracts frequently help small firms purchase inventory needed to complete the contract through the practice of making progress payments. The authors also note that selling to government can help a "new small firm gain credibility, which can help in selling to private customers." Thus government faces the challenge of sustaining and nurturing the image that government business is good business. An important step is to open up the contracting system.

GOVERNMENT NURTURING OF MINORITY AND SMALL BUSINESSES

A small percentage of firms identify their participation in either Minority Business Enterprise (8 percent) or Small Business Enterprise (7 percent) programs as major reasons for selling to government. This finding is consistent with statistics cited in Chapter 2 showing that few governments actually have stringent, mandatory vendor preference policies in place. But where these policies exist, they tend to most affect the construction industry. A great deal of state and local government construction derives at least part of its funding from federal monies, making these recipient governments liable for small and minority business goals.

The firms most likely to cite participation in either MBE or SBE programs as reasons to do business with government are minority-owned firms (see Table 4.1); small, economically disadvantaged firms; newly established, individually owned firms; firms with gross revenues less than $200,000; firms receiving a large part of their gross revenue from government contracts; and construction-related firms. Our statistics also show that when government procurement programs attempt to broaden vendor pools, racial- and ethnic-minority-owned firms are more likely to take advantage of them than small businesses or female-owned businesses.

While a number of studies have reported that participation in official minority contractor programs can help minority business firms succeed,[3] a sizable proportion of small businesses and minority-owned firms do not see participation in MBE or SBE programs as a major reason to do business with government. Instead, they view participation in these programs as too restrictive, limiting the scope of their business and their chances of expansion.[4] For example, Andrea Watson in *Black Enterprise* warns that while many minority entrepreneurs have flourished as a result of government set-aside programs, these programs can "serve as a double-edged sword for Black business owners who allow themselves to be painted into a 'set-aside corner,' where they are limited to a certain portion of work." Furthermore, a survey of the chief executive officers of the 500 largest Hispanic companies, published in the April 1990 issue of *Hispanic Business*, found "great antipathy" among the CEOs to Small Business Administration programs.

Some small businesses believe many of the special government procurement programs conflict with each other, thereby restricting or eliminating business opportunities for small firms.[5] Still other small or minority-owned firms see MBE or SBE programs as poorly administered and too political, frequently letting in businesses that are not legitimate minority or small firms. Nonetheless, small minority-owned firms that have participated in SBE or MBE programs are more positive in their assessments of government contracting than similar firms that have not. The challenge is to broaden the pool of participants in these official enterprise development programs.

OTHER ATTRACTIONS OF GOVERNMENT BUSINESS

More than 10 percent of the firms surveyed identify a reason other than those just reviewed for why they desire to sell to government. An analysis of the responses to this open-ended (fill-in-the-blank) category shows the most common "other" reasons to be:

1. The size of the government market and a chance to expand and diversify a firm's customer base
2. The firm's perception that it is providing a quality public service or good at a good price to the taxpayers
3. Enhancement of the firm's reputation

Size of government market Approximately 70 percent of these "other" reasons are related to the profit motive, the first reason cited above. As predicted in Chapter 1, the sheer volume of government business often attracts a private sector firm to its vendor pool. Some typical comments from our survey:

"Government contracts are generally worth much more $$$ than private contracts" (a large manufacturing corporation in business longer than ten years).
"It's the potential volume of work that is most attractive" (a small service firm).
"The volume of government is simply too large to ignore" (a large, established construction company).
"The large volume of purchases usually compensates for payment problems, except with regard to the federal government and the military" (a large, established retail trade firm). (Chapters 5 and 6 elaborate on the federal government's poor reputation for paying in a timely fashion.)
Government money is "another revenue source that is 'extra,' even if unpredictable because of inconsistencies in volume" (a large wholesale trade firm).

Other firms more specifically identified the opportunity to diversify their customer base. A professional service firm in operation longer than ten years says government business helps it "keep a wide base of clients," although the firm acknowledges "it tries to keep government work at only 10 percent because of a lower profit margin."
A number of firms see government as just another customer. Typical comments:

"We consider government as we would any other customer that uses our product" (a moderate-sized retail trade firm).
"Government is just another source of business, but typically with a lower profit margin" (a communications firm).

In summary, *firms citing diversification of their customer base as a reason for selling to government tend to be those that intentionally restrict government business to a relatively small proportion of their total revenues because of the lower profit margin.*

Quality product Approximately 25 percent of firms that identify "other" as a reason for doing business with government cite the quality of their product. Some comments:

"We offer a quality installed product in excess of what is normally offered by those who are allowed to bid" (a moderate-sized construction-related firm in business six to ten years).
"Government likes our firm because of the quality of our service and our prompt delivery" (a small retail trade firm in operation three to five years).
"We do business with government to help keep taxes lower through our provision of quality goods" (a large, established retail trade firm).

Firm's good reputation The remaining 5 percent of the firms identifying "Other" as a major reason for selling to government see the advantages more in personal terms. Some comments:

It helps "build up bonding capacity based on reports of the quality of my work for the county" (a new, small Hispanic-owned firm).
It's a way of "recovering some of the costs of getting on hundreds of bid lists, but receiving only a few invitations to bid" (a small firm in the durable manufacturing goods business).
"Government business adds credibility and prestige to our firm" (a large, established, wholesale trade corporation from out of state).

As the figures in Table 4.1 show, one type of firm likely to cite the "Other" category among the major reasons it does business with government is the nonprofit organization. Nonprofit organizations are major providers of public services, especially social services.[6] These nonprofit "firms" tend to do business with government because government itself is not able to provide a service efficiently or effectively. Frequently, these organizations deliver social services under subcontracts with governments that have received grants from other levels of government.

While nonprofit organizations often produce a service primarily used by government, they do not see the government market

as their primary raison d'être. A significant number view government contracts as a way to serve greater numbers of worthy, needy, and disadvantaged clients more than as a way to make a profit. (As Rehfuss has noted, however, some see "only a slight difference between nonprofit organizations and their private counterparts, the difference being whether an operating surplus is called profit or a reserve for program support.") Nonprofit organizations also tend to be more up front about acknowledging the linkage between political support and receipt of government contracts than other types of firms.

THE POLITICAL CONNECTION: GOOD RELATIONS WITH ELECTED OFFICIALS

The smallest percentage (5 percent) of the businesses surveyed identify "good relations with elected officials" as a major reason for doing business with government. However, the percentage of firms identifying this item as a major reason is highest among:

- Nonprofit organizations (14 percent)
- Firms in business longer than ten years (5 percent)
- Firms with 1,001 to 5,000 employees (10 percent) or more than 5,000 (9 percent)
- Firms with more than $50 million in gross revenues (7 percent)
- Those securing contracts through either negotiated competitive bidding or sole source contracts (utility, 29 percent; professional services, 17 percent; insurance, 14 percent; finance, 12 percent; or in wholesale trade, 20 percent)
- Minority firms owned by Asians (10 percent) or American Indians (8 percent)
- Firms currently holding government contracts (5 percent)
- Firms with more than half their gross revenues from government contracts
- Firms delivering a service to government (7 percent)

Among nonprofits, the political connection often comes through community influentials who serve on their governing boards. As Rehfuss notes, it is often difficult for government to deny funding to these organizations, particularly the well-established ones, when their "committed volunteers . . . happen to be influential in the community."

It is also not surprising that older, more established firms (which also happen to be larger and owned by nonminorities) are more likely to identify good relations with elected officials as a reason for doing business with government. These firms frequently participate in high-profile business organizations (such as chambers of commerce) that have strong linkages with elected community leaders. These firms also tend to contribute to political campaigns—a factor frequently cited by unsuccessful vendors who see the purchasing system as rigged.

In light of the growing political clout of minorities, particularly of women, blacks, and Hispanics, one might have expected a much larger proportion of minority-owned firms to identify "good relations with elected officials" as a reason for doing business with government. Indeed, many of the governing bodies in the Houston and Tampa metropolitan areas have a sizable number of female and minority council or board members who are interested in recruiting more minorities to compete for government business. The growing number of these firms as well as those classified as small and economically disadvantaged suggest that elected officials must more aggressively seek to broaden their government's vendor pool.

The difficulty with elected officials becoming more aggressive in recruiting businesses is the interpretation of such actions within conflict-of-interest regulations (see Chapter 2). Many elected officials fear being cited for conflict-of-interest violations if they try to expand the vendor pool. Others fear some negative political fallout from the firms not actively recruited—and from those that are recruited but do not win contracts. Regardless of the reason, our survey shows that the "political connection" in contracting is not often cited, at least publicly, as a reason for doing business with government. However, *nothing is inherently wrong with elected officials playing an important role in broadening the vendor pool if that role is properly structured; in most instances, it would better serve the taxpayers by increasing competition.*

SUMMARY

The results of our survey confirm that businesses see the advantages of selling to government almost precisely as Bahls sees them in the *Nation's Business*:

> Doing business with government agencies can be profitable for those familiar with the rules and processes. Red tape may delay your payment for months, but you are sure of payment. And while the government's general insistence on accepting the lowest bid means the profit per item may be marginal, the sheer volume of business can make up for it.

The vast majority (61 percent) do business with government because they are "confident payment will be received"; 33 percent see government revenue as "a predictable revenue source; and 10 percent consider government business attractive because of its volume, its potential for helping them establish and expand their business, and its value as a reward for their offering a high-quality product or service at a good price. Nearly one-fourth (24 percent) view government as their primary market because their firm "produces a service/commodity that is primarily used by government." Another 9 percent, mostly new, small, or minority-owned

firms, see selling to government as "a chance to get established."

A large portion of the firms surveyed say they do business with the public sector because they have learned the rules of the game. Forty-one percent say they sell to government because "they have been doing business with the same governments for years"; 22 percent identify "good relations with the government's purchasing office"; 15 percent cite the fairness of purchasing policies; and 11 percent see government purchasing procedures as efficient and easy to follow.

Other firms do business with government because they have been encouraged by government purchasing practices designed to broaden the vendor pool. Some 12 percent report they were actively "recruited by the government purchasing staff"; 8 percent identify participation in a government Minority Business Enterprise program; and 7 percent point to Small Business Enterprise program participation. However, the businesses most likely to acknowledge that they were recruited by a government purchasing staff are older, larger, more established firms.

In general, businesses do not identify

many reasons for selling to government (the median number identified by each firm was two), and they approach consensus only on one factor: confidence that government will pay its bills. These findings suggest that it will be difficult for government to design public relations campaigns to attract businesses into the public sector vendor pool, yet the primary strategy should be to emphasize the profit, expansion, and experiential opportunities. Campaigns should downplay characteristics of the procurement process. However, as noted in Chapter 2, the public sector desperately needs to develop an educational program to inform the private sector why certain of its procurement practices are more complex than those of the private sector.

The firms that identify the fewest number of reasons for selling to government are those that have heretofore been unsuccessful in winding their way through the government's procurement maze: small, newly established businesses and minority-owned firms. The challenge will be to encourage them to participate in a system they regard as closed. But an even larger problem exists: Businesses of all types see far more negatives than positives in doing business with government.

Notes

1. Our survey found that out-of-state firms, when compared to in-state firms, are more likely to be corporations, firms in business longer than ten years, large firms in terms of number of employees and annual gross revenue, firms in the manufacturing or communications sectors, firms not owned by racial or ethnic minorities, businesses currently holding a government contract, and firms with a large proportion of gross revenue from government contracts.

2. A larger proportion (39 percent) of female-owned businesses in our study have been in operation more than ten years compared to black-owned businesses (23 percent). Although a higher percentage of Hispanics (41 percent) have been in business that long, women-owned businesses generally have been more successful than male-owned racial or ethnic minority firms in securing government contracts, especially state and local government contracts (MacManus, 1990). This is true primarily because women constitute a higher percent of all business owners (27) than blacks (3), Hispanics (2), or Asians (2). See Schwartz, 1988.

3. Cf. O'Neal, 1979; Liburd-Jordan, 1983; Fulwood, 1985; Robson, 1986; Fortune, 1988; Jones, 1988; Engeleiter, 1989; Singletary, 1990; Watson, 1989).

4. Cf. Ross, 1979; Black, 1983, 1989; Isaiah Poole, 1981; Harold Logan, 1983; MacManus, 1990b; Watson, 1989).

5. See Cibinic and Nash, 1986; Kennedy and Trilling, 1988; Cf. Owens, 1987.

6. See Orlans, 1980; De Hoog, 1984; MacManus, 1985; Salamon, 1986, 1989; Rehfuss, 1989. See also Chapter 1.

CHAPTER 5

Problems Businesses Frequently Encounter in Selling to Government

"You have to be meticulous in dealing with the federal government," said a construction contractor. "Once they held up a $50,000 payment because my telephone number was not on the invoice. It was on my cover letter and it was on every other page in my file, which was as thick as a phone book. They could have looked it up or asked the person at the next desk, but they just let the invoice sit there."

"We often find ourselves dealing with people who don't know anything about printing," says the general manager of printing company. "They don't know, for instance, that when you print words in yellow ink, they're hard to read."

BUSINESSES GENERALLY REGARD government purchasing practices as noncompetitive, inefficient, and inequitable (see Chapter 3). But which specific attributes of the public procurement system do businesses see as the most problematic? Do firms agree on the most frequently encountered problems? Do firms differ in their views based upon their size, their industry, or their experience in getting government contracts?

We asked businesses to answer this question:

Which of the following does your firm frequently encounter in contracting with governments? (Check all applicable)

Slow payment cycles

Reluctance to consider new products and services

Confusion as to which government agency or official has the major responsibility for a specific purchasing decision

Difficulty in making contact with the agency or official who will actually use the service/product

Inordinate delays between bid closing and actual contracting decisions

Bid specifications written too narrowly to permit real competition among potential suppliers

Bid specifications written too generally and imprecisely

Mandated labor costs higher than local standards

Mandated minority set-aside requirements

Competition from other firms pushes prices too low for our firm to compete

Difficulty in competing against large firms

Difficulty in competing against small firms

Too many noncompetitive sole source contracts

Government purchasing cycles out of sync with industry cycle

Too much paperwork required for application

Too much paperwork required once contract received

Lack of a written procedures manual available to suppliers

Bid bond requirement

Performance bond requirement

Payment bond requirement

Unrealistic delivery requirements (usually too short a time frame)

Absence of rigorous performance audits to weed out bad or unethical contractors

Inadequate procedures for protests and appeals

Other(s) (Specify):

More Negatives Than Positives

Businesses are much more likely to identify negatives about government purchasing procedures than positives, although no real consensus emerges on which negatives they encounter most frequently. The median number of problems they have identified is four (compared to two positives). Nearly one-third of our respondents identify seven or more negatives. Only 6 percent identify no problems.

Furthermore, an individual business is much more likely to articulate the problem(s) it regards as the most offensive than to elaborate on the reasons it does business with government. We received many detailed comments from firms about their dislikes, more so than their likes; we include many of these responses in this chapter.

The firms most likely to identify a large number of negatives (more than seven) are large corporations; firms in business longer than five years; businesses in the construction, professional services, and wholesale trade sectors; firms that receive more than 10 percent of their gross revenue from government contracts; female- and Hispanic-owned firms; and firms that have had government contracts in the past but no longer do.

The five most frequently encountered problems are:

1. Slow payment cycles (45 percent)
2. Bid specifications written too narrowly to promote competition (36 percent)
3. Difficulty making contact with the actual user of the service/product (32 percent)
4. Too much paperwork required for application (29 percent)
5. Competition from other firms pushes prices too low for our firm to compete (28 percent) (see Figure 5.1)

Less than 10 percent identify other problems, which are in order:

- Too many sole source contracts (10 percent)
- Inadequate procedures for protest and appeals (9 percent)
- Mandated labor costs higher than local standards (8 percent)

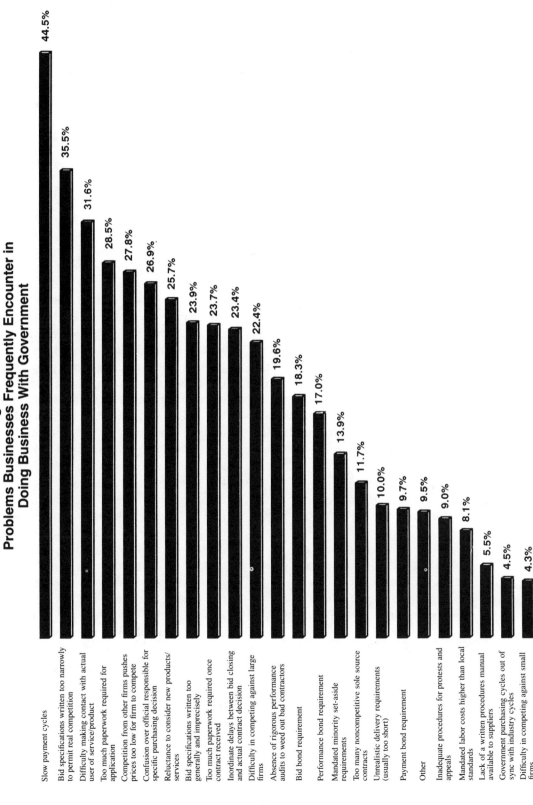

Figure 5.1
Problems Businesses Frequently Encounter in
Doing Business With Government

Slow payment cycles — 44.5%

Bid specifications written too narrowly to permit real competition — 35.5%

Difficulty making contact with actual user of service/product — 31.6%

Too much paperwork required for application — 28.5%

Competition from other firms pushes prices too low for firm to compete — 27.8%

Confusion over official responsible for specific purchasing decision — 26.9%

Reluctance to consider new products/services — 25.7%

Bid specifications written too generally and imprecisely — 23.9%

Too much paperwork required once contract received — 23.7%

Inordinate delays between bid closing and actual contract decision — 23.4%

Difficulty in competing against large firms — 22.4%

Absence of rigorous performance audits to weed out bad contractors — 19.6%

Bid bond requirement — 18.3%

Performance bond requirement — 17.0%

Mandated minority set-aside requirements — 13.9%

Too many noncompetitive sole source contracts — 11.7%

Unrealistic delivery requirements (usually too short) — 10.0%

Payment bond requirement — 9.7%

Other — 9.5%

Inadequate procedures for protests and appeals — 9.0%

Mandated labor costs higher than local standards — 8.1%

Lack of a written procedures manual available to suppliers — 5.5%

Government purchasing cycles out of sync with industry cycles — 4.5%

Difficulty in competing against small firms — 4.3%

121

- Lack of a written procedures manual available to suppliers (6 percent)
- Government purchasing cycles out of sync with industry cycles (5 percent)
- Difficulty in competing against small firms (4 percent) (see Figure 5.1)

These relatively small percentages run somewhat counter to the projections in Chapter 1, which forecast that a sizable number of firms would identify each of these as problems. However, our results do show that some types of firms complain about these problems more than others.

Differences from the Lamm Study of Defense Contractors

Our results vary substantially from Lamm's study of defense contractors cited earlier. His study was based on a survey conducted three years before ours and limited to 427 firms that had refused business or voiced significant problems with the procurement process of the U.S. Department of Defense. Lamm's study found that the most frequently cited problems among federal defense contractors were:

- Burdensome paperwork (69 percent)
- Government bidding methods (57 percent)
- Inflexible procurement policies
- More attractive commercial [private sector] ventures (34 percent)
- Low profitability (32 percent)
- Government attitudes (32 percent)

Problems cited by less than 10 percent of Lamm's defense-related businesses were:

- Inefficient production levels/rates (9 percent)
- Lost business to competitors (9 percent)

- Prime contractor/higher-tier subcontractors methods (8 percent)
- Work set aside for small business (6 percent)
- Not enough defense business (6 percent)
- Government-furnished equipment problems (4 percent)
- Adverse court/board rulings (4 percent)
- Adverse GAO decisions (2 percent)
- Termination of contracts (2 percent)

While our survey instruments are not identical, the differences between Lamm's results and ours are substantial enough to demonstrate that *studies limited to the federal level and/or to one sector yield results different from those based on larger, more inclusive samples.* Most notably, a much higher proportion of the 3,282 businesses in our study report competition-related problems than do defense firms. Furthermore, our survey reveals that a higher proportion of businesses see slow payment cycles, reluctance to consider new products or services, and set-asides (vendor preference policies) as problematic.

The two studies are most alike with regard to the rank ordering of problems related to the procurement process itself (paperwork, specifications, unclear lines of authority, delays in decision making) although, as noted, the wording of the survey questions and choices were different. As we will show, the bulk of these process-related problems occurs in the preaward stage—the stage that is the most exclusionary and has the greatest impact on the size of the potential vendor pool. Again, however, firms vary in their rank orderings of negatives. We turn now to a closer look at the characteristics of the firms most likely to identify specific problems.

SLOW PAYMENT CYCLES

In spite of the proliferation and adoption of model prompt pay laws,[1] *nearly half (45 percent) of the businesses surveyed identify slow payment as one of the biggest hassles of doing business with government.* It ranks at the top of most firms' list of problems most frequently encountered in selling to government (see Table 5.1).

Higher-than-average citations of slow payment as a problem come from firms in business longer than ten years, firms with more than twenty-six employees, firms with gross revenues higher than $1 million, firms in the construction, real estate, retail trade, and professional service sectors, female- and Asian-owned minority firms, firms holding, or having held, government contracts (regardless of the level of government they deal with or the procedures they have used to get one), and out-of-state firms. The common thread here is the breadth of experience a firm has had in dealing with governments: The broader the experience, the more likely the firm is to have experienced slow pay problems.

More important, *nearly one-third (29 percent) of the firms that have never had a government contract see this as a common problem in doing business with government.* These firms no doubt have been influenced by the experiences of their professional peers. Typical comments from our survey respondents include:

"Payment is our biggest problem. Very often it is very slow, and often not at all."

"The county is the only credit account we have. Our other customers pay the day the work is completed."

"Government jobs are the *only* type of job we have a problem collecting on."

"We stopped doing government work several years ago due to low prices, poor coordination, and *slow payment!*"

Thus, government's reputation for slow payment deters the recruitment of more vendors into the vendor pool *and* the retention of others.

RESTRICTION OF COMPETITION

In our survey, firms were asked to cite the frequency of six competition-related outcomes of government purchasing practices. The most negative, and distressing, findings are that more than one-third (36 percent) see competition restricted by bid specifications written too narrowly; 24 percent see bid specifications written too generally and imprecisely (and giving more latitude to government officials); and 22 percent say government procurement practices make it difficult for them to compete against large firms.

The most positive finding is that more than one-fourth (28 percent) of our respon-

dents have frequently encountered government contracting situations in which "competition from other firms pushes prices too low for our firm to compete." This latter finding may be interpreted as evidence that government's procurement system is achieving one of its goals—efficiency. However, a closer analysis of firm responses to the open-ended "other" category shows that many of these firms believe that governments focus too much on cost and not enough on quality. (We will return to this point later in the chapter.)

Results showing that less than 10 percent frequently encounter "too many sole source [noncompetitive] contracts" and only 4 percent have encountered "difficulty in competing against small firms" are also positive for government (see Table 5.1). However, these competition-related assessments vary by firm characteristic.

Bid Specification Problems

Bid specifications too narrow to promote competition is the second most commonly cited problem with government procurement practices. But it ranks as the biggest problem among firms in the wholesale trade and durable manufacturing sectors as well as firms owned by American Indians (one-third of which are in the wholesale trade or manufacturing sectors). This finding is not surprising in light of the fact that the bulk of the standard specifications established by the American Society for Testing and Materials covers items produced by these sectors.[2] Many of the ASTM specifications are viewed as excessively detailed by firms in these sectors.

Higher-than-average (above 36 percent) proportions of firms reporting that they frequently encounter bid specs too narrowly written (see Table 5.1) are those in business less than one year; medium-sized and large firms (more than 1,000 employees, gross revenues higher than $500,000); firms in the wholesale and retail trade, manufacturing, finance, and insurance sectors; firms owned by American Indians or "other" minorities; firms not classified as small or economically disadvantaged; firms currently holding a government contract; those with less than 25 percent of their gross revenues from government contracts but doing business with a wide range of governments; firms delivering a commodity or good to government; and in-state firms. The common threads appear to be experience in doing business with government *and* the degree to which standardized specs exist for certain industries. Firms in the trade, manufacturing, and financial services sectors are most subject to these standards.

Many firms feel strongly about the negative effect of detailed standards on competition. Some feel that government officials purposely exclude certain bidders when they draw up the specs. Typical comments from our survey respondents:

"Bid specs are intentionally designed to allow only one manufacturer's piece of equipment to be bid, usually to a sole source vendor."

"Specifications are purposefully relaxed to accept an inferior product (low bid) or a product that was not on the approved list prior to bid opening."

Other firms believe that those writing the specs are simply incompetent or unaware of current standards. Some survey responses:

"Our firm frequently comes across poorly defined specs that are obscure or technically incorrect."

"Can you believe that a government we do business with is still asking for bids on 'bottled water' which is comparable to asking for bids on the old-fashioned ice box instead of a refrigerator?"

(The shortcomings of government procurement personnel are the most commonly cited "other" problem frequently encountered, a point to be discussed later in the chapter.)

Still other firms feel that narrow specs not only reduce competition but increase price, often at the expense of quality.

"We encounter *over*-specifications in many areas. Many times more importance is placed on the specs (e.g., size of an opening or length of a screw) than to the importance of quality workmanship (e.g., holes or screws are put in the right place). Many times over-speced items prohibit a reasonable bid. When quality workmanship is disregarded, more material will not give a better product!" (a small firm in operation longer than ten years).

"Specifications add to costs with the end result being that government pays for unnecessary requirements" (a large, established durable-goods manufacturing firm).

Several small firms also complain that the mere costs of researching voluminous specs and regulations placed them at a disadvantage and discouraged them from bidding on government jobs.

Too General and Imprecise to Promote Competition

As previously noted, *nearly one-fourth (24 percent) of our respondents frequently encounter bid specs written too generally and imprecisely.* (It is the eighth most commonly cited problem.) The major concern here is that it gives government procurement and elected officials too much latitude in the decision making process. However, as noted in Chapter 2, governments argue that this type of spec is frequently necessary in highly technical and newly emerging fields and actually promotes innovation. Thus, one would expect that firms in the newer, more high-tech sectors would more frequently encounter generally written specs. Our results confirm this hypothesis.

Firms most often reporting a problem with generally written specs (see Table 5.1) are large firms (more than 1,000 employees, with gross revenues higher than $1 million); firms in the mining, manufacturing (durable, nondurable), wholesale trade, construction, and professional service sectors; firms currently holding government contracts and depending on government business to generate more than 10 percent of their gross revenue; and out-of-state firms. Missing from this group are minority-owned firms and small, economically disadvantaged firms, primarily because these firms have had less experience in doing business with government.[3]

Once again it appears that *if a firm does business with governments long and fre-quently enough, it will come across bid specs written too generally.* Firms encountering this situation often find it highly undesirable:

"We frequently encounter contracts prepared by the government that are vague and always interpreted to the government's advantage."

"We have even received IFB's from governments with their usual source already named on the bid, hardly indicative of efforts to promote real competition."

Too Many Sole-Source Contracts

Surprisingly, in light of conventional wisdom, *only a relatively small proportion (10 percent) of firms complain about government issuing too many sole source contracts* (see Chapter 1). Somewhat more predictably, firms in the less competitive and "public good" sectors are most likely to encounter sole source contracts. As the figures in Table 5.1 show, above-average proportions of firms in the mining, communications, finance, and transportation sectors cite this problem. Less predictably, the wholesale trade sector also tends to cite this problem more often than average. However, wholesale trade firms, like most categories of minority-owned firms, are most likely to identify political favoritism among the "other" problems they frequently encounter. This finding indicates that these firms view sole source contracts more as evidence of favoritism than as a supply problem.

Other types of firm likely to cite sole source contracts more frequently than average are those least successful in securing government contracts—i.e., new, small, minority-owned firms. While this percentage is relatively small, the vendor pool could shrink even further if the proportion escalates. This is especially the case since these firms will comprise the majority of all U.S. business firms in the not-too-distant future.

Table 5.1
Problems Businesses Encounter in Selling to Government
by Firm Characteristic

Firm Characteristic	% Citing Problem					
	Slow Payment Cycles	Reluctance to consider new products & services	Confusion over official responsible for specific purchasing decisions	Difficulty making contact with actual user of service/product	Inordinate delays between bid closing & actual contract decision	Bid specs written too narrowly to permit real competition
All Firms	44.5%	25.7%	26.9%	31.6%	23.4%	35.5%
Firm Structure						
Individual owner	40.8	22.6	22.0	30.9	19.9	26.9
Partnership	42.0	19.3	30.7	25.0	19.3	26.1
Nonprofit organization	44.4	13.0	14.8	16.7	9.3	5.6
Corporation	44.9	26.7	27.8	32.5	24.4	37.9
Other	72.7	9.1	18.2	0.0	27.3	27.3
Years in Business						
Less than 1 year	44.4	20.5	15.9	27.3	13.6	43.2
1-2 years	34.1	23.5	27.4	37.4	18.0	27.4
3-5 years	43.2	23.7	28.8	33.4	29.2	35.7
6-10 years	44.1	29.5	24.9	28.7	26.2	38.5
Over 10 years	45.8	25.4	27.2	31.5	22.1	35.3
Number of Employees						
1-25	42.4	23.0	24.5	32.0	21.7	34.7
26-50	46.1	28.2	26.7	28.7	21.2	37.8
51-100	46.2	26.0	30.5	29.8	22.9	30.5
101-500	47.4	29.2	31.7	33.8	31.4	39.1
501-1000	44.7	28.9	28.9	36.8	31.6	32.9
1001-5000	54.2	33.1	33.1	26.3	26.3	38.1
Over 5000	45.2	39.3	38.1	34.5	28.6	42.9

Firm Characteristic	% Citing Problem					
	Bid specs written too generally & imprecisely	Mandated labor costs higher than local standards	Mandated minority set-aside require-ments	Competition from other firms pushes prices too low	Difficulty in competing against large firms	Difficulty in competing against small firms
All Firms	23.9%	8.1%	13.9%	27.8%	22.4%	4.3%
Firm Structure						
Individual owner	17.7	7.0	12.1	26.9	34.4	2.7
Partnership	11.4	9.1	12.5	27.3	25.0	1.1
Nonprofit organization	3.7	13.0	1.9	5.6	9.3	3.7
Corporation	25.9	8.2	14.6	28.3	20.6	4.7
Other	9.1	9.1	9.1	18.2	36.4	0.0
Years in Business						
Less than 1 year	18.2	6.8	0.0	27.3	31.8	0.0
1-2 years	20.1	6.7	8.4	33.0	38.5	2.8
3-5 years	23.4	8.8	14.4	26.9	34.3	2.6
6-10 years	22.2	8.4	11.1	31.0	32.0	1.9
Over 10 years	24.8	8.0	15.3	26.7	15.4	5.6
Number of Employees						
1-25	22.2	7.3	11.0	29.2	31.8	2.3
26-50	23.4	11.6	14.1	25.7	14.9	4.8
51-100	26.3	6.1	16.0	24.4	10.3	4.6
101-500	27.4	10.5	20.6	25.8	8.9	8.0
501-1000	23.7	5.3	21.1	27.6	0.0	9.2
1001-5000	29.7	11.0	23.7	28.8	0.8	13.6
Over 5000	35.7	4.8	16.7	21.4	0.0	13.1

Table 5.1 (continued)

Firm Characteristic	% Citing Problem					
	Too many non-competitive sole source contracts	Government purchasing cycles out of sync with industry cycle	Too much paperwork required for application	Too much paperwork once contract received	Lack of written procedures manual available to suppliers	Bid bond requirement
All Firms	9.7%	4.5%	28.8%	23.7%	5.5%	18.3%
Firm Structure						
Individual owner	6.5	3.2	26.1	16.7	3.5	21.2
Partnership	9.1	1.1	26.1	25.0	9.1	14.8
Nonprofit organization	0.0	1.9	27.8	25.9	9.3	5.6
Corporation	10.5	4.9	29.3	24.7	5.6	18.4
Other	0.0	9.1	0.0	9.1	0.0	9.1
Years in Business						
Less than 1 year	9.1	2.3	31.8	18.2	13.6	27.3
1-2 years	13.4	3.9	23.5	15.6	10.6	21.8
3-5 years	10.7	5.1	25.3	19.0	5.6	23.0
6-10 years	10.9	4.6	29.1	19.7	4.8	23.8
Over 10 years	8.8	4.5	30.0	26.6	4.9	15.2
Number of Employees						
1-25	10.2	3.9	26.5	20.7	5.4	20.8
26-50	11.1	4.8	30.0	27.0	3.0	18.1
51-100	8.8	4.2	31.7	28.2	7.3	14.5
101-500	8.0	7.4	32.6	28.3	7.1	16.0
501-1000	6.6	6.6	27.6	27.6	3.9	13.2
1001-5000	10.2	4.2	33.9	28.8	5.9	10.2
Over 5000	4.8	6.0	41.7	28.6	7.1	4.8

Firm Characteristic	% Citing Problem					
	Performance bond requirement	Payment bond requirement	Unrealistic delivery requirements	Absence of rigorous performance audits to eliminate bad contractors	Inadequate procedures for problems & appeals	Other
All Firms	17.0%	10.0%	11.7%	19.6%	9.0%	9.5%
Firm Structure						
Individual owner	21.5	13.2	9.9	12.4	7.3	10.5
Partnership	9.1	3.4	13.6	15.9	6.8	8.0
Nonprofit organization	3.7	1.9	13.0	7.4	11.1	2.8
Corporation	17.0	10.0	12.1	21.2	9.3	9.3
Other	18.2	9.1	9.1	9.1	0.0	9.1
Years in Business						
Less than 1 year	20.5	15.9	11.4	15.9	4.5	6.8
1-2 years	22.3	12.8	10.6	12.3	6.1	8.9
3-5 years	21.6	14.2	9.5	17.9	10.4	9.3
6-10 years	22.2	13.8	11.3	20.1	11.5	10.3
Over 10 years	14.0	7.7	12.4	20.6	8.4	9.4
Number of Employees						
1-25	19.2	11.7	10.4	18.3	7.7	9.9
26-50	17.6	10.3	13.6	20.7	10.6	11.1
51-100	13.4	7.6	8.4	19.8	8.8	6.5
101-500	15.1	6.5	15.7	23.7	12.9	8.3
501-1000	10.5	5.3	14.5	22.4	6.6	9.2
1001-5000	11.0	7.6	16.9	21.2	16.9	6.8
Over 5000	3.6	3.6	15.5	20.2	7.1	9.5

Table 5.1 (continued)

	% Citing Problem					
Firm Characteristic	Slow Payment Cycles	Reluctance to consider new products & services	Confusion over official responsible for specific purchasing decisions	Difficulty making contact with actual user of service/product	Inordinate delays between bid closing & actual contract decision	Bid specs written too narrowly to permit real competition
Firm Gross Revenues ('88)						
Below $200,000	40.0%	20.3%	23.3%	32.0%	17.5%	25.8%
$200,000-499,999	40.8	22.5	25.1	31.6	20.0	32.9
$500,000-999,999	41.7	23.5	24.0	29.4	22.8	40.9
$1-$10 Million	45.8	26.2	26.5	30.0	24.7	36.0
$11-$25 Million	50.5	29.5	29.0	35.2	28.6	37.1
$26-$50 Million	52.4	35.2	38.1	41.0	26.7	40.0
Over $50 Million	48.4	35.5	36.2	35.5	31.7	44.6
Industry Classification						
Retail trade	48.5	25.1	28.0	34.7	19.1	37.6
Wholesale trade	42.8	32.9	27.7	41.4	25.7	45.7
Finance	41.2	58.8	23.5	5.9	47.1	41.2
Insurance	42.9	28.6	14.3	28.6	28.6	42.9
Utility	28.6	28.6	28.6	42.9	14.3	14.3
Construction	46.7	22.1	23.5	18.5	29.6	32.6
Manufacturing	46.5	25.6	32.6	30.2	27.9	41.9
Manufacturing-durable	39.5	34.3	37.3	39.5	26.6	44.2
Manufacturing-nondurable	36.1	36.1	33.7	43.4	24.1	43.4
Real estate	48.4	19.4	12.9	16.1	16.1	25.8
Communications	42.2	24.1	30.1	41.0	15.7	32.5
Service	43.0	17.8	22.4	27.7	16.1	24.4
Agriculture	38.5	15.4	26.9	34.6	11.5	23.1
Mining	50.0	25.0	50.0	25.0	0.0	25.0
Transportation	42.6	12.8	25.5	21.3	17.0	21.3
Professional Service	48.3	22.8	27.6	25.9	31.9	21.6
Owner						
Minority-owned	43.7	22.4	22.4	33.3	22.1	30.4
Not minority-owned	44.8	26.6	28.2	31.2	24.0	37.0

Firm Characteristic	% Citing Problem					
	Bid specs written too generally & imprecisely	Mandated labor costs higher than local standards	Mandated minority set-aside requirements	Competition from other firms pushes prices too low	Difficulty in competing against large firms	Difficulty in competing against small firms
Firm Gross Revenues ('88)						
Below $200,000	13.5%	6.7%	6.7%	27.3%	44.5%	1.1%
$200,000-499,999	19.3	7.4	7.2	28.1	36.2	2.1
$500,000-999,999	23.5	8.3	12.3	27.5	28.9	2.9
$1-$10 Million	28.3	9.6	16.9	30.1	15.4	4.1
$11-$25 Million	26.7	8.1	20.0	26.2	11.0	9.0
$26-$50 Million	29.5	10.5	21.9	20.0	2.9	8.6
Over $50 Million	32.1	5.6	21.3	26.8	6.7	11.5
Industry Classification						
Retail trade	22.1	2.9	6.0	36.0	28.0	2.2
Wholesale trade	31.5	2.7	11.0	30.9	22.3	1.6
Finance	17.6	0.0	5.9	5.9	17.6	0.0
Insurance	14.3	0.0	14.3	28.6	0.0	0.0
Utility	14.3	0.0	14.3	28.6	14.3	0.0
Construction	24.8	23.7	31.7	23.2	18.5	7.5
Manufacturing	16.3	7.0	14.0	20.9	34.9	4.7
Manufacturing-durable	30.5	6.0	15.9	21.5	12.9	5.2
Manufacturing-nondurable	31.3	1.2	9.6	26.5	14.5	7.2
Real estate	12.9	0.0	9.7	35.5	19.4	0.0
Communications	16.9	3.6	7.2	21.7	19.3	4.8
Service	17.2	7.9	9.7	30.2	21.7	5.6
Agriculture	3.8	7.7	3.8	23.1	15.4	3.8
Mining	50.0	0.0	50.0	0.0	0.0	0.0
Transportation	19.1	0.0	8.5	25.5	12.8	2.1
Professional Service	24.1	8.6	19.0	21.6	30.6	3.4
Owner						
Minority-owned	18.7	8.1	6.8	34.3	44.3	2.8
Not minority-owned	25.5	8.1	15.8	26.3	16.6	4.8

Table 5.1 (continued)

Firm Characteristic	% Citing Problem					
	Too many non-competitive sole source contracts	Government purchasing cycles out of sync with industry cycle	Too much paperwork required for application	Too much paperwork once contract received	Lack of written procedures manual available to suppliers	Bid bond requirement
Firm Gross Revenues ('88)						
Below $200,000	8.4%	3.4%	27.1%	16.6%	7.1%	21.5%
$200,000-499,999	9.5	3.7	27.8	19.3	5.3	20.0
$500,000-999,999	11.8	4.4	24.0	24.0	5.4	21.3
$1-$10 Million	10.0	4.0	29.0	26.4	3.8	18.0
$11-$25 Million	8.6	6.7	33.8	27.6	8.6	18.1
$26-$50 Million	7.6	8.6	29.5	25.7	7.6	11.4
Over $50 Million	9.4	6.6	36.6	31.0	6.6	11.8
Industry Classification						
Retail trade	9.6	4.9	20.6	16.1	4.0	17.0
Wholesale trade	10.6	5.2	28.6	16.0	5.6	14.6
Finance	29.4	0.0	11.8	17.6	5.9	23.5
Insurance	0.0	0.0	42.9	28.6	0.0	14.3
Utility	0.0	0.0	28.6	14.3	0.0	0.0
Construction	7.1	5.0	32.8	43.1	3.4	32.6
Manufacturing	7.0	9.3	39.5	27.9	14.0	20.9
Manufacturing-durable	9.0	3.4	35.6	26.6	6.9	14.6
Manufacturing-nondurable	9.6	3.6	37.3	24.1	9.6	10.8
Real estate	6.5	9.7	29.0	22.6	3.2	12.9
Communications	18.1	7.2	30.1	14.5	4.8	18.1
Service	8.3	2.7	24.8	16.6	4.3	14.9
Agriculture	0.0	7.7	26.9	23.1	3.8	23.1
Mining	25.0	25.0	0.0	0.0	0.0	0.0
Transportation	10.6	2.1	19.1	14.9	6.4	14.9
Professional Service	8.2	2.2	37.5	32.3	8.2	12.5
Owner						
Minority-owned	9.5	4.2	29.4	19.0	7.5	26.0
Not minority-owned	10.1	6.0	28.8	24.9	5.0	16.2

Firm Characteristic	% Citing Problem					
	Performance bond requirement	Payment bond requirement	Unrealistic delivery requirements	Absence of rigorous performance audits to eliminate bad contractors	Inadequate procedures for problems & appeals	Other
Firm Gross Revenues ('88)						
Below $200,000	20.4%	11.4%	8.2%	14.8%	7.7%	10.3%
$200,000-499,999	16.9	10.7	11.8	14.8	6.5	10.7
$500,000-999,999	20.3	11.5	10.3	23.5	9.6	10.0
$1-$10 Million	17.3	11.0	12.0	21.3	9.9	9.6
$11-$25 Million	16.2	7.6	11.9	21.4	8.6	6.7
$26-$50 Million	15.2	4.8	18.1	22.9	11.4	7.6
Over $50 Million	9.8	7.0	16.4	23.3	12.9	8.7
Industry Classification						
Retail trade	13.6	7.4	12.3	12.8	7.6	8.5
Wholesale trade	11.9	5.4	14.2	17.6	6.3	7.7
Finance	17.6	11.8	11.8	11.8	11.8	0.0
Insurance	0.0	0.0	28.6	14.3	0.0	14.3
Utility	0.0	0.0	14.3	28.6	0.0	28.6
Construction	35.1	28.7	9.8	27.8	12.1	9.8
Manufacturing	16.3	4.7	4.7	18.6	4.7	4.7
Manufacturing-durable	13.3	4.7	13.3	17.2	10.7	10.3
Manufacturing-nondurable	10.8	3.6	18.1	15.7	8.4	8.4
Real estate	6.5	6.5	12.9	16.1	9.7	9.7
Communications	12.0	8.4	3.6	15.7	9.6	8.4
Service	15.9	6.2	9.7	19.3	6.8	10.6
Agriculture	19.2	11.5	0.0	19.2	0.0	7.7
Mining	0.0	0.0	0.0	75.0	0.0	0.0
Transportation	10.6	6.4	6.4	14.9	8.5	6.4
Professional Service	14.2	6.0	15.1	22.8	11.2	14.2
Owner						
Minority-owned	25.6	15.1	9.6	17.2	10.1	10.7
Not minority-owned	14.7	8.6	12.4	20.6	8.9	9.1

Table 5.1 (continued)

Firm Characteristic	% Citing Problem					
	Slow Payment Cycles	Reluctance to consider new products & services	Confusion over official responsible for specific purchasing decisions	Difficulty making contact with actual user of service/product	Inordinate delays between bid closing & actual contract decision	Bid specs written too narrowly to permit real competition
Minority Owner-Gender[1]						
Female	49.6%	23.7%	24.6%	34.3%	23.4%	33.1%
Male	36.8	23.1	21.4	34.7	20.3	31.4
Minority Owner-Race[1]						
Black	33.9	13.9	13.0	29.3	15.5	20.7
Hispanic	38.5	24.6	28.5	36.2	23.8	30.8
Asian	55.9	29.4	17.6	32.4	26.5	29.4
American Indian	21.4	14.3	14.3	14.3	21.4	35.7
Other	33.3	26.7	33.3	33.3	13.3	46.7
Size-Economic Classification						
Small, economically disadvantaged	41.4	24.3	26.0	34.3	22.5	30.1
Not small, economically disadvantaged	44.9	26.4	27.4	30.8	23.8	37.2
Current Contract Status						
Has contract with government	46.3	26.1	27.3	30.2	24.9	36.1
No contract with government	36.6	24.9	25.9	37.2	19.0	33.7
No Government Contracts at Present[2]						
Have had one in past	47.5	23.9	27.9	33.6	23.1	33.8
Have not had one in past	28.8	24.4	22.2	38.9	15.5	32.3

[1] Question was answered only by the subset of the respondents meeting the definitional criterion (minority-owned).

[2] Question was answered only by the subset of the respondents meeting the definitional criterion (firm does not have a government contract at the present).

134

Firm Characteristic	Bid specs written too generally & imprecisely	Mandated labor costs higher than local standards	Mandated minority set-aside require-ments	Competition from other firms pushes prices too low	Difficulty in competing against large firms	Difficulty in competing against small firms
			% Citing Problem			
Minority Owner-Gender[1]						
Female	22.5%	7.7%	6.8%	36.7%	40.2%	3.0%
Male	16.1	9.3	0.8	32.2	50.0	0.0
Minority Owner-Race[1]						
Black	7.8	8.6	6.0	36.2	55.2	0.0
Hispanic	17.7	13.1	7.7	31.5	46.2	3.8
Asian	20.6	2.9	2.9	32.4	50.0	0.0
American Indian	14.3	0.0	7.1	21.4	35.7	0.0
Other	20.0	6.7	6.7	40.0	46.7	6.7
Size-Economic Classification						
Small, economically disadvantaged	18.4	7.6	8.3	31.6	42.4	2.2
Not small, economically disadvantaged	25.5	8.2	15.5	26.7	16.7	5.0
Current Contract Status						
Has contract with government	26.3	7.6	14.5	28.0	19.8	4.8
No contract with government	17.3	10.1	10.8	28.5	31.0	2.3
No Government Contracts at Present[2]						
Have had one in past	17.9	13.9	16.2	29.6	27.1	3.5
Have not had one in past	15.0	5.3	7.5	25.2	35.8	3.1

[1] Question was answered only by the subset of the respondents meeting the definitional criterion (minority-owned).

[2] Question was answered only by the subset of the respondents meeting the definitional criterion (firm does not have a government contract at the present).

Table 5.1 (continued)

Firm Characteristic	% Citing Problem					
	Too many non-competitive sole source contracts	Government purchasing cycles out of sync with industry cycle	Too much paperwork required for application	Too much paperwork once contract received	Lack of written procedures manual available to suppliers	Bid bond requirement
Minority Owner-Gender[1]						
Female	10.4%	6.5%	32.5%	20.1%	7.4%	21.9%
Male	8.5	5.9	28.0	20.3	6.8	31.4
Minority Owner-Race[1]						
Black	6.0	4.3	23.3	13.8	2.6	40.5
Hispanic	10.8	4.6	28.5	25.4	10.0	29.2
Asian	17.6	2.9	35.3	17.6	5.9	17.6
American Indian	14.3	7.1	0.0	0.0	0.0	35.7
Other	13.3	6.7	33.3	20.0	0.0	26.7
Size-Economic Classification						
Small, economically disadvantaged	9.6	4.2	28.7	20.8	6.6	25.2
Not small, economically disadvantaged	9.6	4.7	29.0	24.6	5.3	16.5
Current Contract Status						
Has contract with government	8.9	4.2	27.4	23.7	5.6	18.3
No contract with government	11.6	5.7	33.6	23.6	5.6	18.2
No Government Contracts at Present[2]						
Have had one in past	12.7	5.5	34.6	32.1	7.2	19.4
Have not had one in past	11.1	6.2	34.5	16.8	6.2	19.0

[1] Question was answered only by the subset of the respondents meeting the definitional criterion (minority-owned).

[2] Question was answered only by the subset of the respondents meeting the definitional criterion (firm does not have a government contract at the present).

136

Firm Characteristic	% Citing Problem					
	Performance bond requirement	Payment bond requirement	Unrealistic delivery requirements	Absence of rigorous performance audits to eliminate bad contractors	Inadequate procedures for problems & appeals	Other
Minority Owner-Gender[1]						
Female	19.2%	10.9%	8.3%	18.0%	9.8%	11.2%
Male	29.7	21.2	10.2	11.9	7.6	8.5
Minority Owner-Race[1]						
Black	43.1	27.6	12.9	12.9	7.8	9.5
Hispanic	30.0	16.2	9.2	23.1	13.1	10.0
Asian	14.7	11.8	0.0	2.9	5.9	8.8
American Indian	35.7	28.6	0.0	21.4	7.1	14.3
Other	20.0	6.7	6.7	20.0	0.0	33.3
Size-Economic Classification						
Small, economically disadvantaged	24.8	16.7	9.9	15.7	8.8	12.2
Not small, economically disadvantaged	14.9	8.1	12.4	20.8	9.2	8.6
Current Contract Status						
Has contract with government	16.7	9.7	12.7	20.5	9.8	10.0
No contract with government	17.8	10.8	8.4	16.9	6.8	8.3
No Government Contracts at Present[2]						
Have had one in past	20.4	13.4	8.5	22.9	8.2	8.7
Have not had one in past	16.4	9.7	7.5	11.9	5.8	8.4

[1] Question was answered only by the subset of the respondents meeting the definitional criterion (minority-owned).

[2] Question was answered only by the subset of the respondents meeting the definitional criterion (firm does not have a government contract at the present).

Table 5.1 (continued)

Firm Characteristic	% Citing Problem					
	Slow Payment Cycles	Reluctance to consider new products & services	Confusion over official responsible for specific purchasing decisions	Difficulty making contact with actual user of service/product	Inordinate delays between bid closing & actual contract decision	Bid specs written too narrowly to permit real competition
Level of Government Firm Does Business With (Multiple Responses)						
Federal	49.2%	27.7%	29.9%	34.1%	26.7%	37.2%
State	47.9	27.9	28.1	33.2	25.4	37.1
City	48.0	27.9	28.4	32.2	25.4	37.5
County	47.1	27.0	28.1	31.3	24.8	36.5
Transit Authority	51.3	30.4	28.9	34.2	29.8	37.4
School district	48.8	27.3	29.2	33.0	24.9	37.6
Hospital district	51.1	30.1	32.1	34.9	25.4	39.1
Other special district	55.9	29.4	31.9	34.3	31.9	31.4
Other	34.5	21.0	26.8	41.0	18.0	33.8
% of Gross Revenues From Government Contracts						
Less than 10%	40.3	26.5	27.2	35.0	19.5	37.3
10-25%	49.4	26.3	27.3	29.4	23.8	37.5
26-50%	49.2	25.1	26.1	30.1	29.8	33.4
51-75%	50.8	23.0	28.3	24.1	31.6	27.8
76-90%	51.3	18.8	23.9	21.4	31.0	31.6
Over 90%	51.2	25.2	21.3	17.3	37.8	27.6

% Citing Problem

Firm Characteristic	Bid specs written too generally & imprecisely	Mandated labor costs higher than local standards	Mandated minority set-aside require-ments	Competition from other firms pushes prices too low	Difficulty in competing against large firms	Difficulty in competing against small firms
Level of Government Firm Does Business With (Multiple Responses)						
Federal	26.9%	8.9%	15.7%	27.2%	17.2%	4.6%
State	26.5	7.9	15.3	28.3	18.9	4.6
City	26.8	8.1	15.5	28.2	19.2	4.5
County	26.0	7.9	15.1	28.8	20.1	4.4
Transit Authority	28.9	7.5	16.9	30.5	16.1	4.9
School district	26.5	8.0	14.9	29.8	18.8	4.8
Hospital district	29.3	8.2	14.1	30.1	16.2	5.1
Other special district	25.5	10.8	19.6	20.6	15.2	3.4
Other	11.5	12.2	12.2	23.7	46.0	1.4
% of Gross Revenues From Government Contracts						
Less than 10%	19.5	6.7	11.8	27.9	22.6	3.9
10-25%	31.4	8.4	12.9	29.6	21.2	5.0
26-50%	27.4	9.7	16.7	27.8	21.4	4.7
51-75%	30.5	12.3	23.5	25.7	20.3	5.9
76-90%	28.2	13.7	26.5	32.5	23.9	3.4
Over 90%	28.3	7.9	20.5	23.6	29.1	4.7

Table 5.1 (continued)

Firm Characteristic	% Citing Problem					
	Too many non-competitive sole source contracts	Government purchasing cycles out of sync with industry cycle	Too much paperwork required for application	Too much paperwork once contract received	Lack of written procedures manual available to suppliers	Bid bond requirement
Level of Government Firm Does Business With (Multiple Responses)						
Federal	10.6%	5.4%	30.1%	26.6%	6.3%	17.4%
State	9.6	5.3	29.4	25.6	6.1	17.8
City	9.4	5.2	29.1	24.9	5.3	18.7
County	9.4	4.8	28.7	24.2	5.6	18.6
Transit Authority	10.8	5.9	28.4	25.7	4.5	18.4
School district	10.0	5.2	29.4	24.4	5.3	18.2
Hospital district	11.0	5.7	29.2	25.2	6.4	16.1
Other special district	8.3	7.4	28.9	26.0	3.9	14.7
Other	14.4	3.6	41.7	28.8	6.5	22.3
% of Gross Revenues From Government Contracts						
Less than 10%	9.8	4.4	31.2	23.0	5.8	15.7
10-25%	10.1	4.5	25.6	23.1	4.8	19.0
26-50%	11.0	5.7	25.1	24.4	5.4	19.1
51-75%	7.0	3.2	29.9	30.5	6.4	24.6
76-90%	8.5	5.1	27.4	24.8	6.0	27.4
Over 90%	5.5	4.7	19.7	20.5	3.9	29.9

Firm Characteristic	% Citing Problem					
	Performance bond requirement	Payment bond requirement	Unrealistic delivery requirements	Absence of rigorous performance audits to eliminate bad contractors	Inadequate procedures for problems & appeals	Other
Level of Government Firm Does Business With (Multiple Responses)						
Federal	16.0%	9.5%	13.2%	21.9%	10.5%	9.9%
State	16.1	9.6	12.8	20.8	10.1	9.5
City	17.1	10.1	13.1	21.4	9.5	9.2
County	17.2	9.9	12.4	20.9	9.5	9.0
Transit Authority	17.2	9.5	15.4	21.0	9.9	8.9
School district	16.0	9.4	13.3	21.0	9.6	9.4
Hospital district	13.5	8.2	13.9	19.8	10.3	9.2
Other special district	11.8	7.8	13.7	28.9	6.4	15.7
Other	23.7	14.4	7.9	13.7	7.9	13.7
% of Gross Revenues From Government Contracts						
Less than 10%	14.2	8.7	9.5	16.7	7.1	8.6
10-25%	16.0	9.8	14.4	21.5	10.2	8.6
26-50%	17.1	9.4	14.0	24.7	12.0	13.4
51-75%	26.2	13.9	15.0	25.1	13.4	11.8
76-90%	33.3	17.1	12.8	31.6	15.4	12.0
Over 90%	29.9	18.9	17.3	21.3	11.0	12.6

Table 5.1 (continued)

Firm Characteristic	% Citing Problem					
	Slow Payment Cycles	Reluctance to consider new products & services	Confusion over official responsible for specific purchasing decisions	Difficulty making contact with actual user of service/product	Inordinate delays between bid closing & actual contract decision	Bid specs written too narrowly to permit real competition
Procedures for Getting Government Contract (Multiple Responses)						
Formal competitive bid (with negotiation)	51.2%	30.0%	33.0%	32.0%	32.9%	41.3%
Formal competitive bid (sealed)	47.0	28.0	27.3	31.0	27.0	41.5
Local vendor preference	47.7	31.5	32.9	37.9	23.9	41.8
Request for Proposal (competitive negotiation)	50.4	28.3	32.1	31.1	33.7	35.0
Government solicitation of written quote	50.0	28.3	32.4	35.7	29.3	39.3
Government solicitation of telephone quote	50.5	31.2	33.1	40.6	28.0	40.7
Participation in Minority Business Enterprise Program	42.5	18.5	25.3	32.9	31.5	32.9
Participation in Small Business program	49.6	25.6	39.1	39.8	38.3	43.6
Other procedure	47.9	22.7	28.2	35.0	17.8	22.7
Type of Product Delivered to Government (Multiple Responses)						
Service	45.6	22.8	26.6	28.5	23.1	32.2
Commodity/good	45.2	31.1	30.8	38.9	23.9	43.1
Construction	45.4	21.6	23.6	20.4	28.2	31.9
Geographical Location						
In-State	43.2	26.1	26.0	30.5	22.5	35.8
Out-of-State	51.7	22.9	31.8	37.8	28.9	34.6

Source: Random sample survey of businesses listed on the Harris County (Houston), Texas vendor mailing list (conducted May–June, 1989) and mail survey of all businesses listed on the Hillsborough County (Tampa), Florida vendor registration list (conducted June–July, 1989)

142

Firm Characteristic	% Citing Problem					
	Bid specs written too generally & imprecisely	Mandated labor costs higher than local standards	Mandated minority set-aside require-ments	Competition from other firms pushes prices too low	Difficulty in competing against large firms	Difficulty in competing against small firms
Procedures for Getting Government Contract (Multiple Responses)						
Formal competitive bid (with negotiation)	30.4%	8.1%	15.4%	31.3%	17.2%	5.0%
Formal competitive bid (sealed)	30.2	8.5	15.3	30.5	19.8	4.9
Local vendor preference	28.1	7.3	11.2	33.2	23.0	4.3
Request for Proposal (competitive negotiation)	30.2	7.7	16.0	30.1	21.7	5.1
Government solicitation of written quote	30.4	7.1	14.4	30.7	19.8	4.8
Government solicitation of telephone quote	32.1	5.8	12.2	31.5	22.3	3.6
Participation in Minority Business Enterprise Program	19.2	14.4	13.0	45.9	50.0	4.1
Participation in Small Business program	32.3	6.8	19.5	35.3	33.8	2.3
Other procedure	16.0	7.4	8.6	19.0	27.6	1.2
Type of Product Delivered to Government (Multiple Responses)						
Service	22.9	7.8	10.9	28.4	24.2	4.3
Commodity/good	28.3	4.3	10.2	30.8	21.0	3.6
Construction	24.9	21.9	28.7	24.6	19.6	7.6
Geographical Location						
In-State	23.4	8.7	14.2	28.4	23.7	4.4
Out-of-State	26.1	4.0	12.4	23.6	14.4	4.0

Source: Random sample survey of businesses listed on the Harris County (Houston), Texas vendor mailing list (conducted May–June, 1989) and mail survey of all businesses listed on the Hillsborough County (Tampa), Florida vendor registration list (conducted June–July, 1989)

Table 5.1 (continued)

Firm Characteristic	Too many non-competitive sole source contracts	Government purchasing cycles out of sync with industry cycle	Too much paperwork required for application	Too much paperwork once contract received	Lack of written procedures manual available to suppliers	Bid bond requirement
Procedures for Getting Government Contract (Multiple Responses)						
Formal competitive bid (with negotiation)	11.9%	6.4%	32.3%	27.2%	6.2%	20.3%
Formal competitive bid (sealed)	10.2	5.2	28.9	24.8	4.9	21.8
Local vendor preference	11.6	5.4	28.1	20.7	5.1	18.3
Request for Proposal (competitive negotiation)	11.8	5.1	30.7	27.1	7.4	17.1
Government solicitation of written quote	11.1	5.9	31.3	23.6	5.9	19.7
Government solicitation of telephone quote	11.8	4.8	26.3	20.9	5.9	18.5
Participation in Minority Business Enterprise Program	11.6	6.2	35.6	26.7	6.8	33.6
Participation in Small Business program	16.5	3.8	39.1	32.3	9.8	28.6
Other procedure	12.9	3.1	30.1	22.1	9.2	12.3
Type of Product Delivered to Government (Multiple Responses)						
Service	9.9	4.3	27.2	22.7	5.7	17.4
Commodity/good	11.5	5.6	28.7	20.6	6.3	16.2
Construction	7.6	5.0	30.6	38.7	4.2	29.9
Geographical Location						
In-State	9.8	4.6	27.8	23.0	5.6	18.3
Out-of-State	8.5	4.2	36.8	28.4	5.7	18.9

Source: Random sample survey of businesses listed on the Harris County (Houston), Texas vendor mailing list (conducted May–June, 1989) and mail survey of all businesses listed on the Hillsborough County (Tampa), Florida vendor registration list (conducted June–July, 1989)

144

Firm Characteristic	% Citing Problem					
	Performance bond requirement	Payment bond requirement	Unrealistic delivery requirements	Absence of rigorous performance audits to eliminate bad contractors	Inadequate procedures for problems & appeals	Other
Procedures for Getting Government Contract (Multiple Responses)						
Formal competitive bid (with negotiation)	19.5%	10.4%	15.3%	23.3%	12.6%	8.4%
Formal competitive bid (sealed)	20.2	11.7	13.5	22.9	9.8	8.8
Local vendor preference	15.4	8.4	13.5	21.7	9.8	9.8
Request for Proposal (competitive negotiation)	15.4	7.8	14.9	24.6	11.7	11.9
Government solicitation of written quote	17.5	9.3	13.8	22.4	10.0	9.6
Government solicitation of telephone quote	16.0	8.6	14.3	21.0	9.2	8.2
Participation in Minority Business Enterprise Program	34.9	24.7	13.0	25.3	11.6	13.7
Participation in Small Business Program	26.3	18.0	20.3	23.3	14.3	8.3
Other procedure	9.8	6.1	9.8	13.5	9.2	20.9
Type of Product Delivered to Government (Multiple Responses)						
Service	16.2	8.8	11.8	20.7	10.2	10.4
Commodity/good	13.6	6.3	12.3	18.4	8.8	9.1
Construction	31.9	25.6	10.1	28.9	12.1	9.3
Geographical Location						
In-State	17.0	10.6	11.7	20.3	9.1	9.8
Out-of-State	17.2	6.2	11.9	15.7	8.7	7.7

Source: Random sample survey of businesses listed on the Harris County (Houston), Texas vendor mailing list (conducted May–June, 1989) and mail survey of all businesses listed on the Hillsborough County (Tampa), Florida vendor registration list (conducted June–July, 1989)

145

Competition with Large Firms

Almost one-fourth (22 percent) of the firms responding to our survey report that they frequently encounter "difficulty in competing against large firms" for government business. (This was the eleventh most cited problem.) As noted throughout the book, small firms often have a more difficult time competing for government business because they have less money and staff to expend on the preparation of application materials. Also, the sheer volume of some government contracts effectively prohibits small firms from competing for them. Some complaints by small firms:

Government procurement practices "fail to split large volume contracts into smaller parts, permitting small vendors to compete."

"Some big companies bid a government contract as a tax break, and they don't mind to lose 40 percent or 50 percent of the total bid price. It is impossible for small firms to bid competitively in this situation."

Other small firms are critical of large-firm "lobbying" efforts. One small service firm complains "There is too much 'wining and dining' of government procurement officials by large competitors which frequently interferes with procurement officials' decision to send a service out for bid." The proprietor notes that when his firm comes across such activities, it chooses "not to compete" for government business.

Predictably, the problem of competing against large firms for government business ranks higher than eleventh among individually owned firms (they rank it second); businesses in operation one to two years (they rank it first); and firms in operation less than one year or between three and ten years (each ranks it third). Competition against large firms also ranks much higher than eleventh among small firms. It ranks fourth among firms with one to twenty-five employees, first among firms taking in gross revenues less

than \$200,000, second among firms with gross revenues of \$200,000–499,999, and fourth among firms generating \$500,000–999,999. Frequently, these firms are in the retail trade, real estate, and professional services sectors.

Minority-owned firms also rank the inability to compete against larger firms for government contracts higher than eleventh, primarily because a significant number of them are new, small firms.[4] Minority firms as a whole rank it first. Black-, Hispanic-, American Indian-, and minority male-owned firms rank it first, while female- and Asian-owned firms rank it second. Small, economically disadvantaged firms also rank it first.

Another category of firm more prone to complain about the inability to compete against large firms is the group that currently does not have a government contract. Almost one-third (31 percent) of those currently without a contract and 36 percent of those that have never had a government contract report difficulty in competing against large firms. This difficulty ranks as the second most commonly cited problem among the firms that have never done business with government, which is particularly significant.[5] Thus, one big deterrent to broadening the vendor pool is the perception among small firms that they cannot compete.

Clearly, a major deterrent to broadening the vendor pool is the perception that large firms have the upper hand, fairly or unfairly, in the procurement system. For many state and local governments, this general perception unfortunately appears to be heavily influenced by publicity surrounding the federal procurement system. (This will become clearer in Chapter 6.)

Competition with Small Firms

Only 4 percent of our survey respondents report that in doing, or attempting to do, business with government they frequently have "difficulty in competing against small firms." In fact, *this is the least commonly cited problem of any in the survey* (see Figure 5.1). Not surprisingly, the largest firms are more likely to say they frequently have difficulty competing against small firms for government contracts, although the percentages are still extremely small (see Table 5.1). Significantly higher-than-average proportions of firms with more than 1,000 employees (more than 13 percent) and firms generating more than $50 million in gross revenue (12 percent) cite small-firm competition difficulties. It is likely that this happens most often when the contract's dollar volume is relatively small or when the IFB calls for purchase of commodities from firms that can supply parts or service for the items after purchase, thereby giving the advantage to local vendors. (A sizable proportion of the largest corporations are out-of-state firms.[6]) Nonetheless, a smaller percentage of large firms have difficulty competing with small firms than vice versa.

Competition Reduces Competition

More than one-fourth of our respondents (28 percent) report they frequently encounter situations in which "competition from other firms pushes prices too low for our firm to compete." In fact, this was the fifth most commonly encountered outcome of firm involvement in the government procurement process. For free market enthusiasts, this is a highly desirable finding—actually, the essence of the free market. But some vendors see it differently.

Firms in business a relatively short period of time, with relatively small work forces and gross revenues, are the most likely to say low prices force them to bow out of competition for government work (see Table 5.1). These types of firms rank this problem higher than fifth. They tend to be clustered in the retail trade, wholesale trade, utility, real estate, and service sectors. (With the exception of

utilities and wholesale trade, the other sectors are characterized by larger proportions of small firms.) In general, though, the relationship is less clear cut between this low-prices factor and firm characteristics such as years in business, number of employees, firm gross revenue, and government contract status.

More clear-cut is the higher proportion of minority-owned firms and small, economically disadvantaged firms that find government purchasing practices "pushing prices too low" for them to compete. Why don't more of these firms see themselves as competitive? Past research suggests that many of them do not have the expertise in developing cost estimates that the more experienced firms do. Another reason, usually expressed by opponents of minority vendor preference policies, is that less experienced minority firms submit inflated price estimates, speculating that preference policies will land them the contract anyway. Importantly, nearly two-thirds of the minority firms responding to our survey perceive they *are* competitive when it comes to government contracting situations. Still, a third do not—too large a percentage in light of our nation's socioeconomic trends.

Regardless of firm characteristics, businesses that see themselves as noncompetitive tend to lay the blame on the procurement process, not themselves. As noted earlier, *they believe they would be competitive if* government purchasing decisions were based on more than just price. We received many comments to this effect from our survey respondents.

"There is too much emphasis on low price; as a result, good companies don't want to bother with the paperwork, slow payment, dictatorial edicts of buyers, and the stupidity of the system" (a service firm).

"We have lost bids to other vendors with inferior products or which do not meet specifications. Products that are deemed 'equal' are often not equal" (a medium-sized retail trade firm).

Firms often see the exclusive emphasis on price as costing government more in the long run, especially if service of the good after purchase is not figured into total price calculations. According to a carpet company:

"There are a lot of carpet companies that do not know how to properly bid and many times the low bidder is one that made a gross error. This costs the government a lot of money if the company is unable to do the job and all the *legitimate* bidders have wasted their time. More than just lowest price should be considered in awarding bids. Quality products and quality installation should be a main consideration. Anyone can sell carpet, but proper installation should be a key factor to be considered, too."

LACK OF INFORMATION ABOUT THE PROCESS

Three choices in our "frequently encountered problems" question were designed to determine the extent to which firms have difficulty obtaining information that would help them decide whether to compete for government business. Businesses cite two informational shortcomings fairly often:

1. "Difficulty in making contact with the actual user of the service/product (cited by 32 percent of the firms, making it the third most frequently encountered problem)
2. "Confusion over the official responsible for a specific purchasing decision" (identified by 27 percent and ranked sixth among the twenty-four problems offered for assessment).

The third choice is not often a problem; only 6 percent of the respondents say "lack of a written procedures manual available to suppliers" is a commonly experienced facet of government procurement.

Difficulty Making Contact with Actual User of Firm's Product

This problem best exemplifies the often divergent viewpoints of the public and private sectors about what constitutes a legitimate business activity. Public sector procurement specialists are advised by their professional groups to limit the contact between a potential vendor and a potential user as much as possible. The Council of State Governments and the National Association of State Purchasing Officials warn: "In addition to creating demand for needs that many not exist, and stimulating unwarranted preferences for particular brands or sellers, the practice frequently has the improper consequences of a seller drafting or writing a purchase specification."

For businesses, not being able to direct their sales pitches at potential users contradicts what they regard as a normal business practice. Not surprisingly, then, a sizable proportion of our respondents (32 percent) cite this factor as a common frustration of the public sector procurement process. Firms most likely to identify this shortcoming are firms in operation between one and two years and out-of-state firms (it is the second most commonly cited problem among these groups). By industry, the problem is cited often by firms in the nondurable and durable manufacturing sectors (the problem ranks first and second, respectively), utilities (ranks first), the communications sector (ranks second), and the agricultural sector (ranks second). It is the single most cited problem among firms not currently holding a government contract.

Since little relationship exists between industrial classification and a firm's government contract status,[7] we can speculate that these firms have slightly different reasons for their frustrations. Newly established firms and those that have been unsuccessful in winning contracts probably have more limited knowledge of the procurement process in general; out-of-state firms often do not know the specifics of the process in a particular location.

In contrast, firms in the manufacturing, communications, and agricultural sectors are more likely to have new products or services to market. Therefore they may be more likely to perceive that they are getting the runaround from central purchasing office staff who are merely trying to avoid excluding these firms from competing for new business because of perceived conflict-of-interest violations.

Apparently a sizable number of firms are frustrated with what they perceive to be a general lack of coordination within the governmental arena, making it almost impossible to deal directly with users of their products (whom they regard as much more knowledgeable than central purchasing staff). Consider these comments:

"Most of those in responsible positions do not know the product or service they are dealing with."

"Personnel involved in purchasing have insufficient background on the items being purchased and insufficient understanding of specifications and requirements. This is a serious problem and costs government *and* suppliers a great deal of money."

"We frequently encounter a lack of coordination between the purchasing office and the official who actually uses our service."

Confusion over Who Makes a Specific Purchasing Decision

As shown in Figure 5.1, *more than one-fourth (27 percent) of our respondents frequently experience confusion over who is* *responsible for making a specific purchasing decision when they attempt to sell to government.* The problem is most commonly cited by firms that sell to many different governments. These firms are particularly frustrated about the lack of standardization, most notably with regard to the application process and its requirements. As one respondent said:

"The application process in general is confusing. The process is not standardized either within the federal government (each agency has a different commodity book), or across states or local governments. This makes it extremely difficult for companies to stay on bidder lists" to compete for contracts.

Firms most likely to identify confusion over who makes a decision are the larger, more experienced firms with histories of contracting with a wide range of governments and having secured government contracts through a multiplicity of procedures. Out-of-state firms have a particularly difficult time because they typically deal with governments in all fifty states and occasionally even foreign governments. It is the fragmented nature of government purchasing that most frustrates these firms.

Confusion over who makes a specific purchasing decision also plagues firms selling goods to governments but for a different reason (see Table 5.1). For these firms, the confusion relates more to their difficulty in identifying potential users than the lack of standardization in the application process: 57 percent of the firms frequently confused over which official decides on the purchase say they have trouble contacting the person who will actually use the product or service.

Lack of a Written Procedures Manual for Suppliers

"A procedures manual," according to the Council of State Governments and the

National Association of State Purchasing Officials, "documents or prescribes all of the steps of the procurement process, from the origin of an acquisition concept to the final conclusion of a project or disposition of an item." *Only a small percentage of firms (6 percent) say they frequently encounter situations in which such manuals are unavailable from the public sector.* This finding reflects the emphasis of professional purchasing groups on making such manuals available to vendors. Recall from Chapter 2 that professional purchasing groups such as NASPO strongly recommend making these manuals available; forty-three states have such requirements in place. Of course, manuals only describe the basic steps in a jurisdiction's procurement process; they do *not* identify the specific individuals to contact. This explains why a much higher percentage of firms identify problems with contact persons rather than manuals.

Firms reporting higher-than-average incidences of manual unavailability include non-profit organizations, partnerships, those in business less than five years, nondurable manufacturing and professional services firms, minority-owned firms (especially female-owned and Hispanic-owned firms), small and economically disadvantaged firms, firms doing business with the federal or state governments or hospital districts, and those that sell commodities.

The most common thread here is a firm's lack of experience in doing business with government. A sizable number of the firms citing manual unavailability also report difficulty in identifying the potential user of their good or service (56 percent) or confusion over who makes a specific purchasing decision (50 percent). Still, relatively few firms mention that the absence of a procedures manual frequently hampers them in doing business with government. In frequency, this problem ranks twenty-second out of twenty-four.

Informational Shortcomings of Government Purchasing Staff

The Council of State Governments and the National Association of State Purchasing Officials state: "Purchasing professionals need to communicate to the publics they serve, a clear understanding of the level of knowledge, the personal and public discipline, and the range of responsibility and accountability which the purchasing activity requires." Yet a sizable number of our respondents cite deficiencies in information supplied to them by the government procurement staff as a problem in the "other" category.

Some firms criticize the unavailability of purchasing agents. Typical comments come from two firms:

"It is very difficult to get assistance from government purchasing employees. I usually get transferred seven to ten times before someone will take responsibility for helping me."

"Purchasing officials are difficult or impossible to contact by phone."

Others criticize purchasing agents for failing to communicate contract or telephone numbers in correspondence with vendors and potential vendors. A firm selling software complains "When we receive an order for software, the ordering government frequently does not provide a phone number or the name of a contact person. It is always useful to a firm to have the name and phone number of the purchasing agent and the person who initiated the order in case there are problems. It would save government a lot of time and money in the long run."

Another firm says it too is frequently annoyed by "federal government agencies that mail 'mystery paperwork' with no way to contact the originators for more information."

Some firms complain of the general incompetence of public purchasing officials, as shown by these comments:

"We frequently find government supervisory/inspection personnel totally unqualified, resulting in an inordinate number of delays and costly problems."

"We deal with incompetent staffs far too often; they are very frustrating to work with."

"We constantly deal with simple personnel incompetence, ranging from constantly busy telephone lines and unreturned phone calls to unwillingness to act and ignorance. Personnel are particularly ignorant of most aspects regarding *quality* of professional services."

Other firms question the objectivity of purchasing staff and their general lack of professionalism. Typical comments:

"The purchasing person has a closed mind on other products out in the cycle of goods and pretty much has made up his mind on what he will purchase before sending out information on sealed bids."

"We find purchasing agents to be unprofessional and unable to stand behind what is exchanged verbally."

"We find it unconscionable that purchasing personnel frequently leak information to our competitors about prices."

"We often deal with purchasing agents who have no idea what they are purchasing and cannot answer rudimentary questions."

One Asian-owned firm complains of racial bias among purchasing personnel: "As a minority firm, if you are not either black or Spanish you don't get government jobs. People in charge of purchasing decisions are either black or Spanish."

Others complain of the apparent inability of purchasing staff to make a definitive statement. Typical comments:

"We frequently find that there are too many people in the purchasing office that are afraid to answer questions and who are always passing the buck so they do not have to assume responsibility."

"One hand doesn't know what the other hand is doing. There is no coordination between agencies handling the same contract."

A few firms blame high turnover rates among government purchasing officials for their inability to get accurate information from (or to) the government in a timely fashion. A firm in the health insurance business details the consequences of this problem:

We are a broker-dealer with a full-blown life and health division. My current largest municipality has had considerable difficulty in retaining an individual to handle the employees benefits contract and currently has an individual who is not qualified or in-tune with how carriers function in respect to employee benefits. He also is not a believer of free-enterprise which is to the detriment of the employers. The individual goes out of his way to prevent individuals from being able to quote on the specifications. If he remains with this municipality, the situation will only worsen as he continues to operate with blinders.

A significant number of firms complain that the staff does not distribute enough information on how to get on bid lists or on bidding opportunities.

"Our main difficulty is finding out when and if bids are to be sent out. We still do not know how to contact the right people to be sure our company is on the bid lists" (a relatively young service firm).

"We would bid for more government work if it was easier to find out what they need" (a moderate-sized construction firm).

"I would like to do government work but lack knowledge of how to get on bid lists" (a new female-owned construction firm).

A sizable number of firms complain that government purchasing officials often disseminate bid information on short notice, giving firms far too little time to assemble bid applications. This problem most often affects small firms.

"The local public university procurement office does not provide enough lead time on upcoming bids. A few days or even one week is not enough time to receive and submit a bid" (a small female-owned retail trade firm).

Some firms complain that government purchasing office staff often are not willing to share information on previous bids with potential vendors:

"We find that government is reluctant to provide abstracts on quotes so that we can see how our prices compare to the marketplace. This would enable us to study and compare ourselves to our competitors."

Minority-owned firms frequently complain that purchasing officials do not make it easy for prime contractors or government agencies to get listings of minority firms.

"Local governments in our service area make it next to impossible to get a listing of women-owned businesses" (the female owner of a wholesale trade firm).

Minority-owned firms also complain that governments are unwilling to try new ways of reaching minority vendors.

"Purchasing officials are reluctant to consider a minority newspaper in their efforts to reach minority vendors who might be interested in bidding on government business" (a black-owned communications firm).

Importantly, the proportion of firms identifying problems with government procurement personnel is smaller than that proportion saying they have good relations (see Chapter 4). However, those having problems tend to be the newer, smaller, less expe-rienced firms—precisely the firms that must be attracted to the public sector vending pool if the system's competitiveness is to be improved.

Government Procurement Personnel Shortages

In fairness to government purchasing personnel, it should be noted that most governments have small full-time professional purchasing staffs (see Table 5.2). A 1989 survey by the National Institute of Governmental Purchasing found that more than 50 percent of all governments have full-time professional purchasing staffs with four or fewer buyers. Less than one-fifth (17 percent) have staffs with more than twenty employees.

Salaries for government procurement personnel are relatively low, especially in light of the fact that more and more governments require that these individuals have advanced degrees or graduate from professional certi-fication programs.[8] In 1989, according to the National Institute of Governmental Purchasing, only 10 percent of the beginning buyers made more than $25,000 annually; only 31 percent made more than $20,000. Less than half (44 percent) of the fully qualified buyers (not supervisors) made more than $24,000. And only one-third of the chief procurement officers (with supervisory authority) made more than $35,000 annually.

These salaries reflect the rather low esteem that purchasing as a function holds in many governmental entities and master's degree programs in public administration pro-grams.[9] Procurement scandals are changing this picture—fast! From the perspective of many business owners, this change cannot come too soon. Inexperienced staffs have frustrated many firms, especially those with new products or services to offer.

Table 5.2
Full-Time Professional Purchasing Employees by Jurisdiction Type

Full-Time Professional Employees	Type of Government						
	Federal/State Provincial Central	City Municipality Town/Village	County Region Parish	School System University College	State Provincial Special Authority	City County Health	Total
	(n=65)	(n=272)	(n=120)	(n=85)	(n=57)	(n=18)	(n=617)
Over 50	21.5%	5.1%	3.3%	16.5%	8.8%	11.1%	8.6%
21-50	23.1	7.0	2.5	5.9	19.3	5.6	8.8
11-20	12.3	4.0	5.0	3.5	3.5	27.8	5.7
5-10	26.2	15.1	33.3	22.4	15.8	11.1	20.7
1-4	16.9	68.8	55.8	51.8	52.6	44.4	56.2
Totals[1]	100.0	100.0	99.9	100.1	100.0	100.0	100.0

[1] Totals may not equal 100.0% due to rounding.

Source: National Institute of Government Purchasing, *Results of the 1989 Procurement Research Survey*. Falls Church, VA: NIGP, P. 2.

RELUCTANCE TO CONSIDER NEW PRODUCTS OR SERVICES

When doing business with government, one-fourth (26 percent) of our respondents frequently experience a reluctance to consider new products or services—computers, telecommunications equipment, pharmaceuticals, for example. This problem is the seventh (out of twenty-four) most commonly cited problem. It supports the views of some that the government procurement process, as currently operative, stymies innovation. As a consequence, governments end up paying more for products and services that operate less efficiently or effectively than the latest available on the market.

This problem particularly frustrates individually owned firms, moderate-sized corporations and extremely large firms in operation six to ten years; and firms in the wholesale trade, finance, insurance, utility, durable and nondurable manufacturing, mining, retail trade, and communications sectors. It also frustrates firms doing business with federal, state, or city government, and all types of special district governments; in-state firms; and firms securing or attempting to secure contracts through local vendor preferences.

Each of these categories of firms ranks "reluctance to consider new products or services" higher than the seventh most frequently occurring procurement problem. In fact, finance firms rank it first, which is not surprising in light of the rapidly changing character of the finance industry. Few gov-

ernments have employees with the expertise to deal with complex, innovative financial products (see the comments from the health insurance firm quoted earlier).

A somewhat different complaint comes from durable manufacturing firms. Several wrote "Governments are reluctant to consider commercially available (nonspecification) items." This reluctance has become a major issue, particularly at the federal level, and legislators are increasingly stepping in to mandate purchase of off-the-shelf items to save money.[10]

As the figures in Table 5.1 show, larger, more established corporations, especially in the finance, manufacturing, and wholesale trade sectors, complain the most about government's reluctance to consider new products and services. Contract status, proportion of revenue generated from government contracts, and the owner's gender or race do not relate as strongly to the problem as the type of industry in which a firm is engaged. New product development occurs most often in the finance and manufacturing sectors. And frequently the largest corporations develop new products since they typically have the resources to devote to research and development activities. Often these firms are nearly as frustrated with burdensome paperwork associated with government contracting as they are with the reluctance to consider new products or services.

PAPERWORK, PROCEDURES, AND RULES OF THE GAME

A number of the responses to our question about the difficulties firms encounter in selling to government reflect the private sector's view that the world of government purchasing is overly bureaucratic and cumbersome. Excessive paperwork leads the list of this type of complaint.

Paperwork Problems (Application)

More than one-fourth (29 percent) of the firms responding to our survey say one problem in selling to government is "too much paperwork required for application" (the fourth most frequently cited problem). This finding supports the general public's perceptions of government inefficiency. Typical complaints:

"The bid requests are huge volumes that are hard to wade through" (a construction firm).

"For a $1,000 order, the paperwork is what might be expected for a million dollar order. This is particularly true of the federal government. Bidding is simply not cost-effective for many firms" (a small nondurable manufacturing firm).

"There is far too much paperwork for simple orders and simple problems."

"Governments do not understand the cost of preparing for an RFP. Only large firms have the staff and resources to remain in the competition" (a small professional services firm).

Application paperwork ranks even higher than fourth among nonprofit organizations; relatively large firms; firms in the insurance, construction, manufacturing—nondurable, real estate, and professional services sectors; Asian-owned firms; out-of-state firms; firms that had a government contract in the past but do not have one now; and firms that have never had a government contract. Paperwork, aside from deterring new vendors from applying for government business work, chases away experienced vendors.

For some firm types cited above that utilize many subcontractors (such as construction firms), the paperwork can feel especially burdensome. For firms in sectors where specifications tend to be highly detailed (manufacturing and finance), the paperwork necessary to demonstrate that a firm's product or service can meet the specifications can be exhaustive.

Higher-than-average proportions of firms citing excessive paperwork problems also come from the youngest businesses, those in operation less than a year. While many of these firms see government as a primary market for their goods (Chapter 4), they tend to feel frustrated by the application process—the paperwork—especially in light of their small staffs and limited resources. As the experienced contractors know, the paperwork continues to pile up after the firm signs the contract.

Paperwork Problems (*Once Contract Received*)

Nearly one-fourth (24 percent) of our respondents complained of frequently having "too much paperwork once the contract has been received." This ranks as the ninth most commonly experienced problem. The firms most frequently citing this problem are those that have been in business longer than ten years; those with more than fifty employees and annual gross revenues of more than $10 million; firms in the construction, insurance, and professional services sectors, and firms that held government contracts in the past but not now. For the latter group, the paperwork undoubtedly has squelched their interest in selling to government. For the others, the heavy volume of paperwork more likely arises from their prime contractor status or the intergovernmental nature of their government funding. Both situations subject private sector contractors to complex auditing requirements necessitated by federal and state guidelines.

SHORTCOMINGS OF GOVERNMENT PURCHASING PROCEDURES

Various aspects of specific government purchasing procedures often frustrate businesses. These problems typically include "inordinate delays between bid closing and the actual contract decision" (23 percent), "unrealistic delivery requirements, usually too short" (12 percent), "inadequate procedures for protests and appeals" (9 percent), "the absence of rigorous performance audits to weed out bad/unethical contractors" (20 percent), and various other "annoyances."

Delays Between Bid Closing and Contract Decision

Delays of weeks or months between bid closing and the actual contract award are generally perceived by businesses as unfair. These delays too often result in firms losing money because of price changes. We received a lot of comments describing this problem.

"U.S. government bids take too long between submittal and award. Prices sometimes change twice during that period and yet we cannot change submittal price lists" (a medium-sized wholesale trade firm).

"The delivery on the County jail was September, 1989. The order for the equipment was placed in August, 1987. I have absorbed price increases due to this *two*-year delivery lapse. If the government ran like a business must run to survive, I'm sure these problems would not exist" (a new small female-owned wholesale trade firm).

Firms complaining most about delays in making contract awards are the more established, moderate-to-large firms in the finance, professional services, construction, manufacturing, insurance, and wholesale trade sectors as well as Asian-owned firms (49 percent of which are in the sectors just cited) and out-of-state firms. (Out-of-state firms are more likely to get government business through competitive bids.)

The best predictor of a firm's problems with delays is the proportion of its gross revenues generated through government contracts. For firms heavily dependent on government contracts, delays can be particularly frustrating since they make it difficult to meet payrolls or pay expenses already incurred in anticipation of government's disbursement of funds.

Unrealistic Delivery Requirements

Unrealistic delivery requirements can be exasperating for a firm, particularly if the government does not provide enough lead time. This problem particularly frustrates a local firm dependent upon another firm to supply it with the good before it can deliver the product to government. For these firms, many of which are small, it is not cost-effective to have large stocks on hand. This means they need some advance time to secure the product.

Unrealistic delivery requirements can also be a problem for the large manufacturer or distributor located some distance from the purchasing government. These firms, too, often rely on other firms (transportation or communications firms) for timely delivery of products to governments. Thus, *for all types of firms, unrealistic delivery requirements can wreak havoc with their inventory and cash management plans—and profit margins.*

As the figures in Table 5.1 show, the firms most commonly experiencing unrealistic delivery requirements are large firms; firms generating higher percentages of their revenues from government contracts; and firms in the manufacturing, wholesale and retail trade, insurance, and professional services sectors. Manufacturing and trade firms undoubtedly experience the inventory-related problems cited above. In the case of insurance and professional services, short time periods for delivery often do not give them enough time to obtain approval from corporate headquarters or underwriters or to transfer necessary personnel from regional or corporate offices.

Inadequate Procedures for Protests and Appeals

A relatively small proportion (9 percent) of our respondents report having to deal with inadequate protest and appeals procedures.

As noted in Chapter 2, the high incidence of litigation in government procurement in recent years has sensitized most governments to the need for clearly and firmly established protest appeals procedures. The firms most likely to cite problems are those with the greatest dependence on government contracts that tend to do business with a wide range of governments. Since their primary market is the public sector, their frustration may stem more from the outcome of a protest or appeal procedure than from the absence of one.

No Rigorous Performance Audits of Contractors

Nearly one-fifth of our respondents complain that government does not adequately audit the performance of its contractors, thereby permitting incompetent or unethical contractors to remain in the vendor pool to compete against reputable firms. Above-average percentages of firms citing this failure are corporations; medium-sized and large firms; firms in the construction, utility, professional services, and mining sectors; Hispanic and American Indian-owned firms; firms taking in a sizable portion of their total revenues from government contracts; and firms that once had a government contract but no longer do. However, the concern for the lack of procedures to get rid of "bad apples" occurs fairly consistently across all types of firms.

In fairness to government, we must point out that agency staffs frequently experience a shortage of audit personnel. Second, measuring the *quality* of performance is often extremely difficult and often results in negatively appraised firms challenging government's assessment in court. Nonetheless, governments *must not abandon* efforts to develop quality standards. Without such measures, government will fall short of achieving one of the major goals of purchasing: buying quality goods at the lowest and fairest price.

Other Procedural Annoyances

Although respondents cite procurement staff problems most often in the "other" category, several other procedural annoyances surface in the survey.

Slow payment of subcontractors Many nonprofit organizations and construction firms are actually subcontractors to prime contractors (holding the government contract). A number of them complain about the lack of procedures, or little enforcement of existing procedures, to make prime contractors pay their "subs" on time.

"The number one problem for a subcontractor is that they are not protected to collect for labor from a prime contractor" (a small new construction-related firm).

"Direct contracting with government agencies is fine, but the nightmare comes when you become the sub to a general contractor. The government pays the prime contractor in a timely fashion, but the prime forgets the subs. The sub has no contact with government agencies and ends up in court trying to get the money out of the prime. This is a *major* problem in the construction trade" (a female-owned construction firm).

"We bid to general contractors and find they use our bid to get the job, then use our price to get lower bids on the sub work after they get the job. They should be required to name their subcontractors and their price within their bid."

"Competition pushes the price very low and after a general contractor is awarded a contract, he frequently wants to renegotiate his contract with the minority sub at that price" (Hispanic-owned construction firm).

While some see this activity as evidence that government purchasing policies are working as intended, since competition results in lower prices, the losing firms find such practices are inequitable and inhibit them from competing for government contracts.

Unrealistic inspection procedures *Firms complaining about inspection procedures tend to criticize both the procedures and the competency of those doing the inspections.*

"Source inspections on standard commercial products are ridiculous, costly, and counterproductive" (wholesale trade firm).

"Government inspection personnel are totally unqualified, resulting in an inordinate number of delays and costly problems" (large construction firm).

Insufficient procedures for recruiting new vendors *Newly established, frequently minority-owned firms complain that governments do not have adequate procedures to recruit new vendors.* One small firm in business less than five years reproaches government for its "reluctance to ask for bids from new vendors." But even established firms sometimes see the system as closed. A large durable goods manufacturing firm in business longer than ten years complains that "agencies won't send bids to us even though we are on their bid lists. They call only on a few regular suppliers."

Politics and favoritism Some firms speak of cronyism, as these comments reveal:

"Our prices are given to our competitors so that they can get the bid. These are companies that have developed friendships with county government officials" (small retail trade firm).

"People who are in charge and are the decision makers are often 'bought' by other vendors who do things for the government employees at no charge, such as buying them lunch, giving gifts, and offering 'trade outs' " (female-owned transportation firm).

"We frequently encounter favoritism, the 'good ole' boy routine, and collusion" (female-owned demolition firm).

Graft and fraud A few firms allude to improper and illegal activity.

"We don't sell to government units because they beat your price down, then want kickbacks to boot" (moderate-sized retail trade firm).

"Our contracts for professional services frequently depend entirely on the size of our political contribution."

Inefficient and unfair change order policies The National Institute of Governmental Purchasing defines a change order as "a written modification to a contract or purchase order, which normally establishes the cost impact on the contract." According to *State and Local Government Purchasing*, changes occur more commonly in construction and public works contracts than in contracts for equipment, supplies, or services. Typically, the change orders adjust prices and quantities, depending upon the type of contract and the change clause in the contract.

In change orders, contractors often complain that governments take too long to give their okay, as these comments show:

"It takes far too long for a change order approval. Many times it hasn't been approved by the time the required work is done."

"It is not unusual to wait 90 to 180 days for payment on extra work" as a consequence of delayed change order approval.

Other firms criticize governments for using change orders in a manner disadvantageous to firms. One complains that it frequently receives "unfair reviews of honest change order requests or time extension requests." Another alleges:

"We find that government agencies often have not anticipated the problems that occur after a contract is awarded on the basis of a specified bid price for a specific quantity. The work is completed, then government wants more service at no additional cost. If we don't do it, we won't get more contracts in the future."

Businesses with experience in dealing with government contracts are highly critical of change order pricing or costing methodologies. The best account of this problem comes from a construction firm that receives more than 90 percent of its gross revenues from government contracts:

> The rub with the typical pricing procedure is the method that the contract requires the contractor to use in computing his "cost" and the mark-up allowed. . . . Typically, they do not allow the contractor to include in his "cost" such critical items as supervisory time; field overhead (job site trailers, phones, rest rooms, and related facilities); clerical staff; estimating time and costs; delay and impact costs. All of these costs are assumed to be picked up by the

mark-up allowance. To add insult to injury, the mark-up allowance is very outdated. Most contracts limit the contractor to a 10 percent mark-up on his "costs" and some only 5 percent on subcontractor costs. This is terribly outdated. Strict adherence to the above method of calculating cost and mark-up allowance results in the contractor completing the revised work actually below his true cost and losing money! Nice situation! It is a misguided notion that Change Orders are lucrative for contractors. I am sure that the vast majority of contractors would prefer than no Change Orders be necessary. My suggestion is that the "cost" sections be revised to allow for all field and related costs in performing the extra work. The mark-up should be adjusted to allow a 15 percent mark-up for overhead and then a 10 percent fee. Using this method, we would actually realize a 4 to 5 percent profit, which is a reasonable figure.

RULES OF THE GAME

Several problems frequently encountered by business can be classified as difficulties stemming from rules of the public purchasing game. Governments set rules such as "mandated minority set-aside requirements" and "mandated labor costs higher than local standards" to regulate the marketplace. Governments require surety bonds to qualify a firm for competing for government business. Relatively small percentages of firms cite problems related to these rules. The biggest differences among firms occur in their experiences with set-aside and bonding requirements.

Mandated Minority Set-Asides

A relatively small percentage (14 percent) of firms surveyed report they regularly confront mandated minority set-aside requirements. This is consistent with the statistics reported in Chapter 2, showing that only 13 percent of all governments have imposed such require-

ments. (Most vendor preference policies are more "voluntary" than mandatory.)

Higher-than-average percentages of older, larger firms, doing a sizable amount of business with governments, and in the construction, mining, or professional services fields say they frequently encounter these set-asides. This occurrence most likely stems from the larger proportion of their business that comes from the federal government or the likelihood that the contract (in construction especially) is at least partially funded by the federal government. A higher-than-average proportion of firms that no longer do business with government also say they frequently encountered these mandates (25 percent of these firms are in the construction, mining, or professional services fields). Thus, one explanation for the disappearance of these firms from government contractor status might be their negative experience with set-asides.

We received a number of written comments criticizing government socioeconomic policies in general as being unfair. One large retail trade firm complains that "having to deal with minority-owned and small business mandates from the federal government makes it difficult for corporations to deal with some agencies, such as the Air Force!" But most of the complainants are small firms. One small firm argues that government-imposed "affirmative action programs advantage large corporations." Most small firms simply criticize these policies on the grounds that they limit competition. Typical comments:

"Why should an $80 million MBE be protected? Large MBE or SBE firms shoot us out of the water."

"Minority/women competitors receive 'points' for this status, which is unrealistic. A firm's past performance and ability should be the only reason for selection."

"Minority business programs eliminate fair competition."

"We have lost government jobs because we are not a minority even when we were low bidder."

Much lower-than-average proportions of minority-owned firms of all types report that they often come across mandatory set-asides for minority vendors. But several complain that when they encounter these policies, they are unfairly implemented. Some comments:

Government is "making a mockery of set-aside contracts for minorities." "Large, white-owned firms almost always utilize blacks/minorities only as FRONTS for such set-aside contracts, a real bastardization of the set-aside policy" (black-owned construction company).

"Some government entities interpret minority good faith efforts to please themselves and rarely meet the goal. When contested,

they say a good faith effort was made when it was not" (Hispanic-owned service firm).

Other vendor preference policies   *A modest number of firms criticize local vendor policies—primarily their absence.*

"Out-of-state competition drives down the service level and quality of the product neither of which is included in the bid specifications" (medium-sized wholesale trade firm).

The state gives "no preference to firms having their place of business in Florida."

These criticisms of local vendor preference policies surface in responses to our "other" problems category. In general, however, few complain about local vendor preference policies, even fewer than about mandated labor costs.

Mandated Labor Cost Problems

Only 8 percent of our respondents reported frequently coming across "mandated labor costs higher than local standards" (see Figure 5.1). This problem occurs more often among firms doing business with the federal government (because of the Davis–Bacon Act and other federal regulations).[11] Thus, the firms most likely to cite mandated costs as a reoccurring problem are large construction firms generating a relatively large percentage of their business from government contracts (most likely federal or federally funded projects).

Bid, Performance, and Payment Bond Requirements

Businesses encounter bid and performance bond requirements more often than payment bonds. *Nearly one-fifth (18 percent) report they commonly come across bid bond requirements, 17 percent often face performance bond requirements, but only 10 percent say they frequently must secure a payment bond in order to sell to government* (see Figure 5.1). The differences arise primarily in the nature of the bonds.

Recall from Chapter 2 that a *bid bond* guarantees that the business will accept the contract, as bid, if it is awarded. A *performance bond* protects the government from loss if the bidder cannot complete the contract as agreed. A *payment bond*, which is used almost exclusively for construction contracts, guarantees that the bidder will pay material suppliers and subcontractors.

Small and minority-owned firms frequently see these bond requirements as impeding their competitiveness in the public sector marketplace, according to the Council of State Governments and NASPO. These guarantees cost a firm money; the extra expense often means that small firms cannot offer competitively priced bids. One established black construction firm charges: "Prequalification standards [including bonding requirements] are unfair to fledgling MBE/SBE firms that seek to work with government agencies such as the Department of Labor, Department of Defense, or the Department of Transportation."

Our results (see Table 5.1) support these claims. Above-average percentages of firms having to meet bond requirements were individually owned firms; those in business less than ten years; those in the construction, agriculture, and finance sectors; minority-owned firms; and firms classified as small and economically disadvantaged. In all likelihood, the majority of these firms see these requirements as burdensome, not helpful.

On the other hand, more established firms often believe bond requirements prevent incompetent contractors from bidding. A moderate-sized corporation in business longer than ten years says: "The absence of rigorous performance audits to weed out bad or unethical contractors is our utmost problem. Bidders do not have to qualify to bid and sometimes no bonds are required. This lets anyone in and causes real problems to reputable firms."

Other Rules-of-the-Game Problems

Poor timing *Five percent of the firms surveyed identify "government purchasing cycles out of sync with industry cycles."* Businesses that commonly see this factor as problematic tend to be extremely large firms in the real estate, mining, and, to a lesser extent, communications and agricultural sectors. (These are among the more cyclical and seasonal sectors.) Some comments:

"Due to fiscal year funding and purchasing cycles, we suffer an overabundance of work or no work at all. Government employees tend to schedule work for bidders during summer months and make proposals due immediately after holidays to facilitate their own schedules" (a communications firm).

"We frequently are involved in contracts where different trades are working on top of each other."

A somewhat higher-than-average proportion of firms currently without government contracts, especially those that have never had one, cite out-of-sync purchasing cycles as a common problem. (Approximately 9 percent of firms that have never had a government contract are in the sectors listed above.) For these firms, the timing of government purchases of their goods or services may be a major deterrent to their competing for government business.

Large, unrealistic insurance requirements Some representative comments:

"Insurance and legal requirements are so costly they eliminate small firms from small jobs."

"Professional liability insurance requirements of $1 million or more are unrealistic."

"Some governments require the bidder to hold the entity free from all liability from any cause in the operation of the equipment—an area over which we have no control."

Bidder-fee requirements   Paying a fee to bid presents a problem for firms doing business with a wide range of governments. One firm complains that such requirements can unfairly cut into one's profit margin: "We estimate that our firm will expend $12,500 annually if Florida adopts a standard $25 bidder fee," a rather sizable amount just for the privilege of selling to government.

Fixed-price contracts   Firms complaining about fixed-price contracts argue:

"Price guarantees for one year are not realistic."

"Most government bids now are for a one-year period. With inflation and rapidly rising costs it is very difficult to maintain bid prices for a twelve-month period. Our firm usually declines these bids."

"There's no way our firm would be interested in price guarantees for a year."

In general, businesses complain far less about the type of contract than the bidding process itself. When they criticize the bidding process, the complaints most often come from proprietors selling low-cost items or services. These businesses point out that requiring completion of standard forms for all purchases, regardless of dollar volume, is highly cost-ineffective:

"Bidding procedures and requirements, including bid bonds, notarized forms, etc., are *ridiculous* for small orders of a few hundred dollars. They're okay if you're building a school, but too cumbersome for our firm's orders, which never exceed $1000."

These firms oppose standardization of the bidding process across all dollar-volume amounts, but, as we have seen in this chapter—at least among firms doing business with multiple governments—many wish for more standardization.

SUMMARY

Among the 3,282 firms responding to our survey, the problems of doing business with government are, in order:

1. Slow payment cycles (45 percent)
2. Bid specifications written too narrowly to promote competition (36 percent)
3. Difficulty making contact with the actual user of their firm's product or service (32 percent)
4. Too much paperwork required for the application (29 percent)
5. Competition pushes prices too low for a firm to compete (28 percent)
6. Confusion over who is responsible for making a specific purchasing decision (27 percent)
7. Reluctance to consider new products or services (26 percent)
8. Bid specifications written too generally (24 percent)
9. Too much paperwork once contract is received (24 percent)
10. Inordinate delays between bid closing and the actual contract decision (23 percent)
11. Difficulty competing against large firms (22 percent)
12. Absence of rigorous performance audits to weed out bad or unethical contractors (20 percent)

13. Bid bond requirements (18 percent)
14. Performance bond requirements (17 percent)
15. Mandated minority set-aside requirements (14 percent)
16. Unrealistic delivery requirements, usually too short a time frame (12 percent)
17. Payment bond requirements (10 percent)
18. Too many sole source contracts (10 percent)
19. Other (10 percent)
20. Inadequate procedures for protests and appeals (9 percent)
21. Mandated labor costs higher than local standards (8 percent)
22. Lack of a written procedures manual to assist suppliers (6 percent)
23. Government purchasing cycles out of sync with industry cycles (5 percent)
24. Difficulty in competing against small firms (4 percent)

The rank ordering of these problems and the proportions of firms citing them as common vary considerably across different categories of firm characteristics.

The most common "other" problems fall into two major categories: (1) deficiencies of government purchasing personnel (unavailability, incompetence, lack of objectivity, inability to make a decision, failure to distribute information to vendors in a comprehensive and timely fashion) and (2) deficiencies related to procurement procedures and rules (lack of concern for slow/nonpayment of subcontractors by prime contractors, unrealistic inspection procedures, the lack of procedures to recruit new vendors, favoritism in the letting of contracts, graft and fraud, inefficient and unfair change order policies and procedures, large and unrealistic insurance requirements, bidder-fee requirements, fixed-price contracts).

Businesses identify more negatives about government purchasing practices than positives, although no consensus exists about the negatives they encounter most frequently when selling to government. The median number of problems identified in our survey was four (compared to two positives).

The firms most likely to encounter the widest range of problems in selling to government are, naturally: (1) those firms that have had the most experience in government contract work (selling to a wider range of governments and securing government business through many different procedures) and (2) firms that once had government contracts but no longer do (the most alienated firms).

While new, small, and minority-owned firms have not had the breadth of experience in the government contracting world as larger, more established, nonminority-owned firms, higher proportions of them cite competition-restricting problems as common in their dealings, or attempted dealings, with government procurement systems. Most notably, higher proportions of these firms say they frequently have difficulty competing with large firms or are in situations in which competition from other firms pushes prices too low for them to compete. Higher proportions of these firms are also likely to see the system as somewhat closed; they tend to complain about sole source contracts, inadequate procedures for protests and appeals, and political favoritism. These small, relatively new firms are also more likely to experience difficulties in obtaining information about contracting opportunities from government purchasing offices.

Among firms that have never had a government contract (11 percent of our respondents), the most commonly encountered problems are, in order: (1) difficulty in making contact with the actual user of their firm's products or services; (2) difficulty in competing against large firms; (3) the paperwork involved in applying for government business; (4) bid specifications written too narrowly to promote competition; (5) slow payment; and (6) competition forcing prices too low for them to compete.

In developing strategies to broaden the vendor pool, analysts should carefully scrutinize the problems identified by: (1) firms that have heretofore not been well represented, including small and minority-owned businesses and (2) firms that have been alienated from government contracting (those that once held contracts but no longer do and those that have never held a government contract).

The most positive aspect of our findings is that, in spite of these firms' specific criticisms of government procurement, a large proportion still would like to do business with government, although they perceive that some types of government are better to do business with than others.

Notes

1. Cf. Coalition for Prompt Pay, 1987, 1989; GAO, March 1989.
2. Cf. ASTM, 1990.
3. Not much difference occurs between minority- and nonminority-owned firms in the proportion concentrated in the more high-tech sectors. For example, among minority-owned firms, 10 percent are in professional services, 0.2 percent in finance, 3 percent in communications, and 0.9 percent in transportation. Among nonminority-owned firms, 9 percent are in professional services, 0.7 percent in finance, 4 percent in communications, and 2 percent in transportation.
4. For example, 60 percent of the minority-owned firms responding to our survey take in gross revenues below $500,000 compared to 24 percent of our nonminority firms; 85 percent of our minority-owned firms have 1–25 employees compared to 53 percent of our nonminority-owned firms; and 43 percent of the minority-owned firms have been in business five years or less compared to only 17 percent of the nonminority-owned firms. Among small, economically disadvantaged firms, 56 percent have annual gross revenues below $500,000; 82 percent have 1–25 employees; and 38 percent have been in business five years or less; 55 percent of these small, economically disadvantaged firms are minority-owned.
5. Forty percent of the respondents who have never had a government contract have been in business five years or less; 80 percent have 1–25 employees; and 58 percent have annual gross revenues below $500,000. Firms that have never had a government contract are somewhat less likely than minority-owned or small, economically disadvantaged firms to have been in business five years or less. But they closely resemble minority and small, economically disadvantaged firms in their size. (Of the firms that have never had a government contract, 36 percent are minority-owned and 31 percent are small, economically disadvantaged firms.)
6. Of our respondents with gross revenues higher than $50 million, 26 percent are out-of-state vendors. (Among out-of-state vendors, 74 percent have gross revenues more than $50 million compared to only 26 percent of the in-state vendors.)
7. Of the firms in our survey that currently have government contracts, 19 percent are in retail trade, 17 percent in wholesale trade, 0.8 percent in finance, 0.4 percent in insurance, 0.3 percent in utility, 16 percent in construction, 9 percent in durable manufacturing, 3 percent in nondurable manufacturing, 1 percent in real estate, 3 percent in communications, 18 percent in service, 0.7 percent in agriculture, 0.3 percent in mining, 2 percent in transportation, and 10 percent in professional services. Comparable figures for firms currently without a government contract are retail trade, 17 percent; wholesale trade, 15 percent; finance, 0 percent; insurance, 0 percent; utility, 0.3 percent; construction, 17 percent; durable manufacturing, 8 percent; nondurable manufacturing, 2 percent; real estate, 0.8 percent; communications, 3 percent; services, 24 percent; agriculture, 2 per-

cent; mining, 0.3 percent; transportation, 2 percent; and professional services, 8 percent.

8. The Universal Public Purchasing Certification program, endorsed by public purchasing groups such as the National Institute of Governmental Purchasing, National Association of State Purchasing Officials, National Contract Management Association, and the National Association of Purchasing Managers, has two levels of professional competence. The first level is the Professional Public Buyer (PPB), which "signifies an individual is competent as a buyer in public purchas-ing"; the second is the Certified Public Purchasing Officer (CPPO), "an individual who has attained a prescribed competence in the management and supervision of purchasing in governmental agencies, jurisdictions, and public institutions or authorities" (The Council of State Governments and NASPO, 1988).

9. See MacManus and Watson, 1990.

10. Cf. Short, 1979; U.S. Senate Subcommittee on Oversight of Government Management of the Committee on Governmental Affairs, 1989; Goldstein, 1989.

11. See Page, 1987.

CHAPTER 6

Which Type of Government
Is the Best to Do
Business with?

"I've worked with some excellent government people at times," says the owner of a construction company, "like the GSA contracting officer in Fort Worth, the Navy avionics office in Indiana, and the lady who was in charge at the Coast Guard in Miami."

"If I have a choice," says a self-employed training consultant, "I will choose a state contract over a federal one every time."

ARE SOME TYPES of governments easier to do business with than others? Or are they all equally difficult to deal with? These are legitimate questions, especially for firms that have never ventured into government contracting. Knowing which governments make the best customers can be as important a business decision as knowing which bank offers the best financing. Some firms, of course, have few options; the nature of their products or services determines which governments they will do business with. Even so, they often can do better planning when they know the reputations of prospective government customers.

In spite of the aggravations of selling to government, do a fairly large proportion of American businesses still welcome such an opportunity? Do these assessments vary

among different types of private sector firms?

To discern the views of businesses, our survey asked three series of questions. The first series focused on the prompt-pay issue. We suspected that businesses would complain about slow payment, but to determine whether the problem is worse with certain governments, we asked:

What is the average time it takes for your firm to get reimbursed by each of these governments (county, city, school board, state government, federal government[1]): 1–30 days; 31–60 days; 61–90 days; or over 90 days?

Our hypothesis, based on accounts published in business journals, was that the

166

slowest payer would be the federal government.

Our second series of questions asked for an overall appraisal of different governments' purchasing practices:

From your own experience and experiences of other firms like yours, how do you rate the overall purchasing policies and procedures of each of the following governments (county, city, school board, state government, federal government[2]): Excellent, Good, Fair, or Poor?

Again, based on general business accounts of contracting with government, we expected that only a small percentage would rate any of the governments' practices "Excellent." We also expected that the largest proportion of "Poor" ratings would be given to the federal government's procurement practices.

The third series of questions sought to identify which governments had such bad purchasing practices (or a reputation for such) that a business would rather not have it as a customer. We asked:

Which of the following types of government is your firm *not* interested in doing business with—Federal, State, City, County, Transit Authority, School Board, Hospital District, Other Special District?[3]

We expected that among the general purpose governments (federal, state, county, city), the greatest proportion of firms would identify the federal government as an undesirable customer. We had no expectations about business assessments of special purpose governments (transit authority, school board, hospital district, other special districts) because no contracting studies have focused on their purchasing practices. In fact, to our knowledge, this is the first comparative study of business ratings of government purchasing practices. The results produced some surprises and suggest that, with some modifications to their purchasing practices, governments could considerably expand their vendor pools.

WHO PAYS BILLS IN A TIMELY FASHION?

A basic premise of every model procurement law or ordinance (see Chapter 2 and Appendix C) is that governments should pay their bills in a timely manner. But what is considered "timely"? *The Model State Prompt Pay Law* (*which also covers local governments*) *and the federal Prompt Payment Act generally call for payment of bills within thirty calendar days of receipt of invoice* (both appear in Appendix D). But for certain perishable products (meat and meat products, fish and shellfish, poultry, fresh eggs) bills should be paid within seven calendar days. For other perishables (such as groceries, vegetables, fresh fruits, dairy products, edible fats or oils), bills should be paid within ten calendar days. Furthermore, for small purchases ($500 or less in state and local government; under $25,000 federal), government should pay by cash or check on delivery or within ten days after receipt or acceptance of the good or service.

The Model State Prompt Pay Law recommends that if common industry payment practices are to pay within less than thirty days, government should pay within the same time frame. These prompt pay laws (federal and state) call for prime contractors to pay their subcontractors promptly. The prime contractor is expected to pay its subcontractor within seven days of receiving payment (see Model State Prompt Pay Act and Federal Prompt Pay Regulation, Appendix D). But are governments generally successful in meeting these standards?

Who Pays Within 30 Days?

School districts, counties, and cities (in that order) are more likely than the state or federal government to pay their bills within thirty days, according to our respondents (see Figure 6.1). Even so, only 35 percent report that the average reimbursement time for school districts is one to thirty days; comparable figures for the other types of government are county, 32 percent; city, 31 percent; state, 23 percent; and federal, only 19 percent. In other words, nearly two-thirds of our respondents report that local governments do not pay within the recommended time frame. Nearly three-fourths of them find that state government does not pay promptly. More than 80 percent allege that the federal government falls short of the prompt pay regulation.

Who Takes 31–60 Days?

The most common reimbursement time for all types of government is one to two months (see Figure 6.1). *Half of our respondents report they are reimbursed within thirty-one to sixty days by the county (54 percent), the city (54 percent), the state (53 percent), and the school district (51 percent).* Somewhat unexpectedly, nearly half (48 percent) of those with experience selling to the federal government say they are reimbursed within this time frame as well.

Who Pays in 61–90 Days?

Some firms report it takes an average of between sixty-one and ninety days to get reimbursed. Such delays are encountered by twice as many firms dealing with the federal government (20 percent) or the state (18 percent) as by those dealing with county (10 percent), city (10 percent), or school board (11 percent). These are still relatively small percentages—unless your firms happens to

be one of those regularly experiencing these rather long payment delays.

The firms most likely to report longer reimbursement times (see Table 6.1) are nonprofit organizations and large, experienced firms. These firms are in the following industries, by type of contract:

- Federal government—real estate, insurance, agriculture, mining, finance, professional service, communications, and durable manufacturing sectors
- State government—insurance, real estate, transportation, professional service, service, and durable manufacturing sectors
- County—insurance, utility, manufacturing, communications, service, and professional service sectors
- City—construction, durable manufacturing, real estate, service, and professional service
- School district—finance, durable manufacturing, mining, and professional service sectors

Industry sector is strongly related to reimbursement time, regardless of the type of government contract, although the affected sectors differ somewhat. As a common pattern, however, firms in the more high-tech fields (such as finance, insurance, communications, professional services, and durable manufacturing) tend to experience the longest reimbursement periods when they sell to government. We can only speculate that the pattern has something to do with purchasing agents' lack of familiarity with these fields, absence of established specifications, or a shortage of adequately trained inspection personnel.

Who Takes More Than 90 Days to Pay?

The good news for businesses contemplating selling to government is that only a small

Figure 6.1
Average Reimbursement Time by Type of Government

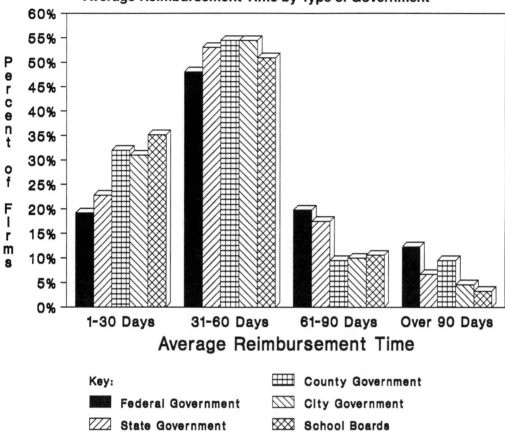

proportion of firms complain that govern-ments take more than ninety days to pay. Predictably, however, the federal government is more likely to pay so late (12 percent of the firms report it generally takes the feds that long to pay them). Only 7 percent of our respondents say it takes state government longer than 90 days to pay them; comparable figures for the county, city, and school district were 10 percent, 5 percent, and 3 percent respectively (see Figure 6.1). Higher proportions of firms in the industry sectors cited above also are most likely to experience average reimbursement times in excess of ninety days.

The relationship between payment delays and other firm characteristics appears slight. However, in the case of the federal govern-ment, a fairly strong relationship exists be-tween the firm's size and excessive payment delays: The larger the firm, the longer it takes the feds to pay. This relationship proba-bly occurs as a consequence of the dollar volume and complexity of the federal con-tracts normally held by extremely large firms.

Small and Minority-Owned Businesses' Ratings

From the perspective of broadening the ven-dor pool, the results offer government pro-curement officials a reason to be somewhat optimistic. *Higher-than-average proportions*

Table 6.1
Average Reimbursement Time by Type of Government and Firm Characteristic

Firm Characteristic	FEDERAL				STATE				COUNTY			
	1-30 Days	31-60 Days	61-90 Days	Over 90 Days	1-30 Days	31-60 Days	61-90 Days	Over 90 Days	1-30 Days	31-60 Days	61-90 Days	Over 90 Days
All Firms	19.9%	48.0%	19.8%	12.3%	22.8%	53.0%	17.5%	6.7%	32.0%	54.4%	9.5%	4.1%
Firm Structure												
Individual owner	26.3	46.1	13.5	14.1	32.0	51.2	8.4	8.4	42.1	46.2	5.4	6.3
Partnership	16.3	41.9	30.2	11.6	17.0	57.5	17.0	8.5	32.1	53.6	10.7	3.6
Nonprofit organization	30.0	26.7	25.3	20.0	32.3	41.9	19.3	6.5	47.1	44.1	5.9	2.9
Corporation	19.1	49.0	20.0	11.9	22.0	53.1	18.6	6.3	30.2	55.9	10.1	3.8
Other	0.0	50.0	25.0	25.0	11.1	66.7	11.1	11.1	0.0	100.0	0.0	0.0
Years in Business												
Less than 1 year	14.3	50.0	21.4	14.3	33.3	55.5	5.6	5.6	48.0	44.0	0.0	8.0
1-2 years	34.6	50.0	11.6	3.8	32.0	60.0	5.3	2.7	49.5	39.8	4.3	6.4
3-5 years	25.9	51.1	16.1	6.9	24.8	51.7	17.4	6.1	31.7	55.6	10.3	2.4
6-10 years	22.6	45.6	20.5	11.3	23.3	54.9	16.0	5.8	37.7	52.8	7.2	2.3
Over 10 years	17.8	47.9	20.5	13.8	21.6	52.3	18.8	7.3	28.8	56.1	10.5	4.6
Number of Employees												
1-25	24.3	50.2	15.6	9.9	26.5	52.4	15.2	5.9	36.9	52.3	7.5	3.3
26-50	17.5	46.8	25.1	10.6	19.0	55.8	17.8	7.4	28.0	58.0	10.9	3.1
51-100	17.1	51.3	19.6	12.0	23.3	54.0	18.4	4.3	25.4	58.6	9.6	6.4
101-500	12.4	46.5	23.9	17.2	14.5	58.0	17.4	10.1	22.4	60.2	10.9	6.5
501-1000	18.2	45.5	25.4	10.9	14.8	59.3	18.5	7.4	21.3	55.3	17.0	6.4
1001-5000	15.2	40.5	22.8	21.5	15.8	40.8	30.3	13.1	21.9	46.6	24.7	6.8
Over 5000	13.7	33.3	28.8	24.2	20.3	42.4	33.9	3.4	27.3	58.2	10.9	3.6

Firm Characteristic	CITY				SCHOOL BOARD			
	1-30 Days	31-60 Days	61-90 Days	Over 90 Days	1-30 Days	31-60 Days	61-90 Days	Over 90 Days
All Firms	31.0%	54.4%	10.0%	4.6%	35.2%	50.9%	10.6%	3.3%
Firm Structure								
Individual owner	38.2	44.6	9.6	7.6	43.3	46.6	4.7	5.4
Partnership	24.4	64.5	11.1	0.0	33.3	58.3	2.8	5.6
Nonprofit organization	40.0	35.0	25.0	0.0	54.5	40.9	46.0	0.0
Corporation	30.3	55.6	9.7	4.4	34.2	51.2	11.5	3.1
Other	25.0	50.0	25.0	0.0	16.7	66.6	16.7	0.0
Years in Business								
Less than 1 year	31.5	57.9	5.3	5.3	27.8	55.6	16.6	0.0
1-2 years	42.2	16.9	6.3	4.6	45.5	47.0	1.5	6.0
3-5 years	38.8	50.0	8.0	3.2	38.7	52.3	7.7	1.3
6-10 years	34.2	52.5	8.3	5.0	39.2	48.9	9.7	2.2
Over 10 years	28.2	56.0	11.0	4.8	33.1	51.4	11.7	3.8
Number of Employees								
1-25	36.2	50.9	8.4	4.5	42.2	47.5	7.4	2.9
26-50	25.1	59.2	11.7	4.0	30.4	50.9	15.0	3.7
51-100	27.0	58.1	10.6	4.3	27.2	56.6	13.3	2.9
101-500	21.9	61.0	11.2	5.9	28.5	53.3	12.1	6.1
501-1000	27.3	56.8	9.1	6.8	16.7	63.9	16.7	2.7
1001-5000	25.0	51.5	17.6	5.9	17.7	54.9	23.5	3.9
Over 5000	28.3	56.6	13.2	1.9	18.7	64.6	14.6	2.1

Table 6.1 (continued)

Firm Characteristic	FEDERAL				STATE				COUNTY			
	1-30 Days	31-60 Days	61-90 Days	Over 90 Days	1-30 Days	31-60 Days	61-90 Days	Over 90 Days	1-30 Days	31-60 Days	61-90 Days	Over 90 Days
Firm Gross Revenues ('88)												
Below $200,000	36.7%	42.4%	11.5%	9.4%	38.5%	48.9%	9.3%	3.3%	45.2%	44.7%	6.5%	3.6%
$200,000-499,999	22.1	51.9	16.6	9.4	25.4	53.5	13.8	7.3	39.8	52.0	6.7	1.5
$500,000-999,999	26.1	50.7	14.5	8.7	24.5	52.7	17.0	5.8	31.9	52.2	11.1	4.8
$1-$10 Million	18.4	49.7	20.7	11.2	20.8	53.6	18.4	7.2	28.9	58.7	8.1	4.3
$11-$25 Million	16.0	45.6	21.7	16.7	20.6	56.8	15.1	7.5	28.8	53.0	12.1	6.1
$26-$50 Million	10.4	55.8	22.1	11.7	15.6	51.6	23.4	9.4	17.6	64.9	14.0	3.5
Over $50 Million	14.0	40.6	27.0	18.4	14.8	52.1	26.3	6.8	20.5	56.8	17.3	5.4
Industry Classification												
Retail trade	19.5	52.6	15.1	12.8	27.8	51.4	16.7	4.1	37.6	51.7	7.3	3.4
Wholesale trade	19.5	48.2	21.0	11.3	18.5	59.6	15.7	6.2	31.0	60.7	6.0	2.3
Finance	22.2	22.2	33.3	22.2	37.5	37.5	12.5	12.5	42.9	57.1	0.0	0.0
Insurance	0.0	33.3	66.7	0.0	0.0	25.0	25.0	50.0	25.0	0.0	25.0	50.0
Utility	25.0	75.0	0.0	0.0	28.6	71.4	0.0	0.0	16.6	66.7	16.6	0.0
Construction	24.2	50.6	15.2	10.0	25.6	52.8	15.6	6.0	23.5	58.2	9.9	8.4
Manufacturing-durable	16.0	47.9	25.7	10.4	21.1	57.8	18.8	2.3	31.6	55.6	12.0	0.8
Manufacturing-nondurable	11.8	60.8	17.6	9.8	28.2	53.8	10.3	7.7	28.9	63.2	5.3	2.6
Real estate	29.4	29.4	11.8	29.4	25.0	35.0	20.0	20.0	52.2	34.8	8.7	4.3
Communications	7.3	41.5	24.4	26.8	20.0	55.5	17.8	6.7	24.5	62.2	11.1	2.2
Service	27.7	37.5	18.8	16.0	26.0	48.8	18.3	6.9	36.4	48.3	10.1	5.2
Agriculture	0.0	33.3	50.0	16.7	15.4	69.2	7.7	7.7	25.0	68.7	6.3	0.0
Mining	0.0	50.0	50.0	0.0	0.0	100.0	0.0	0.0	66.7	33.3	0.0	0.0
Transportation	30.5	43.5	13.0	13.0	17.9	46.4	25.0	10.7	50.0	41.2	5.9	2.9
Professional Service	11.3	50.0	25.5	13.2	16.4	44.0	23.2	16.4	23.7	50.0	22.7	3.6
Owner												
Minority-owned	27.2	45.9	16.8	10.1	29.6	50.5	13.4	6.5	39.4	50.3	6.1	4.2
Not minority-owned	18.6	48.5	20.1	12.8	21.4	53.3	18.5	6.8	30.3	55.5	10.1	4.1

172

Firm Characteristic	CITY				SCHOOL BOARD			
	1-30 Days	31-60 Days	61-90 Days	Over 90 Days	1-30 Days	31-60 Days	61-90 Days	Over 90 Days
Firm Gross Revenues ('88)								
Below $200,000	44.0%	45.3%	6.9%	3.8%	47.6%	45.5%	4.8%	2.1%
$200,000-499,999	39.5	49.5	6.8	4.2	47.3	42.4	6.5	3.8
$500,000-999,999	32.3	52.5	10.3	4.9	39.9	50.7	7.0	2.4
$1-$10 Million	28.5	56.5	10.4	4.6	33.4	50.7	12.8	3.1
$11-$25 Million	26.0	56.3	11.8	5.9	26.5	56.4	10.3	6.8
$26-$50 Million	23.1	59.6	11.5	5.8	32.7	48.1	15.4	3.8
Over $50 Million	22.4	60.1	12.7	4.6	17.5	62.4	17.4	2.7
Industry Classification								
Retail trade	34.0	53.0	9.1	3.9	35.0	52.4	10.1	2.5
Wholesale trade	30.3	59.1	6.7	3.9	35.8	52.9	8.6	2.7
Finance	42.9	42.9	0.0	14.2	50.0	33.3	16.7	0.0
Insurance	100.0	0.0	0.0	0.0	0.0	100.0	0.0	0.0
Utility	80.0	20.0	0.0	0.0	60.0	40.0	0.0	0.0
Construction	24.7	55.9	12.8	6.6	35.1	52.1	8.7	4.1
Manufacturing-durable	28.0	57.0	12.0	3.0	25.6	57.0	15.1	2.3
Manufacturing-nondurable	25.8	61.2	6.5	6.5	28.6	60.0	8.6	2.8
Real estate	38.4	23.1	15.4	23.1	41.7	41.7	8.3	8.3
Communications	15.6	71.9	9.4	3.1	23.8	61.9	9.5	4.8
Service	35.3	49.0	12.3	3.4	39.5	44.3	10.3	5.9
Agriculture	15.4	76.9	7.7	0.0	40.0	40.0	20.0	0.0
Mining	50.0	50.0	0.0	0.0	33.3	66.7	0.0	0.0
Transportation	37.5	50.0	8.3	4.2	56.3	31.3	6.2	6.2
Professional Service	26.3	56.3	13.7	3.7	35.9	43.6	16.7	3.8
Owner								
Minority-owned	39.1	48.0	7.7	5.2	41.3	44.5	10.5	3.6
Not minority-owned	29.6	55.6	10.3	4.5	33.9	52.2	10.6	3.3

Table 6.1 (continued)

Firm Characteristic	FEDERAL				STATE				COUNTY			
	1-30 Days	31-60 Days	61-90 Days	Over 90 Days	1-30 Days	31-60 Days	61-90 Days	Over 90 Days	1-30 Days	31-60 Days	61-90 Days	Over 90 Days
Minority Owner-Gender[1]												
Female	22.2%	45.2%	20.0%	12.6%	28.6%	48.9%	18.0%	4.5%	36.3%	53.3%	6.6%	3.8%
Male	33.6	45.6	12.8	8.0	33.3	50.4	7.8	8.5	44.4	46.0	4.8	4.8
Minority Owner-Race[1]												
Black	50.0	32.5	10.0	7.5	42.3	44.2	3.9	9.6	50.0	38.6	4.6	6.8
Hispanic	24.2	54.8	17.8	3.2	27.3	56.1	12.1	4.5	41.5	47.7	4.6	6.2
Asian	26.7	46.7	13.3	13.3	14.3	64.3	0.0	21.4	37.5	50.0	12.5	0.0
American Indian	40.0	50.0	0.0	0.0	57.1	28.6	0.0	14.3	50.0	50.0	0.0	0.0
Other	33.3	0.0	33.3	33.3	62.5	25.0	12.5	0.0	57.1	28.6	14.3	0.0
Puerto Rican	0.0	100.0	0.0	0.0	0.0	50.0	50.0	0.0	66.7	33.3	0.0	0.0
Size-Economic Classification												
Small, economically disadvantaged	27.2	47.3	18.8	6.7	30.2	50.4	14.0	5.4	37.8	49.6	8.7	3.9
Not small, economically disadvantaged	18.2	48.0	20.1	13.7	21.1	53.3	18.6	7.0	30.4	55.9	9.7	4.0
Current Contract Status												
Has contract with government	21.3	48.3	19.3	11.1	23.3	52.9	17.6	6.2	32.3	54.9	8.8	4.0
No contract with government	13.4	47.8	20.6	18.2	20.1	52.4	18.0	9.5	30.6	53.1	11.5	4.8
No Government Contracts at Present[2]												
Have had one in past	14.0	44.6	21.5	19.9	22.5	48.3	18.7	10.5	23.9	55.6	13.2	7.3
Have not had one in past	17.2	46.8	17.2	18.8	15.2	60.7	16.5	7.6	38.2	47.0	11.3	3.5

[1] Question was answered only by the subset of the respondents meeting the definitional criterion (minority-owned).

[2] Question was answered only by the subset of the respondents meeting the definitional criterion (firm does not have a government contract at the present).

174

Firm Characteristic	CITY				SCHOOL BOARD			
	1-30 Days	31-60 Days	61-90 Days	Over 90 Days	1-30 Days	31-60 Days	61-90 Days	Over 90 Days
Minority Owner-Gender[1]								
Female	40.3%	49.6%	5.8%	4.3%	43.0%	43.7%	9.9%	3.4%
Male	39.2	47.7	8.4	4.7	42.7	42.7	11.5	3.1
Minority Owner-Race[1]								
Black	50.0	38.1	4.8	7.1	40.0	46.6	6.7	6.7
Hispanic	34.0	54.0	8.0	4.0	39.6	43.4	15.1	1.9
Asian	33.3	41.7	25.0	0.0	42.9	57.1	0.0	0.0
American Indian	40.0	60.0	0.0	0.0	50.0	50.0	0.0	0.0
Other	20.0	60.0	20.0	0.0	100.0	0.0	0.0	0.0
Puerto Rican	50.0	50.0	0.0	0.0	100.0	0.0	0.0	0.0
Size-Economic Classification								
Small, economically disadvantaged	35.3	52.5	8.8	3.4	40.4	45.9	10.0	3.7
Not small, economically disadvantaged	29.9	55.1	10.1	4.9	33.6	52.5	10.6	3.3
Current Contract Status								
Has contract with government	32.1	54.8	9.1	3.9	35.6	50.9	10.7	2.8
No contract with government	26.8	52.0	12.8	8.4	32.7	51.8	9.4	6.1
No Government Contracts at Present[2]								
Have had one in past	21.0	56.5	15.0	7.5	33.1	49.5	12.5	4.9
Have not had one in past	28.1	58.5	7.3	6.1	31.9	52.1	11.7	4.3

[1] Question was answered only by the subset of the respondents meeting the definitional criterion (minority-owned).

[2] Question was answered only by the subset of the respondents meeting the definitional criterion (firm does not have a government contract at the present).

Table 6.1 (continued)

Firm Characteristic	FEDERAL				STATE				COUNTY			
	1-30 Days	31-60 Days	61-90 Days	Over 90 Days	1-30 Days	31-60 Days	61-90 Days	Over 90 Days	1-30 Days	31-60 Days	61-90 Days	Over 90 Days
Level of Government Firm Does Business With (Multiple Responses)												
Federal	20.6%	48.9%	19.0%	11.5%	21.9%	53.5	18.6	6.0	30.2	56.9%	9.1%	3.8%
State	18.3	48.6	20.5	12.6	21.7	54.1	17.7	6.5	30.7	56.2	9.0	4.1
City	17.7	49.6	20.6	12.1	20.5	54.8	17.8	6.9	30.8	56.1	9.1	4.0
County	17.8	49.6	20.4	12.2	21.9	53.8	17.6	6.7	32.0	55.0	9.0	4.0
Transit Authority	17.1	48.8	21.9	12.2	22.0	54.8	18.7	4.5	33.0	54.2	8.5	4.3
School district	17.6	48.9	20.6	12.9	21.5	53.2	18.6	6.7	32.1	55.4	8.0	4.5
Hospital district	17.5	46.0	23.0	13.5	22.1	52.7	19.4	5.8	30.9	55.4	9.0	4.7
Other special district	18.0	45.3	24.2	12.5	17.8	52.6	19.2	10.4	31.1	49.6	15.6	3.7
Other	17.3	31.0	31.0	20.7	12.9	38.7	35.5	12.9	26.1	47.8	21.7	4.4
% of Gross Revenues From Government Contracts												
Less than 10%	19.5	47.6	18.4	14.5	22.2	53.5	17.5	6.8	31.5	55.5	9.2	3.8
10-25%	16.2	49.6	21.6	12.6	19.4	57.2	17.4	6.0	31.0	56.4	8.8	3.8
26-50%	22.3	44.1	23.5	10.1	24.7	47.4	18.1	9.8	33.7	51.5	10.2	4.6
51-75%	21.2	60.6	13.1	5.1	20.0	53.6	19.2	7.2	33.0	53.9	8.7	4.4
76-90%	25.4	57.6	11.9	5.1	28.4	51.3	17.6	2.7	34.8	45.5	13.6	6.1
Over 90%	31.9	30.4	26.1	11.6	41.5	35.4	15.4	7.7	23.1	58.4	10.8	7.7
Procedures for Getting Government Contract (Multiple Responses)												
Formal competitive bid (with negotiation)	16.8	48.7	21.8	12.7	19.8	52.6	20.9	6.7	26.9	58.6	10.7	3.8
Formal competitive bid (sealed)	19.3	48.6	20.8	11.3	21.5	54.3	18.0	6.2	29.5	56.4	9.8	4.3
Local vendor preference	17.7	48.4	22.9	11.0	24.2	53.9	17.3	4.6	34.3	55.3	7.8	2.6
Request for Proposal (competitive negotiation)	17.1	47.8	24.0	11.1	19.3	53.5	18.2	9.0	28.5	55.6	12.1	3.8
Government solicitation of written quote	17.6	49.2	21.1	12.1	20.5	57.0	16.5	6.0	29.9	57.6	8.2	4.3
Government solicitation of telephone quote	18.8	51.3	20.2	9.7	22.6	56.9	17.2	3.3	33.6	56.1	7.1	3.2
Participation in Minority Business Enterprise Program	22.1	50.6	20.8	6.5	28.1	57.3	9.0	5.6	31.2	53.8	7.5	7.5
Participation in Small Business Program	24.5	48.0	21.6	5.9	19.3	60.2	14.8	5.7	27.0	62.2	6.8	4.0
Other procedure	18.0	42.3	26.9	12.8	24.4	46.7	22.2	6.7	40.9	46.6	11.4	1.1

Firm Characteristic	CITY				SCHOOL BOARD			
	1-30 Days	31-60 Days	61-90 Days	Over 90 Days	1-30 Days	31-60 Days	61-90 Days	Over 90 Days
Level of Government Firm Does Business With (Multiple Responses)								
Federal	30.4%	54.8%	10.5%	4.3%	32.3%	53.1%	11.1%	3.5%
State	29.6	56.4	9.6	4.4	32.5	52.4	11.8	3.3
City	31.3	55.5	9.4	3.8	33.7	51.8	11.2	3.3
County	31.3	55.4	9.3	4.0	34.8	51.6	10.7	2.9
Transit Authority	30.0	55.5	11.4	3.1	31.5	53.7	11.5	3.3
School district	30.4	55.0	9.4	5.2	35.9	50.5	10.3	3.3
Hospital district	28.0	56.1	10.2	5.7	31.5	52.1	12.3	4.1
Other special district	25.9	58.9	9.8	5.4	31.1	51.9	14.2	2.8
Other	17.9	46.4	25.0	10.7	30.8	50.0	7.7	11.5
% of Gross Revenues From Government Contracts								
Less than 10%	30.3	55.8	9.4	4.5	34.4	52.2	10.0	3.4
10-25%	29.5	57.7	8.7	4.1	32.8	55.3	9.5	2.4
26-50%	33.8	45.2	14.0	7.0	39.5	42.1	15.1	3.3
51-75%	28.1	57.3	10.1	4.5	34.9	47.7	11.6	5.8
76-90%	40.7	49.1	5.1	5.1	51.3	35.9	10.3	2.5
Over 90%	32.7	50.9	12.7	3.7	41.0	48.7	7.7	2.6
Procedures for Getting Government Contract (Multiple Responses)								
Formal competitive bid (with negotiation)	29.0	55.9	10.7	4.4	28.7	55.5	12.8	3.0
Formal competitive bid (sealed)	30.6	55.1	9.7	4.6	34.6	52.0	10.6	2.8
Local vendor preference	33.6	54.9	7.7	3.8	35.4	53.8	8.4	2.4
Request for Proposal (competitive negotiation)	28.3	58.0	10.1	3.6	32.5	52.1	12.3	3.1
Government solicitation of written quote	29.5	57.2	9.1	4.2	33.0	53.3	10.5	3.2
Government solicitation of telephone quote	33.4	54.8	7.9	3.9	35.4	54.6	7.1	2.9
Participation in Minority Business Enterprise Program	33.3	51.4	9.7	5.6	46.0	44.5	7.9	1.6
Participation in Small Business Program	30.7	54.7	10.6	40.0	32.3	55.4	9.2	3.1
Other procedure	32.8	48.4	14.1	4.7	39.1	45.3	12.5	3.1

Table 6.1 (continued)

Firm Characteristic	FEDERAL				STATE				COUNTY			
	1-30 Days	31-60 Days	61-90 Days	Over 90 Days	1-30 Days	31-60 Days	61-90 Days	Over 90 Days	1-30 Days	31-60 Days	61-90 Days	Over 90 Days
Type of Product Delivered to Government (Multiple Responses)												
Service	21.1%	46.7%	19.0%	13.2%	21.8%	50.8%	18.8%	8.6%	33.2%	52.2%	10.3%	4.3%
Commodity/good	17.5	50.4	19.5	12.6	21.3	56.7	16.7	5.3	31.5	58.3	7.9	2.3
Construction	22.3	46.5	21.6	9.6	22.3	54.6	18.1	5.0	24.8	56.4	10.5	8.3
Geographical Location												
In-State	21.0	47.9	19.7	11.4	22.9	52.5	17.7	6.9	32.0	54.3	9.5	4.2
Out-of-State	15.4	47.7	20.3	16.6	19.3	59.1	16.4	5.2	30.0	55.3	10.7	4.0

Source: Random sample survey of businesses listed on the Harris County (Houston), Texas vendor mailing list (conducted May–June, 1989) and mail survey of all businesses listed on the Hillsborough County (Tampa), Florida vendor registration list (conducted June–July, 1989)

Firm Characteristic	CITY				SCHOOL BOARD			
	1-30 Days	31-60 Days	61-90 Days	Over 90 Days	1-30 Days	31-60 Days	61-90 Days	Over 90 Days
Type of Product Delivered to Government (Multiple Responses)								
Service	31.7%	52.9%	10.7%	4.7%	35.6%	49.7%	11.2%	3.5%
Commodity/good	30.2	56.3	9.8	3.7	31.6	54.8	10.8	2.8
Construction	27.5	55.3	11.6	5.6	36.0	51.5	9.6	2.9
Geographical Location								
In-State	31.2	54.3	9.9	4.6	36.1	50.6	10.3	3.0
Out-of-State	27.6	55.9	11.0	5.5	26.9	52.3	14.6	6.2

Source: Random sample survey of businesses listed on the Harris County (Houston), Texas vendor mailing list (conducted May-June, 1989) and mail survey of all businesses listed on the Hillsborough County (Tampa), Florida vendor registration list (conducted June-July, 1989)

of individually owned firms, firms in business a relatively short time, small firms (fewer than twenty-five employees and gross revenues below $200,000), minority-owned firms (especially those owned by blacks and American Indians), and small, economically disadvantaged firms report they are paid within thirty days (see Table 6.1). However, the proportions are still relatively small, as they are for all types of firms. And greater proportions of small and minority firms judge the overall quality of government purchasing practices "Poor" rather than "Excellent."

WHOSE PURCHASING PRACTICES ARE HIGH-QUALITY?

The vast majority of our respondents do not rate the purchasing practices of any type of government "Excellent" (see Figure 6.2). However, local governments are rated more positively than either the state or federal government. School boards are given an "Excellent" rating by 14 percent of our respondents; county government, 13 percent; and city government, 10 percent, compared to 9 percent for the state government and a low 8 percent for the federal government.

Surprisingly, nearly half of our respondents give all but the federal government "Good" ratings (see Figure 6.2). In fact, if the proportions of "Excellent" or "Good" ratings are combined, 59 percent of our firms judge the overall quality of school board procurement positively. Comparable positive ratings for the other types of government are county government, 58 percent; city government, 54 percent; state government, 53 percent; and the federal government, 45 percent. Of course, one's interpretation of these figures is somewhat analogous to interpreting whether a half-filled glass of water is half-full or half-empty.

At the other extreme, one-fifth of our respondents rate the overall quality of the federal government's purchasing practices "Poor." City governments don't fare much better; 17 percent of our respondents rate their practices "Poor." Comparable figures for the other governments rated "Poor" are 15 percent for county government; 14 percent, state government; and 14 percent, school district. If we combine "Fair" and "Poor" ratings and view the aggregate figure as a negative rating, we find that more than half of our firms give the federal government a negative rating and nearly half also give the other governments a negative rating.

What these figures show is that businesses have mixed feelings about the overall quality of different governments' procurement policies, based on their personal experiences and those of other businesses with whom they regularly interact. But several things are clear: First, the most common response category for each type of government is "Good." Second, with the exception of the federal government, more than half of the firms rate the purchasing practices of all governments either "Good" or "Excellent." However, a larger proportion of firms rate practices of all governments (except school districts) "Poor" rather than "Excellent." As expected, the federal government gets the worst overall ratings.

Many firms that have never investigated the possibility of doing business with government are heavily influenced by the federal government's bad reputation. The next section explains why. (See Figure 6.3)

Contract Status: The Best Predictor of a Firm's Ratings

Firms that have never had a government contract tend to rate government procurement practices more harshly than those with contracts. In rating the federal government's procurement system, *two-fifths (41 percent) of*

Figure 6.2
Business Rating of Overall Quality of Purchasing Practices
by Type of Government

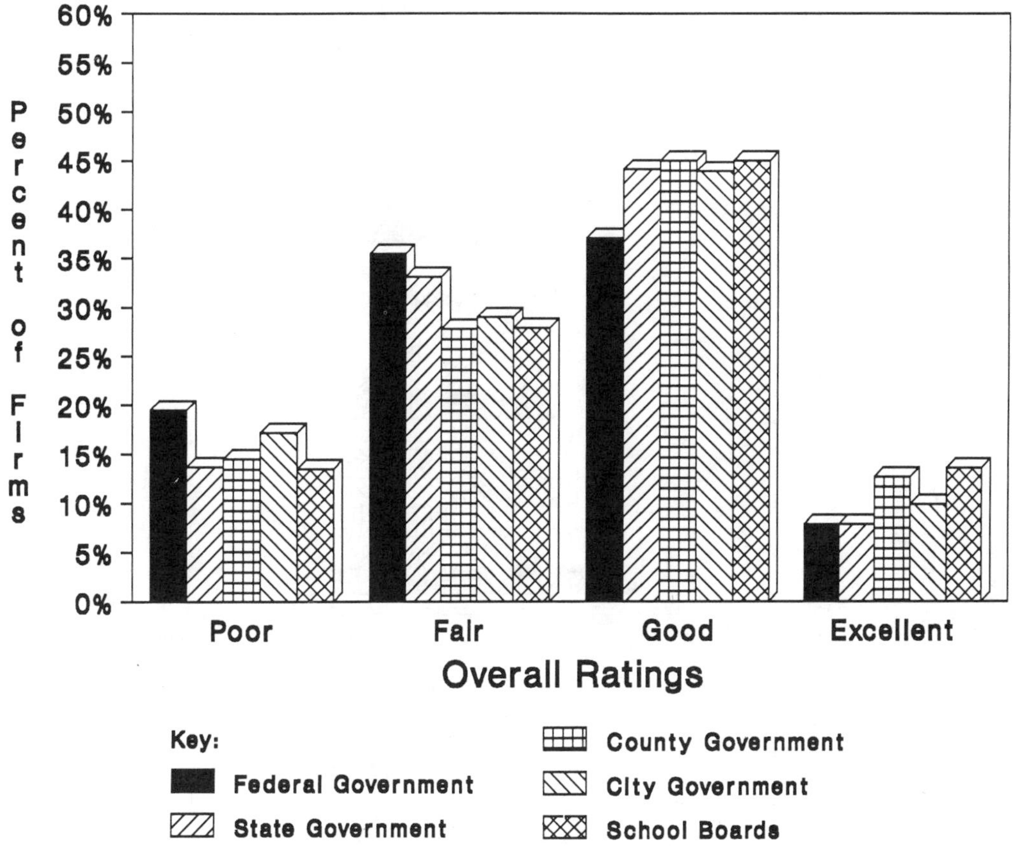

Key:
- ■ Federal Government
- ▨ State Government
- ▦ County Government
- ▧ City Government
- ▩ School Boards

the firms that have never had a government contract judge the overall quality "Poor," compared to only 17 percent of those with a contract. Combining "Fair" with "Poor" ratings raises these proportions even more sharply: Nearly three-fourths (71 percent) of the firms never having a contract rate federal purchasing practices "Fair" or "Poor" compared to 52 percent of those with contracts. But it is the magnitude of the "Poor" rating that helps explain the negative impact of businesses' perceptions of the federal government on efforts to attract new vendors into public procurement pools.

The same pattern appears in the two groups' ratings of other governments, though not so clearly (see Figure 6.3). *Among firms that have never had a government contract, more than half rate the quality of each other type of government "Poor" or only "Fair."* The figures are: state government, 60 percent; county, 54 percent; city, 60 percent; and school district, 54 percent.

In contrast, *among firms with a government contract, less than half judge the purchasing policy quality of any type of government, except the federal government, as only "Fair" or "Poor"* (see Figure 6.3). The variations in quality ratings between these two groups is related to the firm characteristics, shown in Table 6.2.

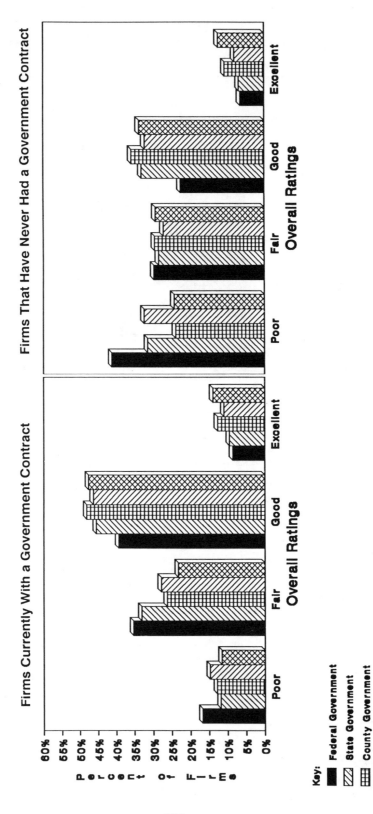

Figure 6.3
Businesses Without Government Contracts
Rate Government Purchasing Practices Differently

Business Firm Characteristics by Contract Status

Firms with and without government contracts differ markedly. Those without government contracts are more likely to be individually owned;[4] be in business less than five years;[5] have fewer than twenty-six employees;[6] have gross revenues below $500,000 annually;[7] be in the retail trade, communications, service, or agricultural sectors;[8] if owned by a minority, be owned by a black or Asian male;[9] and be classified as a small, economically disadvantaged firm.[10] Thus the relationship between a firm's contract status and its quality assessments is stronger than the relationship between specific firm characteristics and quality ratings. Nonetheless, the relative quality ratings of minority-owned firms and of small businesses is important because these two groups represent the greatest potential for expanding vendor pools in the future.

Quality Ratings by Minority-Owned Firms

Minority-owned firms express less enthusiasm about the overall quality of government purchasing practices than nonminority-owned firms (see Table 6.2). The percentages of minority-owned firms rating each government's procurement system either "Good" or "Excellent" are 54 percent for school boards; 54 percent for counties; 50 percent for state governments; 49 percent for cities; and 46 percent for the federal government. Comparable figures for nonminority-owned firms are generally higher: 60 percent for school boards; 58 percent for counties; 54 percent for state governments; 55 percent for cities; and—the exception—45 percent for the federal government. While the percentages vary only marginally, the rank order is somewhat different. Minority-owned firms rate the quality of state purchasing higher than the

city's; the reverse is true among nonminority-owned firms. *Both rate the school district's system as the best and the federal government's as the worst.* But the assessments of minority firms differ by gender and race and do not always reflect mere success in securing government contracts.

Female-owned firms Women-owned businesses are slightly more positive in their ratings of school district, county, state, and city purchasing practices, but more negative in their ratings of federal procurement than minority-owned firms in general. (However, the rank order is identical.) Among female-owned businesses, school district purchasing practices head the list at 58 percent. Comparable percentages for the other types of government are county, 56 percent; state, 55 percent; city, 52 percent; and federal government, 44 percent. There is some evidence that contract success may influence these relative rankings. Among the female-owned firms in our study, higher proportions are currently doing business with state and local governments than with the federal government.[11]

Black-owned firms The assessments by these firms vary considerably from other minority firms. More than half (59 percent) rate federal procurement practices "Good" or "Excellent." Less than half judge either the state or any local government positively. Figures, in rank order, are school districts 48 percent, city 44 percent, and state 43 percent. County government ranks at the bottom; only 40 percent of black-owned firms see county purchasing practices positively.

The relative quality assessments by black-owned firms do not as closely parallel their contract status as is the case among women business owners.[12] For example, among the black-owned firms responding to our survey, only 26 percent report they are currently doing business with the federal government, compared to 50 percent with city govern-

Table 6.2
Business Rating of Overall Quality of Purchasing Policies and Procedures by Type of Government and Firm Characteristics

Firm Characteristic	FEDERAL				STATE				COUNTY			
	Poor	Fair	Good	Excellent	Poor	Fair	Good	Excellent	Poor	Fair	Good	Excellent
All Firms	19.5%	35.5%	37.1%	7.9%	13.7%	33.1%	44.1%	9.1%	14.5%	27.8%	45.0%	12.7%
Firm Structure												
Individual owner	25.1	25.6	41.7	7.6	16.0	27.2	45.6	11.2	20.7	22.3	41.0	16.0
Partnership	8.5	29.8	53.2	8.5	11.8	29.4	51.0	7.8	11.9	16.9	50.9	20.3
Nonprofit organization	8.1	29.7	46.0	16.2	0.0	24.3	59.5	16.2	2.9	25.7	57.1	14.3
Corporation	19.4	37.1	35.7	7.8	13.8	34.4	43.2	8.6	14.0	29.1	45.1	11.8
Other	0.0	40.0	60.0	0.0	0.0	25.0	62.5	12.5	0.0	28.6	42.8	28.6
Years in Business												
Less than 1 year	13.1	39.1	39.1	8.7	16.0	40.0	40.0	4.0	7.7	26.9	53.9	11.5
1-2 years	20.0	28.8	40.0	11.2	24.3	34.6	34.6	6.5	18.7	24.4	39.8	17.1
3-5 years	19.2	37.5	33.0	10.3	18.7	32.7	38.9	9.7	20.3	25.9	41.9	11.9
6-10 years	21.1	35.9	34.5	8.5	14.0	35.0	42.0	9.0	10.5	30.2	44.3	15.0
Over 10 years	19.4	35.5	38.0	7.1	11.5	32.7	46.5	9.3	14.0	27.8	46.3	11.9
Number of Employees												
1-25	19.7	35.1	35.6	9.6	15.1	33.4	40.7	10.8	15.6	27.4	42.4	14.6
26-50	23.8	36.5	32.5	7.2	16.2	31.7	45.3	6.8	13.7	26.3	49.6	10.4
51-100	16.7	30.2	45.3	7.8	7.3	28.7	52.2	11.8	10.9	27.6	48.9	12.6
101-500	20.2	36.8	37.3	5.7	11.2	36.4	47.2	5.2	14.6	27.4	49.8	8.2
501-1000	13.0	33.3	50.0	3.7	7.3	32.7	58.2	1.8	8.3	27.1	62.5	2.1
1001-5000	15.3	44.7	36.5	3.5	13.9	38.4	41.9	5.8	16.5	34.1	37.6	11.8
Over 5000	14.1	38.0	45.1	2.8	7.9	31.8	54.0	6.3	11.5	31.1	49.2	8.2

Firm Characteristic	CITY				SCHOOL BOARD			
	Poor	Fair	Good	Excellent	Poor	Fair	Good	Excellent
All Firms	17.2%	29.0%	43.9%	9.9%	13.5%	27.9%	45.0%	13.6%
Firm Structure								
Individual owner	24.5	23.6	39.6	12.3	17.8	26.5	37.9	17.8
Partnership	7.8	21.6	60.8	9.8	5.1	18.0	61.5	15.4
Nonprofit organization	12.0	20.0	52.0	16.0	7.2	10.7	46.4	35.7
Corporation	16.5	30.3	43.8	9.4	13.3	28.7	45.4	12.6
Other	25.0	0.0	75.0	0.0	0.0	33.3	50.0	16.7
Years in Business								
Less than 1 year	4.3	34.8	47.8	13.1	8.7	34.8	47.8	8.7
1-2 years	25.0	30.0	35.0	10.0	22.0	28.6	39.5	9.9
3-5 years	17.6	30.6	40.0	11.8	16.3	28.6	38.3	16.8
6-10 years	16.5	28.2	46.2	9.1	14.2	32.3	37.0	16.5
Over 10 years	17.6	30.5	40.5	11.4	12.2	26.7	48.3	12.8
Number of Employees								
1-25	19.0	28.9	40.6	11.5	15.7	26.9	40.9	16.5
26-50	18.6	27.9	47.0	6.5	12.1	29.3	47.8	10.8
51-100	13.6	29.2	46.0	11.2	9.8	22.2	54.9	13.1
101-500	15.3	29.7	45.9	9.1	10.6	34.6	46.8	8.0
501-1000	10.2	30.6	53.1	6.1	5.1	33.4	56.4	5.1
1001-5000	7.8	29.9	57.1	5.2	7.0	29.8	54.4	8.8
Over 5000	13.6	28.8	52.5	5.1	15.7	27.5	52.9	3.9

Table 6.2 (continued)

Firm Characteristic	FEDERAL				STATE				COUNTY			
	Poor	Fair	Good	Excel-lent	Poor	Fair	Good	Excel-lent	Poor	Fair	Good	Excel-lent
Firm Gross Revenues ('88)												
Below $200,000	22.7%	34.5%	32.0%	10.8%	18.7%	33.2%	35.2%	12.9%	17.7%	26.3%	40.0%	16.0%
$200,000-499,999	19.8	33.6	36.2	10.4	15.8	31.1	41.4	11.7	14.9	27.8	40.1	17.2
$500,000-999,999	16.9	33.1	41.1	8.9	14.0	32.7	44.9	8.4	18.4	25.4	42.0	14.2
$1-$10 Million	21.0	36.4	34.3	8.3	13.3	34.1	43.1	9.5	14.0	27.9	47.7	10.4
$11-$25 Million	20.0	37.9	35.2	6.9	10.1	30.8	50.9	8.2	12.3	30.8	45.2	11.7
$26-$50 Million	13.7	37.5	46.3	2.5	10.8	33.8	54.0	1.4	10.6	21.2	63.7	4.5
Over $50 Million	17.2	38.0	41.2	3.6	9.3	36.6	48.8	5.3	13.0	32.5	47.0	7.5
Industry Classification												
Retail trade	15.9	31.3	46.1	6.7	11.6	29.5	48.9	10.0	9.3	26.1	49.2	15.4
Wholesale trade	21.9	35.7	35.7	6.7	13.2	36.1	43.7	7.0	12.1	28.6	47.8	11.5
Finance	12.5	50.0	25.0	12.5	0.0	33.3	55.6	11.1	25.0	25.0	25.0	25.0
Insurance	0.0	50.0	0.0	50.0	0.0	50.0	0.0	50.0	50.0	50.0	0.0	0.0
Utility	0.0	50.0	50.0	0.0	14.3	57.1	28.6	0.0	0.0	83.3	16.7	0.0
Construction	17.6	34.0	39.2	9.2	11.1	35.1	45.8	8.0	20.0	30.8	40.7	8.5
Manufacturing	21.4	42.9	28.6	7.1	4.4	30.4	56.5	8.7	19.2	3.9	42.3	34.6
Manufacturing-durable	17.8	46.6	31.3	4.3	7.0	40.1	44.4	8.5	9.7	26.1	49.3	14.9
Manufacturing-nondurable	23.2	33.9	39.3	3.6	17.8	24.5	53.3	4.4	19.5	14.7	58.5	7.3
Real estate	15.8	42.1	36.8	5.3	30.4	30.4	30.4	8.7	0.0	12.5	58.3	29.2
Communications	25.0	41.7	31.2	2.1	17.6	29.4	47.1	5.9	10.6	27.7	53.2	8.5
Service	20.1	30.7	38.6	10.6	16.8	29.2	43.1	10.9	16.1	27.5	42.3	14.1
Agriculture	25.0	50.0	25.0	0.0	15.4	46.1	30.8	7.7	6.2	37.5	31.3	25.0
Mining	0.0	100.0	0.0	0.0	0.0	33.3	66.7	0.0	0.0	0.0	66.7	33.3
Transportation	14.8	44.5	33.3	7.4	16.7	33.3	43.3	6.7	11.1	25.0	47.2	16.7
Professional Service	16.5	41.0	36.7	5.8	18.4	38.2	36.2	7.2	24.7	31.5	34.9	8.9
Owner												
Minority-owned	23.0	31.3	33.7	12.0	18.8	31.0	39.4	10.8	20.6	25.7	39.9	13.8
Not minority-owned	18.3	36.4	38.2	7.1	12.5	33.6	45.3	8.6	13.4	28.2	46.2	12.2

Firm Characteristic	CITY				SCHOOL BOARD			
	Poor	Fair	Good	Excellent	Poor	Fair	Good	Excellent
Firm Gross Revenues (88)								
Below $200,000	23.0%	27.7%	34.6%	14.7%	22.6%	25.0%	35.6%	16.8%
$200,000-499,999	19.1	29.1	39.1	12.7	15.8	28.8	38.3	17.1
$500,000-999,999	21.7	26.4	40.7	11.2	13.6	28.1	41.3	17.0
$1-$10 Million	16.7	29.4	45.7	8.2	12.2	26.5	47.8	13.5
$11-$25 Million	11.8	34.5	43.4	10.3	8.3	34.8	47.0	9.9
$26-$50 Million	14.8	22.9	55.7	6.6	11.7	28.3	51.7	8.3
Over $50 Million	11.6	30.5	52.1	5.8	9.5	30.4	56.3	3.8
Industry Classification								
Retail trade	14.2	28.1	47.9	9.8	11.8	25.2	45.6	17.4
Wholesale trade	15.0	33.8	42.8	8.4	9.7	26.9	50.0	13.4
Finance	33.4	22.2	22.2	22.2	28.6	0.0	42.8	28.6
Insurance	0.0	0.0	0.0	100.0	0.0	0.0	100.0	0.0
Utility	0.0	0.0	80.0	20.0	0.0	20.0	60.0	20.0
Cons'ruction	22.3	27.7	43.2	6.8	14.0	31.3	45.7	9.0
Manufacturing-durable	13.0	30.4	46.1	10.5	14.6	26.1	45.8	13.5
Manufacturing-nondurable	21.1	18.4	57.9	2.6	13.5	13.5	62.2	10.8
Real estate	31.3	31.3	25.0	12.5	15.4	15.4	46.1	23.1
Communications	18.9	24.3	48.7	8.1	11.9	31.0	47.6	9.5
Service	19.7	24.7	42.9	12.7	18.4	27.3	40.4	13.9
Agriculture	14.3	28.6	42.8	14.3	10.0	40.0	30.0	20.0
Mining	0.0	0.0	50.0	50.0	33.3	0.0	66.7	0.0
Transportation	17.9	25.0	46.4	10.7	19.1	23.8	47.6	9.5
Professional Service	16.6	35.7	42.1	5.6	15.0	36.4	34.6	14.0
Owner								
Minority-owned	21.4	29.5	37.4	11.7	20.6	25.4	41.3	12.7
Not minority-owned	16.4	28.8	45.4	9.4	12.0	28.3	46.0	13.7

Table 6.2 (continued)

Firm Characteristic	FEDERAL				STATE				COUNTY			
	Poor	Fair	Good	Excel-lent	Poor	Fair	Good	Excel-lent	Poor	Fair	Good	Excel-lent
Minority Owner-Gender[1]												
Female	23.7%	32.4%	31.2%	12.7%	16.4%	28.8%	41.3%	13.5%	17.7%	26.5%	37.2%	18.6%
Male	21.5	29.4	37.4	11.7	21.3	31.4	37.9	9.4	22.9	26.1	43.3	7.7
Minority Owner-Race[1]												
Black	12.7	28.6	33.3	25.4	24.6	32.9	38.4	4.1	33.8	26.2	36.9	3.1
Hispanic	15.7	27.1	44.3	12.9	15.6	33.7	36.4	14.3	14.9	27.0	50.0	8.1
Asian	30.4	43.5	17.4	8.7	33.3	29.2	37.5	0.0	26.1	26.1	47.8	0.0
American Indian	8.3	8.3	50.0	33.3	12.5	25.0	62.5	0.0	20.0	20.0	40.0	20.0
Other	20.0	60.0	20.0	0.0	33.3	22.2	33.3	11.1	33.3	33.3	33.3	0.0
Puerto Rican	20.0	20.0	40.0	20.0	20.0	40.0	40.0	0.0	20.0	40.0	40.0	20.0
Size-Economic Classification												
Small, economically disadvantaged	19.9	32.6	37.1	10.4	17.4	32.4	40.2	10.0	18.9	25.6	41.5	14.0
Not small, economically disadvantaged	19.1	36.2	37.5	7.2	12.3	33.3	45.6	8.8	13.3	28.3	46.1	12.3
Current Contract Status												
Has contract with government	16.8	35.3	39.3	8.6	11.9	33.1	45.5	9.5	12.9	26.3	48.1	12.7
No contract with government	29.4	35.6	28.8	6.2	20.9	32.7	39.4	7.0	20.2	31.7	36.0	12.1
No Government Contracts at Present[2]												
Have had one in past	27.3	37.9	28.6	6.2	16.3	40.2	35.6	7.9	20.6	33.8	36.0	9.6
Have not had one in past	41.1	29.8	22.6	6.5	31.5	28.5	33.1	6.9	23.9	29.6	35.8	10.7

[1] Question was answered only by the subset of the respondents meeting the definitional criterion (minority-owned).

[2] Question was answered only by the subset of the respondents meeting the definitional criterion (firm does not have a government contract at the present).

	CITY				SCHOOL BOARD			
Firm Characteristic	**Poor**	**Fair**	**Good**	**Excel-lent**	**Poor**	**Fair**	**Good**	**Excel-lent**
Minority Owner-Gender[1]								
Female	17.2%	31.1%	38.9%	12.8%	15.8%	26.0%	40.1%	18.1%
Male	24.5	27.9	36.7	10.9	23.7	23.7	45.2	7.4
Minority Owner-Race[1]								
Black	27.0	28.6	34.9	9.5	29.2	22.9	47.9	0.0
Hispanic	18.8	28.1	42.2	10.9	17.1	28.6	45.7	8.6
Asian	31.6	36.8	31.6	0.0	26.3	21.0	47.4	5.3
American Indian	28.6	42.8	14.3	14.3	40.0	20.0	40.0	0.0
Other	33.3	44.5	22.2	0.0	50.0	12.5	25.0	12.5
Puerto Rican	0.0	40.0	40.0	20.0	0.0	33.3	66.7	0.0
Size-Economic Classification								
Small, economically disadvantaged	21.6	27.7	39.6	11.1	19.8	23.3	42.5	14.4
Not small, economically disadvantaged	15.9	29.2	44.9	10.0	11.8	29.2	45.6	13.4
Current Contract Status								
Has contract with government	14.8	27.9	46.3	11.0	11.6	28.8	47.6	14.0
No contract with government	25.3	32.5	35.2	7.0	20.6	31.0	36.0	12.4
No Government Contracts at Present[2]								
Have had one in past	26.6	34.9	32.1	6.4	20.3	32.9	36.6	10.2
Have not had one in past	32.4	27.2	32.3	8.1	24.3	29.4	33.8	12.5

[1] Question was answered only by the subset of the respondents meeting the definitional criterion (minority-owned).

[2] Question was answered only by the subset of the respondents meeting the definitional criterion (firm does not have a government contract at the present).

Table 6.2 (continued)

Firm Characteristic	FEDERAL				STATE				COUNTY			
	Poor	Fair	Good	Excellent	Poor	Fair	Good	Excellent	Poor	Fair	Good	Excellent
Level of Government Firm Does Business With (Multiple Responses)												
Federal	14.3%	33.2%	41.9%	8.6%	10.9%	31.4%	48.3%	9.4%	12.6%	26.2%	49.6%	11.6%
State	16.6	35.0	40.3	8.1	10.2	32.6	47.6	9.6	12.2	27.1	48.0	12.7
City	17.8	35.2	39.4	7.6	11.7	33.7	45.7	8.9	12.6	26.8	48.0	12.6
County	17.9	34.7	39.3	8.1	11.8	33.1	45.7	9.4	12.4	27.2	47.1	13.3
Transit Authority	15.9	35.9	40.4	7.8	11.3	32.1	46.3	10.3	13.0	25.1	47.8	14.1
School district	18.2	35.2	39.1	7.5	11.3	32.4	46.8	9.5	11.7	26.8	49.2	12.3
Hospital district	16.3	33.4	41.5	8.8	10.8	31.9	47.8	9.5	11.2	26.4	49.8	12.6
Other special district	11.8	43.0	35.6	9.6	10.4	37.9	40.0	11.7	19.3	24.0	43.3	13.4
Other	43.6	30.8	21.8	3.8	43.8	25.0	25.0	6.2	43.1	31.6	17.9	7.4
% of Gross Revenues From Government Contracts												
Less than 10%	24.8	37.3	33.1	4.8	16.6	34.6	41.7	7.1	14.9	29.8	44.0	11.3
10-25%	12.4	36.1	40.5	11.0	10.2	31.1	47.8	10.9	10.3	25.3	49.9	14.5
26-50%	14.4	26.3	48.0	11.3	10.2	31.9	47.8	10.1	10.8	27.4	48.6	13.2
51-75%	12.6	39.6	39.6	8.2	13.1	40.0	40.8	6.1	21.4	22.2	44.5	11.9
76-90%	10.8	23.1	50.7	15.4	5.4	24.3	54.1	16.2	21.6	21.6	41.9	14.9
Over 90%	13.1	38.2	31.6	17.1	6.7	33.3	40.0	20.0	19.4	29.2	33.3	18.1
Procedures for Getting Government Contract (Multiple Responses)												
Formal competitive bid (with negotiation)	14.4	36.4	41.9	7.3	11.7	31.7	48.4	8.2	11.7	25.2	51.0	12.1
Formal competitive bid (sealed)	18.1	36.2	38.0	7.7	12.1	33.8	45.6	8.5	13.1	28.5	47.1	11.3
Local vendor preference	17.3	34.9	38.8	9.0	11.6	31.9	45.6	10.9	12.2	24.7	48.9	14.2
Request for Proposal (competitive negotiation)	14.8	35.6	42.6	7.0	12.4	33.3	46.2	8.1	13.7	27.0	46.3	13.0
Government solicitation of written quote	16.0	36.7	39.3	8.0	10.6	34.2	46.6	8.6	11.5	25.3	50.4	12.8
Government solicitation of telephone quote	14.5	36.3	41.9	7.3	9.0	33.7	48.5	8.8	11.8	21.8	52.2	14.2
Participation in Minority Business Enterprise Program	13.4	37.8	36.6	12.2	9.7	30.1	47.3	12.9	19.5	17.1	56.1	7.3
Participation in Small Business program	11.9	30.7	46.5	10.9	5.4	36.9	45.7	12.0	13.2	21.0	51.3	14.5
Other procedure	25.0	32.6	34.8	7.6	17.8	36.6	35.7	9.9	17.9	29.5	32.6	20.0

Firm Characteristic	CITY				SCHOOL BOARD			
	Poor	Fair	Good	Excel-lent	Poor	Fair	Good	Excel-lent
Level of Government Firm Does Business With (Multiple Responses)								
Federal	14.6%	27.8%	48.5%	9.1%	11.6%	26.7%	48.8%	12.9%
State	14.5	28.1	47.4	10.0	10.5	28.1	47.3	14.1
City	13.7	28.7	46.5	11.1	11.2	28.2	46.6	14.0
County	15.0	28.3	46.1	10.6	11.1	27.9	46.7	14.3
Transit Authority	14.6	26.9	44.7	13.8	12.4	26.8	47.0	13.8
School district	14.6	29.1	46.5	9.8	9.4	26.1	48.9	15.6
Hospital district	12.8	27.9	48.5	10.8	10.2	25.9	49.9	14.0
Other special district	19.5	29.7	38.3	12.5	11.6	23.2	48.2	17.0
Other	48.8	29.3	19.5	2.4	45.2	28.8	20.5	5.5
% of Gross Revenues From Government Contracts								
Less than 10%	19.2	31.6	41.9	7.3	15.8	30.3	44.0	9.9
10-25%	13.1	26.3	47.2	13.4	9.3	24.8	49.1	16.8
26-50%	12.4	24.3	50.3	13.0	8.0	27.0	42.9	22.1
51-75%	24.8	25.7	42.6	6.9	16.3	21.7	45.7	16.3
76-90%	14.9	19.4	47.8	17.9	8.3	29.2	43.8	18.7
Over 90%	9.4	29.7	40.6	20.3	10.6	19.2	46.8	23.4
Procedures for Getting Government Contract (Multiple Responses)								
Formal competitive bid (with negotiation)	13.2	27.1	49.1	10.6	9.0	25.7	52.5	12.8
Formal competitive bid (sealed)	12.1	21.6	33.7	7.6	11.8	28.1	47.1	13.0
Local vendor preference	13.8	26.5	48.2	11.5	10.5	27.2	44.9	17.4
Request for Proposal (competitive negotiation)	13.9	27.0	47.0	12.1	11.6	25.0	49.3	14.1
Government solicitation of written quote	14.5	27.6	47.0	10.9	9.9	26.4	50.4	13.3
Government solicitation of telephone quote	13.5	24.6	48.9	13.0	9.3	24.4	51.7	14.6
Participation in Minority Business Enterprise Program	16.2	21.2	48.8	13.8	11.4	27.2	50.0	11.4
Participation in Small Business program	7.8	23.4	54.5	14.3	10.8	23.0	48.6	17.6
Other procedure	21.2	32.5	38.8	7.5	20.0	31.8	27.0	21.2

Table 6.2 (continued)

Firm Characteristic	FEDERAL				STATE				COUNTY			
	Poor	Fair	Good	Excel-lent	Poor	Fair	Good	Excel-lent	Poor	Fair	Good	Excel-lent
Type of Product Delivered to Government (Multiple Responses)												
Service	18.9%	34.5%	37.8%	8.8%	16.0%	33.7%	41.0%	9.3%	14.2%	29.1%	43.3%	13.4%
Commodity/good	20.1	36.0	37.2	6.7	12.0	32.9	46.4	8.7	11.3	26.7	49.1	12.9
Construction	18.0	33.7	37.6	10.7	12.1	33.6	44.4	9.9	18.5	30.7	41.6	9.2
Geographical Location												
In-State	20.6	34.8	36.3	8.3	14.7	34.3	42.3	8.7	15.6	28.7	43.5	12.2
Out-of-State	13.6	39.5	41.7	5.2	4.4	23.5	62.8	9.3	1.9	17.3	64.2	16.6

Source: Random sample survey of businesses listed on the Harris County (Houston), Texas vendor mailing list (conducted May–June, 1989) and mail survey of all businesses listed on the Hillsborough County (Tampa), Florida vendor registration list (conducted June–July, 1989)

192

Firm Characteristic	CITY				SCHOOL BOARD			
	Poor	Fair	Good	Excel-lent	Poor	Fair	Good	Excel-lent
Type of Product Delivered to Government (Multiple Responses)								
Service	17.8%	29.3%	42.7%	10.2%	14.8%	29.6%	41.1%	14.5%
Commodity/good	15.3	29.7	45.4	9.6	12.0	26.3	48.4	13.3
Construction	19.4	27.3	43.7	9.6	14.7	29.0	45.2	11.1
Geographical Location								
In-State	18.1	29.7	42.5	9.7	14.2	28.6	43.7	13.5
Out-of-State	5.2	20.0	63.7	11.1	4.4	19.9	61.0	14.7

Source: Random sample survey of businesses listed on the Harris County (Houston), Texas vendor mailing list (conducted May–June, 1989) and mail survey of all businesses listed on the Hillsborough County (Tampa), Florida vendor registration list (conducted June–July, 1989)

193

ment and 47 percent with the county. It appears that the more negative quality assessments by black businesses of state and local government purchasing practices are attributable to other factors, such as perceptions of local government favoritism, inability to compete, and bonding requirements (see Chapter 5).

Hispanic-owned firms The assessments by Hispanic-owned firms vary considerably from those of minority-owned firms at large and black-owned firms. Hispanic firms tend to rate the quality of various government procurement practices higher than black firms do. The proportion of Hispanic-owned firms rating purchasing practices either "Good" or "Excellent" are, in rank order, county, 58 percent; federal government, 57 percent; school district, 54 percent; city, 53 percent; and state, 51 percent. But, like black-owned firms, their relative assessments do not closely parallel the proportions in which they deal with different governments. They too have been less successful in securing federal contracts than in securing state, county, or municipal government contracts. Among the Hispanic-owned firms responding to our survey, 65 percent currently do business with the county, 55 percent with the city, and 49 percent with the state, compared to 41 percent with the federal government and 40 percent with the school district. Again, the relative quality assessments of each government's purchasing practices by Hispanic-owned firms most likely reflect their perceived competitiveness, efficiency, and equivocality of each.

Asian-owned firms Asian-owned firms are much more critical of government purchasing practices than black- or Hispanic-owned firms, most likely because they have had less success than the others in securing government contracts. (Only 50 percent of the Asian-owned firms responding to our survey currently have a government contract,

compared to 66 percent of the Hispanic-owned firms, 60 percent of the black-owned firms, and 65 percent of the female-owned firms.)

Asian-owned firms have the best impressions of the procurement practices of school districts (53 percent rate them positively) and county government (48 percent). Asian-owned firms rate the federal government at the bottom of the barrel (only 26 percent regard federal purchasing as "Good" or "Excellent"); city governments are not viewed much better (only 32 percent regard municipal purchasing positively).

Again, these relative quality rankings do not closely parallel the proportions of business relationships. High proportions (64 percent) of the Asian-owned firms with contracts currently do business with the city and county; lower proportions deal with the other governments: 47 percent with the school district, 44 percent with the state, and 33 percent with the federal government.

American Indian-owned firms Of all the minority groups, American Indian proprietors are the most positive in their ratings. They tend to view federal and state practices more favorably than local government practices. The proportion of American-Indian owned firms rating each government's purchasing practices "Good" or "Excellent" are: federal government, 83 percent; state government, 63 percent; county, 60 percent; school district, 40 percent; and city government, a low 29 percent. The higher ratings for federal and state governments are probably attributable to these governments' more extensive product and vendor preference policies expressly targeted at Native American firms.

Summary of minority ratings Minority-owned firms differ considerably in their opinions about which type of government is the most desirable business partner. This difference of opinion stems largely from the experiences of minority firms in dealing with a particular type of government. Consistent with the findings reported in Chapter 5, minority firms are frequently as critical of government purchasing practices as nonminority firms, although they may identify slightly different aspects as their biggest sore points. But the fact remains that a rather large proportion of these firms do not regard the purchasing practices of any government to be outstanding. Nor do small businesses.

Quality Ratings by Small Businesses

Small businesses (defined for the purpose of analysis as those with gross revenues below $200,000) *are more critical of government purchasing policies in general than the largest firms* (those with gross revenues higher than $50 million). The rank order of the two types of firm also differ. Among the smallest firms, the rank order and the percentage judging a government's purchasing practices "Good" or "Excellent" are county government, 56 percent; school district, 52 percent; city government, 49 percent; state government, 48 percent; and the federal government, 43 percent. In other words, small businesses are much more likely to give higher ratings to those governments closest to home—i.e., local governments.

The largest firms are also more likely to give higher overall quality ratings to local governments, although the order is somewhat different and the percentages slightly higher. Their ratings are: school district, 60 percent; city 58 percent; county, 55 percent; state government, 54 percent; and the federal government, 49 percent. These slightly more positive ratings no doubt stem from differences in contract status. Large firms are more likely to have government contracts with a wider range of governments than small firms. (Among businesses currently without a government contract, 32 percent have gross revenues below $200,000, compared to four percent of the firms grossing more than $50 million.)

General Rating: Medium-Grade

In summary, few businesses of any type judge the purchasing practices of any government to be of high quality (an "Excellent" rating). Most judge government purchasing systems to be of only moderate quality, especially if we define as "moderate" the percent rating purchasing practices "Good" or "Fair." Using this definition, three-fourths of our respondents classify the quality of government procurement practices as medium-grade. The figures are: school district, 73 percent; city government, 73 percent; county government, 73 percent; state government, 78 percent; and federal government, 73 percent. But does this medium-grade rating suggest that certain types of businesses will be less likely to do business with some types of governments than with others?

WHICH GOVERNMENTS ARE UNDESIRABLE CUSTOMERS?

In spite of the many deficiencies of government procurement practices identified by our respondents and discussed throughout the book, the bottom line is that *only a small percentage identify any type of government as an undesirable customer* (see Figure 6.4). However, among the businesses reporting that they do not want government as a customer, the most commonly expressed reasons are those delineated in Chapter 5: slow pay, paperwork, and an inability to compete against firms with more economic and political resources.

A small proportion of firms report they do

Figure 6.4
Type of Government Not Desired by Business as a Customer

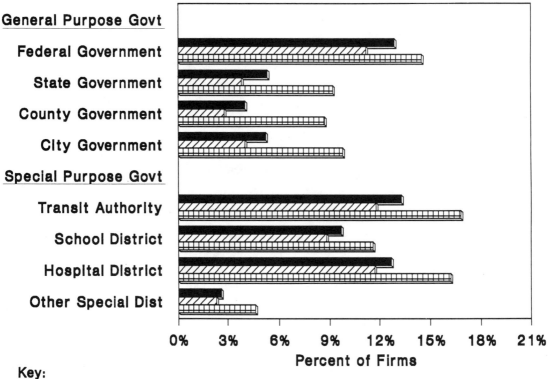

Key:

■ All Firms

▨ Firms Currently with Government Contract

▦ Firms That Have Never Had
Government Contract

not want *any* government as a customer. Typical responses are:

"We are not interested in doing business with any government. We lose money doing business with the county and the only reason we do business with it is because we have compassion for the people being helped. We cannot afford any more 'credit customers,' which is what governments are" (a small appliance and air-conditioning repair firm).

"Government contracts almost put my company out of business and I refuse to do business with any of them. They will have to change their way of doing business before I'll consider bidding a job again" (a small female-owned construction firm).

"We are not interested in doing business with any government. They don't pay and we simply cannot afford to do business with government again" (a nondurable goods manufacturing firm).

More commonly, a firm is interested in doing business with any government, so long as it meets certain conditions. Typical of this perspective are these comments:

"Our company will do business with any government who will pay us and let us make money" (a durable goods manufacturing firm).

"We will do business with any government as long as it is mutually beneficial" (a service firm).

"We take the good with the bad" (a construction firm).

"We are interested in doing business with any government that will fund the service we provide without forcing us to compromise our integrity or lose our sense of purpose" (a nonprofit organization).

Quite a few firms say they would like to do business with any government that would give them a chance. Comments reflecting this perspective include:

"We would love to do business with all types of government but it is almost impossible for small businesses to do so. Governments' applications are too vague. Some governments even charge to get on their bid lists and if you don't respond on every bid, you are dropped from their list. The only way one can get business from government is to find an 'in' and then you can get something sometime" (a retail trade firm).

"Despite registering with Hillsborough County, Pinellas County, the State of Florida, and other local governments, we have *never* received any information on any government contract. We would like to do business with government but just had not had any luck" (a small, professional services firm).

Thus it appears that few firms let past failures to win contracts totally discourage them from selling to government, although a few do. For other firms, the "bad reputation," especially of federal agencies, deters them from competing for government business.

The Undesirables: General Ratings

Among general purpose governments, the federal government is most likely to be identified as an undesirable customer (13 percent of our respondents), followed by state government (5 percent), city government (5 percent), and county government (4 percent).

Special purpose governments are viewed slightly more harshly than the general purpose governments, mostly because these governments do not purchase the goods or services produced by certain types of firms, but also because fewer firms know the workings of these governments. Even so, the percentages of our respondents identifying any one of these as an undesirable business partner are small: transit authorities, 13 percent; hospital districts, 13 percent; school districts, 10 percent; and other special districts 3 percent.

Predictably, a larger proportion of firms that have never had a government contract identify governments they do not want to sell to, but even these percentages are relatively small (see Figure 6.4). Of these firms, 15 percent say they do not want to do business with the federal government; 9 percent with the state or county; and 10 percent with the city. Sixteen percent do not want to sell to transit authorities or hospital districts; 12 percent do not want school districts as customers; and 5 percent do not want to do business with other special district governments (housing, water, mosquito control, health, airport, park).

Governments interested in expanding their vendor pools and in improving their purchasing policies should carefully study the characteristics of firms identifying them as undesirable customers (see Table 6.3).

Who Doesn't Want to Sell to the Federal Government?

Not surprisingly, the type of firm most likely to see the federal government as an undesirable customers (13 percent of all firms) is a small, relatively new firm, individually owned, with a more local market, and most likely from the finance, insurance, manufacturing, agricultural, or transportation sectors (see Table 6.3).

Who Doesn't Want to Sell to State Government?

The type of firm most likely to see the state as an undesirable customer (only 5 percent of all firms) is also small, individually owned, and in business a relatively short time. The firm is probably in the agricultural, nondurable manufacturing, construction, finance, or retail trade business. The major reason for not wanting to do business with the state is slow pay. A higher proportion of firms in these sectors rate slow pay as a major problem of government procurement than firms in other sectors (see Chapter 5). A higher proportion also say they have experienced excessively long average reimbursement timetables in dealing with state government (see Table 6.1).

Who Doesn't Want to Sell to County Government?

Firms less enthusiastic about doing business with county governments (4 percent of all firms identify the county as an undesirable customer) include relatively small, individually owned firms that have been in business a while and come from the same sectors (finance, nondurable manufacturing, and agriculture). Among firms in these sectors, slow pay is the major shortcoming of nearly every type of government (see Table 6.1).

Who Doesn't Want to Sell to City Government?

A less clear-cut pattern emerges in the type of firm identifying city government as an undesirable trading partner (only 5 percent of all firms). However, relatively small firms, whether individually owned or partnerships, in the finance, construction, and nondurable manufacturing sectors seem the most hostile toward selling to city government (see Table 6.3). Again, slow pay is the most likely culprit.

Who Doesn't Want to Sell to School Districts?

Firms less interested in selling to school districts (10 percent of all firms) tend to be small-to-moderate-sized firms in sectors selling products and services that school districts are less likely to need: construction, manufacturing of all types, real estate, transportation, and professional services. This is not to say that school districts do not use goods or services produced by these sectors, only that firms in these sectors may perceive that they can make more money selling to higher-volume general purpose governments than to school districts.

Who Doesn't Want to Sell to Transit Authorities?

Somewhat similar patterns occur among the firms identifying transit authorities as undesirable customers (13 percent of all firms). Firms least likely to see transit authorities as an important marketplace for their goods or services are nonprofit organizations and firms in the utility, nondurable manufacturing, real estate, agricultural, and professional services businesses (see Table 6.3).

Who Doesn't Want to Sell to Hospital Districts?

Firms not interested in selling to hospital districts (13 percent of all firms) are more likely to be new firms or firms in the agricultural, transportation, professional service, utility, real estate, and manufacturing (nondurable) sectors. Again, firms in these sectors are not likely to see hospital districts as an important marketplace for their products.

Table 6.3
Type of Government Not Desired by Business as a Customer by Firm Characteristic

Firm Characteristic	% Citing Government as an Undesirable Customer							
	Federal Government	State Government	County Government	City Government	Transit Authority	School Board	Hospital District	Other Special Districts
All Firms	12.9%	5.3%	4.0%	5.2%	13.3%	9.7%	12.7%	2.6%
Firm Structure								
Individual owner	14.4	7.2	5.5	7.2	16.5	10.2	12.3	3.4
Partnership	16.1	3.2	3.2	8.1	19.4	17.7	19.4	6.5
Nonprofit organization	0.0	0.9	2.2	4.4	26.7	0.5	3.1	0.0
Corporation	13.0	5.1	3.8	4.7	12.3	9.5	12.4	2.3
Other	0.0	12.5	12.5	12.5	12.5	0.0	0.0	0.0
Years in Business								
Less than 1 year	16.1	9.7	3.2	3.2	2.6	12.9	19.4	0.0
1-2 years	10.8	5.0	5.0	7.5	15.0	9.2	11.7	3.3
3-5 years	11.5	6.3	3.8	5.6	12.9	11.5	14.6	1.4
6-10 years	14.4	5.4	3.2	5.4	15.7	10.6	11.2	2.2
Over 10 years	13.0	4.9	4.1	4.8	12.4	9.1	12.6	2.9
Number of Employees								
1-25	14.3	6.1	4.6	5.7	14.4	10.3	13.9	3.3
26-50	15.1	6.1	3.6	5.4	13.3	9.4	10.1	0.7
51-100	10.5	4.1	2.9	3.5	10.5	9.3	12.2	1.7
101-500	10.5	4.4	4.4	4.8	13.2	7.9	12.7	3.1
501-1000	5.8	0.0	0.0	3.8	11.5	11.5	13.5	1.9
1001-5000	9.0	2.2	2.2	4.5	10.1	10.1	7.9	0.0
Over 5000	6.3	1.6	1.6	3.2	7.9	6.3	11.1	3.2

Table 6.3 (continued)

Firm Characteristic	Federal Government	State Government	County Government	City Government	Transit Authority	School Board	Hospital District	Other Special Districts
Firm Gross Revenues ('88)								
Below $200,000	13.9%	6.1%	5.4%	4.8%	14.6%	11.2%	16.0%	4.1%
$200,000-499,999	15.4	8.2	6.4	9.7	20.6	10.9	13.5	3.7
$500,000-999,999	12.7	4.0	3.3	3.6	13.5	8.0	12.4	2.5
$1-$10 Million	13.6	5.7	3.2	4.8	10.6	9.4	11.6	1.4
$11-$25 Million	11.6	5.2	3.9	4.5	13.5	9.7	12.3	4.5
$26-$50 Million	11.5	4.9	6.6	6.6	13.1	13.1	18.0	3.3
Over $50 Million	8.3	1.8	1.8	3.2	11.1	9.2	10.6	1.8
Industry Classification								
Retail trade	12.8	6.2	3.8	4.5	10.0	6.2	10.4	1.7
Wholesale trade	14.2	4.6	2.3	2.6	12.2	6.3	7.9	1.3
Finance	23.1	7.7	7.7	7.7	7.7	7.7	7.7	7.7
Insurance	20.0	0.0	0.0	0.0	0.0	0.0	0.0	0.0
Utility	0.0	0.0	0.0	0.0	20.0	0.0	20.0	0.0
Construction	15.8	8.6	5.3	6.9	13.2	14.2	13.5	3.0
Manufacturing-durable	9.9	3.1	2.5	5.0	12.4	10.6	13.7	1.9
Manufacturing-nondurable	8.8	8.8	8.8	7.0	24.6	14.0	15.8	5.2
Real estate	9.5	0.0	0.0	4.8	14.3	14.3	14.3	0.0
Communications	10.9	3.6	3.6	5.5	12.7	5.4	7.3	1.8
Service	9.9	4.2	4.5	5.4	13.9	8.1	12.7	3.6
Agriculture	21.1	15.8	5.3	5.3	26.3	5.3	31.6	5.3
Mining	0.0	0.0	0.0	0.0	0.0	0.0	0.0	0.0
Transportation	22.7	4.5	0.0	4.5	13.6	22.7	22.7	4.5
Professional Service	8.8	3.8	2.5	5.0	17.0	17.0	21.4	3.8

% Citing Government as an Undesirable Customer

	% Citing Government as an Undesirable Customer							
Firm Characteristic	Federal Government	State Government	County Government	City Government	Transit Authority	School Board	Hospital District	Other Special Districts
Owner								
Minority-owned	11.6%	5.2%	3.1%	3.9%	12.9%	8.2%	12.4%	3.4%
Not minority-owned	13.1	5.1	4.0	5.3	13.4	10.0	12.7	2.3
Minority Owner-Gender[1]								
Female	11.7	5.4	3.6	4.1	12.2	8.1	12.6	3.6
Male	10.4	7.5	4.5	3.8	17.9	9.0	10.4	3.0
Minority Owner-Race[1]								
Black	8.2	1.6	1.6	0.0	13.1	3.3	11.5	3.3
Hispanic	10.7	4.0	4.0	5.3	10.7	9.3	10.7	2.7
Asian	7.4	7.4	3.7	3.7	11.1	14.8	18.5	0.0
American Indian	9.1	0.0	0.0	0.0	0.0	0.0	0.0	9.1
Other	0.0	0.0	0.0	0.0	0.0	12.5	12.5	0.0
Size-Economic Classification								
Small, economically disadvantaged	11.0	5.5	4.3	4.3	12.0	9.8	11.3	2.5
Not small, economically disadvantaged (n	13.5	5.1	3.9	5.4	13.6	9.6	12.9	2.5
Current Contract Status								
Has contract with government	11.2	3.8	2.8	4.0	11.8	8.8	11.7	2.3
No contract with government	19.2	10.0	7.9	9.2	18.2	13.0	16.0	3.2
No Government Contracts at Present[2]								
Have had one in past	19.2	9.2	7.7	7.7	14.0	11.8	14.8	3.0
Have not had one in past	14.5	9.2	8.7	9.8	16.8	11.6	16.2	4.6

[1] Question was answered only by the subset of the respondents meeting the definitional criterion (minority-owned).

[2] Question was answered only by the subset of the respondents meeting the definitional criterion (firm does not have a government contract at the present).

Table 6.3 (continued)

Firm Characteristic	% Citing Government as an Undesirable Customer							
	Federal Govern-ment	State Govern-ment	County Govern-ment	City Govern-ment	Transit Authority	School Board	Hospital District	Other Special Districts
Level of Government Firm Does Business With (Multiple Responses)								
Federal	5.2%	3.2%	3.1%	4.5%	12.0%	9.6%	12.0%	2.6%
State	9.6	2.9	3.0	3.7	13.2	9.1	12.4	2.6
City	11.7	3.8	2.5	2.7	11.3	8.4	12.2	2.0
County	12.4	3.9	2.2	3.4	11.8	8.8	11.9	2.2
Transit Authority	9.8	2.9	2.3	3.1	3.6	6.7	9.0	1.9
School district	12.9	4.4	3.0	4.2	10.3	2.9	8.8	1.5
Hospital district	9.9	2.3	1.9	3.8	10.1	4.4	2.5	1.0
Other special district	11.6	2.7	2.0	2.0	13.6	10.9	13.6	2.0
Other	19.0	12.4	10.2	10.2	19.0	12.4	12.4	4.4
% of Gross Revenues From Government Contracts								
Less than 10%	15.7	6.8	4.4	5.7	13.3	9.5	10.8	2.3
10-25%	11.7	3.9	3.7	5.1	11.0	8.1	10.3	1.5
26-50%	7.1	1.5	1.0	2.0	13.3	5.6	12.2	2.0
51-75%	7.4	6.6	3.3	5.0	12.4	9.9	20.7	1.7
76-90%	8.3	1.2	3.6	3.6	10.7	13.1	21.4	4.8
Over 90%	9.8	2.2	3.3	3.3	30.4	25.0	28.3	8.7

Firm Characteristic	% Citing Government as an Undesirable Customer							
	Federal Government	State Government	County Government	City Government	Transit Authority	School Board	Hospital District	Other Special Districts
Procedures for Getting Government Contract (Multiple Responses)								
Formal competitive bid (with negotiation)	8.3%	2.6%	3.4%	3.4%	11.5%	10.0%	12.1%	2.8%
Formal competitive bid (sealed)	13.2	4.7	3.0	4.2	12.1	9.3	11.4	2.3
Local vendor preference	8.5	3.3	1.9	3.8	11.5	7.3	10.1	2.3
Request for Proposal (competitive negotiation)	9.2	2.6	2.3	3.0	10.9	9.0	13.9	2.1
Government solicitation of written quote	8.8	2.8	2.4	2.9	11.4	7.3	10.8	2.1
Government solicitation of telephone quote	6.8	2.9	2.0	1.8	8.6	5.4	9.5	2.3
Participation in Minority Business Enterprise Program	8.0	2.3	3.4	2.3	6.8	10.2	14.8	1.1
Participation in Small Business program	1.2	1.2	1.2	2.4	12.2	8.5	14.6	1.2
Other procedure	10.8	6.7	7.5	10.0	20.0	13.3	18.3	5.0
Type of Product Delivered to Government (Multiple Responses)								
Service	12.4	4.7	3.7	5.3	12.7	9.0	12.3	3.1
Commodity/good	12.1	4.4	3.0	4.3	12.4	7.1	10.4	1.6
Construction	15.8	7.3	5.4	6.3	12.9	13.4	12.4	3.2
Geographical Location								
In-State	13.9	5.6	4.2	5.4	12.8	9.4	12.2	2.4
Out-of-State	7.0	3.3	3.0	3.3	17.8	11.9	15.6	3.7

Source: Random sample survey of businesses listed on the Harris County (Houston), Texas vendor mailing list (conducted May–June, 1989) and mail survey of all businesses listed on the Hillsborough County (Tampa), Florida vendor registration list (conducted June–July, 1989)

In summary, firms identify certain types of governments as less than desirable customers for two distinctly different reasons: (1) poor purchasing practices of a specific government and (2) a mismatch in the marketplace—i.e., the firm does not perceive a specific type of government as a major-volume customer. Therefore, to broaden vendor pools, governments may have to develop different types of marketing strategies for different economic sectors.

Minority-Owned Firms' Views

In spite of their more negative assessments of the overall quality of most governments' purchasing practices, *minority-owned firms are less likely to identify any type of government as an undesirable customer than nonminority-owned firms* (see Table 6.3). Asian-owned firms are the exception. A

higher-than-average percentage of Asian-owned firms say they do not want to sell to state government, hospital districts, school boards, or transit authorities. The primary reason may be the purchasing policies of these governments rather than the marketplace. (Only a small proportion of Asian-owned firms are in the sectors not likely to see special purpose governments as a major market.) As noted in Chapter 6, Asian proprietors generally feel discriminated against relative to other minority firms, especially black- and Hispanic-owned firms.

In general, however, the overwhelming majority of all categories of minority-owned and nonminority-owned firms *want* governments of all types as customers. The challenge to individual governments is to devise strategies to attract, and keep, more of them in their vendor pools.

SUMMARY

Business judgments of which type of government makes the best customer vary considerably according to a firm's contract status, the economic sector in which it is located, the size of the firm, and the gender, race, or ethnicity of the firm's owner. However, contract status makes the most difference. Firms that currently have government contracts are generally less negative in their assessments than firms that have never had a government contract.

Overall, governments do not reimburse firms in a timely fashion, in accordance with standard recommended timetables. Nearly two-thirds of our respondents report that local governments do not reimburse them within the recommended thirty-day time frame; nearly three-fourths report that state governments do not pay within the thirty-day window; and more than 80 percent say they rarely receive payment from the federal government within this period. More than half the firms report that they are likely to be paid

somewhere between thirty-one and sixty days after submitting their reimbursement or payment requests. Firms in the newer and more technical sectors such as insurance, professional services, finance, communications, real estate, and durable goods manufacturing sectors report the longest average payment delays. Agricultural firms are also more likely to report excessive delays in spite of federal, state, and local prompt-payment regulations calling for even shorter reimbursement periods for agricultural products, especially perishables.

Local government purchasing policies are generally rated higher in quality than the purchasing practices of the state or federal governments. But nearly three-fourths of all private sector firms rate the purchasing policies of each type of government "Fair" or "Good" (medium-grade). Higher proportions rate more government procurement practices "Poor" than "Excellent." Among firms that have never contracted with any government, the assessments are even more negative, particularly of the federal procurement system; 41 percent of these firms judge the federal system "Poor," compared to only 17 percent of those with a government contract of some sort.

The quality assessments by small and minority-owned businesses are usually more critical than those by large and nonminority-owned firms. Female- and Asian-owned businesses are most critical of the federal procurement system; black-owned firms are most critical of county purchasing; Hispanic-owned firms, of state government procurement; and American Indian-owned firms, of local government purchasing systems. Small firms are most critical of the federal procurement system. Nonetheless, an overwhelming majority of minority-owned firms and small businesses do not regard the purchasing practices of any type of government "Excellent."

In spite of the rather medium-grade ratings that businesses give to all government procurement practices, only a small percentage identify any government as an undesirable customer. Only 13 percent identify the federal government an undesirable customer, and 5 percent say that state government is not a desirable business partner. The percentages for other governments are 5 percent, city government; 4 percent, county government; 13 percent, transit authorities and hospital districts; 10 percent school districts; and 3 percent, other special districts. The relatively higher percentages saying they do not wish to do business with special purpose governments may reflect the specialized goods and services these firms produce and their lack of knowledge of the workings of these special governments.

The good news is that minority-owned firms are less likely than nonminority-owned firms to identify any type of government as an undesirable customer. The bad news is that new, small firms are more likely to identify all types of government as undesirable customers. However, the percentages are still relatively small. Regardless of size, years in business, or owner gender, race, or ethnicity, and regardless of the shortcomings of public sector procurement practices at all levels, the bottom line is that businesses want to sell to governments of all types.

It is not too late for all types of governments to improve their purchasing practices in order to expand their vendor pools and increase competition. Surveys of a government's potential vendor pool can be extremely useful tools in helping an entity restructure and improve its procurement system. Today, the potential vendor pool extends beyond the limited geographic boundaries of a specific government, in a specific county, metropolitan area, or state.

Because of the global nature of the world's economy, the vendor pool frequently includes foreign businesses. American governments at all levels must analyze the effectiveness of their purchasing practices in reaching these potential vendors. Conversely, American businesses interested in doing business with foreign governments must develop knowledge of their public procurement practices, an even more monumental task than mastering the complex U.S. public sector. Chapter 7 summarizes the results of this extensive study of the private sector's views of government purchasing practices and concludes with a forecast of the future of public-private business dealings in a rapidly changing nation and world.

NOTES

1. The question specifically asked firms sampled from the Hillsborough County vendor registration list to rate Hillsborough County, the City of Tampa, and the State of Florida. It asked firms sampled from the Harris County vendor mailing list to rate Harris

County, the City of Houston, and the State of Texas.

2. Ibid.

3. Unlike the preceding two questions, this question did not list the names of specific governments.

4. Firm structure among our respondents currently with government contracts breaks down into the following categories: 11 percent are individually owned; 3 percent are partnerships; 2 percent are nonprofit organizations; 84 percent are corporations; and 0.4 percent are other entities. Among those currently without government contracts, 19 percent are individually owned; 4 percent are partnerships; 2 percent are nonprofit organizations; 75 percent are corporations; and 0.4 percent are other entities.

5. For years in business among our respondents currently with government contracts, 1 percent have been in operation less than one year, 5 percent one to two years, 13 percent three to five years, 16 percent six to ten years, and 65 percent longer than ten years. Among the firms without a government contract, 3 percent have been in business less than one year, 10 percent one to two years, 18 percent three to five years, 17 percent six to ten years, and 53 percent longer than ten years.

6. The number of employees reported among our respondents currently with a government contract were: 53 percent have 1–25 employees, 14 percent have 26–50 employees, 9 percent have 51–100 employees, 13 percent have 101–500 employees, 3 percent have 501–1,000 employees, 5 percent have 1,001–5,000 employees, and 4 percent have more than 5,000 employees. Comparable figures for firms without a government contract are: 1–25 employees, 78 percent; 26–50 employees, 9 percent; 51–100 employees, 5 percent; 101–500 employees, 5 percent; 501–1,000 employees, 1 percent; 1,001–5,000 employees, 1 percent; and more than 5,000 employees, 0.7 percent.

7. Gross revenues among our respondents currently with a government contract consisted of: 12 percent have gross revenues below $200,000; 14 percent, $200,000–$499,999; 14 percent, $500,000–$999,999; 36 percent $1–$10 million; 9 percent, $11–$25 million; 4 percent, $26–$50 million; and 12 percent, more than $50 million. Among the firms currently without a government contract, 32 percent have gross revenues below $200,000; 19 percent, $200,000–$499,999; 14 percent, $500,000–$999,999; 27 percent, $1–$10 million; 3 percent, $11–$25 million; 1 percent, $26–$50 million; and 4 percent, more than $50 million.

8. See note 7, Chapter 5.

9. Among our minority-firm respondents currently with a government contract, 57 percent are owned by females; 18 percent are owned by blacks; 22 percent are owned by Hispanics; 5 percent are owned by Asians; 3 percent are owned by American Indians; the remainder are owned by other racial or ethnic minorities or Caucasian females. Among the minority-owned firms without a government contract, 54 percent are owned by females; 21 percent are owned by blacks; 20 percent are owned by Hispanics; 8 percent are owned by Asians; 2 percent are owned by American Indians; and the remainder are owned by other racial or ethnic minorities or Caucasian females.

10. In size and economic classification, 20 percent of our respondents currently with a government contract are classified as small, economically disadvantaged firms. Among those without a government contract, 28 percent are classified as small, economically disadvantaged firms.

11. Of the female-owned firms responding to our survey, 66 percent report having done business with a county government, 59 percent with a city, 53 percent with a state government, 45 percent with a school district, but only 34 percent with the federal government.

12. Of the female-owned firms responding to our survey, 5 percent are owned by black females, 5 percent by Hispanic females, 1 percent by Asian females, 1 percent by American Indian females, 0.8 percent by Puerto Rican females, and 1 percent by females of other races and ethnicities.

CHAPTER 7

Challenges for the Future: Revamping Public Purchasing Practices to Promote Greater Competition, Efficiency, and Equity

"If you're interested in getting government contracts," says the owner of a construction firm, "my advice is to work with someone who's done it before."

"Talk with a knowledgeable person in the originating agency to make sure you understand what the job is," says the general manager of a printing company.

"Before submitting a bid, ask yourself whether you really want the contract," says the director of a drug treatment center. "Make sure you have the management ability and administrative time to do a good job."

ENTERING THE 1990s, business and government will continue to build relationships as trading partners. Businesses can expect government at all levels to keep turning to the private sector for goods and services as a way of coping with fiscal stress. In both the private and the public sectors, leaders will seek ways not only to reduce costs and improve efficiency but also to boost economic development. Our study of what businesses think of government procurement sheds new light on future challenges and suggests strategies for attracting more vendors to compete for government business.

207

CHALLENGES IN PUBLIC SECTOR PROCUREMENT

The vast majority of U.S. businesses do not currently sell to government. According to one estimate, less than 2 percent of all firms sell to the federal government. When state and local governments are considered, the percentage no doubt increases somewhat, although not substantially. (The exact percentage has yet to be reported in any study of government procurement.)

Government's Reputation as a Business Partner

Businesses don't think too highly of government as a business partner. As our survey has shown, only 35 percent believe that public purchasing practices attract first-rate vendors to compete for contracts; only 30 percent perceive that government purchasing practices result in government purchases of quality goods and services at the lowest cost; and just 34 percent view government procurement as fair and impartial.

Negative assessments are particularly acute among firms that have never had a government contract. Perhaps they have applied for contracts and failed, or perhaps they rely on hearsay in the business community. Whatever the source of their disfavor, firms must come to believe that selling to government can be a worthwhile business venture. Business should look at government contracts with more of an open mind, and government must improve its image as a business partner.

Explain why public procurement differs
One message government must relay more clearly to the taxpayers and the business community is how and why public procurement differs from private procurement. Governments must show how certain seemingly onerous aspects of public procurement (such as excessive paperwork and slow payment

patterns due to lengthy testing, inspection, or auditing) frequently protect both government and business.

Businesses should recognize that not only do government purchasing practices differ, even within the same state and metropolitan area, but also some governments may be better trading partners than others. Our study shows that 59 percent of all firms judge the overall quality of school district procurement "Excellent" or "Good." The proportions for other types of government, in descending order, are: county, 58 percent; city, 54 percent; state 53 percent; and, at the bottom, the federal government, 45 percent. Our study also shows that some governments pay more promptly than others. School districts, counties, and cities (in that order) are more likely than the state or federal governments to pay their bills within thirty days, the recommended standard. (Not surprisingly, these rank orderings parallel the overall quality ratings that business gives these governments.)

Many businesses seem to base their negative perceptions of all government procurement on their views of the federal procurement system. The harshest critics usually have never done any business with government. As we have reported, 41 percent of the firms that have never had a government contract judge the overall quality of the federal government's procurement system "Poor," compared to only 17 percent of those with a contract.

Firms with no history of government contracting generally regard local governments in a more positive light. Local governments should take advantage of this more favorable attitude in their vendor recruitment efforts. They may not have done so in the past because of the paucity of studies of procurement practices at the state and local levels of government.

Emphasize the advantages of doing business with government Businesses agree more on what they like about selling to government than what they dislike about it. The vast majority (61 percent) sell to government because they feel confident they will be paid. Similarly, one-third cite the predictability of government contracts as a revenue source. They view government business as a less elastic, more stable revenue source than private sector contracts. Nearly one-fourth (24 percent) sell to government because it is a primary market for the good or service they offer. Another 10 percent specifically cite the profit motive.

Many small, newly established firms see government business as a way to get established. For others, government business comes as a natural outgrowth of participating in Minority Business Enterprise, Women Business Enterprise, or Small Business Enterprise programs.

Contrary to conventional wisdom, few firms (only 5 percent) cite "good connections with elected officials" as a major reason for selling to government. Therefore government vendor-recruitment strategies should emphasize the profit, expansion, and experiential opportunities afforded to businesses that sell to government.

At the same time, businesses should recognize that relatively small proportions of firms identify any one of the specific shortcomings of government procurement as a problem. Not one of the five most frequently encountered problems is cited by a majority of the firms responding to our survey. Not even half (45 percent) identify slow payment cycles, and roughly a third identify too-narrow bid specifications and difficulty in making contact with the actual user of the service or product. Only about one-fourth complain of "too much paperwork to apply," and 28 percent say that competition from other firms frequently pushes prices too low for them to compete. Contrary to popular opinion, less than 10 percent identify too many sole source contracts or inadequate procedures for protest and appeals as common occurrences. Interestingly, the most complaints come from businesses with the most experience in selling to government, yet few acknowledge that the cost (of the aggravations) outweighs the benefit (profit).

Exploit the universal desire to do business with government Governments should expand vendor-recruitment efforts, taking advantage of the finding that the vast majority of all businesses would like to have government contracts. Our survey shows that in spite of their less-than-laudatory evaluations of governments as customers, only 13 percent of all businesses say they do not want to sell to the federal government, 5 percent do not want to sell to the state or city, and 4 percent do not want to sell to county government. While the percentages not wanting to do business with special purpose governments (school districts, hospital districts) are slightly higher, the most negative is still only 13 percent (transit authorities). The higher negative ratings may reflect the more specialized goods and services these special purpose governments require.

Conduct more in-depth studies When significant portions of any type of business say they don't want a specific government as a customer, that government should do in-depth research to determine why. The findings may prove helpful in revamping purchasing practices and devising strategies to attract alienated firms into the vendor pool. The government should analyze the firms that have done business with it in the past but not currently. The opinions of these firms' owners can be valuable in identifying (and then addressing) specific shortcomings of a government's procurement practices. A government should analyze the opinions of firms that have never done business with it before. These firms, by far the majority of all businesses, remain at bay for some reason, and vendor pools cannot be increased substantially without knowing why.

menting better training and certification programs for purchasing personnel.

Improving Esteem of Procurement Staff

Governments at all levels must deal with the relatively low esteem associated with procurement compared to other staff functions such as budgeting and financial management, planning, and personnel administration. The procurement process is extremely complex (and will become more so), yet the purchasing staff is frequently small and poorly paid, and they often lack expertise in the highly technical legal, accounting, and auditing aspects of procurement. Each of these aspects has become a crucial dimension of sound public purchasing. Many governments are paying the price for the antiquated notions that purchasing is nothing more than buying and that anybody can buy.

Even within government, the purchasing function is not perceived as working as well as it could. A 1991 survey of the employees of the city of Clearwater, Florida (Table 7.1) found that more than 76 percent believe that purchasing decisions take too long and end up costing the city more money. They point to the inefficiencies caused by high turnover and low pay of purchasing staff as well as the tendency to leave key purchasing personnel out of the financial management decision loop. *Governments should consider revising their organizational structures and imple-*

Accomplishing the Goals of Public Purchasing

The biggest challenge in the years ahead is how to accomplish each of the goals of public purchasing (competition, efficiency, fairness, and openness) at a time when society and business are changing rapidly and substantially. The public procurement system clearly could be more competitive, efficient, and equitable if vendor pools are enlarged and designed to attract a wider range of firms to compete for government business.

The difficulty lies in how to increase the number and type of firms in the vendor pool without violating the competition and fairness principles of purchasing. Firms currently in the system often view the special efforts by government to bring in new classes of vendors as noncompetitive and unfair. At the same time, firms currently underrepresented in the vendor pool see government's failure to restructure current purchasing practices as equally noncompetitive and inequitable. Nonetheless, as our study has shown, neither category of firm rates government procurement practices, as currently structured, as either highly competitive or equitable. Most businesses agree that public sector vendor pools are too small, although often for different reasons.

ATTRACTING DIFFERENT TYPES OF BUSINESSES INTO THE VENDOR POOL

Business and government could benefit from intensified efforts to recruit vendors into doing business with government. But our study has shown that standardized outreach strategies simply will not work. Governments must diversify their efforts according to industry, the length of time a firm has been in business, its size and experience in dealing

with public contracting, and the gender, race, or ethnicity of the owner. As we have seen in this study, business assessments vary concerning the advantages and shortcomings of selling to different types of governments.

We turn now to a closer examination of small and minority-owned firms' assessments of government purchasing practices.

Table 7.1
Government Employees' Views of Public Purchasing:
Inefficient and Costly[1]

Employee Background	Purchasing Decisions Take Too Long and Cost City Money (n=719)
All Employees	76.5%
By Job Function	
Service	80.1%
Clerical/Clerks	65.1
Professional/technical	83.7
Managerial/administrative/supervisory	63.1
By Work Group	
Administrative/Support[2]	66.7%
Administrative Services[3]	51.4
Fire	82.2
Gas	88.2
General Services[4]	82.9
Library	70.0
Marine	54.6
Parks & Recreation	60.0
Planning & Development	56.5
Police	92.7
Public Works[5]	71.4

[1] Respondents were asked to respond to this statement: "Purchasing decisions generally take too long, which ends up costing the city more money."

[2] Administrative/support work groups includes personnel in: City Manager's office, Economic Development, Internal Audit, Affirmative Action, Legal, City Clerk, Personnel, and Public Information.

[3] Administrative Services work group includes personnel in office of Management and Budget, Finance, Risk Management, Data Information Services, Purchasing, and Utility Customer Support.

[4] General Services work group includes personnel in Administration, Building and Maintenance, Energy, and Fleet Maintenance.

[5] Public Works work group includes personnel in Engineering, Environmental Management, Pollution Control, Sanitation/Solid Waste, Sewers/Streets/Infrastructure, Storm Water, Transportation, and Water.

Source: City of Clearwater, Florida Employee Survey, May 9–15, 1991. Conducted by Institute of Government, University of South Florida, Tampa. (n = 954)

Our intention is to suggest recruitment and retention strategies that could enlarge the vendor pool to reflect current demographics.

Small Businesses: Government's Largest Untapped Vendor

Definitions vary about what constitutes a "small business."[1] As noted in Chapter 1, the federal government defines a small business as an independently owned and operated enterprise, not dominant in the field in which it is bidding. But the U.S. Small Business Administration in the President's report on *The State of Small Business: A Report of the President*, acknowledges that for statistical comparisons, size is usually measured in terms of employment, assets, or receipts.

The Office of Advocacy of the U.S. Small Business Administration defines size as follows: "very small" (fewer than 20 employees); "small" (20–99 employees); "medium-sized" (100–499 employees); and "large" (500 or more employees). Nationally, 87 percent of all firms are "very small," and 98 percent are either "very small" or "small," according to *The State of Small Business*.

The Small Business Administration does not make such precise size classifications using assets or receipts. Nonetheless, SBA and Census data show that more than one-fourth of all enterprises have annual sales less than $100,000, and 70 percent have receipts less than $500,000. As might be expected, a high correlation exists between employment and assets. Of the firms with receipts less than $100,000, 98 percent have fewer than twenty employees. Of those with assets less than $500,000, 97 percent have fewer than twenty employees.

Small firms (less than a hundred employees) make up a majority of all firms in the construction (86 percent), agriculture (79 percent), wholesale trade (60 percent), retail trade (60 percent), and services sectors (51 percent). Almost half (48 percent) of all firms in the finance, insurance, and real estate sector have fewer than 100 employees. And more than one-third of the firms in the mining (38 percent) and manufacturing (36 percent) sectors are small, as are 32 percent of all firms in the transportation, communications, and public utilities industries. Actually, firms in certain sectors are very small. Nearly half of all firms in the agriculture and construction industries employ fewer than twenty people, as do about one-third of the firms in the wholesale trade industry.[2]

In the 1980s, industries dominated by small firms generated new jobs at faster rates than those dominated by large firms. In *The State of Small Business*, analysts predict that in the 1990s "Small firms will continue to have an impact on American society. They employ and train a majority of the Nation's new workers, and they will retrain many workers for new occupations in the years ahead." Small businesses, especially new ones, also stimulate innovation. The report concludes: "Whatever the short-term outlook may be, small firms will continue to bring innovation and competitive strength to the economy over the long term provided government continues to recognize small business' importance to the Nation's vitality."

The bulk of all business establishments in the United States are relatively small, regardless of the precise definition used, and the vast majority do not do business with government. In spite of rather aggressive efforts by the federal government, only 14 to 16 percent of all federal procurement goes to small businesses.[3] Thus, any plans to expand the vendor pool must begin with a close review of our smallest businesses' assessments of government purchasing practices.

Unable to compete   A recap of the assessments by the smallest firms in our study (those with gross receipts less than $200,000[4]) shows that they generally regard government purchasing practices as unfair or partial, and they see themselves as unable to compete in the system, as currently structured. Nearly half of these firms report that they have difficulty competing against larger firms for government business. They do not know how to get (and stay) on vendor mailing and bidder lists; they have little expertise in accurately costing or pricing goods and services; frequently they do not have the cash to pay bidding fees or to meet various bonding requirements; and often they do not have the staff to prepare bids on short notice (see Figure 7.1).

The bottom line is that most small firms simply do not have the resources (time, money, staff, or expertise) to figure out how to successfully deal with government or even to fill out the paperwork to participate in government-sponsored Small Business En-

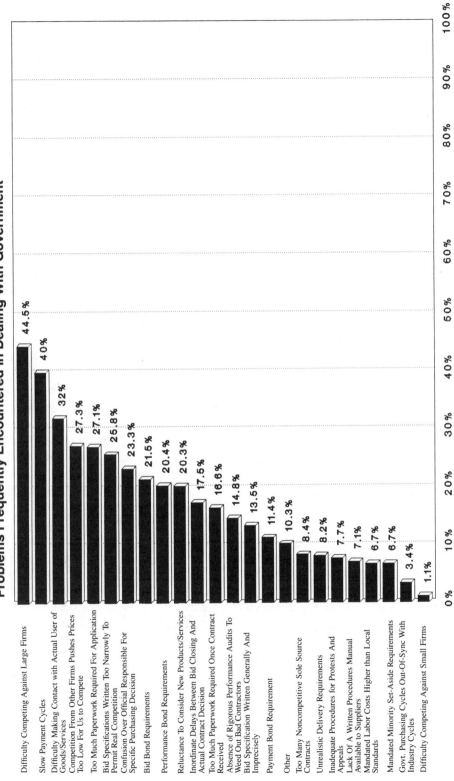

Figure 7.1
The Small Business Owner's Perspective:*
Problems Frequently Encountered in Dealing With Government

Difficulty Competing Against Large Firms — 44.5%
Slow Payment Cycles — 40%
Difficulty Making Contact with Actual User of Goods/Services — 32%
Competition From Other Firms Pushes Prices Too Low For Us to Compete — 27.3%
Too Much Paperwork Required For Application — 27.1%
Bid Specifications Written Too Narrowly To Permit Real Competition — 25.8%
Confusion Over Official Responsible For Specific Purchasing Decision — 23.3%
Bid Bond Requirements — 21.5%
Performance Bond Requirements — 20.4%
Reluctance To Consider New Products/Services — 20.3%
Inordinate Delays Between Bid Closing And Actual Contract Decision — 17.5%
Too Much Paperwork Required Once Contract Received — 16.6%
Absence of Rigorous Performance Audits To Weed Out Bad Contractors — 14.8%
Bid Specification Written Generally And Imprecisely — 13.5%
Payment Bond Requirement — 11.4%
Other — 10.3%
Too Many Noncompetitive Sole Source Contracts — 8.4%
Unrealistic Delivery Requirements — 8.2%
Inadequate Procedures for Protests And Appeals — 7.7%
Lack Of A Written Procedures Manual Available to Suppliers — 7.1%
Mandated Labor Costs Higher than Local Standards — 6.7%
Mandated Minority Set-Aside Requirements — 6.7%
Govt. Purchasing Cycles Out-Of-Sync With Industry Cycles — 3.4%
Difficulty Competing Against Small Firms — 1.1%

* (Firms With Gross Receipts Under $200,000)

213

terprise or Minority Business Enterprise programs. As Gumpert and Timmons noted a decade ago:

> Whereas large corporations have staffs to learn in advance where the red tape lies, small businesses do not. Learning the government's procedures and making initial sales are difficult. . . . Often those small businesses that decide to brave the regulatory maze come to wish they hadn't. They are likely to have trouble finding out which agencies buy what, submitting the requisite voluminous forms, and understanding the even more voluminous replies and contract language. And it doesn't take long for the small business manager to discover that up-and-coming bureaucrats feel more comfortable with big company suppliers.

Apprehensive about slow payment Governments' slow payment patterns greatly deter small vendors. Less than half report that any government regularly reimburses them within thirty days of requisition or payment due date. This protracted payment pattern discourages new, small businesses from selling to government. These businesses often operate on margin and cannot afford long delays in payment just to do business with government.

Unenthusiastic about quality of system Small businesses tend to criticize purchasing practices of local governments less than those of the federal or state government. Still, only slightly more than half judge *any* government's procurement system "Good" or "Excellent" (county government and school districts receive the most positive ratings).

In spite of this lukewarm rating of government purchasing practices, our study shows that most small firms would like to do business with any type of government—if they could somehow overcome the adver-

sities cited above. However, some caution is in order.

Findings from a related study The percentages of small businesses that want to sell to government are probably inflated in light of the fact that our 3,282 respondents were generated from government vendor mailing or registration lists. (But recall from Chapter 1 that businesses do not always put themselves on these lists or even know that they are on the lists.) At the outset of the study, we suspected that small firms, when compared to firms in general, might be more positively inclined to do business with government. To test this hypothesis, we studied a random sample of firms generated from a general business directory of firms in Hillsborough and Pinellas counties (Florida).[5] Our suspicion was confirmed.

Among small businesses selected from the directory, more than one-fourth saw no reason why they should do business with any government.[6] When asked which government they would like to do business with, 42 percent said none.[7] Of those that were interested, less than half (48 percent) said they would like to sell to city government, 35 percent to the state, 32 percent to the county, 29 percent to the federal government, 23 percent to the school district, 19 percent to the hospital district, 16 percent to the transit authority, and 3 percent to other special districts.

However, the results of the two surveys are remarkably similar with regard to what small firms see as the major disadvantages and advantages of selling to government. Among the firms selected from the business directory, the most frequently anticipated problems of doing business with government are, in descending order: slow payment cycles, 44 percent; application paperwork, 44 percent; difficulty in making contact with the agency or official that will actually use the product or service, 34 percent; too much paperwork after one gets the contract, 34 percent; confusion over which government agency or official has the major responsibility for a specific purchasing decision, 31 percent; inordinate delays between bid closing and the actual contract decision, 28 percent; and difficulty competing against large firms, 22 percent. These concerns are much like those of businesses selected from vendor lists in our study.

The same similarities exist with regard to the two groups' ratings of the positive aspects of doing business with government. Among the firms from the directory, the most likely reasons, in descending order, were confidence about being paid, 36 percent; predictable revenue source, 24 percent; opportunity to get established, 15 percent; provision of a service or commodity primarily used by government, 12 percent; and participation in a SBE program, 12 percent.

These comparisons show that the percentage of small businesses not wanting to sell to government is probably higher than indicated in our survey of 3,282 businesses on official vendor lists. Even so, the same basic patterns of likes and dislikes persist among small businesses.

Provide more information Small businesses need more (and more intelligible) information on how to do business with government. Both business and government would benefit from a master list of government contracting opportunities in a metropolitan area. Particularly useful would be information on how to get and stay on vendor mailing and bidder lists.

Groups such as the chamber of commerce, small business organizations, and professional associations should consider developing such a publication and distributing it. Dissemination of this information through channels other than government would certainly reach more potential vendors than simple newspaper advertisements or mailings of contracting opportunity announcements to businesses already on vendor registration or bidder lists.

Governments should seriously consider standardizing procedures and forms Such an effort would require tremendous cooperation among governments, but it would be immensely valuable to small businesses.

Reduce the paperwork Governments must redouble their efforts in reducing the paperwork they require during the entire purchasing process, from bid to payment.

Governments should focus on small purchases, in particular, and simplify the paperwork they involve. In our survey, businesses complained about "having to fill out the same voluminous form to bid on a million-dollar contract as on a fifty-dollar purchase."

Pay bills on time Governments must improve their bill-paying procedures and bring them in line with recommended standards. Any efforts to attract, and retain, more small businesses as vendors will flounder as long as government persists with long delays in payment.

Improve outreach Governments must do a better job of attracting small businesses to the public procurement arena. This outreach, which might resemble a marketing or public relations campaign in the private sector, should show how government contracting can be good business.

As part of this outreach, government agencies must offer better technical assistance, especially in techniques of costing and documenting a firm's eligibility, quality, and ability to meet contract specifications. While this may cost governments more in the short term (because they would have to hire more and better-trained staff), it will save in the long term as the quantity and quality of vendors improves.

Develop better, more objective ways of measuring quality As this study has shown, small firms often feel they cannot compete because of the widespread notion that a low bid always wins, without regard for quality and longevity of a good or service. Many small firms believe they lose out in the bidding wars because government is concerned only with price, not quality. Small firms are generally convinced that the quality of their good or service is superior to that of large firms. Business owners must work together with government officials to develop better ways of measuring quality—of a firm, its products, and its performance.

Women-Owned Businesses: The Fastest-Growing Segment

Government reports indicate that women-owned businesses constitute the fastest-growing segment of the small business community.[8] Women-owned businesses have higher-than-average success rates and steadier revenues than other sole proprietors, although they are no less likely to take business risks than male owners.

In 1986, women made up almost 30 percent of all nonfarm sole proprietors. (According to the SBA, this figure actually underestimates the total business ownership of women because it does not include women-owned corporations and partnerships.) The percentage of women-owned businesses will continue to escalate. In fact, one report, quoted by Lori Balsam in *National Business Woman*, has predicted: "By the year 2000, women should own 50 percent of all small businesses in the United States."

The Women's Bureau of the U.S. Department of Labor offers three major reasons for the tremendous surge in the number of women-owned businesses:

1. Increasing numbers of women have acquired skills and experience as wage and salary workers that can be translated into entrepreneurship.
2. More women are preparing themselves through education and training for business opportunities in expanding fields such as aerospace, telecommunications, electronics, biomedical engineering, and skilled crafts.
3. The expanding role of small business in the economic growth of the United States, particularly in the service sector, has provided many entrepreneurial opportunities.

A number of other studies have also examined the rise of the woman entrepreneur.[9]

Since most women-owned businesses are relatively new, they are also very small. Census figures show that on average they employ just over four employees. A third reported a net income of less than $5,000 in 1982, according to an article by Joe Schwartz in *American Demographics*. The average income figure has since increased. But, like small businesses in general, a sizable proportion of women-owned firms generate less than $100,000 in sales annually. Until recently, women entrepreneurs tended to concentrate in industries with lower profit margins, to operate smaller businesses, and to operate more part-time enterprises.[10] But they are increasingly entering more lucrative fields.

The latest figures available show that the largest proportion of women-owned businesses (80 percent) are clustered in the services and retail trade sectors. But women have increased their share of business ownership in each major industry division over the past several decades. The fastest growth has been in the construction, manufacturing, agricultural services, and transportation fields, along with the more traditional services and retail trade industries.[11]

In spite of the impressive gains in ownership and government policies promoting the growth and development of women-owned businesses and encouraging purchases from women-owned firms,[12] women have not been overly successful in securing government contracts. *The State of Small Business* reports that women-owned firms win less than 1 percent of total federal prime contract awards. They do somewhat better at selling to local governments, although they tend to get relatively small dollar-volume contracts.[13]

Problems they face   A number of studies have examined the problems that newly created, women-owned businesses are most likely to experience. These problems include obtaining funds to start and operate the business; operational problems in the areas of recordkeeping, financial management, and advertising; and tensions emanating from work–home role conflicts.[14] Once established, women business owners face such problems as "finding and keeping qualified professional staff; finding and keeping qualified skilled labour; making the business profitable; and government paperwork," according to an article by Stanley Brown and Phyllis Segal in the *Canadian Banker*. These patterns help explain the responses of women-owned firms to our government purchasing survey (44 percent of our respondents have been in business five years or less, 58 percent longer than five years).

Why female-owned firms sell to government   Women-owned companies do business with government primarily because they feel confident they will be paid (61 percent). A higher-than-expected proportion (27 percent) report a major reason is their participation in MBE programs, a reason that ranks higher than participation in SBE programs (14 percent). Women-owned businesses are less prone to see government contracts as a way to get established (only 17 percent), but this finding may reflect the sizable proportion (65 percent) that already have a government contract, most likely with a state or local government. If we examine the responses of women-owned businesses that have been in operation only a short while (less than two years), the percentage increases (39 percent).

Our study shows that women-owned businesses have been far more successful in contracting with state and local governments than the federal government. Among our respondents, only 34 percent report they are currently doing business with the federal government, compared to 66 percent with the county, 59 percent with the city, 53 percent with the state, and 54 percent with a school district. (Smaller proportions do business with other special purpose governments for reasons cited in Chapter 6: that these governments are frequently less likely to be markets for their products and business owners are less likely to be familiar with what these governments do or how to interact with them.)

Among women-owned firms that have never had a contract with any government, many (43 percent) see a major advantage of doing business with government as the opportunity to gain experience or to participate in either an MBE (36 percent) or SBE (12 percent) program. This finding is somewhat consistent with the findings of other studies of women entrepreneurs. These studies have shown that a much higher proportion of women take advantage of business seminars, courses, or workshops. Schwartz reports:

> Women who own businesses are not more likely to have attended college than are some other entrepreneurs, but they are the most likely to attend business seminars, courses or workshops. Sixty-three percent of women business owners have taken courses, compared with 60 percent of white-male owners, 56 percent of black owners, 48 percent of Asian owners, and 45 percent of Hispanic owners.[15]

Women entrepreneurs, according to Brown and Segal, are also more likely to consult lawyers and accountants for advice at start-up: "Women attempt to minimize the risks that they are taking by learning from the experiences of others. They realize their initial deficiencies in business training and experience and attempt to compensate for it by 'doing their homework' better."

A study by George Nelson in the *Journal of Small Business Management* found that female entrepreneurs have the following information needs, in rank order: (1) how to prepare a budget; (2) tax advice and information; (3) how to prepare and package a business plan; (4) how to define and forecast the market; (5) financial book- and record-keeping; (6) legal aspects of the business; (7) sources of financing; (8) how to make presentations to investors; (9) insurance requirements; (10) personnel management; (11) licensing requirements; (12) supervisory methods; and (13) production techniques.

Offer technical assistance The willingness of women entrepreneurs to learn how to do business suggests that governments could encourage more women-owned firms to compete for government business by offering technical assistance. A sizable proportion of women-owned firms perceive that they cannot compete against large firms or submit winning bids that still let them make a profit. Furthermore, one-third of these women-owned firms complain about excessive application paperwork and narrowly written bid specifications. We have already documented that the vast majority of these firms do not have the staff or resources necessary to devote to learning the complex government procurement maze on their own.

Pay bills promptly Slow payment by government, especially the federal government, ranks at the top of women's complaints (see Figure 7.2). The better reimbursement records of state and local governments no doubt

explain why female-owned firms rate local procurement practices ahead of the federal government's. But nearly half judge the pay records of all governments as anything but stellar.

Timely payments are extremely critical for newly established women-owned firms. A number of studies have found that women business owners are far more likely to start their businesses without borrowing any money and to begin as part-time entrepreneurs. According to Schwartz, 72 percent of the businesses owned by women started out with less than $5,000 in capital, compared to 70 percent of black-owned businesses, 64 percent for Hispanic businesses, 60 percent for white males, and 51 percent for Asian-owned firms. If women do borrow money, they will more likely borrow it from family than from commercial lenders. Women's reluctance to borrow money makes timely payments by governments even more imperative and often critical to the survival and expansion of women-owned firms.

Eliminate good old boys Governments must overcome common perceptions that the system works to the advantage of white-male-owned firms. Only 35 percent of our women-owned-business respondents said that government purchasing practices are fair and impartial. Only 11 percent said they do business with government because purchasing policies are administered fairly. These findings suggest that the stereotyping of government procurement systems as "good old boy" networks may be more widespread than our survey shows.

Statistical analyses are one way for a government to show that the system is not biased—so long as that is indeed the case. The growth-rate projections for women-owned businesses over the next decade make urgent the need for governments, especially the federal government, to change the statistics and demonstrate that government purchasing practices are fair.

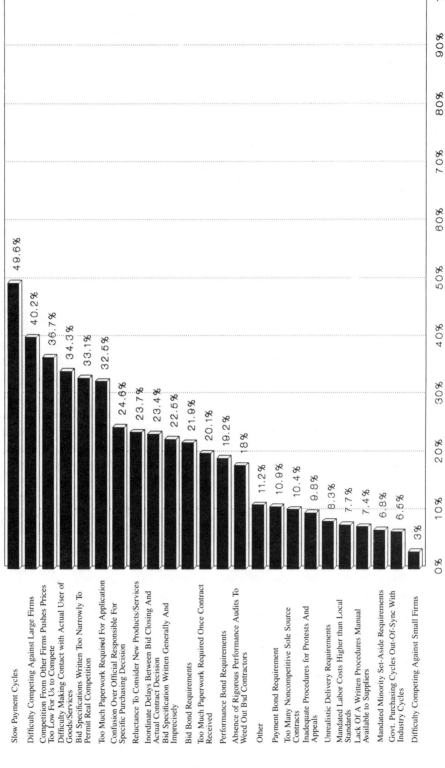

Figure 7.2
The Woman-Owned Business Perspective:
Problems Frequently Encountered in Dealing with Government

219

Minority-Owned Firms: Lagging Behind

The Small Business Administration defines minority-owned businesses as "businesses owned by blacks, persons of Spanish or Latin American ancestry, and persons of American Indian or Asian origin or descent." Despite the fact that one of every five Americans belongs to a minority group, minorities own only a small proportion of all businesses in the United States.[16] According to the U.S. Census Bureau, blacks own 4 percent of all sole proprietorships, Hispanics own 3 percent, and other minorities, including Asians and American Indians, own 3 percent. Among our respondents, 4 percent of the firms are black-owned; 4 percent are Hispanic-owned; 1 percent are Asian-owned; and 0.5 percent are American Indian-owned.

The proportion of minority-owned firms certainly lags behind each group's proportional makeup in the population. According to David Wilson in a *National Journal* article, blacks comprise an estimated 12 percent of the total U.S. population, Hispanics 8 percent, Asians 3 percent, and American Indians, Eskimos, and Aleuts 0.7 percent, each up considerably from a decade ago. By the year 2000, if projections prove true, minorities will comprise a majority of the population in many jurisdictions.

Critical to economic growth   Many experts see the growth and development of minority-owned firms as critical to the future of the U.S. economy. As Michelle Singletary notes in *Black Enterprise*: "In the year 2000 the labor force will be basically made up of minorities. And minorities buy products. If we're going to be able to compete with countries like Japan, we're going to have to buy from minority vendors."

D. J. Miller & Associates, in studying local minority enterprises, observe that "minority business development has a positive rippling effect on the minority unemployment rate, poverty rate, crime rate, and other social and economic indicators of well being."

Schwartz reports: "Minority-owned firms are most likely to hire minorities. . . . Fully 13 percent of the businesses owned by white men who have paid employees have no minority employees, according to the Census Bureau. That compared with only 4 percent of Asian-owned firms, 2 percent of those owned by Hispanics, and 0.3 percent of those owned by Blacks."

Characteristics of minority-owned businesses   The vast majority of all minority-owned firms are small, relatively new sole proprietorships, according to Bruce Cain and D. R. Kiewiet in *Minorities in California*. The SBA reports that of each 1,000 small businesses, Hispanics now own 1.7 firms, blacks 1.3 firms, and Asians 5.5 firms. The figure for American Indian firms is not reported; in fact, there are few analyses of American Indian-owned firms.[17]

According to Schwartz, the fastest growth rates have occurred among Asians, followed by Hispanics and then blacks; again, American Indians are not included. However, other studies have shown that the start-up rate for black firms is flat for reasons we will discuss shortly.[18] In general, according to Cain and Kiewiet, minority businesses tend to have a higher rate of going out of business. Similarly, in an article about small minority businesses in *The Review of Black Political Economy*, Timothy Bates concludes that "relatively high failure rates, less profitability, a high incidence of nonviable firms—these are all characteristics that describe the Black-owned business group."

Studies of minority entrepreneurs show them to be younger and better educated than the population at large. Schwartz's analysis of Census Bureau data indicates:

Only 48 percent of the white men who own businesses are younger than age 45. But fully 60 percent of Asian business owners are younger than age 45, as are 54 percent of Hispanic owners. Black business owners have an age profile similar to that of white men; only 44 percent are younger than age 45. . . . Only 16 percent of all Americans aged 15 and older have completed four or more years of college, compared with 42 percent of Asian business owners, 34 percent of white men who own businesses, 25 percent of black business owners, and 19 percent of Hispanic business owners.

Minority-owned firms tend to be concentrated in the service and retail trade sectors, as is the case with other small businesses. In 1984, according to Cain and Kiewiet, 35 percent of all minority-owned firms were in services, and 34 percent in retail. However, some variation exists among the groups, as noted by Schwartz. Among black-owned businesses, 75 percent are in the services, retail trade, transportation, and public utilities industries. Among Hispanic-owned firms, 74 percent are in services, retail trade, and construction. Of the Asian-owned firms, 76 percent are in services, retail trade, finance, insurance, and real estate industries.

Like women business owners, few minority entrepreneurs borrow money to go into business. Many of them experience difficulties in obtaining credit, for one reason or another, including discrimination.[19]

Problems faced by minority businesses Studies of problems typically confronting minority entrepreneurs identify quite a range. For example, Nathaniel Sheppard in a 1981 article in *Black Enterprise* lists "racism, sexism [in the case of minority women business owners], political contacts, social status, [and] credit." In 1988 Michelle Leder, in an article in the Tampa *Tribune*, reports that for black firms capital was the number-one need, followed by technical assistance. In 1989, Neal Peirce, in an article in the St. Petersburg *Times*, identifies reasons for high failure rates among minority firms

as "lack of management savvy, lack of business connections, and lack of capital." According to an article by Kenneth Smith in the *Wall Street Journal* in February 1989, the executive director of a black business association testified in court that the biggest obstacle to minority [construction] firms winning government contracts is bonding and finance requirements. A common theme is that minority-owned firms simply lack enough capital to meet bonding and bid fee requirements.

Even set-aside programs, designed to help stimulate minority firm growth and development, have not always been successful. A study of the Florida construction industry by Kweku Bentil, reported in the April 21, 1990, issue of the *Orlando Sentinel*, has found that "a lack of qualified companies and red tape hurt state and local programs designed to encourage minority participation." The study identifies such problems as "a lack of projects small enough for minority contractors to bid on; the lack of a program to assist contractor before and after bids are awarded; insufficient funding to administer the program; too much paperwork; and unrealistic goals."

Minority contractors themselves frequently complain about various shortcomings of set-aside programs, especially the SBA's Section 8(a) program.[20] They most commonly criticize slow reimbursement, difficulty in dealing with the federal bureaucracy, including poorly trained federal personnel, and problems associated with prime-subcontractor relationships.[21]

A study by Shelley Green and Paul Pryde in *Black Entrepreneurship in America* refers to the "salt and pepper problem": "Nominally these firms are 50 percent owned by minorities, but the de facto owners and controllers do not belong to minority groups. Adhering to the letter if not the spirit of the law, many nonminority contractors establish 50 percent partnerships with minorities in order to obtain set-asides."

The study also points to inconsistency in set-aside standards. "Standards for firm eligibility vary from agency to agency within the federal government as well as among private corporations and local governments. In particular, the acceptance criteria used by SBA in its 8(a) program have been vague and inconsistent."

Opponents of set-aside programs say more pragmatic approaches to attracting minority vendors would be to guarantee or underwrite loans to minority firms and provide advice on bidding procedures. Even minority firms that might favor set-asides agree with this financial and technical assistance strategy.[22] Sheppard, quoted earlier, acknowledges the utility to minority-owned businesses of technical assistance programs ("on-site visits and evaluations, loan packaging, market development, training/supervision, procurement, plus a wide range of other financial and managerial programs").

Minority entrepreneurial advocates also favor such approaches as waiving bonding requirements for jobs less than $100,000, the establishment of government funds to provide bonding for all small contractors, waiving or reducing charges for bidding documents, and programs to help minority business owners estimate costs and work with suppliers to put together low bids.

As mentioned in Chapter 5, subcontractors often feel they are at the mercy of prime contractors and treated unfairly. Consequently, some minority business owners have proposed that governments bid subcontracts, not just prime contracts. As for slow payment of subcontractors by prime contractors, many minority firms favor the issuance of joint checks to prime and subcontractors.

Overwhelming evidence shows that capital, credit, and the lack of business experience and expertise pose huge problems for many minority entrepreneurs. Even so, discrimination by nonminority contractors continues to be an everyday reality for many minority firms. Proponents of set-asides, for example, say that nonminority-owned firms simply will not use minority contractors unless required. They point to evidence showing drops in the proportion of government contracts let to minorities following abandonment of MBE programs after the *City of Richmond* v. *J. A. Croson* ruling in January 1990.[23]

As noted in Chapter 1, the debate over set-asides presents a dilemma for public procurers. Black journalist William Raspberry, in his nationally syndicated column on February 2, 1990, perhaps states it best:

> The fight over set-asides is merely one aspect of America's philosophical wrangling over the question of racial quotas. It is, at bottom, a contest between theory and pragmatism. Nobody likes quotas, and given a choice between quotas and an open market, hardly anyone would choose quotas. The problem is how to demonstrate that the markets are truly open.

Nonetheless, as our study has shown, not even minority business owners agree that mandatory set-asides are the *sole* solution to the shortage of minority vendors in government contracting pools. Strong evidence shows that the other types of approaches mentioned, such as technical and financial assistance programs, are perceived as equally or more helpful, especially to the long-term growth and development of minority businesses.

In spite of rigorous federal set-asides, small minority-owned firms still receive only 2.6 percent of all federal contracts, according to *The State of Small Business*. While evidence indicates that minority-owned firms do better at getting contracts from state and local governments, they usually get smaller dollar-volume contracts than from the federal government.[24] Evidence also suggests that minority-owned firms frequently do not want to do business with government for many of the same reasons given by Anglo-owned firms.[25]

Minorities increasingly judge the fairness of government contracting policies by their success relative to Anglo contractors and to other minorities.[26] Government procurement efforts in jurisdictions with multiracial and multiethnic constituencies often spark interminority competition and conflict. Minority groups differ in their assessments of the good and bad aspects of government procurement practices. These differences make it particularly difficult to design or revamp public procurement systems that will be satisfactory to each. We turn now to a review of each minority group's assessments.

Black-Owned Businesses

Black business owners generally rate government procurement practices as more competitive and efficient than equitable. Fifty percent agree that government purchasing practices generally attract first-rate vendors to compete for government contracts and ensure that government purchases quality goods and services at the lowest price. But less than one-third (31 percent) see government as fair and impartial in its contracting activities. And only 13 percent say that the fairness of purchasing policies is a reason they do business with government. This problem is not new. A director of a small business development authority in Maryland, quoted by Singletary, acknowledges that "Bringing equity to the table has always been the major problem for minority businesses."

Black-owned firms tend to judge the overall quality of specific governments' procurement practices, especially the federal government's, more positively than do nonminority-owned firms. Importantly, however, with the exception of the federal government, less than half rate the overall quality of any government's purchasing system "Excellent" or "Good."

Why they do business with government   A close look at why black-owned

businesses sell to government shows that the most common reason is their confidence in being paid; 64 percent say this confidence is a major reason, similar to the pattern for almost all types of firms.

But the rank order of the other reasons and the proportion of black-owned firms citing them differs considerably from those of nonminority-owned firms. More than half (56 percent) of the black-owned firms identify participation in an MBE program as a reason; nearly a third (30 percent) identify participation in an SBE program. Like other small businesses, 42 percent say that selling to government is advantageous to new firms because it helps them get established.

Proponents of MBE and SBE programs, which often feature set-asides and vendor preference policies, see these findings as evidence of their effectiveness in attracting new minority vendors into government purchasing pools and in making procurement systems more equitable. The executive director of the National Association of Minority Contractors (NAMC), quoted by Singletary, says: "The reason for creating these programs [is] not to bestow some special privilege on blacks but to take a remedial action to bring us even. Set-asides give us a chance."

However, a sizable proportion of the black business community still does not see MBE or SBE programs as reasons to do business with government. These firms are most likely to be larger, more established firms that are less in need of these programs or that have experienced problems with them and feel they are better off competing on their own, especially if these programs limit their markets. (We will return to this point shortly.) Very small black firms also do not see MBE or SBE programs as reasons for selling to governments because they feel MBE programs shift the advantage to large minority firms.

Problems faced by black-owned businesses   Our study shows that black-owned businesses, like other small businesses, perceive they cannot effectively compete for government contracts (see Figure 7.3). Fifty-five percent of our black-owned firms report that they frequently have difficulty competing against large firms; one-third complain that competition from other firms regularly pushes prices too low for them to compete successfully for government business. As noted in Chapter 5, they frequently lack the money and expertise to maneuver through the government procurement maze.

Our results confirm what black entrepreneurs have alleged for quite some time, that bonding requirements frequently pose problems for black-owned firms. Forty percent of our respondents identified performance and bid bond requirements as obstacles they frequently encounter in doing business with government. Again, these requirements are especially burdensome for small black businesses, which often lack the necessary capital.

Blacks eager to become small business owners face a three-pronged economic problem, according to Robert Hornaday and Bennie Nunnally in an article in *Business Forum*. First, private capital sources are often unwilling to extend necessary credit, making it extremely difficult to acquire start-up expansion capital. Second, if a black firm chooses to locate in a ghetto, "the inability of customers to pay and the high cost of doing business in high-crime areas severely restrict expansion opportunities." Third, more affluent customers from other ethnic groups and other neighborhoods will not do business in the ghetto because of the unattractive socio-economic environment. One clue about why some black businesses are not interested in competing for government set-aside business is that these contracts are often targeted precisely to serving minority communities. As noted by Cain and Kiewiet, this "segregation of markets, a problem for all minorities, is particularly acute for Black business owners." Other scholars have noted: "Black-

owned firms face an economic 'Catch 22.' To generate more sales and more jobs, they must break out of the black neighborhoods and compete in the economic mainstream, but to do this they need start-up and expansion capital which they cannot raise because of socio-economic conditions in the ghetto."[27]

Since "successful black-owned firms are increasingly removed from the ghetto and from serving a minority clientele," according to Bates, *government must loosen the restrictions on set-aside and vendor preference policies and programs* designed to help newly emerging minority businesses. Otherwise, it will increasingly be difficult to attract minority vendors to compete for government business.

Our study has also shown that *government must provide financial management and technical assistance programs* to promote the growth and development of black-owned firms. And, as is true for all categories of minority-owned firms, government has a long way to go to repair its reputation as an inequitable and unfair trading partner.

Hispanic-Owned Businesses

Cain and Kiewiet's study comparing the characteristics of black-, Hispanic-, and Asian-owned firms in California concludes:

> In general, we would characterize the situation facing Latino business owners as resembling the Blacks in certain respects and the Asian-Americans in another. The Latino community like the Black community is economically and educationally disadvantaged, whereas the Asian-American community is not. On the other hand, the stronger family structure in the Latino community and the language difficulties more closely resemble the situation facing the Asian-Americans than the Blacks.

According to Schwartz, Hispanics have been more successful in establishing businesses than blacks but less successful than

Figure 7.3
The Black-Owned Business Perspective:
Problems Frequently Encountered in Dealing with Government

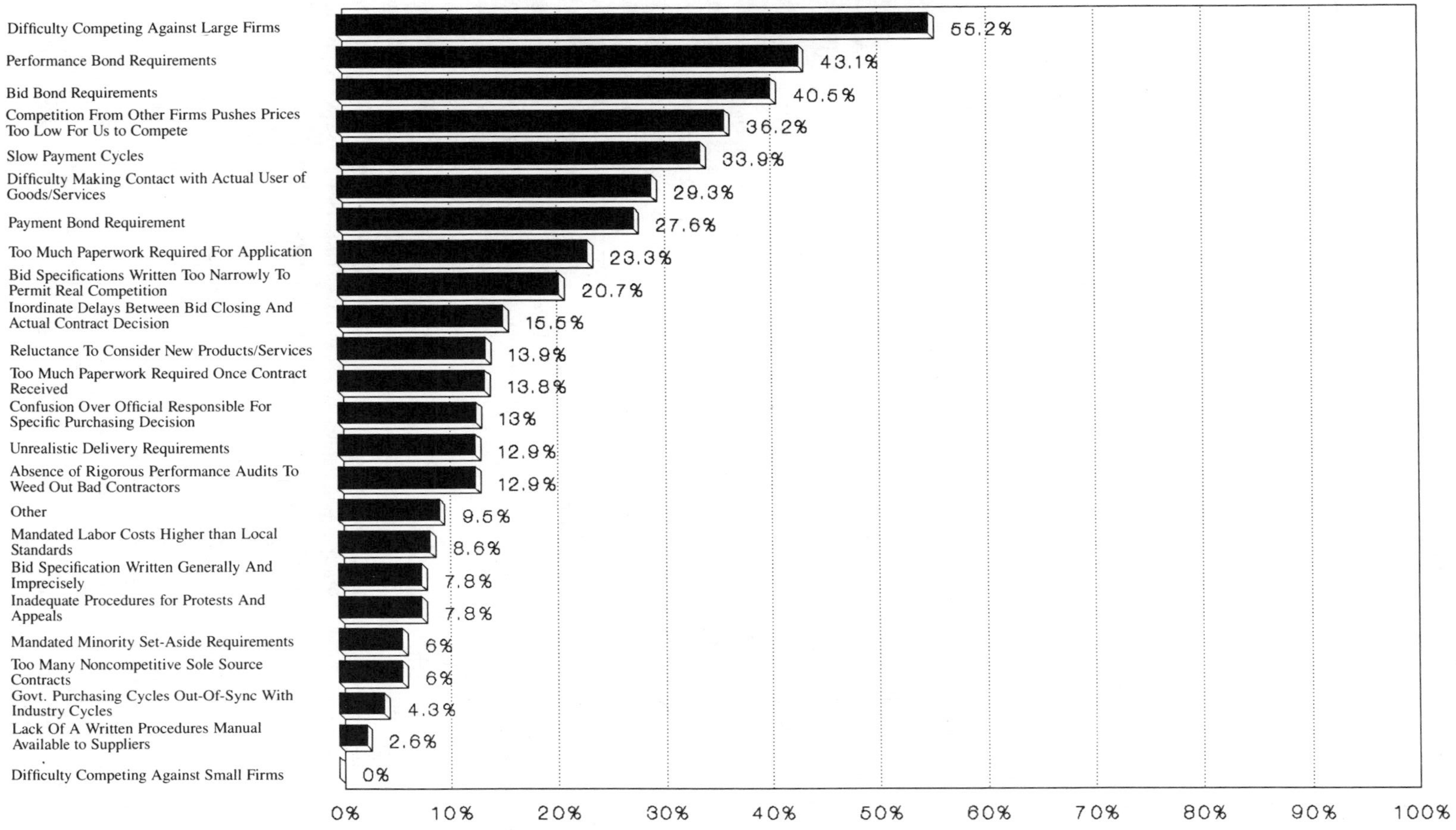

Problem	Percentage
Difficulty Competing Against Large Firms	55.2%
Performance Bond Requirements	43.1%
Bid Bond Requirements	40.5%
Competition From Other Firms Pushes Prices Too Low For Us to Compete	36.2%
Slow Payment Cycles	33.9%
Difficulty Making Contact with Actual User of Goods/Services	29.3%
Payment Bond Requirement	27.6%
Too Much Paperwork Required For Application	23.3%
Bid Specifications Written Too Narrowly To Permit Real Competition	20.7%
Inordinate Delays Between Bid Closing And Actual Contract Decision	16.5%
Reluctance To Consider New Products/Services	13.9%
Too Much Paperwork Required Once Contract Received	13.8%
Confusion Over Official Responsible For Specific Purchasing Decision	13%
Unrealistic Delivery Requirements	12.9%
Absence of Rigorous Performance Audits To Weed Out Bad Contractors	12.9%
Other	9.5%
Mandated Labor Costs Higher than Local Standards	8.6%
Bid Specification Written Generally And Imprecisely	7.8%
Inadequate Procedures for Protests And Appeals	7.8%
Mandated Minority Set-Aside Requirements	6%
Too Many Noncompetitive Sole Source Contracts	6%
Govt. Purchasing Cycles Out-Of-Sync With Industry Cycles	4.3%
Lack Of A Written Procedures Manual Available to Suppliers	2.6%
Difficulty Competing Against Small Firms	0%

Asians. As noted earlier in the chapter, Hispanic business owners are generally younger than black business owners, although less likely to be college graduates. They tend to criticize government business assistance programs more than blacks.

A study of 500 chief executive officers of Hispanic-owned firms in the April 1990 issue of *Hispanic Business* found that few CEOs give high marks to the Small Business Administration in helping them get started. The article begins with this advice to Hispanics contemplating going into business:

> When you start your first business, the only start-up capital you can count on is your own savings and, to a lesser extent, what you get from your family and friends. That's it. Forget about the banks. Forget you even *heard* of the Small Business Administration. Banks and the SBA generally become valuable resources to Hispanic businesses only when they have become well-established.

Another study, *Strategies for Hispanic Business Development*, prepared for the National Chamber Foundation by Richard Arellano, criticizes not only the SBA but other government business assistance programs as well. But the study focuses the harshest criticism at the SBA Section 8(a) program for two major reasons—its overly bureaucratic features and its inequity:

> It is frequently criticized as a bureaucratic nightmare. For many, the long delays in certification for the program and the voluminous paperwork necessary to petition entry into the program are so discouraging that they abandon the program before it can help them. Many who are active in 8(a) find that the paperwork required by the program is counterproductive and becomes a negative influence in their business. They simply cannot spend the time required to satisfy the reporting requirements and still conscientiously engage in business. . . . There is also a widely held perception that what benefits do flow from the 8(a) program are not equi-

tably distributed into the Hispanic business community. It is believed that the amount of government business received by Hispanic firms is not proportional to the representation of Hispanic firms in the total business environment.

The report also criticizes the inequities in the Minority Small Business Investment Companies (MESBIC) program for being oriented more toward black firms than toward Hispanic firms: "The MESBICs that have operated at capacity have been involved permanently with the black community. Compounding the problem is the fact that there are few MESBICS formed by Hispanics, who presumably would have an orientation toward Hispanic business development."

Hispanic business owners resent being compared to black firms generally in the design of government assistance programs. As Arellano states:

> Much of the development assistance work of government agencies relating to the Hispanic business community is accompanied by assumptions that Hispanic businesses are inept, unsophisticated, or "charity cases." This patronizing attitude is readily detected by Hispanics, who are offended and reject the offered assistance as demeaning. They are often reluctant to participate in programs which are seen as "welfare oriented."

Problems they encounter   Hispanic business owners do, however, experience many of the same problems as other minority-owned firms. One, says Arellano, is the bonding requirement:

> A recurring problem facing many Hispanic businesses, particularly those in the construction trades, is that of performance bonding. It is aggravated because companies writing performance bonds require a history of business achievements on which to base their judgment. Most Hispanic businesses are new and do not have the track record necessary to satisfy current bonding require-

ments. The chilling effect on the development of Hispanic businesses that follows from the lack of bonding capacity is serious. It inhibits growth of many deserving Hispanic businesses and retards the economy.

For already established firms, *Hispanic Business* finds that the "biggest business headaches" in rank order are (1) competition, 25 percent; (2) business financing, 19 percent; (3) personnel, 15 percent; (4) obtaining credit, 8 percent; (5) personal problems, 8 percent; (6) liability/litigation, 5 percent; and (7) other, 16 percent.

Reflecting these problems, Arellano in the *Strategies for Hispanic Development* report calls for more small business centers to assist Hispanic firms with new venture counseling and legal, financial, accounting, management, and marketing advice. These centers should advise Hispanic-owned firms: "Hispanic businesses which succeed are those that participate in the main currents of U.S. economic activity. . . . Those Hispanic businesses that are actively in the main flow of commerce are usually the strongest, have the highest levels of income, and evidence the most satisfactory rates of return."

As studies have shown, Hispanic-owned firms, like other minority-owned firms, frequently have trouble getting credit and capital and often need technical assistance. But they are more cynical about government as a solution or as a business partner. The study of Hispanic CEOs by *Hispanic Business* reports that only 13 percent recommend a business apply to the SBA; only 12 percent say they contract with government. A major reason is perceived inequity, as our study confirms.

Similarly, our study has shown that less than one-fourth (24 percent) of Hispanic-owned firms judge the government procurement process to be fair and impartial. Only 16 percent say a reason for doing business with government is fair administration of government purchasing policies. The major

reason they see for selling to government is certainty in getting paid (70 percent).

In spite of animosity toward government assistance programs among the larger, more established firms (the *Hispanic Business* top 500), nearly half of our respondents see participation in an MBE program as an advantage of doing business with government; nearly one-fourth (22 percent) identify SBE program participation as a useful avenue for securing government contracts. And among the Hispanic-owned firms that have been in business two years or less, 56 percent see doing business with government as a way for a new firm to get established. These and other of our findings suggest that newly established firms are more optimistic about the utility of government programs and assistance than the more established ones.

The major problems Hispanic-owned firms experience in doing business with government are those experienced by almost all small firms: difficulties competing against large firms, slow payment cycles, bonding requirements, and difficulties related to the procurement process (knowing who to contact, who makes the decisions, excessive paperwork) (see Figure 7.4). Hispanic-owned firms are slightly less critical than black-owned firms of the overall quality of government purchasing practices of state and local governments. The reason may be that they have been a little more successful in securing state and local government contracts than black-owned firms.

Soon Hispanics will be the largest minority group in the U.S. population. As a first step, *government business development and procurement programs must remedy the rather negative perception that the Hispanic business has regarding their fairness*. Of all the minority groups, Hispanic-owned firms are the least likely to see government purchasing practices as fair and impartial. Traditional approaches to attracting them to sell to government will not be particularly effective. The problem is confounded by

Figure 7.4
The Hispanic-Owned Business Perspective:
Problems Frequently Encountered in Dealing with Government

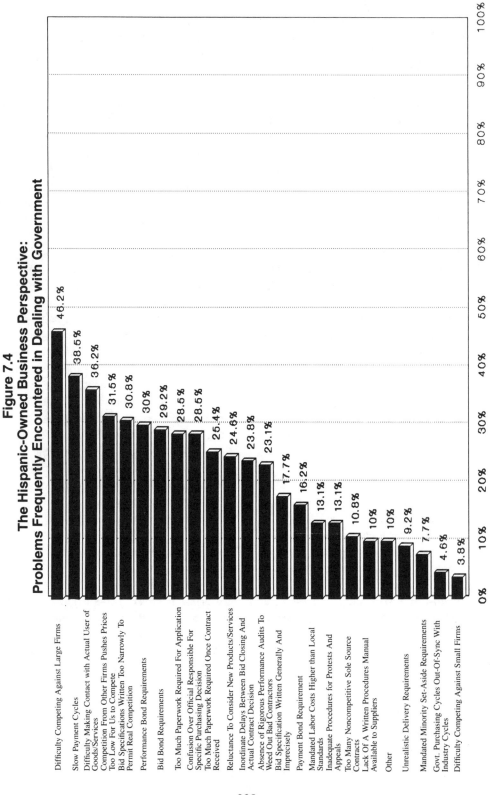

significant differences in the socioeconomic conditions and political perspectives of groups labeled *Hispanic* (e.g., Mexican-Americans, Cuban-Americans, and Puerto Ricans). These differences make it extremely difficult to develop successful strategies.

Asian-Owned Businesses

"Self-employed Asians are outperforming nonminorities and Blacks," concludes Bates' comparative study of Asian, nonminority, and black-owned businesses. The study finds "In terms of such success measures as firm survival rates, profitability, and growth, Asian-male small businesses consistently rank ahead of nonminority males and Black males, even in marginal enterprises such as small scale retailing and personal services."

Asian business owners are generally younger and more educated; they have more start-up capital at the point of small business formation. As Bates says, these "two traits—high financial capital inputs and highly educated owners—are particularly useful for identifying small business start-ups that are likely to survive and prosper." The traits help explain the higher business formation rate of Asian-owned firms.[28]

Problems they face In spite of the advantage that Asian-Americans seem to have over less well-educated groups such as Latinos or blacks, a comparative study of minority businesses in California by Cain and Kiewiet identifies some special problems that Asians have in the business world:

1. While it is true that Asian-Americans enjoy a higher family income, their per capita income is much lower, and in the case of the Koreans and the Filipinos, closer to the Blacks and Latinos than the whites. A control for the number of workers in the family lessens the apparent income advantage that Asian-Americans enjoy over the rest of the population.

2. Many of the Asian-Americans in the retail area rely on unpaid family members and long hours of work to keep them in business.

3. Many of these businesses, because of language problems, depend upon members of their own ethnic community to be their customers and employees. Language can be a barrier to business expansion for them.

4. Asian-American business owners have been slow to take advantage of government programs that might aid them such as SBA loans and procurement opportunities.

Our study confirms what the California study has found: A smaller proportion of Asian- than black- or Hispanic-owned firms identifies participation in either MBE programs (35 percent) or SBE programs (7 percent) as a reason to do business with government. Our Asian firm respondents are much more critical of the overall procurement practices of *all* types of governments, except school districts, than black- or Hispanic-owned firms. Like all other firms, their major reason for selling to government is confidence they will be paid (62 percent), although they are much more critical of the prompt payment practices than other minority groups. Slow payment is the problem they experience most in doing business with government (56 percent).

Like other minority-owned firms, Asian firms report difficulty in competing for government business: 51 percent say they have difficulty competing against large firms and 32 percent say that competition from other firms frequently pushes prices too low for their firms to compete. But Asian-owned firms are more likely to complain about the inefficiencies of the process (paperwork, narrowly written bid specifications, reluctance of governments to consider new products and services) than other minority-owned firms. They are less likely to cite bond requirements as problematic, probably because of their slightly better capital and credit positions on average (see Figure 7.5).

A stereotype as "less needy"   Owners of small, new Asian firms frequently complain of the stereotype of them as better off and less needy of government assistance and business than other minorities. As evidence, they point to conclusions of studies like the one by Bates, who states: "From a policy standpoint, an essential factor stands out: self-employed Asians are *not* a disadvantaged group; their eligibility for government minority business set-aside and preferential procurement programs, financial assistance, subsidized technical assistance, and so forth is completely inappropriate."

Such stereotyping has made Asian business owners cynical of government as a desirable business partner. As our study has shown, only 32 percent of our Asian-owned firm respondents see government procurement practices as fair or impartial. And only a small proportion (17 percent) say they sell to government because purchasing practices are fairly administered.

Public purchasing officials face an uphill battle in devising strategies to attract Asian-owned firms as vendors. First, Asians feel strongly that government programs and practices benefit other minority groups more than them. Second, the socioeconomic situations of different Asian groups (Japanese, Chinese, Vietnamese, Filipinos, Koreans) differ considerably. But the fast-growing nature of the Asian population in a number of states and communities and a sharp increase in the number of Asian-owned firms selling to the U.S. market make it critical for governments at all levels to devise strategies to attract Asian-owned firms to compete for government business.

American Indian-Owned Businesses

An estimated two million American Indians, including Alaskan natives, live in the United States. Between 1980 and 1988 their population grew 19 percent, faster than the U.S. population at large. By 1988, they made up 0.7 percent of the nation's inhabitants. At present, there are 309 federally recognized Indian tribes. A 1989 Bureau of Indian Affairs survey counted 949,055 American Indians living on these reservations.[29]

Few studies have looked at American Indian-owned firms, although they comprise a formally recognized category of small business. These studies show that American Indian-owned firms resemble other small businesses: 88 percent are sole proprietorships and 9 percent are partnerships. They are concentrated in services, wholesale trade, and retail trade industries, although a higher proportion are concentrated in construction than of U.S. small firms in general, according to an article by Marie Humphreys and Jacquetta McClung in the *Texas Business Review*. The educational level of American Indian business owners is much higher than for other small businesses or the population at large.

As is true among other minority groups, Indian business owners criticize government efforts to assist Indian-owned firms. (The Buy Indian Act and the SBA Section 8(a) program are examples of programs designed to aid Indian entrepreneurs.) The economic development coordinator of the Association on American Indian Affairs, quoted by Carol Riggs in an article in *D&B Reports*, complains that "though the federal government has historically made a number of attempts to help Indians become economically independent, results have been on the whole unsatisfactory. There are both cultural and funding problems in the way some of the programs were set up. So they don't always achieve their intended goals."

A unique problem   American Indian entrepreneurs face a rather unique problem—that of tribal ownership, which often causes

Figure 7.5
The Asian-Owned Business Perspective:
Problems Frequently Encountered in Dealing with Government

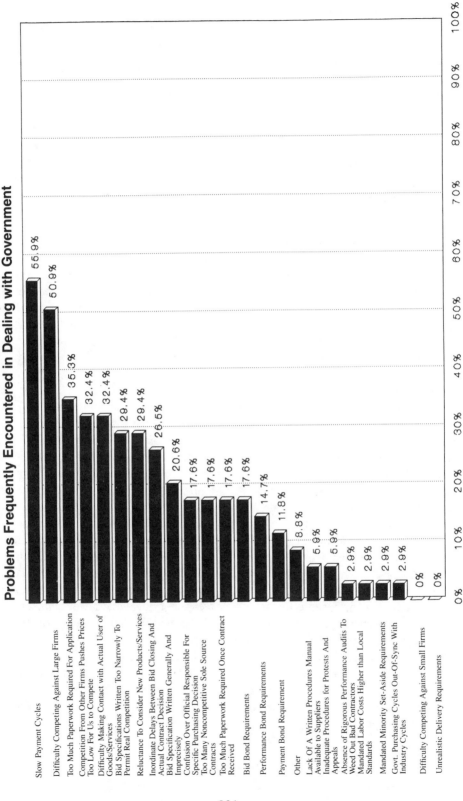

problems in borrowing capital and in management.[30] As Riggs notes:

> When you go to traditional lending institutions and they realize there's tribal ownership, they start worrying about a thing called "sovereign immunity." That's a factor that comes out of Indian law: the status of a tribe as a sovereign that cannot be sued without its consent. Commercial banks begin to wonder, "If there's a default here, will I be able to collect on my loan?" So they oftentimes want a security from the tribe which might not be required in other instances. That sometimes causes problems. Unfortunately, people elected to tribal councils don't always have business backgrounds. We are not yet used to dealing in the world of high finance.

But Indian-owned firms also have some of the same problems as other small, minority firms: obtaining capital, lack of equity and collateral, lack of previous business experience, and the need to expand their market. Like other small, new businesses, they sorely need technical assistance and marketing research.[31]

Unlike the other minorities, only a small percentage of American Indians (16 percent) identify discrimination as a major or moderate obstacle in obtaining loans. A greater barrier is their own Indian cultural heritage, which Humphreys and McClung say is often "antithetical to the development of entrepreneurial aspirations." "Indian values have not customarily included the amassing of valuables for private benefit because of the ingrained tradition of sharing that is part of the Indian culture. Motivation, individualism, and drive for 'success,' as defined by the standards of the dominant society in the United States, do not reflect traditional Indian values." However, evidence suggests this attitude is changing.

Entrepreneurship among both American Indian tribes and individuals has increased since the passage of the Self-Determination and Education Assistance Act in 1975. The study of American Indian entrepreneurs in the Southwest by Humphreys and McClung has found: "Business enterprises owned and managed by the tribes are being developed on and off the reservations, and many tribal economic development programs include loans and management assistance programs for business enterprise development." In addition, Riggs reports that some Indian businesses are being developed as joint ventures with major corporations and have Defense Department contracts.

How they view government purchasing The mainstreaming of American Indian firms undoubtedly helps explain the similarity between their assessments of government purchasing practices and those of other small, minority-owned firms. A majority of these firms do not see public sector procurement practices as competitive, equitable, or efficient.

American Indian-owned firms particularly criticize the inefficiencies, probably because of the disproportionate number of construction firms among them. (Our study has shown that construction firms are more critical of government purchasing practices than firms in other sectors.) Only 13 percent think that government purchases quality goods and services at the lowest cost.

American Indian-owned firms generally rate the quality of government purchasing practices of the federal and state government higher than do other minority firms, but they are more critical of city governments, probably because they have had less success in that arena.

Smaller proportions of American Indian-owned firms identify specific reasons why they do business with government. The pattern differs somewhat from that of other minority-owned firms. The reason may be that a larger proportion of the American Indian-owned firms have been in business longer. In addition to the usual confidence that they will be paid (46 percent) and participation in MBE or SBE programs (39 and 31 percent respectively), one-third cite experience in government contracting and good relations with the government purchasing staff as reasons to sell to government.

Among American Indian firms, the most commonly delineated problems are those identified by most small businesses: difficulty competing against large firms, bond requirements, narrowly written bid specifications, and excessive paperwork (see Figure 7.6). On the other hand, slow payment does not appear as high on the list; only 21 percent say slow payment is a common consequence of doing business with government. American Indian-owned firms are generally less intense in their criticism of specific government purchasing practices than other minority-owned firms.

Public purchasing officials will find it difficult to broaden the pool of American Indian vendors because so few of these firms exist and so little research has been done on American Indian entrepreneurs. Even so, government purchasers must address the perceived problems, particularly in state and local jurisdictions in the Southwest (where the most American Indians live), according to Humphreys and McClung. At the same time, the federal government, which has formal set-asides for American Indian businesses, cannot stand idly by.

The challenge to governments is particularly thorny because American Indians form a less cohesive group than Hispanics and Asians. The needs and priorities of American Indians vary among different tribes. (The ten largest tribes are, in descend-ing order: Cherokee, Navajo, Sioux, Chippewa, Choctaw, Pueblo, Iroquois, Apache, Lumbee, and Creek.) As W. John Moore notes in the *National Journal*: "Tribes are divided by culture and geography—many tribes live in the nation's poorest and most remote areas—and have a long history of being played off against one another." Differences in needs and perspectives also exist between businesses owned by tribes and those owned by individuals of American Indian descent.

Summary of minority businesses In short, all types of minority businesses are confronted with the standard problems facing all small business owners. But they have special difficulties as well, as noted by Cain and Kiewiet: "lack of required business skills and experience, restrictions to markets with lower purchasing power, limited access to capital, and discrimination." As our study has shown, a sizable proportion criticize government as a business partner, as the system currently stands. Many regard the public procurement process as unfair, ineffective, and inefficient.

Unfortunately, perceptions of unfairness frequently stem from one minority group's assessment of its success relative to that of another minority group, or even a group within its own racial or ethnic category. This problem will intensify as more foreign firms compete with U.S. firms. On the other hand, U.S. minority-owned firms may find themselves at an advantage in the procurement practices of other nations. We conclude with a look at the international public procurement environment.

MOVING U.S. BUSINESSES INTO THE INTERNATIONAL PROCUREMENT ARENA

Increasingly, federal, state, and local economic development strategies are targeting foreign markets.[32] These strategies normally take two forms: (1) encouraging foreign companies to invest in American businesses and (2) asking foreign governments to open their markets to American businesses.

Figure 7.6
The Native American-Owned Business Perspective:
Problems Frequently Encountered in Dealing with Government

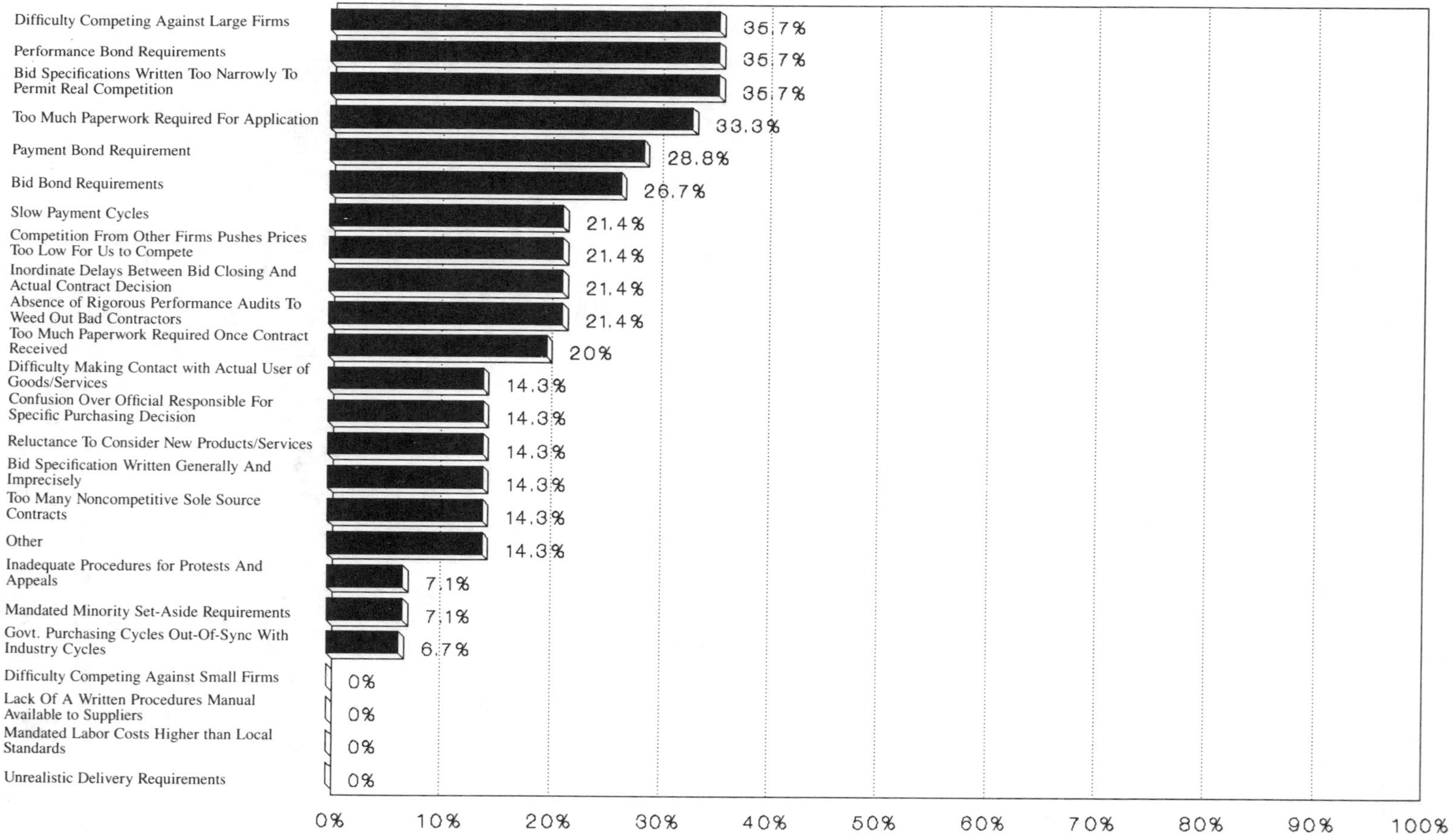

Problem	Percentage
Difficulty Competing Against Large Firms	35.7%
Performance Bond Requirements	35.7%
Bid Specifications Written Too Narrowly To Permit Real Competition	35.7%
Too Much Paperwork Required For Application	33.3%
Payment Bond Requirement	28.8%
Bid Bond Requirements	26.7%
Slow Payment Cycles	21.4%
Competition From Other Firms Pushes Prices Too Low For Us to Compete	21.4%
Inordinate Delays Between Bid Closing And Actual Contract Decision	21.4%
Absence of Rigorous Performance Audits To Weed Out Bad Contractors	21.4%
Too Much Paperwork Required Once Contract Received	20%
Difficulty Making Contact with Actual User of Goods/Services	14.3%
Confusion Over Official Responsible For Specific Purchasing Decision	14.3%
Reluctance To Consider New Products/Services	14.3%
Bid Specification Written Generally And Imprecisely	14.3%
Too Many Noncompetitive Sole Source Contracts	14.3%
Other	14.3%
Inadequate Procedures for Protests And Appeals	7.1%
Mandated Minority Set-Aside Requirements	7.1%
Govt. Purchasing Cycles Out-Of-Sync With Industry Cycles	6.7%
Difficulty Competing Against Small Firms	0%
Lack Of A Written Procedures Manual Available to Suppliers	0%
Mandated Labor Costs Higher than Local Standards	0%
Unrealistic Delivery Requirements	0%

Foreign investment in U.S. business
Foreign businesses may receive incentives for investing directly in U.S. businesses or locating some of their operations in the United States, ideally as joint ventures with American business partners. Table 7.2 shows the success of this strategy over the past two decades.

Direct foreign investment in the United States has jumped from $13 billion in 1970 to $329 billion in 1988. In 1988, according to the Census Bureau, 1,090 foreign businesses had directly invested in U.S. businesses; of these 674 (62 percent) were foreign investors with U.S. affiliates. These figures are actually conservative, since they only cover investments in U.S. business enterprises with assets of more than $1 million or ownership of 200 acres of U.S. land.

The bulk of foreign investment in the United States has been in the manufacturing industry (37 percent in 1988). However, since 1980 the biggest increase (77 percent) has occurred in the wholesale and retail trade sector (Table 7.2).

Table 7.2
Foreign Direct Investment Position in the United States— Value by Area and Industry, 1970 to 1988

[In millions of dollars. Book value at year end. 1970 covers U.S. firms, including real estate investments in which foreign interest or ownership was 25 percent or more; thereafter, ownership of 10 percent or more. Minus sign (−) indicates a negative position. See also *Historical Statistics, Colonial Times to 1970,* series U 47–74]

AREA AND INDUSTRY	1970	1975	1980	1981	1982	1983	1984	1985	1986	1987	1988, prel.
All areas [1]	13,270	27,662	83,046	108,714	124,677	137,061	164,583	184,615	220,414	271,788	328,850
Petroleum	2,992	6,213	12,200	15,246	17,660	18,209	25,400	28,270	29,094	35,598	34,704
Manufacturing	6,140	11,386	32,993	40,533	44,065	47,665	51,802	59,584	71,963	94,745	121,434
Finance and insurance	2,256	3,152	12,027	14,748	17,933	10,934	24,881	27,429	34,978	35,675	39,829
Trade, wholesale and retail	994	4,844	15,210	20,537	23,604	26,513	31,219	35,873	42,920	50,009	64,929
Canada	3,117	5,352	12,162	12,116	11,708	11,434	15,286	17,131	20,318	24,013	27,361
Petroleum	190	596	1,817	1,801	1,550	1,391	1,544	1,589	1,432	1,426	1,614
Manufacturing	1,836	3,061	5,227	3,376	3,500	3,313	4,115	4,607	6,108	7,636	9,391
Finance and insurance	324	341	1,612	1,808	1,801	1,061	3,245	4,008	4,283	5,426	5,051
Europe	9,554	18,584	54,688	72,377	83,193	92,936	108,211	121,413	144,181	186,076	216,418
Petroleum	2,777	5,478	10,137	12,854	15,071	16,326	23,142	25,636	26,139	32,957	31,536
Manufacturing	4,091	6,673	21,953	30,897	33,032	36,866	39,083	45,841	56,016	73,981	91,932
Finance and insurance	1,805	2,088	8,673	10,084	12,601	8,450	15,945	17,022	21,787	25,835	27,328
United Kingdom	4,127	6,331	14,105	18,585	28,447	32,152	38,387	43,555	55,935	79,669	101,909
Petroleum	1,220	(D)	−257	−124	5,444	5,955	10,991	12,155	11,758	(D)	18,779
Manufacturing	1,391	1,833	6,159	7,602	8,504	9,221	9,179	11,687	16,500	27,061	37,021
Finance and insurance	1,141	932	3,350	4,569	5,661	3,777	5,485	6,483	10,163	(D)	11,402
Netherlands	2,151	5,347	19,140	26,824	26,191	29,182	33,728	37,056	40,717	49,115	48,991
Petroleum	1,311	(D)	9,265	11,547	8,098	8,646	9,981	11,481	(D)	(D)	(D)
Manufacturing	652	1,345	4,777	9,018	9,901	11,222	12,497	13,351	13,293	16,137	17,153
Switzerland	1,545	2,138	5,070	5,474	6,378	7,464	8,146	10,568	12,058	14,686	15,896
Manufacturing	1,147	1,308	3,116	3,278	3,584	4,165	4,774	6,881	7,520	7,996	8,072
Finance and insurance	351	365	1,033	1,059	1,473	1,830	(D)	5,425	2,517	(D)	(D)
West Germany	680	1,408	7,596	9,459	9,850	10,845	12,330	14,816	17,250	20,315	23,845
Manufacturing	(NA)	894	3,875	4,199	4,239	4,487	4,389	6,015	7,426	9,294	13,268
Finance and insurance	(NA)	(D)	1,248	1,339	1,426	1,416	1,902	(D)	1,962	2,646	1,443
Other Europe [2]	1,051	3,360	8,777	12,035	12,327	13,293	15,620	15,417	18,221	22,291	25,777
Petroleum	(NA)	490	991	1,315	1,380	1,679	2,080	(D)	(D)	(D)	(D)
Manufacturing	(NA)	1,293	4,026	6,800	6,804	7,771	7,704	7,907	11,277	13,493	16,418
Finance insurance	(NA)	(D)	1,193	546	429	−908	(D)	(D)	(D)	(D)	(D)
Japan	229	591	4,723	7,697	9,677	11,336	16,044	19,313	26,824	35,151	53,354
Other areas	370	3,135	11,472	16,524	20,099	21,356	25,043	26,758	29,091	26,547	31,717

D Withheld to avoid disclosure of data of individual companies.   NA Not Available.   [1] Area totals include industries not shown separately.   [2] Direct investments in 1988 (in millions of dollars): Belgium and Luxembourg, 4,549; France, 11,364; Italy, 667; and Sweden, 5,263.

Source: U.S. Bureau of Economic Analysis, *Survey of Current Business,* August 1989, and earlier issues.

Opened foreign markets Most U.S. governments' economic development strategies focus on persuading foreign governments to open their markets to American businesses. As the figures in Table 7.3 show, U.S. governments have had some success at this tactic. Investment in foreign businesses increased from $215 billion in 1980 to $327 billion in 1988 (a 34 percent increase). Some 40 percent of the investments of U.S. firms have been in the manufacturing sector (1988), mostly in developed countries. Three-fourths of all U.S. business investment has occurred in the developed countries, primarily because their markets are larger and they are generally perceived as less protectionist. Furthermore, a large portion of the developed countries subscribe to principles of the General Agreement on Tariffs and Trade, or GATT.

Exports are another indicator of the effectiveness of U.S. governments in promoting U.S. businesses abroad. In 1990, exports of U.S. merchandise totaled $394 billion (see Figure 7.7). The biggest buyers were the European Economic Community and Canada (see Figure 7.8).

Barriers to Foreign Trade

The 1974 and 1988 trade acts require the Office of the United States Trade Representative to submit to the President and Congress an annual report on significant foreign barriers to, and distortions of, trade. One of the eight categories of trade barriers identified by the Trade Representative's Office is government procurement. Unfair government procurement practices occur when governments adopt "policies and practices that afford protection to domestic products and exclude foreign suppliers." The other barriers are:

- Import policies (e.g., tariffs and other import charges, quantitative restrictions, import licensing, customs barriers)

- Standards, testing, labeling, and certification (e.g., necessarily restrictive application of phytosanitary standards, refusal to accept U.S. manufacturers' self-certification of conformance to foreign product standards)
- Export subsidies (e.g., export financing on preferential terms and agricultural export subsidies that displace U.S. exports in third country markets)
- Lack of intellectual property protection (e.g., inadequate patent, copyright, and trademark regimes)
- Services barriers (e.g., regulation of international data flows, restrictions on the use of foreign data processing)
- Investment barriers (e.g., limitation on foreign equity participation, local content and export performance requirements, and restrictions on transferring earnings and capital)
- Other barriers (e.g., barriers that encompass more than one category listed above or that affect a single sector)

In general, according to the Trade Representative's Office, the goal of U.S. trade policy is to "open markets, expand trade, and eliminate unfair trade practices." The primary vehicle for working toward this goal is the General Agreement on Tariffs and Trade: GATT.

GATT was formed after World War II to promote free trade among nations principally through rules designed to cut tariffs. Since its formation, seven rounds of tariff cuts have occurred under GATT rules. Beginning in the 1960s, the focus shifted as nations began to rely less on tariff protection and more on nontariff barriers such as subsidies and product dumping.

By the late 1980s, ninety nations throughout the world had joined the GATT pact. Unfortunately, many newly developing nations have not and therefore do not abide by GATT rules. Moreover, GATT rules have not kept pace with commercial realities. The

Table 7.3
U.S. Investment Position Abroad by Country, 1980 to 1988

[In millions of dollars. Direct investments represent private enterprises in one country owned or controlled by investors in another country or in the management of which foreign investors have an important role. Negative position occurs when U.S. parent company's liabilities to the foreign affiliate are greater than its equity in, and loans to the foreign affiliate. See also *Historical Statistics, Colonial Times to 1970*, series U 41–46]

COUNTRY	1980	1984	1985	1986	1987	1988 Total[1]	1988 Manufacturing	1988 Petroleum	1988 Finance[2]
All countries	215,375	211,480	230,250	259,800	307,983	326,900	133,819	59,658	60,604
Developed countries	158,214	157,123	172,058	194,280	232,690	245,498	108,850	40,299	43,240
Canada	45,119	46,730	46,909	50,629	58,377	61,244	28,141	11,711	10,377
Europe[3]	96,287	91,589	105,171	120,724	146,243	152,232	67,930	21,323	29,810
Austria	524	530	493	715	714	1,167	95	127	30
Belgium	6,259	4,584	5,038	5,006	6,757	7,224	3,897	551	780
Denmark	1,266	1,144	1,281	1,085	1,091	1,191	265	(D)	174
France	9,347	6,406	7,643	8,952	11,771	12,495	8,047	926	446
Greece	347	265	210	87	132	194	107	45	(D)
Ireland	2,319	2,869	3,693	4,308	5,135	5,743	4,138	−9	1,662
Italy	5,397	4,594	5,906	7,426	9,008	9,075	6,561	401	481
Luxembourg	652	424	690	802	787	756	456	3	93
Netherlands	8,039	5,839	7,129	11,643	14,361	15,367	6,073	2,212	3,178
Norway	1,679	2,841	3,215	3,216	3,844	3,834	36	3,276	119
Portugal	257	205	237	288	412	425	194	(D)	(D)
Spain	2,678	2,139	2,281	2,707	3,789	4,368	2,626	96	26
Sweden	1,474	844	933	918	1,111	1,089	627	(D)	50
Switzerland	11,280	14,725	15,766	16,441	19,518	18,672	1,734	(D)	7,718
Turkey	207	228	234	215	207	193	62	41	–
United Kingdom	28,460	28,553	33,024	35,389	42,031	47,991	18,867	9,327	12,850
West Germany	15,415	14,823	16,764	20,932	24,792	21,673	14,200	2,043	1,921
Japan	6,225	7,936	9,235	11,472	14,671	16,868	7,876	3,468	1,258
Australia, New Zealand, and South Africa	10,583	10,868	10,743	11,455	13,399	15,154	4,903	3,798	1,795
Australia	7,654	8,918	8,772	9,340	11,143	13,058	4,178	3,089	1,685
New Zealand	579	510	576	598	732	826	217	(D)	41
South Africa	2,350	1,440	1,394	1,517	1,524	1,270	508	(D)	69
Developing countries	53,206	49,153	52,764	61,072	70,676	76,837	24,969	16,007	17,364
Latin America	38,761	24,627	28,261	36,851	44,905	49,283	17,850	4,974	14,535
South America[3]	16,342	18,714	17,623	19,813	20,690	21,687	12,378	2,421	1,741
Argentina	2,540	2,753	2,705	2,913	2,673	2,390	1,215	405	176
Brazil	7,704	9,237	8,893	9,268	10,288	11,810	9,004	244	1,272
Chile	536	47	88	265	343	731	9	71	220
Colombia	1,012	2,111	2,148	3,291	3,241	2,429	710	399	(D)
Ecuador	322	371	361	413	466	448	154	189	(D)
Peru	1,665	1,902	1,243	1,103	1,084	1,064	61	348	(D)
Venezuela	1,908	1,761	1,588	1,987	2,036	2,273	1,141	634	6
Central America	10,193	9,853	9,658	10,698	11,657	12,441	5,224	1,593	3,227
Mexico	5,986	4,597	5,088	4,623	4,898	5,516	4,586	60	20
Panama	3,170	4,474	3,959	5,525	6,131	6,140	248	1,419	3,221
Other[3]	1,037	782	611	549	629	785	390	114	26
Costa Rica	303	158	113	113	141	174	128	1	9
El Salvador	105	94	73	50	51	57	18	22	3
Guatemala	229	240	213	181	174	203	110	42	18
Honduras	288	288	171	167	185	231	92	28	−3
Other Western Hemisphere[3]	12,226	−3,941	980	6,341	12,558	15,155	248	960	9,567
Bahamas, The	2,712	3,331	3,795	2,991	2,706	2,244	33	206	882
Bermuda	11,045	13,019	13,116	15,373	19,100	19,880		114	19,265
Dominican Republic	316	239	212	199	156	141	66	27	2
Jamaica	407	257	122	106	102	156	70	(D)	(D)
Netherlands Antilles	−4,336	−24,664	−20,499	−16,969	−14,257	−11,796	24	(D)	12,055
Trinidad and Tobago	951	667	484	424	388	429	10	(D)	4
Other Africa[3]	3,778	4,456	4,497	3,999	4,488	4,603	311	3,548	365
Egypt	1,038	1,538	1,926	1,807	1,680	1,705	50	1,405	2
Libya	575	348	325	241	310	312	–	299	–
Nigeria	18	327	44	781	1,159	1,342	58	1,214	–
Middle East[3]	2,163	5,025	4,606	4,891	4,589	4,090	522	2,317	779
Israel	379	733	717	427	653	722	228	58	133
Saudi Arabia	1,037	2,352	2,442	2,460	2,140	2,047	252	731	575
United Arab Emirates	384	981	792	840	703	680	22	562	(D)
Bahrain	−16	790	440	320	91	−324	–	−49	−2
Other Asia and Pacific	8,505	15,045	15,400	15,332	16,694	18,860	6,286	5,168	1,685
China: Taiwan	498	736	750	869	1,280	1,546	1,161	(D)	(D)
Hong Kong	2,078	3,253	3,295	3,912	4,390	5,028	594	237	1,253
India	398	329	383	421	439	457	415	5	2
Indonesia	1,314	4,093	4,475	3,217	3,050	3,006	92	2,638	46
Malaysia	632	1,101	1,140	1,021	1,019	1,363	521	735	29
Philippines	1,259	1,263	1,032	1,299	1,220	1,305	612	127	145
Singapore	1,204	1,932	1,874	2,256	2,462	3,005	2,000	559	35
South Korea	575	716	743	782	1,003	1,302	497	10	137
Thailand	361	1,081	1,074	1,078	1,274	1,126	326	596	(D)
Other	186	541	635	476	556	721	68	(D)	3
China: Mainland	−6	209	311	167	207	310	61	110	–
International	3,955	5,204	5,428	4,448	4,617	4,565	–	3,351	–
Addendum—OPEC[4]	6,090	10,481	10,383	10,235	10,143	10,229	1,721	6,383	728

- Represents zero.   D = Suppressed to avoid disclosure of data of individual companies.   [1] Includes industries not shown separately.   [2] Includes insurance.   [3] Includes countries not shown separately.   [4] OPEC = Organization of Petroleum Exporting Countries. Includes Algeria, Ecuador, Gabon, Indonesia, Iran, Kuwait, Libya, Qatar, Saudi Arabia, United Arab Emirates, and Venezuela.

Source: U.S. Bureau of Economic Analysis, *Survey of Current Business,* August 1989.

237

Figure 7.7
Composition of U.S. Merchandise Trade With the World

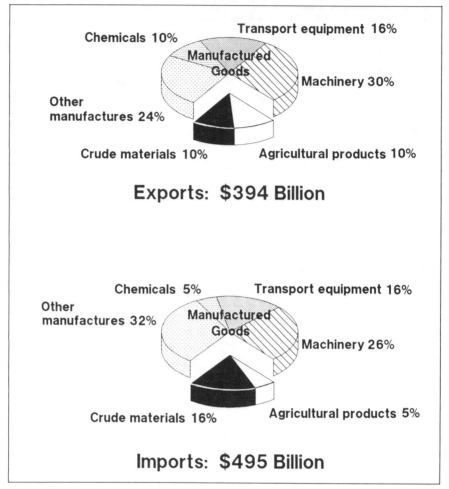

Chemicals 10%

Transport equipment 16%

Manufactured Goods

Machinery 30%

Other manufactures 24%

Crude materials 10%   Agricultural products 10%

Exports: $394 Billion

Chemicals 5%   Transport equipment 16%

Other manufactures 32%   Manufactured Goods

Machinery 26%

Crude materials 16%   Agricultural products 5%

Imports: $495 Billion

U.S. Trade Representative's Office estimates that "one-third of world trade—or more than $1 trillion in goods and services—is not adequately covered by internationally agreed rules of fair play." Areas inadequately covered (such as agriculture) or areas not covered at all (such as services, investment, and intellectual property) particularly concern U.S. entrepreneurs.

The government procurement barrier

With regard to other nations' government procurement policies, the United States seeks, in the words of the Trade Representa-

tive's Office, "adoption of competitive procurement procedures, elimination of any measures which favor domestic procedures, and the provision of predictable non-discriminatory treatment for U.S. suppliers."

As for its own procurement policies, the United States subscribes to the GATT Government Procurement Code (to be discussed shortly), which took effect on January 1, 1981. However, the U.S. government comes in for its own share of criticism from other nations for restrictive trade practices, according to an article by Martin Golub and Sandra Fenske in the *George Washington*

Figure 7.8
Direction of U.S. Merchandise Trade With the World

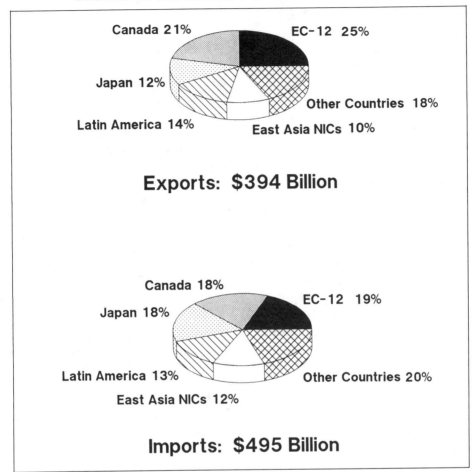

Canada 21%   EC-12 25%

Japan 12%

Other Countries 18%

Latin America 14%   East Asia NICs 10%

Exports: $394 Billion

Canada 18%   EC-12 19%

Japan 18%

Latin America 13%   Other Countries 20%

East Asia NICs 12%

Imports: $495 Billion

Journal of International Law & Economics. For example, U.S. policies such as the Buy American Act and Balance of Payment Program encourage the purchase of domestic goods for public use. And we have seen that various state and local governments also have local vendor preference policies, although the Buy American Act of 1988 and the Trade Act of 1988 restrict these practices somewhat.[33]

The GATT Agreement on Government Procurement

The GATT Agreement on Government Procurement, or Government Procurement

Code, was the first internationally accepted agreement on government procurement. (For an excellent description of the Code, see Michael Janik's 1987 article in the *George Washington Journal of International Law & Economics.*) According to Janik:

The Code is comprehensive in its scope, covering the entire bidding process from qualification of suppliers to notification of contract awards.[34] The framers sought to achieve their goal of eliminating prejudicial treatment of foreign countries by mandating a "transparent procurement process" [bidders can see all applicable rules and decision-making] whereby all bidders, both potential and actual, can reasonably assess the government's needs and reasonably understand the applicable procurement procedures.

The GATT Government Procurement Code establishes four criteria for determining whether a government contract should be subject to the Code. Most of these criteria are highly discretionary or subjective in their interpretation, says Janik, which has led to international debates regarding the fairness of government procurement:

The first criterion is that the contract must primarily be a supply (rather than a service) contract.

Second, the contract value must exceed a specified threshold value, defined in terms of the International Monetary Fund's official unit of account, the Special Drawing Right.

Third, the contract must be awarded by a government agency not exempted from the Code. The Code applies to "procurement by the entities under the direct or substantial control of Parties to this agreement and other designated entities, with respect to their procurement procedures and practices. As Janik notes: "The 'direct or substantial control' language can create confusion as to whether quasi-autonomous governmental entities or public corporations are subject to the Code." Each government determines the agencies it wants covered by the Code. As of 1987, the United States had designated fifty-four agencies covered under the Code.[35]

The fourth criterion is that the contract must not otherwise be subject to an exemption to the Code. There are two general exemptions: (1) procurements "indispensable for national security or for national defense purposes," and (2) procurements based on social policies. The latter may work to the advantage of minority-owned U.S. firms if foreign countries choose to implement procurement policies favoring foreign businesses that share a common cultural or historical heritage. It may also work to the advantage of women and minority-owned firms at home if the U.S. government mandates adherence to its own social policies.[36]

Different nations' interpretations of the inclusiveness of the Code to their governmental purchasing decisions explain the lower-than-projected benefits to U.S. businesses of the Code's adoption. Janik reports: "Although the U.S. government originally estimated that $20 to $25 billion in foreign government procurement would become available to U.S. firms as a result of the Code, the available data indicates that only approximately $4 billion in procurement has been made available." Even this amount is inflated "because it represents all foreign procurements opened to U.S. companies, and not just those procurements that were opened . . . solely as a result of the Code."

The Uruguay Round of international trade talks, begun in 1986, attempted to address GATT shortcomings but did not resolve them. The Uruguay Round collapsed in December 1990. One major reason was the changing world political and economic order that made many nations more protectionist. As stated in an article in the March–April 1991 *Harvard Business Review*:

When GATT's focus shifted from its early tariff cutting to eliminating nontariff barriers to trade, members stumbled into intractable conflicts over their sovereign rights. Each nation understandably insisted on setting its own economic and social priorities and would not—on many issues could not—give way to a more international vision.

These problems demonstrate that government-imposed policies, whether at home or abroad, often restrict the ability or willingness of businesses to sell to other governments.

Dealing with Foreign Government Procurement Systems

A number of scholars have examined government procurement policies in foreign countries. In one notable series appearing in the *George Washington Journal of International Law and Economics* in 1987,[37] editor John Cibinic, Jr., identifies the common problems businesses share in selling to any government, regardless of its prevailing ideological or economic structure:

> Selling to governments is a complex and risky business with many legal snares that can entrap unwary contractors. Dealing with sovereigns presents many unique problems. Sovereign immunity from suits, the power to expropriate property within the sovereign's territory, and limited authority of governmental officials can have a devastating impact on the most well-planned transaction. In addition, virtually all governments have adopted relatively complex rules designed to guide their officials in the contracting process, protect the public interest, and advance national goals.

One can find many similarities in the way the government procurement processes work (see note 34). As Cibinic observes, "the requirement of competition and the use of sealed bids or formal tenders predominates, but negotiation or limited competition may be used when appropriate conditions arise."

One can also find differences in each government's procurement practices. Predictably, these differences stem from variations in legal and economic systems as well as cultural norms. For example, some countries have fairly informal procurement rules, while others have much more formal practices.[38] As one might expect, marked differences can occur, depending on the extent to which a nation's private sector is developed or relied upon by government to provide public services.

A worldwide trend toward privatization began in the 1980s.[39] While the emphasis on markets and competition has grown even among socialist and communist nations, it has been difficult for any nation to adopt a totally free and competitive market. Often the most serious opposition comes from within. In the United States, for example, opposition to governments' buying from foreign businesses[40] has come especially from small U.S. vendors who already feel governments' purchasing practices cut them out of the competition for public sector business.

Businesses and governments view the world's changing political and economic order,[41] particularly the emergence of strong regional economic organizations, with mixed emotions. On the one hand, rapid globalization makes it urgent for nations to further open the international market. On the other hand, it may become more difficult to abandon "domestic" protectionist policies aimed at promoting the success of giant trade entities. The Office of the U.S. Trade Representative has stated the dilemma well: "As the 20th Century enters its last decade, the world trading system stands at a crossroads, poised between further liberalization and expansion on the one hand, and protection and contraction on the other."

Government procurement policies are either the cause of, or the solution to, this dilemma, depending on one's point of view. One thing is certain: government procurement policies must attract a larger, more diverse number of vendors to compete for government business. Otherwise the world's economy will suffer in the long run.

How to Sell to Foreign Governments and Industries

Many federal agencies play an integral role in helping U.S. businesses sell abroad.

U.S. Department of Commerce The Department of Commerce's International Trade Administration (ITA) offers an excellent starting place to learn about the complex system. ITA promotes exports of American products and helps American businesses increase their international sales. It also helps formulate foreign policy and monitors international agreements. ITA serves businesses through the forty-seven district offices and twenty-one branch offices of its U.S. and Foreign Commercial Services (US & FCS). (See Appendix G for a list of these offices.)

For information about trade potential by country, businesses should contact country desk officers in ITA's International Economic Policy Unit. These officers keep up to date on the economic and commercial conditions in their assigned countries. Each officer collects information on the country's regulation, tariffs, business practices, economic and political developments, trade, trends, market size, and growth. These officers also work to remove obstacles to U.S. commercial activities in their assigned countries. (See Appendix G for a list of country desk officers in ITA.)

For information about trade potential by industry, businesses should contact industry officers in ITA's Trade Development Unit. These officers promote exports of their assigned industries through marketing seminars, foreign buyer groups, executive trade missions, trade fairs, and business counseling. They also work directly with trade associations and state development agencies. (See Appendix G for a list of ITA industry desk officers.)

The Department of Commerce's Bureau of Export Administration (BXA) is responsible for coordinating and administering U.S. national security, foreign policy, and short-supply export controls. BXA administers the Export Administration Act by developing export control policy, processing export license applications, and enforcing U.S. export control laws. BXA operates eight field offices and a western regional office. (See Appendix G for a list.)

A number of other Department of Commerce agencies also offer export-related services:

- The U.S. Travel and Tourism Administration (USTTA) promotes U.S. export earnings through trade in tourism.
- The National Institute of Standards and Technology (NIST) provides businesses information about foreign standards and certification systems and maintains a GATT hotline.
- The Minority Business Development Agency provides special assistance to minority-owned businesses.
- The Office of Metric Programs gives exporters guidance and assistance on foreign metric import regulations.
- The National Oceanic and Atmospheric Administration (NOAA) assists seafood exporters in securing entry to foreign markets.
- The National Marine Fisheries Service (NMFS) inspects and certifies U.S. fish exports.

Information sources   The Department of Commerce publishes a number of information sources about foreign trade opportunities:

- *Commerce Business Daily* (CBD). Regularly reports opportunities for foreign sales, along with the name and address of the contact person.
- *Business America*. Issued biweekly, provides helpful interpretations of U.S. government policies and programs that may affect international business decisions. Also gives concise, up-to-date information on worldwide trade and investment trends and includes a special section on business leads. In 1991 *Business America* published an invaluable Directory of Export Services (included in Appendix G).
- The National Trade Data Bank (NTDB). Contains more than 90,000 international trade and economic entries gathered

from fifteen U.S. federal government agencies. (For a description of this data base, see Melissa Malhame's article in the special edition of *Business America*.) Updated monthly, the data base is available in a CD-ROM (electronic data base) format on a monthly or annual subscription basis from the U.S. Department of Commerce, Office of Business Analysis, HCHB Rm. 4885, Washington, D.C. 20230; telephone (202) 377-1986. It is also available at the nearly 700 federal depository libraries throughout the United States.

- *The Export Yellow Pages.* Published by the Office of Export Trading Company Affairs (OETCA); designed to help U.S. firms locate export service providers, trading companies, and manufacturers. It lists international trade service providers alphabetically by the type of service provided, by Standard Industrial Classification (SIC) code, and by state.

Financial assistance The U.S. Export-Import Bank (Eximbank) is the principal government agency responsible for firms through a variety of loan, guarantee, and insurance programs. (These programs are described in the Department of Commerce's Export Guide in Appendix G.) Many of Eximbank's programs are targeted to small businesses.

The Small Business Administration's Office of International Trade offers a wide range of assistance programs to small businesses desiring to sell abroad. The U.S. Trade Development Program, the U.S. Department of Agriculture's Commodity Credit Corporation, the Overseas Private Investment Corporation, and the Agency for International Development are other sources of financial assistance to U.S. firms. (See *Business America*, March 25, 1991, for a detailed discussion of each agency's loan programs.)

Other federal agencies A number of other federal agencies offer foreign trade-related assistance to U.S. businesses. (See Appendix G for descriptions of their activities, addresses, and telephone numbers.) These agencies include:

- U.S. Department of Agriculture's Foreign Agricultural Services (FAS)
- U.S. Department of State's country desks and its Bureau of Economic and Business Affairs
- Overseas Private Investment Corporation
- Office of the U.S. Trade Representative
- Agency for International Development
- Trade and Development Program

State and local government assistance Most state governments now offer services intended to help their businesses sell abroad. Whether the agency responsible is called a state trade development office, a state economic development agency, or a state foreign trade office, the purpose is the same. (For a list of state trade development offices, see Appendix G.)

In addition, many states have established offices abroad designed to promote goods or services produced by firms in their states to foreign governments and businesses. Even some local governments, usually the largest ones, send delegations of officials to other countries in an effort to stimulate economic development.

Some observers see the multitudinous, and often competitive, marketing efforts of U.S. governmental units in the international marketplace as counterproductive, while others believe such efforts are crucial to success. The issue boils down to whether one views centralized efforts as superior to decentralized efforts, a debate that has raged for decades.

PERSISTING DILEMMAS IN PUBLIC PROCUREMENT

Our investigation of government procurement highlights some seemingly inevitable conflicts and contradictions in the American system. One dilemma is how to ensure that government buys from ethical vendors that provide quality goods and services at a reasonable price while at the same time avoiding a regulatory system so complex and onerous that it deters good vendors from competing for government business. This dilemma reflects the basic difference between public and private purchasing priorities. For the public sector, the number-one priority is accountability to the taxpayers. For the private sector, the priority is profit.

A second dilemma is how to expand vendor pools to reflect the changing ownership patterns of American industry without violating the fairness principle of public procurement. As we have shown, small businesses and those owned by women and minorities clearly differ in their opinions of the public purchasing system. Strategies to attract them to compete for government business must differ to be effective. Yet designing rules and procedures to benefit a certain type of firm by definition creates an aura of unfairness among all the others. Compounding this dilemma is the sparsity of empirical data to demonstrate that efforts thus far to broaden vendor pools have made the purchasing system more efficient or effective.

Furthermore, efforts to expand the list of businesses interested in selling to government may ultimately shrink the vendor pool unless the actual contract *recipient* pool is also expanded. Thus formal competitive bidding processes designed to yield one "winning" firm to produce a good or service at the lowest cost over time may create private monopolies if these processes drive away all firms but one.

Another dilemma reflecting public–private sector differences centers on the profit to be made by businesses from selling to government. The purpose of the competition principle of public purchasing is to obtain a quality good or service at the lowest possible price. This conflicts with the private sector's profit-making priority. As our study has shown, many businesses believe that the current public procurement process greatly limits the amount of profit they can make, especially when the paperwork is excessive and the payments slow. These phenomena, along with other irritants in the system, frequently dampen a firm's interest in public sector business.

At a more micro level, public procurement officials face the dilemma of writing specifications narrowly to assure that they get precisely what they want or broadly to allow flexibility and encourage innovation. Our study shows that businesses question the objectivity of those drawing up the specs, regardless of the path taken. Ironically, criticisms of specs is greatest among those that have been the most successful in securing government contracts, probably because they have experienced the change-order phenomenon emanating from badly written specs.

These dilemmas, while challenging, are not insurmountable. Business and government can fashion mutually acceptable solutions, but only through more open communication and joint restructuring ventures. After all, when each plays the role of purchaser, both government and business want to get the best product at the lowest price. And both agree that competition and openness in purchasing make this possible.

NOTES

1. Cf. Kennedy and Trilling, 1988.
2. See *The State of Small Business: A Report of the President*, 1989.
3. Ibid. The federal government has created a number of different requirements and programs designed to bolster this percentage such as total set-asides, partial set-asides, set-asides under the Defense Appropriations Acts of 1987 and 1988, Small Business Innovation Research Set Asides, small business subcontracting preferences, and assistance to small businesses owned and controlled by socially and economically disadvantaged firms under the Small Business Act Section 8(a). (See Kennedy and Trilling, 1988; *The State of Small Business: A Report of the President*, 1989, for excellent descriptions of these programs.)

   As our study has shown, few small firms cite participation in SBE programs as a reason for doing business with government; and a rather large proportion rate the federal procurement system worse than that of any other type of government. Even the federal Prompt Payment Act Amendments of 1988 have not been very effective. Nearly two-thirds (63 percent) of the small firms estimate that it takes longer than the standard thirty days to get reimbursed by the federal government— the worst of all the different types of government rated.
4. We chose to use this definition of small because 97 percent of these firms also have 1–25 employees. In other words, it best captures the two measures of size: number of employees and assets.
5. See note 3, Chapter 3 for a description of the survey of firms not on government vendor lists. The cover letter and survey instrument for this survey varied slightly from the larger, vendor-list-based survey. Both survey instruments appear in Appendix A.
6. The survey of nongovernment vendor-list businesses added another response category to the question asking businesses to identify the reasons they do/would like to do business with government: "None of the above. We don't like to do business with government" (see survey instrument, Appendix A).

7. The overall failure rate for new ventures started each year is 70 percent (Balsam, 1987:1). Four of five new businesses fail within five years (Therrien, Carson, Hamilton, and Hurlock, 1986:81).
8. Cf. U.S. Department of Labor, Women's Bureau, 1987; U.S. Small Business Administration, Office of Women's Business Ownership, March 1987; Schwartz, 1988; *The State of Small Business: A Report of the President*, 1989.
9. Cf. Charboneau, 1981; Hisrich and Brush, 1985; Bowen and Hisrich, 1986; Scott, 1986; Stevenson, 1986; Balsam, 1987; Suchenski, 1987; Aldrich, 1989; Bowman-Upton, 1989; Brockhaus, 1989; Brophy, 1989; Fried, 1989; Hagan, Rivchun, and Sexton, 1989; Nelton, 1989; Sexton, 1989a,b.
10. See Longstreth, Stafford, and Mauldin, 1987.
11. See U.S. Department of Labor, Women's Bureau, 1987; Nelton, 1989.
12. There is no program exclusively authorizing federal contract set-asides for women-owned businesses (as there are for small businesses and businesses owned by racial and ethnic minorities). However, a presidential executive order requires most federal contracts larger than $10,000 to include a clause under which the contractor agrees to use its best efforts to give women-owned small businesses the "maximum practicable opportunity" to participate in contracts "to the fullest extent consistent with the efficient performance of its contract" (Kennedy and Trilling, 1988:59).

   To help stimulate the growth and development of women-owned firms, The Women's Business Ownership Act of 1988 calls for improved data collection on women's business ownership, improved accessibility of certain SBA programs to women entrepreneurs, and broadening the application of the Equal Credit Opportunity Act to certain business credit applications (*The State of Small Business: A Report of the President*, 1989:27).
13. See MacManus, 1990b.
14. See Hisrich, 1989:8; also see Balsam, 1987;

Therrien, Carson, Hamilton, and Hurlock, 1986; Nelton, 1987; Buttner and Rosen, 1988; Stoner, Hartman, and Arora, 1990; Brown and Segal, 1989.

15. The U.S. Department of Labor, Women's Bureau's Facts on Working Women series (1989) reports that in 1982, 92.5 percent of all women-owned sole proprietorships were owned by white women; 3.8 percent by black women; 2.1 percent by women of Hispanic origin; 1.6 percent by Asian women; and 7.5 percent by other races, including American Indian women. Among our respondents, 4.9 percent of the women-owned firms are owned by blacks, 5.1 percent by Hispanics, 1.4 percent by American Indians, and 1.1 percent by Asians.

16. See Engeleiter, 1989.

17. For exceptions, see Humphreys and McClung, 1982; Riggs, 1987.

18. Cf. O'Hare and Suggs, 1986; Hornaday and Nunnally, 1987.

19. Cf. Bates and Bradford, 1979; Bates, 1989a,b.

20. The major set-aside program aiding small minority-owned firms is the U.S. Small Business Administration's Section 8(a) Program. "Officially entitled the Minority Small Business and Capital Ownership Development program, it opens doors to promising minority-owned small businesses by providing opportunities to contract with the federal government for a limited period of time" (Engeleiter, 1989:1).

The Business Opportunity Development Reform Act of 1988 made a number of changes and improvements to the 8(a) program, most notably requirements that 8(a) firms compete for government manufacturing contracts larger than $5 million and all other government contracts above $3 million, regulations calling for an accelerated application process and better-trained SBA personnel to assist minority-owned firms and provide to them quality management, technical and financial assistance, among others. (See *The State of Small Business: A Report of the President*, 1989: 150-151, and Engeleiter, 1989:2.)

21. Cf. Ross, 1979; Isaiah Poole, 1980, 1981; Harold Logan, 1983; Dingle, 1985; Owens,

1987; Black, 1989; Engeleiter, 1989; Watson, 1989; Green and Pryde, 1990; and Singletary, 1990.

22. Cf. Sheppard, 1981; Watson, 1989.

23. Cf. McCall, 1989.

24. See National Institute for Governmental Purchasing, 1982.

25. Cf. Ross, 1979; Isaiah Poole, 1981; Harold Logan, 1983; Cain and Kiewiet, 1986; Andrews, 1988; MacManus, 1990b.

26. See Arellano, 1984; Cain and Kiewiet, 1986; MacManus, 1990b.

27. See Hornaday and Nunnally, 1987:35; O'Hare and Suggs, 1986; Bates, 1989a,b.

28. See Schwartz, 1988; Bates, 1989b.

29. See Wilson, 1990; Riggs, 1987; Moore, 1990.

30. Cf. Vinje, 1985; Riggs, 1987.

31. See Sorkin, 1978.

32. Cf. Bradley, 1990; Chanis, 1990; Cohen, 1990; Culbertson, 1990; Deardorff and Stern, 1990; Dunn's Marketing Service, 1990; Ebel and Marks, 1990; Kincaid, 1990; Liner, 1990; Macchiarola, 1990a; Madarassy, 1990; McCulloch, 1990; Nelson, 1990; O'Neill, 1990; Ostry, 1990; Sanderson and Hayes, 1990; Schwab, 1990; Spicer's Centre for Europe, 1990; Spiro, 1990; Strauss, 1990; Tommy Thompson, 1990; Vernon, 1990; and Wendt, 1990; Aronoff, 1991; Bailey and Teske, 1991; *Business America*, 1991; Collins and Doorley, 1991; Duesterberg, 1991; Farren, 1991; Hagigh, 1991; Jelacic, 1991; H.S. Jones, 1991; R. Johnson, 1991; Kozitsyn and Johnson, 1991; Lewis, 1991; Litman, 1991; Masterson, 1991; McCreary, 1991; Menes and Carson, 1991; Nelson, 1991; Powers and Elliott, 1991; Saunders, 1991; Stillman, 1991; Straetz, 1991; Treinen, 1991; Vial, 1991; Watson, 1991; Wright, 1991).

33. Vaughan (1989:604) describes the goals of the Buy American Act of 1988: "First, the Act attempts to secure stricter compliance with the terms of the [GATT] Procurement Agreement by parties who have not opened their markets accordingly. A second goal . . . is to discourage discrimination in government procurement against U.S. suppliers by countries not party to the Procurement Agreement, and concurrently encourage

countries to become signatories." But Vaughan concludes that the effectiveness of the 1988 revisions to the Buy American Act has been limited because certain provisions, such as the time limit placed on dispute resolution, conflict with the GATT Procurement Code.

34. The GATT Government Procurement Code includes a number of rather standard (from the U.S. perspective) purchasing rules (Janik, 1987). Among them are rules related to a government agency's procurement announcement, or notice. Each notice must contain information describing the items being procured, the due date for obtaining a bid, and the identity and address of the government agency doing the purchasing. A summary of the notice must be written in one of the official languages of the GATT.

Other rules govern tender documentation (IFB). The Code requires that the following be clearly delineated: the address to which bids should be submitted; the address from which supplementary information can be obtained; the language in which a bid must be submitted; the closing date for the receipt of bids; a full description of any special economic or technical requirements that must be satisfied; a full description of the products that are being purchased, including their technical specifications and any necessary documents that a bidder needs to fully understand technical requirements; the contract award criteria, including any specific factors other than price that will be considered in evaluating the bid; and explanations of how transport, insurance, customs duties, and other such items are to be handled in government evaluations of price.

Another rule is that the period for submission of bids must be reasonable. The time between the purchase announcement and the actual purchase must not be less than thirty days (except in the case of an "urgency duly substantiated" by the government agency doing the purchasing).

The bids must be submitted in writing, either directly or by mail. The Code permits bidders to correct unintentional errors during the period between the submission of bids and the contract award so long as the govern-

ment agency does not grant such permission in a discriminatory fashion. The Code also permits consideration of late bids under extraordinary circumstances.

The Code calls for the contract to be awarded to the bidder submitting the most advantageous offer as defined by the evaluation criteria specified by the government agency, unless it is in the public interest not to award a contract.

The Code also contains requirements for notification of, and protest and appeals rights of, unsuccessful bidders. Unsuccessful bidders must be notified by written communication or publication within seven working days after the date of the contract award. Upon a request from an unsuccessful bidder, the government agency must provide information as to why its bid was not accepted, including the characteristics and relevant advantages of the bid selected and the name of the awardee. Government agencies must establish a contact point to hear any disputes arising out of the rejection of bids and the contact point must have established procedures for hearing and reviewing such complaints.

The Code addresses the problem of bid specifications too narrowly written to promote competition. The Code prohibits the drafting of technical specifications that create obstacles to international trade. The Code also requires that specifications be drafted in terms of performance requirements rather than design requirements, when possible, and that they be based upon internationally or nationally recognized or adopted standards. The use of brand-name specifications is prohibited unless there is no other precise way of describing an agency's requirements.

With regard to supplier certification or qualification, the Code prohibits rules that discriminate against foreign companies or foreign goods. If a supplier has asked to be included on a qualified vendor list, the government agency must advise the vendor when it has been accepted. The agency must also inform a supplier if it has been deleted from a list of if the list was terminated.

Finally, the Code establishes a formal GATT dispute process. However, it is a government-to-government arrangement not directly involving the complainant firm. As outlined by Janik (1987:501–502), if there is a complaint, the parties to the Code must enter into formal consultations to try to resolve the conflict. If this doesn't work, a party may request the Committee on Government Procurement created by the Code to review the complaint. If the committee is unsuccessful, it will appoint a disputes panel to examine the matter. This panel is required to submit a report back to the committee, at which time it issues its factual findings, recommendations, and other rulings. If either party does not accept the committee's recommendations, the committee may authorize a party or parties to suspend temporarily, in whole or in part, the application of the Code to any other party or parties, if the committee judges the circumstances to be serious enough. In summary, the Code is similar to the codes of many U.S. governments.

35. See Golub and Fenske, 1987.
36. Cf. Goode, 1985.
37. These two volumes contain articles on government procurement laws in Sweden (Linder, 1987); Belgium (Verbist, 1987); Canada (Barton and Unger, 1987); Germany (Cleesattel, 1987); Japan (Toyama, Nakatani, and Mattei, 1987); Saudi Arabia (Wisner, 1988); the United Kingdom (Blyth, 1987); Switzerland (Von Meiss, 1987); the United States (Golub and Fenske, 1987); and France (Goldman, 1987).

    The two volumes also contain articles on government procurement within the North Atlantic Treaty Organization (Kuckelman, 1987); the European Economic Community (Thys and Henry, 1987); the General Agreement on Tariffs and Trade (Janik, 1987); alternative dispute resolution in international government contracting (Green and Jordan-Walker, 1987), and military procurement (Mayer, 1987).

    Other articles addressing the GATT or other aspects of international government procurement include Cao, 1980, 1981; Peterson, 1980; Anthony and Hagerty, 1981; Brown, 1981; Bourgeois, 1982; Dempsey, 1982; Pomeranz, 1982; Rothlein and Schooner, 1983; Barovick, 1984; Pavlovitz, 1984; Alexander, 1986; Frignani, 1986; Silber-

man, 1986; Fried, 1987; Wooldridge, 1987; Nymark, 1989; Watson, 1988; Weiss, 1988; Bisopoulos, 1989; Korbel and Brescia, 1989; McAfee and McMillan, 1989; McKinney, 1989; Riga, 1989; Saba, 1989; Vaughan, 1989; *Business America* (May 21, 1990); Deardorff and Stern, 1990; Fernandez and Mashatt, 1990; and Whitehurst, Gaughan, and Yachnin, 1990.

38. Cf. Cibinic, 1987.
39. The privatization efforts of other countries are discussed in Caves and Christensen, 1980; Borcherding, 1982; Bellante, 1983; McDavid, 1985; Stanley, 1985; Deschamps, 1986; Kay and Thompson, 1986; Mac-Manus, 1986; Sakoh, 1986; Wynne, 1986; Young, 1986, 1987; Burton, 1987; Hanke, 1987; Jacquillat, 1987; King, 1987; Maule, 1987; Roth, 1987b; Wildman and Siwek, 1987; Fraser, 1988; Hemming and Mansoor, 1988; Ryser, 1988; Sandler, 1988; Seguiti and Pitsvada, 1988; Shirley, 1988; Waterman, 1988; Lim and Moore, 1989; Lowenstein, 1989; MacAvoy et al., 1989; Molz, 1989; Ray Smith, 1989; Van Oudenhoven and Pieter, 1989; Vernon, 1989; Ash, 1990; Barham, 1990; *The Economist*, 1985, 1988, 1990a,b,c; Fairlamb, 1990; Gomez-Ibañez and Meyer, 1990; Madarassy, 1990; Nankani, 1990; Peagam, 1990; Rigg and Leach, 1990; Lerner, 1990; Shoreham, 1990; Sington, 1990; and Westlake, 1990.
40. Cf. Harrigan, 1987; Tolchin and Tolchin, 1988; Stokes, 1990a.
41. Excellent overviews of the changing international economic order and the rise of regionalism, especially in Europe and Asia, can be found in Macchariola, 1990; Bisopoulos, 1989; Choplick, 1989; Emerson, 1989; Korbel and Brescia, 1989; Lamoriello, 1989; Toma, 1989; Michael Williams, 1989; Wolf, 1989; Bradley, 1990; Chanis, 1990; Cohen, 1990; Culbertson, 1989, 1990; Deardorff and Stern, 1990; Dornsbusch, 1990; Ebel and Marks, 1990; Farrell and Schares, 1990; Goette, 1990; Green, 1990; Kelso, 1990; Kuttner, 1990; Marshall, 1990; McCulloch, 1990; Sachs, 1990; Schneider, 1990a,b,c; Spievack, 1990; Stanfield, 1990; Stokes, 1990a,b,c,d; and Whitehead, 1990.

Survey Instruments

Survey Instrument: Business Selected from Business Directory

Survey
Business Views of Government Contracting Policies
and Procedures

Directions: This survey is part of a national study examining private sector evaluations of government contracting policies and procedures. **Even if your firm does not do business with government, we are interested in your opinions. It will take no more than 5 minutes of your time.** All questions require only a ✔ for an answer.

1. Businesses like yours generally believe that government purchasing policies and procedures are effective in attracting first rate vendors to compete for contracts.
   _____ Yes   _____ No   _____ No opinion

2. Businesses like yours believe that government purchasing policies and procedures result in government purchases of quality goods & services at the lowest cost.
   _____ Yes   _____ No   _____ No opinion

3. Businesses like yours believe that government policies and procedures are fair and impartial.
   _____ Yes   _____ No   _____ No opinion

4. What is the structure of your firm? (**Check one**)
   _____ Individual owner   _____ Nonprofit organization
   _____ Partnership   _____ Corporation
                           _____ Other (specify) _____

5. How many years has your firm been in business? (**Check one**)
   _____ Less than 1 year
   _____ 1–2 years
   _____ 3–5 years
   _____ 6–10 years
   _____ over 10 years

6. How many employees does your firm have? (**Check one**)
   _____ 1–25   _____ 501–1000
   _____ 26–50   _____ 1001–5000
   _____ 51–100   _____ over 5000
   _____ 101–500

7. What was the gross revenue for your firm in 1988? (**Check one**)
   _____ Below $200,000   _____ $11–25 million
   _____ $200,000–499,999   _____ $26–50 million
   _____ $500,000–999,999   _____ over $50 million
   _____ $1–10 million

8. Which of the following industry classifications characterizes your firm? (**Check one**)
   _____ Retail trade   _____ Construction   _____ Service
   _____ Wholesale trade   _____ Manufacturing   _____ Agriculture
   _____ Finance   _____ Durable goods   _____ Mining
   _____ Insurance   _____ Nondurable Goods   _____ Transportation
   _____ Utility   _____ Real Estate   _____ Professional
                                 _____ Communications

9. Is your firm classified as a minority-owned (51%) business?
   _____ Yes   If Yes, is the owner a:
   _____ No   _____ Woman   _____ Black   _____ Puerto Rican
                        _____ Man   _____ Hispanic   _____ Eskimo
                                             _____ Asian   _____ American Indian
                                                                  _____ Other (specify) _____
                                                                  _____

10. Is your firm classified as a small and economically disadvantaged business?
    _____ Yes   _____ No

11. Does your firm currently contract with any government?
    _____ Yes   If yes, which type? (**check all applicable**)
    _____ No
                                   _____ Federal   _____ School District
                                   _____ State   _____ Hospital District
                                   _____ City   _____ Other Special District
                                   _____ County   (specify) _____
                                   _____ Transit Authority   _____ None of the above

12. Has your firm contracted with governments in the past?
    _____ Yes   If yes, which type? (**check all applicable**)
    _____ No
                                   _____ Federal   _____ School District
                                   _____ State   _____ Hospital District
                                   _____ City   _____ Other Special District
                                   _____ County   (specify) _____
                                   _____ Transit Authority   _____ None of the above

13. Has your firm ever submitted a bid to secure a government contract and *not* been awarded the
    contract?
    _____ Yes   _____No
    If yes, why, in your opinion were your efforts unsuccessful? (**check all applicable**)
    _____ My bid was too high
    _____ My firm was judged as not having experience as a contractor
    _____ Bidding process was not genuinely competitive
    _____ It was my firm's first effort and we did not do a good job in putting the bid proposal together
    _____ We received no help or guidelines from the purchasing office in the preparation of the bid

14. Which of the following are the major reasons your firm would like to do business with government if given an opportunity? (**check all applicable**)

_____ Confident that payment will be received

_____ Predictable revenue source

_____ Firm produces service/commodity primarily used by government

_____ As a new business firm, government contracts offer an opportunity to get established

_____ Actively recruited by government purchasing staff

_____ Participation in Minority Business Enterprise program

_____ Participation in Small Business Enterprise program

_____ Have been doing business with same governments for years

_____ Good relations with government purchasing office

_____ Good relations with elected officials

_____ Purchasing procedures are efficient and easy to follow

_____ Purchasing policies are administered fairly

_____ Other (specify) _____

_____ None of the above. We do not like to do business with government.

15. Which of the following are typical problems with government contracting that might make your firm prefer **not** to contract with governments? (**check all applicable**)

_____ Slow payment cycles

_____ Reluctance to consider new products and services

_____ Confusion as to which government agency or official has the major responsibility for a specific purchasing decision

_____ Difficulty in making contact with the agency or official who will actually use the service/product

_____ Inordinate delays between bid closings and actual contracting decisions

_____ Bid specifications written too narrowly to permit real competition among potential suppliers

_____ Bid specifications written too generally and imprecisely

_____ Mandated labor costs higher than local standards

_____ Mandated minority set-aside requirements

_____ Competition from other firms pushes prices too low for our firm to compete

_____ Difficulty in competing against large firms

_____ Difficulty in competing against small firms

_____ Too many noncompetitive sole source contracts

_____ Government purchasing cycles out-of-sync with industry cycle

_____ Too much paperwork required for application

_____ Too much paperwork required once contract received

_____ Lack of a written procedures manual available to suppliers

_____ Bid bond requirement

_____ Performance bond requirement

_____ Payment bond requirement

_____ Unrealistic delivery requirements (usually too short a time frame)

_____ Absence of rigorous performance audits to weed out bad/or unethical contractors

_____ Inadequate procedures for protests and appeals

_____ Other(s) (specify) _____

_____ None of the above. We like to do business with government.

16. *Locally*, which of the following specific governments has a reputation among businesses like yours for having *poor* overall purchasing policies and procedures? (**check all applicable**)

_____ City of Tampa   _____ Pinellas School District

_____ City of St. Petersburg   _____ State of Florida

_____ Hillsborough County   _____ Federal Government

_____ Pinellas County   _____ Other

_____ Hillsborough School District   _____ None of the above

17. *In general*, which of the following levels of government has a reputation among businesses like yours for having *poor* overall purchasing policies and procedures? (**check all applicable**)

_____ City   _____ Transit Authority

_____ County   _____ Hospital District

_____ School District   _____ Other (list) _____

_____ State Government   _____ None of the above

_____ Federal Government

18. *In general*, which of the following levels of government has a reputation among businesses like yours for having *excellent* overall purchasing policies and procedures? (**check all applicable**)

_____ Federal   _____ School District

_____ State   _____ Hospital District

_____ City   _____ Other Special

_____ County   District (specify) _____

_____ Transit Authority   _____ None of the above

19. Which of the following types of government is your firm interested in doing business with? (**check all applicable**)

_____ Federal   _____ School District

_____ State   _____ Hospital District

_____ City   _____ Other Special

_____ County   District (specify) _____

_____ Transit Authority   _____ None of the above

THANK YOU FOR YOUR COOPERATION!

Return survey in the enclosed envelope **no later than August 25, 1992,** to:

Dr. Susan A. MacManus
Public Administration Program/SOC 107
University of South Florida
Tampa, Florida 33620

Survey Instrument: Business on Harris County, Texas, Vendor Mailing List

Survey
Business Views of Government Contracting Policies and Procedures

Directions: This survey is part of a national study examining private sector evaluations of government contracting policies and procedures. **It will take no more than 5 minutes of your time.** All questions require only a ✔ for an answer.

1. Businesses like yours generally believe that government purchasing policies and procedures are effective in attracting first rate vendors to compete for contracts.

   _____ Yes   _____ No   _____ No opinion

2. Businesses like yours believe that government purchasing policies and procedures result in government purchases of quality goods & services at the lowest cost.

   _____ Yes   _____ No   _____ No opinion

3. Businesses like yours believe that government policies and procedures are fair and impartial.

   _____ Yes   _____ No   _____ No opinion

4. What is the structure of your firm? (**Check one**)

   _____ Individual owner   _____ Nonprofit organization
   _____ Partnership   _____ Corporation
                                        _____ Other (specify) _____

5. How many years has your firm been in business? (**Check one**)

   _____ Less than 1 year
   _____ 1–2 years
   _____ 3–5 years
   _____ 6–10 years
   _____ over 10 years

6. How many employees does your firm have? (**Check one**)

   _____ 1–25   _____ 501–1000
   _____ 26–50   _____ 1001–5000
   _____ 51–100   _____ over 5000
   _____ 101–500

7. What was the gross revenue for your firm in 1988? (**Check one**)

   _____ Below $200,000   _____ $11–25 million
   _____ $200,000–499,999   _____ $26–50 million
   _____ $500,000–999,999   _____ over $50 million
   _____ $1–10 million

8. Which of the following industry classifications characterizes your firm? (**Check one**)

   _____ Retail trade   _____ Construction   _____ Service
   _____ Wholesale trade   _____ Manufacturing   _____ Agriculture
   _____ Finance   _____ Durable goods   _____ Mining
   _____ Insurance   _____ Nondurable Goods   _____ Transportation
   _____ Utility   _____ Real Estate   _____ Professional
                                _____ Communications

9. Is your firm classified as a minority-owned (51%) business?

_____ Yes ➤ If Yes, is the owner a:
_____ No   _____ Woman
                 _____ Man   _____ Black   _____ Puerto Rican
                                      _____ Hispanic   _____ Eskimo
                                      _____ Asian   _____ American Indian
                                                             _____ Other (specify) _____

10. Is your firm classified as a small and economically disadvantaged business?
_____ Yes   _____ No

11. Does your firm currently contract with any government?
_____ Yes
_____ No ➤ If no, has your firm contracted with governments in the past?
              _____ Yes   _____ No

12. Which of the following types of government does your firm currently do business with? (**check all applicable**)
_____ Federal   _____ School District
_____ State   _____ Hospital District
_____ City   _____ Other Special
_____ County   District (specify) _____
_____ Transit Authority   _____ None of the above

13. What percentage of your firm's gross revenue is currently generated from government contracts? (**Check one**)
_____ Less than 10%   _____ 51–75%
_____ 10–25%   _____ 76–90%
_____ 26–50%   _____ over 90%

14. Through which of the following procedures has your firm secured a government contract? (**check all applicable**)
_____ Formal competitive bidding with negotiation
_____ Formal competitive bid (sealed)
_____ Local vendor preference policy
_____ Request for proposal (RFP/Competitive negotiation)
_____ Government solicitation of a written quote from your firm
_____ Government solicitation of a telephone quote from your firm
_____ Through participation in a Minority Business Enterprise program
_____ Through participation in a Small Business program
_____ Other (specify) _____

15. How would you categorize the nature of work you deliver to government? (**check all applicable**)
_____ Service
_____ Commodity/Good
_____ Construction

16. Which of the following are the major reasons your firm does business with government (**check all applicable**)
_____ Confident that payment will be received
_____ Predictable revenue source
_____ Firm produces service/commodity primarily used by government
_____ As a new business firm, government contracts offer an opportunity to get established

_____ Actively recruited by government purchasing staff
_____ Participation in Minority Business Enterprise program
_____ Participation in Small Business Enterprise program
_____ Have been doing business with same governments for years
_____ Good relations with government purchasing office
_____ Good relations with elected officials
_____ Purchasing procedures are efficient and easy to follow
_____ Purchasing policies are administered fairly
_____ Other (specify) _____

17. Which of the following does your firm frequently encounter in contracting with governments? **(check all applicable)**
_____ Slow payment cycles
_____ Reluctance to consider new products and services
_____ Confusion as to which government agency or official has the major responsibility for a specific purchasing decision
_____ Difficulty in making contact with the agency or official who will actually use the service/product
_____ Inordinate delays between bid closings and actual contracting decisions
_____ Bid specifications written too narrowly to permit real competition among potential suppliers
_____ Bid specifications written too generally and imprecisely
_____ Mandated labor costs higher than local standards
_____ Mandated minority set-aside requirements
_____ Competition from other firms pushes prices too low for our firm to compete
_____ Difficulty in competing against large firms
_____ Difficulty in competing against small firms
_____ Too many noncompetitive sole source contracts
_____ Government purchasing cycles out-of-sync with industry cycle
_____ Too much paperwork required for application
_____ Too much paperwork required once contract received
_____ Lack of a written procedures manual available to suppliers
_____ Bid bond requirement
_____ Performance bond requirement
_____ Payment bond requirement
_____ Unrealistic delivery requirements (usually too short a time frame)
_____ Absence of rigorous performance audits to weed out bad/or unethical contractors
_____ Inadequate procedures for protests and appeals
_____ Other(s) (specify) _____

18. What is the average time it takes for your firm to get reimbursed by each of these governments **(check all applicable)**

	Government				
	Harris County	City of Houston	School District	State of Texas	Fed. Govt.
1–30 days	_____	_____	_____	_____	_____
31–60 days	_____	_____	_____	_____	_____
61–90 days	_____	_____	_____	_____	_____
over 60 days	_____	_____	_____	_____	_____
over 90 days	_____	_____	_____	_____	_____

19. From your own experience and experiences of other firms like yours, how do you rate the overall purchasing policies and procedures of each of the following governments?

| | Government | | | | |
Rating	Harris County	City of Houston	School District	State of Texas	Fed. Govt.
Excellent	____	____	____	____	____
Good	____	____	____	____	____
Fair	____	____	____	____	____
Poor	____	____	____	____	____

20. Which of the following types of government is your firm **not** interested in doing business with?

_____ Federal _____ School District
_____ State _____ Hospital District
_____ City _____ Other Special
_____ County District (specify) _____
_____ Transit Authority _____ None of the above

THANK YOU FOR YOUR COOPERATION!

Return survey in the enclosed envelope **no later than May 15, 1992,** to:

Dr. Susan A. MacManus
Research Associate
Rice Institute for Policy Analysis
Rice University
Post Office Box 1892
Houston, TX 77251

Survey Instrument: Business on Hillsborough County, Florida, Vendor Mailing List

Survey
Business Views of Government Contracting Policies and Procedures

Directions: This survey is part of a national study examining private sector evaluations of government contracting policies and procedures. **Even if your firm does not do business with government, we are interested in your opinions. It will take no more than 5 minutes of your time.** All questions require only a ✔ for an answer.

1. Businesses like yours generally believe that government purchasing policies and procedures are effective in attracting first rate vendors to compete for contracts.
   _____ Yes   _____ No   _____ No opinion

2. Businesses like yours believe that government purchasing policies and procedures result in government purchases of quality goods & services at the lowest cost.
   _____ Yes   _____ No   _____ No opinion

3. Businesses like yours believe that government policies and procedures are fair and impartial.
   _____ Yes   _____ No   _____ No opinion

4. What is the structure of your firm? (**Check one**)
_____ Individual owner   _____ Nonprofit organization
_____ Partnership   _____ Corporation
                              _____ Other (specify) _____

5. How many years has your firm been in business? (**Check one**)
_____ Less than 1 year
_____ 1–2 years
_____ 3–5 years
_____ 6–10 years
_____ over 10 years

6. How many employees does your firm have? (**Check one**)
_____ 1–25   _____ 501–1000
_____ 26–50   _____ 1001–5000
_____ 51–100   _____ over 5000
_____ 101–500

7. What was the gross revenue for your firm in 1988? (**Check one**)
_____ Below $200,000   _____ $11–25 million
_____ $200,000–499,999   _____ $26–50 million
_____ $500,000–999,999   _____ over $50 million
_____ $1–10 million

8. Which of the following industry classifications characterizes your firm? (**Check one**)
_____ Retail trade   _____ Construction   _____ Service
_____ Wholesale trade   Manufacturing   _____ Agriculture
_____ Finance   _____ Durable goods   _____ Mining
_____ Insurance   _____ Nondurable Goods   _____ Transportation
_____ Utility   _____ Real Estate   _____ Professional
                          _____ Communications

9. Is your firm classified as a minority-owned (51%) business?

_____ Yes ➔ | If Yes, is the owner a:
_____ No | _____ Woman   _____ Black   _____ Puerto Rican
              | _____ Man   _____ Hispanic   _____ Eskimo
              | _____ Asian   _____ American Indian
              | _____ Other (specify) _____
              | _____

10. Is your firm classified as a small and economically disadvantaged business?
_____ Yes   _____ No

11. Does your firm currently contract with any government?

_____ Yes ➔ | If Yes, which type? (**Check all applicable**)
_____ No | _____ Federal   _____ School District
              | _____ State   _____ Hospital District
              | _____ City   _____ Other Special District
              | _____ County   (specify) _____
              | _____ Transit Authority   _____ None of the above

12. Has your firm contracted with governments in the past?

_____ Yes ➤ If Yes, which type? (**Check all applicable**)
_____ No

_____ Federal	_____ School District
_____ State	_____ Hospital District
_____ City	_____ Other Special District
_____ County	(specify) _____
_____ Transit Authority	_____ None of the above

13. Has your firm ever submitted a bid to secure a government contract and *not* been awarded the contract?

_____ Yes   _____ No

If yes, why, in your opinion were your efforts unsuccessful? (**check all applicable**)
_____ My bid was too high
_____ My firm was judged as not having experience as a contractor
_____ Bidding process was not genuinely competitive
_____ It was my firm's first effort and we did not do a good job in putting the bid proposal together
_____ We received no help or guidelines from the purchasing office in the preparation of the bid

14. Which of the following are the major reasons your firm would like to do business with government if given an opportunity? (**check all applicable**)
_____ Confident that payment will be received
_____ Predictable revenue source
_____ Firm produces service/commodity primarily used by government
_____ As a new business firm, government contracts offer an opportunity to get established
_____ Actively recruited by government purchasing staff
_____ Participation in Minority Business Enterprise program
_____ Participation in Small Business Enterprise program
_____ Have been doing business with same governments for years
_____ Good relations with government purchasing office
_____ Good relations with elected officials
_____ Purchasing procedures are efficient and easy to follow
_____ Purchasing policies are administered fairly
_____ Other (specify) _____
_____ None of the above. We do not like to do business with government.

15. Which of the following are typical problems with government contracting that might make your firm prefer **not** to contract with governments? (**check all applicable**)
_____ Slow payment cycles
_____ Reluctance to consider new products and services
_____ Confusion as to which government agency or official has the major responsibility for a specific purchasing decision
_____ Difficulty in making contact with the agency or official who will actually use the service/product
_____ Inordinate delays between bid closings and actual contracting decisions
_____ Bid specifications written too narrowly to permit real competition among potential suppliers
_____ Bid specifications written too generally and imprecisely

_____ Mandated labor costs higher than local standards
_____ Mandated minority set-aside requirements
_____ Competition from other firms pushes prices too low for our firm to compete
_____ Difficulty in competing against large firms
_____ Difficulty in competing against small firms
_____ Too many noncompetitive sole source contracts
_____ Government purchasing cycles out-of-sync with industry cycle
_____ Too much paperwork required for application
_____ Too much paperwork required once contract received
_____ Lack of a written procedures manual available to suppliers
_____ Bid bond requirement
_____ Performance bond requirement
_____ Payment bond requirement
_____ Unrealistic delivery requirements (usually too short a time frame)
_____ Absence of rigorous performance audits to weed out bad/or unethical contractors
_____ Inadequate procedures for protests and appeals
_____ Other(s) (specify) _____
_____ None of the above. We like to do business with government.

16. *Locally*, which of the following specific governments has a reputation among businesses like yours for having *poor* overall purchasing policies and procedures? (**check all applicable**)

_____ City of Tampa	_____ Pinellas School District
_____ City of St. Petersburg	_____ State of Florida
_____ Hillsborough County	_____ Federal Government
_____ Pinellas County	_____ Other
_____ Hillsborough School District	_____ None of the above

17. *In general*, which of the following levels of government has a reputation among businesses like yours for having *poor* overall purchasing policies and procedures? (**check all applicable**)

_____ City	_____ Transit Authority
_____ County	_____ Hospital District
_____ School District	_____ Other (list) _____
_____ State Government	_____ None of the above
_____ Federal Government	

18. *In general*, which of the following levels of government has a reputation among businesses like yours for having *excellent* overall purchasing policies and procedures? (**check all applicable**)

_____ Federal	_____ School District
_____ State	_____ Hospital District
_____ City	_____ Other Special
_____ County	District (specify) _____
_____ Transit Authority	_____ None of the above

19. Which of the following types of government is your firm interested in doing business with? (**check all applicable**)

_____ Federal	_____ School District
_____ State	_____ Hospital District
_____ City	_____ Other Special
_____ County	District (specify) _____
_____ Transit Authority	_____ None of the above

THANK YOU FOR YOUR COOPERATION!

Return survey in the enclosed envelope **no later than August 3, 1992,** to:

Dr. Susan A. MacManus
Public Administration Program/SOC 107
University of South Florida
Tampa, Florida 33620

Breakdown of Respondent Characteristics: Survey of Firms on Hillsborough County, Florida, and Harris County, Texas, Vendor Lists

Table B.1
Breakdown of Respondent Characteristics: Survey of Firms on Hillsborough County, Florida, and Harris County, Texas, Vendor Lists, 1989

Characteristics	Hillsborough Co. Florida (n = 2576) %	Harris Co. Texas (n = 706) %
Firm Structure		
Individual owner	13.0%	11.6%
Partnership	3.1	2.8
Nonprofit organ.	1.1	5.2
Corporation	81.6	78.3
Other	0.4	0.4
Not reported	0.8	1.6
Yrs. in Business		
Less than 1 yr.	2.0%	0.6%
1–2 yrs.	7.4	2.1
3–5 yrs.	16.5	6.9
6–10 yrs.	17.0	10.5
Over 10 yrs.	56.9	79.3
Not reported	0.2	0.6
No. of Employees		
1–25	60.6%	54.1%
26–50	12.9	12.0
51–100	8.0	8.9
101–500	9.5	13.5
501–1000	2.1	3.7
1001–5000	3.7	3.5
Over 5000	2.7	3.3
Not reported	0.4	1.0
Firm Gross Rev. ('88)		
Below $200,000	17.9%	12.2%
$200,000–499,999	14.5	13.3
$500,000–999,999	13.6	12.6
$1–$10 Million	31.6	35.1
$11–$25 Million	6.7	6.9
$26–$50 Million	3.0	4.4
Over $50 Million	8.9	10.3
Not reported	3.8	5.1
Industry Classification		
Retail trade	13.9%	17.6%
Wholesale trade	13.7	15.6
Finance	0.5	0.4
Insurance	0.3	0.1
Utility	0.3	8.6
Construction	15.6	3.3
Manufacturing	0.9	9.8
Manufacturing-durable	7.0	3.8

Breakdown of Respondent Characteristics: Survey of Firms on Hillsborough County, Florida, and Harris County, Texas, Vendor Lists, 1989

Characteristics	Hillsborough Co. Florida (n = 2576) %	Harris Co. Texas (n = 706) %
Industry Classification		
Manufacturing-nondurable	2.4%	2.3%
Real estate	0.8	4.8
Communications	2.4	14.4
Service	17.5	0.6
Agriculture	1.0	0.3
Mining	0.2	2.0
Transportation	1.4	6.5
Professional service	7.9	0.1
Not reported	14.4	9.8
Owner		
Minority-owned	22.8%	13.0%
Not minority owned	75.1	84.1
Not reported	2.1	2.8
Minority Owner-Gender[1]	(n = 587)	(n = 88)
Female	54.2%	63.6%
Male	20.8	18.8
Not reported	25.0	21.6
Minority Owner-Race[1]	(n = 583)	(n = 89)
Black	19.7%	14.6%
Hispanic	23.3	7.0
Puerto Rican	1.4	0
Asian	5.1	10.1
American Indian	2.2	2.2
Other	1.9	5.6
None of the above/not report. (includes Caucasians—Female)	53.6	58.4
Size-Econ. Class.		
Small econ. disadv.	22.4%	19.1%
Not small econ. dis.	74.5	75.8
No response	3.1	5.1
Current Contract Status		
Has contract w/ govt.	71.6%	64.7%
No contract w/ govt.	25.1	31.0
No response	3.3	4.2
No. Govt. Contract Presently[2]	(n = 562)	(n = 212)
Have had one in past	51.8%	61.8
Have not had one in past	48.2	38.2

Table B.1 (*continued*)
Breakdown of Respondent Characteristics: Survey of Firms on Hillsborough County, Florida, and Harris County, Texas, Vendor Lists, 1989

Characteristics	Hillsborough Co. Florida (n = 2576) %	Harris Co. Texas (n = 706) %
Level of Govt. Firm Does Business		
With (Mult. Resp.)		
Federal	46.3%	51.3%
State	62.2	61.8
City	69.4	66.1
County	74.8	65.2
Transit authority	22.4	25.8
School district	49.2	58.2
Hospital district	22.9	32.4
Other spec. district	5.9	7.5
None of the above	8.3	7.1
Total of Gross Rev. from Govt.		
Contracts		
Less than 10%	50.7%	58.2%
10–25%	19.3	16.6
26–50%	10.0	6.5
51–75%	6.1	4.4
76–90%	4.0	2.1
Over 90%	3.9	4.0
No response	6.1	8.2
Procedure for Getting Govt.		
Contracts (Mult. Resp.)		
Formal competitive bid (with negotiation)	29.0%	22.8%
Formal competitive bid (sealed)	67.5	56.2
Local vendor preference	20.8	17.4
Request for Proposal		
(competitive negotiation)	27.8	19.8
Govt. solicitation of written quote	36.0	37.7
Govt. solicitation of telephone quote	25.6	26.3
Participation in Min. Business		
Enterprise program	5.2	2.0
Participation in Small Business program	4.3	3.3
Other procedure	4.8	6.9
No response		
Type of Product Delivered to Government		
(Mult. Resp.)		
Service	50.7%	39.7%
Commodity/good	49.5	59.3
Construction	20.8	11.9

Notes:
[1] Question was answered only by the subset of the respondents meeting the definitional criteria (minority owned firm).

[2] Question was answered only by the subset of the respondents meeting the definitional criteria (firm does not have a government contract at the present).

Mult. Resp.: Question asked the respondent to "check all applicable". Because of multiple responses, totals for the question add to greater than 100 percent.

Sources: Random sample mail survey of businesses on the Harris County, Texas vendor mailing list (conducted May–June, 1989). Survey of all businesses on Hillsborough County, Florida vendor registration list (conducted June–July, 1989).

Outline of Contents of Model Procurement Codes (American Bar Association; National Institute of Municipal Law Officers)

SUMMARY TABLE OF CONTENTS

CHAPTER 2 — PROCUREMENT ORGANIZATION

CHAPTER 3 — SOURCE SELECTION AND CONTRACT FORMATION

Regulation 3-502 — Approval of Accounting Systems

Regulation 3-503 — Multi-Term Contracts

CHAPTER 4 — SPECIFICATIONS

Regulation 4-101 — Definitions

Regulation 4-201 — General Provisions

Regulation 4-202 — Chief Procurement Officer's Responsibilities

CHAPTER 5 — PROCUREMENT OF CONSTRUCTION, ARCHITECT-ENGINEER AND LAND SURVEYING SERVICES

Regulation 5-301 — Bid Bonds

Regulation 5-302 — Performance and Payment Bonds

CHAPTER 6 — MODIFICATION AND TERMINATION OF CONTRACTS FOR SUPPLIES AND SERVICES

Regulation 6-101 — Contract Clauses for Supply and
Service Contracts

CHAPTER 7 — COST PRINCIPLES

Regulation 7-101 — Cost Principles

CHAPTER 8 — SUPPLY MANAGEMENT

Regulation 8-101 — Definitions

Regulation 8-201 — Supply Management and Disposition

Regulation 8-301 — Disposition of Proceeds

CHAPTER 9 — LEGAL AND CONTRACTUAL REMEDIES

Regulation 9-101 — Protest Resolution by the Chief Procurement Officer
or the Head of a Purchasing Agency

CHAPTER 10 — INTERGOVERNMENTAL RELATIONS

CHAPTER 11 — ASSISTANCE TO SMALL AND DISADVANTAGED BUSINESSES; FEDERAL ASSISTANCE OR CONTRACT PROCUREMENT REQUIREMENTS

CHAPTER 12 — ETHICS IN PUBLIC CONTRACTING

Regulation 12-101 — Definitions

Regulation 12-201 — Statement of Policy

Regulation 12-202 — General Standards of Ethical Conduct

Regulation 12-203 — Criminal Sanctions

Regulation 12-204 — Conflict of Interest

Regulation 12-205 — Disclosure of Benefit from Contract

Regulation 12-206 — Gratuities and Kickbacks

Regulation 12-207 — Contingent Fees

Regulation 12-208 — Employment Prohibitions and Restrictions

Regulation 12-209 — Use of Confidential Information

Regulation 12-301 — Civil and Administrative Remedies Against Employees Who Breach Ethical Standards

APPENDICES

Table of Contents

Page

Appendix 9-506 — Rules of Procedure of the Procurement Appeals Board
for the Protest of Solicitations or Awards

Appendix 9-508 — Rules of Procedure of the Procurement Appeals Board for the Resolution of Contract and Breach of Contract Controversies

APPENDIX 10 — INTERGOVERNMENTAL RELATIONS

Appendix 10-201 — Cooperative Purchasing Agreements

Appendix 10-203 — Agreement for Cooperative Use of Services

Appendix 10-204 — Agreements for Joint Use of Facilities

Appendix 10-205 — Agreements to Supply Personnel, Information, and
Technical Services

Appendix 10-301 — Agreement Designating State Procurement Appeals Board
to Hear and Resolve Controversies

Source: American Bar Association, Section of Urban, State and Local Government Law and Section of Public
Contract Law, *The Model Procurement Code for State and Local Governments*. Chicago, IL: American Bar
Association, 1981. Reprinted with permission of the American Bar Association.

TABLE OF CONTENTS

ARTICLE 2—OFFICE OF THE PURCHASING AGENT

ARTICLE 3—SOURCE SELECTION AND CONTRACT FORMATION

Part A—Methods of Source Selection

Part B—Qualifications and Duties

Part C—Types of Contracts and Contract Administration

ARTICLE 4—SPECIFICATIONS

ARTICLE 5—PROCUREMENT OF CONSTRUCTION, ARCHITECT-ENGINEER AND LAND SURVEYING SERVICES

Part A—Management of Construction Contracting

Part B—Bid Security and Performance Bonds

Part C—Fiscal Responsibility

Part D—Architect-Engineer and Land Surveying Services

ARTICLE 6—DEBARMENT OR SUSPENSION

ARTICLE 7—COST PRINCIPLES
[Reserved]

ARTICLE 8—SUPPLY MANAGEMENT
[Reserved]

ARTICLE 9—APPEALS AND REMEDIES

ARTICLE 10—COOPERATIVE PURCHASING
[Reserved]

ARTICLE 11—ASSISTANCE TO SMALL AND DISADVANTAGED BUSINESSES
[Reserved]

ARTICLE 12—ETHICS IN PUBLIC CONTRACTING

APPENDIX—PROCUREMENT UNDER FEDERAL ASSISTANCE AGREEMENTS

Source: American Bar Association, Section of Public Contract Law and Section of Urban, State and Local Government Law. *The Model Procurement Ordinance for Local Governments.* Chicago, IL: American Bar Association, August, 1982. Reprinted with permission by the American Bar Association.

National Institute of Municipal Law Officers

NIMLO MODEL PURCHASING ORDINANCE— ANNOTATED

TABLE OF CONTENTS

NIMLO MODEL PURCHASING ORDINANCE—
ANNOTATED*

[EDITOR'S NOTE: Nearly one-third of the expenditures for current operations of the average municipality are made for procuring the supplies, materials, equipment and contractual services necessary to carry on its various activities. In an effort to bring efficiency to this tremendous volume of governmental buying municipalities are adopting the techniques of centralized purchasing which American industry has employed so successfully. The authorities are agreed that installation of the sound procurement methods which centralized purchasing stands for can bring savings to a municipality of not less than 15 per cent.

Modern, centralized purchasing embodies the following essential principles:

1. Centralization of authority over purchases.
2. Employment of competent purchasing personnel.
3. Standardization and specification to reduce commodities to a minimum and assure the quality of goods.
4. Consolidation of requirements into bulk purchases in order to obtain quantity prices.
5. Stimulation of competitive bidding to reduce prices.
6. Inspection and testing of goods delivered to enforce compliance with specifications and terms of contracts.
7. Centralized control over supplies in storerooms and warehouses.
8. Centralized control over excess, obsolete and salvage goods.
9. Market analysis, assuring purchases when market conditions are favorable.
10. Prompt payment of all bills, thereby earning cash discounts.
11. Transfer of usable supplies from one using agency to another.
12. Reduction of unnecessary sales effort and expense.
13. Elimination of unnecessary purchases.
14. Elimination of unnecessary paper work.
15. Elimination of favoritism and connivance in public purchasing.

The NIMLO Model Purchasing Ordinance constitutes an effort on the part of the National Institute of Municipal Law Officers, in cooperation with the National Institute of Governmental Purchasing, to assist municipalities in adopting centralization techniques by making available to them ''guide'' provisions based on the principles enumerated above.

It is recommended that the NIMLO Model Purchasing Ordinance be read in conjunction with three important NIMLO companion studies:

(1) *The Law of Municipal Contracts—With Annotated Model Forms,* 1952. An outline of the *law of the field* in which city purchasing agents work.

(2) Generally, Rhyne, MUNICIPAL LAW (1957).

(3) *The NIMLO Model Administrative Code.* Section 1-301 of the **NIMLO MODEL ORDINANCE SERVICE.** An ordinance prescribing **administrative policy and procedures and setting forth the general powers and duties of city officials.**

The annotations accompanying this Model Ordinance are a departure from normal Model Ordinance Service policy, and are offered in order to acquaint the purchasing novice with some of the ramifications of policy and method underlying a given provision.

It is generally recommended that ordinance provisions concerned with purchasing be flexible, including only broad requirements and authorizations with power in the Purchasing Agent to work out the myriad details. Where the Model appears more particularized than might be advisable, it

---

* See annotations immediately following ordinance.

will in many instances, be the result of an effort to thus acquaint the reader with a suggested consideration.

An Ordinance Establishing a Department of Purchases in the Administrative Service of the City of ....;[1] Creating the Office of City Purchasing Agent; Setting Forth the Powers and Duties of the City Purchasing Agent; Creating a Committee on Standardization and Specifications; Establishing Purchasing Procedures; and Prescribing Penalties for the Violation of Its Provisions.[2]

BE IT ORDAINED BY THE COUNCIL OF THE CITY OF ....:

---

[1] Information for blank spaces found herein must be supplied, and all reference to bodies and officials must be revised, according to the governing facts and requirements of the given municipality.

[2] The titles of the ordinances studied in preparing this model ordinance varied in accordance with the requirements of constitutional, charter or legislative provisions covering each particular city. Attorneys for each city must therefore rewrite the title of the model ordinance so as to satisfy any local, constitutional, charter or statutory directive requiring that every provision of an ordinance be specifically indicated in its title.

Source: National Institute of Municipal Law Officers, 1000 Connecticut Avenue, N.W., Suite 902, Washington, D.C. 20036. Reprinted by permission of the National Institute of Municipal Law Officers.

Federal Prompt Pay Regulations Summary Model State Prompt Pay Law

SUMMARY OF FEDERAL PROMPT PAY REGULATIONS

On March 31, 1989, the final rules for implementing the Prompt Payment Act Amendments of 1988 were published in the *Federal Acquisition Regulation* (FAR).

The following is a summary of those regulations. To order a copy of the regulations, see **Order Form for Additional Copies of This Report and Additional Publications** at the end of this book.

Applicability of the Prompt Pay Rules

The new rules apply to all contracts awarded, renewed, and options exercised on or after April 1, 1989.

Foreign Vendors Excluded
From Interest Provisions of the Act
[FAR:32.901]

Contracts awarded to foreign vendors doing business outside the U.S. are not covered by the interest penalty provisions.

Elimination of All "Grace" Periods
[FAR:32.907-1(a)(4)]

In accordance with the Prompt Pay Act Amendments of 1988, all "grace" periods have been eliminated. "Grace" periods are the extra days beyond the normal 30, 10 or 7 days Federal agencies have to pay their bills before interest payments are due. (This was accomplished by removing all references to the 15 extra days on 30-day invoices and the 3 and 5 extra days on the 7-day and 10-day invoices.)

Temporary Unavailability of Funds No Excuse
for Nonpayment of Interest
[FAR: 32.903]

If an agency is temporarily out of funds to make payments, the agency must pay the late interest penalty when funds become available.

Determination of the 30-Day Payment Due Date
[FAR: 32.905(a)]

Due Date of an invoice is:

(1) The 30th day from the date the designated billing office receives a proper invoice or the 30th day after Government acceptance of goods or services, whichever is later, or

(2) The 30th day from the date of the invoice if the designated billing office fails to date-stamp the invoice on the date it was first received.

Constructive Acceptance
or the 7-Day Acceptance Period
[FAR: 32.905(a)(ii)]

"Constructive acceptance" is a term used to describe the 7 extra days given to the government to accept goods or services after delivery before the 30-day payment "clock" begins. This actually gives the government 38 days to pay an invoice if acceptance of the goods or services occurs after the proper invoice is received and properly date-stamped.

For "constructive acceptance" to occur in 7 or less days, there must be no disagreement over quantity, quality or contract compliance.

If the government accepts the goods or services before the end of the 7-day constructive acceptance period, then the 30-day payment clock begins on the date of acceptance (if this occurs after receipt of a proper invoice that has been properly date-stamped).

The government may take more than 7 days to receive goods and services, but unless this longer period has been negotiated into the contract, the time clock begins 7 days after delivery. The contract file must indicate the reasons for extending the constructive acceptance period beyond 7 days.

The government cannot take longer than 7 days to accept brand-name commercial items which are to be resold (in commissaries, etc.).

On final invoices where payment is subject to contract settlement actions, acceptance occurs on the date of the contract settlement.

Due Date When No Invoice Is Required
If the contract does not require an invoice, the due date is as specified in the contract.

Payment Date
[FAR:32.902 Definitions and Proposed Circular A-125:4.l.]

The payment date is the date written on the payment check or the date on which an electronic funds transfer is made. The proposed Circular A-125 further defines the electronic funds transfer date by providing that the funds must be received by the contractor's financial institution on the "established due date."

Other Payment Due Dates
[FAR:32.905(d)]

Meat and Fresh Eggs
The due date for meat or meat food products, including any edible fresh or frozen poultry meat or poultry food products, fresh eggs and any perishable egg products is the 7th day after delivery.

Perishable Agricultural Commodities
The due date for perishable agricultural commodities is the 10th day after delivery, unless another date is specified in the contract.

Dairy and Edible Oils
The due date for dairy products, edible fats or oils and food products prepared from edible oils is the 10th day after the date on which a proper invoice has been received.

Proper Invoice
[FAR:32.905(e)]

A proper invoice must include the following:
(1) Name and address of the contractor
(2) Invoice date
(3) Contract number or other authorization
(4) Description of goods or services
(5) Shipping and payment terms
(6) Name and address of contractor official to whom payment is to be sent — must be same person as that in contract
(7) Name (where practicable), title, phone number and mailing address of person to be notified in event of a defective invoice
(8) Any other information or documentation required by the contract

Notification of an Improper Invoice
[FAR:32.905(e)]

If an invoice is missing required information, the designated billing office must notify the contractor within 7 days after the receipt of the invoice. For meat and meat products this notification period is 3 days; for perishable agricultural commodities, dairy products, edible fats or oils and food products this notification period is 5 days.

The reason that the invoice is improper or defective must be included in this notification.

Interest Penalty
[FAR:32.907-1]

Interest To Be Paid Automatically [32.907.1(a)]
Interest must be paid automatically without a request from the contractor when:
(1) A proper invoice was received

(2) Receiving report was processed and there was no disagreement over quantity, quality or contract compliance
(3) In the case of a final invoice, the payment amount was not subject to further contract actions between the Government and the contractor
(4) Payment was made after the due date

Periods for Which Government Will Not Pay Interest
The Government will not pay interest for:
[32.907-1(b)]
(1) The time taken to notify the contractor of a defective invoice (unless this time exceeds 7 days after the receipt of an invoice)
(2) The time taken by the contractor to correct the invoice

Interest is not due under the Prompt Payment Act [32.907-1(e)]:
(1) After contractor files claim under the Contract Disputes Act
(2) For more than one year

Other Circumstances Under Which Interest Is Not Due:
(1) If penalty is less than one dollar ($1.00). [FAR:32.907-1(e)]
(2) On disputed invoices or on amounts temporarily withheld or retained in accordance with the terms of the contract. Claims involving disputes, and any interest due to the contractor, are to be resolved in accordance with the Contract Disputes Act. [FAR:32.907-1(f)]

Failure to Notify Contractor of Defective Invoice Within Time Designated [FAR:32.907-1(b)]
If the designated payment office fails to notify the contractor of a defective invoice within time permitted for the specific contract, then the amount of days taken beyond the specified time is subtracted from the number of days in the payment due date. (e.g. If an agency takes 10 days to notify a contractor on a 30-day payment period, then 3 days are subtracted from 30 days giving the agency 27 days to pay the invoice — after the agency receives a corrected invoice.)

Interest to Be Paid Automatically on Improperly Taken Discount [FAR: 32.907-1(c)]
If the Government agency takes a discount after the date for taking such a discount, the Government must automatically pay an interest penalty from the date after the expiration of the discount until the date the contractor is paid.

Effective Interest Rate [FAR:32.907-1(d)]
The interest to be paid is the "Renegotiation Board Interest Rate" in effect on the day after payment is due and is to be paid during the entire period for

which interest is due. Interest is compounded monthly.

This interest rate is published semiannually in the *Federal Register* on or about January 1 and July 1 of each year. This rate can be obtained by calling 202/566-5651.

Notice to Accompany Late Payment [FAR:32.907-1(d)]
Effective October 1, 1989, all late payments must be accompanied with a notice stating:
(1) Amount of interest paid
(2) Interest rate
(3) Period for which interest is being paid

[NOTE: The FAR has this provision effective April 1, 1989. The Office of Management and Budget's (OMB) Circular A-125 has this provision effective October 1, 1989.]

No Interest Due on Late Contract Financing Payments
[FAR: 32.907-2]
Interest is not due on late contract financing payments. Contract financing payments, as used in this section of the FAR, are payments to a contractor before government acceptance of supplies or services. Contract financing payments do not include invoice payments or payments for partial deliveries. [FAR:32.902]

Date to be Used When Taking Discounts
[FAR:52.232-8(b)]
When taking a discount, the discount period must be calculated from the date of the invoice. In other words, the contractor determines both when the discount period begins and ends.

Added Penalty for Nonpayment of Interest
[FAR:32.907-1(g)]
If the Government agency fails to pay the interest penalty automatically, the contractor is due, in addition to the interest penalty, an added penalty if:
(1) He is owed an interest penalty
(2) The Government agency does not pay the interest penalty within 10 days after the date the invoice is paid, i.e., the date of the check
(3) The contractor makes a written demand not later than 40 days after the date of the check

[NOTE: The FAR has this provision effective October 1, 1989. However, OMB has this provision effective 30 days after the publication of the final Circular A-125.]

Calculation of the Penalty
The Prompt Payment Act Amendments of 1989 gave OMB the authority to set the added penalty for nonpayment of the interest penalty.

In its proposed revision of Circular A-125 [*Federal Register,* April 14, 1989, Section 11.(b), page 15060] OMB set the rates at:
(1) Fifty percent of the original late payment interest penalty for the period April 1, 1989 through September 30, 1989
(2) One hundred percent of the original late payment interest penalty beginning October 1, 1989.

Since this was the proposed revision of the circular and the not the final circular, contractors should call OMB at 202/395-3066 to obtain the latest information on the amount of the added penalty. Additionally, this provision is effective 30 days after the publication of the final version of Circular A-125, in the summer of 1989.

Help for Small Businesses
[FAR:32.909 and 19.201(c)(5)]
Small businesses may obtain additional help in getting their bills paid, interest due or information on the Prompt Payment Act from their local Office of Small and Disadvantaged Business. For this information call 1/800/368-5855 or 1/202/634-7532.

Contractor Inquiries
[FAR:32.909]
All questions concerning late payments should be directed to the designated billing office or designated payment office.

All questions concerning payment amounts and timing of payments should be directed to the contracting officer.

Fast Payment Procedure
[FAR:52.232-25(c)]
Due date for payment under the "Fast Payment Procedure" is 15 days after the receipt of the invoice.

Fast Payment Procedure [FAR:13.3]
This procedure is to be used for small purchases (under $25,000). In addition:
(1) Title vests in Government upon:
(a) Delivery to Post Office or Common Carrier or
(b) Receipt by Government if shipment is by means other than Postal Service or Common Carrier
(2) Contractor agrees to replace, repair or correct damaged supplies, or supplies not conforming to contract

Fast Payment Procedure is utilized when there is a geographic separation between the disbursing and receiving activities.

Partial Payment for Partial Delivery
[FAR:32.903 and Proposed Circular A-125: 8.a.(2)]

Government agencies must pay for partial deliveries unless the contract specifically prohibits such payment.

Due Dates for Payments for Fixed-Price Architect-Engineer Contracts
[FAR:32.905(b)]

For invoice payments the due date is:
 (1) The later of:
  (a) The 30th day from the day the designated billing office receives a proper invoice, or
  (b) The 30th day after Government approval of contractor estimates of work or services performed (includes the definition of "constructive acceptance" as described under **Determination of the 30-Day Payment Due Date**), or
 (2) The 30th day from the date of the invoice if Government fails to date-stamp invoice

For progress payments:
 (1) The 30th day after Government approval of contractor estimates of work or services. (Includes the definition of "constructive acceptance" as described under **Determination of the 30-Day Payment Due Date**.)
 (2) The 30th day from the date of the invoice if Government fails to date-stamp invoice

Due Dates for Construction Contracts
[FAR:32.905(c)]:

The due date for progress payments to prime contractors under construction contracts is:
 (1) The 14th day from the receipt of a proper payment request, or
 (2) The 14th day from the date of the payment request if the Government fails to date-stamp the invoice

A longer period may be specified in the solicitation and contract if more time is needed to adequately inspect work. The contract file must specify the reasons for extending the due date beyond 14 days.

Additionally, progress payment requests cannot be approved unless contractor has certified and substantiated the amounts requested.

The due date for payment of retained amounts to prime contractors under construction contracts is:
 (1) As specified in the contract, or
 (2) Thirty (30) days after approval by the contracting officer for release to the contractor

The due date for final payments (including retained amounts) and partial payments for partial delivery to prime contractors under construction contracts is:
 (1) The later of:

(a) The 30th day from the receipt of a proper invoice, or
(b) The 30th day after Government acceptance of work or services completed (includes the definition of "constructive acceptance" as described under **Determination of the 30-Day Payment Due Date**), or
(2) The 30th day from the date of the invoice if the Government fails to date-stamp invoice, or
(3) On the effective date of the contract settlement where the payment amount is subject to contract settlement actions on a final invoice

Progress Payments May Include Reimbursement for Bond Premiums
[FAR: 52.232-5(g)]

Requests for progress payments may include reimbursement for premiums paid for performance and payment bonds.

Substantiation of Progress Payments Requests
[FAR:52.232-5(b)]

Prime contractor must provide an itemization of the specific amounts requested to provide a basis for payment. Contracting officer may require more detail if necessary to substantiate payment request.

Certification of Progress Payment Requests
[FAR:52.232-5(c)]

In addition to substantiating his request for a progress payment, the prime contractor must certify to the Government:
 (1) The payment request covers only amounts earned according to specifications, terms and conditions of the contract
 (2) The prime contractor has paid all subcontractors for satisfactory performance from previous progress payments and will make timely payments to subcontractors from proceeds covered by this certification
 (3) This request for payment does not include any amounts the prime contractor intends to withhold or retain from the subcontractors

Discovery of Deficiency in Work Performed by Contractor After Request for Progress Payment
[FAR:52.232-5(d)]

If, after submitting a request for a progress payment, the contractor discovers that all or part of his request constitutes a payment for deficient performance by the contractor (hereafter referred to as an "unearned amount"), the contractor must:
 (1) Notify the contracting officer
 (2) Pay interest on the "unearned amounts"

Interest is due on the "unearned amounts" from the date of the prime contractor's receipt of payment until the date the prime contractor notifies the contracting officer that the deficiency has been corrected or until the date the money is returned to the agency by reducing subsequent payment requests equal to the "unearned amount."

The rate of interest applicable is the 91-day Treasury bill rate in effect at the time of the prime contractor's discovery of a deficiency.

Extension of the Prompt Payment Act to All Tiers of Subcontractors
[FAR: 52.232-27(c)]

Each prime contractor is required to include in all subcontracts the following clauses:

(1) Payment clause which obligates the prime contractor to pay the subcontractor not later than 7 days after the prime contractor receives payment

(2) Interest penalty clause which obligates the prime contractor to pay interest on overdue payments

Subcontractors must include the same payment and interest penalty clauses in all their subcontracts.

Retainage by Prime Contractor and Subcontractors
[FAR:52.232-27(d)(1)]

Prime contractors and subcontractors may retain a specified percentage of each progress payment according to the terms of their contracts.

Withholding for Cause by the Prime Contractor or Subcontractor
[FAR: 52.232-27(d)(2)&(3)]

Prime contractors and subcontractors may determine that part or all of the subcontractor's request for payment should be withheld in accordance with terms of the subcontract. No interest penalty is required if notice is sent to subcontractor and contracting officer.

Discovery of Deficiency in Work Performed by Subcontractor After Request for Progress Payment but Before Subcontractor is Paid
[FAR:52.232-27 (e)]

If, after submitting a request for progress payment, the contractor discovers a deficiency in subcontractor's performance that is cause for withholding under the subcontract, the contractor must:
(1) Notify the subcontractor
(2) Give copy of notice to contracting officer
(3) Reduce subcontractor's payment by amount specified in notice
(4) Pay the subcontractor as soon as possible once deficiency is corrected

If subcontractor is not paid within 7 days after correction of a deficiency or 7 days after contractor receives payment from the Government, then the contractor must pay a late payment interest penalty.

The contractor must notify the contracting officer when he/she is reducing his/her request for payment of the amount withheld. The contractor must also notify the contracting officer when payment of the withheld amounts is made, the amount withheld, and the dates such funds were withheld.

The contractor must pay interest on the withheld funds beginning on the 8th day after the contractor receives such funds until the day the deficiency is corrected or the date the withheld amount has been deducted from a payment request.

Miller Act — Withholding by the Contractor
[FAR:52.232-27(f)]

A second-tier subcontractor, in accordance with the Miller Act, may give written notice to the prime contractor of a deficiency in a first-tier subcontractor's performance. If the prime contractor, who may be ultimately liable for the deficiency, determines that all or part of the future payments should be withheld according to subcontract provisions, he/she may withhold such payments without incurring any obligation to pay interest.

The prime contractor must furnish a written notice to the first-tier subcontractor and may withhold the amount specified in the notice from the first-tier's next available progress payment.

The amount withheld must be paid no later than 7 days after the prime contractor has received written notice that the deficiency has been corrected or the prime contractor must pay interest.

Contents of Written Notice
[FAR:52.232-27(g)]

The written notice to be sent to subcontractors for withholding must include:
(1) Amount withheld
(2) Specific reasons for withholding according to terms of subcontract
(3) Remedial actions needed to be taken for payment

Electronic Funds Transfer (EFT) Payment Methods
[FAR:52.232-28]

Payment is to be made by check or electronic funds transfer. Government agencies may use either the Treasury Fedline System (FEDLINE) or the Automated Clearing House (ACH) for electronic funds transfer.

At least 14 days before an invoice or contract financing request is submitted, the contractor must designate a financial institution to receive electronic funds transfer payments to the contracting officer or other designated Government official.

For payment through FEDLINE, the contractor must submit the following information:

(1) Name, address and telegraphic abbreviation of the financial institution to receive payment.

(2) The American Bankers Association 9-digit identifying number for wire transfers for the contractor's designated financial institution, if the institution has access to the Federal Reserve Communications System.

(3) Contractor's account number at the designated financial institution where funds are to be transferred.

(4) If designated financial institution does not have access to Federal Reserve Communications System, contractor must provide the name, address, telegraphic abbreviation and American Bankers Association identifying number of the correspondent financial institution through which contractor's financial institution obtains wire transfer activity.

For payment through ACH, the contractor must supply the following information:

(1) Routing transit number of the contractor's finan-cial institution to receive payment. This number is the same as the American Bankers Association identifying number used for FEDLINE.

(2) Number of contractor's account to which funds are to be deposited.

(3) Type of depositor account — "C" for checking, "S" for savings.

(4) If the contractor has never used the ACH system, a "Payment Information Form," SF3881 must be completed before payment can be processed.

Change of Financial Institution by Contractor

If a contractor decides to change the financial institution to which electronic funds transfer payments are to be made, he must notify the appropriate Government official 30 days prior to the date such a change is to take effect.

Documentation

Documents furnishing the information for electronic funds transfer payment must contain the signature, title, and telephone number of the contractor official authorized to provide information, as well as contractor's name and contract number.

Failure to provide complete information required may delay payment.

Source: Coalition for Prompt Pay, *Guide to Getting Paid Promptly by State and Local Agencies*, 3150 Spring Street, Fairfax, VA 22031, 703/273-7200: Coalition for Prompt Pay, 1989, pp. 47–52. Reprinted by permission of Coalition for Prompt Pay.

MODEL STATE PROMPT PAY LAW

(1) "Public entity" means all state or commonwealth departments, institutions, agencies, cities, towns, counties, school districts, projects supported in whole or in part by public funds, public corporations created by charter, statute, or executive order and any political subdivisions thereof.

(2) It is the policy of this state or commonwealth that all bills owed by any public entity shall be paid promptly. No public entity shall be exempt from the provisions of this statute.

(3) All bills shall be paid within 30 calendar days of receipt of invoice, except as provided in (4) and (11).

(4) Where any public entity purchases:

(a) Meat and meat products, fish and shellfish, edible fresh or frozen poultry, poultry meat food products, fresh eggs and perishable egg products, bills shall be paid within 7 calendar days.

(b) Groceries, vegetables, fresh fruits, dairy products, edible fats or oils, food products made from edible fats or oils and other perishables, bills shall be paid within 10 calendar days.

(c) Other products with common industry payment practices of less than 30 calendar days, the state or commonwealth shall comply with industry terms.

(5) Interest penalties shall be paid automatically when bills become overdue. It shall be up to each public entity to calculate and pay interest automatically at the time payment is made on the principal. Interest payments shall accompany payment of net due for goods and services. Agencies shall not require companies to petition, invoice, bill or wait any additional days to receive interest due.

(6) When a public entity is required to pay an interest penalty, the payment must be accompanied by a notice stating:

(a) The amount of interest paid.

(b) The interest rate used.

(c) The period for which interest is being paid.

(d) The contract and invoice numbers to assist the vendor or contractor in reconciling the payment.

(7) If any public entity fails to pay the interest penalty automatically, the vendor or contractor, in addition to the interest penalty, shall be entitled to an added penalty if:

(a) The vendor or contractor is owed an interest penalty.

(b) The public entity does not pay the interest penalty within 10 days after the date the invoice is paid.

(c) The vendor or contractor makes a written demand not later than 40 days after the date on the invoice.

The added penalty shall be equal to 100 percent of the original interest penalty.

(8) No public entity shall request any vendor or contractor to waive his or her rights, under this Act, to recover a penalty for late payment as a condition of or inducement to enter into any contract for goods or services.

(9) Partial payment shall be made on partial deliveries. Each complete item or service must be paid for within 30 calendar days or in accordance with (4) above.

(10) All proper deliveries and completed services shall be received or accepted promptly and proper receiving and acceptance reports shall be forwarded to payment offices within 3 days of delivery of goods or completion of services.

(11) Payment due date is:

(a) Day on which the agency or office designated by the agency to first receive such invoice actually receives the invoice or day on which government agency receives the goods or services, whichever is later, or

(b) Date of the invoice if the office designated to first receive such invoice fails to date-stamp the invoice on date it was received.

The 30-, 10- and 7-calendar day periods shall be considered as "grace periods" during which all proper invoices shall be paid.

(12) The rate of interest paid by the public entity shall be the one commonly charged to all the vendor's or contractor's customers. The rate of interest charged by the vendor or contractor may be equal to the vendor's or contractor's cost of short-term money, but not higher. Vendor or contractor is required to state the interest rate on the invoice.

(13) Unpaid interest penalties owed to vendors or contractors shall compound every month.

(14) These rules shall apply to all purchases, leases, rentals, contracts for services, construction, repairs, and remodeling.

(15) No discount offered by a vendor or contractor shall be taken by a public entity unless full payment is made within the discount period.

When taking a discount, the discount period must be calculated from the date of the vendor's or contractor's invoice.

In the event a discount is taken later, interest shall accrue on the unpaid balance from the day the discount offer expired.

(16) Interest shall be paid from funds already appropriated to the offending public entity. If more than one department, institution or agency has caused a late payment, each shall bear a proportional share of the interest penalty. No interest shall be charged directly back to the public entity's general funds.

(17) In instances where an invoice is filled out incorrectly, or where there is any defect or impropriety in an invoice submitted, the public entity shall contact the vendor or contractor in writing within 7 days of receiving the invoice, stating the reason(s) the invoice is defective or improper.

An error on the vendor's or contractor's invoice, if corrected by the vendor or contractor within 5 working days of being contacted by the agency, shall not result in the vendor or contractor being paid late.

(18) Checks shall be mailed or transmitted on the same day for which the check is dated.

Payments made by electronic fund transfer (EFT) mechanism must be made so as to be received by the vendor's or contractor's financial institution on the established due date.

(19) This statute authorizes no new appropriation to cover interest penalties. No public entity shall seek to increase appropriations for the purpose of obtaining funds to pay interest penalties.

(20) Payment of interest penalties may be postponed when payment on principal is delayed because of disagreement between the public entity and the vendor or contractor. However, in the event of a dispute, the dispute shall be settled within 30 days after interest penalties could begin to be assessed. At the resolution of any dispute, vendors or contractors shall automatically receive interest on all proper invoices not paid for as provided in sections (3) and (4).

(21) On small purchases of $500 or less, the public entity shall:

(a) Make payment by cash-on-delivery or check-on-delivery, or

(b) Make payment by 10 calendar days after receipt or acceptance of the goods or services.

(22) This statute shall in no way be construed to prohibit any public entity from making advance payments, pro-gress payments, or from prepaying where circumstances make such payments appropriate. All such payments shall be made promptly and are subject to interest penalties when payment is late.

(23) Where construction, repair and remodeling payments are subject to retainage, interest penalties shall accrue on retained amounts beginning 30 calendar days after substantial completion by the contractor(s) unless otherwise provided by the contract. When a prime contractor withholds retainage from a subcontractor or supplier, the rate of such retainage shall be no higher than the rate the public entity withheld from the prime contractor.

(24) Any contract awarded by any public entity shall include:

(a) A payment clause which obligates the prime contractor to pay each subcontractor (including a materials supplier) within 7 days out of amounts paid to the contractor by the public entity for work performed by the subcontractor or supplier under that contract.

(b) An interest clause which obligates the prime contractor to pay interest to the subcontractor or supplier as provided by sections (5) and (12) of this Act, if payment is not made within 7 days.

Any contract awarded by any public entity shall further require the prime contractor to include in each of its subcontracts a provision requiring each subcontractor to include the same payment and interest penalty clause with each lower-tier subcontractor or supplier.

A contractor's obligation to pay an interest penalty to a subcontractor pursuant to the payment clause in this section may not be construed to be an obligation of the public entity. A contract modification may not be made for the purpose of providing reimbursement of such interest penalty. A cost reimbursement claim may not include any amount for reimbursement of such interest penalty.

However, if the contractor is paid interest earned due to late pay by the public entity on work done by a subcontractor, that interest shall be forwarded by the contractor to the subcontractor.

(25) Each department, institution and agency head shall be responsible for prompt payments. In all instances where a payment is made late, the head of the agency shall submit to the proper committee of the public entity's legislative body an explanation of why the bill was paid late and what is being done to solve the late payment problem.

(26) Whenever a vendor or contractor brings formal administrative action or judicial action to collect interest due under this act, should the vendor or contractor prevail, the public entity is required to pay any reasonable attorney fees.

(27) Each public entity making purchases for projects using Federal funds shall make no purchases without final assurance of Federal funds to cover cost of purchases. Where the date of payment to vendors or contractors is contingent on the receipt of Federal funds or Federal approval, the solicitation of bids for contracts and any contracts awarded shall clearly state that payment is contingent on such conditions.

(28) Where a procurement involves the expenditure of Federal assistance or contract funds, the public entity shall comply with such Federal laws and authorized regulations as are mandatorily applicable and are not reflected in this code, except that requirements of this Act which are more restrictive than Federal requirements shall apply.

(29) Each January, the Governor shall submit a report to the state or commonwealth legislature summarizing the state or commonwealth's payment record for the preceding year. Included in the report shall be:

(a) The number and dollar amount of late payments by department, institution, or agency,

(b) The amounts of interest paid,

(c) The percents (a) and (b) are of the total number of purchases and the total dollars spent on procurement of all goods and services, and

(d) Specific steps being taken to reduce the incidence of late payments.

Each January, the head of each political subdivision of the state, shall submit a report to the legislative body of the political subdivision summarizing the public entity's payment record for the preceding year. The report may include:

(a) The number and dollar amount of late payments by department, institution, or agency,

(b) The amounts of interest paid,

(c) The percents (a) and (b) are of the total number of purchases and the total dollars spent on procurement of all goods and services, and

(d) Specific steps being taken to reduce the incidence of late payments.

(30) This statute shall be effective at the beginning of the state's or commonwealth's next fiscal year and shall apply to all payments due on or after that date.

Prepared by:

Coalition for Prompt Pay
Attn: **Kenton Pattie**, *Director*
3150 Spring Street
Fairfax, VA 22031-2399
Phone: 703/273-7200

Source: Coalition for Prompt Pay, *Guide to Getting Paid Promptly by State and Local Agencies*, 3150 Spring Street, Fairfax, VA 22031, 703/273-7200: Coalition for Prompt Pay, 1989, pp. 43–45. Reprinted by permission of Coalition for Prompt Pay.

Contacts for Selling to Governments in the U.S.

GSA Business Service Center Regional Offices

Areas and Office Locations

District of Columbia and nearby Maryland and Virginia
7th and D Streets, S.W.
Room 1050
Washington, D.C. 20407
(202) 472-1804

Maine, Vermont, New Hampshire, Massachusetts, Connecticut, Rhode Island
John W. McCormack Post Office and Courthouse
10 Causeway Street
Boston, MA 02222
(617) 565-8100

New York, New Jersey, Puerto Rico, Virgin Islands
26 Federal Plaza
New York, N Y 10278
(212) 264-1234

Pennsylvania, Delaware, West Virginia, Maryland, Virginia
9th and Market Streets
Room 1300
Philadelphia, PA 19107
(215) 597-9613

North Carolina, South Carolina, Georgia, Tennessee, Kentucky, Florida, Alabama, Mississippi
Richard B. Russell Federal Building and Courthouse
Atlanta, GA 30303
(404) 221-5103/3032

Ohio, Indiana, Illinois, Michigan, Minnesota, Wisconsin
230 South Dearborn Street
Chicago, IL 60604
(312) 353-5383

Missouri, Iowa, Kansas, Nebraska
1500 East Bannister Road
Kansas City, MO 64131
(816) 926-7201

Arkansas, Louisiana, Texas, New Mexico, Oklahoma
819 Taylor Street
Fort Worth, TX 76102
(817) 334-3284

Colorado, North Dakota, South Dakota, Utah, Montana, Wyoming
Building 41
Denver Federal Center
Denver, CO 80225
(303) 234-2216

Northern California, Hawaii, all of Nevada except Clark County
525 Market Street
San Francisco, CA 94105
(415) 454-9000

Los Angeles, Southern California, Arizona and Clark County, Nevada
300 North Los Angeles Street
Los Angeles, CA 90012
(213) 688-3210

Washington, Oregon, Idaho, Alaska
GSA Center, Room 2413
15th and C Streets, S.W.
Auburn, WA 98001
(206) 931-7956

Source: U.S. Small Business Administration, *Women Business Owners: Selling to the Federal Government*, Washington, D.C.: U.S. Small Business Administration, Office of Women's Business Ownership, June, 1990, p. 40

Defense Logistics Agency (DLA) Supply Centers

Defense Construction Supply Center
3990 East Broad Street
Columbus, OH 43215
(614) 236-3541

Defense Electronics Supply Center
1507 Wilmington Pike
Dayton, OH 45444
(513) 296-5231

Defense Fuel Supply Center
Cameron Station, Building 8
5010 Duke Street
Alexandria, VA 22314
(202) 274-7428

Defense General Supply Center
Bellwood, Petersburg Pike
Richmond, VA 23297
(804) 275-3617 or 275-2387

Defense Industrial Supply Center
700 Robbins Avenue
Philadelphia, PA 19111
(215) 697-2747

Defense Personnel Support Center
2800 South 20th Street
Philadelphia, PA 19101
(215) 952-2321

Source: U.S. Small Business Administration, *Women Business Owners: Selling to the Federal Government*, Washington, D.C.: U.S. Small Business Administration, Office of Women's Business Ownership, June, 1990, p. 50.

Defense Contract Administration Services (DCAS) Regional Offices

805 Walker Street
Marietta, GA 30060
(404) 424-6000, Ext. 231

666 Summer Street
Boston, MA 02210
(617) 542-6000, Ext. 886

O'Hare International Airport
P.O. Box 66475
Chicago, IL 60666
(312) 649-6390

Federal Office Building
Room 1821
1240 East Ninth Street
Cleveland, OH 44199
(216) 522-5122 or 522-5150

500 South Ervay Street
Dallas, TX 75201
(214) 670-9205

11099 South La Cienega
Boulevard
Los Angeles, CA 90045
(213) 643-0620 or 643-0621

60 Hudson Street
New York, NY 10013
(212) 374-9090 or 374-9091

2800 South 20th Street
P.O. Box 7478
Philadelphia, PA 19101
(215) 271-4006

1136 Washington Avenue
St. Louis, MO 63101
(314) 263-6617

Source: U.S. Small Business Administration, *Women Business Owners: Selling to the Federal Government*, Washington, D.C.: U.S. Small Business Administration, Office of Women's Business Ownership, June, 1990, p. 51.

GSA Small Business Information Offices

Alabama
Birmingham
(205) 254-1755
Huntsville
(205) 895-5326
Mobile
(205) 690-2361
Montgomery
(205) 832-7310

Alaska
Anchorage
(907) 271-3650

Arizona
Phoenix
(602) 261-3294
Tucson
(602) 792-6301

Arkansas
Little Rock
(501) 378-5526
Ft. Smith
(501) 782-1934

California
Fresno
(209) 487-5069
Sacramento
(916) 440-3171
San Diego
(714) 293-6640

Colorado
Colorado Springs
(303) 635-8911
Ext. 3243

Connecticut
Hartford
(203) 244-3540
New Haven
(203) 773-2345

Florida
Jacksonville
(904) 791-2791
Miami
(305) 350-5751
Tampa
(813) 228-2351

Georgia
Savannah
(912) 944-4208
Thomasville
(912) 226-2716

Hawaii
Honolulu
(808) 546-7516

Idaho
Boise
(208) 384-1242

Illinois
Springfield
(217) 492-4270

Indiana
Indianapolis
(317) 269-6234

Iowa
Des Moines
(515) 384-4114

Kentucky
Covington
(513) 684-1393
Louisville
(502) 582-6436

Louisiana
New Orleans
(504) 589-6601
Shreveport
(318) 226-5006

Maine
Augusta
(207) 622-6171
Ext. 252

Maryland
Baltimore
(301) 922-7611

Massachusetts
Andover
(617) 681-5504
Worcester
(617) 793-0408

Michigan
Detroit
(313) 226-4910

Minnesota
Twin Cities
(612) 725-4015

Mississippi
Jackson
(601) 960-4449
Tupelo
(601) 842-0613

Montana
Billings
(406) 657-6279
Helena
(406) 449-5285
Missoula
(406) 329-3117

Nevada
Las Vegas
(702) 385-6444
Reno
(702) 784-5302

New Hampshire
Manchester
(603) 666-7581

New Jersey
Newark
(201) 645-2416
Trenton
(609) 989-2082

New Mexico
Albuquerque
(505) 766-2101
Santa Fe
(505) 988-6361

New York
Albany
(518) 472-5447
Brooklyn (NYC)
(212) 330-7474
Buffalo
(716) 846-4588
Plattsburg
(518) 563-0860
Rochester
(716) 263-6288
Syracuse
(315) 423-5424

North Carolina
Asheville
(704) 258-2850
Raleigh
(919) 755-4680

North Dakota
Bismarck
(701) 255-4011
Ext. 4316
Fargo
(701) 237-5771
Ext. 5453

Ohio
Cincinnati
(513) 684-2306
Cleveland
(216) 522-4220
Columbus
(614) 469-6824

Oklahoma
Muskegee
(918) 687-2283
Oklahoma City
(405) 231-4706
Tulsa
(918) 581-7755

Oregon
Eugene
(503) 687-6640

Pennsylvania
Erie
(814) 452-2903

Puerto Rico
Hato Rey
(809) 753-4370

Rhode Island
Providence
(401) 528-4492

South Carolina
Charleston
(803) 724-4233
Columbia
(803) 765-5581

South Dakota
Aberdeen
(605) 225-0250
Ext. 301
Pierre
(605) 224-5852

Tennessee
Memphis
(901) 521-3675
Nashville
(615) 251-5221
Oak Ridge
(615) 576-0583

Texas
Beaumont
(713) 839-2501
Dallas
(214) 767-0084
El Paso
(915) 541-7714
Laredo
(512) 723-6642
Lubbock
(806) 762-7401
San Antonio
(512) 229-6040

Utah
Ogden
(801) 625-6764

Vermont
Burlington
(802) 951-6364

Virginia
Richmond
(804) 771-2101
Roanoke
(703) 982-6174

Washington
Bellingham
(206) 676-8440

Spokane
(509) 456-4663

West Virginia
Parkersburg
(304) 422-8551
Ext. 1276

Wisconsin
Milwaukee
(414) 291-3035

Wyoming
Casper/Mills
(307) 265-5550
Ext. 5427
Cheyenne
(307) 778-2220
Ext. 2341

Source: U.S. Small Business Administration, *Women Business Owners: Selling to the Federal Government*, Washington, D.C.: U.S. Small Business Administration, Office of Women's Business Ownership, June, 1990, p. 39.

Small Business Administration Regional Offices

Maine, New Hampshire, Rhode Island,
Massachusetts, Vermont, Connecticut
60 Batterymarch, 10th Floor
Boston, MA 02110
(617) 451-2030

New York, New Jersey, Puerto Rico, Virgin Islands
26 Federal Plaza
New York, NY 10278
(212) 264-7772

Pennsylvania, Maryland, West Virginia,
Virginia, Delaware, District of Columbia
231 St. Asaphs Rd., Suite 640-West Lobby
Bala Cynwyd, PA 19004
(215) 596-5889

North Carolina, South Carolina, Georgia,
Florida, Mississippi, Alabama, Kentucky,
Tennessee
1375 Peachtree St., N.E., 5th Floor
Atlanta, GA 30367-8102
(404) 347-2797

Ohio, Illinois, Indiana, Wisconsin, Michigan,
Minnesota
230 S. Dearborn St., Rm. 510
Chicago, IL 60604-1779
(312) 353-0359

Texas, Louisiana, Arkansas, Oklahoma,
New Mexico
8625 King George Dr., Building C
Dallas, TX 76235
(214) 767-7643

Kansas, Missouri, Nebraska, Iowa
911 Walnut St., 23rd Floor
Kansas City, MO 64106
(816) 374-5288

Colorado, Wyoming, Utah, Montana,
North Dakota, South Dakota
999 18th St.,Suite 701
Denver, CO 80202
(303) 294-7001

California, Hawaii, Nevada, Guam, Arizona
415 Golden Gate Avenue
San Francisco, CA 94102
(415) 556-7487

Oregon, Idaho, Washington, Alaska
2615 4th Avenue, Rm. 440
Seattle, WA 98121
(206) 442-5676

Source: U.S. Department of Commerce, *How to Sell to the United States Department of Commerce*, Washington, D.C.: U.S. Government Printing Office, April 1988, p. 16.

Federal Offices of Small and Disadvantaged Business Utilization (OSDBU)

The following offices offer small businesses information and guidance on procurement procedures, how to be placed on a bidder's mailing list, and identification of both prime and subcontracting opportunities.

DEPARTMENTS

Department of Agriculture
14th & Independence Ave, SW
Room 124 W
Washington, DC 20250
Telephone: (202) 447-7117

Department of Commerce
14th & Constitution Ave, NW
Room 6411
Washington, DC 20230
Telephone: (202) 377-1472

Department of Defense
The Pentagon, Room 2A340
Washington, DC 20301-3061
Telephone: (202) 694-1151

Department of the Air Force
The Pentagon, Room 5E271
Washington, DC 20330-5040
Telephone: (202) 697-4126

Department of the Army
The Pentagon, Room 2A712
Washington, DC 20310-0106
Telephone: (202) 695-9800

Department of the Navy
Crystal Plaza #5
Room 120
Washington, DC 20360-5000
Telephone: (202) 692-7122

Defense Logistics Agency
Cameron Station
Room 4C112
Alexandria, VA 22304-6100
Telephone: (703) 274-6471

Department of Education
400 Maryland Ave, SW
Room 4149
Washington, DC 20202-0521
Telephone: (202) 732-4500

Department of Energy
1000 Independence Ave, SW
Mail-Stop MA-401
Washington, DC 20585
Telephone: (202) 586-8201

Department of Health & Human Services
200 Independence Ave, SW
Room 517-D
Washington, DC 20201
Telephone: (202) 245-7300

Department of Housing & Urban Development
7th & D Streets, SW
Room 10232
Washington, DC 20410
Telephone: (202) 755-1428

Department of the Interior
18th & C Streets, NW
Room 2727
Washington, DC 20240
Telephone: (202) 343-8493

Department of Justice
Patrick Henry Building
Room 7014
Washington, DC 20530
Telephone: (202) 724-6271

Department of Labor
200 Constitution Ave, NW
Room S 1004
Washington, DC 20210
Telephone: (202) 523-9148

Department of State
Room 212 (SA-6)
Washington, DC 20520
Telephone: (703) 875-6823

Department of Transportation
400 7th Street, SW
Room 9414
Washington, DC 20590
Telephone: (202) 366-1930

Department of the Treasury
1500 Pennsylvania Ave, NW
Room 6101
Washington, DC 20220
Telephone: (202) 566-9616

The majority of Independent Agencies do not have designated offices of Small and Disadvantaged Business utilization. However, they do have specific personnel available to assume such responsibilities.

Independent Agencies

ACTION
1100 Vermont Ave, NW
Suite 2101
Washington, DC 20525
Telephone: (202) 634-9150

Administrative Office of the
U.S. Courts
719 13th Street, NW
5th Floor
Washington, DC 20544
Telephone: (202) 633-6239

AID
Room 1400-A, SA-14
Washington, DC 20523
Telephone: (703) 875-1551

Civil Aeronautics Board
1825 Connecticut Ave, NW
Washington, DC 20428
Telephone: (202) 673-5260

Commodity Futures Trading
Commission
2033 K Street, NW
Washington, DC 20581
Telephone: (202) 254-9735

U.S. Consumer Product Safety
Commission
1111 18th Street, NW
Room 240
Washington, DC 20207
Telephone: (202) 492-6621

Federal Mediation & Conciliation
Service
2100 K Street, NW
Room 100
Washington, DC 20427
Telephone: (202) 653-5310

Environmental Protection Agency
401 M Street, SW
Code A-149C
Washington, DC 20460
Telephone: (202) 557-7777

Federal Maritime Commission
1100 L Street, NW
Room 10101
Washington, DC 20573
Telephone: (202) 523-5911

Federal Emergency Management
Agency
Federal Center Plaza
500 C Street, SW
Room 728
Washington, DC 20472
Telephone: (202) 646-3744

Federal Trade Commission
6th & Pennsylvania Ave, NW
Room 706
Washington, DC 20580
Telephone: (202) 326-2258

Foreign Claims Settlement
Commission of the United States
1111 20th Street, NW
Washington, DC 20579
Telephone: (202) 653-6159

General Services Administration
18th and F Streets, NW
Room 6029
Washington, DC 20405
Telephone: (202) 566-1021

International Communication
Agency
1717 H Street, NW
Room 613
Washington, DC 20547
Telephone: (202) 653-5570

Interstate Commerce
Commission
12th & Constitution Ave, NW
Room 3119
Washington, DC 20423
Telephone: (202) 275-7597

National Aeronautics and Space
Administration
Headquarters Code K
Room 116
Washington, DC 20546
Telephone: (202) 453-2088

National Endowment for the
Humanities
1100 Pennsylvania Ave, NW
Room 503
Washington, DC 20506
Telephone: (202) 786-0438

National Labor Relations Board
1717 Pennsylvania Ave, NW
Room 400
Washington, DC 20570
Telephone: (202) 254-9200

National Science Foundation
1800 G Street, NW
Room 1250-I
Washington, DC 20550
Telephone: (202) 357-9666

Nuclear Regulatory Commission
Maryland National Bank Bld
Room 7217
Washington, DC 20555
Telephone: (202) 492-4665

Office of Personnel Management
1900 E Street, NW
Room 1342
Washington, DC 20415
Telephone: (202) 632-6274

Peace Corps
806 Connecticut Ave, NW
Room P-300
Washington, DC 20526
Telephone: (202) 254-3513

Pennsylvania Avenue
Development Corporation
425 13th Street, NW
Washington, DC 20004
Telephone: (202) 724-9068

U.S. Government Printing Office
North Capitol & H St. NW
Room A-332
Washington, DC 20401
Telephone: (202) 275-2470

U.S. Postal Service
475 L'Enfant Plaza W., SW
Room 4131
Washington, DC 20260-6201
Telephone: (202) 268-4633

Railroad Retirement Board
2000 L Street, NW
Suite 558
Washington, DC 20036
Telephone: (202) 653-9540

Smithsonian Institution
955 L'Enfant Plaza SW
Suite 3120
Washington, DC 20024
Telephone: (202) 287-3343

Small Business Administration
Office of Procurement Assistance
1441 L Street, NW
Room 624
Washington, DC 20416
Telephone: (202) 653-6588

Tennessee Valley Authority
1000 Commerce Union Bank
Building
Chattanooga, TN 37401
Telephone: (615) 751-2624

Veterans Administration
810 Vermont Avenue, NW
Washington, DC 20420
Telephone: (202) 376-6996

Source: U.S. Small Business Administration, *Women Business Owners: Selling to the Federal Government*, Washington, D.C.: U.S. Small Business Administration, Office of Women's Business Ownership, June, 1990, p. 45–46.

Minority Business Development Agency
Minority Business Development Centers (MBDC)

State	Firm	Address	Telephone
Alabama	Birmingham MBDC	2100 16th Ave., South, Suite 203 Birmingham, AL 35205	205-930-9254
	Mobile MBDC	801 Executive Park Drive, Suite 104 Mobile, AL 36606	205-471-5165
	Montgomery MBDC	770 S. McDonough St., Suite 207 Montgomery, AL 36104	205-834-7598
Alaska	Alaska MBDC	1577 C St., Plaza, Suite 200 Anchorage, AK 99501	907-274-5400
Arizona	Arizona IBDC	2111 East Baseline Road, Suite F-8 Tempe, AZ 85283	602-831-7524
	Phoenix MBDC	1661 East Camelback, Suite 210 Phoenix, AZ 85016	602-277-7707
Arkansas	Little Rock MBDC	One Riverfront Place, Suite 416 North Little Rock, AR 72114	501-372-7312
California	Anaheim MBDC	5 Hutton Center Dr., Suite 1050 Santa Ana, CA 92707	714-542-2700
	Bakersfield MBDC	218 South H St., Suite 103 Bakersfield, CA 93304	805-837-0291
	California IBDC	9650 Flair Dr., Suite 303 El Monte, CA 91731	818-442-3701
	Fresno MBDC	2010 N. Fine, Suite 103 Fresno, CA 93727	209-252-7551
	Los Angeles 2 MBDC	3807 Wilshire Blvd., Suite 700 Los Angeles, CA 90010	213-380-9471
	Oxnard MBDC	451 W. Fifth St. Oxnard, CA 93030	805-483-1123
	Stockton MBDC	5361 N. Pershing Ave., Suite F Stockton, CA 95207	209-477-2098
	Riverside MBDC	1060 Cooley Dr., Suite F Colton, CA 92324	714-824-9695
	Sacramento MBDC	630 Bercut Drive, Suite C & D Sacramento, CA 95814	916-443-0700
	Salinas MBDC	123 Capital St., Suite B Salinas, CA 93901	408-754-1061
	San Francisco MBDC	One California St., Suite 2100 San Francisco, CA 94111	415-989-2920
	San Jose MBDC	150 Almaden Blvd., Suite 600 San Jose, CA 95150	408-275-9000
	Santa Barbara MBDC	4141 State St., Suite B-4 Santa Barbara, CA 93110	805-964-1136
Colorado	Denver MBDC	4450 Morrison Road Denver, CO 80219	303-937-1006
Connecticut	Connecticut MBDC	410 Asylum St., Suite 243 Hartford, CT 06103	203-246-5371
District of Columbia	Washington MBDC	1133-15th St., NW, Suite 1120 Washington, DC 20005	202-785-2886

323

State	Firm	Address	Telephone
Florida	Jacksonville MBDC	333 N. Laura St., Suite 465 Jacksonville, FL 32202-3508	904-353-3826
	Miami/Ft. Lauderdale MBDC	1200 N.W. 78th Ave., Suite 301 Miami, FL 33126	305-591-7355
	Orlando MBDC	132 E. Colonial Dr., Suite 211 Orlando, FL 32801	407-422-6234
	Tampa/St. Petersburg MBDC	5020 W. Cypress, Suite 217 Tampa, FL 33607	813-228-7555
	West Palm Beach MBDC	2001 Broadway, Suite 301 Riveria Beach, FL 33404	407-393-2530
Georgia	Atlanta MBDC	75 Piedmont Ave., N.E. Suite 256 Atlanta, GA 30303	404-586-0973
	Augusta MBDC	1208 Laney Walker Blvd. Augusta, GA 30901-2796	404-722-0994
	Columbus MBDC	1214 First Ave., Suite 430 Columbus, GA 31902-1696	404-324-4253
	Savannah MBDC	31 W. Congress St., Suite 201 Savannah, GA 31401	912-236-6708
Hawaii	Honolulu MBDC	1001 Bishop St., Suite 2900 Honolulu, HI 98813	808-536-0066
Illinois	Chicago 1 MBDC	35 E. Wacker Dr., Suite 790 Chicago, IL 60601	312-977-9190
	Chicago 2 MBDC	600 Prudential Plaza Chicago, IL 60601	312-585-4710
Indiana	Gary MBDC	567 Broadway Gary, IN 48402	219-883-5802
	Indianapolis MBDC	617 Indiana Ave., Suite 319 Indianapolis, IN 46202	317-685-0055
Kentucky	Louisville MBDC	835 W. Jefferson St., Suite 103 Louisville, KY 40202	502-589-7401
Louisiana	Baton Rouge MBDC	2036 Woodale Blvd., Suite D Baton Rouge, LA 70806	504-924-0186
	New Orleans MBDC	1683 North Clayborne New Orleans, LA 70116	504-947-1491
	Shreveport MBDC	202 North Thomas Drive, Suite 16 Shreveport, LA 71108	318-226-4931
Maryland	Baltimore MBDC	2901 Druid Park Drive, Suite 201 Baltimore, MD 21215	301-383-2214
Massachusetts	Boston MBDC	985 Commonwealth Ave. Boston, MA 02215	617-353-7060
Michigan	Detroit MBDC	65 Cadillac Square, Suite 3701 Detroit, MI 48228-2822	313-961-2100
Minnesota	Minneapolis MBDC	2021 E. Hennepin Ave., Suite 370 Minneapolis, MN 55413	612-378-0361
	Minnesota IBDC	3045 Farr Ave. Cass Lake, MN 56633	218-335-8583
Mississippi	Jackson MBDC	1350 Livingston Lane, Suite A Jackson, MS 39213	601-362-2260

State	Firm	Address	Telephone
Missouri	Kansas City MBDC	1000 Walnut St., Suite 1000 Kansas City, MO 64106	816-221-6504
	St. Louis MBDC	500 Washington, Ave., Suite 1200 St. Louis, MO 63101	314-621-6232
Nevada	Las Vegas MBDC	716 South Sixth St. Las Vegas, NV 89101	702-384-3293
New Jersey	New Brunswick MBDC	134 New St., Room 102 New Brunswick, NJ 08901	201-247-2000
	Newark MBDC	60 Park Place, Suite 1404 Newark, NJ 07102	201-623-7712
New Mexico	Albuquerque MBDC	718 Central S.W. Albuquerque, NM 87102	505-843-7114
	New Mexico IBDC	2401 Twelfth St., N.W. Albuquerque, NM 87197-6507	605-889-9092
New York	Bronx MBDC	349 E. 149th St., Suite 702 Bronx, NY 10451	212-665-8583
	Brooklyn MBDC	16 Court St., Room 1903 Brooklyn, NY 11201	718-522-5880
	Buffalo MBDC	523 Delaware Ave. Buffalo, NY 14202	716-885-0336
	Manhattan MBDC	51 Madison Ave., Suite 2212 New York, NY 10010	212-779-4360
	Nassau/Suffolk MBDC	150 Broad Hollow Road, Suite 304 Melville, NY 11747	516-649-5454
	Queens MBDC	110-29 Horace Harding Expwy. Corona, NY 11368	718-699-2400
	Rochester MBDC	111 East Ave., Suite 215 Rochester, NY 14604	715-232-6120
	Williamsburg/Brooklyn MBDC	12 Heywood St. Brooklyn, NY 11211	718-522-5620
North Carolina	Charlotte MBDC	700 East Stonewall St., Suite 360 Charlotte, NC 28202	704-334-7522
	Cherokee IBDC	Alquoni Rd., Box 1200 Cherokee, NC 28719	704-497-9335
	Cherokee IBDC	185 French Broad Ave. Asheville, NC 28801	704-252-2516
	Fayetteville MBDC	114-1/2 Anderson St. Fayetteville NC 28302	919-483-7513
	Raleigh/Durham MBDC	817 New Bern Ave., Suite 8 Raleigh, NC 27601	919-833-8122
North Dakota	North Dakota IBDC	3315 University Dr. Bismarck, ND 58501-7598	710-255-3225
Ohio	Cleveland MBDC	801 Lakeside, Suite 335 Cleveland, OH 44114	216-664-4150
	Cincinnati MBDC	113 W. Fourth St., Suite 800 Cincinnati, OH 45202	513-381-4770
	Columbus MBDC	37 North High St. Columbus, OH 43215	614-225-6959

State	Firm	Address	Telephone
Oklahoma	Oklahoma City MBDC	1500 N.E. 4th St., Suite 101 Oklahoma City, OK 73117	405-235-0430
	Oklahoma IBDC	5727 Garnett, Suite H Tulsa, OK 74146	918-250-5950
	Tulsa MBDC	240 East Apache St. Tulsa, OK 74106	918-592-1995
Oregon	Portland MBDC	8959 S.W. Barbur Blvd., Suite 102 Portland, OR 97219	503-245-9253
Pennsylvania	Philadelphia MBDC	801 Arch St. Philadelphia, PA 19107	215-629-9841
	Pittsburgh MBDC	Nine Parkway Center, Suite 250 Pittsburgh, PA 15220	412-921-1155
Puerto Rico	Mayaguez MBDC	70 West Mendez Bigo Mayaguez, PR 00708	809-833-7783
	Ponce MBDC	19 Salud St. Ponce, PR 00731	809-840-8100
	San Juan MBDC	207 O'Neill St. San Juan, PR 00936	809-753-8484
South Carolina	Charleston MBDC	701 E. Bay St., Suite 1539 Charleston, SC 29403	803-724-3477
	Columbia MBDC	2700 Middleburg Drive Columbia, SC 29204	803-256-0528
	Greenville/Spartanburg MBDC	300 University Ridge, Suite 200 Greenville, SC 29601	803-271-8753
Tennessee	Memphis MBDC	5 North Third St., Suite 2000 Memphis, TN 38103	901-527-2298
	Nashville MBDC	404 J. Robertson Pkwy., Suite 1920 Nashville, TN 37219	615-255-0432
Texas	Austin MBDC	301 Congress Ave., Suite 1020 Austin, TX 78701	512-476-9700
	Beaumont MBDC	550 Fannin, Suite 106A Beaumont, TX 77701	409-836-1377
	Corpus Christi MBDC	3649 Leopard, Suite 514 Corpus Christi, TX 78404	512-887-7961
	Dallas/Ft. Worth MBDC	1445 Ross Ave., Suite 800 Dallas, TX 75202	214-855-7373
	Houston MBDC	1200 Smith St., Suite 2800 Houston, TX 77002	713-650-3831
	Laredo MBDC	777 Calledelhorte No. 2 Laredo, TX 78401	512-725-5177
	Lubbock/Midland-Odessa MBDC	1220 Broadway, Suite 509 Lubbock, TX 79401	806-762-6232
	McAllen MBDC	1701 W. Bus., Hwy. 83, Suite 1108 McAllen, TX 78501	512-687-5224
	San Antonio MBDC	UTSA, Hemisphere Tower San Antonio, TX 78285	512-224-1945

State	Firm	Address	Telephone
Utah	Salt Lake City MBDC	350 East 500 South, Suite 101 Salt Lake City, UT 84111	810–328–8181
Virgin Islands	Virgin Islands MBDC	81–AB Princess Gade St. Thomas, VI 00804	809–774–7215
Virginia	Newport News MBDC	6060 Jefferson Ave., Suite 6016 Newport News, VA 23605	804–245–8743
	Norfolk MBDC	355 Crawford Parkway, Suite 808 Portsmouth, VA 23701	804–399–0888
Washington	Seattle MBDC	155 N.E. 100th Ave., Suite 401 Seattle, WA 98125	206–525–5617
Wisconsin	Milwaukee MBDC	3929 N. Humboltd Blvd. Milwaukee, WI 53212	414–332–6288

Source: U.S. Small Business Administration, *Women Business Owners: Selling to the Federal Government*, Washington, D.C.: U.S. Small Business Administration, Office of Women's Business Ownership, June, 1990, p. 40–44

SBA Women's Business Ownership Coordinators and Representatives

REG	TYPE	CITY	ST	ZIP	ADDRESS		PUBLIC PHONE
01	RO	BOSTON	MA	02110	60 BATTERYMARCH STREET	10TH FLOOR	(617)451-2023
01	DO	AUGUSTA	ME	04330	40 WESTERN AVENUE	ROOM 512	(207)622-8378
01	DO	BOSTON	MA	02222-1093	10 CAUSEWAY STREET	ROOM 265	(617)565-5590
01	DO	CONCORD	NH	03301-1257	55 PLEASANT STREET	ROOM 210	(603)225-1400
01	DO	HARTFORD	CT	06106	330 MAIN STREET	2ND FLOOR	(203)240-4700
01	DO	MONTPELIER	VT	05602	87 STATE STREET	ROOM 205	(802)828-4474
01	DO	PROVIDENCE	RI	02903	380 WESTMINISTER MALL	5TH FLOOR	(401)528-4561
01	BO	SPRINGFIELD	MA	01103	1550 MAIN STREET	ROOM 212	(413)785-0268
02	RO	NEW YORK	NY	10278	26 FEDERAL PLAZA	ROOM 31-08	(212)264-7772
02	POD	ALBANY	NY	12207	445 BROADWAY	ROOM 222	(518)472-6300
02	POD	CAMDEN	NJ	08104	2600 MT. EPHRAIN AVE.		(609)757-5183
02	POD	ROCHESTER	NY	14614	100 STATE STREET	ROOM 601	(716)263-6700
02	POD	ST. CROIX	VI	00820	4C & 4D ESTE SION FRM	ROOM 7	(809)778-5380
02	POD	ST. THOMAS	VI	00801	VETERANS DRIVE	ROOM 283	(809)774-8530
02	DO	HATO REY	PR	00918	CARLOS CHARDON AVE.	ROOM 691	(809)753-4002
02	DO	NEW YORK	NY	10278	26 FEDERAL PLAZA	ROOM 3100	(212)264-4355
02	DO	NEWARK	NJ	07102	60 PARK PLACE	4TH FLOOR	(201)645-2434
02	DO	SYRACUSE	NY	13260	100 S. CLINTON STREET	ROOM 1071	(315)423-5383
02	BO	BUFFALO	NY	14202	111 W. HURON STREET	ROOM 1311	(716)846-4301
02	BO	ELMIRA	NY	14901	333 E. WATER STREET	4TH FLOOR	(607)734-8130
02	BO	MELVILLE	NY	11747	35 PINELAWN ROAD	ROOM 102E	(516)454-0750
03	RO	KING PRUSSIA	PA	19406	475 ALLENDALE ROAD	SUITE 201	(215)962-3750
03	DO	BALTIMORE	MD	21202	10 N. CALVERT STREET	3RD FLOOR	(301)962-4392
03	DO	CLARKSBURG	WV	26301	168 W. MAIN STREET	5TH FLOOR	(304)623-5631
03	DO	KING PRUSSIA	PA	19406	475 ALLENDALE ROAD	SUITE 201	(215)962-3846
03	DO	PITTSBURGH	PA	15222	960 PENN AVENUE	5TH FLOOR	(412)644-2780
03	DO	RICHMOND	VA	23240	400 N. 8TH STREET	ROOM 3015	(804)771-2617
03	DO	WASHINGTON	DC	20036	1111 18TH STREET, NW	6TH FLOOR	(202)634-1500
03	BO	CHARLESTON	WV	25301	550 EAGAN STREET	SUITE 309	(304)347-5220
03	BO	HARRISBURG	PA	17101	100 CHESTNUT STREET	SUITE 309	(717)782-3840
03	BO	WILKES-BARRE	PA	18701	20 N. PENNSYLVANIA AVE.	ROOM 2327	(717)826-6497
03	BO	WILMINGTON	DE	19801	920 N.KING STREET	ROOM 412	(302)573-6294
04	RO	ATLANTA	GA	30367-8102	1375 PEACHTREE ST., NE	5TH FLOOR	(404)347-2797
04	POD	STATESBORO	GA	30458	52 N. MAIN STREET	ROOM 225	(912)489-8719
04	POD	TAMPA	FL	33602	700 TWIGGS STREET	ROOM 607	(813)228-2594
04	POD	W. PALM BEACH	FL	33407	5601 CORPORATE WAY	SUITE 402	(407)689-3922
04	DO	ATLANTA	GA	30309	1720 PEACHTREE RD, NW	6TH FLOOR	(404)347-2441
04	DO	BIRMINGHAM	AL	35203-2398	2121 8TH AVE. N.	SUITE 200	(205)731-1344
04	DO	CHARLOTTE	NC	28202	222 S. CHURCH STREET	ROOM 300	(704)371-6563
04	DO	COLUMBIA	SC	29202	1835 ASSEMBLY STREET	ROOM 358	(803)765-5376
04	DO	CORAL GABLES	FL	33146	1320 S. DIXIE HIGHWAY	SUITE 501	(305)536-5521
04	DO	JACKSON	MS	39269-0396	101 W. CAPITOL STREET	SUITE 322	(601)965-4378
04	DO	JACKSONVILLE	FL	32256-7504	7825 BAYMEADOWS WAY	SUITE 100-B	(904)443-1950
04	DO	LOUISVILLE	KY	40202	600 M. L. KING, JR. PL.	ROOM 188	(502)582-5976
04	DO	NASHVILLE	TN	37228-1500	50 VANTAGE WAY	2ND FLOOR	(615)736-5850
04	BO	GULFPORT	MS	39501-7758	ONE HANCOCK PLAZA	SUITE 1001	(601)863-4449
05	RO	CHICAGO	IL	60604-1593	230 S. DEARBORN STREET	ROOM 510	(312)353-0359
05	POD	EAU CLAIRE	WI	54701	500 S. BARSTOW COMMO	ROOM 37	(715)834-9012
05	DO	CHICAGO	IL	60604-1779	219 S. DEARBORN STREET	ROOM 437	(312)353-4528
05	DO	CLEVELAND	OH	44199	1240 E. 9TH STREET	ROOM 317	(216)522-4180
05	DO	COLUMBUS	OH	43215	85 MARCONI BLVD.	ROOM 512	(614)469-6860
05	DO	DETROIT	MI	48226	477 MICHIGAN AVE.	ROOM 515	(313)226-6075
05	DO	INDIANAPOLIS	IN	46204-1584	575 N. PENNSYLVANIA ST.	ROOM 578	(317)226-7272
05	DO	MADISON	WI	53703	212 E. WASHINGTON AVE.	ROOM 213	(608)264-5261
05	DO	MINNEAPOLIS	MN	55403-1563	100 N. 6TH STREET	STE 610	(612)370-2324
05	BO	CINCINNATI	OH	45202	550 MAIN STREET	ROOM 5028	(513)684-2814
05	BO	MARQUETTE	MI	49885	300 S. FRONT ST.		(906)225-1108
05	BO	MILWAUKEE	WI	53203	310 W. WISCONSIN AVE.	SUITE 400	(414)291-3941
05	BO	SPRINGFIELD	IL	62704	511 W. CAPITOL STREET	SUITE 302	(217)492-4416

RO=REGIONAL OFFICE   DO=DISTRICT OFFICE   BO=BRANCH OFFICE   POD=POST OF DUTY

DAO=DISASTER AREA OFFICE

SBA FORM 348 (2/01/90)   PREVIOUS EDITIONS ARE OBSOLETE, DESTROY OLD STOCK

REG	TYPE	CITY	ST	ZIP	ADDRESS		PUBLIC PHONE
06	RO	DALLAS	TX	75235-3391	8625 KING GEORGE DR.	BLDG. C	(214)767-7643
06	POD	AUSTIN	TX	78701	300 E. 8TH STREET	ROOM 520	(512)482-5288
06	POD	MARSHALL	TX	75670	505 E. TRAVIS	ROOM 103	(214)935-5257
06	POD	SHREVEPORT	LA	71101	500 FANNIN STREET	ROOM 8A-08	(318)226-5196
06	DO	ALBUQUERQUE	NM	87100	5000 MARBLE AVE., NE	ROOM 320	(505)262-6171
06	DO	DALLAS	TX	75242	1100 COMMERCE STREET	ROOM 3C-36	(214)767-0605
06	DO	EL PASO	TX	79902	10737 GATEWAY W.	SUITE 320	(915)541-7586
06	DO	HARLINGEN	TX	78550	222 E. VAN BUREN ST.	ROOM 500	(512)427-8533
06	DO	HOUSTON	TX	77054	2525 MURWORTH	SUITE 112	(713)660-4401
06	DO	LITTLE ROCK	AR	72201	320 W. CAPITOL AVE.	ROOM 601	(501)378-5871
06	DO	LUBBOCK	TX	79401	1611 TENTH STREET	SUITE 200	(806)743-7462
06	DO	NEW ORLEANS	LA	70112	1661 CANAL STREET	SUITE 2000	(504)589-6685
06	DO	OKLAHOMA CITY	OK	73102	200 N. W. 5TH STREET	SUITE 670	(405)231-4301
06	DO	SAN ANTONIO	TX	78216	7400 BLANCO ROAD	SUITE 200	(512)229-4535
06	BO	CORPUS CHRISTI	TX	78401	400 MANN STREET	SUITE 403	(512)888-3331
06	BO	FT. WORTH	TX	76102	819 TAYLOR STREET	ROOM 10A27	(817)334-3777
07	RO	KANSAS CITY	MO	64106	911 WALNUT STREET	13TH FLOOR	(816)426-2989
07	DO	CEDAR RAPIDS	IA	52402-3118	373 COLLINS ROAD NE	ROOM 100	(319)399-2571
07	DO	DES MOINES	IA	50309	210 WALNUT STREET	ROOM 749	(515)284-4422
07	DO	KANSAS CITY	MO	64106	1103 GRAND AVE.	6TH FLOOR	(816)374-3419
07	DO	OMAHA	NB	68154	11145 MILL VALLEY RD.		(402)221-4691
07	DO	ST. LOUIS	MO	63101	815 OLIVE STREET	ROOM 242	(314)539-6600
07	DO	WICHITA	KS	67202	110 E. WATERMAN ST.	1ST FLOOR	(316)269-6571
07	BO	SPRINGFIELD	MO	65802-3200	620 S. GLENSTONE ST.	SUITE 110	(417)864-7670
08	RO	DENVER	CO	80202	999 18TH STREET	SUITE 701	(303)294-7001
08	DO	CASPER	WY	82602-2839	100 EAST B. STREET	ROOM 4001	(307)261-5761
08	DO	DENVER	CO	80202-2599	721 19TH STREET	ROOM 407	(303)844-2607
08	DO	FARGO	ND	58108-3086	657 2ND AVE. N.	ROOM 218	(701)239-5131
08	DO	HELENA	MT	59626	301 S. PARK	ROOM 528	(406)449-5381
08	DO	SALT LAKE CITY	UT	84138-1195	125 S. STATE STREET	ROOM 2237	(801)524-5800
08	DO	SIOUX FALLS	SD	57102-0527	101 S. MAIN AVE.	SUITE 101	(605)336-4231
09	RO	SAN FRANCISCO	CA	94102	450 GOLDEN GATE AVE.		(415)556-7489
09	POD	RENO	NV	89505	50 S. VIRGINIA ST.	ROOM 238	(702)784-5268
09	POD	TUCSON	AZ	85701	300 W. CONGRESS ST.	ROOM 3V	(602)629-6715
09	DO	FRESNO	CA	93727-1547	2719 N. AIR FRESNO DR.		(209)487-5189
09	DO	HONOLULU	HI	96850	300 ALA MOANA BLVD.	ROOM 2213	(808)541-2990
09	DO	LAS VEGAS	NV	89125	301 E. STEWART ST.	ROOM 301	(702)388-6611
09	DO	GLENDALE	CA	91203	330 N. GRAND BLVD.		(213)894-2956
09	DO	PHOENIX	AZ	85004	2005 N. CENTRAL AVE.	5TH FLOOR	(602)379-3737
09	DO	SAN DIEGO	CA	92188	880 FRONT STREET	STE. 4-S-29	(619)557-5440
09	DO	SAN FRANCISCO	CA	94105-1988	211 MAIN STREET	4TH FLOOR	(415)974-0649
09	BO	AGANA	GM	96910	PACIFIC DAILY NEWS BDG	ROOM 508	(671)472-7277
09	BO	SACRAMENTO	CA	95814-2413	660 J STREET	ROOM 215	(916)551-1426
09	DO	SANTA ANA	CA	92703	901 W. CIVIC CTR DR	ROOM 160	(714)836-2494
09	POD	VENTURA	CA	93003-4459	6477 TELEPHONE RD.	SUITE 10	(805)642-1866
10	RO	SEATTLE	WA	98121	2615 4TH AVENUE	ROOM 440	(206)442-5676
10	DO	ANCHORAGE	AK	99501	222 W. 8th AVE.	ROOM 67	(907)271-4022
10	DO	BOISE	ID	83702	1020 MAIN STREET	SUITE 290	(208)334-1696
10	DO	PORTLAND	OR	97201-6605	222 S. W. COLUMBIA	SUITE 500	(503)326-2682
10	DO	SEATTLE	WA	98174-1088	915 SECOND AVE.	ROOM 1792	(206)442-5534
10	DO	SPOKANE	WA	99204	W.601 FIRST AVENUE	10TH FLOOR	(509)353-2807
CO	DAO1	NIAGARA FALLS	NY	14302	360 RAINBOW BLVD S.	3RD FLOOR	(716)282-4612
CO	DAO2	ATLANTA	GA	30308	120 RALPH McGILL ST.	14TH FLOOR	(201)794-8195
CO	DAO3	FT. WORTH	TX	76155	4400 AMON CARTER BLVD	SUITE 102	(817)267-1888
CO	DAO4	SACRAMENTO	CA	95825	1825 BELL STREET	SUITE 208	(916)978-4578

RO=REGIONAL OFFICE   DO=DISTRICT OFFICE   BO=BRANCH OFFICE   POD=POST OF DUTY

DAO=DISASTER AREA OFFICE

Source: U.S. Small Business Administration, *Women Business Owners: Selling to the Federal Government*, Washington, D.C.: U.S. Small Business Administration, Office of Women's Business Ownership, June, 1990, p. 33–34.

Standard Federal Application Forms for Vendors

SF 129, Solicitation Mailing List
Application

SF 18, Request for Quotations

SF 33, Solicitation, Offer and Award

SOLICITATION MAILING LIST APPLICATION	1. TYPE OF APPLICATION ☐ INITIAL ☐ REVISION	2. DATE	FORM APPROVED OMB NO. 3090-0009

NOTE—Please complete all items on this form. Insert N/A in items not applicable. See reverse for Instructions.

3. NAME AND ADDRESS OF FEDERAL AGENCY TO WHICH FORM IS SUBMITTED (Include ZIP code)	4. NAME AND ADDRESS OF APPLICANT (Include county and ZIP code)

5. TYPE OF ORGANIZATION (Check one)
☐ INDIVIDUAL   ☐ NON-PROFIT ORGANIZATION
☐ PARTNERSHIP   ☐ CORPORATION, INCORPORATED UNDER THE LAWS OF THE STATE OF:

6. ADDRESS TO WHICH SOLICITATIONS ARE TO BE MAILED (If different than Item 4)

7. NAMES OF OFFICERS, OWNERS, OR PARTNERS

A. PRESIDENT	B. VICE PRESIDENT	C. SECRETARY
D. TREASURER	E. OWNERS OR PARTNERS	

8. AFFILIATES OF APPLICANT (Names, locations and nature of affiliation. See definition on reverse.)

9. PERSONS AUTHORIZED TO SIGN OFFERS AND CONTRACTS IN YOUR NAME (Indicate if agent)

NAME	OFFICIAL CAPACITY	TELE. NO. (Include area code)

10. IDENTIFY EQUIPMENT, SUPPLIES, AND/OR SERVICES ON WHICH YOU DESIRE TO MAKE AN OFFER (See attached Federal agency's supplemental listing and instructions, if any)

11A. SIZE OF BUSINESS (See definitions on reverse)	11B. AVERAGE NUMBER OF EMPLOYEES (Including affiliates) FOR FOUR PRECEDING CALENDAR QUARTERS	11C. AVERAGE ANNUAL SALES OR RECEIPTS FOR PRECEDING THREE FISCAL YEARS
☐ SMALL BUSINESS (If checked, complete items 11B and 11C) ☐ OTHER THAN SMALL BUSINESS		$

12. TYPE OF OWNERSHIP (See definitions on reverse) (Not applicable for other than small businesses)
☐ DISADVANTAGED BUSINESS   ☐ WOMAN-OWNED BUSINESS

13. TYPE OF BUSINESS (See definitions on reverse)
☐ MANUFACTURER OR PRODUCER   ☐ REGULAR DEALER (Type 1)   ☐ CONSTRUCTION CONCERN   ☐ SURPLUS DEALER
☐ SERVICE ESTABLISHMENT   ☐ REGULAR DEALER (Type 2)   ☐ RESEARCH AND DEVELOPMENT

14. DUNS NO. (If available)	15. HOW LONG IN PRESENT BUSINESS?

16. FLOOR SPACE (Square feet)		17. NET WORTH	
A. MANUFACTURING	B. WAREHOUSE	A. DATE	B. AMOUNT $

18. SECURITY CLEARANCE (If applicable, check highest clearance authorized)

FOR	TOP SECRET	SECRET	CONFIDENTIAL	C. NAMES OF AGENCIES WHICH GRANTED SECURITY CLEARANCES (Include dates)
A. KEY PERSONNEL				
B. PLANT ONLY				

CERTIFICATION — I certify that information supplied herein (Including all pages attached) is correct and that neither the applicant nor any person (Or concern) in any connection with the applicant as a principal or officer, so far as is known, is now debarred or otherwise declared ineligible by any agency of the Federal Government from making offers for furnishing materials, supplies, or services to the Government or any agency thereof.

19. NAME AND TITLE OF PERSON AUTHORIZED TO SIGN (Type or print)	20. SIGNATURE	21. DATE SIGNED

NSN 7540-01-152-8086
PREVIOUS EDITIONS UNUSABLE

129-106

STANDARD FORM 129 (REV. 10-83)
Prescribed by GSA
FAR (48 CFR) 53.214(c)

INSTRUCTIONS

Persons or concerns wishing to be added to a particular agency's bidder's mailing list for supplies or services shall file this properly completed and certified Solicitation Mailing List Application, together with such other lists as may be attached to this application form, with each procurement office of the Federal agency with which they desire to do business. If a Federal agency has attached a Supplemental Commodity list with instructions, complete the application as instructed. Otherwise, identify in Item 10 the equipment supplies and/or services on which you desire to bid. (Provide Federal Supply Class or Standard Industrial Classification Codes if available.) The application shall be submitted and signed by the principal as distinguished from an agent, however constituted.

After placement on the bidder's mailing list of an agency, your failure to respond (submission of bid, or notice in writing, that you are unable to bid on that particular transaction but wish to remain on the active bidder's mailing list for that particular item) to solicitations will be understood by the agency to indicate lack of interest and concurrence in the removal of your name from the purchasing activity's solicitation mailing list for the items concerned.

SIZE OF BUSINESS DEFINITIONS
(See Item 11A.)

a. Small business concern—A small business concern for the purpose of Government procurement is a concern, including its affiliates, which is independently owned and operated, is not dominant in the field of operation in which it is competing for Government contracts and can further qualify under the criteria concerning number of employees, average annual receipts, or other criteria, as prescribed by the Small Business Administration. (See Code of Federal Regulations, Title 13, Part 121, as amended, which contains detailed industry definitions and related procedures.)

b. Affiliates—Business concerns are affiliates of each other when either directly or indirectly (i) one concern controls or has the power to control the other, or (ii) a third party controls or has the power to control both. In determining whether concerns are independently owned and operated and whether or not affiliation exists, consideration is given to all appropriate factors including common ownership, common management, and contractual relationship. (See Items 8 and 11A.)

c. Number of employees—(Item 11B) In connection with the determination of small business status, "number of employees" means the average employment of any concern, including the employees of its domestic and foreign affiliates, based on the number of persons employed on a full-time, part-time, temporary, or other basis during each of the pay periods of the preceding 12 months. If a concern has not been in existence for 12 months, "number of employees" means the average employment of such concern and its affiliates during the period that such concern has been in existence based on the number of persons employed during each of the pay periods of the period that such concern has been in business.

TYPE OF OWNERSHIP DEFINITIONS
(See Item 12.)

a. "Disadvantaged business concern"—means any business concern (1) which is at least 51 percent owned by one or more socially and economically disadvantaged individuals; or, in the case of any publicly owned business, at least 51 percent of the stock of which is owned by one or more socially and economically disadvantaged individuals; and (2) whose management and daily business operations are controlled by one or more of such individuals.

b. "Women-owned business"—means a business that is at least 51 percent owned by a woman or women who are U.S. citizens and who also control and operate the business.

TYPE OF BUSINESS DEFINITIONS
(See Item 13.)

a. Manufacturer or producer—means a person (or concern) owning, operating, or maintaining a store, warehouse, or other establishment that produces, on the premises, the materials, supplies, articles, or equipment of the general character of those listed in Item 10, or in the Federal Agency's Supplemental Commodity List, if attached.

b. Service establishment—means a concern (or person) which owns, operates, or maintains any type of business which is principally engaged in the furnishing of nonpersonal services, such as (but not limited to) repairing, cleaning, redecorating, or rental of personal property, including the furnishing of necessary repair parts or other supplies as part of the services performed.

c. Regular dealer (Type 1)—means a person (or concern) who owns, operates, or maintains a store, warehouse, or other establishment in which the materials, supplies, articles, or equipment of the general character listed in Item 10, or in the Federal Agency's Supplemental Commodity List, if attached, are bought, kept in stock, and sold to the public in the usual course of business.

d. Regular dealer (Type 2)—In the case of supplies of particular kinds (at present, petroleum, lumber and timber products, machine tools, raw cotton, green coffee, hay, grain, feed, or straw, agricultural liming materials, tea, raw or unmanufactured cotton linters and used ADPE), Regular dealer means a person (or concern) satisfying the requirements of the regulations (Code of Federal Regulations, Title 41, 50-201.101(a)(2)) as amended from time to time, prescribed by the Secretary of Labor under the Walsh-Healey Public Contracts Act (Title 41 U.S. Code 35-45). For coal dealers see Code of Federal Regulations, Title 41, 50-201.604(a).

● COMMERCE BUSINESS DAILY—The Commerce Business Daily, published by the Department of Commerce, contains information concerning proposed procurements, sales, and contract awards. For further information concerning this publication, contact your local Commerce Field Office.

REQUEST FOR QUOTATIONS
(THIS IS NOT AN ORDER)

The Notice of Small Business-Small Purchase Set-Aside on the reverse of this form ☐ is ☐ is not applicable.

| PAGE | OF | PAGES |

| 1. REQUEST NO. | 2. DATE ISSUED | 3. REQUISITION/PURCHASE REQUEST NO. | 4. CERT. FOR NAT. DEF. UNDER BDSA REG. 2 AND/OR DMS REG. 1 ▶ | RATING |

5A. ISSUED BY

6. DELIVER BY (Date)

5B. FOR INFORMATION CALL: *(Name and telephone no.)* *(No collect calls)*

7. DELIVERY

☐ FOB DESTINATION ☐ OTHER *(See Schedule)*

8. TO: NAME AND ADDRESS, INCLUDING ZIP CODE

9. DESTINATION *(Consignee and address, Including ZIP Code)*

10. PLEASE FURNISH QUOTATIONS TO THE ISSUING OFFICE ON OR BE-FORE CLOSE OF BUSINESS *(Date)*

11. BUSINESS CLASSIFICATION *(Check appropriate boxes)*

☐ SMALL ☐ OTHER THAN SMALL ☐ DISADVANTAGED ☐ WOMEN-OWNED

IMPORTANT: This is a request for information, and quotations furnished are not offers. If you are unable to quote, please so indicate on this form and return it. This request does not commit the Government to pay any costs incurred in the preparation of the submission of this quotation or to contract for supplies or services. Supplies are of domestic origin unless otherwise indicated by quoter. Any representations and/or certifications attached to this Request for Quotations must be completed by the quoter.

12. SCHEDULE *(Include applicable Federal, State and local taxes)*

ITEM NO. (a)	SUPPLIES/SERVICES (b)	QUANTITY (c)	UNIT (d)	UNIT PRICE (e)	AMOUNT (f)

| 13. DISCOUNT FOR PROMPT PAYMENT ▶ | 10 CALENDAR DAYS % | 20 CALENDAR DAYS % | 30 CALENDAR DAYS % | CALENDAR DAYS % |

NOTE: Reverse must also be completed by the quoter.

| 14. NAME AND ADDRESS OF QUOTER *(Street, city, county, State and ZIP Code)* | 15. SIGNATURE OF PERSON AUTHORIZED TO SIGN QUOTATION | 16. DATE OF QUOTATION |
| | 17. NAME AND TITLE OF SIGNER *(Type or print)* | 18. TELEPHONE NO. *(Include area code)* |

NSN 7540-01-152-8084
PREVIOUS EDITION NOT USABLE

18-118

STANDARD FORM 18 (REV. 10-83)
Prescribed by GSA
FAR (48 CFR) 53.215-1(a)

334

REPRESENTATIONS, CERTIFICATIONS, AND PROVISIONS

The following representation applies when the contract is to be performed inside the United States, its territories or possessions, Puerto Rico, the Trust Territory of the Pacific Islands, or the District of Columbia.

52.219-1 SMALL BUSINESS CONCERN REPRESENTATION (Apr 84)

The quoter represents and certifies as part of its quotation that it ☐ is, ☐ is not a small business concern and that ☐ all, ☐ not all supplies to be furnished will be manufactured or produced by a small business concern in the United States, its possessions, or Puerto Rico. "Small business concern, as used in this provision, means a concern, including its affiliates, that is independently owned and operated, not dominant in the field of operation in which it is bidding on Government contracts, and qualified as a small business under the criteria and size standards in 13 CFR 121.

The following provision is applicable if required on the face of the form:

52.219-2 Notice of Small Business-Small Purchase Set-Aside (Apr 84)

Quotations under this acquisition are solicited from small business concerns only. Any acquisition resulting from this solicitation will be from a small business concern. Quotations received from concerns that are not small businesses shall not be considered and shall be rejected.

335

SOLICITATION, OFFER AND AWARD

1. CERTIFIED FOR NATIONAL DEFENSE UNDER BDSA REG. 2 AND/OR DMS REG. 1 ▶	**RATING** / **PAGE OF** PAGES

2. CONTRACT NO.	3. SOLICITATION NO.	4. TYPE OF SOLICITATION	5. DATE ISSUED	6. REQUISITION/PURCHASE NO.
		☐ ADVERTISED (IFB) ☐ NEGOTIATED (RFP)		

7. ISSUED BY	CODE	8. ADDRESS OFFER TO (If other than Item 7)

NOTE: In advertised solicitations "offer" and "offeror" mean "bid" and "bidder".

SOLICITATION

9. Sealed offers in original and _____ copies for furnishing the supplies or services in the Schedule will be received at the place specified in Item 8, or if handcarried, in the depository listed in _____ until _____ local time _____
(Hour)   (Date)

CAUTION — LATE Submissions, Modifications, and Withdrawals: See Section I, Provision No. 52.214-7 or 52.215-10. All offers are subject to all terms and conditions contained in this solicitation.

10. FOR INFORMATION CALL: ▶	A. NAME	B. TELEPHONE NO. (Include area code) (NO COLLECT CALLS)

11. TABLE OF CONTENTS

(✓)	SEC.	DESCRIPTION	PAGE(S)	(✓)	SEC.	DESCRIPTION	PAGE(S)
		PART I — THE SCHEDULE				**PART II — CONTRACT CLAUSES**	
	A	SOLICITATION/CONTRACT FORM			I	CONTRACT CLAUSES	
	B	SUPPLIES OR SERVICES AND PRICES/COSTS				**PART III — LIST OF DOCUMENTS, EXHIBITS AND OTHER ATTACH.**	
	C	DESCRIPTION/SPECS./WORK STATEMENT			J	LIST OF ATTACHMENTS	
	D	PACKAGING AND MARKING				**PART IV — REPRESENTATIONS AND INSTRUCTIONS**	
	E	INSPECTION AND ACCEPTANCE			K	REPRESENTATIONS, CERTIFICATIONS AND OTHER STATEMENTS OF OFFERORS	
	F	DELIVERIES OR PERFORMANCE					
	G	CONTRACT ADMINISTRATION DATA			L	INSTRS., CONDS., AND NOTICES TO OFFER	
	H	SPECIAL CONTRACT REQUIREMENTS			M	EVALUATION FACTORS FOR AWARD	

OFFER (Must be fully completed by offeror)

NOTE: Item 12 does not apply if the solicitation includes the provisions at 52.214-16, Minimum Bid Acceptance Period.

12. In compliance with the above, the undersigned agrees, if this offer is accepted within _____ calendar days (60 calendar days unless a different period is inserted by the offeror) from the date for receipt of offers specified above, to furnish any or all items upon which prices are offered at the price set opposite each item, delivered at the designated point(s), within the time specified in the schedule.

13. DISCOUNT FOR PROMPT PAYMENT (See Section I, Clause No. 52-232-8) ▶	10 CALENDAR DAYS %	20 CALENDAR DAYS %	30 CALENDAR DAYS %	CALENDAR DAYS %

14. ACKNOWLEDGMENT OF AMENDMENTS (The offeror acknowledges receipt of amendments to the SOLICITATION for offerors and related documents numbered and dated:)	AMENDMENT NO.	DATE	AMENDMENT NO.	DATE

15A. NAME AND ADDRESS OF OFFEROR	CODE	FACILITY	16. NAME AND TITLE OF PERSON AUTHORIZED TO SIGN OFFER (Type or print)

15B. TELEPHONE NO. (Include area code)	15C. CHECK IF REMITTANCE ADDRESS IS DIFFERENT FROM ABOVE ENTER SUCH ADDRESS IN SCHEDULE ☐	17. SIGNATURE	18. OFFER DATE

AWARD (To be completed by Government)

19. ACCEPTED AS TO ITEMS NUMBERED	20. AMOUNT	21. ACCOUNTING AND APPROPRIATION

22. SUBMIT INVOICES TO ADDRESS SHOWN IN ▶ ITEM (4 copies unless otherwise specified)	23. NEGOTIATED PURSUANT TO ☐ 10 U.S.C. 2304(a) ( ) ☐ 41 U.S.C. 252(c) ( )

24. ADMINISTERED BY (If other than Item 7)	CODE	25. PAYMENT WILL BE MADE BY	CODE

26. NAME OF CONTRACTING OFFICER (Type or print)	27. UNITED STATES OF AMERICA (Signature of Contracting Officer)	28. AWARD DATE

IMPORTANT — Award will be made on this Form, or on Standard Form 26, or by other authorized official written notice.

NSN 7540-01-152-8064
PREVIOUS EDITION NOT USABLE

33-132

STANDARD FORM 33 (REV. 10-83)
Prescribed by GSA
FAR (48 CFR) 53.214(c)

REPRESENTATIONS, CERTIFICATIONS AND ACKNOWLEDGMENTS

REPRESENTATIONS *(Check or complete all applicable boxes or blocks.)*
The offeror represents as part of his offer that:

1. SMALL BUSINESS *(See par. 14 on SF 33-A.)*

He ☐ is, ☐ is not, a small business concern. If offeror is a small business concern and is not the manufacturer of the supplies offered, he also represents that all supplies to be furnished hereunder ☐ will, ☐ will not, be manufacturered or produced by a small business concern in the United States, its possessions, or Puerto Rico.

2. MINORITY BUSINESS ENTERPRISE

He ☐ is, ☐ is not, a minority business enterprise. A minority business enterprise is defined as a "business, at least 50 percent of which is owned by minority group members or, in case of publicly owned businesses, at least 51 percent of the stock of which is owned by minority group members." For the purpose of this definition, minority group members are Negroes, Spanish-speaking American persons, American-Orientals, American-Indians, American Eskimos, and American-Aleuts.

3. REGULAR DEALER — MANUFACTURER *(Applicable only to supply contracts exceeding $10,000.)*

He is a ☐ regular dealer in ☐ manufacturer of, the supplies offered.

4. CONTINGENT FEE *(See par. 15 on SF 33-A.)*

(a) He ☐ has, ☐ has not, employed or retained any company or persons *(other than a full-time bona fide employee working solely for the offeror)* to solicit or secure this contract, and (b) he ☐ has, ☐ has not, paid or agreed to pay any company or person *(other than a full-time bona fide employee working solely for the offeror)* any fee, commission, percentage, or brokerage fee contingent upon or resulting from the award of this contract; and agrees to furnish information relating to (a) and (b) above, as requested by the Contracting Officer. *(Interpretation of the representation, including the term "bona fide employee," see Code of Federal Regulations, Title 41, Subpart 1-1.5.)*

5. TYPE OF BUSINESS ORGANIZATION

He operates as ☐ an individual, ☐ a partnership, ☐ a nonprofit organization, ☐ a corporation, incorporated under the laws of the State of _____ .

6. AFFILIATION AND IDENTIFYING DATA *(Applicable only to advertised solicitations.)*

Each offeror shall complete (a) and (b) if applicable, and (c) below:

(a) He ☐ is, ☐ is not, owned or controlled by a parent company. *(See par. 16 on SF 33-A.)*

(b) If the offeror is owned or controlled by a parent company, he shall enter in the blocks below the name and main office address of the parent company:

NAME OF PARENT COMPANY AND MAIN OFFICE ADDRESS *(Include ZIP code)* ▶	

(C) EMPLOYER'S IDENTIFICATION NUMBER *(SEE PAR. 17 on SF 33-A)*	OFFEROR'S E I NO	PARENT COMPANY'S E I NO

7. EQUAL OPPORTUNITY

(a) He ☐ has, ☐ has not, participated in a previous contract or subcontract subject either to the Equal Opportunity clause herein or the clause originally contained in section 301 of Executive Order No. 10925, or the clause contained in Section 201 of Executive Order No. 11114; that he ☐ has, ☐ has not, filed all required compliance reports; and that representations indicating submission of required compliance reports, signed by proposed subcontractors, will be obtained prior to subcontract awards. (The above representation need not be submitted in connection with contracts or subcontracts which are exempt from the equal opportunity clause.)

(b) The bidder (or offeror) represents that (1) he ☐ has developed and has on file, ☐ has not developed and does not have on file, at each establishment affirmative action programs as required by the rules and regulations of the Secretary of Labor (41 CFR 60-1 and 60-2) or (2) he ☐ has not previously had contracts subject to the written affirmative action programs requirement of the rules and regulations of the Secretary of Labor. *(The above representation shall be completed by each bidder (or offeror) whose bid (offer) is $50,000 or more and who has 50 or more employees.)*

CERTIFICATIONS *(Check or complete all applicable boxes or blocks)*

1. BUY AMERICAN CERTIFICATE

The offeror certifies as part of his offer, that: each end product, except the end products listed below, is a domestic end product (as defined in the *clause* entitled "Buy American Act"); and that components of unknown origin have been considered to have been mined, produced, or manufactured outside the United States.

EXCLUDED END PRODUCTS	COUNTRY OF ORIGIN

2. **CLEAN AIR AND WATER** *(Applicable if the bid or offer exceeds $100,000, or the contracting officer has determined that orders under an indefinite quantity contract in any year will exceed $100,000, or a facility to be used has been the subject of a conviction under the Clean Air Act (42 U.S.C. 1857c-8(c)(1)) or the Federal Water Pollution Control Act (33 U.S.C.1319(c)) and is listed by EPA, or is not otherwise exempt.)*

The bidder or offeror certifies as follows:

(a) Any facility to be utilized in the performance of this proposed contract ☐ has, ☐ has not, been listed on the Environmental Protection Agency List of Violating Facilities.

(b) He will promptly notify the contracting officer, prior to award, of the receipt of any communication from the Director, Office of Federal Activities, Environmental Protection Agency, indicating that any facility which he proposes to use for the performance of the contract is under consideration to be listed on the EPA list of Violating Facilities.

(c) He will include substantially this certification, including this paragraph (c), in every nonexempt subcontract.

3. **CERTIFICATION OF INDEPENDENT PRICE DETERMINATION** *(See par. 18 on SF 33-A)*

(a) By submission of this offer, the offeror certifies, and in the case of a joint offer, each party thereto certifies as to its own organization, that in connection with this procurement:

(1) The prices in this offer have been arrived at independently, without consultation, communication, or agreement, for the purpose of restricting competition, as to any matter relating to such prices with any other offeror or with any competitor;

(2) Unless otherwise required by law, the prices which have been quoted in this offer have not been knowingly disclosed by the offeror and will not knowingly be disclosed by the offeror prior to opening in the case of an advertised procurement or prior to award in the case of a negotiated procurement, directly or indirectly to any other offeror or to any competitor; and

(3) No attempt has been made or will be made by the offeror to induce any other person or firm to submit or not to submit an offer for that purpose of restricting competition.

(b) Each person signing this offer certifies that:

(1) He is the person in the offeror's organization responsible within that organization for the decision as to the prices being offered herein and that he has not participated, and will not participate, in any action contrary to (a)(1) through (a)(3), above; or

(2) (i) He is not the person in the offeror's organization responsible within that organization for the decision as to the prices being offered herein but that he has been authorized in writing to act as-agent for the persons responsible for such decision in certifying that such persons have not participated and will not participate, in any action contrary to (a)(1) through (a)(3) above, and as their agent does hereby so certify; and (ii) he has not participated, and will not participate, in any action contrary to (a)(1) through (a)(3) above.

4. **CERTIFICATION OF NONSEGREGATED FACILITIES** *(Applicable to (1) contracts, (2) subcontracts, and (3) agreements with applicants who are themselves performing federally assisted construction contracts, exceeding $10,000 which are not exempt from the provisions of the Equal Opportunity clause.)*

By the submission of this bid, the bidder, offeror, applicant, or subcontractor certifies that he does not maintain or provide for his employees any segregated facilities at any of his establishments, and that he does not permit his employees to perform their services at any location under his control, where segregated facilities are maintained. He certifies further that he will not maintain or provide for his employees any segregated facilities at any of his establishments, and that he will not permit his employees to perform their services at any location, under his control, where segregated facilities are maintained. The bidder, offeror, applicant, or subcontractor agrees that a breach of this certification is a violation of the Equal Opportunity clause in this contract. As used in this certification, the term "segregated facilities" means any waiting rooms, work areas, rest rooms and wash rooms, restaurants and other eating areas, time clocks, locker rooms and other storage or dressing areas, parking lots, drinking fountains, recreation or entertainment areas, transportation, and housing facilities provided for employees which are segregated by explicit directive or are in fact segregated on the basis of race, color, religion or national origin, because of habit, local custom, or otherwise. He further agrees that (except where he has obtained identical certifications from proposed subcontractors for specific time periods) he will obtain identical certifications from proposed subcontractors prior to the award of subcontracts exceeding $10,000 which are not exempt from the provisions of the Equal Opportunity clause; that he will retain such certifications in his files; and that he will forward the following notice to such proposed subcontractors (except where the proposed subcontractors have submitted identical certifications for specific time periods):

Notice to prospective subcontractors of requirement for certifications of nonsegregated facilities.

A Certification of Nonsegregated Facilities must be submitted prior to the award of a subcontract exceeding $10,000 which is not exempt from the provisions of the Equal Opportunity clause. The certification may be submitted either for each subcontract or for all subcontracts during a period (i.e., quarterly, semiannually, or annually). *NOTE: The penalty for making false offers is prescribed in 18 U.S.C. 1001.*

ACKNOWLEDGMENT OF AMENDMENTS The offeror acknowledges receipt of amendments to the Solicitation for offers and related documents numbered and dated as follows:	AMENDMENT NO	DATE	AMENDMENT NO	DATE

NOTE: Offers must set forth full, accurate and complete information as required by this Solicitation (including attachments). The penalty for making false statements in offers is prescribed in 18 U.S.C. 1001.

Standard Form 33 Page 3 (REV 3-77)

338

SOLICITATION INSTRUCTIONS AND CONDITIONS

1. DEFINITIONS.

As used herein:

(a) The term "solicitation" means Invitation for Bids (IFB) where the procurement is advertised, and Request for Proposal (RFP) where the procurement is negotiated.

(b). The term "offer" means bid where the procurement is advertised, and proposal where the procurement is negotiated.

(c) For purposes of this solicitation and Block 2 of Standard Form 33, the term "advertised" includes Small Business Restricted Advertising and other types of restricted advertising.

2. PREPARATION OF OFFERS.

(a) Offerors are expected to examine the drawings, specifications, Schedule, and all instructions. Failure to do so will be at offeror's risk.

(b) Each offeror shall furnish the information required by the solicitation. The offeror shall sign the solicitation and print or type his name on the Schedule and each Continuation Sheet thereof on which he makes an entry. Erasures or other changes must be initialed by the person signing the offer. Offers signed by an agent are to be accompanied by evidence of his authority unless such evidence has been previously furnished to the issuing office.

(c) Unit price for each unit offered shall be shown and such price shall include packing unless otherwise specified. A total shall be entered in the Amount column of the Schedule for each item offered. In case of discrepancy between a unit price and extended price, the unit price will be presumed to be correct, subject, however, to correction to the same extent and in the same manner as any other mistake.

(d) Offers for supplies or services other than those specified will not be considered unless authorized by the solicitation.

(e) Offeror must state a definite time for delivery of supplies or for performance of services unless otherwise specified in the solicitation.

(f) Time, if stated as a number of days, will include Saturdays, Sundays and holidays.

(g) Code boxes are for Government use only.

3. EXPLANATION TO OFFERORS.
Any explanation desired by an offeror regarding the meaning or interpretation of the solicitation, drawings, specifications, etc., must be requested in writing and with sufficient time allowed for a reply to reach offerors before the submission of their offers. Oral explanations or instructions given before the award of the contract will not be binding. Any information given to a prospective offeror concerning a solicitation will be furnished to all prospective offerors as an amendment of the solicitation, if such information is necessary to offerors in submitting offers on the solicitation or if the lack of such information would be prejudicial to uninformed offerors.

4. ACKNOWLEDGMENT OF AMENDMENTS TO SOLICITATIONS.
Receipt of an amendment to a solicitation by an offeror must be acknowledged (a) by signing and returning the amendment, (b) on page three of Standard Form 33, or (c) by letter or telegram. Such acknowledgment must be received prior to the hour and date specified for receipt of offers.

5. SUBMISSION OF OFFERS.

(a) Offers and modifications thereof shall be enclosed in sealed envelopes and addressed to the office specified in the solicitation. The offeror shall show the hour and date specified in the solicitation for receipt, the solicitation number, and the name and address of the offeror on the face of the envelope.

(b) Telegraphic offers will not be considered unless authorized by the solicitation; however, offers may be modified or withdrawn by written or telegraphic notice, provided such notice is received prior to the hour and date specified for receipt. (However, see paragraphs 7 and 8.)

(c) Samples of items, when required, must be submitted within the time specified, and unless otherwise specified by the Government, at no expense to the Government. If not destroyed by testing, samples will be returned at offeror's request and expense, unless otherwise specified by the solicitation.

6. FAILURE TO SUBMIT OFFER.
If no offer is to be submitted, do not return the solicitation unless otherwise specified. A letter or postcard shall be sent to the issuing office advising whether future solicitations for the type of supplies or services covered by this solicitation are desired. Failure of the recipient to offer, or to notify the issuing office that future solicitations are desired, may result in removal of the name of such recipient from the mailing list for the type of supplies or services covered by the solicitation.

7. LATE BIDS, MODIFICATIONS OF BIDS, OR WITHDRAWAL OF BIDS.

(a) Any bid received at the office designated in the solicitation after the exact time specified for receipt will not be considered unless it is received before award is made and either:

(1) It was sent by registered or certified mail not later than the fifth calendar day prior to the date specified for the receipt of bids (e.g., a bid submitted in response to a solicitation requiring receipt of bids by the 20th of the month must have been mailed by the 15th or earlier) ; or

(2) It was sent by mail (or telegram if authorized) and it is determined by the Government that the late receipt was due solely to mishandling by the Government after receipt at the Government installation.

(b) Any modification or withdrawal of a bid is subject to the same conditions as in (a), above. A bid may also be withdrawn in person by a bidder or his authorized representative, provided his identity is made known and he signs a receipt for the bid, but only if the withdrawal is made prior to the exact time set for receipt of bids.

(c) The only acceptable evidence to establish:

(1) The date of mailing of a late bid, modification, or withdrawal sent either by registered or certified mail is the U.S. Postal Service postmark on both the envelope or wrapper and on the original receipt from the U.S. Postal Service. If neither postmark shows a legible date, the bid, modification, or withdrawal shall be deemed to have been mailed late. (The term "postmark" means a printed, stamped, or otherwise placed impression (exclusive of a postage meter machine impression) that is readily identifiable without further action as having been supplied and affixed on the date of mailing by employees of the U.S. Postal Service. Therefore, offerors should request the postal clerk to place a hand cancellation bull's-eye "postmark" on both the receipt and the envelope or wrapper.)

(2) The time of receipt at the Government installation is the time-date stamp of such installation on the bid wrapper or other documentary evidence of receipt maintained by the installation.

(d) Notwithstanding (a) and (b) of this provision, a late modification of an otherwise successful bid which makes its terms more favorable to the Government will be considered at any time it is received and may be accepted.

Note: The term "telegram" includes mailgrams.

8. LATE PROPOSALS, MODIFICATIONS OF PROPOSALS, AND WITHDRAWALS OF PROPOSALS.

(a) Any proposal received at the office designated in the solicitation after the exact time specified for receipt will not be considered unless it is received before award is made, and:

(1) It was sent by registered or certified mail not later than the fifth calendar day prior to the date specified for receipt of offers (e.g., an offer submitted in response to a solicitation requiring receipt of offers by the 20th of the month must have been mailed by the 15th or earlier) ;

(2) It was sent by mail (or telegram if authorized) and it is determined by the Government that the late receipt was due solely to mishandling by the Government after receipt at the Government installation ; or

(3) It is the only proposal received.

(b) Any modification of a proposal, except a modification resulting from the Contracting Officer's request for "best and final" offer, is subject to the same conditions as in (a)(1) and (a)(2) of this provision.

(c) A modification resulting from the Contracting Officer's request for "best and final" offer received after the time and date specified in the request will not be considered unless received before award and the late receipt is due solely to mishandling by the Government after receipt at the Government installation.

(d) The only acceptable evidence to establish:

(1) The date of mailing of a late proposal or modification sent either by registered or certified mail is the U.S. Postal Service postmark on both the envelope or wrapper and on the original receipt from the U.S. Postal Service. If neither postmark shows a legible date, the proposal or modification shall be deemed to have been mailed late. (The term "postmark" means a printed, stamped, or otherwise, placed impression (exclusive of a postage meter machine impression) that is readily identifiable without further action as having been supplied and affixed on the date of mailing by employees of the U.S. Postal Service. Therefore, offerors should request the postal clerk to place a hand cancellation bull's-eye "postmark" on both the receipt and the envelope or wrapper.)

(2) The time of receipt at the Government installation is the time-date stamp of such installation on the proposal wrapper or other documentary evidence of receipt maintained by the installation.

STANDARD FORM 33–A (Rev. 1–78)
Prescribed by GSA, FPR (41 CFR) 1-16.101

(e) Notwithstanding (a), (b), and (c), of this provision, a late modification of an otherwise successful proposal which makes its terms more favorable to the Government will be considered at any time it is received and may be accepted.

(f) Proposals may be withdrawn by written or telegraphic notice received at any time prior to award. Proposals may be withdrawn in person by an offeror or his authorized representative, provided his identity is made known and he signs a receipt for the proposal prior to award.

Note: The term "telegram" includes mailgrams.

Note: The alternate late proposals, modifications of proposals and withdrawals of proposals provision prescribed by 41 CFR 1-3.802-2(b) shall be used in lieu of provision 8, if specified by the contract.

9. DISCOUNTS.

(a) Notwithstanding the fact that a blank is provided for a ten (10) day discount, prompt payment discounts offered for payment within less than twenty (20) calendar days will not be considered in evaluating offers for award, unless otherwise specified in the solicitation. However, offered discounts of less than 20 days will be taken if payment is made within the discount period, even though not considered in the evaluation of offers.

(b) In connection with any discount offered, time will be computed from date of delivery of the supplies to carrier when delivery and acceptance are at point of origin, or from date of delivery at destination or port of embarkation when delivery and acceptance are at either of those points, or from the date correct invoice or voucher is received in the office specified by the Government, if the latter date is later than date of delivery. Payment is deemed to be made for the purpose of earning the discount on the date of mailing of the Government check.

10. AWARD OF CONTRACT.

(a) The contract will be awarded to that responsible offeror whose offer conforming to the solicitation will be most advantageous to the Government, price and other factors considered.

(b) The Government reserves the right to reject any or all offers and to waive informalities and minor irregularities in offers received.

(c) The Government may accept any item or group of items of any offer, unless the offeror qualifies his offer by specific limitations. UNLESS OTHERWISE PROVIDED IN THE SCHEDULE, OFFERS MAY BE SUBMITTED FOR ANY QUANTITIES LESS THAN THOSE SPECIFIED; AND THE GOVERNMENT RESERVES THE RIGHT TO MAKE AN AWARD ON ANY ITEM FOR A QUANTITY LESS THAN THE QUANTITY OFFERED AT THE UNIT PRICES OFFERED UNLESS THE OFFEROR SPECIFIES OTHERWISE IN HIS OFFER.

(d) A written award (or Acceptance of Offer) mailed (or otherwise furnished) to the successful offeror within the time for acceptance specified in the offer shall be deemed to result in a binding contract without further action by either party.

The following paragraphs (e) through (h) apply only to negotiated solicitations:

(e) The Government may accept within the time specified therein, any offer (or part thereof, as provided in (c) above), whether or not there are negotiations subsequent to its receipt, unless the offer is withdrawn by written notice received by the Government prior to award. If subsequent negotiations are conducted, they shall not constitute a rejection or counter offer on the part of the Government.

(f) The right is reserved to accept other than the lowest offer and to reject any or all offers.

(g) The Government may award a contract, based on initial offers received, without discussion of such offers. Accordingly, each initial offer should be submitted on the most favorable terms from a price and technical standpoint which the offeror can submit to the Government.

(h) Any financial data submitted with any offer hereunder or any representation concerning facilities or financing will not form a part of any resulting contract; provided, however, that if the resulting contract contains a clause providing for price reduction for defective cost or pricing data, the contract price will be subject to reduction, if cost or pricing data furnished hereunder is incomplete, inaccurate, or not current.

11. GOVERNMENT-FURNISHED PROPERTY. No material, labor, or facilities will be furnished by the Government unless otherwise provided for in the solicitation.

12. LABOR INFORMATION. General information regarding the requirements of the Walsh-Healey Public Contracts Act (41 U.S.C.

35-45), the Contract Work Hours Standards Act (40 U.S.C. 327-330), and the Service Contract Act of 1965 (41 U.S.C. 351-357) may be obtained from the Department of Labor, Washington, D.C. 20210, or from any regional office of that agency. Requests for information should include the solicitation number, the name and address of the issuing agency, and a description of the supplies or services.

13. SELLER'S INVOICES. Invoices shall be prepared and submitted in quadruplicate (one copy shall be marked "original") unless otherwise specified. Invoices shall contain the following information: Contract and order number (if any), item numbers, description of supplies or services, sizes, quantities, unit prices, and extended totals. Bill of lading number and weight of shipment will be shown for shipments made on Government bills of lading.

14. SMALL BUSINESS CONCERN. A small business concern for the purpose of Government procurement is a concern, including its affiliates, which is independently owned and operated, is not dominant in the field of operation in which it is submitting offers on Government contracts, and can further qualify under the criteria concerning number of employees, average annual receipts, or other criteria, as prescribed by the Small Business Administration. (See Code of Federal Regulations, Title 13, Part 121, as amended, which contains detailed industry definitions and related procedures.)

15. CONTINGENT FEE. If the offeror, by checking the appropriate box provided therefor, has represented that he has employed or retained a company or person (other than a full-time bona fide employee working solely for the offeror) to solicit or secure this contract, or that he has paid or agreed to pay any fee, commission, percentage, or brokerage fee to any company or person contingent upon or resulting from the award of this contract, he shall furnish, in duplicate, a complete Standard Form 119, Contractor's Statement of Contingent or Other Fees. If offeror has previously furnished a completed Standard Form 119 to the office issuing this solicitation, he may accompany his offer with a signed statement (a) indicating when such completed form was previously furnished, (b) identifying by number the previous solicitation or contract, if any, in connection with which such form was submitted, and (c) representing that the statement in such form is applicable to this offer.

16. PARENT COMPANY. A parent company for the purpose of this offer is a company which either owns or controls the activities and basic business policies of the offeror. To own another company means the parent company must own at least a majority (more than 50 percent) of the voting rights in that company. To control another company, such ownership is not required; if another company is able to formulate, determine, or veto basic business policy decisions of the offeror, such other company is considered the parent company of the offeror. This control may be exercised through the use of dominant minority voting rights, use of proxy voting, contractual arrangements, or otherwise.

17. EMPLOYER'S IDENTIFICATION NUMBER. (Applicable only to advertised solicitations.) The offeror shall insert in the applicable space on the offer form, if he has no parent company, his own Employer's Identification Number (E.I. No.) (Federal Social Security Number used on Employer's Quarterly Federal Tax Return, U.S. Treasury Department Form 941), or, if he has a parent company, the Employer's Identification Number of his parent company.

18. CERTIFICATION OF INDEPENDENT PRICE DETERMINATION.

(a) This certification on the offer form is not applicable to a foreign offeror submitting an offer for a contract which requires performance or delivery outside the United States, its possessions, and Puerto Rico.

(b) An offer will not be considered for award where (a)(1), (a)(3), or (b) of the certification has been deleted or modified. Where (a)(2) of the certification has been deleted or modified, the offer will not be considered for award unless the offeror furnishes with the offer a signed statement which sets forth in detail the circumstances of the disclosure and the head of the agency, or his designee, determines that such disclosure was not made for the purpose of restricting competition.

19. ORDER OF PRECEDENCE. In the event of an inconsistency between provisions of this solicitation, the inconsistency shall be resolved by giving precedence in the following order: (a) the Schedule; (b) Solicitation Instructions and Conditions; (c) General Provisions; (d) other provisions of the contract, whether incorporated by reference or otherwise; and (e) the specifications.

Source: U.S. Small Business Administration, *Women Business Owners: Selling to the Federal Government,* Washington, D.C.: U.S. Small Business Administration, Office of Women's Business Ownership, June 1990, Appendix 1, pps. 20-29.

Contacts for Selling to Foreign Governments and Industries

ALABAMA
*Birmingham**—Rm. 302, Berry Bldg., 2015 2nd Ave. North, 35203, (205) 731-1331

ALASKA
Anchorage—World Trade Center, 4201 Tudor Centre Dr., Suite 319, 99508, (907) 261-4237

ARIZONA
Phoenix—Federal Bldg., 230 North 1st Ave., Rm. 3412, 85025, (602) 379-3285

ARKANSAS
Little Rock—Suite 811, Savers Fed. Bldg., 320 W. Capitol Ave., 72201, (501) 324-5794

CALIFORNIA
Los Angeles—Rm. 9200, 11000 Wilshire Blvd., 90024, (213) 575-7104.
Santa Ana—116-A W. 4th St., Suite #1, 92701, (714) 836-2461
San Diego—6363 Greenwich Dr., Suite 145, 92122, (619) 557-5395
*San Francisco**—Fed. Bldg., Box 36013, 450 Golden Gate Ave., 94102, (415) 556-5860

COLORADO
*Denver**—Suite 680, 1625 Broadway, 80202, (303) 844-3246

CONNECTICUT
*Hartford**—Rm. 610-B, Fed. Office Bldg., 450 Main St., 06103, (203) 240-3530

DELAWARE
Serviced by Philadelphia District Office

DISTRICT OF COLUMBIA
*Washington, D.C.**—(Baltimore District) Rm. 1066 HCHB, Department of Commerce, 14th St. & Constitution Ave., N.W. 20230, (202) 377-3181

FLORIDA
Miami—Suite 224, Fed. Bldg., 51 S.W. First Ave., 33130, (305) 536-5267
*Clearwater**—128 North Osceola Ave. 34615, (813) 461-0011
*Orlando**—College of Business Administration, CEBA II, Rm. 346, University of Central Florida, 32816, (407) 648-6235
*Tallahassee**—Collins Bldg., Rm. 401, 107 W. Gaines St., 32304, (904) 488-6469

GEORGIA
Atlanta—Plaza Square North, 4360 Chamblee Dunwoody Rd., 30341, (404) 452-9101
Savannah—120 Barnard St., A-107, 31401, (912) 944-4204

HAWAII
Honolulu—P.O. Box 50026, 400 Ala Moana Blvd., 96850, (808) 541-1782

IDAHO
*Boise (Portland District)**—2nd Flr., Joe R. Williams Bldg., 700 W. State St., 83720, (208) 334-3857

ILLINOIS
Chicago—Rm. 1406, 55 East Monroe St., 60603, (312) 353-4450
Wheaton—Illinois Institute of Technology, 201 East Loop Rd., 60187, (708) 353-4332
*Rockford**—515 North Court St., P.O. Box 1747, 61110-0247, (815) 987-8123

INDIANA
Indianapolis—One North Capitol Ave., Suite 520, 46204, (317) 226-6214

---

* DENOTES REGIONAL OFFICE WITH SUPERVISORY REGIONAL RESPONSIBILITIES
* DENOTES TRADE SPECIALIST AT A BRANCH OFFICE

IOWA
Des Moines—817 Fed. Bldg., 210 Walnut St., 50309, (515) 284-4222
*Cedar Rapids**—424 First Ave. N.E. 52401, (319) 362-8418

KANSAS
*Wichita**—(Kansas City, Mo., District) 151 N. Volutsla, 67214-4695 (316) 269-6160

KENTUCKY
Louisville—Rm. 636B, Gene Snyder Courthouse and Customhouse Bldg., 601 W. Broadway, 40202, (502) 582-5066

LOUISIANA
New Orleans—432 World Trade Center, No. 2 Canal St., 70130, (504) 589-6546

MAINE
*Augusta**—(Boston District) 77 Sewall St., 04330, (207) 622-8249

MARYLAND
Baltimore—413 U.S. Customhouse, 40 South Gay and Lombard Sts., 21202, (301) 962-3560

MASSACHUSETTS
Boston—World Trade Center, Suite 307 Commonwealth Pier Area, 02210, (617) 565-8563

MICHIGAN
Detroit—1140 McNamara Bldg., 477 Michigan Ave., 48226, (313) 226-3650
*Grand Rapids**—300 Monroe N.W., 49503, (616) 456-2411

MINNESOTA
Minneapolis—108 Fed. Bldg., 110 S. 4th St., 55401, (612) 348-1638

MISSISSIPPI
Jackson—328 Jackson Mail Office Center, 300 Woodrow Wilson Blvd., 39213, (601) 965-4388

MISSOURI
*St. Louis**—7911 Forsyth Blvd., Suite 610, 63105, (314) 425-3302
Kansas City—Rm. 635, 601 East 12th St., 64106, (816) 426-3141

MONTANA
Serviced by Portland District Office

NEBRASKA
Omaha—11133 "O" St., 68137, (402) 221-3664

NEVADA
Reno—1755 E. Plumb Ln., #152, 89502, (702) 785-5203

NEW HAMPSHIRE
Serviced by Boston District Office

NEW JERSEY
Trenton—3131 Princeton Pike Bldg., #6, Suite 100, 08648, (609) 989-2100

NEW MEXICO
*Albuquerque** (Dallas District)—625 Silver SW., 3rd Fl., 87102, (506) 766-2070
*Sante Fe** (Dallas District)—c/o Economic Develop and Tourism Dept., 1100 St. Francis Drive, 87503, (505) 988-6261

NEW YORK
Buffalo—1312 Fed. Bldg., 111 West Huron St., 14202, (716) 846-4191
*Rochester**—111 East Ave., Suite 220, 14604, (716) 263-6480
New York—Fed. Office Bldg., 26 Fed. Plaza, Rm. 3718, Foley Sq., 10278, (212) 264-0600

NORTH CAROLINA
*Greensboro**—324 W. Market St., Room 203, P.O. Box 1950, 27402, (919) 333-5345

NORTH DAKOTA
Serviced by Omaha District Office

OHIO
*Cincinnati**—9504 Fed. Office Bldg., 550 Main St., 45202, (513) 684-2944
Cleveland—Rm. 600, 668 Euclid Ave., 44114 (216) 522-4750

OKLAHOMA
Oklahoma City—6601 Broadway Extension, 73116, (405) 231-5302
*Tulsa**—140 S. Houston St., 74127, (918) 581-7650

OREGON
Portland—Suite 242, One World Trade Center, 121 S.W. Salmon St., 97204, (503) 326-3001

PENNSYLVANIA
Philadelphia—475 Allendale Road, Suite 202, King of Prussia, Pa., 19406, (215) 962-4980
Pittsburgh—2002 Fed. Bldg., 1000 Liberty Ave., 15222, (412) 644-2850

PUERTO RICO
San Juan (Hato Rey)—Rm. G-55 Fed. Bldg., 00918, (809) 766-5555

RHODE ISLAND
*Providence**—(Boston District) 7 Jackson Walkway, 02903, (401) 528-5104, ext. 22

SOUTH CAROLINA
Columbia—Strom Thurmond Fed. Bldg., Suite 172, 1835 Assembly St., 29201 (803) 765-5345
*Charleston**—JC Long Bldg., Rm. 128, 9 Liberty St., 29424, (803) 724-4361

SOUTH DAKOTA
Serviced by Omaha District Office

TENNESSEE
Nashville—Suite 1114, Parkway Towers, 404 James Robertson Parkway, 37219-1505, (615) 736-5161
*Knoxville**—301 E. Church Ave., 37915, (615) 549-9268
*Memphis**—The Falls Building, Suite 200, 22 North Front St., 38103, (901) 544-4137

TEXAS
*Dallas**—Rm. 7A5, 1100 Commerce St., 75242-0787, (214) 767-0542
*Austin**—P.O. Box 12728, 816 Congress Ave., Suite 1200, 78711, (512) 482-5939
Houston—2625 Fed. Courthouse, 515 Rusk St., 77002, (713) 229-2578

UTAH
Salt Lake City—Suite 105, 324 South State St., 84111, (801) 524-5116

VERMONT
Serviced by Boston District Office

VIRGINIA
Richmond—8010 Fed. Bldg., 400 North 8th St., 23240, (804) 771-2246

WASHINGTON
Seattle—3131 Elliott Ave., Suite 290, 98121, (206) 553-5615
*Spokane**—West 808 Spokane Falls Blvd., Suite 625, 99201, (509) 456-2922

WEST VIRGINIA
Charleston—405 Capitol St., Suite 809, 25301, (304) 347-5123

WISCONSIN
Milwaukee—Fed. Bldg., U.S. Courthouse, Rm. 606, 517 E. Wisc. Ave., 53202, (414) 297-3473

WYOMING
Serviced by Denver District Office

Source: U.S. Department of Commerce, *How to Sell to the United States Department of Commerce*, Washington, D.C.: U.S. Government Printing Office, April 1988.

Listing of Country Desk Officers

Country	Desk Officer	Phone (202)	Room	Country	Desk Officer	Phone (202)	Room
A				**E**			
Afghanistan	Stanislaw Bilinski	377-2954	2029B	East Caribbean	Robert Dormitzer	377-2527	3021
Albania	Elizabeth Brown/EEBIC	377-2645	6043	Ecuador	Laurie McNamara	377-1659	3025
Algeria	Jeffrey Johnson	377-4652	2039	Egypt	Thomas Sams	377-4441	2039
Angola	Stephen Lamar	377-5148	3317	El Salvador	Theodore Johnson	377-2527	3020
Anguilla	Robert Dormitzer	377-2527	3021	Equatorial	Jeffrey Hawkins	377-5148	3317
Argentina	Randy Mye	377-1548	3021	Guinea			
Aruba	Thomas Wilde	377-2527	3020	Ethiopia	Chandra Watkins	377-4564	3317
ASEAN	George Paine	377-3875	2308	European	Charles Ludolph	377-5276	3036
Antigua/Barbuda	Robert Dormitzer	377-2527	3021	Community			
Australia	Simone Altfeld	377-3875	2308				
Austria	Philip Combs	377-2920	3029	**F**			
				Finland	Maryanne Lyons	377-3254	3413
B				France	Kelly Jacobs/	377-8008	3042
Bahamas	Mark Siegelman	377-2527	3021		Elena Mikalis		
Bahrain	Claude Clement	377-5545	2039				
Bangladesh	Stanislaw Bilinski	377-2954	2029B	**G**			
Barbados	Robert Dormitzer	377-2527	3021	Gabon	Jeffrey Hawkins	377-5148	3317
Belgium	Simon Bensimon	377-5373	3046	Gambia	Reginald Biddle	377-4388	3317
Belize	Robert Dormitzer	377-2527	3021	Germany	Velizar Stanoyevitch/	377-2434	3409
Benin	Reginald Biddle	377-4388	3317		Brenda Fisher/	377-2435	3409
Bermuda	Robert Dormitzer	377-2527	3021		Joan Kloepfer	377-2841	3409
Bhutan	Stanislaw Bilinski	377-2954	2029B	Ghana	Reginald Biddle	377-4388	3317
Bolivia	Laura Zeiger	377-2521	3029	Greece	Ann Corro	377-3945	3044
Botswana	Stephen Lamar	377-5148	3317	Grenada	Robert Dormitzer	377-2527	3021
Brazil	Roger Turner/	377-3871	3017	Guadeloupe	Robert Dormitzer	377-2527	3021
	Larry Farris			Guatemala	Theodore Johnson	377-2527	3020
Brunei	Alison Lester	377-3875	2308	Guinea	Philip Michelini	377-4388	3317
Bulgaria	Elizabeth Brown/EEBIC	377-2645	6043	Guinea-Bissau	Philip Michelini	377-4388	3317
Burkina Faso	Philip Michelini	377-4388	3317	Guyana	Robert Dormitzer	377-2527	3021
Burma	George Paine	377-3875	2308				
(Myanmar)				**H**			
Burundi	Jeffrey Hawkins	377-5148	3317	Haiti	Mark Siegelman	377-2527	3021
				Honduras	Theodore Johnson	377-2527	3020
C				Hong Kong	JeNelle Matheson	377-3583	2317
Cambodia	Hong-Phong B. Pho	377-3875	2308	Hungary	Russell Johnson/EEBIC	377-2645	6043
Cameroon	Jeffrey Hawkins	377-5148	3317				
Canada	Kathleen Keim/	377-3101	3033	**I**			
	Joseph Payne			Iceland	Maryanne Lyons	377-3254	3037
Cape Verde	Philip Michelini	377-4388	3317	India	John Simmons/	377-2954	2029B
Caymans	Robert Dormitzer	377-2527	3020		John Crown/		
Central Africa	Jeffrey Hawkins	377-5148	3317		Tim Gilman		
Rep.				Indonesia	Karen Goddin	377-3875	2308
Chad	Jeffrey Hawkins	377-5148	3317	Iran	Claude Clement	377-5545	2039
Chile	Randy Mye	377-1548	3017	Iraq	Thomas Sams	377-4441	2039
Colombia	Laurie MacNamara	377-1659	3025	Ireland	Boyce Fitzpatrick	377-5401	3039
Comoros	Chandra Watkins	377-4564	3317	Israel	Kate FitzGerald-Wilks	377-4652	2039
Congo	Jeffrey Hawkins	377-5148	3317	Italy	Noel Negretti	377-2177	3045
Costa Rica	Theodore Johnson	377-2527	3020	Ivory Coast	Philip Michelini	377-4388	3317
Cuba	Mark Siegelman	377-2527	3021				
Cyprus	Ann Corro	377-3945	3044	**J**			
Czechoslovakia	Shelley Galbraith/EEBIC	377-2645	6043	Jamaica	Mark Siegelman	377-2527	3021
				Japan	Ed Leslie/	377-2425	2318
D					Cantwell Walsh/		
Denmark	Maryanne Lyons	377-3254	3413		Eric Kennedy		
D'Jibouti	Chandra Watkins	377-4564	3317	Jordan	Corey Wright	377-2515	2039
Dominica	Robert Dormitzer	377-2527	3021				
Dominican Rep.	Mark Siegelman	377-2527	3021				

The area code for telephoning these desk officers from outside Washington, D.C. is 202. Letters should be addressed to the individual at his or her room number, U.S. Department of Commerce, Washington, D.C. 20230.

Country	Desk Officer	Phone (202)	Room
K			
Kenya	Chandra Watkins	377-4564	3317
Korea	Ian Davis/ Dan Duvall	377-4957	2327
Kuwait	Corey Wright	377-2515	2039
L			
Laos	Hong-Phong B. Pho	377-3875	2308
Lebanon	Corey Wright	377-2515	2039
Lesotho	Stephen Lamar	377-5148	3317
Liberia	Reginald Biddle	377-4388	3317
Libya	Claude Clement	377-5545	2039
Luxembourg	Simon Bensimon	377-5373	3046
M			
Macao	Rosemary Gallant	377-3583	2317
Madagascar	Chandra Watkins	377-4564	3317
Malawi	Stephen Lamar	377-5148	3317
Malaysia	Alison Lester	377-3875	2308
Maldives	Stanislaw Bilinski	377-2954	2029B
Mali	Philip Michelini	377-4388	3317
Malta	Robert McLaughlin	377-3748	3049
Martinique	Robert Dormitzer	377-2527	3021
Mauritania	Philip Michelini	377-4564	3317
Mauritius	Chandra Watkins	377-4564	3317
Mexico	Elise Pinkow/ Andrew Lowry/ Ingrid Mohn	377-4464	3028
Mongolia	Rosemary Gallant	377-3583	2317
Montserrat	Robert Dormitzer	377-2527	3314
Morocco	Claude Clement	377-5545	2039
Mozambique	Stephen Lamar	377-5148	3317
N			
Namibia	Emily Solomon	377-5148	3317
Nepal	Stanislaw Bilinski	377-2954	2029B
Netherlands	Boyce Fitzpatrick	377-5401	3039
Netherlands Antilles	Robert Dormitzer	377-2527	3021
New Zealand	Simone Altfeld	377-3975	2308
Nicaragua	Theodore Johnson	377-2527	3021
Niger	Philip Michelini	377-4388	3317
Nigeria	Reginald Biddle	377-4388	3317
Norway	James Devlin	377-4414	3037
O			
Oman	Claude Clement	377-5545	2039
P			
Pacific Islands	Karen Goddin	377-3875	2308
Pakistan	Cheryl McQueen	377-2954	2029B
Panama	Theodore Johnson	377-2527	3020
Paraguay	Randy Mye	377-1548	3021
People's Rep. of China	Christine Lucyk	377-3583	2317
Peru	Laura Zeiger	377-2521	3029
Philippines	George Paine	377-3875	2308
Poland	Michael Arsenault/ Mary Moskaluk/EEBIC	377-2645	6043
Portugal	Ann Corro	377-3945	3044
Puerto Rico	Mark Seigelman	377-2527	3021
Q			
Qatar	Claude Clement	377-5545	2039
R			
Romania	Lynn Fabrizio/EEBIC	377-2645	6043
Rwanda	Jeffrey Hawkins	377-5148	3317
S			
Sao Tome & Principe	Jeffrey Hawkins	377-5138	3317
Saudi Arabia	Jeffrey Johnson	377-4652	2039
Senegal	Philip Michelini	377-4388	3317
Seychelles	Chandra Watkins	377-4564	3317
Sierra Leone	Reginald Biddle	377-4388	3317
Singapore	Alison Lester	377-3875	2308
Somalia	Chandra Watkins	377-4564	3317
South Africa	Emily Solomon	377-5148	3317
Spain	Mary Beth Double	377-4508	3045
Sri Lanka	Stanislaw Bilinski	377-2954	2029B
St. Barthelemy	Robert Dormitzer	377-2527	3021
St. Kitts-Nevis	Robert Dormitzer	377-2527	3021
St. Lucia	Robert Dormitzer	377-2527	3021
St. Martin	Robert Dormitzer	377-2527	3021
St. Vincent– Grenadines	Robert Dormitzer	377-2527	3021
Sudan	Chandra Watkins	377-4564	3317
Suriname	Robert Dormitzer	377-2527	3021
Swaziland	Stephen Lamar	377-5148	3317
Sweden	James Devlin	377-4414	3037
Switzerland	Philip Combs	377-2920	3039
Syria	Corey Wright	377-2515	2039
T			
Taiwan	Laura Scogna/ Dan Duvall	377-4957	2308
Tanzania	Stephen Lamar	377-5148	3317
Thailand	Jean Kelly	377-3875	2308
Togo	Reginald Biddle	377-4564	3021
Trinidad & Tobago	Robert Dormitzer	377-2527	3021
Tunisia	Corey Wright	377-2515	2039
Turkey	Noel Negretti	377-2177	3045
Turks & Caicos Islands	Mark Siegelman	377-2527	3021
U			
Uganda	Chandra Watkins	377-4564	3317
United Arab Emirates	Claude Clement	377-5545	2039
United Kingdom	Robert McLaughlin	377-3748	3045
Uruguay	Mark Siegelman	377-1495	3021
USSR	Susan Lewenz/ Leslie Brown/ Linda Nemac	377-4655	3318
V, W			
Venezuela	Herbert Lindow	377-4303	3029
Vietnam	Hong-Phong B. Pho	377-3875	2308
Virgin Islands (UK)	Robert Dormitzer	377-2527	3020
Virgin Islands (US)	Mark Siegelman	377-2527	3021
X, Y			
Yemen, Rep. of	Corey Wright	377-2515	2039
Yugoslavia	Jeremy Keller/EEBIC	377-2645	6043
Z			
Zaire	Jeffrey Hawkins	377-5148	3317
Zambia	Stephen Lamar	377-5148	3317
Zimbabwe	Stephen Lamar	377-5148	3317

EEBIC (Eastern Europe Business Information Center)

Source: *Business America* 112 (Special Edition, 1991), pps. 18–19.

Listing of ITA Industry Desks

INDUSTRY	CONTACT	PHONE (202) 377-
A		
Abrasive Products	Presbury, Graylin	5157
Accounting	Chittum, J Marc	0345
Adhesives/Sealants	Prat, Raimundo	0128
Advertising	Chittum, J Marc	3050
Aerospace Financing Issues	Jackson, Jeff	0222
Aerospace Industry Analysis	Walsh, Hugh	0678
Aerospace Market Development	Bowie, David C	4222
Aerospace-Space Programs	Pajor, Peter	8228
Aerospace Trade Policy	Bath, Sally	4222
Aerospace (Trade Promo)	White, John C	2835
Agribusiness (Major Proj)	Bell, Richard	2460
Agricultural Chemicals	Maxey, Francis P	0128
Agricultural Machinery	Wiening, Mary	4708
Air Couriers	Elliott, Frederick	3734
Air Conditioning Eqpmt	Holley, Tyrena	3509
Air, Gas Compressors	McDonald, Edward	0680
Air, Gas Compressors (Trade Promo)	Zanetakos, George	0552
Air Pollution Control Eqpmt	Jonkers, Loretta	0564
Aircraft & Aircraft Engines	Driscoll, George	8228
Aircraft & Aircraft Engines (Trade Promo)	White, John C	2835
Aircraft Auxiliary Equipment	Driscoll, George	8228
Aircraft Parts (Market Support)	Driscoll, George	8228
Aircraft Parts/Aux Eqpmt (Trade Promo)	White, John C	2835
Airlines	Johnson, C William	5071
Airport Equipment	Driscoll, George	8228
Airport Equipment (Trade Promo)	White, John C	2835
Airports, Ports, Harbors (Major Proj)	Piggot, Deboorne	3352
Air Traffic Control Equip	Driscoll, George	8228
Alcoholic Beverages	Kenney, Cornelius	2428
Alum Sheet, Plate/Foil	Cammarota, David	0575
Alum Forgings, Electro	Cammarota, David	0575
Aluminum Extrud Alum Rolling	Cammarota, David	0575
Analytical Instruments	Podolske, Lewis	3360
Analytical Instruments (Trade Promo)	Manzolillo, Franc	2991
Animal Feeds	Janis, William V	2250
Apparel	Dulka, William	4058
Apparel (Trade Promo)	Molnar, F	2043
Asbestos/Cement Prod	Pitcher, Charles	0132
Assembly Equipment	Abrahams, Edward	0312
Audio Visual Equipment (Trade Promo)	Beckham, Reginald	5478
Audio Visual Services	Siegmund, John	4781
Auto Parts/Suppliers (Trade Promo)	Reck, Robert	5479
Auto Industry Affairs	Keitz, Stuart	0554
Air Transport Services	Johnson, C William	5071
Avionics Marketing	Driscoll, George	8228
B		
Bakery Products	Janis, William V	2250
Ball Bearings	Reise, Richard	3489
Basic Paper & Board Mfg	Smith, Leonard S	0375
Bauxite, Alumina, Prim Alum	Cammarota, David	0575
Beer	Kenney, Neil	2428
Belting & Hose	Prat, Raimundo	0128

INDUSTRY	CONTACT	PHONE (202) 377-
Beryllium	Duggan, Brian	0575
Beverages	Kenney, Cornelius	2428
Bicycles	Vanderwolf, John	0348
Biotechnology	Arakaki, Emily	3888
Biotechnology (Trade Promo)	Gwaltney, G P	3090
Boat Building (Major Proj)	Piggot, Deboorne	3352
Boats, pleasure	Vanderwolf, John	0348
Books	Lofquist, William S	0379
Books (Trade Promo)	Kimmel, Ed	3640
Brooms & Brushes	Harris, John	1178
Breakfast Cereal	Janis, William V	2250
Building Materials & Construction	Pitcher, Charles B	0132
Business Forms	Bratland, Rose Marie	0380
C		
CAD/CAM	McGibbon, Patrick	0314
Cable TV	Plock, Ernest	4781
Canned Food Products	Hodgen, Donald A	3346
Capital Goods (Trade Prom)	Morse, Jerry	5907
Carbon Black	Prat, Raimundo	0128
Cellular Radio Telephone Equip	Gossack, Linda	4466
Cement	Pitcher, Charles	0132
Cement Plants (Major Proj)	White, Barbara	4160
Ceramics (Advanced)	Shea, Moira	0128
Ceramics Machinery	Shaw, Eugene	3494
Cereals	Janis, William V	2250
Chemicals (Liaison & Policy)	Kelly, Michael J	0128
Chemical Plants (Major Proj)	Haraguchi, Wally	4877
Chemicals & Allied Products	Kamenicky, Vincent	0128
Chinaware	Corea, Judy	0311
Civil Aircraft Agreement	Bath, Sally	4222
Civil Aviation Policy	Johnson, C William	5071
Coal Exports	Yancik, Joseph J	1466
Cobalt	Cammarota, David	0575
Cocoa Products	Petrucco-Littleton	5124
Coffee Products	Petrucco-Littleton	5124
Commercial Aircraft (Trade Policy)	Bath, Sally	4222
Commercial Lighting Fixtures	Whitley, Richard A	0682
Commercial/Indus Refrig Eqpmt	Holley, Tyrena	3509
Commercial Printing	Lofquist, William S	0379
Commercialization of Space (Market)	Bowie, David C	8228
Commercialization of Space (Services)	Plock, Ernest	4781
Composites, Advanced	Manion, James	5157
Computer and DP Services	Atkins, Robert G/ Inoussa, Mary C	4781 / 5820
Computer Industry	Miles, Timothy O	2990
Computers (personal)	Woods, R Clay	3013
Computers (Trade Promo)	Fogg, Judy A	4936
Computer Consulting	Atkins, Robert G	4781
Confectionery Products	Kenney, Cornelius	2428
Construction	MacAuley, Patrick	0132
Construction Machinery	Heimowitz, Leonard	0558
Consumer Electronics	Fleming, Howard	5163
Consumer Goods	Boyd, Hayden	0337
Containers & Packaging	Cooperthite, Kim	5159
Cosmetics (Trade Promo)	Kimmel, Ed	3640
Cutlery	Corea, Judy	0311

INDUSTRY	CONTACT	PHONE (202) 377-
D		
Dairy Products	Janis, William V	2250
Data Base Services	Inoussa, Mary C	5820
Data Processing Services	Atkins, Robert G	4781
Desalination/Water Reuse	Greer, Damon	0564
Direct Marketing	Elliott, Frederick	3734
Distilled Spirits	Kenney, Neil	2428
Disk Drives	Kader, Victoria	0571
Dolls	Corea, Judy	0311
Drugs	McIntyre, Leo	0128
Durable Consumer Goods	Ellis, Kevin	1176
E		
Earthenware	Corea, Judy	0311
Education Facilities (Major Proj)	White, Barbara	4160
Educational/Training	Francis, Simon	0350
Electric Industrial Apparatus Nec	Whitley, Richard A	0682
Elec/Power Gen/Transmission & Dist Eqt (Trade Promo)	Brandes, Jay	0560
Electrical Power Plants (Major Proj)	Dollison, Robert	2733
Electrical Test & Measuring	Hall, Sarah	2846
Electricity	Sugg, William	1466
ElectroOptical Instruments (Trade Promo)	Manzolillo, Franc	2991
ElectroOptical Instruments	Podolske, Lewis	3360
Electronic Components	Scott, Robert	2795
Electronic Components/ Production & Test Equip (Trade Promo)	Burke, Joseph J	5014
Electronic Database Services	Inoussa, Mary C	5820
Elevators, Moving Stairways	Wiening, Mary	4708
Employment Services	Francis, Simon	0350
Energy (Commodities)	Yancik, Joseph J	1466
Energy, Renewable	Rasmussen, John	1466
Engineering/Construction Services (Trade Promo)	Ruan, Robert	0359
Entertainment Industries	Siegmund, John	4781
Entertainment Ind.	Plock, Ernest	4781
Explosives	Maxey, Francis P	0128
Export Trading Companies	Muller, George	5131
F		
Fabricated Metal Construction Materials	Williams, Franklin	0132
Farm Machinery	Wiening, Mary	4708
Fasteners (Industrial)	Reise, Richard	3489
Fats and Oils	Janis, William V	2250
Fencing (Metal)	Shaw, Robert	0132
Ferroalloys Products	Presbury, Graylin	5158
Ferrous Scrap	Sharkey, Robert	0606
Fertilizers	Maxey, Francis P	0128
Fiber Optics	McCarthy, James	4466
Filters/Purifying Eqmt	Jonkers, Loretta	0564
Finance & Management Industries	Candilis, Wray O	0339
Fisheries (Major Proj)	Bell, Richard	2460
Flexible Mftg Systems	McGibbon, Patrick	0314
Flour	Janis, William V	2250

345

INDUSTRY	CONTACT	PHONE (202) 377-
Flowers	Janis, William V	2250
Fluid Power	McDonald, Edward	0680
Food Products Machinery	Shaw, Eugene	3494
Food Retailing	Kenney, Cornelius	2428
Footwear	Byron, James	4034
Forest Products	Smith, Leonard S	0375
Forest Products, Domestic Construction	Kristensen, Chris	0384
Forest Products (Trade Policy)	Hicks, Michael	0375
Forgings Semifinished Steel	Bell, Charles	0609
Fossil Fuel Power Generation (Major Proj)	Dollison, Robert	2733
Foundry Eqmt	Comer, Barbara	0316
Foundry Industry	Bell, Charles	0609
Fruits	Hodgen, Donald	3346
Frozen Foods Products	Hodgen, Donald	3346
Fur Goods	Bryon, James	4034
Furniture	Enright, Joe	3459

G

INDUSTRY	CONTACT	PHONE (202) 377-
Gallium	Cammarota, David	0575
Games & Children's Vehicles	Corea, Judy	5479
Gaskets/Gasketing Materials	Reise, Richard	3489
General Aviation Aircraft	Walsh, Hugh	4222
Gen Indus Mach Nec, Exc 35691	Shaw, Eugene	3494
General Industrial Machinery	Harrison, Joseph	5455
Generator Sets/Turbines (Major Proj)	Dollison, Robert	2733
Germanium	Cammarota, David	0575
Glass, Flat	Williams, Franklin	0132
Glassware	Corea, Judy	0311
Gloves (work)	Byron, James	4034
Giftware (Trade Promo)	Beckham, Reginald	5478
Grain Mill Products	Janis, William V	2250
Greeting Cards	Bratland, Rose Marie	0380
Grocery Retailing	Kenney, Neil	2428
Ground Water Exploration & Development	Greer, Damon	0564

H

INDUSTRY	CONTACT	PHONE (202) 377-
Hand Saws, Saw Blades	Shaw, Eugene	3494
Hand/Edge Tools Ex Mach Tl/Saws	Shaw, Eugene	3494
Handbags	Byron, James	4034
Hard Surfaced Floor Coverings	Shaw, Robert	0132
Hardware (Export Promo)	Johnson, Charles E	3422
Health	Francis, Simon	0350
Heat Treating Equipment	Comer, Barbara	0316
Heating Eqmt Ex Furnaces	Holley, Tyrena	3509
Helicopters	Walsh, Hugh	4222
Helicopters (Market Support)	Driscoll, George	8228
High Tech Trade, U.S. Competitiveness	Hatter, Victoria L	3913
Hoists, Overhead Cranes	Wiening, Mary	4708
Home Video	Plock, Ernest	4781
Hose & Belting	Prat, Raimundo	0128
Hotel & Restaurants/Equip (Trade Promo)	Kimmel, Edward K	3640
Hotels And Motels	Sousane, J Richard	4582
Household Appliances	Harris, John M	1178
Household Appliances (Trade Promo)	Johnson, Charles E	3422
Household Furniture	Enright, Joe	3459
Housewares (Export Promo)	Johnson, Charles E	3422
Housing Construction	Cosslett, Patrick	0132
Housing & Urban Development (Major Proj)	White, Barbara	4160

INDUSTRY	CONTACT	PHONE (202) 377-
Hydro Power, Plants (Major Proj)	Healey, Mary Alice	4333

I

INDUSTRY	CONTACT	PHONE (202) 377-
Industrial Controls	Whitley, Richard A	0682
Industrial Drives/Gears	Reise, Richard	3489
Industrial Gases	Kostalas, Antonios	0128
Industrial Organic Chemicals	McIntyre, Leo	0128
Industrial Process Controls	Podolske, Lewis	3360
Industrial Robots	McGibbon, Patrick	0314
Industrial Sewing Machines	Holley, Tyrena	3509
Industrial Structure	Davis, Lester A	4924
Industrial Trucks	Wiening, Mary	4608
Information Services	Inoussa, Mary C	5820
Information Industries	Crupe, Friedrich R	4781
Inorganic Chemicals	Kamenicky, Vincent	0128
Inorganic Pigments	Kamenicky, Vincent	0128
Insulation	Shaw, Robert	0132
Insurance	McAdam, Bruce	0346
Intellectual Property Rights (Services)	Siegmund, John E	4781
International Commodities	Siesseger, Fred	5124
International Major Projects	Thibeault, Robert	5225
Investment Management	Muir, S Cassin	0349
Irrigation Equipment	Greer, Damon	0564
Irrigation (Major Proj)	Bell, Richard	2460

J

INDUSTRY	CONTACT	PHONE (202) 377-
Jams & Jellies	Hodgen, Donald A	3346
Jewelry	Harris, John	1178
Jewelry (Trade Promo)	Beckham, Reginald	5478
Jute Products	Tasnadi, Diani	5124

K

INDUSTRY	CONTACT	PHONE (202) 377-
Kitchen Cabinets	Wise, Barbara	0375

L

INDUSTRY	CONTACT	PHONE (202) 377-
Laboratory Instruments	Podolske, Lewis	3360
Laboratory Instruments (Trade Promo)	Manzolillo, Franc	2991
Lasers (Trade Promo)	Manzolillo, Franc	2991
Lawn & Garden Equip	Vanderwolf, John	0348
Lead Products	Larrabee, David	0575
Leasing: Eqmt & Vehicles	Shuman, John	3050
Leather Tanning	Byron, James E	4034
Leather Products	Byron, James E	4034
Legal Services	Chittum, J Marc	0345
LNG Plants (Major Proj)	Thomas, Janet	4146
Local Area Networks	Spathopoulos, Vivian	0572
Logs, Wood	Hicks, Michael	0375
Luggage	Byron, James	4034
Lumber	Wise, Barbara	0375

M

INDUSTRY	CONTACT	PHONE (202) 377-
Machine Tool Accessories	McGibbon, Patrick	0314
Magazines	Bratland, Rose Marie	0380
Magnesium	Cammarota, David	0575
Major Projects	Thibeault, Robert	5225
Management Consulting	Chittum, J Marc	0345
Manifold Business Forms	Bratland, Rose Marie	0380
Manmade Fiber	Dulka, William	4058
Margarine	Janis, William V	2250
Marine Recreational Equipment (Trade Promo)	Beckham, Reginald	5478
Marine Insurance	Johnson, C William	5012

INDUSTRY	CONTACT	PHONE (202) 377-
Maritime Shipping	Johnson, C William	5012
Materials, Advanced	Cammarota, David	0575
Mattresses & Bedding	Enright, Joe	3459
Meat Products	Hodgen, Donald A	3346
Mech Power Transmission Eqmt	Reise, Richard	3489
Medical Facilities (Major Proj)	White, Barbara	4160
Medical Instruments	Fuchs, Michael	0550
Medical Instruments & Equip (Trade Promo)	Keen, George B	2010
Mercury, Fluorspar	Manion, James J	5157
Metal Building Products	Williams, Franklin	0132
Metal Cookware	Corea, Judy	0311
Metal Cutting Machine Tools	McGibbon, Patrick	0314
Metal Forming Machine Tools	McGibbon, Patrick	0314
Metal Powders	Duggan, Brian	0575
Metals, Secondary	Brueckmann, Al	0606
Metalworking	Mearman, John	0315
Metalworking Eqmt Nec	McGibbon, Patrick	0314
Millwork	Wise, Barbara	0375
Mineral Based Construction Materials (Clay, Concrete, Gypsum, Asphalt, Stone)	Pitcher, Charles B	0132
Mining Machinery	McDonald, Edward	0680
Mining Machinery (Trade Promo)	Zanetakos, George	0552
Mobile Homes	Cosslett, Patrick	0132
Molybdenum	Cammarota, David	0575
Monorails (Trade Promo)	Wiening, Mary	4708
Motion Pictures	Siegmund, John	4781
Motor Vehicles	Warner, Albert T	0669
Motorcycles	Vanderwolf, John	0348
Motors, Electric	Whitley, Richard A	0682
Music	Siegmund, John	4781
Musical Instruments	Corea, Judy	0311
Mutual Funds	Muir, S Cassin	0349

N

INDUSTRY	CONTACT	PHONE (202) 377-
Natural Gas	Gillett, Tom	1466
Natural, Synthetic Rubber	McIntyre, Leo	0128
Newspapers	Bratland, Rose Marie	0380
Nickel Products	Presbury, Graylin	0575
Non-alcoholic Beverages	Kenney, Cornelius	2428
Noncurrent Carrying Wiring Devices	Whitley, Richard A	0682
Nondurable Goods	Simon, Les	0341
Nonferrous Foundries	Duggan, Brian	0610
Nonferrous Metals	Manion, James J	0575
Nonmetallic Minerals Nec	Manion, James J	0575
Nonresidential Constr	MacAuley, Patrick	0132
Nuclear Power Plants/ Machinery	Greer, Damon	0681
Nuclear Power Plants (Major Proj)	Dollison, Robert	2733
Numerical Controls For Mach Tools	McGibbon, Patrick	0314
Nuts, Edible	Janis, William V	2250
Nuts, Bolts, Washers	Reise, Richard	3489

O

INDUSTRY	CONTACT	PHONE (202) 377-
Ocean Shipping	Johnson, C William	5012
Office Furniture	Enright, Joe	3459
Oil & Gas Development & Refining (Major Proj)	Thomas, Janet	4146
Oil & Gas (Fuels Only)	Gillett, Tom	1466
Oil Field Machinery	McDonald, Edward	0680
Oil Field Machinery (Trade Promo)	Miles, Max	0679
Oil Shale (Major Proj)	Thomas, Janet	4146
Operations & Maintenance	Chittum, J Marc	0345
Organic Chemicals	McIntyre, Leo	0128
Outdoor Lighting Fixtures	Whitley, Richard A	0682

INDUSTRY	CONTACT	(202) 377-
Outdoor Power Equip (Trade Promo)	Johnson, Charles E	3422
P		
Packaging & Containers	Copperthite, Kim	0575
Packaging Machinery	Shaw, Eugene	2204
Paints/Coatings	Prat, Raimundo	0128
Paper	Smith, Leonard S	0375
Paper & Board Packaging	Smith, Leonard S	0375
Paper Industries Machinery	Abrahams, Edward	0312
Pasta	Janis, William V	2250
Paving Materials (Asphalt & Concrete)	Pitcher, Charles	0132
Pectin	Janis, William V	2250
Pens/Pencils, etc.	Corea, Judy	0311
Periodicals	Bratland, Rose Marie	0380
Pet Food	Janis, William V	2250
Pet Products (Trade Promo)	Kimmel, Ed	3640
Petrochemicals	McIntyre, Leo	0128
Petrochem, Cyclic Crudes	McIntyre, Leo	0128
Petrochemicals Plants (Major Proj)	Haraguchi, Wally	4877
Petroleum, Crude & Refined Products	Gillett, Tom	1466
Pharmaceuticals	McIntyre, Leo	0128
Pipelines (Major Proj)	Thomas, Janet	4146
Photographic Eqmt & Supplies	Watson, Joyce	0574
Plastic Construction Products (Most)	Williams, Franklin	0132
Plastic Materials	Shea, Moira	0128
Plastic Products	Prat, Raimundo	0128
Plastic Products Machinery	Shaw, Eugene	3494
Plumbing Fixtures & Fittings	Shaw, Robert	0132
Plywood/Panel Products	Wise, Barbara	0375
Point-of-Use Water Treatment	Greer, Damon	0564
Pollution Control Equipment	Jonkers, Loretta	0564
Porcelain Electrical Supplies	Whitley, Richard A	0682
Potatoe Chips	Janis, William	2250
Pottery	Corea, Judy	0311
Poultry Products	Hodgen, Donald A	3346
Power Hand Tools	Abrahams, Edward	0312
Precious Metal Jewelry	Harris, John M	1178
Prefabricated Buildings (Wood)	Cosslett, Patrick	0132
Prefabricated Buildings (Metal)	Williams, Franklin	0132
Prepared Meats	Hodgen, Donald A	3346
Pretzels	Janis, William V	2250
Primary Commodities	Siesseger, Fred	5124
Printing & Publishing	Lofquit, William S	0379
Printing Trade Services	Bratland, Rose Marie	0380
Printing Trades Mach/Eqmt	Kemper, Alexis	5956
Process Control Instruments	Podolske, Lon	3360
Process Control Instruments (Trade Promo)	Marcolillo, Franc	2991
Pulp And Paper Mills (Major Proj)	White, Barbara	4160
Pulpmills	Stanley, Gary	0375
Pumps, Pumping Eqmt	McDonald, Edward	0680
Pumps, Valves, Compressors (Trade Promo)	Zanetakos, George	0552
R		
Radio & TV Broadcasting	Siegmund, John	4781
Radio & TV Communications Eqmt	Gossack, Linda	2872
Recorded Music	Siegmund, John	4781
Recreational Eqmt (Trade Promo)	Beckham, Reginald	5478
Refractory Products	Duggan, Brian	0575
Renewable Energy Eqpmt	Garden, Les	0556

INDUSTRY	CONTACT	(202) 377-
Residential Lighting Fixtures	Whitley, Richard A	0682
Retail Trade	Margulies, Marvin J	5086
Rice Milling	Janis, William V	2250
Roads, Railroads, Mass Trans (Major Proj)	Smith, Jay L	4642
Robots	McGibbon, Patrick	0314
Roofing, Asphalt	Pitcher, Charles	0132
Roller Bearings	Reise, Richard	3489
Rolling Mill Machinery	Comer, Barbara	0316
Rubber	Prat, Raimundo	0128
Rubber Products	Prat, Raimundo	0128
S		
Saddlery & Harness Products	Byron, James	4034
Safety & Security Equip (Trade Promo)	Umstead, Dwight	8410
Space Services	Plock, Ernest	5620
Satellites & Space Vehicles (Marketing)	Bowie, David C	8228
Satellites, Communications	Cooper, Patricia	4466
Science & Electronic (Trade Promo)	Moose, Jake	4125
Scientific Instruments (Trade Promo)	Manzolillo, Franc	2991
Scientific Measurement/ Control Eqmt	Podolske, Lewis	3360
Screw Machine Products	Reise, Richard	3489
Screws, Washers	Reise, Richard	3489
Security & Commodity Brokers	Fenwick, Thomas R	0347
Security Management Svcs.	Chittum, J Marc	0345
Semiconductors (except Japan)	Scott, Robert	2795
Semiconductors, Japan	Nealon, Marguerite	8411
Semiconductor Prod Eqmt & Materials	Hall, Sarah	2846
Service Industries (Uruguay Round)	Dowling, Jay	1134
Services Data Base Development	Atkins, Robert G	4781
Services, Telecom	Shefrin, Ivan	4466
Shingles (Wood)	Wise, Barbara	0375
Silverware	Harris, John	1178
Sisal Products	Manger, Jon	5124
Small Arms, Ammunition	Vanderwolf, John	0348
Snackfood	Janis, William V	2250
Soaps, Detergents, Cleaners	McIntyre, Leo	0128
Software	Hyikata, Heidi	0572
Software (Trade Promo)	Fogg, Judy	4936
Solar Cells/Photovoltaic Devices	Garden, Les	0556
Solar Eqmt Ocean/Biomass/ Geothermal	Garden, Les	0556
Soy Products	Janis, William V	2250
Space Commercialization (Equipment)	Bowie, David C	8228
Space Commercialization (Services)	Plock, Ernest	5820
Space Policy Development	Pajor, Peter	8228
Special Industry Machinery	Shaw, Eugene	3494
Speed Changers	Reise, Richard	3489
Sporting & Athletic Goods	Vanderwolf, John	0348
Sporting Goods (Trade Promo)	Beckham, Reginald	5478
Steel Industry Products	Bell, Charles	0608
Steel Industry	Brueckmann, Al	0606
Steel Markets	Bell, Charles	0608
Storage Batteries	Larrabee, David	5124
Sugar Products	Tasnadi, Diana	5124
Supercomputers	Streeter, Jonathan	0572
Superconductors	Chiarado, Roger	0402
Switchgear & Switchboard Apparatus	Whitley, Richard A	0682

INDUSTRY	CONTACT	(202) 377-
T		
Tea	Janis, William V	2250
Technology Affairs	Shykind, Edwin B	4694
Telecommunications	Stechschulte, Roger	4466
Telecommunications (Major Proj)	Paddock, Richard	4466
Telecommunications (Trade Promo)	Rettig, Theresa E	2952
Telecommunications (Network Equip)	Henry, John	4466
Telecommunications (military communications equip)	Mocenigo, Anthony	4466
Teletext Services	Inoussa, Mary C	5820
Textile Machinery	McDonald, Edward	0680
Textiles	Dulka, William A	4058
Textiles (Trade Promo)	Molnar, Ferenc	2043
Timber Products (Tropical)	Tasnadi, Diana	5124
Tin Products	Manger, Jon	5124
Tires	Prat, Raimundo	0128
Tools/Dies/Jigs/Fixtures	McGibbon, Patrick	0314
Tourism (Major Proj)	White, Barbara	4160
Tourism Services	Sousane, J Richard	4582
Toys	Corea, Judy	0311
Toys & Games (Trade Promo)	Becham, Reginald	5478
Trade Related Employment	Davis, Lester A	4924
Transborder Data Flows	Inoussa, Mary C	5820
Transformers	Whitley, Richard A	0682
Transportation Industries	Alexander, Albert	4581
Tropical Commodities	Tasnadi, Diana	5124
Trucking Services	Sousane, J Richard	4581
Tungsten Products	Manger, Jon	5124
Turbines, Steam	Greer, Damon	0681
U		
Uranium	Sugg, William	1466
V		
Value Added Telecommunications Serv	Atkins, Robert G	4781
Valves, Pipe Fittings (Except Brass)	Reise, Richard	3489
Vegetables	Hodgen, Donald A	3346
Video Services	Plock, Ernest	5820
Videotex Services	Inoussa, Mary C/	5820
	Siegmund, John	4781
W		
Wallets, Billfords, Flatgoods	Byron, James	4034
Warm Air Heating Eqmt	Holley, Tyrena	3509
Wastepaper	Stanley, Gary	0375
Watches	Harris, John	1178
Water and Sewerage Treatment Plants (Major Proj)	Healey, Mary Alice	4643
Water Resource Eqmt	Greer, Damon	0564
Water Supply & Distribution	Greer, Damon	0564
Welding/Cutting Apparatus	Comer, Barbara	0316
Wholesale Trade	Margulis, Marvin	3050
Wine	Kenney, Cornelius	2428
Windmill Components	Garden, Les	0556
Wire & Wire Products	Breuckmann, Al	0606
Wire Cloth, Industrial	Reise, Richard	3489
Wire Cloth	Williams, Franklin	0132
Wood Containers	Hicks, Michael	0375
Wood Preserving	Hicks, Michael	0375
Wood Products	Smith, Leonard S	0375
Wood Working Machinery	McDonald, Edward	0680
Writing Instruments	Corea, Judy	0311
Y		
Yeast	Janis, William V	2250

Source: *Business America* 112 (Special Edition, 1991), pps. 20–22.

347

Bureau of Export Administration Export Enforcement Field Offices

Office of Export Enforcement
International Trade Administration
U. S. Department of Commerce
Room 3704
26 Federal Plaza
NEW YORK, NY 10278
(212) 264-1365
FTS-264-1365
Allen Adrezin, Special Agent
  in Charge

Office of Export Enforcement
International Trade Administration
U.S. Department of Commerce
Suite 201
2501 W. Burbank Boulevard
BURBANK, CA 91505
(818) 904-6019
FTS-983-6019
Wayne Collier, Special Agent
  in Charge

Office of Export Enforcement
International Trade Administration
U.S. Department of Commerce
Room 2008
5285 Port Royal Road
SPRINGFIELD, VA 22161
(703) 487-4950
FTS-737-4950
Robert Rice, Special Agent
  in Charge

Office of Export Enforcement
International Trade Administration
U.S. Department of Commerce
Room 4118
280 South First Street
SAN JOSE, CA 95113-3002
(408) 291-4204
FTS-466-4204
Frank Deliberti, Special Agent
  in Charge

Office of Export Enforcement
International Trade Administration
U.S. Department of Commerce
Room 501
610 S. Canal Street
CHICAGO, IL 60607
(312) 353-6640
FTS-353-6640
William Hendrickson, Special Agent
  in Charge

Office on Export Enforcement
International Trade Administration
U.S. Department of Commerce
New Boston Federal Building
Room 350
10 Causeway Street
BOSTON, MA 02222
(617) 565-6030
FTS-835-6030
Joseph Leone, Special Agent
  in Charge

Office of Export Enforcement
International Trade Administration
U.S. Department of Commerce
Room 211
8070 N.W. 53rd Street
MIAMI, FL 33166
(305) 536-6621
FTS-350-6621
Lyndon Berezowsky, Special Agent
  in Charge

Office of Export Enforcement
International Trade Administration
U.S. Department of Commerce
Room 622
525 Griffin Street
DALLAS, TX 75202
(214) 767-9294
FTS-729-9294
Vacant

Bureau of Export Administration Regional Office

BXA Western Regional Office
  (Export Licensing Assistance)
Newport Irvine Center
Suite 345
3300 Irvine Avenue
Newport Beach, CA 92660
(714) 606-0144

Source: U.S. Department of Commerce, *How to Sell to the United States Department of Commerce*, Washington, D.C.: U.S. Government Printing Office, April 1988, p. 14.

A Directory of Export Services

Do you have questions about the most promising overseas markets for your products and services? About economic conditions in a particular country? About how to get export financing or an export license? About how to obtain an overseas sales representative? About the credit rating of a prospective customer? About how to ship your products? About public works projects in developing countries?

Rest easy. There is plenty of help available free or at nominal cost.

The directory of U.S. Government export services that follows will tell you where to get the information and counseling you need.

The Commerce Department's International Trade Administration (ITA) has the chief responsibility in the federal government for promoting exports. Other Commerce Department agencies also help exporters in specialized ways.

Our directory includes the export services of eight additional federal agencies.

International Trade Administration

The best starting place for getting information about export programs is a district office of the Commerce Department's International Trade Administration (ITA). See inside back cover for a list of the district offices, which form the domestic arm of ITA's U.S. and Foreign Commercial Service (US&FCS). Through a district office, a company has access to all assistance available in the Commerce Department: practical information about overseas market opportunities, developed by commercial officers abroad and by industry and country desk officers in Washington, D.C. The district offices also can direct companies toward other government and private sector export services.

The ITA District Offices

Forty-seven ITA district offices and 21 branch offices in cities throughout the United States and in Puerto Rico provide information and professional export counseling to business people. Each

office is headed by a director, supported by trade specialists and other staff. These professionals can help companies assess the export capacity of their products; target markets; locate and check out potential overseas partners; and counsel on the steps involved in exporting.

Each district office can offer information on:

- Trade and investment opportunities abroad
- Foreign markets for U.S. products and services
- Services to locate and evaluate overseas buyers and representatives
- Financing aid for exporters
- International trade exhibitions
- Export documentation requirements
- Foreign economic statistics
- U.S. export licensing and foreign nation import requirements
- Export seminars and conferences

Most district offices maintain business libraries containing the Commerce Department's latest reports.

The district offices work closely with 51 District Export Councils (DECs), comprised of nearly 1,800 business and trade experts who volunteer to help U.S. firms develop a solid export strategy.

The Overseas Posts

Much of the information about trends and actual trade leads in foreign countries is gathered on-site by the commercial officers of the US&FCS. About half of the approximately 186 American officers working in 67 countries (with 122 offices) have been hired directly from the private sector, many with international trade experience. All understand firsthand the problems encountered by U.S. companies in their efforts to trade abroad. In addition, a valued asset of the US&FCS is a group of about 525 foreign nationals who provide continuing support for commercial programs. US&FCS staff provide a range of services to help companies sell overseas. These include background information on foreign companies, agency-finding services, market research, business counseling, assistance in making appointments with key buyers and government officials, and representations on behalf of companies adversely affected by trade barriers.

The overseas posts seek trade/investment opportunities to benefit U.S. firms.

Country Desk Officers

Country desk officers, in ITA's International Economic Policy unit, are another excellent source of information on trade potential in specific countries. Every country in the world has a country desk officer assigned to it. These specialists can look at the needs of an individual U.S. firm wishing to sell in a particular country in the full context of that country's overall economy, trade policies, and political situation, and also in light of U.S. policies toward that country.

Desk officers keep up-to-date on the economic and commercial conditions in their assigned countries. Each collects information on the country's regulations, tariffs, business practices, economic and political developments, trade data and trends, market size, and growth. Each keeps tabs on the country's potential as a market for U.S. products, services, and investments.

Trade Development Industry Officers

ITA's Trade Development unit promotes U.S. business interests in international trade, and offers information on markets and trade practices worldwide. The organization is grouped into seven units: Aerospace, Automotive Affairs and Consumer Goods, Basic Industries, Capital Goods and International Construction, Science and Electronics, Services, and Textiles and Apparel. A cross-sectoral unit—Trade Information and Analysis—provides data and analyses useful in export promotion. See pages 20-22 for list of these desk officers.

The industry specialists promote exports of their industries through marketing seminars, foreign buyer groups, executive trade missions, trade fairs, business counseling, and information on market opportunities. They work directly with their industries, trade associations, and state development agencies.

For major projects abroad, the International Construction unit assists U.S. planning, engineering, and construction firms with bids and contracts.

The Major Projects Reference Room in the Commerce Department headquarters in Washington, D.C. keeps detailed project documents on multilateral bank and U.S. foreign assistance projects.

Export Services of Commerce's ITA

Export counseling. Trade specialists are available at ITA district and branch offices for individualized export counseling.

Agent/Distributor Service. A customized search for interested and qualified foreign representatives will identify up to six foreign prospects who have examined the U.S. firm's literature and expressed interest in representing it.

Commercial News USA. A monthly magazine that promotes the products or services of U.S. firms to more than 110,000 overseas agents, distributors, government officials, and purchasers. Exporters may submit a black-and-white photo and a brief description of their product or service.

Comparison Shopping. A custom-tailored service that provides firms with key marketing and foreign representation information about their specific products. Commerce Department staff conduct on-the-spot interviews to determine nine key marketing facts about the product, such as sales potential in the market, comparable products, distribution channels, going price, competitive factors, and qualified purchasers.

Foreign Buyer Program. Exporters can meet qualified foreign purchasers for their product or service at trade shows in the United States. The Commerce Department promotes the shows worldwide to attract foreign buyer delegations, manages an international business center, counsels participating firms, and brings together buyer and seller.

Gold Key Service. A custom-tailored service for U.S. firms planning to visit a country. Offered by many overseas posts, it combines several services, such as market orientation briefings, market research, introductions to potential partners, an interpreter for meetings, and assistance in developing a sound market strategy and an effective followup plan.

Trade Opportunities Program. Provides companies with current sales leads from overseas firms seeking to buy or represent their product or service. These leads are available electronically from the Commerce Department and are redistributed by the private sector in printed or electronic form.

World Traders Data Report. Custom reports that evaluate potential trading partners. Includes background information, standing in the local business community, credit-worthiness, and overall reliability and suitability.

Overseas Catalog and Video-Catalog Shows. Companies can gain market exposure for their product or service without the cost of traveling overseas by participating in a catalog or video-catalog show sponsored by the Commerce Department. Provided with the firm's product literature or promotional video, an industry will display the material to select foreign audiences in several countries.

Overseas Trade Missions. Officials of U.S. firms can participate in a trade mission which will give them an opportunity to confer with influential foreign business and government representatives. Commerce Department staff will identify and arrange a full schedule of appointments in each country.

Overseas Trade Fairs. U.S. exporters may participate in overseas trade fairs which will enable them to meet customers face-to-face and also to assess the competition. The Commerce Department creates a U.S. presence at international trade fairs, making it easier for U.S. firms to exhibit and gain international recognition. The Department selects international trade fairs for special endorsement, called certification. This cooperation with the private show organizers enables U.S. exhibitors to receive special services designed to enhance their market promotion efforts. There is a service charge.

Matchmaker Events. Matchmaker Trade Delegations offer introductions to new markets through short, inexpensive overseas visits with a limited objective: to match the U.S. firm with a representative or prospective joint-venture/licensee partner who shares a common product or service interest. Firms learn key aspects of doing business in the new country and meet in one-on-one interviews the people who can help them be successful there.

To take advantage of these export services contact the Commerce Department (International Trade Administration) district office nearest you. See list of district offices on inside back cover.

Export Trading Companies

The Office of Export Trading Company Affairs promotes the formation of export trading companies (ETCs) and export management companies (EMCs) by sponsoring conferences and legal seminars, and by working with U.S. trade associations. It provides a program for registering suppliers, ETCs, and EMCs to help registrants identify and contact potential business partners. The office also administers the Export Trade Certificate of Review program under Title III of the Export Trading Company Act, which extends antitrust protection for joint exporting ventures. Telephone: (202) 377-5131.

Other Commerce Export Services

In addition to ITA, seven other Commerce Department agencies offer export services:

Export Licensing Assistance

Expanded export licensing services and information are available to America's business community from the U.S. Commerce Department's Bureau of Export Administration (BXA). BXA provides high-level direction for national export control policy and administration, strong enforcement of export laws, and improved service to business. U.S. export control laws prevent the unauthorized transfer of high technology that would harm America's national security.

Among improved business services are:

● Electronic licensing by ELAIN: (202) 377-4811;

● Instant status updates on license applications via STELA: (202) 377-2752;

● Information on the status of applications in addition to STELA: (202) 377-2753.

● Export licensing education seminars offered by the Export Seminar Staff: (202) 377-8731;

● Expert detailed guidance on preparing license documents provided by the Exporter Assistance Office: (202) 377-4811.

● Western region exporters (Alaska, Arizona, California, Hawaii, Idaho, New Mexico, Nevada, Oregon, Utah, Washington, and Guam) should contact the BXA Western Regional Office, 3300 Irvine Ave., Suite 345, Newport Beach. Calif. 92660-3198. Office hours are 8:30

a.m. to 5:00 p.m., telephone (714) 660-0144.

Travel and Tourism

The U.S. Travel and Tourism Administration (USTTA) promotes U.S. export earnings through trade in tourism. USTTA stimulates foreign demand, helps to remove barriers, increases the number of small- and medium-size travel businesses participating in the export market, provides timely data, and forms marketing partnerships with private industry and with state and local governments.

To maintain its programs in international markets, USTTA has offices in Toronto, Montreal, Vancouver, Mexico City, Tokyo, London, Paris, Amsterdam, Milan, Frankfurt, and Sydney, as well as in Miami, to serve South America. The International Congress Office in Paris promotes the United States as a site for international meetings and conventions.

Travel development activities in countries without direct USTTA representation are carried out under the direction of USTTA regional directors, who cooperate with "Visit USA" committees, comprised of representatives of the U.S. and foreign travel industry in those countries, and also with the Commerce Department's U.S. and Foreign Commercial Service.

U.S. destinations and suppliers of tourism services interested in the overseas promotion of travel to the United States should call (202) 377-4003.

Foreign Requirements for U.S. Products and Services

For information about foreign standards and certification systems, write: NCSCI, National Institute of Standards and Technology (NIST), Administration Building, A629, Gaithersburg, Md. 20899. The telephone number is (301) 975-4040, 975-4038, or 975-4036.

NIST maintains a GATT Hotline with a recording that reports on the latest notifications of proposed foreign regulations that may affect trade. Hotline number: (301) 975-4041.

Exporters can get information from the non-governmental American National Standards Institute, telephone (212) 354-3300.

Minority Business Development

Minority-owned businesses can receive special assistance from the Minority Business Development Agency (MBDA). Contact: Minority Business Development Agency, U.S. Department of Commerce, Washington, D.C. 20230; telephone (202) 377-2414.

Foreign Metric Regulations

The Office of Metric Programs provides exporters with guidance and assistance on foreign metric import regulations and on matters relating to U.S. transition to the metric system; it can give referrals to state metric contacts. The office's telephone number: (202) 377-3036.

A non-governmental source of information on foreign metric import regulations: American National Metric Council, 1620 I St. N.W., Suite 220, Washington, D.C. 20006, telephone (202) 857-0474.

Fishery Product Exports

The National Oceanic and Atmospheric Administration (NOAA) assists seafood exporters by facilitating access to foreign markets. The National Marine Fisheries Service (NMFS) provides inspection services for fishery exports and issues official U.S. Government certification attesting to the findings.

Contact:
Office of Trade and Industry Services
National Marine Fisheries Service
Room 6490
1335 East-West Highway
Silver Spring, Md. 20910
Telephone: **Trade Matters**
(301) 427-2379 or 2383
Export Inspection
(301) 427-2355
Fisheries Promotion
(301) 427-2379

Census Bureau

Shipper's Export Declarations—tel. (301) 763-5310.
Trade Data—(301) 763-5140

Where to Start

The first point of contact for export information and assistance should be an exporter's local Commerce Department district office. They are listed on the inside back cover of this magazine.

Other Federal Export Assistance

U.S. Export-Import Bank

The Export-Import Bank of the United States (Eximbank) is the principal government agency responsible for aiding the export of U.S. goods and services through a variety of loan, guarantee, and insurance programs.

Eximbank's financial programs generally are available to any U.S. export firm, regardless of size. The following programs, however, are particularly helpful to small business exporters.

Export Credit Insurance. An exporter may reduce its financing risks by purchasing export credit insurance from Eximbank's agent, the Foreign Credit Insurance Association (FCIA). Policies available include insurance for financing or operating leases, medium-term insurance, the new-to-export policy, insurance for the service industry, the umbrella policy, and multibuyer and singlebuyer policies.

Working Capital Guarantee. The Working Capital Loan Guarantee Program assists small businesses in obtaining crucial working capital to fund their export sales. The program guarantees working capital loans extended by banks to eligible U.S. exporters with exportable inventory or export receivables as collateral. ·

Direct and Intermediary Loans. Eximbank provides two types of loans: direct loans to foreign buyers of U.S. exports and intermediary loans to fund responsible parties that extend loans to foreign buyers of U.S. capital and quasi-capital goods and related services. Both the local and guarantee programs cover up to 85 percent of the U.S. export value, with repayment terms of one year or more.

Guarantees. Eximbank's guarantee provides repayment protection for private sector loans to creditworthy buyers of U.S. capital equipment and related services. The guarantee is available alone or with an intermediary loan.

Most guarantees provide comprehensive coverage of both political and commercial risks, but political-risks-only coverage is also available.

Small Business Advisory Service. To encourage small business to sell overseas, Eximbank maintains a special office to provide information on the availability and use of export credit insurance, guarantees, and direct and intermediary loans to finance the sale of

351

U.S. goods and services abroad. Its toll-free number, open all the time, is 1-800-424-5201; or within the Washington, D.C., area or from Alaska and Hawaii, the number is (202) 566-4423.

Briefing Programs. Eximbank offers briefing programs available to small business. For scheduling information, call (202) 566-4490.

Electronic Bulletin Board for Eximbank information. In operation all the time, telephone (202) 566-4699.

The address of the U.S. Export-Import Bank is 811 Vermont Ave., N.W., Washington, D.C. 20571; telephone (202) 566-8990 (public affairs office).

Small Business Administration

Small Business Administration (SBA) serves U.S. small business primarily through its 107 regional, district, and branch offices. The Office of International Trade, located in Washington, D.C., provides assistance related to exporting. Small businesses, which are either already exporting or interested in doing so, can receive information through conferences and seminars, instructional publications, export counseling, and financial assistance.

Export Counseling: International Trade Officers in SBA regional and district offices provide advice and counseling on exporting. These professionals help small businesses locate and utilize various government programs and guide them through the export process.

• **Score Program**—One-on-one assistance is provided by members of the Service Corps of Retired Executives (SCORE), many with years of practical experience in international trade. Specialists assist small firms in evaluating export potential and strengthening domestic operations by identifying financial, managerial, or technical problems.

• **SBDC/SBI Programs**—Basic business counseling and assistance are offered through Small Business Development Centers (SBDCs), some of which are located at colleges and universities. Through Small Business Institutes (SBIs), business students from more than 450 colleges and universities provide in-depth, long-term counseling under faculty supervision to small businesses.

• **Legal advice**—Export Legal Assistance Network (ELAN)—Free, initial consultations to small companies on the legal aspects of exporting through an arrangement with the Federal Bar Association (FBA). Advice is provided by qualified attorneys from the International Law Council of the FBA.

Financial Assistance—The SBA offers direct loan and loan guarantee programs to assist small business exporters. To be eligible for a loan, a business person must first attempt to secure a loan from a private bank, invest a reasonable amount of capital in the business, and demonstrate that the loan can be paid back. The SBA provides guarantees of up to 85 percent of a private lending institution's loan to an eligible small business if the total SBA-guaranteed portion does not exceed the SBA's $750,000 statutory loan guarantee limit. However, the SBA can provide a maximum guarantee of 90 percent for loans less than $155,000.

• **Regular Business Loan Program**—Covers loans for fixed-asset acquisition or expansion and other working capital purposes up to $750,000 and having a maximum maturity of 25 years. Guarantees for general purpose, term working capital loans are usually limited to a maximum maturity of seven years.

• **Export Revolving Line of Credit Program (ERLC)**—The SBA has established this program to encourage more small businesses to export their products and services abroad. Any number of withdrawals and repayments can be made as long as the dollar limit of the credit is not exceeded, and the disbursements are made within the stated maturity period. Proceeds can only finance labor and materials needed for manufacturing or wholesaling for export, or to penetrate or develop foreign markets. The maximum maturity of an ERLC guarantee is 18 months, including all extensions.

• **Small Business Investment Company (SBIC) Financing**—For an export company requiring more than $750,000, an SBIC approved loan is a financial option.

To get SBA help, contact any regional, district, or branch offices. You may also contact: Office of International Trade, U.S. Small Business Administration, Room 501A, 1441 L St. N.W., Washington, D.C. 20416, tel. (800) 368-5855, or (202) 653-7794.

Department of Agriculture (Foreign Agricultural Service)

The export promotion efforts of the U.S. Department of Agriculture (USDA) are centered in the Foreign Agricultural Service (FAS). For information on programs, contact the Director of High Value Products Division, FAS, Room 4647, South Bldg., U.S. Department of

Agriculture, Washington, D.C. 20250; telephone: (202) 447-6343.

FAS provides financial support for U.S. agricultural exports through the Commodity Credit Corporation. Firms may obtain information on financial programs by contacting General Sales Manager, Export Credits, Foreign Agricultural Service, 14th Street and Independence Ave., S.W., Washington, D.C. 20250; telephone: (202) 447-5173. Other USDA contacts:

Minority and Small Business Coordinator ....(202) 447-6343

FAS Commodity and Marketing Divisions

Dairy, Livestock and Poultry
...................(202) 447-8031
Grain and Feed Division
...................(202) 447-6219
Horticulture and Tropical Products
...................(202) 447-6590
Oilseed and Oilseed Products
...................(202) 447-7037
Tobacco, Cotton and Seeds
...................(202) 382-9516
Forest Products ......(202) 382-8138

Department of State

The State Department and Foreign Service professionals provide business persons, including producers of services and farm products, unique insights into problems of foreign marketing and doing business abroad. They direct administration of Commerce Department programs for exporters in more than 82 countries where no Commerce personnel are available and they will brief prospective exporters and investors on political and economic conditions in foreign countries.

Contact a State Department country desk officer—specify the country—telephone (202) 647-4500; or:

Office of Commercial, Legislative and Public Affairs
Bureau of Economic and Business Affairs
U.S. Department of State, Room 6822
Washington, D.C. 20520
(202) 647-1942

Overseas Private Investment Corporation

Through the Overseas Private Investment Corporation (OPIC), the government facilitates U.S. private investments in less developed nations. OPIC is an independent, financially self-supporting corporation, fully owned by the U.S.

Government with offices in Washington, D.C.

OPIC provides political risk insurance and financing to American companies interested in the developing countries. It also offers specialized insurance and financing services for U.S. service contractors and exporters operating in the developing world.

For more information on OPIC programs, a toll-free telephone number may be used: (800) 424-6742 (457-7010 in the Washington, D.C., metropolitan area).
Contact:
Overseas Private Investment Corporation (OPIC)
1615 M St., N.W., Suite 400
Washington, D.C. 20527

Trade Policy (U.S. Trade Representative)

The Office of the U.S. Trade Representative (USTR) is an agency of the Executive Office of the President. The USTR is the President's chief advisor on trade, coordinates trade policy within the U.S. Government, and is the principal negotiator of trade agreements. The USTR also is the U.S. representative to the General Agreement on Tariffs and Trade (GATT) and is responsible for administering some of the laws to prevent unfair trade practices. Individual exporters should contact the USTR's office if they want to file a complaint about unfair trade practices under Section 301 of the Trade Act of 1974 or if they seek relief under Section 201 of that law. Contact:
Office of the U.S. Trade Representative
600 17th St., N.W.
Washington, D.C. 20501
(202) 395-3230

Agency for International Development

The Agency for International Development (AID) administers most of the foreign economic assistance programs for the federal government. AID offers U.S. exporters opportunities to compete in the sales of goods or services supplied to foreign countries under loans and grants made by AID. U.S. exporters can benefit from two AID programs: the Commodity Import Programs and Project Procurements. In both of these programs, AID recipient countries purchase the commodities directly through U.S. suppliers.
Contact:
Office of Business Relations

● Commodities . . . .(703) 875-1590
● Technical Assistance Service
. . . .(703) 875-1551
Agency for International Development (AID/USDBU)
Department of State Building
320 21st St., N.W.
Washington, D.C. 20523

Trade and Development Program

The Trade and Development Program (TDP) is an independent U.S. Government agency that primarily funds feasi-

bility studies for public/private sector projects in developing countries. TDP finances studies mainly in large-scale energy generation and conservation, infrastructure, mineral development, agribusiness, and basic industrial facilities. A major purpose of TDP funding is to help U.S. engineering/planning firms win major consulting contracts overseas.
Contact:
Trade and Development Program
Room 304, SA 16
Department of State
Washington, D.C. 20523-1602
(703) 875-4357

Trade Promotion Coordinating Committee Harnesses U.S. Government Resources to Serve Exporters

Exports are the engine of growth for the U.S. economy, generating 70 percent of GNP growth in the first three quarters of 1990. Exports are also responsible for most of the job creation in the manufacturing sector in the past year. Recognizing the importance of exports to the U.S. economy, and to encourage more American firms to begin exporting, President Bush announced last May a Commercial Opportunities Initiative to better focus and coordinate federal programs to assist U.S. firms.

To implement this initiative, President Bush asked Commerce Secretary Mosbacher to chair a Trade Promotion Coordinating Committee (TPCC) to harness all the resources of the U.S. Government to serve American exporters.

The TPCC, comprised of 16 federal agencies, operates through a Sub-Cabinet Committee. The TPCC Sub-Cabinet Committee is implementing its mandate through ten interagency Working Groups which are focusing their efforts on specific regions, sectors, and programs. The Working Groups will coordinate, streamline, and increase the effectiveness of federal trade promotion efforts by: increasing communication among agencies; exchanging and sharing information on business support activities; developing multi-agency trade promotion activities; developing and maintaining a coordinate federal trade promotion events calendar; and reducing overlap and eliminating duplication of trade promotion activities.

To increase awareness among American exporters of the wide variety of export services and programs available to them, Secretary Mosbacher has announced a national export initiative, comprised of a series of seminars in U.S. cities over the next several months. The seminars will embody the Trade Promotion Coordinating Committee goals, taking the federal government programs and resources to the local level. Each event will be followed up with community activities to further support and encourage local exporters.

President Bush, citing his reason for creating the Trade Promotion Coordinating Committee, said: "As the winds of freedom blow down old barriers and liberalize markets from Managua to Warsaw, we must be prepared to take advantage of this historic opportunity to compete and to win."

Committee members include the Departments of Commerce, State, Treasury, Agriculture, Defense, Energy, and Transportation; the Office of Management and Budget; the Office of the U.S. Trade Representative; the Council of Economic Advisers; the Export-Import Bank of the United States; the Overseas Private Investment Corporation; the U.S. Information Agency; the Agency for International Development; the Trade and Development Program; and the Small Business Administration. Other agencies will be included, as appropriate. The committee will operate within existing resource levels and legal authorities.

Source: *Business America* 112 (Special Edition, 1991), pps 8–12.

Where to Get Market Information and Trade Leads

U.S. Department of Commerce/US&FCS Commercial Information Management System/National Trade Data Bank—Local Commerce District Office specialists can tailor information packages drawing from statistical trade and economic data, market research reports, and foreign traders indices. CIMS/NTDB house all relevant international trade publications published by ITA, including Foreign Economic Trends reports, Overseas Business Reports, and Industry Sector Analyses.
Contact: For your nearest Department of Commerce District Office, call (202) 377-4767, or see local telephone directory under U.S. Department of Commerce listing

U.S. Department of Commerce/Comparison Shopping Service—A custom-tailored service provides firms with targeted information on marketing and foreign representation for specific products in specific countries. Fee varies.
Contact: For your nearest Department of Commerce District Office, call (202) 377-4767, or see local telephone directory under U.S. Department of Commerce listing

U.S. Department of Commerce/Agent/Distributor Service—A customized search helps identify agents, distributors, and foreign representatives for U.S. firms based on the foreign companies' examination of U.S. product literature. A fee of $125 per country is charged.
Contact: For your nearest Department of Commerce District Office, call (202) 377-4767, or see local telephone directory under U.S. Department of Commerce listing

U.S. Department of Commerce/Trade Opportunities Program—TOP provides companies with current sales leads from international firms seeking to buy or represent their products or services. TOP leads are printed daily in leading commercial newspapers and are also distributed electronically via the Economic Bulletin Board. The fee varies.
Contact: For your nearest Department of Commerce District Office, call (202) 377-4767, or see local telephone directory under U.S. Department of Commerce listing; for the Department of Commerce Economic Bulletin Board, call (202) 377-1986

U.S. Department of Commerce/Minority Business Development Agency/Minority Export Development Consultants Program—This program helps develop marketing plans, identify potential overseas markets, and trade leads for minority business. It also provides assistance in documentation, short-term financing and shipping.
Contact: Business Development Specialist, (202) 377-2414

U.S. Department of Agriculture/Economic Research Service—The staff provides economic data, models, and research information about agricultural economies and policies of foreign countries and bilateral agricultural trade and development relationships.
Contact: Bob Robinson, (202) 219-0700

U.S. Department of Agriculture/Trade and Marketing Information Centers—These centers, part of the National Agricultural Library, help locate relevant material from their large collection on trade and marketing and provide copies of research and data from their AGRICOLA database.
Contact: Mary Lassanyi, (301) 344-3704

U.S. Department of Energy/Coal and Technology Export Program—This program promotes the export of U.S. clean coal products and services, by acting as an information source on coal and coal technologies.
Contact: Peter Cover, (202) 586-7297

U.S. Department of Energy/Fossil Energy-AID Database—The Office of Fossil Energy forwards prospective energy-related leads to AID for inclusion in its growing trade opportunities database in an effort to reach an extended audience seeking energy-related trade opportunities.
Contact: Denise Swink, (202) 586-9680

Small Business Administration/Export Information System—Data reports provide specific product information on the top 25 world markets and market growth trends for the past five years.
Contact: Luis Saldarriaga, (404) 542-5760

Agency for International Development/Trade and Investment Monitoring System—TIMS, a user-friendly computer-based system, provides a broad array of trade and investment information to potential U.S. investors and exporters on 42 developing countries, e.g., general economic and business data; trade and investment policies and prospects; government regulation and incentives; sources of funding and corporate tax structures; production and labor forces; and business facilities and infrastructure.
Contact: Tracy L. Smith, (202) 647-3805

Overseas Private Investment Corporation/Investor Information Service—This information clearinghouse provides "one-stop-shopping" for basic economic, business, and political information and data from a variety of sources on 118 developing countries and 16 geographic regions. This service is available for purchase in country- and region-specific kits.
Contact: Daven Oswalt, Manager, Public Affairs, (202) 457-7087

Overseas Private Investment Corporation/Investor Services—A new OPIC initiative designed to assist smaller U.S. firms with their overseas investment planning and implementation needs. Fee-based services provide counseling to American firms on business plan development, project structuring, joint-venture partner identification, and location of project financing services.
Contact: Dan Riordan, Director, Investor Services, (202) 457-7091

Overseas Private Investment Corporation/Opportunity Bank—This computer data system matches a U.S. investor's interest with specific overseas opportunities. A modest fee is charged.
Contact: Daven Oswalt, Manager, Public Affairs, (202) 457-7087

Source: *Business America* 112 (March 25, 1991), p. 17.

State Offices That Provide Export Assistance

For some time, governors have guided and stimulated economic development and job creation in their states. In the past 10 years, this activism extended beyond state and national borders. Today, many governors lead overseas trade missions that are an important part of state economic development programs.

President Bush told the National Governors' Association that governors ''are becoming our economic envoys and ambassadors of democracy. You are a new force in restoring American international competitiveness and expanding world markets for American goods and services.''

Most states have trade programs that serve as catalysts and brokers in the international arena. States provide technical assistance—from seminars on the ''how to's'' of trade, to individual exporter counseling, to dissemination of specific trade leads. They promote joint ventures, seek foreign investment, and encourage international travel to the United States.

Forty-one states maintain offices in 24 different countries. Seven states have export finance programs. Others provide information on non-state sources of financing.

The top international trade officials in the 50 states, the District of Columbia, and Puerto Rico are listed below, with their addresses and telephone numbers.

Alabama

Alabama Development Office
Fred Denton, Dir., Int'l Mktg. Div.
State Capitol
Montgomery, Ala. 36130
(205) 263-0048

Alaska

State of Alaska
Governor's Office of Intl. Trade
Director
3601 C St., Ste. 798
Anchorage, Alaska 99503
(907) 561-5585

Arizona

Arizona Dept. of Commerce
Peter Cunningham, Intl. Trade Dir.
3800 N. Central
Phoenix, Ariz. 85012
(602) 280-1371

Arkansas

Ark. Industrial Dev. Commission
Charles Sloan, Mkting. Dir.
#1 State Capitol Mall
Little Rock, Ark. 72201
(501) 682-1121

California

Calif. State World Trade Commission
Robert DeMartini, Dir., Export Dev.
1121 L St., Ste. 310
Sacramento, Calif. 95814
(916) 324-5511

Colorado

Colo. Intl. Trade Office
Morgan Smith, Dir.
1625 Broadway, Ste. 680
Denver, Colo. 80202
(303) 892-3850

Connecticut

Conn. Dept. Econ. Devel. Intl. Division
Matthew J. Broder, Dir.
865 Brook St.
Rocky Hill, Conn. 06067-3405
(203) 258-4256

Delaware

Delaware Dev. Office
Business Dev. Office
Donald Sullivan, Dir.
P.O. Box 1401
Dover, Del. 19903
(302) 739-4271

District of Columbia

D.C. Office of Intl. Business
Rosa Whitaker, Dir.
1250 I St.
Ste. 1003
Washington, D.C. 20005
(202) 727-1576

Florida

Florida Dept. of Commerce
Bureau of Intl. Trade and Dev.
Tom Slattery, Dir.
331 Collins Building
Tallahassee, Fla. 32399-2000
(904) 488-6124

Georgia

Georgia Dept. of Industry and Trade
Kevin Langston, Dir.
285 Peachtree Center Ave.
Stes. 1000 and 1100
P.O. Box 1776
Atlanta, Ga. 30301-1776
(404) 656-3571

Hawaii

State of Hawaii
Dept. of Bus. and Econ. Dev.
Trade and Ind. Dev. Branch
Dennis Ling, Chief
P.O. Box 2359
Honolulu, Hawaii 96804
(808) 548-7719

Idaho

Division of Intl. Business
David P. Christensen, Administrator
Idaho Dept. of Commerce
700 W. State St.
Boise, Idaho 83720
(208) 334-2470

Illinois

Ill. Dept. of Commerce and Community Affairs
Nan K. Hendrickson, Mgr.,
Intl. Business Div.
310 S. Michigan Ave., Ste. 1000
Chicago, Ill. 60604
(312) 814-7164

Indiana

Indiana Dept. of Commerce
Maria Mercedes Plant, Dir. of Intl. Trade, Business Dev. Div.
One N. Capitol, Ste. 700
Indianapolis, Ind. 46204-2288
(317) 232-8845

Iowa

Iowa Dept. of Econ. Dev.
Michael Doyle, Bureau Chief, Intl. Mkting. Div.
200 E. Grand Ave.
Des Moines, Iowa 50309
(515) 242-4743

Kansas

Kansas Dept. of Commerce
Trade Development Div.
Jim Beckley, Dir.
400 SW 8th St., Ste. 500
Topeka, Kans. 66603
(913) 296-4027

Kentucky

Ky. Cabinet for Econ. Dev.
Michael Hayes, Dir., Office of Intl. Mkting.
Capital Plaza Tower
Frankfort, Ky. 40601
(502) 564-2170

Louisiana

Office of Intl. Trade, Finance and Devel.
William Jackson, Dir.
P.O. Box 94185
Baton Rouge, La. 70804-9185
(504) 342-4320

Maine

Maine State Dev. Office
Lynn Wachtel, Commissioner
State House, Station 59
Augusta, Maine 04333
(207) 289-2656

Maryland

Md. Office of Intl. Trade (MOIT)
Eric Feldman. Exec. Dir.
7th Floor, World Trade Center
401 E. Pratt St.
Baltimore, Md. 21202
(301) 333-8180

Massachusetts

Mass. Office of Intl. Trade
Gwen Pritchard, Exec. Dir.
100 Cambridge St., Ste. 902
Boston, Mass. 02202
(617) 367-1830

Michigan

Mich. Dept. of Commerce
Gene Ruff, Actg. Dir.,
World Trade Services Div.
P.O. Box 30225
Lansing, Mich. 48909
(517) 373-1054

Minnesota

Minn. Trade Office
Director
1000 World Trade Center
30 E. 7th St.
St. Paul, Minn. 55101
(612) 297-4227

Mississippi

Miss. Dept. of Econ. & Community Dev.
Elizabeth Cleveland, Dir., Export Office
P.O. Box 849
Jackson, Miss. 39205
(601) 359-3618

Missouri

Missouri Dept. of Commerce
Intl. Business Office
Robert Black, Dir.
P.O. Box 118
Jefferson City, Mo. 65102
(314) 751-4855

Montana

Mont. Dept. of Commerce
Business Dev. Div.
Matthew Cohn, Dir., Intl. Trade Office
1429-9th Ave.
Helena, Mont. 59620
(406) 444-4380

Nebraska

Nebraska Dept. of Econ. Devel.
Steve Buttress, Dir.
301 Centennial Mall S.
Lincoln, Neb. 68509
(402) 471-4668

Nevada

(State of) Nevada
Commission on Econ. Dev.
Julie Wilcox, Dir.
Las Vegas Mail Room Complex
Las Vegas, Nev. 89158
(702) 486-7282

New Hampshire

(State of) New Hampshire
Dept. of Resources and Econ. Dev.
William Pillsbury, Dir.
Office of Industrial Trade
P.O. Box 856
Concord, N.H. 03301
(603) 271-2591

New Jersey

(State of) N.J. Div. of Intl. Trade
Philip Ferzen, Dir.
P.O. Box 47024
153 Halsey St., 5th Floor
Newark, N.J. 07102
(201) 648-3518

New Mexico

(State of) New Mexico
Economic Dev. and Tourism Dept.
Trade Division
Roberto Castillo, Dir.
1100 St. Francis Dr.,
Joseph M. Montoya Bldg.
Santa Fe. N.M. 87503
(505) 827-0307

New York

N.Y. State Dept. of Commerce
Dept. of Econ. Dev.
Intl. Trade Div.,
Stephen Koller, Dir.
1515 Broadway
New York, N.Y. 10036
(212) 827-6200

North Carolina

N.C. Dept. of Econ. and Community Dev., Intl. Division
Richard (Dick) Quinlan, Dir.
430 N. Salisbury St.
Raleigh, N.C. 27611
(919) 733-7193

North Dakota

N.D. Econ. Devel. Commission
L.R. Minton, Dir.
Liberty Memorial Bldg.
State Capital Grounds
Bismarck, N.D. 58505
(701) 224-2810

Ohio

Ohio Dept. of Dev.
Intl. Trade Division
Dan Waterman, Dep. Dir.
77 S. High St., 29th Floor
Columbus, Ohio 43215
(614) 466-5017

Oklahoma

Oklahoma Dept. of Commerce
Gary H. Miller, Dir.
6601 Broadway Extension
Oklahoma City, Okla. 73116
(405) 841-5217

Oregon

Oregon Econ. Devel. Dept.,
Intl. Trade Division
Glenn Ford, Dir.
One World Trade Center
121 SW Salmon, Ste. 300
Portland, Ore. 97204
(503) 229-5625

Pennsylvania

Pa. Dept. of Commerce
Office of Intl. Dev.
Paul Haugland, Dir.
433 Forum Bldg.
Harrisburg, Pa. 17120
(717) 787-7190

Puerto Rico

P.R. Department of Commerce
Jorge Santiago, Secy.
P.O. Box 4275
San Juan, P.R. 00905
(809) 725-7254

Rhode Island

R.I. Dept. of Econ. Dev.
Intl. Trade Div.
Christine Smith. Dir.
7 Jackson Walkway
Providence, R.I. 02903
(401) 277-2601 x47

South Carolina

S.C. State Dev. Board
Frank Newman, Assoc. Dir., Intl. Business Division
P.O. Box 927
Columbia, S.C. 29202
(803) 737-0403

South Dakota

S.D. Governor's Office of Econ. Dev., Export, Trade & Mktg. Div.
David Brotzman, Dir.
Capitol Lake Plaza
Pierre, S.D. 57501
(605) 773-5735

Tennessee

Tenn. Export Office
Ms. Leigh Wieland, Dir.
320 6th Ave. N.
7th Floor
Nashville, Tenn. 37219-5308
(615) 741-5870

Texas

Texas Dept. of Commerce
Office of Intl. Trade
Deborah Hernandez, Mgr.

P.O. Box 12728, Capitol Sta.
816 Congress
Austin, Tex. 78711
(512) 320-9439
The Department maintains export assistance centers in a number of Texas cities.

Utah

Utah Dept. of Community & Econ. Devel.
Dan Mabey, Actg. Dir., Intl. Dev.
Ste. 200
324 S. State St.
Salt Lake City, Utah 84111
(801) 538-8736

Vermont

(State of) Vermont Agency of Dev. and Community Affairs
Ron Mackinnon, Commissioner
Pavillion Office Bldg.
109 State St.
Montpelier, Vt. 05602
(802) 828-3221

Virginia

Va. Dept. of Econ. Dev.
Stuart Perkins, Dir.,
Export Dev.
1021 East Cary St.
Richmond Va. 23206
(804) 371-8242

Washington

Wash. State Dept. of Trade and Econ. Dev.
Importing/Exporting Office
Paul Isaki, Dir.
2001 Sixth Ave.,
26th Floor
Seattle, Wash. 98121
(206) 464-7143

West Virginia

Governor's Office of Community and Ind. Dev.
Stephen Spence, Dir.,
Intl. Division
Room 517, Building #6
1900 Washington St. E.
Charleston, W. Va. 25305
(304) 348-2234

Wisconsin

Wis. Dept. of Development
Bureau of Intl. Dev.
Ralph Graner, Dir.
P.O. Box 7970
123 W. Washington Ave.
Madison, Wis. 53707
(608) 266-9487

Wyoming

(State of) Wyoming
Office of the Governor
Richard Lindsey, Dir.
Capitol Building
Cheyenne, Wyo. 82002
(307) 777-6412

Source: *Business America* 112 (Special Edition, 1991), pps. 24–25.

Bibliography

Adams, Gordon (1981). *The Politics of Defense Contracting*. New Brunswick, N.J.: Transaction Books.

Addison, Eric (1989). "HUD: The Real Scandal," *Journal of Housing* 46 (November/December): 287–295.

Adler, Theodore A. (1982). "State and Local Procurement" (annual survey of significant developments in Pennsylvania law), *Pennsylvania Bar Association Quarterly* 53 (July): 154–163.

Advisory Commission on Intergovernmental Relations (1967). *A Handbook for Interlocal Agreements and Contracts*. Washington, D.C.: ACIR, Report M–29.

Advisory Commission on Intergovernmental Relations (1985). *Intergovernmental Service Arrangements for Delivering Local Public Services: Update 1983*. Washington, D.C.: ACIR, Report A–102 (October).

Advisory Commission on Intergovernmental Relations (1988). *Governments at Risk: Liability Insurance and Tort Reform*. Washington, D.C.: ACIR, Report SR–7.

Advisory Commission on Intergovernmental Relations (1988). *Metropolitan Organization: The St. Louis Case*. Washington, D.C.: ACIR, Report M–158 (September).

Advisory Commission on Intergovernmental Relations (1989). *Residential Community Associations: Private Governments in the Intergovernmental System?* Washington, D.C.: ACIR, Report A–112 (May).

Ager, R. L. (1966). "State Public Works Contract Bond Problems," *The Forum* 1 (April): 23–38.

Ahern, Charlotte F. (1989). "Despite Court Ruling Firm Won't 'Go Away,' " *City & State* 6 (January 30): 21.

Ahlbrandt, Robert S., Jr. (1973). "Efficiency in the Provision of Fire Services," *Public Choice* 16 (Fall): 1–15.

Ahlbrandt, Robert S., Jr. (1974). "Implications of

Contracting for Public Service," *Urban Affairs Quarterly* 9 (March): 337–357.

Aldrich, Howard (1989). "Networking Among Women Entrepreneurs," in Oliver Hagan, Carol Rivchun, and Donald Sexton, eds., *Women-Owned Businesses*. New York: Praeger: 103–132.

Alexander, Albert N. (1986). "GATT Explores Extension of Government Procurement Code Coverage to Services," *Business America* 9 (February 3): 14–15.

Alexander, James, Jr. (1981). "Cooperative Purchasing: A Tool to Consider," *Current Municipal Problems* 8 (Summer): 33–37.

Alexander, Laurence B. (1989). "An Update on the Minority Preference at the Federal Communications Commission," *National Black Law Journal* 11 (Spring): 249–260.

Alijan, George W., ed. (1982). *Purchasing Handbook*, 4th ed. Falls Church, Va.: The National Institute of Governmental Purchasing.

Allen, Joan W. (1989a). "Use of the Private Sector for Service Delivery in State Parks and Recreation Areas," in Joan W. Allen et al., eds., *The Private Sector in State Service Delivery: Examples of Innovative Practices*. Washington, D.C.: The Urban Institute Press: 45–71.

Allen, Joan W. (1989b). "Use of the Private Sector for State Transportation Activities," in Joan W. Allen et al., eds., *The Private Sector in State Service Delivery: Examples of Innovative Practices*. Washington, D.C.: The Urban Institute Press: 139–162.

Allen, Joan W. (1989c). "Use of the Private Sector in Corrections Service Delivery," in Joan W. Allen et al., eds., *The Private Sector in State Service Delivery: Examples of Innovative Practices*. Washington, D.C.: The Urban Institute Press: 13–44.

Allen, Joan W., Keon S. Chi, Kevin A. Devlin, Mark Fall, Harry P. Hatry, and Wayne Masterman, eds. (1989). *The Private Sector in State Service Delivery: Examples of Innovative Practices.* Washington, D.C.: The Urban Institute Press.

Alpha Center for Public/Private Initiative (n.d.). *Pragmatic Visions: The Privatization of Human Services.* New York: Alpha Center for Public/Private Initiative.

Alston, Frank M. (1989). "Government Contracting: A New Strategy for a New Climate," *Price Waterhouse Review* 33 (2):4–13.

Amdur, Meredith (1989). "Quality Federal Style," *Government Executive* 21 (June): 54–56, 70.

American Bar Association (1970). *Survey of State Procurement and Protest Procedures.* Chicago: American Bar Association (June).

American Bar Association (1979). *The Model Procurement Code for State and Local Governments.* Chicago: American Bar Association.

American Bar Association (1980). *The Model Procurement Code for State and Local Governments: Recommended Regulations.* Chicago: American Bar Association.

American Bar Association (1982). *The Model Procurement Ordinance for Local Governments.* Chicago: American Bar Association.

American Bar Association (1984). *Identifying and Prosecuting Fraud and Abuse in State and Local Contracting.* Chicago: American Bar Association.

American Bar Association (1987). *Annotations to the Model Procurement Code for State and Local Governments.* Chicago: American Bar Association.

American Bar Association (1988). *First Supplement, Annotations of the Model Procurement Code for State and Local Governments with Analytical Summary of State Enactments.* Chicago: American Bar Association.

American City & County (1983). "Contract Management Keeps Vehicles Moving for Less," 98 (July): 35–36.

American Federation of State, County, and Municipal Employees (1983). *Passing the Bucks.* Washington, D.C.: AFSCME.

American Federation of State, County, and Municipal Employees (n.d.). *Private Profit, Public Risk.* Washington, D.C.: AFSCME.

American Federation of State, County, and Municipal Employees (1987). *When Public Services Go Private: Not Always Better, Not Always Honest, There May Be a Better Way.* Washington, D.C.: AFSCME.

American Law Institute and National Conference of Commissioners of Uniform State Laws (1987). *Uniform Commercial Code*, 10th ed. Philadelphia and Chicago: American Law Institute and National Conference of Commissioners on Uniform State Laws.

American Management Association (n.d.). *Purchasing Department Organization and Authority.* American Management Association Research Study No. 45. New York.

American Society for Testing and Materials (1990). *Selected ASTM Standards for the Purchasing Community*, 2nd ed. Philadelphia: ASTM.

Ammer, O. S. (1973). "Is Your Purchasing Department a Good Buy?" *Harvard Business Review* 52 (March/April): 36.

Amsun Associates (1977). *Socioeconomic Analysis of Asian American Business Patterns: A Study.* Washington, D.C.: Department of Commerce, Office of Minority Business Enterprise.

Ancel, Louis (1961). "Municipal Contracts," *University of Illinois Law Forum* 961 (Fall): 357–376.

Anderson, Robert L. and Kathleen P. Anderson (1988). "A Comparison of Women in Small and Large Companies," *American Journal of Small Business* 12 (Winter): 23–33.

Anderson, T. L. and Peter J. Hill (1983). "Privatizing the Commons," *Southern Economic Journal* 50 (October): 438–450.

Anderson, Terry L., ed. (1983). *Water Rights: Scarce Resource Allocation, Bureaucracy, & Environment.* Cambridge, Mass.: Ballinger Publishing Company.

Andrews, Edmund L. (1988). "Financing: This Helping Hand Can Stunt Growth," *Venture* 10 (June): 72–76.

Anthony, David V. and Carol K. Hagerty (1981). "Cautious Optimism as a Guide to Foreign Government Procurement," *Public Contract Law Journal* 12 (May 1981): 1–39.

Antitrust Committee, National Association of Attorneys General and the Committee on Competitive Governmental Purchasing, National Association of State Purchasing Officials (1963). *Impediments to Competitive Bidding—*

How to Detect and Combat Them. Lexington, Ky.: The Council of State Governments.

Anton, James J. and Dennis A. Yao (1987). "Second Sourcing and the Experience Curve: Price Competition in Defense Procurement," *Rand Journal of Economics* 18 (Spring): 57–76.

Appel, Steven J. (1987). "S Corporation Benefits for Small Business," *Business Forum* 12 (Fall): 18–21.

Arellano, Richard G. (1984). *Strategies for Hispanic Business Development: Agenda for Action: Recommendations.* Washington, D.C.: National Chamber Foundation.

Arieff, Irwin B. (1983). "Defense Fraud Crackdown Misguided, Lawyers Say," *Legal Times* 5 (January 24): 2.

Armendaris, Alex (1975). "New Trends in Minority Enterprise Development," *Journal of Small Business Management* 13 (July): 18–22.

Armington, R. Q. and William D. Ellis, eds. (1984). *This Way Up: The Local Official's Handbook for Privatization & Contracting.* Chicago: Regnery Gateway.

Arnett, R. and G. Trapnell (1984). "Private Insurances: New Measures of a Complex and Changing Industry," *Health Care Financing Review* 6: 31–42.

Arnold, David S. (1987). "Purchasing and Risk Management," in J. Richard Aronson and Eli Schwartz, eds., *Management Policies in Local Government Finance.* Washington, D.C.: International City Management Association: 364–382.

Aronoff, Arthur (1991). "Complying with the Foreign Corrupt Practices Act," *Business America* 112 (February 11): 10–11.

Aronson, J. Richard and Eli Schwartz, eds. (1987). *Management Policies in Local Government Finance.* Washington, D.C.: International City Management Association.

Arthurs, Rich (1984a). "Contract Bar Puzzles over New Acquisition Regs," *Legal Times* 6 (March 26): 4.

Arthurs, Rich (1984b). "Contractors Fume as Air Force Takes off After Rights to Data," *Legal Times* 6 (February 27): 1.

Ascher, Kate (1987). *The Politics of Privatization: Contracting Out Public Services.* New York: St. Martin's Press.

Ash, Nigel (1990). "Turkey: Foreign Invest-

ment—Too Little Too Late?" *Euromoney* (March): 21–28.

Ashe, George (1969). "New Developments in Statutory Bond Law, Part One—Classification," *Commercial Law Journal* 74 (May): 114–118.

Ashe, George (1969). "New Developments in Statutory Bond Law, Part Two—Payment and Application," *Commercial Law Journal* 74 (June): 141–144.

Atherton, Cliff and Duane Windsor (1987). "Privatization of Urban Services," in Calvin A. Kent, ed., *Entrepreneurship and the Privatizing of Government.* New York: Quorum Books: 81–100.

Atkins, George L. (1989). "Humana, Inc.— A Business Perspective on Health Care," in Lawrence K. Finley, ed., *Public Sector Privatization: Alternative Approaches to Service Delivery.* New York: Quorum Books: 121–140.

Auster, Ellen R. and Howard Aldrich (1984). "Small Business Vulnerability, Ethnic Enclaves, and Ethnic Enterprise," in Robin Ward and Richard Jenkins, eds., *Ethnic Communities in Business.* Cambridge, MA: Cambridge University Press: 39–54.

Austin, Harry A. (1988). "A Questionable Expansion of the Government Contract Defense" (case note), *Georgia Law Review* 23 (Fall): 227–256.

Aviation Week (1985). "Planned Bill Will Favor Private Sector," 122 (February 18): 50.

Aviation Week (1987). "Independent Study Recommends Additional Acquisition Reforms to Save $50 Billion per Year," 126 (April 13): 102.

Aviation Week & Space Technology (1988). "Canadians Debate Privatization of Air Canada," 129 (August 15): 113.

Ayres, D. (1975). "Municipal Interfaces in the Third Sector: A Negative View," *Public Administration Review* 35 (September/October): 459–467.

Baber, Walter F. (1987). "Privatizing Public Management: The Grace Commission," in Steve H. Hanke, ed., *Prospects for Privatization.* New York: *Proceedings of the Academy of Political Science* 36 (3): 153–163.

Babin, James C. (1982–83). "Federal Source Selection Procedures in Competitive Negotiated

Acquisitions," *Air Force Law Review* 23 (Summer-Fall): 318–369.

Bacas, Harry (1988). "Economic Development: The Appeal of Privatization," *Nation's Business* 76 (May): 42A–42J.

Baden, John and Laura Rosen (1983). "The Environmental Justification," *Environment* 25 (October): 7, 38–43.

Bahls, Jane Easter (1990). "A Demanding Customer," *Nation's Business* 78 (March): 29–30.

Bailey, Robert W. (1987). "Uses and Misuses of Privatization," in Steve H. Hanke, ed., *Prospects for Privatization.* New York: *Proceedings of the Academy of Political Science* 36 (3): 138–152.

Bailey, Victor B. and Gary B. Teske (1991). *U.S. Foreign Trade Highlights 1990.* Washington, D.C.: U.S. Department of Commerce (April).

Baim, Dean (1985). *Comparison of Privately Owned Sports Arenas and Stadiums.* Chicago: Heartland Institute (August 19).

Bain, J. Adam (1986). "The Affirmative Action Obligations of Government Contractors in Indiana" (case note), *Indiana Law Journal* 61 (Fall): 793–807.

Bain, James W. and Alvin M. Cohen (1987). "The Potential and Perils of Colorado Public Construction Contracting," *Colorado Lawyer* 16 (December): 2131–2140.

Baker, John L. (1985). "Use of Private Contracting in Highway Maintenance," in American Society of Civil Engineers, *Urban Transportation Performance*, proceedings of a speciality conference. New York: ASCE.

Balsam, Lori (1987). "Women in Finance, Part II: Women Entrepreneurs," *National Business Woman* 68 (June/July): 1, 6.

Banker, Stephen (1989). "The Search for Compatibility," *Government Executive* 21 (May): 42–45.

Baram, M. S. (1966). "Buy American Policies," *Boston College Industrial and Commercial Law Review* 7 (Spring): 269.

Barham, John (1990). "Brazil: Banking on the Almighty," *Banker* 140 (February): 69–70.

Barker, Robert (1984). "Identity Crisis: It Has Been a Big Liability to Minority Banks," *Barron's* 64 (May 14): 16, 53.

Barnes, John A. (1986). "The Failure of Privatization," *National Review* 38 (July 18): 38–40, 61.

Baron, David P. and David Besanko (1978). "Monitoring, Moral Hazard, Asymmetric Information and Risk Sharing in Procurement Contracting," *Rand Journal of Economics* 18 (Winter): 509–532.

Barovick, Richard L. (1984). "Opening Government Markets," *Business America* 7 (September 3): 2–7.

Barron, Paul A. (1968). "Administrative Resolution of Breaches; Service Contract Developments, Incentive Contract Changes; Application of Freedom of Information Act to Procurement," *Federal Bar Journal* 28 (Summer): 1961–1964.

Bartik, Timothy J. (1989). "Small Business Start-Ups in the United States: Estimates of the Effects of Characteristics of States," *Southern Economic Journal* 55 (April): 1004–1018.

Barton, S. L. (1989). "Small Firm Financing: Implications from a Strategic Management Perspective," *Journal of Small Business Management* 27 (January): 1–7.

Barton, Wayne D. and Richard G. Ungar (1987). "Government Procurement in Canada," *George Washington Journal of International Law & Economics* 21 (1): 27–58.

Barzey, Rachel (1991a). "Help for Firms Seeking Kuwait Contracts Increases," *Black Enterprise* 21 (June): 29.

Barzey, Rachel (1991b). "Operation Contract Procurement," *Black Enterprise* 21 (July): 53, 54, 56–57.

Baskerville, Dawn M. (1991a). "Black Businesses on the Rise," *Black Enterprise* 21 (April): 45.

Baskerville, Dawn M. (1991b). "Keys to Small-Business Success," *Black Enterprise* 21 (June): 80.

Bates, Timothy (1973a). "The Potential of Black Capitalism," *Public Policy* 21 (Winter): 135–148.

Bates, Timothy (1973b). "An Econometric Analysis of Lending to Black-Owned Businesses," *The Review of Economics and Statistics* 55 (August): 272–283.

Bates, Timothy (1973c). *Black Capitalism: A Qualitative Analysis.* New York: Praeger.

Bates, Timothy (1974). "Financing Black Enterprise," *Journal of Finance* 29 (June): 747–762.

Bates, Timothy (1986). "Characteristics of Minorities Who Are Entering Self-Employment,"

The Review of Black Political Economy 15 (Fall): 31–49.

Bates, Timothy (1989a). "Small Business Viability in the Urban Ghetto," *Journal of Regional Science* 29 (November): 625–643.

Bates, Timothy (1989b). "The Changing Nature of Minority Business: A Comparative Analysis of Asian, Nonminority, and Black-Owned Businesses," *The Review of Black Political Economy* 19 (Fall): 25–42.

Bates, Timothy (1989c). *The Role of Black Enterprise in Urban Development.* Washington, D.C.: Joint Center for Political Studies.

Bates, Timothy and Donald Hester (1977). "Analysis of a Commercial Bank Minority Lending Program," *Journal of Finance* 32 (December): 1783–1790.

Bates, Timothy and William Bradford (1979). *Financing Black Economic Development.* New York: Academic Press.

Baumback, C. M. and K. Lawyer (1988). *How to Organize and Operate Small Business.* Englewood Cliffs, N.J.: Prentice-Hall.

Baxter, Murray B. (1986). "Application of the Debt Collection Act of 1982—Restraining the Beast," *Army Lawyer* (June): 64–65.

Bayard, Michael J. and Bryan C. Jackson (1989). "California's Minority Goals After 'Croson,' " *The Los Angeles Daily Journal* 102 (April): 7.

Bean, Richard C. (1988). "Practical Considerations in ADP Acquisition," *Air Force Law Review* 29 (Fall): 265–276.

Bearse, Peter J. (1983). *An Econometric Analysis of Minority Entrepreneurship.* Washington, D.C.: U.S. Department of Commerce, Minority Business Development Agency.

Beattie, L. Elisabeth (1984). "The Entrepreneurial Woman," *Business & Economic Review* 31 (October): 3–6.

Beauregard, Robert A. (1990). "Tenacious Inequalities: Politics and Race in Philadelphia," *Urban Affairs Quarterly* 25 (March): 420–434.

Bedell, Robert P. (1988). "The Agendas of the Office of Federal Procurement Policy," *National Contract Management Journal* 21 (Winter): 1–7.

Bedingfield, James P. and A. J. Stagliano (1990). "A Developing Picture of Business Ethics and Accountability: The Defense Industry Initiative," *Government Accountants Journal* 39 (Spring): 59–65.

Bekey, Michelle (1989). "The Rocky Road to Launching a Business," *Working Woman* (June): 41–44.

Bell, A. Fleming (1989). "City of Richmond v. J. A. Croson Company: The Decision and Some of Its Implications," *School Law Bulletin* 20 (Fall): 22–29.

Bell, Hubert J., Jr. and Charles W. Surasky (1982). "Georgia" (recent developments in state and local public contract law), *Public Contract Newsletter* 18 (Fall): 8.

Bell, S. R. (1986). "Tapping the Money Pool," *Black Enterprise* 16 (June): 231.

Bellante, Don (1983). "Breaking the Political Barriers to Privatization, Private Alternatives to Social Security: The Experience of Other Countries," *Cato Journal* 3 (2): 575–580.

Bellush, Sandra Mokuvos (1985). "Private Choices," *American City & County* 100 (October): 62–65.

Belmonte, Robert M. (1969). "Voluntary Joint Public Bidding," *The American City* 84 (October): 162, 164–165.

Bendic, Mark, Jr. (1984). "Privatization of Public Services: Recent Experience," in Harvey Brooks, Lance Liebman, and Corrine S. Schelling, eds., *Public-Private Partnership: New Opportunities for Meeting Social Needs.* Cambridge, Mass.: Ballinger Publishing Company: 153–171.

Benimadhu, Prem (1989). "Industrial Relations Update: Consultation, Co-Operation, and Confrontation," *Canadian Business Review* 16 (Autumn): 42–44.

Benjamin, Joyce Holmes (1989). "The Supreme Court Decision and the Future of Race-Conscious Remedies," *Government Finance Review* 5 (April): 21–24.

Bennett, James T. and Manuel W. Johnson (1980). "Tax Reduction Without Sacrifice: Private-Sector Production of Public Services," *Public Finance Quarterly* 8 (October): 363–396.

Bennett, James T. and Manuel W. Johnson (1981). *Better Government at Half the Price: Private Production of Public Services.* Ottawa, IL: Caroline House.

Bennett, James T. and Thomas J. DiLorenzo (1983a). "Public Employee Unions and Privatization of 'Public' Services," *Journal of Labor Research* 4 (Winter): 33–45.

Bennett, James T. and Thomas J. DiLorenzo

(1983b). "Public Employee Unions, Privatization, and the New Federalism," *Government Union Review* 4 (Winter): 58–73.

Bennett, James T. and Thomas J. DiLorenzo (1987). "The Role of Tax-Funded Politics," in Steve H. Hanke, ed., *Prospects for Privatization*. New York: *Proceedings of the Academy of Political Science* 36 (3): 14–23.

Bennett, Robert S. and Alan Kriegel (1986). "Negotiating Global Settlements of Procurement Fraud Cases," *Public Contract Law Journal* 16 (August): 30–46.

Benson, Frank and M. T. Vaziri (1987). "What Tax Reform Means for Small Business," *Business Forum* 12 (Fall): 14–17.

Benson, Robert (1985). *Privatizing Public Services*. Washington, D.C.: *Congressional Quarterly*, Editorial Research Reports 2: 559–576.

Bentil, Kweku K. (1979). "The Minority Contractor and His Effect on the Construction Costs of Federally Funded Projects," *AACE Transactions*: J6.1–6.5

Berenyi, Eileen B. (1981). "Contracting Out Refuse Collection: The Nature and Impact of Change," *Urban Interest* 3 (Spring): 30–42.

Berenyi, Eileen Brettler and Barbara J. Stevens (1988). "Does Privatization Work? A Study of the Delivery of Eight Local Services," *State and Local Government Review* 20 (Winter): 11–20.

Berger, C. Jaye (1982). "Minority Set-Aside Programs on Public Building Projects: The Current State of the Law," *Construction Lawyer* 3 (Fall): 213–225.

Berger, Renee A. (1986). "Private-Sector Initiatives in the Reagan Administration," in Perry Davis, ed., *Public-Private Partnerships: Improving Urban Life*. New York: Academy of Political Science: 14–30.

Berger, Renee A. (1988). "U.S. Government–Business Cooperation (A Critique)," *National Civic Review* 77 (January-February): 34–41.

Bergsman, Steve (1990). "Movers & Shakers: Political Empowerment is Opening the Doors for Hispanics in Chicago," *Hispanic Business* 12 (May): 24–32.

Bernard, Paul (1989). "Managing Vendor Performance," *Production and Inventory Management Journal* (1): 1–7.

Berne, Robert and Richard Schramm (1986). *The Financial Analysis of Governments*. Englewood Cliffs, N.J.: Prentice-Hall.

Berney, Karen (1988). "Where Women Are Welcome," *Nation's Business* 76 (August): 26R–27R.

Bernstein, Amy (1990). "Act Now to Avoid Procurement Protests Later," *Government Executive* 22 (July): 48–50.

Best, Judah, Jeffrey P. Moran, and Cary K. Williams (1984). "Civil RICO" (Racketeer Influenced and Corrupt Organizations), in American Bar Association, *Identifying and Prosecuting Fraud and Abuse in State and Local Contracting*. Chicago: ABA: 87–101.

Bibber, David W. (1984). "Private Sector Fire Protection: A Fire Chief's Point of View," *The International Fire Chief* 50 (February): 24–27.

Binnbaum, Owen (1956). "Government Contracts: The Role of the Comptroller General," *American Bar Association Journal* 42 (May): 433–436.

Birley, Sue (1989). "Female Entrepreneurs: Are They Really Any Different?" *Journal of Small Business Management* 27 (January): 32–37.

Birley, Sue, Caroline Moss, and Peter Saunders (1987). "Do Women Entrepreneurs Require Different Training?" *American Journal of Small Business* 12 (Summer): 27–35.

Bish, Robert and Robert Warren (1972). "Scale and Monopoly Problems in Urban Government Services," *Urban Affairs Quarterly* 8 (September): 92–122.

Bish, Robert L. and David W. Rasmussen (1987). "Federalism: A Market Economics Perspective; Federalism from a Market Perspective," *Cato Journal* 7 (Fall): 377–402.

Bisopoulos, Tasos (1989). "Government Procurement and the Single Market," *International Financial Law Review* (UK) 8 (October): 34–36.

Black, Dennis E. (1983). "Effectiveness of the Mandatory Minority Business Set-Aside Contracting Goals: A Regression Analysis," *Evaluation Review* 7 (June): 321–336.

Black, Dennis E. (1989). "Socioeconomic Contract Goal Setting Within the Department of Defense: Promises Still Unfulfilled," *National Contract Management Journal* 22 (Winter): 67–82.

Black Enterprise (1988). "Defining a New Generation," 18 (June): 103–139.

Black Enterprise (1991). "Are Blacks Getting A Fair Share?" 21 (March): 76.

Blake, Daniel (1987). "Are Set-Aside Programs Helping Anybody?" *D & B Reports* 35 (July/August): 38–39.

Blake, Daniel (1988). "Privatization: Is It a Panacea?" *D & B Reports* 36 (January/February): 41–44.

Blasky, H. F. (1968). "Equal Employment in the Construction Industry," *William and Mary Law Review* 10 (Fall): 3–17.

Blechman, William J. (1982). "Agent Orange and the Government Contract Defense: Are Military Manufacturers Immune from Product Liability?" *University of Miami Law Review* 36 (May): 489–532.

Blow, James L. (1991). "US&FCS Joins the Staff of the U.S. Mission to the European Communities," *Business America* 112 (February 25): 19.

Blyth, Alfred H. (1987). "Government Procurement in the United Kingdom," *George Washington Journal of International Law & Economics* 21 (1): 127–149.

Boney, P. (1964). "Public Relations in Public Purchasing," *Purchasing Magazine* 56 (June 1): 71–72.

Boorman, John T. (1974). *The Recent Loan Loss Experience of New Minority-Owned Commercial Banks.* Washington, D.C.: Federal Deposit Insurance Corporation, Working Paper No. 74-6.

Boorman, John T. and Myron L. Kwast (1974). "The Start-Up Experience of Minority-Owned Commercial Banks: A Comparative Analysis," *The Journal of Finance* 29 (September): 1123–1141.

Borcherding, T. E. et. al. (1982). "Comparing the Efficiency of Private and Public Production: The Evidence From Five Countries," *Journal of Economics*, supplement 2: 127–156.

Borchers, Patrick J. and Paul F. Dauer (1988). "Taming the New Breed of Nuclear Free Zone Ordinances: Infirmities in Local Procurement Ordinances Blacklisting the Producers of Nuclear Weapons Components," *Hastings Law Journal* 40 (November): 87–118.

Bourgeois, J. H. J. (1982). "The Tokyo Round Agreements on Technical Barriers and on Government Procurement in International and EEC Perspective," *Common Market Law Review* 19 (March): 5–33.

Bovbjerg, Randall R., Philip J. Held, and Mark V. Pauly (1987). "Privatization and Bidding in the Health-Care Sector," *Journal of Policy Analysis and Management* 6 (December): 666–673.

Bowen, Donald D. and Robert D. Hisrich (1986). "The Female Entrepreneur: A Career Development Perspective," *Academy of Management Review* 11 (April): 393–407.

Bower, Joe (1990). "Council's Role: Discuss, Inform on Privatization," *City & State* 7 (June 4): 17.

Bowman-Upton, Nancy. (1989). "Transition Planning and Business Succession for Women Entrepreneurs," in Oliver Hagan, Carol Rivchun, and Donald Sexton, eds., *Women-Owned Businesses.* New York: Praeger: 151–182.

Bowytz, R. B. (1971). "Federal Contractor: A Survey of Government Contract Law," *Commercial Law Journal* 76 (January): 16–17; (February): 45–48; (March): 73–75; (April): 108–110; (May): 138–139; (June): 168–170; (September): 324–326.

Boyd, Roger N. (1985). "The Changing World of Sole Source Negotiated Procurement," *ALI-ABA Course Materials Journal* 9 (February): 21–34.

Boyd, Roger N. and Richard L. Beizer (1984). "State Prosecutions for Conspiracy," in American Bar Association, *Identifying and Prosecuting Fraud and Abuse in State and Local Contracting.* Chicago: ABA: 41–45.

Bozeman, Barry (1987). *All Organizations Are Public.* San Francisco: Jossey-Bass.

Bozeman, Barry (1988). "Exploring the Limits of Public and Private Sectors: Sector Boundaries as Maginot Line," *Public Administration Review* 48 (March/April): 672–674.

Bradford, William D. (1974). "Minority Financial Institutions, Inner-City Economic Development, and the Hunt Commission Report," *The Review of Black Political Economy* 4 (Spring): 47–62.

Bradford, William D. and Alfred E. Osborne, Jr. (1976). "The Entrepreneurship Decision and Black Economic Development," *The American Economic Review* 66 (May): 316–319.

Bradley, Bill (1990). "Building a Pacific Coalition," in Frank J. Macchiarola, ed., *International Trade: The Changing Role of the United States.* New York: The Academy of Political Science: 1–8.

Brailsford, Daniel T. and Barbara McMillan (1982). "South Carolina" (recent developments in state and local public contract law), *Public Contract Newsletter* 18 (Fall): 9–10.

Branch, Eleanor (1988). "Competing for Contracts," *Black Enterprise* 18 (February): 204–208.

Brannen, K. C. and J. C. Gard (1985). "Grantsmanship and Entrepreneurship: A Partnership Opportunity Under the Small Business Innovation Development Act," *Journal of Small Business Management* 23 (July): 44–49.

Briese, Garry L. (1984). "An Overview of the Private Sector Fire Service," *The International Fire Chief* 50 (February): 16–19.

Brimmer, Andrew F. (1990). "A Battleplan for Fairness," *Black Enterprise* (November): 45–46.

Brimmer, Andrew F. and Henry S. Terrell (1971). "The Economic Potential for Black Capitalism," *Public Policy* 19 (Spring): 289–308.

Brockhaus, Robert H., Sr. (1989). "Appendix: Sources of Assistance to Women Entrepreneurs," in Oliver Hagan, Carol Rivchun, and Donald Sexton, eds., *Women-Owned Businesses.* New York: Praeger: 195–216.

Bromberg, Michael D. and Mark J. Brand (1984). "Privatization of Hospitals," in Raymond Q. Armington and William D. Ellis, eds., *This Way Up.* Chicago: Regnery Gateway: 113–123.

Brooks, Harvey, Lance Liebman, and Corrine S. Schelling, eds. (1984). *Public-Private Partnership: New Opportunities for Meeting Social Needs.* Cambridge, Mass.: Ballinger.

Brophy, David J. (1989). "Financing Women-Owned Entrepreneurial Firms," in Oliver Hagan, Carol Rivchun, and Donald Sexton, eds., *Women-Owned Businesses.* New York: Praeger: 55–76.

Brown, Alan C. (1984a). "Bribery," in American Bar Association, *Identifying and Prosecuting Fraud and Abuse in State and Local Contracting.* Chicago: ABA: 47–48.

Brown, Alan C. (1984b). "Civil Remedies for Official Corruption," in American Bar Association, *Identifying and Prosecuting Fraud and Abuse in State and Local Contracting.* Chicago: ABA: 57–61.

Brown, Pamela Clark (1989). "A Risk-Averse Buyer's Contract Design," *European Economic Review* (Netherlands) 33 (October): 1527–1544.

Brown, Ronald Wellington (1981). "The New International Government Procurement Code Under GATT," *New York State Bar Journal* 53 (April): 198.

Brown, Stanley A. and Phyllis Segal (1989). "Female Entrepreneurs in Profile," *Canadian Banker* 96 (July/August): 32–34.

Browne, M. Neil (1981). "The Promise of Federal Procurement for the Implementation of Incomes Policy," *University of Toledo Law Review* 12 (Winter): 347–367.

Browne, Robert S. (1971). "Cash Flows in a Ghetto Community," *The Review of Black Political Economy* 1 (Spring): 28–39.

Bruce, Charles M. (1971). "Reform of the Renegotiation Process in Government Contracting," Editorial Notes, *George Washington Law Review* 39 (July): 1141–1166.

Bruggink, Thomas H. (1982). "Public Versus Regulated Private Enterprise in the Municipal Water Industry: A Comparison of Operating Costs," *Quarterly Review of Economics and Business* 22 (Spring): 111–125.

Brunette, Robert A. (1989). "U.S. Congress Requires Limitations on Competition for Innovative Defense Contractors and Subcontractors," *National Contract Management Journal* 23 (Summer): 85–89.

Buerk, Susan C. (1978). "Women's Opportunity . . . Starting Your Own Business," *Vital Speeches* 44 (February 1): 230–232.

Buford, J. J. (1959). "Notice Requirement Under Government Construction Contracts," *Minnesota Law Review* 44 (December): 275–287.

Bullock, Bob (1986). "New Law May Change the Way You Do Business," *City and County Financial Management Systems* (March): 1–5.

Buonocore, Vincent (1987). "Implementing a Procurement Fraud Program: Keeping the Contractors Honest," *Army Lawyer* (June): 14–19.

Burton, John (1987). "Privatization: The Thatcher Case," *Managerial & Decision Economics* (UK) 8 (March): 21–29.

Busby, David, Morton Pomeranz, Alfred R. McCauley, and Bruce Davis (1980). "Procurement" (U.S. Court of Customs and Patent Appeals, Judicial Conference, 1979), *Federal Rules Decisions* 84 (March): 573–579.

Business America (1990). "USTR Issues Reports

on Procurement and Intellectual Property Protection," 111 (May 21): 15–16.

Business America (1991a). "A Directory of Export Services," 112 (special edition): 8–12.

Business America (1991b). "Practical Tips on How to Succeed in Exporting," 112 (special edition): 6–7.

Business America (1991c). "Much Assistance Is out There for the Inexperienced Exporter," 112 (special edition): 23.

Business America (1991d). "The International Trade Administration Has Many Services to Help U.S. Exporters," 112 (special edition): 15–16.

Business America (1991e). "USA: ABCs of Exporting," 112 (special edition): 2–5.

Business America (1991f). "European Community '92 UPDATE," 112 (February 25): 2–5.

Business America (1991g). "Economic Report of the President: Economies in Transition Around the World," 112 (March 11): 2–8.

Business America (1991h). "Financing," 112 (March 25): 18–23.

Business America (1991i). "Market Entry Strategy," 112 (March 25): 12–16.

Business America (1991j). "The Global Economic Expansion Is Forecast to Continue This Year and to Gain Renewed Strength in 1992," 112 (June 3): 18–22.

Business Week (1978). "More Aid for Minority Business," (Industrial Edition) 2530 (April 17): 146, 149.

Business Week (1979a). "Minority Contracting Gets a Federal Overhaul," 2571 (February 5): 32.

Business Week (1979b). "The Boomerang Effect of a Procurement Law," (Industrial Edition) 2598 (August 13): 29, 32.

Business Week (1980). "Women Rise as Entrepreneurs," (Industrial Edition) 2625 (February 25): 85–86, 91.

Business Week (1981). "Minority Job Quotas Go Local," (Industrial Edition) 2686 (May 4): 134F, 134H.

Butler, James P. (1984). "Public Housing," in Raymond Q. Armington and William D. Ellis, eds., *This Way up.* Chicago: Regnery Gateway: 48–64.

Butler, Katherine (1991). "Grooming Business Coaches," *Government Executive* 23 (June): 17–18.

Butler, Stuart M. (1984). "Public Housing: From Tenants to Homeowners." *Heritage Backgrounder* 359 (June 12).

Butler, Stuart M. (1985). *Privatizing Federal Spending: A Strategy to Eliminate the Deficit.* New York: Universe Books.

Butler, Stuart M. (1987). "Changing the Political Dynamics of Government," in Steven H. Hanke, ed., *Prospects for Privatization.* New York: *Proceedings of the Academy of Political Science* 36 (3): 4–13.

Butler, Stuart M. (1988). "Privatization of Government Assets," *Vital Speeches* 54 (April 1): 375–379.

Butler, Stuart M., ed. (1985). *The Privatizing Option: A Strategy to Shrink the Size of the Government.* Washington, D.C.: Heritage Foundation.

Buttner, E. Holly and Benson Rosen (1988). "Bank Loan Officers' Perceptions of the Characteristics of Men, Women, and Successful Entrepreneurs," *Journal of Business Venturing* 3 (Summer): 249–258.

Buttner, E. Holly and Benson Rosen (1989). "Funding New Business Ventures: Are Decision Makers Biased Against Women Entrepreneurs?" *Journal of Business Venturing* 4 (July): 249–261.

Byers, Karen (1983). "Recognizing Personal Services Contracts," *Army Lawyer* (January): 8–14.

Byers, Karen S. (1983). "Contracting with the Federal Government: An Overview," *Illinois Bar Journal* 71 (May): 552–557.

Cain, Bruce E. and D. R. Kiewiet (1986). *Minorities in California.* Pasadena: California Institute of Technology, Division of Humanities and Social Services.

Calamari, Joseph A. (1982). "The Aftermath of Gonzalez and Horne on the Administrative Debarment and Suspension of Government Contractors," *New England Law Review* 17 (Fall): 1137–1174.

Caldwell, Charles W. and Judith K. Welch (1989). "Applications of Cost-Volume-Profit Analysis in the Governmental Environment," *Association of Government Accountants Journal* (Summer): 3–8.

Callahan, J. W. (1967). "Liability of the Surety When Contractor Withdraws Bid," *Federation of Insurance Counsel* 17 (Summer): 80.

Callison, C. H., J. Baden, and L. Rosen (1983). "The Fallacies of Privatization," *Environment* 25 (October): 7, 17–20, 37.

Camp, Camille, G. and George M. Camp (1983). *Private Sector Involvement in Prison Services and Operations.* New York: Criminal Justice Institute.

Campbell, A. K. (1986). "Private Delivery of Public Services: Sorting out the Policy and Management Issues," *PM Public Management* 68 (December): 5.

Campbell, Bebe Moore (1983). "Five Cents Gas Tax Promises Business Opportunities for Blacks," *Black Enterprise* 13 (July): 21.

Campbell, Bebe Moore (1984). "These Women Mean Business," *Black Enterprise* 14 (June): 224–228.

Campbell, Colin A. (1984). "Private Sector Fire Protection: A Threat or a Challenge?" *The International Fire Chief* 50 (February): 18.

Cantor, J. A. (1989). "The Small Business in the Federal Marketplace—A Study of Barriers," *Journal of Small Business Management* 27 (January): 74–77.

Cao, A. D. (1980). "Government Procurement Policies: An Invisible Barrier to U.S. Exports," *Journal of Purchasing & Materials Management* 16 (Fall): 28–32.

Cao, A. D. (1981). "Government Procurement Policies: An Invisible Barrier to U.S. Exports in the 1980s," *National Contract Management Journal* 15 (Summer): 68–73.

Caponiti, Fred and Ed Booher (1986). "Parking Privatization—An Enforcement Alternative," *Parking Professional* (November).

Carlson, Barbara (1983). "This Women's Bank Sheds a Little Bit of Its Female Image," *New England Business* 5 (May 2): 20–22.

Carmichael, Jane (1981). "This Is Not a Chicken-Plucking Operation," *Forbes* 128 (August 17): 51–52.

Caron, Arthur J., Jr. (1970). "Federal Procurement and the Freedom of Information Act," *Federal Bar Journal* 29 (Summer): 271–286.

Carrizosa, Philip (1985). "Free-Market Ideas Play Novel Role in PUC Bias Case; Pacific Bell Is Target," *The Los Angeles Daily Journal* 98 (December 30): 1.

Carroll, Barry J., Ralph W. Conant, and Thomas A. Easton, eds. (1987). *Private Means—Public Ends: Private Business in Social Service Delivery.* New York: Praeger.

Carroll, James (1987). "Public Administration in the Third Century of the Constitution: Supply Side Management, Privatization, or Public Investment?" *Public Administration Review* 47 (January/February): 106–114.

Carsrud, Alan L., Connie Marie Gaglio, and Kenneth W. Olm (1987). "Entrepreneurs—Mentors, Networks, and Successful New Venture Development: An Exploratory Study," *American Journal of Small Business* 12 (Fall): 13–18.

Carter, Karen B. (1986). "Private Contracts for Public Work," *Current Municipal Problems* 13 (Fall): 218–227.

Carter, Robert N. (1980/81). "New Women Entrepreneurs Mean Business," *Review of Business* (Winter): 9–10.

Carver, Robert H. (1989). "Examining the Premises of Contracting Out," *Public Productivity & Management Review* 13 (Fall): 27–40.

Catania, Frank (1986). "Contracting Out: Management and Labor at War Under Section 7106 of the Civil Service Reform Act," *Public Contract Law Journal* 16 (August): 287–296.

Caves, D. W. and L. R. Christensen (1980). "The Relative Efficiency of Public and Private Firms in a Competitive Environment; The Case of Canadian Railroads," *Journal of Political Economy* 88 (October): 958–976.

Cavin, Sealy H., Jr. (1984). "Federal Immunity of Government Contractors from State and Local Taxation: A Survey of Recent Decisions and Their Impact on Government Procurement Policies," *Denver Law Journal* 61 (Fall): 797–836.

Cervero, Robert (1988). "Revitalizing Urban Transit," in John C. Weicher, ed., *Private Innovations in Public Transit.* Washington, D.C.: American Enterprise Institute for Public Policy Research: 71–81.

Chandler, Ralph (1986). "The Myth of Private Sector Superiority in Personnel Administration," *Policy Studies Review* 3: 643–653.

Chaney, Barbara (1989). "The Governmental Accounting Standards Board: How It Affects Local Government," in International City Management Association, *The Municipal Year Book 1989.* Washington, D.C.: ICMA: 12–24.

Chanis, Jonathan A. (1990). "United States Trade Policy Toward the Soviet Union: A More Commercial Orientation," in Frank J. Macchiarola, ed., *International Trade: The Changing Role of the United States*. New York: The Academy of Political Science: 110–121.

Chappel, Stephen (1985). "Privatization of Pollution Control Financing: Antitrust Implications," *The Privatization Review* 1 (Summer): 48–59.

Charboneau, F. Jill (1981). "The Woman Entrepreneur," *American Demographics* 3 (June): 21–23.

Checchi, Kathryn Dean (1980). "Federal Procurement and Commercial Procurement Under the U.C.C.: A Comparison," *Public Contract Law Journal* 11 (June): 358–378.

Chemical Week (1967). "How to Build a Better Contract" 27 (April 1): 27–28.

Chi, Keon (1985). *The Private Sector in State Correctional Industries: The Control Data Program in Minnesota*. Lexington, Ky.: Council of State Governments.

Chi, Keon (1986b). "Private-Public Alliances Grow," *State Government News* 29 (January): 10–13.

Chi, Keon (1988). *Privatization and Contracting for State Services: A Guide*. Lexington, Ky.: Council of State Governments, Innovation Report, RM–777.

Chi, Keon S. (1986a). *Alternative Service Delivery and Management Improvement in State Government: A Bibliography*. Iron Works Pike, Ky.: Council of State Governments (January).

Chi, Keon and Kevin M. Devlin (1989). "Use of the Private Sector in Employment and Job Training," in Joan W. Allen et al., eds., *The Private Sector in State Service Delivery: Examples of Innovative Practices*. Washington, D. C.: The Urban Institute Press: 103–118.

Chi, Keon, Kevin M. Devlin and Wayne Masterman (1989). "Use of the Private Sector in Delivery of Human Services," in Joan W. Allen et al., eds., *The Private Sector in State Service Delivery: Examples of Innovative Practices*. Washington, D.C.: The Urban Institute Press: 75–102.

Chicago Daily Law Bulletin (1989). "Minority Set-Aside Plan Struck Down as 'Reverse Bias'," 135 (January 23): 1.

Chinyelu, Mamadou (1991). "N.Y. to Add Small Biz," *Black Enterprise* 21 (January): 15.

Choplick, Jim, Jr. (1989). "Europe 1992—Lifting the Barriers to Trade," *Business Credit* 9 (November): 8–12.

Cibinic, John, Jr. (1987). "Introduction: International Symposium on Government Procurement Law, Part 2," *George Washington Journal of International Law and Economics* 21 (Fall): 1–4.

City & State (1990). "Top 50 Counties: 5th Annual County Financial Report," 7 (July 2): 12.

City of Richmond v. J. A. Croson Co., United States Law Week 57 (January 24, 1989): 4132–4157.

Clark, Asa A. IV, et al., eds. (1984). *The Defense Reform Debate*. Baltimore: The Johns Hopkins University Press.

Clark, Sharon Lynn (1986). "The City of Houston's Minority and Women Business Enterprise Ordinance: Eleemosynary or Free Enterprise Promotion?" *Thurgood Marshall Law Review* 11 (Spring): 393–414.

Clarke, J. Frederick (1980). "AFL-CIO v. Kahn Exaggerates Presidential Power Under the Procurement Act" (case note), *California Law Review* 68 (September): 1044–1069.

Clarkson, Kenneth W. (1972). "Some Implications of Property Rights in Hospital Management," *Journal of Law and Economics* 15 (October): 363–384.

Clarkson, Kenneth W. and Philip E. Fixler, Jr. (1987). *The Role of Privatization in Florida's Growth*. Miami: Law and Economics Center, University of Miami and Local Government Center and the Reason Foundation.

Clawson, Marion (1983). "Reassessing Public Lands Policy," *Environment* 25 (October): 6, 8–17.

Cleary, Terence M. (1989). "Government-Furnished Property: Government-Furnished Problems," *National Contract Management Journal* 22 (Winter): 1–7.

Cleesattel, Norman (1987). "Government Procurement in the Federal Republic of Germany," *George Washington Journal of International Law & Economics* 21 (1): 59–90.

Coalition for State Prompt Pay (1989). *Guide to Getting Paid Promptly by State and Local*

Agencies. Fairfax, Va.: Coalition for State Prompt Pay.

Coalition for State Prompt Pay (1987). *The Model State Prompt Pay Law,* rev. ed., Fairfax, Va.: Coalition for State Prompt Pay.

Coburn, George M. (1988). "How Contractors Can Minimize the Risk of Becoming 'Federal Actors'," *Public Contract Law Journal* 17 (June): 361–387.

Coburn, George M. and Milton Eisenberg (1982a). "Debarment, Suspension Methods Stir Controversy" (government contracts), *Legal Times of Washington* 5 (August 23): 14.

Coburn, George M. and Milton Eisenberg (1982b). "OFPP Letter Doesn't Provide Necessary Safeguards," *Legal Times* 5 (November 1): 13.

Coburn, George M. and Matthew S. Simchak (1989). "Federal Procurement in the Federal Courts 1987–88: A Selective Review," *Public Contract Law Journal* 19 (Fall): 14–115.

Cockerham, John M. (1989). "Whistleblowing on U.S. Defense Contractors Is out of Control," *Aviation Week & Space Technology* 130 (April 10): 99, 101.

Cogan, John P., Jr. (1967). "Are Government Bodies Bound by Arbitration Agreements?" *Arbitration Journal* 22: 151–160.

Cohen, David S. (1989). "The Evidentiary Predicate for Affirmative Action After Croson: A Proposal for Shifting the Burdens of Proof," *Yale Law & Policy Review* 7 (Spring–Summer): 489–515.

Cohen, Stephen D. (1990). "United States–Japan Trade Relations," in Frank J. Macchiarola, ed., *International Trade: The Changing Role of the United States.* New York: The Academy of Political Science: 199–136.

Cohen, Susan I. and Martin P. Loeb (1989). "The Demand for Cost Allocations: The Case of Incentive Contracts Versus Fixed-Price Contracts," *Journal of Accounting & Public Policy* 8 (Fall): 165–180.

Cohen, William S. (1983). "The Competition in Contracting Act," *Public Contract Law Journal* 14 (October): 1–39.

Cohen, William S. and Carl Levin (1981). "Debarment, Suspension Designed to Balance Needs" (discipline of government contractors), *Legal Times of Washington* 4 (September 28): 10.

Colby, Mary (1990a). "Jurisdictions Catch Privatization Wave," *City & State* 7 (June 4): 11, 14.

Colby, Mary (1990b). "Obstacles Clip Wings of Private Airport Drive," *City & State* 7 (June 4): 13.

Colby, Mary (1990c). "Privatization Opens Gates for Operation of Toll Roads," *City & State* 7 (June 4): 12.

Cole, Brian M. (1970). "Misrepresentation in Public Contracts: Allocating the Risk of Loss," Student Notes, *Syracuse Law Review* 21 (Spring): 1004–1025.

Coleman, John J. and David B. Yoffie (1990). "Institutional Incentives for Protection: The American Use of Voluntary Export Restraints," in Frank J. Macchiarola, ed., *International Trade: The Changing Role of the United States.* New York: The Academy of Political Science: 137–150.

Collett, M. (1981). "The Federal Contracting Process," *The Bureaucrat* 10 (2): 18–19.

Collins, Stephen H. (1989). "Minority Contract Program Reformed," *Journal of Accountancy* 167 (January): 97.

Collins, Timothy M. and Thomas L. Doorley (1991). *Teaming Up for the 90s: A Guide to International Joint Ventures and Strategic Alliances.* Homewood, Ill.: Business One Irwin.

Colman, William G. (1989). *State and Local Government and Public-Private Partnerships.* Westport, Conn.: Greenwood Press.

Columbia Law Review (1959). "Disappointed Low Bidder on Public Contract Has Cause of Action Against State Officials and Successful High Bidder for Malicious Interference with Prospective Advantage," Student Note, 59 (June): 953–958.

Comita, Nancy, Rita P. Hull, and Donald W. Hicks (1989). "Strengthening Controls in State Government," *Association of Government Accountants Journal* (Spring): 29–34.

Commission on Governmental Procurement (1972). *Summary of the Report of the Commission on Governmental Procurement.* Washington, D.C.: Government Printing Office (December).

Committee for Economic Development (1982). *Public-Private Partnership: An Opportunity for Urban Communities.* New York: CED.

Consumers' Research Magazine (1988). "Don't Privatize the Post Office," 71 (June): 25.

Conway, J. Edward (1964). "State and Local Contracts and Subcontracts," *Buffalo Law Review* 14 (Fall): 130–139.

Cooper, Joseph A. (1988). "Supply-Tied Economics," *The National Law Journal* 10 (July 25): 13.

Cooper, Phil (1980). "Government Contracts in Public Administration: The Role and Environment of the Contracting Officer," *Public Administration Review* 40 (5): 459–468.

Copeland, Lennie (1988). "Valuing Workplace Diversity," *Personnel Administrator* 33 (November): 38, 40.

Copulos, Milton (1983). "Privatizing Federal Energy Research," *Heritage Backgrounder* 270 (June 7).

Corbett, Sue E. (1989). "All the King's Contractors and All the King's Men," *Oklahoma City University Law Review* 14 (Summer): 499–519.

Corey, E. Raymond (1978). *Procurement Management*. Boston: CBI Publishing Company.

Cornelius, Roger W. and Robert L. Ackley (1985). "The Competition in Contracting Act of 1984," *Army Lawyer* (January): 31–42.

Council of State Governments (1975). *State and Local Government Purchasing*. Lexington, Ky.: Council of State Governments.

Council of State Governments and the National Association of State Purchasing Officials (1988). *State and Local Government Purchasing*, 3rd ed. Lexington, Ky.: The Council of State Governments.

Courter, Jim (1986). "Military Reform: Improving Our Defenses," *Seton Hall Legislative Journal* 9 (Summer): 475–490.

Cox, Gail Diane (1986). "State Contracting for Public Services Crippled by Court; Labor Union Victory" (California), *The Los Angeles Daily Journal* 98 (March 7): 1.

Cox, Gail Diane (1987). "9th Circuit Revives Fraud Probes: General Dynamics Trial Ordered," *The National Law Journal* 9 (April): 10.

Cox, Wendell (1988). "Competitive Contracting and the Strategic Prospects of Transit," in John C. Weicher, ed., *Private Innovations in Public Transit*. Washington, D.C.: American Enterprise Institute for Public Policy Research: 56–61.

Cragg, Lauren C. and H. Felix Kloman (1985).

"Risk Management: A Developed Discipline," in Natalie Wasserman and Dean G. Phelus, eds., *Risk Management Today: A How-to Guide for Local Government*, Washington, D.C.: International City Management Association: 7–21.

Crain, W. Mark and Asghar Zardkoohi (1978). "A Test of the Property Rights Theory of the Firm: Water Utilities in the United States," *Journal of Law and Economics* 21 (October): 395–408.

Crossick, Stanley A. (1987). "European Integration Through the Courts: A Wonderful Opportunity for Lawyers," *New Law Journal* 137 (April 10): 349.

Crowell, Eldon H. and W. Stanfield Johnson (1967). "A Primer on the Standard Form Changes Clause," *William and Mary Law Review* 8 (Summer): 550–572.

Cruce, B. H. (1969). "The Trouble with Municipal Purchasing Agents," *The American City* 84 (November): 101–102.

Crutcher, J. (1984). "Privatizing the U.S. Postal Service," *Government Union Review* 5 (Summer): 11.

Crutcher, John (1988). "Privatizing the U.S. Postal Service," *Vital Speeches* 54 (June): 520–525.

Culbertson, John M. (1990). "Workable Trade Policy for Today's Economic and Political World," in Frank J. Macchiarola, ed., *International Trade: The Changing Role of the United States*. New York: The Academy of Political Science: 151–164.

Culen, Steve (1990). "High Costs, Scandal Raise the Price of Privatization," *City & State* 7 (June 4): 7.

Cummins, J. Michael (1977). "Incentive Contracting for National Defense: A Problem of Optimal Risk Sharing," *Bell Journal of Economics* 8 (Spring): 168–185.

Cuneo, Gilbert A. and Thomas H. Truitt (1967). "Discovery Before the Contract Appeals Board," *William and Mary Law Review* 8 (Summer): 505–549.

Cunningham, William C. and Todd W. Taylor (1985). *Private Security and Police in America*. Portland, Ore.: Chancellor Press.

Curtiss, Frederic R. (1989). "How Managed Care Works," *Personnel Journal* 68 (July): 38–53.

Daly, Mary C. (1988). "Some Runs, Some Hits, Some Errors—Keeping Score in the Affirmative Action Ballpark from Weber to Johnson," *Boston College Law Review* 30 (December): 1–97.

Dantico, Marilyn (1987). "The Impact of Contracting out on Minorities and Women," in *When Public Services Go Private*. Washington, D.C.: AFSCME, AFL-CIO: 25–29.

Danzig, Richard and David Hazelton (1989). "Suspension and Debarment: The End of the Line," *Public Contract Newsletter* 24 (Spring): 3–4, 20–22, 24.

Darr, T. (1987). "Pondering Privatization May Be Good for Your Government," *Governing* 1 (November): 42–50.

Darwent, Charles (1988). "Consultants After the Party," *Management Today* (UK) (January): 70–80.

Dauer, Paul F. (1990). "Potential for Disaster: MBE Programs and Void Public Contracts," *Public Contract Newsletter* 25 (Winter): 3–4.

David, Irwin T. (1988). "Privatization in America," in International City Management Association. *The Municipal Year Book 1988*. Washington, D.C.: ICMA: 43–55.

Davidson, Dan H. and Solon A. Bennett (1980). "Municipal Purchasing Practices," *The Municipal Year Book*. Washington, D.C.: International City Management Association.

Davidson, Jeff (1981–82). "Identifying Minority Business Enterprises," *Bureaucrat* 10 (Winter): 40–41.

Davies, David G. (1971). "The Efficiency of Public Versus Private Firms: The Case of Australia's Two Airlines," *Journal of Law and Economics* 14 (April): 149–165.

Davis, Barton Bolling (1987). "Acquisition of Rights in Computer Software by the Department of Defense," *Public Contract Law Journal* 17 (September): 77–151.

Davis, C. H. and D. D. Jackson (1990). "The Sunset of Affirmative Action? City of Richmond v. J. A. Croson Co.," *National Black Law Journal* 12: 73–87.

Davis, Perry (1986). "Partners for Downtown Development: Creating a New Central Business District in Brooklyn," in Perry Davis, ed., *Public-Private Partnerships: Improving Urban Life*. New York: The Academy of Political Science: 87–99.

Davis, Perry (1986). "Why Partnerships? Why Now?" in Perry Davis, ed., *Public-Private Partnerships: Improving Urban Life*. New York: The Academy of Political Science: 1–3.

Davis, Perry, ed. (1986). *Public-Private Partnerships: Improving Urban Life*. New York: The Academy of Political Science.

Days, Drew S., III (1987). "Fullilove," *Yale Law Journal* 96 (January): 453–485.

DeAlessi, Louis (1974). "An Economic Analysis of Government Ownership and Regulation: Theory and the Evidence From the Electric Power Industry," *Public Choice* 19 (Fall): 1–42.

DeAlessi, Louis (1975). "Some Effects of Ownership on the Wholesale Prices of Electric Power," *Economic Inquiry* 13 (December): 526–538.

DeAlessi, Louis (1982). "On the Nature and Consequence of Private and Public Enterprise," *Minnesota Law Review* 67 (October): 191–209.

DeAlessi, Louis (1987a). "Property Rights and Privatization," in Steve H. Hanke, ed., *Prospects for Privatization*. New York: Proceedings of the Academy of Political Science 36 (3): 24–35.

DeAlessi, Louis (1987b). "Theoretical Foundations of Privatization," in Kenneth W. Clarkson and Philip E. Fixler, Jr., *The Role of Privatization in Florida's Growth*. Miami: Law and Economics Center, University of Miami and Local Government Center and the Reason Foundation: 439–451.

Deardorff, Alan V. and Robert M. Stern (1990). "Options for Trade Liberalization in the Uruguay Round Negotiations," in Frank J. Macchiarola, ed., *International Trade: The Changing Role of the United States*. New York: The Academy of Political Science: 17–27.

Dees, C. Stanley and Stephen D. Knight (1982). "Certification Requirements and the Problems of Contract Claims and Requests for Relief," *Public Contract Law Journal* 12 (March): 162–182.

DeGrazia, Alfred, ed. (1957). *Grass Roots Private Welfare*. New York: New York University Press.

DeHoog, Ruth (1984). *Contracting Out for Human Services: Economic, Political, and Organizational Perspectives*. Albany: State University Press of New York.

Del Duca, Louis F., Patrick J. Falvey, and Theodore A. Adler (1986a). *State and Local Government Procurement: Developments in Legislation and Litigation*. Chicago: American Bar Association.

Del Duca, Louis F., Patrick J. Falvey, and Theodore A. Adler (1986b). "State and Local Government Procurement: Developments in Legislation and Litigation," *The Urban Lawyer* 18 (Spring): 301–367.

Del Duca, Louis F., Patrick J. Falvey, and Theodore A. Adler (1987). *Annotations to the Model Procurement Code for State and Local Governments*. Chicago: American Bar Association.

Del Duca, Louis F., Patrick J. Falvey, Theodore A. Adler, and Larry C. Ethridge (1988). *First Supplement, Annotations to the Model Procurement Code for State and Local Governments with Analytical Summary of State Enactments*. Chicago: American Bar Association.

Deloria, Vine, Jr. (1985). *American Indian Policy in the Twentieth Century*. Norman, Okla.: University of Oklahoma Press.

Demone, Harold W. and Margaret Gibelman (1987). "Privatizing Acute Care General Hospitals," in Barry J. Carroll, Ralph W. Conant, and Thomas A. Easton, eds., *Private Means Public Ends: Private Business in Social Service Delivery*. New York: Praeger: 50–75.

Dempsey, David B. (1982). "Foreign Procurement Under Memoranda of Understanding and the Trade Agreements Act," *Public Contract Law Journal* 12 (March): 221–254.

Dent, David J. (1985). "Double Eagle's Ship Comes in," *Black Enterprise* 15 (June): 236–238.

Denton, J. C. (1965). "The Function of Purchasing," *Journal of Purchasing* 1 (August): 1–5.

DeRose, Louis J. (1986). "Government Procurement Regs Do Not Reflect Reality," *Purchasing World* 30 (July): 32, 35.

DeRose, Louis J. (1989). "Purchasing's Changing Negotiating Roles," *Purchasing World* 33 (December): 39–44.

Deschamps, Jean-Dominique (1986). "Privatization of Water Systems in France," *American Water Works Association Journal* 78 (February): 34–40.

DeThomas, A. R. (1989). "DCF: How a Small Company Outbids Its Competition" (dis-

counted cash flow methods). *Journal of Accountancy* 167 (March): 115–164.

Devlin, Joan C. (1989). "Protests Against Government Awards: Contractor's Rights," *Small Business Reports* 14 (January): 72–75.

Dingle, Derek T. (1985). "B.E. Economists' Report—Black America at a Crossroad," *Black Enterprise* 15 (June): 179–184.

Dingle, Derek T. (1989). "Affirmative Action," *Black Enterprise* 20 (September): 42–48.

Directory of Leading U.S. Export Management Companies (1991). Fairfield, Conn.: Bergano Book Co.

Dixon, Richard B. (1988/1989). "Contracting Out: L.A. County Makes Consultants Worth the Cost," *Business Forum* 14 (Fall/Winter): 32–34.

Dobbs, James C. (1985). "Rebuilding America: Legal Issues Confronting Privatization," *The Privatization Review* 1 (Summer): 28–38.

Dobrovier, William (1989). "Creating a Program That Passes the Croson Test: Minority Set-Asides and the Court: Was the Croson Decision the End of Affirmative Action?" *Legal Times* 11 (May 1): 32.

Doctor, Ronald D. (1986). "Private Sector Financing for Water Systems," *American Water Works Association Journal* 78 (February): 47–48.

Doherty, Ed (1989). "Alternative Delivery of Services in Rochester, New York," in Lawrence K. Finley, ed., *Public Sector Privatization: Alternative Approaches to Service Delivery*. New York: Quorum Books: 25–34.

Doherty, Edward J. (1983). "Private Contracting in Municipal Operations: Rochester, New York," *Urban Resources* 2 (Summer): 29–36.

Doke, Marshall J., Jr. (1964). "Mistakes in Government Contracts," *Southwestern Law Journal* 18 (March): 1–45.

Doke, Marshall J., Jr. (1968). "Contract Formation, Remedies, and Special Problems," *Public Contract Law Journal* 2 (October): 12–19.

Dolive, Henry C., ed. (1985). "Urban Resources: Privatization and Alternative Service Delivery." *Urban Resources* 2 (Summer, special issue).

Dollinger, Marc J., Cathy A. Enz, and Catherine M. Daily (1991). "Purchasing From Minority Small Businesses," *International Journal of*

Purchasing Materials and Management 27 (Spring): 9–14.

Dominguez, J. (1976). *Capital Flows in Minority Areas.* Lexington, Mass.: Lexington Books.

Donahue, John D. (1989). *The Privatization Decision: Public Ends, Private Means.* New York: Basic Books.

Donnally, Robert A. and Mark W. Stone (1987). "The Prompt Payment Act in 1987: Collecting From Uncle Sam," *National Contract Management Journal* 21 (Summer): 45–55.

Dornbusch, Rudiger (1990). "The Dollar and the Adjustment Options," in Frank J. Macchiarola, ed. *International Trade: The Changing Role of the United States.* New York: The Academy of Political Science: 54–66.

Doyle, Frank P. (1990). "People-Power: The Global Human Resource Challenge for the '90s," *Columbia Journal of World Business* 25 (Spring/Summer): 36–45.

Drabkin, Jess H. (1983). "Minority Enterprise Development and the Small Business Administration's Section 8 (a) Program: Constitutional Basis and Regulatory Implementation," *Brooklyn Law Review* 49 (Spring): 433–477.

Drew, Joseph (1984). "The Dynamics of Human Services Subcontracting: Service Delivery in Chicago, Detroit, and Philadelphia," *Policy Studies Journal* 13 (September): 67–89.

Duberstein, Douglas R. (1988). "Validation of Proprietary Data Restrictions: How Contractors Can Protect Their Rights in Technical Data Against Government Challenge," *National Contract Management Journal* 22 (Summer): 25–32.

Dudek & Company (1988). *Privatization and Public Employees: The Impact of City and County Contracting Out on Government Workers.* Washington, D.C.: National Commission for Employment Policy, May.

Duesterberg, Thomas J. (1991). "Prepare Now for the 1992 Export Market," *Business America* 112 (February 25): 8–9.

Duffy, Shannon P. (1990). "Minority Set-Aside Law Found Unconstitutional," *Pennsylvania Law Journal-Reporter* 13 (April): 1.

Dunn's Marketing Services (1990). *Exporters' Encyclopaedia 1990–91 Edition.* Parsippany, N.J.: DMS.

Duquesne Law Review (1963). "Municipal Liability Upon Improperly Executed Contracts," Comments, 1 (Spring): 221–231.

Durenberger, Dave (1984). "Public-Private Partnerships: New Meaning, New Advocates, New Problems," *National Civic Review* 73 (January): 7–10, 23.

Earnest, Ernest (1979). *The Volunteer Fire Company.* New York: Stein & Day.

East Asian Executive Reports (1987). "Government Procurement: Procedures and Trends" (Hong Kong), 9 (September 15): 14.

East Asian Executive Reports (1988). "Foreign Access to Major Construction Projects" (Taiwan), 10 (April 15): 17.

Eastland, T. (1989). "Racial Preferences in Court (Again)," *Commentary* (January): 32–38.

Ebel, Robert D. and Laurence Marks (1990). "American Competitiveness in the World Economy," *International Perspective* 16 (Winter): 5–9.

Eberts, Randall W. and Timothy J. Gronberg (1988). "Can Competition Among Local Governments Constrain Government Spending?" *Economic Review* (Federal Reserve of Cleveland) 24 (1): 2–9.

Echols, James C. (1985). "Use of Private Companies to Provide Public Transportation in Tidewater, Virginia," in Charles A. Lave, ed., *Urban Transit.* Cambridge, Mass.: Ballinger Publishing Company: 79–100.

The Economist (1985). "Privatisation: Everybody's Doing It Differently," 297 (December 21): 71–86.

The Economist (1988). "A Railway for Sale," (UK) 307 (May 21): 61.

The Economist (1990a). "Britain—Water Industry: Paying for Purity," (UK) 314 (March 24): 63–64.

The Economist (1990b). "Privatisation in Eastern Europe: Rediscovering the Wheel," (UK) 315 (April 14): 19–21.

The Economist (1990c). "Privatising Britain's Housing: An Englishman's Council Home," (UK) 314 (February 24): 17–20.

The Economist (1990d). "Did America's Small Firms Ever Get off the Launching Pad?" 315 (June 30): 61–62.

Edgell, David L., Sr. (1990). *International Tourism Policy.* New York: Van Nostrand Reinhold.

Edmond, Alfred J. (1990). "A 'Golden Opportunity' for Black Firms," *Black Enterprise* 20 (April): 33–34.

Edmundson, Brad (1989). "Targeting Black Enterprise," *American Demographics* 11 (November): 26–27.

Edwards, F. R. and B. J. Stevens (1978). "The Provision of Municipal Sanitation Services by Private Firms: An Empirical Analysis of the Efficiency of Alternative Markets," *The Journal of Industrial Economics* 27 (December): 133–147.

Ellsworth, James E. (1988). "Extending Immunity to Private Contractions on Government Contracts" (case note), *Brigham University Law Review* 1988 (Fall): 835–847.

Emerson, Michael (1989). "The Emergence of the New European Economy of 1992," *Business Economics* 24 (October): 5–9.

Engeleiter, Susan S. (1989). "Promoting Minority Enterprise," *Network* 4 (September–October): 1–2.

Engelhardt, Meghan (1981). "Coping With Persistent NLRA Violators: The Potential for Debarment Through Executive Order," *Iowa Law Review* 66 (January): 425–437.

Engineering News-Record (1986). "More Road Maintenance is Being Contracted Out," (May 15).

England, Catherine and John Palffy (1982). "Replacing the FDIC: Private Insurance for Bank Deposits," *Heritage Backgrounder* 229 (December 2).

Etheridge, Larry C. (1982). "Kentucky" (recent developments in state and local public contract law), *Public Contract Newsletter* 18 (Fall): 8–9.

Etheridge, Larry C. and Linda K. Talley (1986). "Annual Survey of State and Local Procurement Law," *The Urban Lawyer* 18 (Fall): 1031–1043.

Etheridge, Larry C. (1984). "A Report on Region IV Model Procurement Code Symposium," *Public Contract Newsletter* 19 (Summer): 7–8.

Failing, Michael E. (1989). "A Layman's Guide to the Federal Fraud Laws," *National Contract Management Journal* 23 (Summer): 37–54.

Fairlamb, David (1990). "The Privatizing of Eastern Europe," *Institutional Investor* 24 (April): 171–178.

Falcioni, John G. (1989). "Businesses Play Legal

Wait and See," *City & State* (January 30): 1–21.

Fall, Mark (1989). "Use of the Private Sector for State Government Passenger Vehicle Maintenance," in Joan W. Allen et al., eds., *The Private Sector in State Service Delivery: Examples of Innovative Practices.* Washington, D.C.: The Urban Institute Press: 119–138.

Farmakides, John B. (1967). "Technical Data in Government Contracts," *William and Mary Law Review* 8 (Summer): 573–588.

Farmanfarmaian, Roxane (1988). "Are Women Starving Their Businesses?" *Working Woman* 13 (October): 114–117.

Farmer, Guy O. and Kevin E. Hyde (1989). "Subcontracting—The Changing Rules," *Employee Relations Law Journal* 15 (Autumn): 225–238.

Farrell, Christopher and Gail Schares (1990). "Blueprints for a Free Market in Eastern Europe," *Business Week* 3144 (February 5): 88–89.

Farrell, Paul V., ed. (1982). *Alijan's Purchasing Handbook*, 4th ed. New York: McGraw Hill.

Farren, J. Michael (1991). "Opportunities and Challenges in the New European Market," *Business America* 112 (February 25): 6–7.

Farrior, Rex J., Jr and John H. Rains III (1982). "Public Sector Competitive Bidding in Florida," *Stetson Law Review* 11 (Spring): 428–453.

Feidelman, Joel R. (1981). "Facts Still Crucial in Stable Law of Bidding 'Mistakes'," *Legal Times of Washington* 4 (July 6): 12.

Feidelman, Joel R. (1982). "Contractors Must Know Nuances of 'Buy American' Laws," *Legal Times of Washington* 4 (January 4): 14.

Feidelman, Joel R. (1985). "86 Defense Act: Signs of Procurement Activism," *Legal Times of Washington* 8 (November): 12.

Feidelman, Joel R. and Dennis J. Riley (1980). "Model Code: A Cure for States' Procurement Malady?" *Legal Times of Washington* 3 (September 15): 14.

Feidelman, Joel R. and Eric J. Zahler (1983). "Controversial Antifraud Principle Issued by Defense," *Legal Times of Washington* 5 (January 24): 16.

Feidelman, Joel R. and Estelle E. Friedman (1983). "Application of U.S. Contracting-Out

Policy Debated," *Legal Times of Washington* 5 (May): 12.

Feidelman, Joel R. and Estelle E. Friedman (1984). "New Act Promises Major Procurement Reforms," *Legal Times of Washington* 7 (September 17): 11.

Feidelman, Joel R. and Estelle E. Friedman (1986). "Competition Advocates Take Root in the Agencies," *Legal Times of Washington* 8 (January 6): 13.

Feidelman, Joel R. and Garry S. Grossman (1985). "Government Contractors' Bids Must be Timely," *Legal Times of Washington* 7 (January 14): 25.

Feidelman, Joel R. and Harold L. Jordan (1982). "SBA's Proposals on Size May Be Counterproductive," *Legal Times of Washington* 5 (July 5): 13.

Feidelman, Joel R. and Jacob B. Pankowski (1981). "U.S. Termination of Contracts: Few Practical Limits," *Legal Times of Washington* 3 (March 16): 19.

Feidelman, Joel R. and Josephine L. Ursini (1982). "Government Held to Stricter Bill-Paying Standards," *Legal Times of Washington* 5 (August 9): 37.

Feidelman, Joel R. and Nathaniel M. Rosenblatt (1981). "Results of Procurement Test Program Still Uncertain," *Legal Times of Washington* 4 (October 19): 14.

Feidelman, Joel R. and Sabdra R. Comenetz (1983). "Congressional Action Aids Small Business Contractors," *Legal Times of Washington* 6 (November 14): 13.

Feidelman, Joel R. and Terry E. Miller (1984). "Weapon System Warrant Acts Trouble Contractors," *Legal Times of Washington* 6 (May 7): 13.

Feidelman, Joel R., Kenneth S. Kramer, and Ray Mabus (1980). "When Must Agencies Use Private Goods, Services?" *Legal Times of Washington* 3 (July 28): 36.

Feidelman, Joel R., Richard A. Sauder, and Estelle E. Friedman (1984). "Debarment Rules Tighten for Errant Contractors," *Legal Times of Washington* 7 (October 29): 12.

Fein, Bruce and William Bradford Reynolds (1989). "A Kinder, Gentler Affirmative Action," *Legal Times of Washington* 11 (February 13): 16.

Feld, Jonathan S. (1990). "Thou Shalt Not Dis-close" (government procurement process), *Criminal Justice* 4 (Winter): 14–20.

Feldman, Roger D. (1986). "Privatization and the State Statutory Framework: A Key to Success," *The Privatization Review* 2 (Winter): 9–15.

Feldman, Steven W. (1983). "The Comptroller General's Authority to Examine Contractor Books and Records After Bowsher v. Merck and Company: The Need for Legislative Reform," *West Virginia Law Review* 86 (Winter): 339–368.

Feldman, Steven W. (1987a). "Interim Suspension Authority of the General Services Board of Contract Appeals in Automatic Data Processing Protests: Illegal and Practical Considerations," *Public Contract Law Journal* 17 (September): 1–30.

Feldman, Steven W. (1987b). "Traversing the Tightrope Between Meaningful Discussions and Improper Practices in Negotiated Federal Acquisitions: Technical Transfusion, Technical Leveling, and Auction Techniques," *Public Contract Law Journal* 17 (September): 211–264.

Feldman, Steven W. (1988). "The Truth in Negotiations Act: A Primer," *National Contract Management Journal* 21 (Winter): 67–81.

Femino, Dominic A., Jr. (1989). "Evaluating Past Performance (in federal acquisitions)," *Army Lawyer* (April): 25–28.

Fenster, Herbert L. and Darryl J. Lee (1982). "The Expanding Audit and Investigative Powers of the Federal Government," *Public Contract Law Journal* 12 (March): 193–220.

Fernandez, Kenneth and Merriam Mashatt (1990). "Procurement Opens Further Under U.S.-Canada FTA; The FTA Encourages Liberalization in Services," *Business America* 111 (February 12): 11–14.

Ferrara, Peter J. (1987). "Social Security and the Private Sector," in Steve H. Hanke, ed., *Prospects for Privatization*. New York: Proceedings of the Academy of Political Science 36 (3): 49–59.

Ferris, J. and E. Graddy (1986). "Contracting Out: For What? With Whom?" *Public Administration Review* 46: 332–344.

Ferris, J. M. (1984). "Coprovision: Citizen Time and Money Donations in public Service Provision," *Public Administration Review* 44 (July/ August): 324–333.

Ficker, H. (1964). "The Buy Immersion Act: A Survey and Analysis," Washington, D.C.: Library of Congress Legislative Reference Service (April).

Fiedler, Terry G. (1987). "Region's Largest Black-Owned Firm Looks to Growth Beyond Federal Contracts," *New England Business* 9 (June 15): 63–64.

Finley, Lawrence K. (1989a). "Alternative Service Delivery, Privatization, and Competition," in Lawrence K. Finley, ed., *Public Sector Privatization: Alternative Approaches to Service Delivery*. New York: Quorum Books: 3–12.

Finley, Lawrence K. (1989b). "Introducing Entrepreneurial Competition Into Public Service Delivery," in Lawrence L. Finley, ed., *Public Sector Privatization: Alternative Approaches to Service Delivery*. New York: Quorum Books: 153–162.

Finley, Lawrence K., ed. (1989c). *Public Sector Privatization: Alternative Approaches to Service Delivery*. New York: Quorum Books.

Finley, Lawrence L. (1984). "Can Your Small Company Acquire Resources as Favorably as the Large Company?" *American Journal of Small Business* 9 (Summer): 19–25.

Finley, Lawrence L. (1987). "An Entrepreneurial Process for Privatization at the Local Level," *The Privatization Review* 3 (Winter): 19–25.

Fiscal Watchdog (1983). "Privatization: Rx for Sick Hospitals," 77 (March): 1–4.

Fiscal Watchdog (1985). "Hospital Privatization and Indigent Care," 109 (November): 3–4.

Fiscal Watchdog (1986). "A Brief Look at Contracting Out Support Services," 120 (October): 4–5.

Fiscal Watchdog (1987). "Privatization Central to Future Public Works," 131 (September): 3–5.

Fisher, Ronald J. (1984). "Megatrends in Urban Transit," *Transportation Quarterly* 38 (January): 87–101.

Fishner, Stanley (1986). *Costing for Negotiated Government Contracts*. Vienna, Va.: Fishner Books.

Fishner, Stanley (1989). *A Report on Government Procurement Practices: What's Needed to Reverse the Trend*. Merrifield, Va.: Camelot Publishers.

Fisk, Donald, H. Kiesling, and Thomas Muller (1978). *Private Provision of Public Services:*

An Overview. Washington, D.C.: The Urban Institute.

Fitch, Lyle (1974). "Increasing the Role of the Private Sector in Providing Public Services," in D. Hawley and D. Rogers, eds., *Improving the Quality of Urban Management*, Sage Urban Affairs Annual Reviews, Vol. 8. Beverly Hills, Calif.: Sage Publications.

Fitch, Lyle C. (1988). "The Rocky Road to Privatization," *American Journal of Economics & Sociology* 47 (January): 1–14.

Fitzgerald, Michael R. (1986). "The Promise and Performance of Privatization: The Knoxville Experience," *Policy Studies Review* 5 (3): 606–613.

Fitzgerald, Randall (1988). *When Government Goes Private*. New York: Universe Books.

Fixler, Philip E., Jr. (1984). "Can Privatization Resuscitate Emergency Medical Service?" *Fiscal Watchdog* 98 (December): 1–4.

Fixler, Philip E., Jr. (1985a). "The Appeal of Private Courts," *Fiscal Watchdog* 99 (January): 1–4.

Fixler, Philip E., Jr. (1985b). "Applying Privatization to Public Housing," *Fiscal Watchdog* 115 (May): 1–4.

Fixler, Philip E., Jr. (1985c). "Contracting Out Professional Services," *Fiscal Watchdog* 108 (October): 1–4.

Fixler, Philip E., Jr. (1985d). "How Privatization Can Ease the Water Crisis," *Fiscal Watchdog* 102 (April): 1–4.

Fixler, Philip E., Jr. (1985e). "The Privatization of Resource Recovery," *Fiscal Watchdog* 104 (June): 1–3.

Fixler, Philip E., Jr. (1985f). *Privatizing Coast Guard Services*. Washington, D.C.: Citizens for a Sound Economy.

Fixler, Philip E., Jr. (1985g). "The Road to Privatization," *Fiscal Watchdog* 105 (July): 1–4.

Fixler, Philip E., Jr. (1986a). "In Search of Educational Cost Savings and Excellence? How About Privatization?" *Fiscal Watchdog* 119 (September): 1–4.

Fixler, Philip E., Jr. (1986b). "Increasing Employee Options Under Privatization," *Fiscal Watchdog* 118 (August): 1–5.

Fixler, Philip E., Jr. (1986c). "New Lessons on Privatizing Emergency Medical Services," *Fiscal Watchdog* 112 (February): 1–3.

Fixler, Philip E., Jr. (1986d). "Private Prisons

Begin to Establish Track Record," *Fiscal Watchdog* 116 (June): 1–4.

Fixler, Philip E., Jr. (1986e). "The Role of Private Landfills in the Waste Disposal Crisis," *Fiscal Watchdog* 114 (April): 1–4.

Fixler, Philip E., Jr. (1986f). "Service-Shedding—A New Option for Local Governments," *The Privatization Review* 2 (Summer): 18–23.

Fixler, Philip E., Jr. (1986g). "Which Police Services Can Be Privatized?" *Fiscal Watchdog* 111 (January): 1–4.

Fixler, Philip E., Jr., and Randolph T. Piper (1986). *Employee Options Under Privatization.* Santa Monica, Calif.: Local Government Center.

Fixler, Philip E., Jr., and Robert W. Poole, Jr. (1986). "The Privatization Revolution: What Washington Can Learn From State and Local Government," *Policy Review* 37 (Summer): 68–73.

Fixler, Philip E., Jr., and Robert W. Poole, Jr. (1987). "Status of State and Local Privatization," in Steve H. Hanke, ed., *Prospects for Privatization.* New York: Proceedings of the Academy of Political Science 36 (3): 164–178.

Fleming, J. E. (1969). "A Systems Approach to Purchasing," *Journal of Purchasing* 5 (February): 5–45.

Flener, Mark H. (1989). "Legal Considerations in Privatization and the Role of Legal Counsel," in Lawrence L. Finley, ed., *Public Sector Privatization: Alternative Approaches to Service Delivery.* New York: Quorum Books: 141–152.

Florestano, Patricia S. and Stephen B. Gordon (1979). "Private Provision of Public Services: Contracting by Large Local Governments," *International Journal of Public Administration* 1 (3): 307–327.

Florestano, Patricia S. and Stephen B. Gordon (1980). "Public Versus Private: Small Government Contracting With the Private Sector," *Public Administration Review* 40 (1): 29–34.

Florestano, Patricia S. and Stephen B. Gordon (1981). "A Survey of City and County Use of Private Contracting," *The Urban Interest* 3 (Spring): 22–29.

Fordham Law Review (1962). "The Surety's Rights to Money Retained From Payments Made on a Public Contract," Student Note, 31 (Spring): 161–178.

Fordham, Gregory L. (1989). "Auditing Unallowable Costs of Government Contracts," *Internal Auditing* 5 (Summer): 12–120.

Forman, Ellen (1989). "Dealing Carefully with Uncle Sam," *Venture* 11 (September): 14, 17.

Fortune, Mark (1988). "Divide and Conquer," *Black Enterprise* 18 (June): 168–175.

Fosler, R. S. and R. Berger, eds. (1982). *Public-Private Partnerships in American Cities.* Lexington, Mass.: Lexington Books.

Foust, Dean (1990). "The Iran-Contra Scandal of the Small Business World," *Business Week* 3162 (June 4): 63.

Fox, J. Ronald (1974). *Arming America.* Cambridge, Mass.: Harvard University Press.

Fox, Paul (1988). "Water Sell-Off Will Hit Consumers," *New Statesman & Society* 1 (July 15): 27.

France, Steve (1990). "The Private War on Pentagon Fraud," *ABA Journal* 76 (March): 46.

Frank, Anthony M. (1988). "The U.S. Postal System: What is Meant by Privatization?" *Vital Speeches* 54 (June 1): 504–506.

Franklin, David S. (1975). *Contracting for Purchase of Services—A Professional Manual.* Washington, D.C.: National Technical Information Service, Report No. SHR-0000705.

Fraser, Robert (1988). *Privatization: The UK Experience and International Trends.* Harlow, Essex: Longman.

Fratoe, Frank A. (1986). "A Sociological Analysis of Minority Business," *The Review of Black Political Economy* 16 (Fall): 30–49.

Frazier, Mark (1980). "Privatizing the City," *Policy Review* 12 (Spring): 91–108.

Freeborn, Michael D. (1971). "Government Contractors Today: Turning Square Corners on a One-Way Street?" Student Note, *Indiana Legal Forum* 4 (Spring): 489–517.

Frenzen, Donald (1968). "The Administrative Contract in the United States," *George Washington Law Review* 37 (December): 270–292.

Fried, Charles (1989). "Comments: Affirmative Action after 'City of Richmond v. J. A. Croson Co.': A Response to the Scholars' Statement," *The Yale Law Journal* 99 (October): 155–162.

Fried, Jonathan T., et al (1987). "Government Procurement: An Annotated Bibliography," *Review of International Business Law* 1 (July): 259–283.

Fried, Lisa I. (1989). "A New Breed of

Entrepreneur—Women," *Management Review* 78 (December): 18–25.

Frignani, Aldo (1986). "The GATT Agreement on Government Procurement," *Journal of World Trade Law* (UK) 20 (September/October): 567–570.

Fulwood, Sam (1985). "Paving the Way for Big Money Contracts," *Black Enterprise* 15 (February): 119–122.

Gabb, Annabella (1989). "Clean Sweep at the Council," *Management Today* (UK) (May): 54–55.

Gabig, Jerome S. and Charles L. Cook (1989). "A Guide to Interpreting Contracts," *National Contract Management Journal* 23 (Summer): 55–64.

Gabig, Jerome S. and Roger J. McAvoy (1988). "The DOD's Rights in Technical Data and Computer Software Clause—Part II," *National Contract Management Journal* 21 (Winter): 37–43.

Gage, John D. (1972). "The Application of Quasi-Contractual Liability Against a Public Entity," Student Note, *Hasting Law Journal* 23 (March): 874–888.

Gallman, Vanessa (1991). "Winning the Government Procurement Game," *Black Enterprise* 21 (February): 153–162.

Gamlin, Joanne (1979). "Minority Hiring Drive Demands Attention of the Risk Manager," *Business Insurance* 13 (May 14): 57–58.

Ganister, Ruth E. (1980). "Government Contracts as Socio-Economic Tools: What Changes Under Reagan Administration?" *Pennsylvania Law Journal* 3 (December 22): 7.

Ganister, Ruth E. (1981). "The Unusual Circumstances Exception to Debarment Under Service Contract Act," *Pennsylvania Law Journal-Reporter* 4 (April 20): 6.

Gansler, Jacques S. (1980). *The Defense Industry.* Cambridge, Mass.: The MIT Press.

Gantt, Paul H. (1967). "Survey of State and Municipal Public Contracts," *Public Contract Law Journal* 1 (July): 41–43.

Garner, Gordon (1986). "Cities and Contracting Out: How Public-Private Partnerships Can Work," *Current Municipal Problems* 12 (Winter): 376–382.

Gaskins, John W. (1963). "Practical Aspects of Changed Conditions Clause Under Government Construction Contracts," *Boston College Industrial and Commercial Law Review* 5 (Fall): 79–87.

Geldon, Fred W. (1986). "Government Contract Law," *Case & Comment* 91 (July–August): 27–36.

Giantris, Philip D. (1989). "Business Perspective—Environmental Infrastructure," in Lawrence K. Finley, ed., *Public Sector Privatization: Alternative Approaches to Service Delivery.* New York: Quorum Books: 47–62.

Giedraitas, John P. and Kielbaso, James J. (1982). "Municipal Tree Management," *Urban Data Service Report* 14 (January): 1–14.

Gifford, James P. (1986). "Partnerships and Public Policy Advocacy," in Perry Davis, ed., *Public-Private Partnerships: Improving Urban Life.* New York: Academy of Political Science: 74–86.

Gilliam, Reginald E. (1981). "Reindustrialization, Deregulation: Opportunity for Minority Economic Development," *ICC Practitioner's Journal* 48 (March–April): 290–293.

Ginsburg, Gilbert and Sandra Boyd (1987). "Justice Department Fails in Challenge of Procurement Law," *Legal Times* 9 (February 16): 13.

Girdner, Bill (1988). "Complex Issues Cloud Prosecution of Defense Cases: Kickbacks Curtailed, Government Moves to Thornier Cases; No More 'Golden Eggs'," *The Los Angeles Daily Journal* 101 (March 25): 1.

Gite, Lloyd (1984). "Partners in Marriage and Business: Johnson Textile and Plastic Co., Dallas, Texas," *Black Enterprise* 14 (April): 40.

Gite, Lloyd (1989a). "Broadcast News," *Black Enterprise* 20 (December): 100–106.

Gite, Lloyd (1989b). "Steering Safely Through Setbacks," *Working Woman* (February): 39–44.

Glasser, Robert and William M. Ray (1988). "Tax Advantages in the Sale of Radio and Television Broadcast Stations to Minorities Section 1071—Deferral of Capital Gains," *Georgia State Bar Journal* 25 (November): 58.

Glazerman, Leon J. (1967). "Doctrine of Substantial Compliance Applicable to Supply Contracts," Case Comment, *Boston University Law Review* 47 (Summer): 441–450.

Gluck, Peter R. (1978). "Citizen Participation in Urban Services: The Administration of a Community-Based Crime Prevention

Program," *Journal of Voluntary Action Research* 7 (Winter–Spring): 33–44.

Goette, Eckart E. (1990). "Europe 1992: Update for Business Planners," *Journal of Business Strategy* 11 (March/April): 10–13.

Goldberg, Stephanie B. (1989). "Commercial Civil Rights: Hispanic Lawyers Told Help Clients with SBA Contracts," *ABA Journal* 75 (January): 24.

Goldman, Claude (1987). "An Introduction to the French Law of Government Procurement Contracts," *George Washington Journal of International Law & Economics* 20 (3): 461–489.

Goldman, Harvey and Sandra Mokuvos (1984). *The Privatization Book*. New York: Arthur Young.

Goldstein, Edward (1980). "Doing Business Under the Agreement on Government Procurement: The Telecommunications Business—A Case in Point," *St. John's Law Review* 55 (Fall): 63–91.

Goldstein, Mark L. (1989). "Uncle Sam: A Tough Customer," *Government Executive* 21 (May): 10–17.

Goldstein, Mark L. (1990a). "The Biggest Buyer," *Government Executive* 22 (August): 7–12.

Goldstein, Mark L. (1990b). "The Computer Diet," *Government Executive* 22 (August): 46–51.

Goldstein, Mark L. (1990c). "Just $105 Million a Day," *Government Executive* 22 (August): 28–30.

Goldstein, Mark L. (1990d). "The Shadow Government," *Government Executive* 22 (May): 30–37, 56–57.

Golub, Martin J. and Sandra Lee Fenske (1987). "U.S. Government Procurement: Opportunities and Obstacles for Foreign Contractors," *George Washington Journal of International Law & Economics* 20 (3): 567–597.

Gomez-Ibañez, Jose A. and John R. Meyer (1990). "Privatizing and Deregulating Local Public Services: Lessons From Britain's Buses," *Journal of the American Planning Association* 56 (Winter): 9–21.

Goode, Victor (1985). "Procurement, International Organizations, and Minority and Women Contractors," *Thurgood Marshall Law Review* 10 (Spring): 483–505.

Goodman, Gary A. and Robert M. Saunders (1985). "U.S. Federal Regulation of Foreign Involvement in Aviation, Government Procurement, and National Security," *Journal of World Trade Law* (UK) 19 (January/February): 54–61.

Goodman, John C. (1987). "Privatizing the Welfare State," in Steve H. Hanke, ed., *Prospects for Privatization*. New York: Proceedings of the Academy of Political Science 36 (3): 36–48.

Goodman, John C., ed. (1986). *Privatization*. Dallas: National Center for Policy Analysis.

Goodrich, Jonathan N. (1988). "Privatization in America," *Business Horizons* 31 (January/February): 11–17.

Goodrich, William W., Jr. and Coralyn G. Mann (1984). "Avoiding Disaster in Federal Supply Schedule Contracts," *Public Contract Law Journal* 15 (August): 1–45.

Goodwin, Glenn R. (1986). "Statutory Resident Bidder Preference Is Constitutional" (annual survey of South Carolina law: January 1–December 31, 1985), *South Carolina Law Review* 38 (Autumn): 21–24.

Gordon, Paul (1984). "Justice Goes Private," *Reason* 17 (September): 23–30.

Gordon, Stephen B. and Stanley D. Zemansky (1981). "Public Purchasing: The Great Debate," *Modern Purchasing* (June).

Goretsky, M. Edward (1986). "Market Planning for Government Procurement," *Industrial Marketing Management* 15 (November): 287–291.

Government Executive (1978). "Small/Minority Business Contracting: Why Government's Program Is a Flop," 10 (November): 38–40.

Government Executive (1979). "Move Over, Big Daddy," 11 (February): 49–50.

Government Executive (1989a). "Nine Contracts to Watch," 21 (May): 50–52.

Government Executive (1989b). "The Domestic Side of Procurement Contracting," 21 (May): 32–37.

Government Executive (1989c). "The Top 10: Profiles of the 10 Companies That Earned 29 Percent of Government's Procurement Dollars," 21 (May): 30–31.

Government Executive (1989d). "The Top 100: Facts and Figures on the Companies That Sold the Most to Uncle Sam in Fiscal 1988," 21 (May): 24–29.

Graham, James J. (1988). "Corporate Criminal

Liability of the Public Contractor—Are Guidelines Needed?" *National Contract Management Journal* 21 (Winter): 9–20.

Grassi, Sebastian V., Jr. (1987). "The Michigan Strategic Fund," *Michigan Bar Journal* 66 (February): 182.

Green, Allen B. and Denice Jordan-Walker (1987). "Alternative Dispute Resolution in International Government Contracting: A Proposal," *George Washington Journal of International Law and Economics* 20 (3): 419–444.

Green, Loretta M., Sharon Skeeter, and Constance Mitchell (1985). "What's Cooking in America's High Tech Hot Spots?" *Black Enterprise* 15 (June): 256–264.

Green, Marshall (1990). "Considerations on the Western Pacific Rim," *Presidential Studies Quarterly* 20 (Summer): 477–480.

Green, Robert L. (1970). "A New Concept of Mitigation in Government Contracts," Editorial Notes, *George Washington Law Review* 38 (March): 463–485.

Green, Shelley and Paul Pryde. (1990). *Black Entrepreneurship in America.* New Brunswick, N.J.: Transaction Publishers.

Greenberg, Max E. (1970). "Problems Relating to Changes and Changed Conditions on Public Contracts," *Public Contract Law Journal* 3 (August): 135–162.

Greenhalgh, L. and R. McKersie (1980). "Cost Effectiveness of Alternate Strategies for Cutback Management," *Public Administration Review* 40 (6): 575–584.

Greenspun, Julian S. (1990). "1988 Amendments to Federal Procurement Policy Act: Did the 'Ill Wind' Bring an Impractical Overreaction That May Run Afoul of the Constitution?" *Public Contract Law Journal* 19 (Winter): 393–404.

Gregory, William H. (1990). "The Defense Procurement Mess," *Internal Auditor* 47 (April): 49–55.

Grenough, Donald S. and Nelson H. Shapiro (1984). "Defective Pricing," in American Bar Association, *Identifying and Prosecuting Fraud and Abuse in State and Local Contracting.* Chicago: ABA: 35–39.

Groarke, Leo (1990). "Affirmative Action as a Form of Restitution," *Journal of Business Ethics* 9 (March): 207–213.

Grossman, J. J. (1971). "Procedural Fairness in Public Contracts: The Procurement Regulations," *Virginia Law Review* 57 (March): 171.

Grossman, Larry (1989). "Competitive, Complex, Controversial," *Government Executive* 21 (May): 18–23.

Gubin, E. K. (1968). "Waiver of the Delivery Schedule in Government Contracts—A Review of the 1967 BCA Decisions," *William and Mary Law Review* 10 (Fall): 58–79.

Guiliano, Genevieve and Robert F. Teal (1985). "Privately Provided Commuter Bus Services: Experiences, Problems, and Prospects," in Charles A. Lave, ed., *Urban Transit.* Cambridge, Mass.: Ballinger Publishing Company: 151–180.

Gumpert, David E. (1988). "Why It Doesn't Always Pay to Be First," *Working Woman* (February): 41–42.

Gumpert, David E. and Jeffry A. Timmons (1982). "Penetrating the Government Procurement Maze," *Harvard Business Review* 60 (May/June): 14–20.

Gunzer, C. R. (1962). *Renegotiation Practice and Procedure.* New Fairfield, Conn.: Gunzer Publications.

Gupta, Udayan (1984). "B. E. Company of the Year: Henderson Industries," *Black Enterprise* 14 (June): 106–114.

Guskind, Robert (1987). "Leave the Driving to Us: UMTA Spreads the Gospel of Privatization," *Planning* 53 (7): 6–11.

Hackett, Judith, et al. (1987). *Issues in Contracting for the Private Operation of Prisons and Jails.* Washington, D.C.: National Institute of Justice Research Report (October).

Hagan, Oliver, Carol Rivchun, and Donald Sexton. (1989). *Women-Owned Businesses.* New York: Praeger.

Hagigh, Sara E. (1991). "The Technical Angle of Trade with the EC: EC Standards, Testing and Certification," *Business America* 112 (February 25): 24–26.

Haider, Donald (1986). Partnerships Redefined: Chicago's New Opportunities," in Perry Davis, ed., *Public-Private Partnerships: Improving Urban Life.* New York: The Academy of Political Science: 137–149.

Haizlip, A. L. (1989). "The Government Contractor Defense in Tort Liability: A Continuing

Genesis," *Public Contract Law Journal* 19 (Fall): 116–145.

Halachmi, Arie (1989). "Ad-Hocracy and the Future of the Civil Service," *International Journal of Public Administration* 12 (4): 617–650.

Hall, David (1990). "Contradictions, Illusions, Ironies and Inverted Realities: The Historical Relevance of the *Richmond v. Croson* Case," *The Urban League Review* 14 (Summer): 9–16.

Hames, Peter (1984). "When Public Services Go Private: There's More Than One Option," *National Civic Review* 73 (June): 278–282.

Hammer, Richard M., Hans H. Hinterhuber, and Justus Lorentz (1989). "Privatization—A Cure for All Ills?," *Long Range Planning* (UK) 22 (December): 19–28.

Hampton, Lynn (1991). "Money Talks: A Government's Financial Muscle Helps Provide Business Opportunities for Minorities and Women," *Government Finance Review* 7 (April): 11–14.

Handel, S. S. and R. M. Paulson (1968). *A Study of Formally Advertised Procurement.* Santa Monica, Calif.: Rand Corporation.

Hanes, Chisman and Sherwood B. Smith, Jr. (1966). "Contracting Officer: Authority to Act and Duty to Act Independently," *Dickinson Law Review* 70 (Spring): 333–355.

Hanke, Steve H. (1980). "Municipal Pricing: A Ship Without a Port," *Water and Sewage Works* 127 (December): 29–30.

Hanke, Steve H. (1982). "The Privatization Debate: An Insider's View," *Cato Journal* 2 (Winter): 653–662.

Hanke, Steve H. (1985). "The Literature on Privatization," in Stuart M. Butler, ed., *The Privatization Option.* Washington, D.C.: The Heritage Foundation: 83–97.

Hanke, Steve H. (1987). "Privatization Versus Nationalization," in Steve H. Hanke, ed., *Prospects for Privatization.* New York: *Proceedings of the Academy of Political Science* 36 (3): 1–3.

Hanke, Steve H. and Barney Dowdle (1987). "Privatizing the Public Domain," in Steve H. Hanke, ed., *Prospects for Privatization.* New York: *Proceedings of the Academy of Political Science* 36 (3): 114–124.

Hanke, Steve H. and Stephen J. K. Walters (1987). "Privatizing Waterworks," in Steve H.

Hanke, ed., *Prospects for Privatization.* New York: *Proceedings of the Academy of Political Science* 36 (3): 104–113.

Hanke, Steve H., ed. (1987). *Prospects for Privatization.* New York: *Proceedings of the Academy of Political Science* 36 (3).

Hanna, Janan (1990). "Minority Set-Aside Program Under Attack," *Chicago Daily Law Bulletin* 136 (February 5): 1.

Hannah, Paul F. (1963). "Government by Procurement," *The Business Lawyer* 18 (July): 997–1016.

Hanrahan, John D. (1983). *Government by Contract.* New York: Norton.

Hanrahan, John D. (1977). *Government for Sale: Contracting Out—The New Patronage.* Washington, D.C.: American Federation of State, County, and Municipal Employees.

Hardwick, Clyde T. (1969). "Regional Purchasing: A Study in Governmental Cooperative Buying," *Journal of Purchasing* 5 (November): 13–19.

Harr, David J. (1989). "Productive Unit Resourcing: A Business Perspective in Governmental Financial Management," *Government Accountants Journal* 38 (Summer): 51–57.

Harrigan, Anthony H., ed. (1987). *Putting America First: A Conservative Trade Alternative.* Washington, D.C.: United States Industrial Council Educational Foundation.

Harrison, Shelia S. and Geraldine D. Jones (1990). "Star Search: The Black Enterprise Executive Recruiter Directory," *Black Enterprise* 20 (April): 74–82.

Hartmann, C. R. (1988). "Big Opportunities in the Small-Purchase World," *D & B Reports* 36 (January/February): 38–40, 44.

Harvard Law Review (1955). "Administration of Claims Against the Sovereign—A Survey of State Techniques," Student Note, 68 (January): 506–517.

Harvard Law Review (1980a). "Statutory Preference for Minority-Owned Businesses," (Supreme Court 1979 term), 94 (November): 125–138.

Harvard Law Review (1988). "The Nonperpetuation of Discrimination in Public Contracting: A Justification for State and Local Minority Business Set-Asides After Wygant" (case note), 101 (June): 1797–1815.

Haslam, C. L. (1980). "The Trade Agreements Act of 1979," *Private Investors Abroad* (Annual): 379–419.

Hatch, Richard C. (1984). "The New Federal Acquisition Regulation: An Improvement?" *New York State Bar Journal* 56 (October): 13–17.

Hatry, Harry P. (1983). *A Review of Private Approaches for Delivery of Public Services.* Washington, D.C.: Urban Institute Press.

Hatry, Harry P. (1985). "Privatization Pros and Cons and Ways to Make Government Agencies More Competitive," *Urban Resources* 2 (September): 15–16.

Hatry, Harry P. (1988). "Privatization Presents Problems," *National Civic Review* 77 (March–April): 112–117.

Hatry, Harry P. (1989). "Introduction," and "Overall Findings and Recommendations," in Joan W. Allen, Keon S. Chi, Kevin M. Devlin, Mark Fall, Harry P. Hatry, and Wayne Masterman, *The Private Sector in State Service Delivery: Examples of Innovative Practices.* Washington, D.C.: The Council of State Governments and The Urban Institute Press.

Hatry, Harry P. and Carl F. Valente (1983). "Alternative Service Delivery Approaches Involving Increased Use of the Private Sector," in International City Management Association, *The Municipal Year Book, 1983.* Washington, D.C.: ICMA: 119–217.

Hatry, Harry P. and Eugene Durman (1985). *Issues in Competitive Contracting for Social Services.* Falls Church, Va.: National Institute of Governmental Purchasing.

Hatry, Harry P., Louis H. Blair, Donald M. Fisk, John M. Greiner, John R. Hall and Philip S. Schaenman (1977). *How Effective Are Your Community Services? Procedures for Monitoring the Effectiveness of Municipal Services.* Washington, D.C.: The Urban Institute.

Hawthorne, Fran (1988). "Is the Muni Market Color-Blind?" *Institutional Investor* 22 (June): 43–47.

Hayes, Edward C. (1986). "Contracting for Services: The Basic Steps," *The Privatization Review* 2 (Winter): 21–27.

Hayes, T. (1984). *Service Contracting.* San Diego: Metro Associates.

Head, L. M. (1962). "Blanket Orders Make Buying Easier," *Purchasing Magazine* 53 (October 8): 86–87.

Hemming, Richard and Ali M. Mansoor (1988). "Is Privatization the Answer?" *Finance & Development* 25 (September): 31–33.

Henderson, L. (1986). "Intergovernmental Service Arrangements and the Transfer of Functions," in International City Management Association, *The Municipal Year Book 1985.* Washington, D.C.: ICMA: 194–202.

Herander, Mark G. (1986). "Discriminatory Government Procurement With a Content Requirement: Its Protective Effects and Welfare Costs," *Atlantic Economic Journal* 14 (March): 20–29.

Herbert, Leo, Larry N. Killough, and Alan Walter Steiss (1984). *Governmental Accounting and Control.* Monterrey, Calif.: Brooks/Cole Publishing Co.

Herbert, R. F. and A. N. Link (1982). *The Entrepreneur, Mainstream Views and Radical Critiques.* New York: Praeger.

Herzlinger, Regina E. and William S. Karasker (1987). "Who Profits from Non-Profits?" *Harvard Business Review* 65 (January–February): 93–106.

Hess, Martha (1989). "Constitutional Law—Equal Protection—Benign Classifications Based on Race Must Be Narrowly Tailored to Achieve a Compelling Governmental Interest" (case note), *St. Mary's Law Journal* 21 (Fall): 493–510.

Hiestand, O. S. (1988). "The U.S. Supreme Court and Federal Procurement Contracts," *Public Contract Newsletter* 23 (Winter): 16–18.

Hiestand, O. S. and Thomas F. Williamson (1985). "The New Federal Procurement System: Is Anyone in Charge?" *Uniform Commercial Code Law Journal* 17 (Spring): 355–375.

Hiestand, O. S., Jr. (1968). "A New Era in Government Construction Contracts," *Federal Bar Journal* 28 (Summer): 165–184.

Higgins, C. Wayne (1989). "American Health Care and the Economics of Change," in Lawrence K. Finley, ed., *Public Sector Privatization: Alternative Approaches to Service Delivery.* New York: Quorum Books: 93–120.

Hill, Paul C. (1970). "The Finality of Acceptance Under Government Supply Contracts," *Public Contract Law Journal* 3 (February): 97–126.

Hill, Roy (1986). "Women-Owned Companies Finally Start Making Their Mark," *International Management* (UK) 41 (May): 66–70.

Hiller, John R. and Robert D. Tollison (1978). "Incentive Versus Cost-Plus Contracts in Defense Procurement," *Journal of Industrial Economics* 26 (March): 239–248.

Hilliard, Sheryl L. and Jube Shiver, Jr. (1989). "Go West, Young Entrepreneur," *Black Enterprise* 19 (June): 110–122.

Hirsch, Werner Z. (1989). "The Economics of Contracting Out: The Labor Cost Fallacy," *Labor Law Journal* 40 (August): 536–542.

Hirschhorn, Larry (1983). *Cutting Back: Retrenchment and Redevelopment in Human and Community Services.* San Francisco: Jossey-Bass.

Hirschman, A. O. (1982). *Shifting Involvements: Private Interest and Public Action.* Princeton, N.J.: Princeton University Press.

Hispanic Business (1990). "CEO's—Charging Into the 90s" 12 (April): 24–34.

Hisrich, Robert D. (1989). "Women Entrepreneurs: Problems and Prescriptions for Success in the Future," in Oliver Hagan, Carol Rivchun, and Donald Sexton, eds., *Women-Owned Businesses.* New York: Praeger: 3–32.

Hisrich, Robert D. and C. G. Brush (1985). *The Woman Entrepreneur: Characteristics and Prescriptions for Success.* Lexington, Mass.: Lexington Books.

Hoch, Charles (1985). "Municipal Contracting in California: Privatizing With Class," *Urban Affairs Quarterly* 20 (March): 303–323.

Hocker, William C. (1990). "New Debentures Bill Should Help MESBICs," *Black Enterprise* 20 (February): 43.

Hodge, Scott A. (1986). *Privatizing Fire Protection.* Chicago: Heartland Institute (May 6).

Hoffer, William (1987). "Businesswomen: Equal but Different," *Nation's Business* 75 (August): 46–47.

Hofmann, Mark A. (1989a). "HMO Bidding Helps City Control Medical Costs," *Business Insurance* 23 (July 31): 1, 12.

Hofmann, Mark A. (1989b). "Surety Market Faces Struggle Despite Profitable '88: Expert," *Business Insurance* 23 (May 22): 67.

Holcombe, Randall G. (1990). "The Tax Cost of Privatization," *Southern Economic Journal* 56 (January): 732–742.

Holcombe, Randall G. (n.d.). "What's Happened to Privatization?," *Madison Op-Ed Series.* Tallahassee, Fla.: The James Madison Institute for Public Policy Studies.

Holding, Willis, Jr. (1976). "Problems of State Procurement," *Public Contract Law Journal* 8 (May): 17–21.

Holding, Willis, Jr. (1978). "Multiple Awards: A View from the States," *Government Executive* 10 (April).

Holmes, Peter A. (1985). "Taking Public Services Private," *Nation's Business* 73 (August): 18–24.

Holsendolph, Ernest (1978). "Washington to Triple Contract 'Pot' for Black Business," *Black Enterprise* 8 (May): 30–31, 33–34, 36.

Holter, Norma (1987). "MRP and Government Contract Costing: Are They Compatible?" *National Contract Management Journal* 21 (Summer): 1–9.

Holtz, Herman (1980). *The $100 Billion Market: How To Do Business With the U.S. Government.* New York: AMACON.

Holtz, Herman (1986). "The $650 Billion Market Opportunity," *Business Marketing* 71 (October): 88–96.

Honesty, Edward F., Jr. (1980). "The Right to Economic Parity" (case note), *Black Law Journal* 6 (Winter–Spring): 276–287.

Honiberg, Scott A. (1990). "Military Contracts Present Growth Opportunities," *Healthcare Financial Management* 44 (April): 38–45.

Honig, David (1984). "The FCC and Its Fluctuating Commitment to Minority Ownership of Broadcast Facilities," *Howard Law Journal* 27 (Summer): 859–877.

Hoogland, K. A. and C. McGlothlen (1989). "City of Richmond v. Croson': A Setback for Minority Set-Aside Programs," *Employee Relations Law Journal* (Summer): 5–19.

Hooks, Benjamin L. (1987). "Government Assistance; Despite Wedtech, Aid to Minorities Is Good Business," *The Los Angeles Daily Journal* 100 (June 25): 4.

Hornaday, Robert W. and Bennie H. Nunnally, Jr. (1987). "Problems Facing Black-Owned Businesses," *Business Forum* 12 (Fall): 34–37.

Horowitz, Steven (1983). "Looking for Mr. Good Bar: In Search of Standards for Federal Debarment," *Public Contract Law Journal* 14 (October): 58–95.

Horton, Len (1989). "Small Firms Seek Big Opportunities: Some Software Firms Work at Learning How to Reach Key Government Contractors," *Software Magazine* 9 (May): 95–96.

Hosch, Dorothea (1973). *Use of the Contract Approach in Public Social Services*. Los Angeles: University of Southern California Regional Research Institute in Social Welfare.

Hoshower, Leon B. (1989). "How Regulatory Ambiguity Frustrates Defense Contractors," *Financial Executive* 5 (September/October): 54–57.

Houlden, Pauline (1985). "Quality and Cost Comparisons of Private Bar Indigent Defense Systems: Contract vs. Ordered Assigned Counsel," *Journal of Criminal Law and Criminology* 76 (Spring): 176–200.

Howard, James S. (1987a). "Can Small Manufacturers Survive?" *D & B Reports* (March/April): 18–21.

Howard, James S. (1987b). "Small Business Presidents Speak Out," *D & B Reports* (November/December): 16–19.

Howard, Robert (1990). "Can Small Business Help Countries Compete?" *Harvard Business Review* (November–December): 88–90, 94, 96–97, 100, 102–103.

Hula, Richard C., ed. (1988). *Market Based Public Policy*. London: Macmillan Press.

Humphreys, Marie Adele and Jacquetta McClung (1982). "American Indian Entrepreneurs in the Southwest," *Texas Business Review* 56 (July/August): 187–192.

Hunt, Raymond G. (1984). "Cross-Purposes in the Federal Contract Procurement System: Military R & D and Beyond," *Public Administration Review* 44 (May/June): 247–256.

Hutchings, Vicky (1988). "The Strangest Privatisation of All," *New Statesman & Society* 1 (June 24): 27.

Hutto, T. Don and Gary E. Vick (1984). "Designing the Private Correctional Facility," *Corrections Today* 46 (April): 78–79.

Ibraheim, A. B. and J. R. Goodwin (1986). "Perceived Causes of Success in Small Business," *American Journal of Small Business* 11 (Fall): 41–50.

Inquiry (1982a). "Getting the Government out of the Environment" (Spring).

Inquiry (1982b). "Selling the Federal Lands" (September).

Institute for Local Self-Government (1977). *Alternatives to Traditional Public Safety Systems: Civilians in Public Safety Services*. Berkeley, Calif.: Institute for Local Self-Government.

Interagency Task Force on Trade (1988). *Exporter's Guide to Federal Resources for Small Business*. Washington, D.C.: U.S. Government Printing Office.

International City Management Association (1971). "Purchasing Through Intergovernmental Agreements," *Management Information Service* 3 (June): S–6.

International City Management Association (1989). "Trends and Issues in the Use of Intergovernmental Agreements and Privatization in Local Government," *Baseline Data Report* 21 (November/December): 1–13.

Irons, E., S. Doctors, and A. Drebin (1975). "The Impact of Minority Banks on Communities," *The Banker's Magazine* 158 (Spring): 84–91.

Jackson, Jesse (1978). "Reparations Are Justified for Blacks," *Regulation* 2 (September/October): 24–29.

Jacoby, Sidney B. (1980). "The Contract Disputes Act of 1978: An Important Development," *Federal Bar Journal* 39 (Summer): 10–22.

Jacquillat, Bertrand (1987). "Nationalization and Privatization in Contemporary France," *Government Union Review* 8 (Fall): 21–50.

James, Herman G. (1946). *The Protection of the Public Interest in Public Contracts*. Chicago: Public Administration Service.

Janik, Michael T. (1987). "A U.S. Perspective on the GATT Agreement on Government Procurement," *George Washington Journal of International Law & Economics* 20 (3): 491–526.

Janis, Lenore (1988). "The Future of Women in Construction," *AACE Transactions*: I.1.1–I.1.3.

Janken, Bruce and Betsy Conrad (1989). "Florence, Kentucky, Adapts to Growth," in Lawrence K. Finley, ed., *Public Sector Privatization: Alternative Approaches to Service Delivery*. New York: Quorum Books: 35–46.

Jelacic, John (1991). "The U.S. Trade Outlook in 1991," *Business America* 112 (April 22): 2–7.

Jenkins, John A. (1968). "Impact of Sovereign Immunity of Subcontractors Dealing with State and Local Government," *Public Contract Law Journal* 2 (October): 27–32.

Jennings, G. W. (1969). *State Purchasing—The Essentials of a Modern Service For Modern Government*. Lexington, Ky.; The Council of State Governments.

Jiminez, Daniel (1981). *Government Contracts with Voluntary Organizations*. National Technical Information Service (November).

Johansen, Eivind H. (1985). "Workshops for the Blind: The Debate Goes on; Law Firm's Practice-Building Efforts Are a Drain on Organization's Time," *Legal Times* 8 (November 4): 7.

Johnsen, K. (1967). "Procurement Study Bill Deferred to 1968," *Aviation Week & Space Technology* 87 (November 27): 77.

Johnson, Charles H., Jr. (1981). "Mitchell v. Freeman et al.: Judicial Enforcement of Affirmative Action Set-Asides—Overcoming the Economic Remnants of Slavery," *Black Law Journal* 7 (Fall): 213–225.

Johnson, Gerald W. and John G. Heilman (1987). "Metapolicy Transition and Policy Implementation: New Federalism and Privatization," *Public Administration Review* 47 (November/December): 468–478.

Johnson, R. Bradley and Bernard H. Ross (1989). "Risk Management in the Public Sector," in International City Management Association, *The Municipal Year Book 1989*, Washington, D.C.: ICMA: 3–11.

Johnson, Russell (1991). "Privatization in Hungary Is Creating Investment Opportunities for U.S. Firms," *Business America* 112 (January 14): 17–18.

Johnson, Verne and Ted Kolderie (1984). "Public-Private Partnerships; Useful but Sterile," *National Civic Review* 73 (November): 503–511.

Johnson, W. Stanfield (1984). "Air Force Collection Practices Ruled Illegal by Board," *Legal Times* 6 (May 7): 13.

Johnston, Joan M. (1983). "Competitive Negotiation Under the Virginia Public Procurement Act," *Virginia Bar Association Journal* 9 (Winter): 19–23.

Johnston, William B. (1991). "Global Work Force 2000: The New World Labor Market," *Harvard Business Review* (March/April): 115–126.

Jones, Heather S. (1991). "Market Opening, Expansion in Civil Aviation Attract U.S. Aerospace Firms to Eastern Europe," *Business America* 112 (January 14): 19–20.

Jones, Mark L. (1984). "The GATT-MIN System and the European Community as International Frameworks for the Regulation of Economic Activity: The Removal of Barriers to Trade in Government Procurement," *Maryland Journal of International Law and Trade* 8 (Summer): 53–121.

Jones, Walter J. (1988). "The Impact of Equal Opportunity Compliance Laws in Government Contracting: The Shelby County, Tennessee Experience," *International Journal of Public Administration* 11 (March): 173–190.

Journal of Accountancy (1988). "New Rules on Government Contractors," 165 (May): 168–170.

Journal of Accountancy (1989). "Challenges Ahead for Small Businesses," 167 (Fall): 84–87.

Kahn, P. D. (1984). "Privatizing Municipal Legal Services," *Local Government Studies* 10: 1–4.

Kamerman, Sheila B. and Alfred J. Kahn, eds. (1989). *Privatization and the Welfare State*. Princeton, N.J.: Princeton University Press.

Kamuchey, Cassandra T. (1989). "False Claims (White Collar Crime: Fifth Survey of Law)," *American Criminal Law Review* 26 (Winter): 815–827.

Kanter, Rosabeth Moss (1989). "From Climbing to Hopping: The Contingent Job and the Post-Entrepreneurial Career," *Management Review* 78 (April): 22–27.

Kaplan, J. Kim (1986). "Agencies Squabble Over Procurement Authority," *Legal Times* 8 (March 24): 2.

Kaplan, M. and R. B. Lillich (1985). "Municipal Conflicts of Interest: Inconsistencies and Patchwork Prohibitions," *Columbia Law Review* 58 (July): 157.

Kapp, Sue (1987). "She's More Than 'Just One of the Guys,' " *Business Marketing* 72 (April): 12, 14.

Karger, Howard Jacob (1989). "Social Service Administration and the Challenge of Unionization," *Administration in Social Work* 13 (3, 4): 199–218.

Kashiwagi, Kaoru, Robert A. Rubin, and Marcy Ressler Harris (1989). "Construction Law and

Practice in Japan," *Construction Lawyer* 9 (January): 1.

Kassenbaum, Gene et al. (1978). *Contracting for Correctional Services in the Community*. Washington, D.C.: National Institute of Law Enforcement and Criminal Justice.

Katz, Jeffrey L. (1991). "Privatizing Without Tears," *Governing* 4 (June): 38–42.

Katzman, Samuel (1969). "Arbitration in Government Contracts: The Ghost at the Banquet," *Arbitration Journal* 24: 133–142.

Kay, J., C. Mayer, and D. Thompson (1986). *Privatization and Regulation: The UK Experience*. Oxford: Clarendon Press.

Keating, J. Michael (1985). *Seeking Profit in Punishment*. Washington, D.C.: American Federation of State, County, and Municipal Employees.

Keller, Bill (1982). "How Congress Spoils Small Business" (from *The Washington Monthly*), *The Los Angeles Daily Journal* 95 (March 19): 4.

Kelley, J. (1984). *Costing Government Services: A Guide for Decision Making*. Washington, D.C.: Government Finance Officers Association.

Kellman, Barry (1986). "De-Coupling the Military-Industrial Complex: The Liability of Weapons Makers for Injuries to Servicemen," *Cleveland State Law Review* 35 (Fall): 351–402.

Kelso, John (1990). "The Pacific Rim: The View from Down Under," *Presidential Studies Quarterly* 20 (Summer): 481–488.

Kemper, Pater and John M. Quigley (1976). *The Economics of Refuse Collection*. Cambridge, Mass.: Ballinger Publishing Company.

Kendall, Richard J. (1967). "The Material and Workmanship Clause in Standard Government Construction Contracts," *George Washington Law Review* 35 (June): 998–1009.

Kennedy, Bingham and Barry J. Trilling (1988). "Pathways and Pitfalls for Small Business: Federal Procurement Socioeconomic Programs," *National Contract Management Journal* 22 (Summer): 55–64.

Kennedy, Morris and Wayne Garcia (1989). "Foundation Weakens for Minority Firms," *The Tampa Tribune* (July 2): 1A, 12A.

Kenney, Robert J., Jr. and Wendy T. Kirby (1985). "A Management Approach to the Procurement Fraud Problem," *Public Contract Law Journal* 15 (July): 345–364.

Kent, C. A., ed. (1987). *Entrepreneurship and the Privatizing of Government*. Westport, Conn.: Greenwood Press.

Kent, Calvin A. (1986). "Privatization of Public Sector," *Heartland Policy Study*, No. 8.

Kenworthy, James Lawrence (1981). "The Constitutionality of State Buy-American Laws," *UMKC Law Review* 50 (Fall): 1–20.

Kettle, D. (1981). "The Fourth Face of Federalism," *Public Administration Review* 41 (3): 366–371.

Kettler, Richard K. (1986). "Federal Employee Challenges to Contracting Out: Is There a Viable Forum?" *Military Law Review* 111 (Winter): 103–166.

Keyes, W. Noel (1984). "Competition and Sole-Source Procurements—A View Through the Unsolicited Proposal Example," *Public Contract Law Journal* 14 (February): 284–312.

Kidd, Yvonne (1988). "Successful Contractors Know the Rules of Competition," *Inform* 2 (October): 8–9.

Kidd, Yvonne (1990). "Federal Ethics Reforms Pose New Dilemmas for Contractors," *Inform* 4 (April): 74, 76.

Kiesling, Herbert and Donald Fisk (1973). *Local Government Privatization/Competition*. Washington, D.C.: The Urban Institute.

Kilgore, Kathleen (1978). "Women's Banks: One Works, The Other Doesn't," *New Englander* 24 (March): 38–40, 42.

Kilgore, Peter G. (1981). "Did 'Fullilove' Settle Quota Issue in Grant Programs?" *Legal Times* 3 (April 20): 12.

Kilgore, Peter G. (1981). "Racial Preferences in the Federal Grant Programs: Is There a Basis for Challenge After Fullilove v. Klutznick?" *Labor Law Journal* 32 (May): 306–314.

Kilgore, Peter G. (1982). "Racial Preference in the Federal Grant Programs: Is There a Basis for Challenge After Fullilove v. Klutznick?" *Florida Bar Journal* 56 (January): 29–34.

Kimbro, Dennis P. (1990). "Dreamers: Black Sales Heroes and Their Secrets," *Success* 37 (May): 40–41.

Kincaid, John (1990). "State and Local Governments Go International," *International Perspective* 16 (Spring): 6–9.

King, Lord (1987). "Lessons of Privatization," *Long Range Planning* (UK) 20/6 (December): 18–22.

Kinley, J. (1956). "Self-Dealing by School Board Members," *Illinois Bar Journal* 45 (November): 168–170.

Kinosky, Barbara A. (1989). "Commentary: Another Perspective on Boyle v. United Technologies Corporation," *National Contract Management Journal* 23 (Summer): 77–83.

Kirby, Ronald F. (1988). "The Prospects for Greater Private Sector Involvement in Urban Transportation," in John C. Weicher, ed., *Private Innovations in Public Transit*. Washington, D.C.: American Enterprise Institute for Public Policy Research: 23–28.

Kirk, Flayo O. (1988). "The Government's Judicial Criminal Remedies Against Fraudulent Contractors," *Air Force Law Review* 29 (Fall): 149–155.

Kirlin, John (1973). "The Impact of Contract Service Arrangements Upon the Los Angeles County Sheriff's Department and Law Enforcement in Los Angeles County," *Public Policy* 21 (Fall): 533–584.

Kirlin, John J. and A. M. Kirlin (1982). "Public/Private Bargaining in Local Development," *Public Choices—Private Resources: Financing California's Growth Through Public-Private Bargaining*. Sacramento: California Tax Foundation: 23–26.

Kirlin, John J., J. D. Ries, and S. Sonenblum (1977). Alternatives to City Departments," in E. S. Savas, ed. *Alternatives for Delivering Public Services*. Boulder, Colo.: Westview: 111–145.

Kirschten, Dick (1990). "Bush Pressed on China's Trade Status," *National Journal* 22 (May 19): 1228–1229.

Kisser, C. E. (1978). "Market Segmentation for Better Purchasing Results," *Journal of Purchasing* 14 (November).

Kitano, Harry H. L. and Roger Daniels (1988). *Asian Americans: Emerging Minorities*. Englewood Cliffs, NJ: Prentice-Hall.

Kitchen, Harry M. (1976). "A Statistical Estimation of an Operating Cost Function for Municipal Refuse Collection," *Public Finance Quarterly* 4 (January): 56–76.

Kitfield, James (1990a). "John Betti: Managing the Decline," *Government Executive* 22 (August): 52–57.

Kitfield, James (1990b). "Stepping Back from Reform," *Government Executive* 22 (August): 18–27.

Kline, Lowry F. (1964). "Government Option Contracts," Comments, *Tennessee Law Review* 31 (Winter): 230–248.

Knauth, Kirstin (1989). "Binding Contract," *Government Executive* 21 (June): 42–43, 74.

Knowlton, Winthrop and Richard Zechhauser, eds. (1986). *American Society: Public and Private Responsibilities*. Cambridge, Mass.: Ballinger Publishing Company.

Kolderie, Ted (1982). *Many Providers, Many Producers: A New View of the Public Service Industry*. Minneapolis: Hubert H. Humphrey Institute of Public Affairs, University of Minnesota (April), No. HHH 82–4.

Kolderie, Ted (1986). "The Two Different Concepts of Privatization," *Public Administration Review* 46 (July/August): 285–291.

Kolderie, Ted and Jody Hauer (1984). "Contracting as an Approach to Public Management," *Municipal Management* (Spring).

Kolodzief, Edward A. (1987). *Making and Marketing Arms*. Princeton, N.J.: Princeton University Press.

Konecky, Nathan (1988). "Legal Changes Affecting the Use of Independent Consultants," *Journal of Systems Management* 39 (August): 42.

Kono, Dayne (1981–1982). "United States–Japan Trade Developments Under the MTN Agreement on Government Procurement," *Fordham International Law Journal* 5 (Winter): 139–183.

Konrad, Walecia (1985). "How Bold Decisions Help a Business Beat the Odds," *Working Woman* 10 (November): 47–49.

Korbel, John J. and Christopher J. Brescia (1989). "Europe 1992: Changing the Rules of the Game," *Price Waterhouse Review* 33 (1): 2–16.

Korneich, Donald B. and Ronald S. Schwartz (1968). "New 'Law' of Government of Service Contracts," *Federal Bar Journal* 28 (Summer): 239–255.

Kosowatz, John J. and Barbara Lamb (1986). "Questions Shroud Privatization: Changing Tax Codes Hamper Private Municipal Sewerage Work," *Engineering News-Record* 216 (January 9): 26–27.

Kostos, Theodore M. (1970). "Government Contracts and the Commercial Code," *Pennsylvania Bar Association Quarterly* 41 (January): 165–172.

Kotz, Nick (1988). *Wild Blue Yonder: Money, Politics, and the B-1 Bomber.* New York: Pantheon.

Kovach, Kenneth A. (1983). "Should the Davis–Bacon Act Be Repealed?," *Business Horizons* 26 (September/October): 33–37.

Kozitsyn, Valentin and William W. Johnson (1991). *1991 Comprehensive Guide to Doing Business in the U.S.S.R.* Southlake, Texas: TAG International.

Krajick, Kevin (1984). "Prisons for Profit," *State Legislatures* 10 (April): 9–14.

Kramer, Ralph and Paul Terrell (1984). *Social Services Contracting in the Bay Area.* Berkeley, Calif.: Institute of Government Studies.

Kuckelman, David J., II (1987). "Contracting with the North Atlantic Treaty Organization," *George Washington Journal of International Law and Economics* 20 (Summer): 527–559.

Kull, Donald C. (1989–90). "Reflections on Third-Party Government," *The Bureaucrat* 18 (Winter): 37–41.

Kuttner, Robert (1983). "Going Private: The Dubious Case for Selling off the State," *The New Republic* 188 (May 30): 29–33.

Kuttner, Robert (1988). "A Public Service Doesn't Always Require a Public Payroll," *Business Week* 3047 (April 18): 20.

Kuttner, Robert (1990). "Managed Trade and Economic Sovereignty," in Frank J. Macchiarola, ed., *International Trade: The Changing Role of the United States.* New York: The Academy of Political Science: 37–53.

Kysiak, Ronald C. (1986). "The Role of the University in Public-Private Partnerships," in Perry Davis, ed., *Public-Private Partnerships: Improving Urban Life.* New York: The Academy of Political Science: 47–59.

Lambert, David M. F. and Joseph J. Petrillo (1982). "SBA Minority Contracting Program Stirs Controversy," *Legal Times of Washington* 5 (June 21): 19.

Lambert, Jeremiah D. and James Richard O'Neill (1988). "Privatization of Municipal Hydroelectric Facilities Under Current Law," *Public Utilities Fortnightly* 12 (February 2): 11–17.

Lamm, David V. (1988). "Why Firms Refuse

DOD Business: An Analysis of Rationale," *National Contract Management Journal* 21 (Winter): 45–55.

Lamoriello, Francine C. (1989). "Trading Concerns," *World* 23 (3): 28–30.

Lane, John, Jr. (1968). "Administrative Resolution of Government Breaches—The Case for an All-Breach Clause," *Federal Bar Journal* 28 (Summer): 199–233.

Langton, S. (1983). "Public-Private Partnerships: Hope or Hoax?" *National Civic Review* 72 (May): 256–261.

Lanson, Gerald (1987). "Graduation Day," *Inc.* 9 (May): 104–108.

Lantry, Terry L. and John D. McConahay (1968). "Pitfalls in Purchasing Under the Uniform Commercial Code," *Journal of Purchasing* 4 (November): 43–51.

Larkin, David (1980). "Congressional Amendments Slowing Federal Contracts," *Office* 91 (January): 93–94.

Lauter, David (1982). "U.S. Must Pay Whistle-Blower's Fees," *The National Law Journal* 4 (April 19): 8.

Lauter, David (1985). "The Plunge Into Private Justice," *The National Law Journal* 17 (March 11): 1.

Lebowitz, Philip H. (1981). "FCC Minority Distress Sale Policy: Public Interest v. the Public's Interest," *Wisconsin Law Review* (March–April): 365–397.

Leder, Michelle (1988). "Government Downshifts Aid to Black Business, Study Says," *The Tampa Tribune* (October 3): 15–D.

Lee, Francis C. and Clay L. Wirt (1983). "Ethical Dilemmas in Public Procurement: A Test for Mayors, Council Members, and County Supervisors," *Current Municipal Problems* 9 (Spring): 406–413.

Lee, Yong S. (1987). "Civil Liabilities of State and Local Government: Myth and Reality," *Public Administration Review* 47 (March/April): 160–170.

Leff, Laurel (1985). "Finding Your Way Through the Government Procurement Maze," *Working Woman* 10 (April): 55.

Legal Research Journal (1983). "A Legal Research Report for Companies Thinking of Doing Business With the Government," 7 (March–April): 1–3.

Legal Research Journal (1985). "Lowest Commercial Price Certificate Requirement in Noncompetitive Contracts for Government Supplies," 9 (Winter): 8–9.

Legal Research Journal (1986). "Lowest Commercial Price Certificate Requirement in Noncompetitive Contracts for Government Supplies," 9 (July–August): 8–9.

Legal Times of Washington (1980). "Lawyers Watch Standing Rule" (government computer procurement), 2 (February 11): 7.

LeGrant, Julian and Ray Robinson, eds. (1984). *Privatization and the Welfare State*. Winchester, Mass.: Allen and Unwin.

Leimkuhler, William F. (1981). "Contracts: Enforcing Social and Economic Policy Through Government Contracts," *Annual Survey of American Law 1980* (April): 539–559.

Lemieux, Denis (1988). "Legal Issues Arising from Protectionist Government Procurement Policies in Canada and the United States," *Les Cahiers de Droit* 29 (June): 369–423.

Lemov, Penelope (1988). "Purchasing Officials Push New Techniques to Get More for Their Money," *Governing* 1 (August): 40–47.

Lempert, Larry (1982a). "DOJ Lawyer Aims at Defense Procurement Fraud," *Legal Times of Washington* 4 (May 10): 4.

Lempert, Larry (1982b). "OFPP Letter Will Spark Court Action," *Legal Times* 5 (July 26): 1.

Leon, Philip and Michael Johnson (1984). "Profiting from Defense," *Black Enterprise* 15 (October): 91–94.

Lerner, Norman C. (1990). "Telecommunications Privatization in Argentina," *Telecommunications* (International Edition) 24 (February): 52–56.

Levin, John (1985). "Programmed to Succeed," *Black Enterprise* 16 (September): 56–60.

Levine, Charles H. (1984). *The Private Delivery of Public Services* (Bibliography). Washington, D.C.: Department of Housing and Urban Development, HUD User 0002308.

Levinson, Robert B. (1976). *Government by Private Contract: Experimentation in South San Francisco*. Davis, Calif.: Institute of Governmental Affairs, University of California.

Levinson, Robert B. (1984). "The Private Sector and Corrections," *Corrections Today* 46 (August): 42.

Levinson, Robert B. (n.d.). *Private Operation of a Correctional Institution*. Washington, D.C.: National Institute of Corrections.

Lewis, Anthony (1989). "Now Is a Time for Healing on the Race Issue" (minority set-asides, City of Richmond v. J. A. Croson Co.), *The Los Angeles Daily Journal* 102 (April 13): 6.

Lewis, Eleanor Roberts (1991). "Legal Protections Provided to U.S. Investors Under the Bilateral Investment Treaty Program," *Business America* 112 (February 11): 12–13.

Lewis, Harold (1989). "Ethics and the Private Non-Profit Human Service Organization," *Administration in Social Work* 13 (2): 1–14.

Lewyn, Mark (1989). "Revolt of Uncle Sam's Paper Pushers," *Business Week* (Industrial/technology edition) 3131 (October 30): 156.

Liburd-Jordan, Sondra (1983). "Fueling His Way to the Top," *Black Enterprise* 13 (June): 169–174.

Lidstone, Herrick K. and Robert D. Witte (1960). "Government Contracts: Disputes and Claims Procedures," *Virginia Law Review* 46 (March): 252–295.

Lieberman, Myron (1986a). *Beyond Public Education*. New York: Praeger.

Lieberman, Myron (1986b). "Market Solutions to the Education Crisis," *Cato Policy Analysis* 75 (July 1).

Lieberman, Myron (1987). "Market Solutions to the Education Crisis: Vouchers, Technology, Contracting Out Instruction," *Journal of Collective Negotiations in the Public Sector* 16 (2): 169–184.

Lieberman, Myron (1988). "Efficiency Issues in Educational Contracting," *Government Union Review* 9 (Winter): 1–24.

Lieblich, Robert E. (1972). "Bidder Pre-Qualification: Theory in Search of Practice," *Public Contract Law Journal* 5 (April): 32–47.

Lillich, Richard B. (1958). "Municipal Conflicts of Interest: Rights and Remedies Under an Invalid Contract," *Fordham Law Review* 27 (Spring): 31–47.

Lim, Gill-Chin and Richard J. Moore (1989). "Privatization in Developing Countries: Ideal and Reality," *International Journal of Public Administration* 12 (January): 137–151.

Linder, Georg (1987). "Government Procurement Law in Sweden," *George Washington*

Journal of International Law & Economics 20 (3): 561–566.

Lindley, J. and E. Selby (1973). "Black Customers—Hidden Market Potential," *The Bankers Magazine* 156 (Summer): 84–87.

Lindquist, Charles A. (1980). "Private Sector in Corrections: Contracting Probation Services From Community Organizations," *Federal Probation* 44 (March): 58–64.

Liner, Blaine (1990). "States and Localities in the Global Marketplace," *International Perspective* 16 (Spring): 11–14.

Linowes, David F. (1988). *Privatization: Toward More Effective Government: Report of the President's Commission on Privatization.* Urbana: University of Illinois Press.

Lipsky, Abbott B., Jr. and William J. Cople III (1985). "Defense Contracting: Is Antitrust the Right Cure?," *Legal Times* 8 (October 14): 8.

Litman, George III (1991). "Opportunities for U.S. Oil and Gas Companies in the U.S.S.R.," *Business America* 112 (June 3): 6–8.

Livingston, Scott A. (1986). "Fair Treatment for Contractors Doing Business with the State of Maryland," *University of Baltimore Law Review* 15 (Winter): 215–250.

Logan, Charles H. (1985a). "Competition in the Prison Business," *The Freeman* 35 (August): 469–78.

Logan, Charles H. (1985b). *Privatization and Corrections: A Bibliography.* Storrs, Conn.: University of Connecticut.

Logan, Hal J. (1983). "Harnessing the Information Explosion," *Black Enterprise* 13 (June): 223–228.

Logan, Harold J. (1983). "Maxima's 8A Dilemma," *Black Enterprise* 13 (January): 42–45.

Logan, Robert J. (1983). "San Jose Choice of Towing Services Does Not Constitute Antitrust Violation," *Municipal Attorney* 24 (May–June): 2–3.

Longenecker, J. G. (1989). "Ethics in Small Business," *Journal of Small Business Management* 27 (January): 27–31.

Longstreth, Molly, Kathryn Stafford, and Theresa Mauldin (1987). "Self-Employed Women and Their Families," *Journal of Small Business Management* 25 (July): 30–37.

Lopez, Raymond A. (1989). "The Vitality of the Government Contractor Defense Continues" (case note), *Mercer Law Review* 40 (Winter): 753–778.

Los Angeles County (1984). *Contract Development Manual.* Los Angeles: Los Angeles County.

Los Angeles County (1985). *Agreements Providing for Services to Cities by the County of Los Angeles.* Los Angeles: Los Angeles County.

Loustaunau, Cherie (1991). "An Update for American Exporters on the U.S.–Israel Free Trade Area Agreement," *Business America* 112 (January 14): 16.

Lovitky, Jeffrey A. (1987). "Understanding the Submission Requirement for Cost or Pricing Data," *National Contract Management Journal* 21 (Summer): 57–65.

Lovitky, Jeffrey A. (1988). "Understanding Causation and Determining the Price Adjustment in Defective Pricing Cases," *Public Contract Law Journal* 17 (June): 407–442.

Lovitky, Jeffrey A. (1989). "Applying the Exemptions to Cost or Pricing Data," *Public Contract Law Journal* 19 (Fall): 146–173.

Low, Charlotte (1980). "Justices Decline to Hear Case on S. F. Minority Program: Set-Aside Was Voided," *The Los Angeles Daily Journal* 93 (December 17): 1.

Lowenstein, Jack (1989). "Indonesia: Private Sector's Banking Ambitions Unleased," *Euromoney, Indonesia Supplement* (December): 41–44.

Luizzo, C. N. (1967). "The Challenge of Municipal Purchasing," *Journal of Purchasing* 3 (February): 52–63.

Luke, Richard (1989). "Pensions: Private Solutions to a Public Problem," *Accountancy* (UK) 10 (June): 67–68.

Lyall, Katharine C. (1986). "Public-Private Partnerships in the Carter Years," in Perry Davis, ed., *Public-Private Partnerships: Improving Urban Life.* New York: The Academy of Political Science: 4–13.

Lydenberg, Steven (1984). "Minority Banks Gasp for Corporate Accounts," *Business and Society Review* 50 (Summer): 30–33.

Lynch, Charles A. and Edward C. Reading (1964). "Formal and Doctrinal Differences Between Government and Private Contracts," Student Note, *San Diego Law Review* 1 (January): 88–99.

Lynch, David J. (1989). "Journeying to Jointness," *Government Executive* 21 (June): 46–47.

Lynch, Edward J. (1989). "Privatization Stand-off," *Government Executive* 21 (December): 18–23.

Lyndon B. Johnson School of Public Affairs (1986). *Contracting Selected State Government Functions: Issues and Next Steps.* Austin, Texas: LBJ School of Public Affairs, The University of Texas at Austin, Policy Research Project Report 75.

Lyndon B. Johnson School of Public Affairs (1987). *Contracting Selected State Government Functions: Legislation and Implementation.* Austin, Texas: LBJ School of Public Affairs, The University of Texas at Austin, Policy Research Project Report 81.

Lyons, Joanne Marie (1989). "New Ground for the Government Contractor Defense" (case note), *North Carolina Law Review* 67 (June): 1172–1190.

Lyons, Robert S., Jr. (1990). "Long-Distance Leap," *Nation's Business* 78 (March): 14, 16.

Lyons, William and Michael R. Fitzgerald (1986). "The City as Purchasing Agent: Privatization and the Urban Polity in America," in Terry N. Clark, ed., *Research in Urban Policy* 2. Greenwich, Conn.: JAI Press: 61–73.

MacAvoy, Paul W. et al., eds. (1989). *Privatization and State-Owned Enterprises: Lessons From the United States, Great Britain, and Canada.* Boston: Kluwer Academic Publishers.

Macchiarola, Frank J. (1986). "Managing Partnerships: A CEO's Perspective," in Perry Davis, ed., *Public-Private Partnerships: Improving Urban Life.* New York: The Academy of Political Science: 127–136.

Macchiarola, Frank J., ed. (1990). *International Trade: The Changing Role of the United States.* New York: The Academy of Political Science.

Macchiarola, Frank J. (1990). "Mexico as a Trading Partner," in Frank J. Macchiarola, ed. *International Trade: The Changing Role of the United States.* New York: The Academy of Political Science, pp. 90–109.

Mackie, Sam A. (1989). "Florida Minority Business Hiring in Light of City of Richmond v. J. A. Croson Co.," *Florida Bar Journal* 63 (June): 11–14.

MacManus, Susan A. (1985). "Staying in the Game: The Reaction of Nonprofit Organizations to Federal Cutbacks," *Western Political Quarterly* 38 (December): 641–651.

MacManus, Susan A. (1986). "A Global View of Fiscal Stress: The Rise of Fiscal Populism," *Society/Transaction* 23 (September/October): 51–53.

MacManus, Susan A. (1989). "A Decade of Decline: A Longitudinal Look at Big City and Big County Strategies to Cope with Declining Revenues," *International Journal of Public Administration* 12 (September): 749–796.

MacManus, Susan A. (1990a). "Financing Federal, State, and Local Governments in the 1990s," *The Annals of the American Academy of Political and Social Science* 509 (May): 22–35.

MacManus, Susan A. (1990b). "Minority Business Contracting with Local Government," *Urban Affairs Quarterly* 25 (March): 455–473.

MacManus, Susan A. (1991). "Why Businesses Are Reluctant to Sell to Government," *Public Administration Review* 51 (July/August): 328–344.

MacManus, Susan A. and Steven A. Watson (1990). "Procurement Policy: The Missing Element in Financial Management Education," *International Journal of Public Administration* 13 (1, 2): 155–179.

Madarassy, Andrea (1990). "Private Investment Rebounds in Developing Countries," *Finance & Development* 27 (June): 48.

Madden, Thomas J. (1982). "Model Procurement Code and Ordinance: Implications for Local Governments," *Public Contract Newsletter* 18 (Fall): 18.

Magnotti, John F., Jr. (1986). "The Small Business Administration's Pilot Program: A Study in Frustration," *National Contract Management Journal* 20 (Summer): 61–65.

Malhame, Melissa (1991). "The National Trade Data Bank: A Valuable Resource for Exporters," *Business America* 112 (special edition): 13–14.

Malarkey, William S. (1989). "Government Contract Fraud (White Collar Crime: Fifth Survey of Law)," *American Criminal Law Review* 26 (Winter): 875–898.

Management Information Services Report (1980). "Contracting with the Private Sector for

Municipal Servicemen Practitioners," 12 (February): 1–17.

Manchester, Lydia (1989). "Alternative Service Delivery Approaches and City Service Planning," in Lawrence K. Finley, ed., *Public Sector Privatization: Alternative Approaches to Service Delivery.* New York: Quorum Books: 13–24.

Manchester, Lydia D. and Geoffrey S. Bogart (1988). *Contracting and Volunteerism in Local Government: A Self-Help Guide.* Washington, D.C.: International City Management Association.

Mandelker, Daniel R. (1951). "Specifications for Public Contracts—A Critique of Competitive Bidding," *Washington Law Quarterly* 1951 (December): 513–536.

The Manhattan Report Policy Forum (1982). "Privatizing Public Lands: The Ecological and Economic Case for Private Ownership of Federal Lands," 2 (May).

Mardikes, George M., Pamela Cone, and Julie Van Horn (1986). "Governmental Leasing: A Fifty State Survey of Legislation and Case Law," *The Urban Lawyer* 18 (Winter): 1–187.

Marlin, John, ed. (1984). *Contracting Municipal Services: A Guide to Purchasing from the Private Sector.* New York: John Wiley and Sons.

Marlowe, Julia (1985). "Private Versus Public Provision of Refuse Removal Service: Measures of Citizen Satisfaction," *Urban Affairs Quarterly* 20 (March): 355–363.

Marsh, James M. (1981). "Bar Assn. Recommends Study of Model Procurement Code for Pa.," *Pennsylvania Law Journal* 4 (January): 2.

Marsh, James M. (1989). "Statewide Procurement Law Could Prevent Corruption," *Pennsylvania Law Journal-Reporter* 12 (August 21): 3.

Marshall, Ray (1990). "Trade-Linked Labor Standards," in Frank J. Macchiarola, ed., *International Trade: The Changing Role of the United States.* New York: The Academy of Political Science: 67–78.

Marshall, Sue A. (1984). *Public Housing and Mediating Structures: The Case for Tenant Control.* Washington, D.C.: American Enterprise Institute (May).

Martin, Dan (1986). "Parking Privatization: A Construction Alternative," *Parking Professional* (November).

Maruca, James and Alexander Leak (1988). *How To Sell to the United States Department of Commerce.* Washington, D.C.: Government Printing Office (April).

Maskin, Arvin (1989). "Understanding the Government Contractor Defense," *ALI–ABA Course Materials Journal* 13 (February): 53–76.

Masters, Kim (1980). "OFCCP Stands by Construction Goals," *Legal Times of Washington* 3 (July 28): 2.

Masters, Robert and Robert Meier (1988). "Sex Differences and Risk-Taking Propensity of Entrepreneurs," *Journal of Small Business Management* 26 (January): 31–35.

Masterson, John T., Jr. (1991). "Source Materials for International Marketing and Distribution Agreements: Getting Started," *Business America* 112 (February 11): 8–9.

Mataxas, T. (1964). "Where You Can Go Wrong on Value Analysis," *Purchasing Magazine* 56 (January 27): 78–79.

Matthews, Roger (1988). "The Privatization of Punishment," *New Statesman & Society* 1 (July 22): 30.

Maule, Christopher J. (1987). "Privatization—The Case of the Urban Transportation Development Corporation Ltd.," *Business Quarterly* (Canada) 52 (Fall): 26–32.

Mayer, Andrew II (1987). "Military Procurement: Basic Principles and Recent Developments," *George Washington Journal of International Law and Economics* 21 (Fall): 165–187.

Mayer, Raymond R. (1972). "Selection of Rules of Thumb in Inventory Control," *Journal of Purchasing* 8 (May): 19–24.

McAfee, R. Preston and John McMillan (1989). "Government Procurement and International Trade," *Journal of International Economics* (Netherlands) 26 (May): 291–308.

McCall, Nathan (1989). "Ruling Delivers Hard Blow to Set-Asides," *Black Enterprise* 19 (April): 17–18.

McCann, Raymond D., Levator Norsworthy, Jr., Robert L. Ackley, Jose Aguirre, Charles B. Mellies, and Earle D. Munns, Jr. (1989). "Recent Developments in Contract Law: 1988 in Review," *Army Lawyer* 1989 (February): 5–39.

McCarthy, John J. (1982). "Contract Medical

Care: Prescription for Change," *Corrections Magazine* 8 (April): 6–14.

McClenahen, John S. (1990). "Should Government Run Like a Business?" *Government Executive* 22 (January): 12–17.

McConaghy, Richard W. (1971). "An Expanded Cause of Action Under the Tucker Act for an Unsuccessful Bidder," Comments, *Temple Law Quarterly* 44 (Summer): 552–563.

McConnell, Margaret E. (1985). "Contracting with the State Under the Newly Enacted Arizona Procurement Code," *Arizona Bar Journal* 21 (June–July): 27.

McCoy, Frank (1990). "B. E. Economists' Report: Standing on Shaky Ground," *Black Enterprise* 20 (January): 55–60.

McCoy, Frank (1991). "The World's Biggest Fire Sale," *Black Enterprise* 21 (June): 267–272.

McCraw, Thomas K. (1984). "The Public and Private Spheres in Historical Perspective," in Harvey Brooks et al., *Public-Private Partnerships*. Cambridge, Mass.: Ballinger Publishing Company: 31–60.

McCreary, Stephen E. (1991). "International Arbitration in Latin America," *Business America* 112 (February 11): 17–18.

McCulloch, Rachel (1990). "The United States–Canada Free Trade Agreement," in Frank J. Macchiarola, ed., *International Trade: The Changing Role of the United States*. New York: The Academy of Political Science: 79–89.

McDavid, James C. (1985). "The Canadian Experience with Privatizing Residential Solid Waste Collection Services," *Public Administration Review* 45 (September/October): 602–608.

McEntee, G. (1986). "Privatization's Financial Arguments Flawed," *City & State Magazine*: 10.

McEntee, Gerald W. (1985). "City Services: Can Free Enterprise Outperform the Public Sector? Privatization Can Lead to Problems," *Business and Society Review* (Fall): 43–47.

McFarlane, Walter A. (1984). "Benign Racial Classifications: A Guide for Transportation Attorneys," *University of Richmond Law Review* 19 (Fall): 29–68.

McFarlane, Walter A. and John J. McCarthy (1984). "Antitrust and State Government Contracting," *Identifying and Prosecuting Fraud and Abuse in State and Local Government Con-*

tracting. Chicago: American Bar Association: 9–29.

McGoldrick, John G. (1981). "Governor Offers Program to Foster Economic Rights," *New York Law Journal* 185 (May 1): 32.

McGrath, Robert L. (1988). "An Introduction to Fiscal Law in Government Contracting," *Air Force Law Review* 29 (Fall): 207–222.

McGuigan, Austin J. and John M. Massameno (1984). "Prosecuting Government Corruption Cases: Dangers and Pitfalls," *Identifying Fraud and Abuse in State and Local Contracting*. Chicago: American Bar Association: 63–67.

McGuire, Robert A. (1984). "Public vs. Private Activity: A New Look at School Bus Transportation," *Public Choice* 42 (1): 25–43.

McKinney, Joseph A. (1989). "Degree of Access to the Japanese Market: 1979 to 1986," *Columbia Journal of World Business* 24 (Summer): 53–59.

McMillan, Richard, Jr. (1982). "Special Problems in Section 2 Sherman Act Cases Involving Government Procurement: Market Definition, Measuring Market Power, and the Government as Monopsonist," *Antitrust Law Journal* 51 (Fall): 689–703.

McMillan, Richard, Jr. (1984). "Special Problems in Section 2 Sherman Act Cases Involving Government Procurement: Market Definition, Measuring Market Power, and the Government as Monopsonist," *Antitrust Law Journal* 14 (February): 262–275.

McNett, John F. (1989). "Nuclear Indemnity for Government Contractors Under the Price–Anderson Act: 1988 Amendments," *Public Contract Law Journal* 19 (Fall): 1–13.

Menes, Jonathan C. (1991). "1991 U.S. Industrial Outlook Predicts Major Role for Exports," *Business America* 112 (January 14): 2–4.

Mennemeyer, Stephen T. and Lois Olinger (1989). "Selective Contracting in California: Its Effect on Hospital Finances," *Inquiry* 26 (Winter): 442–457.

Menninger, Bonar (1989). "Beltway Bandits Regroup," *Government Executive* 21 (May): 46–49.

Mercer, James L. (1983). "Growing Opportunities for Public Service Contracting," *Harvard Business Review* 61 (March/April): 178.

Mercer/Slavin, Inc. (1987). *Findings of a*

National Survey of Local Government Service Contracting Practices. Atlanta: Mercer/Slavin, Inc.

Merrill, Maurice H. (1970). "Our Unrealized Resource—Inter-Municipal Cooperation," *Oklahoma Law Review* 23 (November): 349–389.

Mertz, George J. (1985). "Story on Firm's Successes Leaves 'Misimpression' " (Trilling and Kennedy and Committee for Purchase from the Blind and Other Severely Handicapped), *Legal Times* 8 (September 23): 13.

Mewett, Alan W. (1959). "Formalities in Government Contracts," *Wayne Law Review* 5 (Summer): 303–318.

Mewett, Alan W. (1960). "The Settlement of Government Contract Disputes—A Comparative Study," *Catholic University Law Review* 9 (May): 65–84.

Meyer, Michale E. and David R. Morgan (1979). *Contracting for Municipal Services: A Handbook for Local Officials.* Norman, Okla.: Bureau of Government Research, University of Oklahoma.

Meyers, Edward M. (1989). "Regulation of Federal Contractors' Employment Patterns," *Public Administration Review* 49 (January/February): 52–60.

Middle East Executive Reports (1985a). "How Algiers Buys: A Primer on State Purchasing Procedures," 8 (January): 7–10.

Middle East Executive Reports (1985b). "Iran's New Procurement and Distribution Centers: What They Do (and Where They Are)," 8 (January): 7.

Middle East Executive Reports (1985). "New Tender Law" (Oman), 8 (January): 20–21.

Middleton, Martha (1981). "States and Localities Use Model Procurement Code," *ABA Journal* 67 (December): 1608–1609.

Mikesell, John L. (1991). *Fiscal Administration: Analysis and Applications for the Public Sector*, 3rd ed. Pacific Grove, Calif.: Brooks/Cole Publishing Co.

Miller, D. J. and Associates (1989). *The Hillsborough County Disparity Study: A Study and Methodology to Assist the County of Hillsborough in the Establishment of Minority and Women Business Enterprise Goals for the Minority/Women Business Enterprise Program.* Atlanta: D. J. Miller and Associates.

Miller, G. (1981). *Cities for Contract: The Politics of Municipal Incorporation.* Boston: MIT Press.

Miller, Girard (1986). *Investing Public Funds.* Chicago, IL: Government Finance Officers Association.

Miller, John A. (1971). "Validity of a Municipal Contract Award Where the Bid Specifications Call for Both Design and Construction of the Contract Subject Matter," *University of Pittsburgh Law Review* 33 (Winter): 231–242.

Miller, John Perry (1949). *Pricing of Military Procurements.* New Haven, Conn.: Yale University Press.

Miller, John R. (1987). "Doing More with Less: Is Privatization the Answer?," *Ohio CPA Journal* 46 (Autumn): 57–58.

Miller, John R. and Christopher R. Tufts (1988). "Privatization Crossfire: Privatization Is a Means to 'More With Less,' " *National Civic Review* 77 (March–April): 100–111.

Miller, Paul (1988). "PMG Frank Expresses Interest in Worksharing, Private Contracting," *Catalog Age* 5 (June): 18, 66.

Mills, James (1984). "Contract Street Sweeping Is a Viable Alternative," *American City & County* 99 (July): 48–54.

Milne, Andrew (1988). "Constitutional Law: Nonfederal Government Entities May Use Racial Classifications Only to Remedy Prior Government Discrimination" (the Fourth Circuit Review) (case note), *Washington and Lee Law Review* 45 (Spring): 721–734.

Minnesota Law Review (1980). "State Buy-American Laws: Invalidity of State Attempts to Favor American Producers," 64 (January): 389–412.

Mitchell, Constance (1985). "What's Cooking in America's High-Tech Hot Spots?," *Black Enterprise* 16 (June): 257–264.

Mitchell, Jerry C. (1981). "Contract Wastewater Treatment Plants—Pros and Cons," *Water Pollution Control Federation Highlights* (November).

Moe, Ronald C. (1987). "Exploring the Limits of Privatization," *Public Administration Review* 47 (November/December): 453–460.

Molz, Rick (1990). "Privatization in Developing Countries," *Columbia Journal of World Business* 25 (Spring/Summer): 17–24.

Molz, Rick (1989). "Privatization of Government

Enterprise: The Challenge to Management," *Management International Review* (Germany) 29 (Fourth Quarter): 29–44.

Monczka, Robert M. and Robert J. Trent (1991). "Global Sourcing: A Development Approach," *International Journal of Purchasing Materials and Management* 27 (Spring): 2–8.

Monthly Labor Review (1984). "Significant Decisions in Labor Cases," 101 (August): 46–47.

Moore, Stephen (1986). "Rx for Ailing U.S. Mass Transit Policy: A Dose of Competition," *Heritage Backgrounder* 542 (October 29).

Moore, Stephen (1987). "Contracting Out: A Painless Alternative to the Budget Cutter's Knife," in Steve H. Hanke, ed., *Prospects for Privatization*. New York: *Proceedings of the Academy of Political Science* 36 (3): 60–73.

Moore, W. John (1990). "Tribal Imperatives," *National Journal* 22 (June 9): 1396–1401.

Moorhouse, John C., ed. (1986). *Electric Power: Deregulation and the Public Interest*. San Francisco: Pacific Research Institute.

Morgan, David. R. and Robert E. England (1988). "The Two Faces of Privatization," *Public Administration Review* 48 (November/December): 979–987.

Morgan, Tracy A. (1986). "Toward A State Policy on Privatization," *The Privatization Review* 2 (Summer): 38–45.

Morley, Elaine (1989). "Patterns in the Use of Alternative Service Delivery Approaches," *The Municipal Year Book 1989*. Washington, D.C.: International City Management Association: 33–44.

Morlock, Edward K. and Philip A. Viton (1985). "The Comparative Costs of Public and Private Transit in Urban Transit," in Charles A. Lave, ed., *Urban Transit*. Cambridge, Mass.: Ballinger Publishing Company: 233–254.

Morris, Joe and Terri Stone (1986). "Private Choices for Public Parks," *American City & County* 101 (May): 28, 32, 34, 36, 38.

Morrison, David C. (1990). "Two for the Money," *National Journal* 22 (June 2): 1343–1346.

Mrkvicka, Pam (1980). "Labor Law—Executive Legislation in the Federal Procurement System," Case Note, *Washington Law Review* 55 (June): 717–732.

Mulhern, John J. (1991). "Market Research for Federal Contracting Officers: Key to Procurement Reform," *International Journal of Purchasing and Materials Management* 27 (Winter): 23–26.

Mullen, Joan (1985a). "Corrections and the Private Sector," *The Privatization Review* 1 (Fall): 10–19.

Mullen, Joan (1985b). *Corrections and the Private Sector*. Washington, D.C.: National Institute of Justice (May).

Mullen, Joan, K. J. Chaboter, and D. M. Carrow (1985). *The Privatization of Corrections*. Washington, D.C.: National Institute of Justice.

Mund, Vernon A. (1960). "Identical Bid Prices," *The Journal of Political Economy* 68 (April): 150–169.

Murin, William J. (1985). "Contracting as Method of Enhancing Equity in the Delivery of Local Government Services," *Journal of Urban Affairs* 7 (Spring): 1–10.

Murphy, James J. (1982). "Dunning Uncle Sam: The Prompt Payment Act of 1982," *Journal of the Missouri Bar* 38 (October–November): 531–532.

Murray, Sylvester (1985). "Privatization: Myth and Potential," *Urban Resources* 4 (September): 3–5.

Musell, R. Mark (1987). *Contracting Out: Potential for Reducing Federal Costs*. Washington, D.C.: Congress of the United States, Congressional Budget Office.

Mushkin, S. J., ed. (1972). *Public Prices for Public Products*. Washington, D.C.: Urban Institute.

Muzychenko, J. (1987). "Local Governments at Risk: The Crisis in Liability Insurance," in *The Municipal Year Book, 1987*. Washington, D.C.: International City Management Association: 3–7.

NACA (National Animal Control Association) News (1984). "Contracts: Are They For You?" (June/July).

Nachmias, David and Chava Nachmias (1987). *Research Methods in the Social Sciences*, 3rd ed. New York: St. Martin's Press.

Nadler, David M. (1989). "Suspension and Debarment of Government Contractors: The Current Climate," *National Contract Management Journal* 22 (Winter): 9–16.

Nagle, James F. (1982). "Prompt Payment Discounts in Government Contracts," *Public Contract Law Journal* 13 (July): 108–136.

Nagle, James F. (1987). "Financial Inability in Government Contracts," *Public Contract Law Journal* 17 (September): 320–361.

Nankani, Helen B. (1990). "Lessons of Privatization in Developing Countries," *Finance & Development* 27 (March): 43–45.

Napoleon, Vincent J. (1989). "The Government Contractor Defense: Its Implications in the Wake of Boyle v. United Technologies Corporation," *National Contract Management Journal* 23 (Summer): 65–76.

Nash, Ralph C., Jr. (1966). "Risk Allocation in Government Contracts," *George Washington Law Review* 34 (4): 693–718.

Nash, Ralph C. Jr. and John Cibinic (1985). *Administration of Government Contracts.* Washington, D.C.: Government Contracts Program, National Law Center, George Washington University.

Nathans, Leah J. (1990). "What Do Women Want? A Piece of the Muni Business," *Business Week* (Industrial/technology edition) 3145 (February 12): 66.

Nation's Business (1988). "More Contracting Opportunities," 76 (January): 12.

National Academy of Public Administration (1987). *Third-Party Government and the Public Manager: The Changing Forms of Government Action.* Washington, D.C.: NAPA.

National Academy of Public Administration (1989). *Privatization: The Challenge to Public Management.* Washington, D.C.: NAPA.

National Association of Attorneys General (1977). *Government Purchasing and the Antitrust Laws.* The National Association of Attorneys General (May).

National Association of Counties and International City Management Association (1978). "Contracting for Services," *The County Year Book, 1978.* Washington, D.C.: NACO and ICMA.

National Association of Counties Research Foundation (1982). *Interlocal Agreements/Contracts for Local Officials.* Washington, D.C.: NACO Research Foundation.

National Association of County Officials (1968). *The Case for Cooperative or Centralized Purchasing.* Washington, D.C.: NACO.

National Association of Purchasing Agents, Value Techniques Committee (1964). *Standardization Manual: A Book of Principles and Practices for Purchasing Personnel.* New York: National Association of Purchasing Agents.

National Association of State Purchasing Officials (1966). *Standard Specifications Preparation Manual.* Lexington, Ky.: The Council of State Governments.

National Association of State Purchasing Officials, Committee on Research (1977). *Purchasing by the States.* Lexington, Ky.: The Council of State Governments.

National Association of State Purchasing Officials and The Council of State Governments (1990). *How to Do Business with the States: A Guide for Vendors.* Lexington, Ky.: NASPO and The Council of State Governments.

National Center for Policy Analysis (1985). *Privatization in the U.S.: Cities and Counties.* National Center for Policy Analysis, Policy Report No. 116 (June).

National Institute of Governmental Purchasing (1976). *Value Analysis Program Guide.* Falls Church, Va.: NIGP.

National Institute of Governmental Purchasing (1981a). *"Joint Administrative" (Consolidated) Purchasing.* Falls Church, Va.: NIGP.

National Institute of Governmental Purchasing (1981b). *"Joint Bid" Intergovernmental Cooperative Purchasing.* Falls Church, Va.: NIGP.

National Institute of Governmental Purchasing (1982a). "Fall 1981 Survey of County (50,000+) Governments Regarding Contracts with Other Organizations for the Provision of Non-Professional Housekeeping Services," *Annual Procurement Survey, 1982.* Washington, D.C.: NIGP.

National Institute of Governmental Purchasing (1982b). *Report of a Study of Minority Business Participation in State and Local Government.* Falls Church, Va.: NIGP.

National Institute of Governmental Purchasing (1986). *The NIGP Dictionary of Purchasing Terms*, 4th ed. Falls Church, Va.: NIGP.

National Institute of Governmental Purchasing (1989). *Results of the 1989 Procurement Survey.* Falls Church, Va.: NIGP.

National Institute of Justice (1985). *The Privatization of Corrections.* Washington, D.C.: U. S. Justice Department.

National Institute of Justice (1987). *The Privatization of Corrections.* Washington, D.C.: Department of Justice.

National Institute of Municipal Law Officers (1955). *NIMLO Model Purchasing Ordinance.* Arlington, Va.: National Institute of Governmental Purchasing.

National Office for Social Responsibility (n.d.). *The Private Sector in Juvenile Probation.* Alexandria, Va.: National Office for Social Responsibility.

Nelson, Carl A. (1990). *Global Success: International Business Tactics for the 90's.* Blue Ridge Summit, Pa.: Liberty Hall Press, TAB Books.

Nelson, George W. (1987). "Information Needs of Female Entrepreneurs," *Journal of Small Business Management* 25 (July): 38–44.

Nelson, Mark (1990a). "Discrimination: The Untold Story: California Senate Bill 963 Will Produce Hard Facts Needed to Fight Discrimination," *Hispanic Business* 12 (August): 14.

Nelson, Mark (1990b). "Industrial Strength Border Towns," *Hispanic Business* 12 (March): 12–16.

Nelson, Mark (1991). "U.S.–Mexico Trade: The Curtain Is Going up," *Hispanic Business* 13 (March): 18, 20, 22, 24, 26.

Nelson, Mark A. (1988). "Jakarta Modifies Policies on Government Procurement," *East Asian Executive Reports* 10 (June 15): 20.

Nelson, Richard (1987). "Roles of Government in a Mixed Economy," *Journal of Policy Analysis and Management* 6 (Summer): 541–557.

Nelton, Sharon (1984). "A Business of Her Own," *Nation's Business* 72 (November): 70–72.

Nelton, Sharon (1989). "The Age of the Woman Entrepreneur," *Nation's Business* 77 (May): 22–30.

Nero, Christine T. (1989). "Constitutional Law—Legal Windfalls for Government Procurement Contractors," *Wake Forest Law Review* 24 (3): 745–779.

Netzer, Dick (1985). "Taxes," *Setting Municipal Priorities.* New York: Columbia University Press: 76–114.

New York Law Journal (1980). "Justices Affirm Business Help for Minorities," 184 (July 3): 1.

New York Law Journal (1989). "High Court Weakens Affirmative Action: Strikes Virginia Plan To Aid Minority Businesses," 201 (January 24): 1.

Newman, Richard G. (1967). "A Note on Competitive Bidding," *Journal of Purchasing* 3 (May): 69–83.

Nibley, Stuart B. and Sandra Lee Fenske (1988). "Government Progress Payments Can Be Tricky Business—Seeking Reimbursement of Payments to Subcontractors," *National Contract Management Journal* 22 (Summer): 9–23.

Nicholson, J. (1968). *Identical Bids and How to Combat Them.* Washington, D.C.: National Institute of Governmental Purchasing.

Nicholson, J. W., T. J. Nammacaher, and K. L. Smith (1965). *Guide to Governmental Purchasing.* Minneapolis: Lakewood Publications.

Nieman, Lisa Marie (1982). "Constitutional Law—Strictly Scrutinizing Fullilove v. Klutznick: A Proposed Analytical Model for Supreme Court Review of Congressional Legislation" (case note), *North Carolina Law Review* 60 (March): 681–694.

Noble, Barbara Presley (1986). "Women Entrepreneurs: The New Business Owners/A Sense of Self," *Venture* 8 (July): 33–36.

Northern Kentucky Law Review (1989). "In Search of the Definitive Interpretation of the Government Contractor Defense" (case note), 16 (Fall): 603–629.

Norton, Eleanor Holmes and Edward W. Norton (1989). "A Setback for Minority Businesses; Minority Set-Asides and the Court: Was the Croson Decision the End of Affirmative Action?" *Legal Times* 11 (May 1): 31.

Norton, Gerald P. (1989). "The Questionable Constitutionality of the Suspension and Debarment Provisions of the Federal Acquisition Regulations; What Does Due Process Require?" *Public Contract Law Journal* 18 (June): 633–655.

Nymark, Alan B. (1989). "United States/Canadian Post-Free Trade Agreement Relationship," *Economic Development Review* 7 (Fall): 16–18.

O'Bannon, Donna (1977). "Women as Entrepreneurs," *Executive* 4 (1): 36–38.

O'Connor, Brian W. (1991). "More Woes for Black Businesses," *Black Enterprise* 21 (January): 23.

O'Connor, Philip R. and Wayne P. Olson (1990). "Localizing Federal Power Assets: A Path for the Pacific Northwest," *Public Utilities Fortnightly* 125 (February 1): 7–13.

O'Hara, J. Patrick (1990). "Set-Asides: Carrots Speak Louder Than Words: New Congressional Hispanic Aerospace Awards Elicit an 'Amazing Response,' " *Hispanic Business* 12 (November): 12–13.

O'Hare, William (1989). "In the Black," *American Demographics* 11 (November): 25–26, 28–29.

O'Hare, William and Robert Suggs (1986). "Embattled Black Businesses," *American Demographics* 8 (April): 26–29, 48–49.

O'Neal, Donna J. (1979). "Capturing Defense Dollars," *Black Enterprise* 9 (March): 43–48.

O'Neill, Hugh (1990). "The Role of the States in Trade Development," in Frank J. Macchiarola, ed., *International Trade: The Changing Role of the United States*. New York: The Academy of Political Science: 181–189.

Oakerson, R. (1987). "Local Public Economies: Provision, Production, and Governance," *Intergovernmental Perspective* 13 (Summer–Fall): 20–25.

Office of Federal Procurement Policy (1980). *Proposal for a Uniform Procurement System*. Washington, D.C.: Office of Federal Procurement Policy.

Office of the United States Trade Representative (1990a). *1990 National Trade Estimate Report on Foreign Trade Barriers*. Washington, D.C.: U.S. Government Printing Office.

Office of the United States Trade Representative (1990b). *1990 Trade Policy Agenda and 1989 Annual Report of the President of the United States on the Trade Agreement Program*. Washington, D.C.: U.S. Government Printing Office.

Officer, Lawrence H. (1990). "The International Monetary Fund," in Frank J. Macchiarola, ed., *International Trade: The Changing Role of the United States*. New York: The Academy of Political Science: 28–36.

Ollerman, C. M. (1989). "Recent Developments—Constitutional Law: Equal Protection and Affirmative Action in Local Government Contracting—*City of Richmond v. J. A. Croson Co.*," *Harvard Journal of Law and Public Policy* 12: 1069–1081.

Olson, James C. (1982). "Federal Limitations on State 'Buy America' Laws," *Columbia Journal of Transnational Law* 21 (Winter): 177–210.

Orlando Sentinel (1990). "Minority Programs Face Setback: Study: Red Tape Hinders Participation," (April 21): C–1, C–6.

Orlans, H. ed. (1980). *Nonprofit Organizations, A Government Management Tool*. New York: Praeger.

Orski, C. Kenneth (1988). "New Solutions to Old Problems in Public Transportation," in John C. Weicher, ed., *Private Innovations in Public Transit*. Washington, D.C.: American Enterprise Institute for Public Policy Research: 3–10.

Ostry, Sylvia (1990). "Governments and Corporations in a Shrinking World: Trade and Innovation Policies in the United States, Europe and Japan," *Columbia Journal of World Business* 25 (Spring/Summer): 10–16.

Otterbourg, Susan D. and Michael Timpane (1986). "Partnerships and Schools," in Perry Davis, ed., *Public-Private Partnerships: Improving Urban Life*. New York: The Academy of Political Science: 60–73.

Owens, Major R. (1987). "Federal Contracting: Minority Progress Halted by Majority Greed," *Business & Society Review* 60 (Winter): 41–44.

Owens, Raymond L. (1970). "A Primer of Procurement by Formal Advertising and Relief from Mistakes in Bids," *New York State Bar Journal* 42 (August): 428–435.

Pack, Janet Rothenberg (1987). "Privatization of Public Sector Services in Theory and Practice," *Journal of Policy Analysis and Management* 6 (Summer): 523–540.

Page, Harry Roberts (1987). *Public Purchasing and Materials Management*. Lexington, Mass.: Lexington Books.

Palmer, Tom G. (1983). "Infrastructure: Public or Private?" *Policy Report* 5 (May): 1, 3–5.

Palumbo, Dennis J. (1986). "Privatization and Corrections Policy," *Policy Studies Review* 5 (3): 598–605.

Parker, Jeffrey A. (1988). "Private Financing of Mass Transit," in John C. Weicher, ed., *Private Innovations in Public Transit*. Washington, D.C.: American Enterprise Institute for Public Policy Research: 29–37.

Parker, Myles A. (1989). "Affirmative Action Minority Set-Asides: Future Justification for Implementation at the State and/or Local Government Level," *Mississippi Law Journal* 59 (Spring): 189–208.

Parker, Richard (1990). "All Over the Map," *Hispanic Business* 12 (March): 40–44.

Parry, Edward F. (1968). "Changes Clause in Incentive Contracting," *Federal Bar Journal* 28 (Summer): 256–270.

Parvin, Cordell M. (1984). "Civil Remedies," *Identifying and Prosecuting Fraud and Abuse in State and Local Contracting.* Chicago: American Bar Association, 81–86.

Paschal, Anthony H. (1981). "User Charges, Contracting Out, and Privatization in an Era of Fiscal Retrenchment," *Urban Interest* 3 (Spring): 6–12.

Paschal, Anthony H. and Mark Menchik (1979). *Fiscal Containment: Who Gains? Who Loses?* Santa Monica, Calif.: Rand.

Pasco, Monte (1982). "Libertarian Longing, Privatization and Federalism," *State Government* 55 (4): 111–114.

Pashigan, Peter B. (1976). "Consequences and Causes of Public Ownership of Urban Transit Facilities," *Journal of Political Economy* 84 (December): 1239–1260.

Pasley, Robert S. (1957). "The Non-Discrimination Clause in Government Contracts," *Virginia Law Review* 43 (October): 837–871.

Patten, Thomas L. and Edward J. Shapiro (1984a). "Prosecutions for Fraud and False Pretenses," *Identifying and Prosecuting Fraud and Abuse in State and Local Contracting.* Chicago: American Bar Association: 31–33.

Patten, Thomas L. and Edward J. Shapiro (1984b). "Removal of Government Officials for Misconduct," *Identifying and Prosecuting Fraud and Abuse in State and Local Contracting.* Chicago: American Bar Association: 69–74.

Patterson, Margaret K. (1988). "The New NAF Contracting Regulation" (nonappropriated fund), *Army Lawyer* 1988 (March): 12–16.

Pattie, Kenton H. (1989). "New Prompt Pay Law Relieves Credit Headaches," *Business Credit* 91 (September): 28–30.

Patton, Robert J., Jr. (1967). "Changed Conditions as Misrepresentation in Government Construction Contracts," *George Washington Law Review* 35 (June): 978–987.

Paul, Amy Cohen (1988). "Private Funds: Public Projects," *Baseline Data Report* 20 (March/April), Washington, D.C.: International City Management Association.

Pavlovitz, Gregory John (1984). "United States and Japanese Government Procurement: The Impact on Trade Relations," *Washington University Law Quarterly* 62 (Spring): 127–164.

Peagam, Norman (1990). "Costa Rica: The Banks Sharpen Up," *Euromoney* (March): 24–28.

Peck, Merton J. and Frederic M. Scherer (1962). *The Weapons Acquisition Process.* Boston: Harvard Business School Press.

Peckar, Robert S. (1983). "ABA Model Procurement Code Advances in New Jersey," *Public Contract Newsletter* 18 (Winter): 3–4.

Peirce, Neal R. (1989). "Looking Beyond Set-Asides for Minority Business," *St. Petersburg Times* (February 19).

Pelton, Eric J. (1986). "Privatization of the Public Sector: A Look at Which Labor Laws Should Apply to Private Firms Contracted to Perform Public Services," *Detroit College of Law Review* 1986 (Fall): 805–823.

Pennsylvania Law Journal-Reporter (1988). "Judge Orders Conditional OK of Contractor for Highway Job" (Glasgow, Inc.–Nyleve Co., Pennsylvania), 11 (January 4): 9.

Perlman, Ellen (1989). "Court Rewrites Book on Set-Asides," *City & State* (January 30): 1, 21.

Perlman, Ellen (1990). "Minority Set-Aside Programs Back on Track," *City & State* (November 5): 4.

Perlman, Matthew (1968). "State and Local Contracts Finances with Federal Assistance," *Public Contract Law Journal* 2 (October): 20–26.

Perry, James and Hal Rainey (1988). "The Public-Private Distinction in Organization Theory," *Academy of Management Review* 13 (April): 182–201.

Perry, James L. and Timlynn T. Babitsky (1986). "Comparative Performance in Urban Bus Transit: Assessing Privatization Strategies," *Public Administration Review* 46 (January/February): 57–66.

Peters, W. A. and J. 'In't Veld (1989). "The Use of Alternate Contract Types in Europe as Protection Against Overruns," *National Contract Management Journal* 23 (Summer): 23–35.

Peterson, Deborah J. (1980). "The Trade Agreements Act of 1979: The Agreement on Government Procurement," *Journal of International Law and Economics* 14 (Winter): 321–348.

Peterson, George E. (1984). "Financing the Nation's Infrastructure Requirements," in Royce Hanson, ed., *Perspectives on Urban Infrastructure*. Washington, D.C.: National Academy Press.

Petit, C. L. (1985). "Key Points in NSWMA's New Model Contract," *Waste Age* (October).

Pettit, Walter F. and G. K. Gleason (1971). "Liquidated Damages in Government Contracts: A Comment on Defenses," *Southwestern Law Journal* 25 (May): 264.

Pettit, Walter F. and Allan J. Joseph (1968). "Government's Obligation to Disclose Under the Truth in Negotiations Act," *William and Mary Law Review* 10 (Fall): 18–38.

Phillips, Ragan T. (1990). "The Future of Competitive Power Generation," *Public Utilities Fortnightly* 125 (March 15): 13–16.

Pier, William J., Robert B. Vernon, and John H. Wicks (1974). "An Efficiency Comparison of Government and Private Production," *National Tax Journal* 27 (December): 653–656.

Pirie, Madsen (1985). *Dismantling the State: The Theory and Practice of Privatization*. Dallas: The National Center for Policy Analysis.

Pitts, David (1989). "To Be Young, British, and Black," *Black Enterprise* 20 (December): 86–98.

Pittsburgh Law Review (1965). "The Necessity of Competitive Bidding in Municipal Contracts," Student Note, 27 (October): 117.

Platt, S. F. (1988). "Defense Business Needs Small Business," *Nation's Business* 76 (July): 9.

Platt, T., K. Barnes, and B. Bishop (1983). *Government Not for Profit: The Case Against Contracting Out*. San Francisco: Institute for the Study of Labor and Economic Crises.

Pomeranz, Morton (1982). "Toward a New International Order in Government Procurement," *Public Contract Law Journal* 12 (March): 129–161.

Pontz, Robert W. (1988). "Antitrust Law: Persons Under the Sherman Act" (The Fourth Circuit Review), Case Note, *Washington and Lee Law Review* 45 (Spring): 679–689.

Poole, Isaiah J. (1980). "If Acronyms Could Cure . . . ," *Black Enterprise* 10 (June): 101–108.

Poole, Isaiah J. (1981). "Negotiating the 8A Maze," *Black Enterprise* 11 (July): 39–42.

Poole, Robert W., Jr. (1979). "Leave the Driving to . . . the Private Sector," *Fiscal Watchdog* 28 (January): 1–3.

Poole, Robert W., Jr. (1980). *Cutting Back City Hall*. New York: Universe Books.

Poole, Robert W., Jr. (1981). "Why Hospitals Go Private," *Fiscal Watchdog* 53 (March): 1–4.

Poole, Robert W., Jr. (1982a). "Air Traffic Control: The Private Sector Option," *Heritage Backgrounder* 216 (October).

Poole, Robert W., Jr. (1982b). "Making Bridges Self Supporting," *Fiscal Watchdog* 65 (March): 1–4.

Poole, Robert W., Jr. (1983a). "Airports Take off Under Contracting," *Fiscal Watchdog* 82 (August): 1–4.

Poole, Robert W., Jr. (1983b). "Municipal Services: The Privatization Option," *Heritage Backgrounder* 238 (January).

Poole, Robert W., Jr. (1984a). "Cleaning up Through Contracting Out," *Fiscal Watchdog* 87 (January): 1–4.

Poole, Robert W., Jr. (1984b). "Privatization of Transportation Infrastructure," *Transportation Quarterly* 38 (April): 203.

Poole, Robert W., Jr. (1984c). "Transit Systems," in R. Q. Armington and William D. Ellis, eds., *This Way Up*. Chicago: Regnery Gateway: 20–47.

Poole, Robert W., Jr. (1984d). "Why the Trend Toward Privatization?" *The International Fire Chief* 50 (February): 12–15.

Poole, Robert W., Jr. (1985a). *Privatizing Washington's Airports: Issue Analysis*. Washington, D.C.: Citizens for a Sound Economy.

Poole, Robert W., Jr. (1985b). *Unnatural Monopolies: The Case for Deregulating Public Utilities*. Lexington, Mass.: Lexington Books.

Poole, Robert W., Jr. (1986). "Privatizing the Air Traffic Control System," *Reason Foundation Issue Paper*, part of the Federal Privatization Project. Santa Monica, Calif.: Reason Foundation (November 14).

Poole, Robert W., Jr. (1987). "Privatizing City Services—The Efficiencies of the Private Sector," *Vital Speeches* 53 (July 15): 588–590.

Poole, Robert W. and Philip E. Fixler, Jr. (1987). "Privatization of Public-Sector Services in Practice: Experience and Potential," *Journal of Policy Analysis and Management* 6 (Summer): 612–624.

Poole, Robert W., Jr., ed. (1982). *Instead of*

Regulation: Alternatives to Federal Regulatory Agencies. Lexington, Mass.: Lexington Books.

Porter, David D. and Rosalyn Gist Porter (1983). "The Changing Profile of Charlotte," *Black Enterprise* 13 (June): 178–186.

Posner, Alan R. (1984). *State Government Export Promotion: An Exporter's Guide.* Westport, CT: Quorum Books.

Post, Steven (1986). "The Freedom of Information Act and the Commercial Activities Program," *Army Lawyer* 1986 (May): 9–15.

Powers, Linda F. and Frederick T. Elliott (1991). "EC 92: A Mixed Scorecard for U.S. Service Industries," *Business America* 112 (February 25): 16–17.

Premo, Jerome C. (1988). "Privatization in Practice: The Case of New Jersey Transit," in John C. Weicher, ed., *Private Innovations in Public Transit.* Washington, D.C.: American Enterprise Institute for Public Policy Research: 16–22.

Prescott, Eileen (1989). "How a One-Woman Show Becomes a Big-Bucks Business," *Working Woman* 14 (March): 51–54.

President, The (1990). *The State of Small Business 1990: A Report of the President.* Washington, D.C.: U.S. Government Printing Office.

President's Task Force on Private Sector Initiatives (1984). *Corporate Community Involvement.* New York: President's Task Force on Private Sector Initiatives (distributed by Citizens Forum on Self-Government/National Municipal League).

Presidential Advisory Committee on Small and Minority Business Ownership (annual). *Annual Report.* Washington, D.C.: Presidential Advisory Committee on Small and Minority Business Ownership.

Prestowitz, Clyde V., Jr., Alan Tonel, and Robert W. Jerome (1991). "The Last Gasp of GATTism," *Harvard Business Review* (March–April): 130–138.

Prevost, Richard J. (1985). "Contract Modification vs. New Procurement: An Analysis of General Accounting Office Decisions," *Public Contract Law Journal* 15 (July): 453–462.

Privatization (1986a). "Privatization in Metropolitan Toronto: Snow Removal," 122 (December 12): 1–9.

Privatization (1986b). "Trying a New Way: Fairfield, Calif. Uses Private Employees to Make

Firefighting Economics More Efficient," 117 (July 7): 2–5.

Privatization (1987a). "Contractor Provides Correction Services to State and Federal Agencies," 129 (July 7): 2–3.

Privatization (1987b). "First 'Sludge Privatization' Agreement Reached," 132 (November): 1–2.

Privatization (1987c). "Handling Children and Youth Services Through Contracting," (October): 6–7.

Privatization (1987d). "Jails, Corporate Style," (September 7): 7–8.

Privatization (1987e). "Privatization Abroad: It's Different from America in the Decade of Privatization," (March 21): 1–8.

Privatization (1987f). "Privatization Jolts London Bus Transit: Public Provider Pushed by Competition," (March 7): 1–8.

Privatization (1987g). "Problematic Labor Relations in Privatization," (September 7): 7–10.

Privatization (1987h). "Pros and Cons of Prison Contracting," (June 21): 7–8.

Privatization (1987i). "Some States Lock in Private Prisons, Opponents Worry: Is It Legal?" (April 7): 1–6.

Privatization (1987j). Supporters, Opponents Locked Into Private Prison Debate," (June 7): 17.

Privatization (1987k). "Two Successful Texas Water Projects: Both Flow from Unique Privatization System," (February 7): 1–2.

Privatization Council, The (1986). *Compendium of Privatization Laws.* New York: The Privatization Council (April).

The Privatization Report (1986). "Public Safety Can Be Privately Provided," 5 (May).

Project SHARE (1982). *New Approaches to Meeting Human Service Needs.* Rockville, Md.: Project SHARE.

Pryke, R. (1982). "The Comparative Performance of Public and Private Enterprise," *Fiscal Studies* 3 (No. 2): 68–81.

Public Contract Law Journal (1976). "Symposium: The Model Procurement Code," 8 (May): 1–48.

Public Finance and Accountancy (1991). "Auditing Small Building Works Contracts," (March 15): 14, 16.

Public Lands Council (1983). *Privatizing the Public Lands: Issues Involved in Transferring Fed-*

eral Lands to Private Owners. (n.p.): Public Lands Council, September 20.

Purchasing (1965). "Pre-Pricing Strengthens the Buyer's Hand," 56 (October 7): 70–73.

Purchasing (1967). "Purchasing and Vendor Evaluation," 58 (February 9): 50–52.

Puryear, Alvin N. and Charles A. West (1973). *Black Enterprise, Inc.: Case Studies of a New Experiment in Black Business Development*. Garden City, NY: Anchor Press.

Quinn, K. and M. Olstein (1985). "Privatization: Public/Private Partnerships Provide Essential Services," in Barbara Weiss, ed., *Financing a Commonwealth*. Washington, D.C." Government Finance Officers Association.

Rainey, Hal G., Robert W. Backoff, and Charles H. Levine (1976). "Comparing Public and Private Organizations," *Public Administration Review* 36 (March/April): 233–244.

Ramsey, James B. (1983). "Selling the New York Subways," *National Review* 35 (February 4): 112–116.

Ramsey, James B. (1987). "Selling the New York City Subway: Wild-Eyed Radicalism or the Only Feasible Solution?" in Steve H. Hanke, ed., *Prospects for Privatization*. New York: *Proceedings of the Academy of Political Science* 36 (3): 93–103.

Rans, Lynn (1987). "Starting a Business: The Government Connections," *Business Forum* 12 (Fall): 22–25.

Ransick, Scott E. (1989). "Adverse Impact of the Federal Bankruptcy Law on the Government's Rights in Relation to the Contractor in Default," *Military Law Review* 124 (Spring): 65–110.

Rappaport, Alfred (1990). "The Staying Power of the Public Corporation," *Harvard Business Review* 68 (January/February): 96–104.

Rappleye, Willard C., Jr. (1990). "John S. Lehman, Jr.: Peace Dividend? Or Assessment?" *Financier* 14 (February): 22–26.

Rasnic, Carol D. (1989). "City of Richmond v. J. A. Croson Co.: What Does It Portend for Affirmative Action?" *Creighton Law Review* 23 (Fall): 19–43.

Raspberry, William (1989). "Discrimination Ignored," *The Tampa Tribune* (February 2).

Raubitschek, John H. (1986). "Recent Developments in Government Patent and Data Policy," *Army Lawyer* 1986 (March): 57–60.

Raysman, Richard and Peter Brown (1986). "Government Contracts" (federal regulations governing computer acquisitions), *New York Law Journal* 195 (May 14): 1.

Reagan, Ronald (1989). *The State of Small Business: A Report of the President*. Washington, D.C.: Government Printing Office.

Reason (1981). "Selling the Subways in New York: Wild-Eyed Radicalism or the Only Feasible Solution?" (November).

Reck, Dickson (1954). *Government Purchasing and Competition*. Berkeley, Calif.: University of California Press.

Rehfuss, John A. (1989). *Contracting Out in Government: A Guide to Working with Outside Contractors to Supply Public Services*. San Francisco: Jossey-Bass Publishers.

Rehfuss, John (1990). "Contracting Out and Accountability in State and Local Governments— The Importance of Contract Monitoring," *State and Local Government Review* 22 (Winter): 44–48.

Reichard, Robert S. (1991). "Profile of a Purchasing Pro: A Look at Yourself At The Start of the 1990s," *Purchasing* 110 (March 21): 30–39.

Reinhardt, William G. (1988). "Metcalf and Eddy Builds Privatization Empire," *ENR* 22 (July 21): 24–26.

Reinhardt, William G. (1990). "Construction 2000: All Roads Lead to Privatization," *ENR* 224 (March 15): 28–30.

Renner, Tari (1989). "Trends and Issues in the Use of Intergovernmental Agreements and Privatization in Local Government," *Baseline Data Report* 21 (November/December): 1–15.

Reuben, Richard C. (1989a). "Justices Reject Key Affirmative Action Program; 'Set-Aside' Plans as Remedies Must Focus on Specifics; Conservative Win," *The Los Angeles Daily Journal* 102 (January 24): 1.

Reuben, Richard C. (1989b). "U.S. High Court Sharpens Focus on 'Set-Asides'; 'Croson' Doctrine," *The Los Angeles Daily Journal* 102 (March 7): 1.

Reynolds, L. (1988). "Small Business Grants Spur Innovation," *Management Review* 77 (November): 23–24.

Reynolds, Larry (1989). "When Government Says 'The Check's in the Mail,' " *Management Review* 78 (June): 53–54.

Rice, Mitchell F. (1991). "Government Set-

Asides, Minority Business Enterprises, and the Supreme Court," *Public Administration Review* 51 (March/April): 114–122.

Richardson, Karen L. (1982). "The Application of the Services Contract Act to ADP Service Contracts: A Classic Case in Overregulation," *Public Contract Newsletter* 17 (January): 3–9.

Rickover, Hyman G. (1982). "The Scandals of Military Contracting," *Business and Society Review* 41 (Spring): 48–52.

Riemer, David R. (1990). "Milwaukee's Successful Effort to Control Employee Health Care Costs," *Government Finance Review* 6 (February): 15–17.

Riga, Joseph F. (1989). "Recent Council Directives and Commission Proposals Affecting Public Procurement in the European Communities (Third annual European law issue), *Boston College International and Comparative Law Review* 12 (Summer): 387–421.

Rigg, John and Graeme Leach (1990). "After Privatization—Economic Ideas and the Business Environment," *Long Range Planning* (UK) 23 (February): 151–156.

Riggs, Carol R. (1987). "The Blackfeet Tribe Writes a Success Story," *D&B Reports* 35 (July/August): 22–25.

Ringo, Philip J. (1988). "Privatization in the Transit Industry," in John C. Weicher, ed., *Private Innovations in Public Transit*. Washington, D.C.: American Enterprise Institute for Public Policy Research: 62–70.

Ritenburg, Peter J. (1988). "Task Order Contracts: Popular, but Are They Legal?" *National Contract Management Journal* 22 (Summer): 33–45.

Robbins, Ira P. (1988). "The Impact of the Delegation Doctrine on Prison Privatization," *UCLA Law Review* 35 (June): 911–952.

Robbins, Wayne Lindsey, Jr. (1989). "The Government Contract Defense After Boyle v. United Technologies Corporation," *Baylor Law Review* 41 (Spring): 291–315.

Roberts, Charley (1989). "Black Lawyers Envision Victory Beyond 'Croson'; Invitation to Outrage" (reverse discrimination challenge to set-aside program for minority-owned subcontractors), *The Los Angeles Daily Journal* 102 (March 20): 1.

Roberts, Michael A. (1977). "Affirmative Action Without Reverse Discrimination," *EEO Today* 4 (Autumn): 193–199.

Roberts, S. (1985). "Making It on Your Own," *Black Enterprise* 15 (June): 201–210.

Robson, Britt (1986). "When Private Companies Do Public Work," *Black Enterprise* 16 (February): 140–144.

Rockefeller, David (1986). "Ingredients for Successful Partnerships: The New York City Case," in Perry Davis, ed., *Public-Private Partnerships: Improving Urban Life*. New York: The Academy of Political Science: 122–126.

Roehm, Harper S., Joseph F. Castellano, and David A. Karns (1989). "Contracting Services to the Private Sector: A Survey of Management Practices," *Government Finance Review* 5 (February): 21–25, 52.

Rogers, Jay (1988). "Trends in Transit Financing," in John C. Weicher, ed., *Private Innovations in Public Transit*. Washington, D.C.: American Enterprise Institute for Public Policy Research: 38–46.

Rollins, Timothy J. (1989). "Flawed GSBCA Decision Departs from GAO Precedent in Defining Discussions" (General Services Board of Contract Appeals), *Army Lawyer* 1989 (April): 52–54.

Rosen, Michael (1985). "Constitutionality of State and Local Authority to Implement Minority Business Enterprise Set-Aside Upheld" (case note), *Washington University Journal of Urban and Contemporary Law* 29 (Winter): 247–261.

Rosenbloom, Sandi (1972). "Taxis and Jitneys: The Case for Deregulation," *Reason* 3 (February): 4–17.

Rosenfield, Michel (1989). "Decoding 'Richmond': Affirmative Action and the Elusive Meaning of Constitutional Equality," *Michigan Law Review* 87: 1729–1794.

Ross, Irwin (1979). "The Puny Payoff from Affirmative Action in Small Business," *Fortune* 100 (September 10): 98–108.

Roth, Gabriel (1982). *Private Road Ahead*. London: Adam Smith Institute.

Roth, Gabriel (1987a). "Airport Privatization," in Steve H. Hanke, ed., *Prospects for Privatization*. New York: *Proceedings of the Academy of Political Science* 36 (3): 74–82.

Roth, Gabriel (1987b). *The Private Provision of Public Services in Developing Countries.* New York: Oxford University Press for the World Bank.

Roth, Gabriel (1988). "Private Sector Roles in Urban Public Transport," in John C. Weicher, ed., *Private Innovations in Public Transit.* Washington, D.C.: American Enterprise Institute for Public Policy Research: 109–122.

Roth, Gabriel and Anthony Shepard (1984). *Wheels Within Cities: Private Alternatives to Public Transport.* London: The Adam Smith Institute.

Roth, Gabriel and G. G. Wayne (1982). *Free Enterprise Urban Transportation.* New Brunswick, N.J.: Transaction Books for Council for International Urban Liaison.

Rothlein, Julius and Steven L. Schooner (1983). "The Trade Agreements Act: Installation Procurement and International Government Acquisition Law," *Army Lawyer* 1983 (September): 1–13.

Rowe, Samuel (1990). "The Advantages of Venture Capital Investing," *Black Enterprise* 20 (February): 186–190.

Rozek, Richard P. (1989). "Competitive Bidding in Electricity Markets: A Survey," *Energy Journal* 10 (October): 117–138.

Rudolf, Harold W. (1952). "Performance Bond Servicing of Government Contracts," *Insurance Counsel Journal* 19 (April): 171–177.

Runge, Carlisle Ford (1983). "The Fallacy of 'Privatization'," *The Journal of Contemporary Studies* 7 (Winter): 3–17.

Rushford, Greg (1989). "Staking Their Claim: As Budding Plaintiffs Bar Circles, Defense Contractors Fight Back," *Legal Times* 12 (July 10): 1.

Ryser, Jeffrey (1988). "Getting South America's #!*% Phones to Work: Major Moves to Privatize Scrambled State-Owned Phone Systems," *Business Week* 3047 (April 18): 44.

Saba, Joseph P. (1989). "Iraqi Agents Now Permitted for Government Contracts," *Middle East Executive Reports* 12 (June): 8, 15.

Sabian, Margery (1981). "Impermissible Reverse Discrimination v. Allowable Affirmative Action: The Supreme Court Upholds Racial Classifications," *John Marshall Law Review* 14 (Spring): 4491–4518.

Sabir, Q. (1990). "Affirmative Action Watch," *Black Enterprise* (October): 24.

Sachs, Jeffrey (1990). "Eastern Europe's Economies: What Is to Be Done?" *Economist* (UK) 314 (January 13): 21–26.

Sakoh, Katsuro (1986). *Privatizing State-Owned Enterprises: A Japanese Case Study.* Washington: Heritage Foundation Asian Studies Center.

Salamon, Lester (1981). "Rethinking Public Management: Third-Party Government and the Changing Forms of Government Action," *Public Policy* 12 (Summer): 255–275.

Salamon, Lester (1986). "The Non-Profit Sector in an Era of Retrenchment," *Journal of Public Policy* 6 (No. 11): 1–19.

Salamon, Lester (1989). "The Changing Tools of Government Action," in Lester Salamon, ed., *Beyond Privatization.* Washington, D.C.: The Urban Institute: 7–13.

Salamon, Lester, ed. (1989). *Beyond Privatization.* Washington, D.C.: The Urban Institute.

Sammet, George, Jr., and David E. Green (1990). *Defense Acquisition Management.* Boca Raton: Florida Atlantic University Press.

Sample, Virlindia Albritton (1985). "The Small and Minority Business Assistance Act of 1985: A Unified Approach to Florida Business," *Florida State University Law Review* 13 (Fall): 681–703.

Sanderson, Susan Walsh and Robert H. Hayes (1990). "Mexico—Opening Ahead of Eastern Europe," *Harvard Business Review* (September–October): 32–34, 38, 40–41.

Sandler, Neil (1988). "Israel's Big Inventory Sale," *Business Week* (August 15): 58.

Sandoval, Rodolpho (1990). "An Analysis of the New Legal Model for Establishing Set-Aside Programs for Minority Business Enterprise: The Case of City of Richmond v. J. A. Croson Co." (case note), *Gonzaga Law Review* 25 (January): 141–155.

Sappington, David and Joseph Stiglitz (1987). "Privatization, Information, and Incentives," *Journal of Policy Analysis and Management* 6 (Summer): 567–582.

Saunders, Mary (1991). "EC Testing and Certification Procedures: How Will They Work?," *Business America* 112 (February 25): 27–28.

Savas, E. S. (1977a). "An Empirical Study of Competition in Municipal Service Delivery,"

Public Administration Review 37 (6): 714–717.

Savas, E. S. (1977b). *The Organization and Efficiency of Service Delivery: Solid Waste Collection.* Lexington, Mass.: Lexington Books.

Savas, E. S. (1979). "Public v. Private Refuse Collection: A Critical Review of the Evidence," *Journal of Urban Analysis* 6: 1–13.

Savas, E. S. (1981). "Intracity Competition Between Public and Private Service Delivery," *Public Administration Review* 41 (January/February): 46–52.

Savas, E. S. (1982). *Privatizing the Public Sector: How To Shrink Government.* Chatham, N.J.: Chatham House.

Savas, E. S. (1987). *Privatization: The Key to Better Government.* Chatham, N.J.: Chatham House.

Scadron, Michael (1989). "The New Government Contractor Defense: Will It Insulate Asbestos Manufacturers From Liability for the Harm Caused by Their Insulation Products?" *Idaho Law Review* 25 (Spring): 375–398.

Schaal, Steven D. (1989). "The End of State and Local Set-Aside Plans, as We Know Them" (case note), *Creighton Law Review* 23 (Fall): 129–158.

Scherer, Douglas D. (1990). "Affirmative Action Doctrine and the Conflicting Messages of Croson," *University of Kansas Law Review* 38 (Winter): 281–341.

Scherer, Frederic M. (1964). *The Weapons Acquisition Process: Economic Incentives.* Boston: Harvard Business School Press.

Schlesinger, Mark, Robert A. Dorwart, and Richard T. Pulice (1986/87). "Competitive Bidding and State Purchase of Services: The Case of Mental Health Care in Massachusetts," *Journal of Policy Analysis and Management* 8 (Winter): 245–259.

Schneider, William (1990a). "The New Games of International Power," *National Journal* 22 (June 2): 1374.

Schneider, William (1990b). "Communism's Death: Swift or Slow?" *National Journal* 22 (June 23): 1574.

Schnitzer, Paul and Melvin Rishe (1982a). "A Reasoned Proposal to Reform the Federal Procurement System," *The National Law Journal* 4 (January 11): 42.

Schnitzer, Paul and Melvin Rishe (1982b). "The New 'White Book' Offers Modest Changes in Procurement," *The National Law Journal* 4 (July 12): 18.

Schuerger, William J. (1983). "Antitrust" (Fifth Circuit Survey: July 1981), *Texas Tech Law Review* 14 (February): 83–98.

Schulman, Martha A. (1982). "Alternative Approaches for Delivering Public Services," *Urban Data Service Report* 14 (October): 1–17.

Schussheim, Morton J. (1984). *Selling Public Housing to Tenants: How Feasible?* Washington, D.C.: Library of Congress, Congressional Research Service, December 14.

Schwab, Susan C. (1990). "Building a National Export Development Alliance," *Intergovernmental Perspective* 16 (Spring): 18–20.

Schwartz, Joe (1988). "Who's the Boss?" *American Demographics* 10 (April): 38–41.

Schwartz, Joe and Thomas Exter (1989). "All Our Children: Diverse Destiny," *American Demographics* 11 (May): 35–37.

Schwieterman, Joseph P. (1986). "Efficiency in Mass Transit: An Inquiry into the Effects of Regulation," in John C. Weicher, ed., *Private Innovations in Public Transit.* Washington, D.C.: American Enterprise Institute for Public Policy Research: 82–88.

Scott, Carole E. (1986). "Why More Women Are Becoming Entrepreneurs," *Journal of Small Business Management* 24 (October): 37–44.

Scott, Jill B. (1990). "Will the Supreme Court Continue to Put Aside Local Government Set-Asides as Unconstitutional? The Search for an Answer" (case note), *Baylor Law Review* 42 (Winter): 199–229.

Scott, Matthew S. (1989). "Doing Business on the Home Front," *Black Enterprise* 19 (April): 68–70.

Scott, Matthew S. (1991). "Will Commission Report on Minority Business Make A Difference?" *Black Enterprise* 21 (June): 102.

Scullard, Richard (1989). "Productivity in Local Government," *Management Services* (UK) 33 (January): 38–41.

Seader, D. (1986). "Privatization and America's Cities," *Public Management* 52 (12): 6–7.

Secrest, John R. and Scott R. Torpey (1988). "Government Contractor Defense—Absolute Immunity for the Product Maker," *American Journal of Trial Advocacy* 12 (Summer): 1–18.

Secrest, John R. and Scott R. Torpey (1989a).

"Government Contractor Defense: Absolute Immunity for the Product Maker," *Trial Lawyer's Guide* 32 (Winter): 377–404.

Secrest, John R. and Scott R. Torpey (1989b). "The Government Contractor Defense: Immunity for the Product Maker," *For the Defense* 31 (April): 14–21.

Secrest, John R. and Scott R. Torpey (1989c). "U.S. Supreme Court Adopts and Expands the Government Contractor Defense," *Michigan Bar Journal* 68 (February): 132.

Sedwick, John A. and staff of Envirotech (1984). "Contract Services for Wastewater Treatment," in R. Q. Armington and William D. Ellis, eds., *This Way Up*. Chicago: Regnery Gateway: 124–148.

Seguiti, Maria Laura and Bernard T. Pitsvada (1988). "Comparative Reforms in the Provision of Public Goods in the U.S. and Western European Democracies," *Government Accountants Journal* 37 (Spring): 11–24.

Seidman, Paul J. (1985). "An Overview of Small and Disadvantaged Business Contracting," *National Contract Management Journal* 19 (Summer): 5–19.

Seifert, Timothy D. (1989). "Boyle v. United Technologies Corporation: The Government Contractor Defense," *Saint Louis University Public Law Review* 8 (Spring): 189–206.

Selig, Joel (1990). "Affirmative Action in Employment After 'Croson' and 'Martin': The Legacy Remains Intact," *Temple Law Review* 63: 1–29.

Semmens, John (1985). "Highways: Public Problems, Private Solutions," *Freeman* 35 (March): 172–181.

Sentell, R. Perry, Jr. (1969). "Local Governments and Contracts That Bind," *Georgia Law Review* 3 (Spring): 546–577.

Sexton, Donald L. (1989a). "Growth Decisions and Growth Patterns of Women-Owned Enterprises," in Oliver Hagan, Carol Rivchun, and Donald Sexton, eds., *Women-Owned Businesses*. New York: Praeger: 135–150.

Sexton, Donald L. (1989b). "Research on Women-Owned Businesses: Current Status and Future Direction," in Oliver Hagan, Carol Rivchun, and Donald Sexton, eds., *Women-Owned Businesses*. New York: Praeger: 183–194.

Sharkansy, Ira (1980). "Policymaking and Service Delivery on the Margins of Government: The Case of Contractors," *Public Administration Review* 40 (2): 116–124.

Shea, Thomas E. (1980). "An Introduction to Federal Government Contracts," *Colorado Lawyer* 9 (March): 470–481.

Shedd, Joel P. (1967). "Resolving Ambiguities in Interpretation of Government Contracts," *George Washington Law Review* 36 (October): 1–22.

Shedd, Joel P. (1972). "Principles and Authority of Contracting Officers in Administration of Government Contracts," *Public Contract Law Journal* 5 (April): 88.

Shedd, Joel P. (1982). "Government Contractor's Obligation to Continue Performance in Accordance with Contracting Officer's Decision," *Public Contract Law Journal* 12 (March): 89–28.

Sheppard, Nathaniel (1981). "Women's Work," *Black Enterprise* 11 (February): 57–58.

Sherman, Stanley N. (1981). *Government Procurement Management*. Gaithersburg, Md.: Woodcrafters Publications.

Sherrer, Charles W. (1980). "The Unsolicited Proposal," *Journal of the Missouri Bar* 36 (September): 385–391.

Sherrer, Charles W. (1981). "Predatory Pricing: An Evaluation of Its Potential for Abuse Under Government Procurement Contracts," *The Journal of Corporation Law* 6 (Spring): 531–549.

Shields, Patricia M. (1981). "Public Pricing: One Answer to the Human Service Fiscal Dilemma," *New England Journal Human Services* 14 (Summer): 18–24.

Shillito, Barry J. and David Westermann (1988). "Defense Profit Policy," *National Contract Management Journal* 21 (Winter): 58–65.

Shimek, William G. (1982). "Tennessee" (recent developments in state and local public contract law), *Public Contract Newsletter* 18 (Fall): 10–11.

Shipp, Brian (1989). "Torts: The United States Supreme Court Accepts the Government Contractor Defense" (case note), *Oklahoma Law Review* 42 (Summer): 359–379.

Shirley, Mary (1988). "The Experience with Privatization," *Finance & Development* 25 (September): 34–35.

Shnitzer, Paul and Melvin Rishe (1981). "New

Decision on Direct Actions Opens the Door to Subcontractors," *The National Law Review* 4 (September 14): 28.

Shonick, William and Ruth Roemer (1982). "Private Management of California County Hospitals: Expectations and Performance," *Public Affairs Report* 23 (February): 1–11.

Shoreham, Diana (1990). "Latin America: Privatization Gains New Momentum," *Euromoney* (UK) 105–109.

Short, John (1978). "Contracting for Services," *Governmental Purchasing* (May).

Short, John (1979). *What GSA Could Learn from State Purchasing in Commercial Products.* National Contract Management Association (December).

Short, John (1980). "The Model Procurement Code . . . Don't Adopt It, Adapt It," *Government Purchasing* (May).

Short, John (1987). *The Contract Cookbook for Purchase of Services.* Falls Church, Va.: National Institute of Governmental Purchasing.

Shulman, M. (1982). "Alternative Ways for Delivering Public Services," *Urban Data Service Reports* 14 (10): 2–6.

Silberman, Wendy (1986). "GATT Strengthens Government Procurement Code; New Regulations To Be Implemented Jan. 1, 1988," *Business America* 9 (December 8): 16.

Simms, Margaret C. (1990). "Rebuilding Set-Aside Programs," *Black Enterprise* (September): 33.

Simonson, G. R. (1988). "Measurements of Defense Profits," *National Contract Management Journal* 21 (Summer): 47–53.

Singletary, Michelle L. (1990). "How to Profit in the Post-Croson Era," *Black Enterprise* 20 (February): 179–183.

Sington, Philip (1990). "Little Market, Big Future," *Euromoney* (UK) supplement (February): 14–16.

Slawsky, N. and J. DeMarco (1980). "Is the Price Right? State and Local Government Architect and Engineer Selection," *Public Administration Review* 40 (3): 269–275.

Sloane, Todd (1990). "Will Ecorse Stumble Back to Its Old Course?" *City & State* 7 (June 4): 11, 14.

Slover, William L. (1984). "Dulles Bus Bidding Overturned," *ICC Practitioner's Journal* 51 (May–June): 418.

Smith, Douglas J. (1989a). "Electric Utilities Turn to Bidding for New Capacity," *Power Engineering* 93 (October): 17.

Smith, Douglas J. (1989b). "Is Competitive Bidding the Answer for New Capacity?" *Power Engineering* 93 (October): 30–33.

Smith, Emily T. and Naomi Freundlich (1989). "The Women Who Are Scaling High Tech's Heights; Making Science More Seductive to Women on Campus," *Business Week* (Industrial/technology edition) 3121 (August 28): 86–89.

Smith, Fred L., Jr. (1987). "Privatization at the Federal Level," in Steve H. Hanke, ed., *Prospects for Privatization.* New York: Proceedings of the Academy of Political Science 36 (3): 179–189.

Smith, G. Nelson III (1988). "Defective Military Aircraft and the Government Contractor Defense: The Constitutional Difficulties That Arise Even After Boyle v. United Technologies Corp.," *Journal of Air Law and Commerce* 54 (Winter): 439–498.

Smith, Kenneth. (1989). "Richmond Built Set-Asides on Shaky Foundation," *Wall Street Journal* (February).

Smith, Ray (1989). "New Zealand Special Report: Deregulation Forces Speedy Telecom Overhaul," *Telephone Engineer & Management* 93 (May 1): 60–64.

Smith, Richard (1983). "Public Procurement Act" (Virginia), *Public Contract Newsletter* 18 (Summer): 7–8.

Smith, Robert J. (1982). "Privatizing the Environment," *Policy Review* 20 (Spring): 11–50.

Solomon, Charlene Marmer (1990). "Careers Under Glass," *Personnel Journal* 69 (April): 96–105.

Sonfield, Matthew C. (1987). "An Attitudinal Comparison of Black and White Small Businessmen," *American Journal of Small Business* 12 (January): 38–45.

Sorett, Stephen M. (1984). "Debarment and Suspension," *Identifying and Prosecuting Fraud and Abuse in State and Local Contracting.* Chicago: American Bar Association: 75–79.

Sorkin, Alan L. (1978). *The Urban American Indian.* Lexington, Mass.: D. C. Heath and Company.

Southwestern Law Journal (1970). "A New Liability for Government Contractors," Student Note, 24 (December): 852.

Spann, R. M. (1977). "Public Versus Private Provision of Government Services," in T. E. Borcherding, ed. *Budgets and Bureaucrats: The Sources of Government Growth.* Durham, N.C.: Duke University Press: 71–89.

Speck, William H. II (1982). "Government Claims Against Contractors," *Public Contract Law Journal* 13 (July): 137–168.

Speck, William H. (1963). "Enforcement of Nondiscrimination Requirements for Government Contract Work," *Columbia Law Review* 63 (February): 243.

Speckman, Robert E. (1991). "U.S. Buyers' Relationship with Pacific Rim Sellers," *International Journal of Purchasing and Materials Management* 27 (Winter): 2–10.

Spector, Louis (1971). "Public Contract Claims Procedure—A Perspective," *Federal Bar Journal* 30 (Winter): 1–12.

Spector, Louis (1980). "The Contract Disputes Act of 1978—Some Observations and Predictions," *Federal Bar Journal* 39 (Summer): 1–9.

Spicer's Centre for Europe (1990). *Opportunities in European Financial Services: 1992 and Beyond.* New York: John Wiley.

Spievack, Edwin B. (1990). "Telecommunications Trade: Evolving Markets and Opportunities," *Telecommunications* (North American edition) 24 (January): 36–38.

Spiro, Peter J. (1990). "The Limits of Federalism in Foreign Policymaking," *Intergovernmental Perspective* 16 (Spring): 32–34.

Spitzer, Stephen and Andrew T. Scull (1977). "Privatization and Capitalist Development: The Case of the Private Police," *Social Problems* 25 (1): 18–29.

Spivack, Tommy J. (1989). "Constitutional Law—Fourteenth Amendment—Supreme Court Adopts Strict Scrutiny Standard to Review the Constitutionality of Affirmative Action Measures" (case note), *Seton Hall Law Review* 20 (Fall): 205–227.

Splitt, David A. (1988). "Here's the Fine Print: A Guide to Procurement Law in the District (District of Columbia)," *Washington Lawyer* 2 (May–June): 24.

Spratlen, T. (1978). "The Impact of Affirmative Action Purchasing," *Journal of Purchasing and Materials Management* 14: 8–11.

Squiers, Deborah (1990). "Panel Rejects Asbestos-Suit Appeal: Military Contractor Loses Defense Linked to Government Order," *New York Law Journal* 203 (February 22): 1.

Stainback, John P. (1990). "Privatization Is the Answer, But There Is No Free Lunch," *Real Estate Finance* 6 (Winter): 63–69.

Stamps, Robert F. (1989). "The Department of Defense Balance of Payments Program: A Brief History and Critique," *Public Contract Law Journal* 18 (June): 528–543.

Stanfield, Rochelle L. (1990). "Fixing Foreign Aid," *National Journal* 22 (May 19): 1223–1226.

Stanley, Guy (1985). "Could Markets Run the Social Services? Probably and Transform the Welfare State in the Process," *Canadian Business Review* 12 (Spring): 48–50.

Stanley, Ralph (1988). "Privatization and the Challenge of Urban Mobility," in John C. Weicher, ed. *Private Innovations in Public Transit.* Washington, D.C.: American Enterprise Institute for Public Policy Research: 11–15.

Stansberry, James W. (1978). "Minority Businesses Taking Wing Under the Air Force," *Defense Management Journal* 14 (January): 40–43.

Starr, Paul (1987). "The Limits of Privatization," in Steve H. Hanke, ed., *Prospects for Privatization.* New York: Proceedings of the Academy of Political Science 36 (3): 124–137.

State Factor, The (n.d.). "Privatizing Transportation Infrastructure," 10 (no. 6): 1–10.

Stead, W. Edward, Dan L. Worrell, and Jean Garner Stead (1990). "An Integrative Model for Understanding and Managing Ethical Behavior in Business Organizations," *Journal of Business Ethics* 9: 233–242.

Steinberg, Norman (1989/1990). "A Policy Framework for Privatization," *Optimum* (Canada) 20 (3): 38–50.

Steinhauer, Raleigh F. (1972). "IGCP: The Wave of the Future," *Journal of Purchasing* 8 (August): 34–45.

Steiss, Alan Walter (1989). *Financial Management in Public Organizations.* Pacific Grove, Calif.: Brooks/Cole Publishing Co.

Stenzel, Sandra (1988). "A Government Procurement Outreach Center as an Existing Business Development Tool," *Economic Development Review* 6 (Winter): 33–35.

Stevens, Barbara J. (1978). "Scale, Market Structure, and the Cost of Refuse Collection," *Review of Economics and Statistics* 60 (August): 438–448.

Stevens, Barbara J. (1984). "Comparing Public and Private Sector Productive Efficiency: Analysis of Eight Activities," *National Productivity Review* 3 (Autumn): 395–406.

Stevens, Barbara J. and E. S. Savas (1977). "The Cost of Residential Refuse Collection and the Effect of Service Arrangement," *The Municipal Year Book, 1977.* Washington, D.C.: International City Management Association: 200–205.

Stevens, Barbara J., ed. (1984). *Delivering Municipal Services Efficiently: A Comparison of Municipal and Private Service Delivery*, report prepared for the U.S. Department of Housing and Urban Development. New York: Ecodata, Inc. (June).

Stevenson, Lois A. (1986). "Against All Odds: The Entrepreneurship of Women," *Journal of Small Business Management* 24 (October): 30–36.

Steward, James F. and Daniel R. Boyd (1988). "Teaching Entrepreneurs: Opportunities for Women and Minorities," *Business Forum* 13 (Summer): 8–10.

Stewart, David Overlock and Robert B. Gordon (1990). "New Jersey's Casino Set-Aside Program After Croson," *Seton Hall Legislative Journal* 13 (Winter): 155–179.

Stewart, Rodney D. (1988). *Managing Millions: An Inside Look at Hi-Tech Government Spending.* New York: Wiley.

Stillman, Thomas H. (1991). "Export Controls in a Changing World," *Business America* 112 (February 11): 3–4.

Stimpson, Wesley E. (1989). "Fast Tracking Military Waste," *Civil Engineering* 59 (April): 36–39.

Stokes, Bruce (1990a). "GATT Going," *National Journal* 22 (May 12): 1150–1155.

Stokes, Bruce (1990b). "High-Tech Tussle," *National Journal* 22 (June 2): 1338–1342.

Stokes, Bruce (1990c). "Mexico Trade Pact Looming," *National Journal* 22 (May 19): 1235.

Stokes, Bruce (1990d). "Opening Eastern Gates," *National Journal* 22 (June 23): 1531–1534.

Stokes, Bruce (1990e). "Trade Talks with Mexico Face Hurdles," *National Journal* 22 (June 16): 1486–1487.

Stoltenberg, John (1988). "High-Tech Women Entrepreneurs Turning Problems Into Profits," *Working Woman* 13 (May): 55–57.

Stone, Clarence N. (1986). "Partnership New South Style: Central Atlanta Progress," in Perry Davis, ed. *Public-Private Partnerships: Improving Urban Life.* New York: The Academy of Political Science: 100–110.

Stoner, Charles R., Richard I. Hartmann, and Raj Arora (1990). "Work-Home Role Conflict in Female Owners of Small Businesses: An Exploratory Study," *Journal of Small Business Management* 28 (January): 30–38.

Strasser, Fred (1986). "Defending Contractors Against the Pentagon," *The National Law Journal* 8 (March 3): 1.

Strasser, Fred (1988). "Pentagon Probe Defense Emerges: Insider Trading, Washington Style?" *The National Law Journal* 10 (July 4): 3.

Strassfeld, Robert N. (1983). "Corporate Standing to Allege Race Discrimination in Civil Rights Actions," *Virginia Law Review* 69 (September): 1153–1181.

Strauss, Robert P. (1990). "The EC Challenge to State and Local Governments," *International Perspective* 16 (Winter): 13–14.

Straussman, Jeffrey and John Farie (1981). "Contracting for Social Services at the Local Level," *The Urban Interest* 3 (Spring): 43–49.

Stump, Michael M. (1986). "Private Operation of U.S. Water Utilities," *American Water Works Association Journal* 78 (February): 49–51.

Suchenski, Karen (1987). "Women and Finance: Part 1: Working Toward Financial Emancipation," *National Business Woman* 68 (April/May): 1–2.

Suggs, Robert E. (1985). "Minorities and Privatization: Issues of Equity," *Focus* (Washington, D.C.: Joint Center for Political Studies) 13 (February): 3, 6, 14–15.

Suggs, Robert E. (1986). "Minorities and Privatization: Issues of Equity," *Public Management* 68 (December): 14–15.

Suggs, Robert E. (1990). "Rethinking Minority Business Development Strategies," *Harvard Civil Rights—Civil Liberties Law Review* (Winter): 101–145.

Sullivan, Harold J. (1987). "Privatization of Public Services: A Growing Threat to Constitutional Rights," *Public Administration Review* 47 (November/December): 461–467.

Sullivan, James C. (1989). "The Government Contractor Defense: Extending Sovereign Immunity to the Limits" (case note), *UMKC Law Review* 57 (Spring): 655–664.

Sullivan, Matthew J. (1989). "Tort Law—Products Liability—Military Contractors Who Comply with Elements of Government Contractor Defense Are Immune from Products Liability Suits Stemming from Design Defects" (case note), *St. Mary's Law Journal* 20 (Summer): 993–1012.

Sullivan, N. and J. Marietta (1987). "New Strategies for a New Game: Privatizing Water and Wastewater Treatment Plants," *The Privatization Review* 3 (3): 56–63.

Sutton, James O. III (1988). "Conflicts of Interest in the Acquisition Process," *Air Force Law Review* 29 (Fall): 165–168.

Talley, W. K. and E. E. Anderson (1986). "An Urban Transit Firm Providing Transit, Paratransit, and Contracted-Out Service," *Journal of Transport Economics and Policy* 20, No. 3: 353–368.

Taylor, James W. and B. Alan Dickson (1984). "Organizational Conflicts of Interest Under the Federal Acquisition Regulation," *Public Contract Law Journal* 15 (August): 107–121.

Teal, Roger F. (1985). "Private Enterprise in Public Transportation: The Case of the Taxi Industry," *Transportation Quarterly* 39 (April): 235–252.

Teal, Roger F. (1988). "Contracting for Transit Service," in John C. Weicher, ed. *Private Innovations in Public Transit*. Washington, D.C.: American Enterprise Institute for Public Policy Research: 47–55.

Teal, Roger F. (1989). "Privatization of Transportation Services," in Lawrence K. Finley, ed. *Public Sector Privatization: Alternative Approaches to Service Delivery*. New York: Quorum Books: 63–76.

Teal, Roger F., G. M. Guiliano, J. Golob, and E. W. Morlok (1988). *Cost Impacts of Public Service Transit Service Contracting*, final report to the Urban Mass Transportation Administration. Washington, D.C.: U.S. Government Printing Office.

Terrell, Paul (1979). "Private Alternatives to Public Human Services Administration," *Social Service Review* 53 (March): 56–74.

Terrell, Paul and Ralph M. Kramer (1984). "Contracting with Nonprofits," *Public Welfare* 42 (Winter): 31–37.

Therrien, Lois, Teresa Carson, Joan O'Connor Hamilton, and Jim Hurlock (1986). "What Do Women Want? A Company They Can Call Their Own," *Business Week* (Industrial/technology edition) 2978 (December 22): 60–62.

Thigpen, Julia Grace (1981). "Do Affirmative Action Fians Require Congressional Authorization?" (case note), *Washington and Lee Law Review* 38 (Fall): 1315–1332.

Thomas, R. Roosevelt, Jr. (1990). "From Affirmative Action to Affirming Diversity," *Harvard Business Review* 90 (March/April): 107–117.

Thomas, Ralph C. III (1988). "Minority Participation in Government Construction Projects: Developing New Approaches," *Construction Lawyer* 8 (August): 15–21.

Thompson, Kevin D. (1988). "Special Report: Black Women in Corporate America—Starting Over," *Black Enterprise* 19 (August): 58–61.

Thompson, Kevin D. (1990). "Married . . . with Business," *Black Enterprise* 20 (April): 46–54.

Thompson, Tommy G. (1990). "Going Global: A Governor's Perspective," *International Perspective* 16 (Spring): 15–17.

Thybony, William B. (1987). *Government Contracting Based on the Federal Acquisition Regulation (FAR) and the Competition in Contracting Act of 1984*, 2nd rev. Falls Church, Va.: The National Institute of Governmental Purchasing.

Thybony, William B. (1988). *The FAR Primer*, FAR Monograph No. 1. Falls Church, Va.: The National Institute of Governmental Purchasing.

Thys, Patrice J. and Patrick Henry (1987). "Government Procurement Regulations of the European Economic Community," *George Washington Journal of International Law & Economics* 20 (Summer): 445–460.

Tobin, Gary A. (1983). "The Public/Private Sector Partnership in the Redevelopment Process," *Policy Studies Journal* 11 (March): 473–482.

Tolchin, Edward (1988). "To Clean up Military Procurement Fraud, Call on Adam Smith: Charges of Bribery and Bid Collusion Are Mounting Against Defense Contractors. Could a Dose of Free-Market Economics Have Prevented This Costly Scandal?," *Legal Times* 11 (December 12): 16.

Tolchin, Martin and Susan Tolchin (1988). *Buying Into America: How Foreign Money Is Changing the Face of Our Nation.* New York: Times Book.

Tolle, John R. (1986). "A Review of the First Year of ADP Bid Protests and the GSBCA," *Public Contract Law Journal* 16 (August): 120–160.

Tolley, George S. (1988). "What If Transit Markets Were Freed?" in John C. Weicher, ed., *Private Innovations in Public Transit.* Washington, D.C.: American Enterprise Institute for Public Policy Research: 89–100.

Toma, Darrell M. (1989). "Free Trade Implications for Consultants," *Journal of Management Consulting* (Netherlands) 5 (1): 5–9.

Touche Ross (1987a). *Financing Infrastructure in America.* Washington, D.C.: Touche Ross.

Touche Ross (1987b). *Privatization in America: An Opinion Survey of City and County Governments on Their Use of Privatization and Their Infrastructure Needs.* Washington, D.C.: Touche Ross.

Touche Ross and Co. (1985). *The Infrastructure Crisis.* Washington, D.C.: Touche Ross.

Toyama, Kozo, Eiichiro Nakatani, and Ivan E. Mattei II (1987). "Government Procurement Procedures of Japan," *George Washington Journal of International Law and Economics* 21 (Fall): 91–113.

Treinen, Marie (1991). "Deepening or Broadening? The European Community in the 1990s," *Business America* 112 (February 25): 20–21.

Trial Lawyer's Guide (1990). "Eleventh Circuit Reverses Verdict for Plaintiff on Issue of Design Defect or Manufacturing Defect," 33 (Winter): 596–601.

Trilling, Barry J. and Kennedy Bingham (1985). "Challengers Raise Legitimate Issues Before President's Purchase Panel," *Legal Times* 8 (November 4): 7.

Trout, Robert V., Eric L. Wilson, and Mary Ellen Amaral (1989). "Reaping the Rewards of the Federal Procurement Process," *Colorado Lawyer* 18 (October): 1903–1912.

Turner, John A. (1989). "Privatization of Fire Protection and Beyond by Rural/Metro," in Lawrence K. Finley, ed., *Public Sector Privatization: Alternative Approaches to Service Delivery.* New York: Quorum Books: 77–92.

Turro, John (1988). "FCC Tax Certificates Give Minority Broadcasters a Boost," *Tax Notes* 40 (September 26): 1340–1341.

Tzanis, Joanne (1986). "More Prosecutions of Minority Fronts Sought," *Pennsylvania Law Journal-Reporter* 9 (August): 1.

U.S. Bureau of Reclamation, Division of Acquisition and Property Management (1988). *How to Survive the Acquisition Process in the Bureau of Reclamation.* Washington, D.C.: Bureau of Reclamation, Division of Acquisition and Property Management, Acquisition Management Branch, Engineering and Research Center.

U.S. Bureau of the Census (1990). *Statistical Abstract of the United States 1990,* 110th ed. Washington, D.C.: U.S. Government Printing Office.

U.S. Commission on Minority Business Development (1990). *Historically Underutilized Businesses: Interim Report 1990.* Washington, D.C.: U.S. Commission on Minority Business Development.

U.S. Comptroller General (1973). *Limited Success of Federally Financed Minority Businesses in Three Cities.* Washington, D.C.: U.S. Government Printing Office.

U.S. Comptroller General (1976). *Governmental Buy: National Practices of the United States and Other Countries: An Assessment; Report to the Congress.* Washington, D.C.: General Accounting Office.

U.S. Comptroller General (1979). *Civil Agencies Can Do a Better Job of Negotiating Noncompetitive Contracts Priced over $100,000.* Washington, D.C.: General Accounting Office.

U.S. Comptroller General (1980a). *Controls Over Consulting Service Contract at Federal Agencies Need Tightening.* Washington, D.C.: U.S. General Accounting Office.

U.S. Comptroller General (1980b). *Implementation of Federal Policy on Acquiring and Distributing Commercial Products Is Faltering Badly: Report to the Congress.* Washington, D.C.: General Accounting Office.

U.S. Comptroller General (1981). *Civil Servants*

and Contract Employees: Who Should Do What for the Federal Government? Washington, D.C.: U.S. General Accounting Office.

U.S. Comptroller General (1985). *Information From Previous Reports on Various Aspects of Contracting Out Under OMB Circular A-76.* Washington, D.C.: U.S. General Accounting Office.

U.S. Comptroller General (1986). *Contracts With Employee Organizations Should Be Terminated.* Washington, D.C.: U.S. General Accounting Office.

U.S. Congress (1983). *An Act To Revise the Authority and Responsibility of the Office of Federal Procurement Policy, To Authorize Appropriations for the Office of Federal Procurement Policy for an Additional Four Fiscal Years, and for Other Purposes (Public Law 98–191).* Washington, D.C.: U.S. Government Printing Office.

U.S. Congress (1984). *Small Business and Federal Procurement Competition Enhancement Act of 1984* (Public Law 98–577). Washington, D.C.: U.S. Government Printing Office.

U.S. Congress (1985a). *Defense Procurement Conflict of Interest Act: Report Together with Dissenting Views* (to accompany H.R. 2554). Washington, D.C.: U.S. Government Printing Office.

U.S. Congress (1985b). *Socioeconomic Regulations and the Federal Procurement Market: A Study Prepared for the Use of the Joint Economic Committee, Congress of the United States.* Washington, D.C.: U.S. Government Printing Office.

U.S. Congress (1987). *Buy American Act of 1987: Report Together With Additional and Dissenting Views.* Washington, D.C.: U.S. Government Printing Office.

U.S. Congress (1988a). *An Act to Amend Chapter 39 of Title 31, United States Code, To Require the Federal Government To Pay Interest on Overdue Payments, and for Other Purposes (Public Law 101–496).* Washington, D.C.: U.S. Government Printing Office.

U.S. Congress (1988b). *Business Opportunity Development Reform Act of 1988: Conference Report* (to accompany H.R. 1807). Washington, D.C.: U.S. Government Printing Office.

U.S. Congress (1989a). *An Act to Delay the Effective Date of Section 27 of the Office of Federal Procurement Policy Act* (Public Law 101–28). Washington, D.C.: U.S. Government Printing Office.

U.S. Congress (1989b). *An Act to Make Technical Corrections to the Businesss Opportunity Development Reform Act of 1988.* Washington, D.C.: U.S. Government Printing Office.

U.S. Congressional Budget Office (1987). *Contracting Out: Potential for Reducing Federal Costs.* Washington, D.C.: Congressional Budget Office.

U.S. Department of Agriculture, Food and Nutrition Service, Food Distribution Division (1985, 1986). *USDA Food Service Technical Assistance Purchasing Manuals. Catalog of Food Specifications,* Vol. I; *Contract Purchasing,* Vol. II; *Food Facts,* Vol. III; *Directory of Food Information Sources,* Vol. IV; *Storage and Care of Food Products,* Vol. V; *Purchasing French-Fry Potatoes,* Vol. VI; *Description of the USDA-FNS Donated Foods Program,* Vol. VII; *Purchasing Guidelines and Meal Cost Management,* Vol. VIII; *Food Purchasing for Elderly Programs,* Vol. IX; and *Food Identifications and Standards,* Vol. X. Washington, D.C.: USDA.

U. S. Department of Agriculture, Forest Service, Intermountain Region (1981). *$elling to the Forest Service.* Ogden, Utah: USDA.

U. S. Department of Commerce (1986). *Women and Business Ownership: An Annotated Bibliography.* Washington, D.C.: U. S. Government Printing Office (July).

U. S. Department of Commerce (1987). *Directory of Women Business Owners: Megamarketplace East/West.* Washington, D.C.: U. S. Department of Commerce.

U. S. Department of Commerce (1988). *How to Sell to the U. S. Department of Commerce.* Washington, D.C.: U. S. Government Printing Office (April).

U. S. Department of Commerce, Economics and Statistics Administration, Bureau of the Census (August 1990–June 1991). *1987 Survey of Minority-Owned Business Enterprises.* Vol. 1—*Black;* Vol. 2—*Hispanic;* Vol. 3—*Asian Americans, American Indians, and other Minorities.* Washington, D.C.: U. S. Government Printing Office.

U. S. Department of Commerce, Minority Business Development Agency (1991). *MBDA*

Annual Business Assistance Report for Fiscal Year 1990. Washington, D.C.: U. S. Government Printing Office.

U. S. Department of Commerce, Office of Minority Business Enterprise (1977). *Minority Enterprise Corporate Involvement.* Washington, D.C.: Department of Commerce.

U. S. Department of Defense, Assistant Secretary of Defense, Installations and Logistics (1975). *Armed Services Procurement Regulation Manual: Contract Pricing.* Washington, D.C.: Department of Defense.

U. S. Department of Defense, Assistant Secretary of Defense, Installations and Logistics (1976). *Armed Services Procurement Regulation: Small Purchase Manual.* Washington, D.C.: Department of Defense.

U. S. Department of Defense, Assistant Secretary of Defense, Installations and Logistics (1977). *Armed Services Procurement Regulations: Supplement No. 1: Guide for Conducting Contractor Procurement System Review (CPSR).* Washington, D.C.: Department of Defense.

U. S. Department of Defense (1980). *A Guide to Resources and Sources of Information for Acquisition Research.* Washington, D.C.: Department of Defense.

U. S. Department of Defense, Department of the Army (1976). *Army Procurement Procedure.* Washington, D.C.: Department of Defense.

U. S. Department of Labor, Office of Federal Contract Compliance Programs (1984). *Employment Patterns of Minorities and Women in Federal Contractor and Noncontractor Establishments, 1974–1980.* Washington, D.C.: Department of Labor.

U. S. Department of Labor (1987). *What the U. S. Department of Labor Buys.* Washington, D.C.: Department of Labor.

U. S. Department of Labor, Employment Standards Administration, Wage and Hour Division (1987). *The Walsh–Healey Public Contracts Act, as Amended.* Washington, D.C.: Department of Labor.

U. S. Department of Labor, Region 2 (1989). *Major Laws Administered by the U. S. Department of Labor Which Affect Business.* Washington, D.C.: Department of Labor (January).

U. S. Department of Labor, Women's Bureau (1985). *Business Development Opportunities in the U. S. for Women in Other Countries.* Washington, D.C.: Department of Labor (July: 1–3).

U. S. Department of Labor, Women's Bureau (1987). "Women Business Owners," *Facts on U. S. Working Women.* Washington, D.C.: Department of Labor (87–2): 1–4.

U. S. Department of Labor, Women's Bureau (1988). "Women and Workforce 2000," *Facts on U. S. Working Women.* Washington, D.C.: Department of Labor (88–1) (January): 1–4.

U. S. Department of Labor, Women's Bureau (1989a). "American Indian Women Business Owners," *Facts on Working Women.* Washington, D.C.: Department of Labor (89–10): 1–4.

U. S. Department of Labor, Women's Bureau (1989b). "Asian American Women Business Owners," *Facts on Working Women.* Washington, D.C.: Department of Labor (89–9): 1–4.

U. S. Department of Labor, Women's Bureau (1989c). "Black Women Business Owners," *Facts on Working Women.* Washington, D.C.: Department of Labor (89–7) (September): 1–3.

U. S. Department of Labor, Women's Bureau (1989d). "Hispanic Women Business Owners," *Facts on Working Women.* Washington, D.C.: Department of Labor (89–8): 1–4.

U. S. Department of Labor, Women's Bureau (1989e). "Women in Management," *Facts on Working Women.* Washington, D.C.: Department of Labor (89–4) (December): 1–8.

U. S. Department of Labor, Women's Bureau (1989f). "Women of Hispanic Origin in the Labor Force," *Facts on Working Women.* Washington, D.C.: Department of Labor (89–1) (August): 1–4.

U. S. Department of State (1988). *General Agreement on Tariffs and Trade: Government Procurement: Agreement Between the United States of America and Other Governments Done at Geneva April 12, 1979.* Washington, D.C.: Department of State.

U. S. Department of State, Office of Small and Disadvantaged Business Utilization (annual). *A Guide to Doing Business with the Department of State.* Washington, D.C.: Department of State.

U. S. Department of Transportation, Office of Private Sector Initiatives (1986). *New Directions in Urban Transportation Private/Public*

Partnerships. Washington, D.C.: Department of Transportation (November).

U. S. Energy Research and Development Administration (1975). *Selling to ERDA.* Washington, D.C.: ERDA (May).

U. S. Environmental Protection Agency, Office of Water and Waste Management (1979). *Collection of Data Pertinent to the EPA's Development of Guidelines for Government Procurements of Paper Products Containing Recycled Materials.* Washington, D.C.: EPA.

U. S. Executive Office of the President, Office of Management and Budget (1979). *Costing Methods and Models for Acquisition Planning, Budgeting and Contracting.* Washington, D.C.: OMB, Office of Federal Procurement Policy, Federal Acquisition Institute.

U. S. Executive Office of the President, Office of Management and Budget (1985). *Procedures Governing Implementation of Certain Unconstitutional Provisions of the Competition in Contracting Act of 1984.* Washington, D.C.: OMB.

U. S. General Accounting Office (1977). *Ineffective Management of GSA's Multiple Award Schedule Program—A Costly, Serious, and Longstanding Problem.* Washington, D.C.: GAO (September 30).

U. S. General Accounting Office (1978). *Special Procurement Procedures Help Prevent Wage Busting Under Federal Service Contracts in the Cape Canaveral Area.* Washington, D.C.: GAO.

U. S. General Accounting Office (1979). *GSA Needs To Strengthen Its Inspection and Testing to Make Sure the Government Gets the Quality It Pays for.* Washington, D.C.: GAO.

U. S. General Accounting Office (1980). *Government Contract Principles Compiled in the Office of the General Counsel.* Washington, D.C.: GAO.

U. S. General Accounting Office (1983). *Data Collection Under the International Agreement on Government Procurement Could Be More Accurate and Efficient.* Washington, D.C.: GAO.

U. S. General Accounting Office (1984). *Compensation by Twelve Aerospace Contractors.* Washington, D.C.: GAO (October).

U. S. General Accounting Office (1986a). *Government Contracting: Assessment of the Study of Defense Contractor Profitability.* Washington, D.C.: GAO (December).

U. S. General Accounting Office (1986b). *Minority Business Enterprises Awarding of Cooperative Agreement to Operate Development Centers: Briefing Report to Congressional Requesters.* Washington, D.C.: GAO (November).

U. S. General Accounting Office (1986c). *Small Business Act: GSA's Disadvantaged Business Advocate Reports to Property Management Level: Report to the Administrator of General Services.* Washington, D.C.: GAO.

U. S. General Accounting Office (1986d). *Small Business Act: HUD's Disadvantaged Business Advocate Reports to Proper Management Level: Report to the Secretary, Department of Housing and Urban Development.* Washington, D.C.: GAO.

U. S. General Accounting Office (1987a). *Procurement: Small Business Suspension and Debarment by the Department of Defense: Briefing Report of the Senate Committee on Small Business.* Washington, D.C.: GAO.

U. S. General Accounting Office (1987b). *Procurement: Suspension and Debarment Procedures: Briefing Report to the Chairman, Committee on Government Operations, House of Representatives.* Washington, D.C.: GAO.

U. S. General Accounting Office (1989). *Prompt Payment: State Laws Are Similar to the Federal Act But Less Comprehensive.* Washington, D.C.: GAO (March).

U. S. General Services Administration (1989). *Doing Business with the Federal Government.* Washington, D.C.: GAO.

U. S. House of Representatives, Acquisition Policy Panel of the Committee on Armed Services (1987, 1988). *Implementation of Section 1207—the 5 Percent Goal for Awards to Small and Disadvantaged Business* (of the National Defense Authorization Act for FY 1987, Public Law 99–661), 100th Congress, 1st and 2nd sessions (October 29, November 4–5, 1987; January 29, February 5, 10–12, March 14, August 12, 1988). Washington, D.C.: U. S. Government Printing Office.

U. S. House of Representatives, Committee on Armed Services (1986). *Laws Relating to*

Federal Procurement (as amended through February 28, 1986). Washington, D.C.: U. S. Government Printing Office.

U. S. House of Representatives, Committee on Armed Services (1987). *Laws Relating to Federal Procurement* (as amended through April 21, 1987). Washington, D.C.: U. S. Government Printing Office.

U. S. House of Representatives, Committee on Armed Services (1989). *Laws Relating to Federal Procurement* (as amended through December 31, 1988). Washington, D.C.: U. S. Government Printing Office.

U. S. House of Representatives, Committee on Government Operations (1986). *Efforts by Federal Agencies to Circumvent the Competition in Contracting Act; Hearing*, 99th Congress, 2nd session. Washington, D.C.: U. S. Government Printing Office.

U. S. House of Representatives, Committee on Government Operations (1988a). *Amendments to the Prompt Payment Act; Hearings*, 100th Congress, 2nd session, March 17, 23, 1988. Washington, D.C.: U. S. Government Printing Office.

U. S. House of Representatives, Committee on Government Operations (1988b). *Legislation Needed To Curb Secrecy Contracts: Fifty-Ninth Report*. Washington, D.C.: U. S. Government Printing Office.

U. S. House of Representatives, Committee on Small Business (1980). *Government Procurement From Small and Small Disadvantaged Businesses* (Public Law 95–507), 96th Congress, 2nd session. Washington, D.C.: U. S. Government Printing Office.

U. S. House of Representatives, Committee on Small Business (1981, 1982). *Small and Minority Business in the Decade of the 90s: Hearings Before the Committee*, 97th Congress, 1st session (September 1, 1981, Phoenix, and January 18, 1982, Atlanta). Washington, D.C.: U. S. Government Printing Office.

U. S. House of Representatives, Committee on Small Business (1982). *Small and Minority Business in the Decade of the 80's: Hearings*, 97th Congress, 1st session (March 15, 1982, Philadelphia). Washington, D.C.: U. S. Government Printing Office.

U. S. House of Representatives, Committee on Small Business (1988a). *Summary of Major Provisions of Public Law 100–656, The Business Opportunity Development Reform Act of 1988*, 100th Congress, 2nd session. Washington, D.C.: U. S. Government Printing Office.

U. S. House of Representatives, Committee on Small Business (1988b). *H.R. 2703 and Related Size Standards Issues: Hearings*, 100th Congress, 2nd session (March 22–24, 1988). Washington, D.C.: U. S. Government Printing Office.

U. S. House of Representatives, House Committee on the Judiciary (1985, 1986). *Hearings on the Privatization of Corrections*, 99th Congress, 1st session (November 13, 1985 and March 18, 1986). Washington, D.C.: U. S. Government Printing Office.

U. S. House of Representatives, Subcommittee on Administrative Law and Governmental Relations of the Committee on the Judiciary (1986). *Defense Procurement Conflict of Interest Act: Hearings*, 99th Congress, 2nd session (January 29–30, 1986). Washington, D.C.: U. S. Government Printing Office.

U. S. House of Representatives, Subcommittee on Administrative Law and Governmental Relations of the Committee on the Judiciary (1988a). *Amendment of the Miller Act: Hearing*, 100th Congress, 2nd session (May 12, 1988). Washington, D.C.: U. S. Government Printing Office.

U. S. House of Representatives, Subcommittee on Administrative Law and Governmental Relations of the Committee on the Judiciary (1988b). *Federal Procurement Liability Reform Act of 1987: Hearing*, 100th Congress, 1st session (October 29, 1988). Washington, D.C.: U. S. Government Printing Office.

U. S. House of Representatives, Subcommittee on Exports, Tourism, and Special Problems of the Committee on Small Business (1987). *Prompt Payment: Hearing*, 100th Congress, 1st session (July 30, 1987). Washington, D.C.: U. S. Government Printing Office.

U. S. House of Representatives, Subcommittee on Government Procurement and International Trade of the Committee on Small Business (1976a). *Government Procurement Within Military and Civilian Agencies: A Report of the Subcommittee*. Washington, D.C.: U. S. Government Printing Office (October).

U. S. House of Representatives, Subcommittee on

Government Procurement and International Trade of the Committee on Small Business (1976b). *Government Procurement Within Military And Civilian Agencies: Hearings*, 94th Congress, 2nd session (June 29 and 30, 1976). Washington, D.C.: U. S. Government Printing Office.

U. S. House of Representatives, Subcommittee on Human Resources of the Committee on Post Office and Civil Service (1986). *Defense Procurement Conflict of Interest Act: Hearing*, 99th Congress, 2nd session (February 26, 1986). Washington, D.C.: U. S. Government Printing Office.

U. S. House of Representatives, Subcommittee on Oversight and Investigations of the Committee on Energy and Commerce (1989). *Contract Fraud Within DOE: Hearing*, 100th Congress, 2nd session (September 29, 1988). Washington, D.C.: U. S. Government Printing Office.

U. S. House of Representatives, Subcommittee on Procurement, Innovation, and Minority Enterprise Development of the Committee on Small Business (1987a). *A Bill to Reform the Capital Ownership Development Program: Hearings*, 100th Congress, 1st session (May 12, 18–21, June 4, 1987). Washington, D.C.: U. S. Government Printing Office.

U. S. House of Representatives, Subcommittee on Procurement, Innovation, and Minority Enterprise Development of the Committee on Small Business (1987b). *Examining the Rule of Two: Hearings*, 100th Congress, 1st session (May 7 and 13, 1987). Washington, D.C.: U. S. Government Printing Office.

U. S. House of Representatives, Subcommittee on Procurement, Innovation, and Minority Enterprise Development of the Committee on Small Business (1988). *Minority Business Development Act of 1988—H.R. 1769: Hearing*, 100th Congress, 2nd session (June 30, 1988). Washington, D.C.: U. S. Government Printing Office.

U. S. House of Representatives, Subcommittee on SBA and SBIC Authority, Minority Enterprise, and General Small Business Problems of the Committee on Small Business (1985). *H.R. 1178—Small Business Size Standards: Hearings*, 99th Congress, 1st session (July 30–August 1, 1985). Washington, D.C.: U. S. Government Printing Office.

U. S. House of Representatives, Subcommittee on SBA and SBIC Authority, Minority Enterprise, and General Small Business Problems of the Committee on Small Business (1986). *Participation of California's Small Businesses in the Federal Procurement System*, 99th Congress, 2nd session (April 3, 1986, Los Angeles). Washington, D.C.: U. S. Government Printing Office.

U. S. House of Representatives, Subcommittee on SBA and SBIC Authority, Minority Enterprise, and General Small Business Problems of the Committee on Small Business (1987). *Minority Enterprise and General Small Business Problems: Hearings*, 99th Congress, 2nd session (Santa Fe, N.M., September 8, 1986). Washington, D.C.: U. S. Government Printing Office.

U. S. Office of Federal Procurement Policy (1985). *Procurement Policy Letters: A Compilation of Policies Issued by the Office of Federal Procurement Policy, Office of Management and Budget, Executive Office of the President.* Washington, D.C.: Office of Federal Procurement Policy.

U. S. Office of Management and Budget (1976). *Interagency Report on the Federal Minority Business Development Programs.* Washington, D.C.: U. S. Government Printing Office.

U. S. President's Commission on Privatization (1988). *Privatization: Toward More Effective Government: Report of the President's Commission on Privatization.* Washington, D.C.: U. S. Government Printing Office.

U. S. Senate (1985). "Testimony Regarding Privatizing Public Housing," *Congressional Record* 131 (February 7): S1291–5.

U. S. Senate (1988). *Prompt Payment Act Amendments of 1988: Report* (to accompany S. 328). Washington, D.C.: U. S. Government Printing Office.

U. S. Senate, Committee on Commerce, Science, and Transportation (1988). *Minority Business Development Act of 1987: Hearing*, 100th Congress, 2nd session (March 3, 1988). Washington, D.C.: U. S. Government Printing Office.

U. S. Senate, Committee on Governmental Affairs (1983). *Competition in Contracting Act of 1983: Report.* Washington, D.C.: U. S. Government Printing Office.

U. S. Senate, Committee on Governmental

Affairs (1987). *Prompt Payment Act Amendments of 1987: Committee Report* (together with additional views to accompany S. 328, to amend chapter 39 of Title 31, United States Code, to clarify and strengthen the Prompt Payment Act of 1982). Washington, D.C.: U. S. Government Printing Office.

U. S. Senate, Committee on Governmental Affairs (1988). *Prompt Payment Act Amendments of 1987: Hearing*, 100th Congress, 1st session (March 19, 1987). Washington, D.C.: U. S. Government Printing Office.

U. S. Senate, Committee on Small Business (1986a). *An Act to Extend Through Fiscal Year 1988 Pilot Programs Under Section 8 of the Small Business Act: Report of the Committee.* Washington, D.C.: U. S. Government Printing Office.

U. S. Senate, Committee on Small Business (1986b). *A Bill to Extend the Authorization for Not-For-Profit Organizations Operated in the Interest of Handicapped and Blind Individuals to Receive Procurement Contracts Under the Small Business Act: Report.* Washington, D.C.: U. S. Government Printing Office.

U. S. Senate, Committee on Small Business (1986c). *Implementation of the Prompt Pay Act: Hearing*, 99th Congress, 1st session (Norfolk, Va. December 2, 1985). Washington, D.C.: U. S. Government Printing Office.

U. S. Senate, Committee on Small Business (1986d). *Implementation of the Prompt Payment Act: Impact on Small Business Contractors: Hearing*, 99th Congress, 2nd session (June 19, 1986). Washington, D.C.: U. S. Government Printing Office.

U. S. Senate, Committee on Small Business (1986e). *S. 2147, A Bill to Reauthorize the Eligibility of Sheltered Workshops to Compete on Federal Procurement Contracts: Hearing*, 99th Congress, 2nd session (March 26, 1986). Washington, D.C.: U. S. Government Printing Office.

U. S. Senate, Committee on Small Business (1988a). *Minority Business Development Program Reform Act of 1988: Hearings*, 100th Congress, 2nd session (February 2 and 25, 1988). Washington, D.C.: U. S. Government Printing Office.

U. S. Senate, Committee on Small Business (1988b). *Minority Business Development Program Reform Act of 1988: Report of the Committee.* Washington, D.C.: U. S. Government Printing Office.

U. S. Senate, Subcommittee on Federal Services, Post Office, and Civil Service of the Committee on Governmental Affairs (1988). *Commercial Activities Contracting Act of 1987: Hearings*, 100th Congress, 1st and 2nd sessions (December 17, 1987; March 30, 1988). Washington, D.C.: U. S. Government Printing Office.

U. S. Senate, Subcommittee on Intergovernmental Relations of the Committee on Government Operations (1986). *Minority Business Development Administration: Hearing*, 94th Congress, 2nd session (April 13, 1976). Washington, D.C.: U. S. Government Printing Office.

U. S. Senate, Subcommittee on International Trade of the Committee on Finance (1982). *Oversight on Government Procurement Code and Related Agreements: Hearing*, 97th Congress, 2nd session (June 9, 1982). Washington, D.C.: U. S. Government Printing Office.

U. S. Senate, Subcommittee on Oversight of Government Management, Senate Committee on Governmental Affairs (1988). *Wedtech: A Review of Federal Procurement Decisions.* Washington, D.C.: U. S. Government Printing Office.

U. S. Senate, Subcommittee on Oversight of Government Management of the Committee on Governmental Affairs (1989a). *DOD's Inadequate Use of Off-the-Shelf Items: Report*, 101st Congress, 1st session. Washington, D.C.: U. S. Government Printing Office.

U. S. Senate, Subcommittee on Oversight of Government Management of the Committee on Governmental Affairs (1989b). *Oversight of DOD's Inadequate Use of Off-The-Shelf Items: Hearings*, 101st Congress, 1st session (May 16, June 1, 1989). Washington, D.C.: U. S. Government Printing Office.

U. S. Senate, Subcommittee on Oversight of Government Management of the Committee on Governmental Affairs (1989c). *Oversight of DOD's Management of Inside Information in the Acquisition Process: Hearing*, 101st Congress, 1st session (February 24, 1989). Washington, D.C.: U. S. Government Printing Office.

U. S. Small Business Administration (1974).

Study of Minority Borrowers and Firms Prior and Subsequent to SBA Assistance. Washington, D.C.: U. S. Government Printing Office.

U. S. Small Business Administration (1980). *Government Procurement Opportunities for Small Business.* Washington, D.C.: SBA.

U. S. Small Business Administration (1989). *The States and Small Business: A Directory of Programs and Activities.* Washington, D.C.: U. S. Government Printing Office.

U. S. Small Business Administration (1990). "The Annual Report on Small Business and Competition of the U. S. Small Business Administration," in The President, *The State of Small Business 1990: A Report of the President*, Washington, D.C.: U. S. Government Printing Office.

U. S. Small Business Administration, Office of Women's Business Ownership, Interagency Committee on Women's Business Enterprise (1990). *Women Business Owners: Selling to the Federal Government.* Washington, D.C.: SBA (June).

Usher, Harry L. (1964). "California's Buy American Policy: Conflict With GATT and the Constitution," Student Note, *Stanford Law Review* 17 (November): 119–137.

University of Pennsylvania Law Review (1981). "Requests for Proposals in State Government Procurement," 130 (November): 179–219.

Valente, Carl F. and Lydia D. Manchester (1984a). "Building Code Inspection and Enforcement," in International City Management Association, *Rethinking Local Services: Examining Alternative Delivery Approaches.* Washington, D.C.: ICMA.

Valente, Carl F. and Lydia D. Manchester (1984b). "Fleet Management and Vehicle Maintenance," in International City Management Association, *Rethinking Local Services: Examining Alternative Delivery Approaches.* Washington, D.C.: ICMA.

Valente, Carl F. and Lydia D. Manchester (1984c). "Rethinking Local Services: Examining Alternative Delivery Systems," *Management Information Service Special Report, No. 12.* Washington, D.C.: International City Management Association.

Villareal, Roberto E., Norma G. Hernandez, and Howard D. Neighbor, eds. (1988). *Latino Empowerment: Progress, Problems, and Prospects.* New York: Greenwood Press.

Vom Baur, F. Trowbridge (1970). "Fifty Years of Government Contract Law," *Federal Bar Journal* 29 (Fall): 305–358.

Von Meiss, Florian (1987). "Government Procurement in Switzerland," *George Washington Journal of International Law and Economics* 21 (Fall): 151–163.

Wacht, Richard F. (1987). *A New Approach to Capital Budgeting for City and County Governments*, 2nd ed. Atlanta: Business Publishing Division, College of Business Administration, Georgia State University.

Walder, Jay H. (1985). "Private Commuter Vans in New York," in Charles A. Lave, ed. *Urban Transit.* Cambridge, Mass.; Ballinger Publishing Company: 101–120.

Waldinger, Roger, Howard Aldrich, and Robin Ward (1990). *Ethnic Entrepreneurs: Immigrant Businesses in Industrial Societies.* Newbury Park, CA: Sage Publications.

Wallick, Robert D. (1982). "Excelsior" (government procurement), *Public Contract Newsletter* 17 (Summer): 2.

Wallick, Robert D. (1983a). "The Chairman on Ideals" (in government procurement), *Public Contract Newsletter* 18 (Summer): 2.

Wallick, Robert D. (1983b). "Chairman's Ruminations on Glaciations" (thoughts on government procurement), *Public Contract Newsletter* 18 (Winter): 2.

Wallick, Robert D., Peter L. Wellington, and Jerald S. Howe, Jr. (1990). "Procurement Integrity: Pondering Some Imponderables," *Public Contract Law Journal* 19 (Winter): 349–381.

Walters, A. A. (1987). "Ownership and Efficiency in Urban Buses," *Prospects for Privatization.* New York: *Proceedings of the Academy of Political Science* 36 (3): 83–92.

Walters, A. A. (1988). "Privatization in British Transport Policy," in John C. Weicher, ed., *Private Innovations in Public Transit.* Washington, D.C.: American Enterprise Institute for Public Policy Research: 101–108.

Walzer, N. (1970). "Price Index for Municipal Purchasing," *National Tax Journal* 23 (December): 441–447.

Ward, Dale (1988). "United States Supreme Court Launches Government Contractor

Defense Into Orbit" (case note), *Washburn Law Journal* 28 (Winter): 753–778.

Wasserman, Natalie and Dean G. Phelus, eds. (1985). *Risk Management Today: A How-To Guide for Local Government.* Washington, D.C.: International City Management Association.

Warren, James D. (1983). "Procurement Activities," (District of Columbia), *Public Contract Newsletter* 18 (Summer): 6.

Waterman, David (1988). "World Television Trade: The Economic Effects of Privatization and New Technology," *Telecommunications Policy* (UK) 12 (June): 141–151.

Watson, Andrea M. (1989). "Maneuvering Through the Vendor Maze," *Black Enterprise* 19 (February): 154–158.

Watson, Arthur R. (1991). "Exon-Florio: Two Years Later," *Business America* 112 (February 11): 14–16.

Watson, Brian and Wiley M. Woodard (1988). "Entrepreneurship: Still Making It," *Black Enterprise* 19 (November): 65–72.

Watson, Peter S. (1988). "Buy American, or Else" (procedures for reducing discriminatory foreign government procurement policies), *The Los Angeles Daily Journal* 101 (December 30): 5.

Weckstein, Kenneth B. and Daniel B. Abrahams (1989). "Doing Business with the U. S. Government," *Compleat Lawyer* 6 (Winter): 50–53.

Wedel, Kenneth R. (1980). "Purchase of Service Contracting in Human Services," *Journal of Health and Human Resources Administration* 2 (February): 327–342.

Wedel, Kenneth R., Arthur Katz, and Ann Weick (1979). *Social Services by Government Contract: A Policy Analysis.* New York: Praeger.

Weeden, Daniel (1989). " 'City of Richmond v. J. A. Croson' and the Aborted Affirmative Action Plan," *Southern University Law Review* 16: 73–100.

Weicher, John C., ed. (1988). *Private Innovations in Public Transit.* Washington, D.C.: American Enterprise Institute for Public Policy Research.

Weidenbaum, Murray (1991). "Business and Government: Fences Make Good Neighbors," *Business and Society Review* (Spring): 22–25.

Weinberger, Michael (1983). "Government Con-

tract Defense," *Corporation Law Review* 6 (Fall): 371–373.

Weisbrod, Burton (1988). *The Nonprofit Economy.* Cambridge, Mass.: Harvard University Press.

Weiss, Charles A. (1982). "An Anatomy of the Federal Contract Disputes Act of 1978," *Journal of the Missouri Bar* 38 (June): 232–243.

Weiss, Friedl (1988). "Public Procurement in the EEC: Public Supply Contracts," *European Law Review* 13 (October): 318–334.

Welch, J. Edward (1968). "Patent Infringement in Government Procurement: GAO's Role," *William and Mary Law Review* 10 (Fall): 1.

Wendt, Timothy (1990). "Strategic Trade: Protecting American Economic and Political Interests," in Frank J. Macchiarola, ed., *International Trade: The Changing Role of the United States.* New York: The Academy of Political Science: 165–180.

Wesemann, E. (1981). *Contracting for City Services.* Pittsburgh: Innovations Press.

Westerhoff, Garret P. (1986). "An Engineer's View of Privatization: The Chandler Experience," *American Water Works Association Journal* 78 (February): 41–46.

Western Reserve Law Review (1963). "Rights of the Unsuccessful Low Bidder on Government Contracts," Student Note, 15 (December): 208–226.

Westlake, Michael (1990). "Local Turbulence: PIA Aims for Partial Privatisation," *Far Eastern Economic Review* (Hong Kong) 147 (January 18): 39.

Whelan, J. W. (1964). "Purse Strings, Payment and Procurement," *Public Law* 322 (Winter): 322.

Whelan, John W. and George H. Gnoss (1968). "Government Contracts: Subcontractors and Privity," *William and Mary Law Review* 10 (Fall): 80–117.

Whitcomb, C. (1983). *Contracting for Residential Services.* McLean, Va.: Community Systems and Services, Inc.

White, Kenneth R. and James A. Vander (1988). "Minimizing Discrimination Practices," *Personnel Administrator* 33 (August): 92–95.

Whitehead, John C. (1990). "The New Freedom in the Soviet Union and Eastern Europe," *Presidential Studies Quarterly* 20 (Summer): 471–476.

Whitehouse, J. David and Bob G. Rogers (1986). "Privatization in Kentucky: Before and After Enabling Legislation," *The Privatization Review* 2 (Summer): 46–50.

Whitehurst, Catherine, Laura Gaughan, and Mara Yachnin (1990). "New Opportunities for Small Businesses Under the FTA; A Review of FTA Provisions Going into Force in 1990; Business Opportunities in Atlantic Canada; Commerce Department Helps U. S. Firms Do Business in Canada," *Business America* 111 (February 12): 27–34.

Whitfield, D. (1983). *Making It Public: Evidence and Action Against Privatization*. London: Pluto Press.

Whittemore, Meg (1989). "Franchising's Appeal to Women," *Nation's Business* 77 (November): 63–64.

Wickham, DeWayne (1985). "Are They Doing It Better in Baltimore?" *Black Enterprise* 15 (June): 266–274.

Wilde, Bruce R. (1990). "FCC Tax Certificates for Minority Ownership of Broadcast Facilities: A Critical Re-Examination of Policy," *University of Pennsylvania Law Review* 138 (January): 979–1026.

Wilder, Clinton (1990). "Outsourcing: Fad or Fantastic?" *Computerworld* 24 (December 25): 8.

Wildman, Steven S. and Stephen E. Siwek (1987). "The Privatization of European Television: Effects on International Markets for Programs," *Columbia Journal of World Business* 22 (Fall): 71–76.

William and Mary Law Review (1970). "Government Contracts: The Consequences of an Improper Award," Student Note, 11 (Spring): 706–722.

Williams, Charles B. (1980). *Contracting for City Services: An Annotated Bibliography*. Norman, Okla.: Bureau of Government Research, University of Oklahoma (July).

Williams, Fred (1989). "Funds Ease Requirements: Minority Firms Able To Compete for $1.4 Billion," *Pensions & Investment Age* 17 (December 11): 3, 45.

Williams, Ian (1990). "Wall Street's Huntresses," *Business* (UK) (April): 107–108.

Williams, K. (1988). "Small Business: A Boon to the U. S. Economy," *Management Accountancy* 70 (August): 16.

Williams, Michael (1989). "Bidding for Japanese Business," *Industry Week* 238 (November 20): 56, 61.

Williams, Michael (1991). "State Profile: Putting a New Face on Virginia's Future," *Black Enterprise* 21 (June): 284–292.

Williams, Walter B. (1989). "Government Requirements Met Through Software Enhancements," *Production & Inventory Management Review and APICS News*," 9 (August): 41–42.

Williams, Walter E. (1981). "Freedom To Contract: Blacks and Labor Organizations," *Government Union Review* 2 (Summer): 28–47.

Willis, Eric (1990). "White Collar Crime: Fact or Fiction?: The Alternative Approach to Solving the Problem of Fraud," *Management Accounting* (UK) 68 (March): 24–27.

Wilson, David L. (1990). "The U. S. Melting Pot Is Still Bubbling," *National Journal* 22 (June 23): 1565.

Wilson, M. Victoria (1987). "Set-Asides of Local Government Contracts for Minority Owned Businesses: Constitutional and State Law Issues," *New Mexico Law Review* 17 (Spring): 337–359.

Wingerter, Eugene J. (1986). "Refuse Collection: The Private Alternative," *The Privatization Review* 2 (Winter): 29–37.

Winston, D. C. (1969). "Industry To Support Procurement Study: Proposed In-Depth Review of Government Procurement Policies," *Aviation Week & Space Technology* 90 (April 21): 23.

Wise, Charles R. (1989). "Whither Federal Organizations: The Air Safety Challenge and Federal Management's Response," *Public Administration Review* 49 (January/February): 17–28.

Wise, Charles R. (1990). "Public Service Configurations and Public Organizations: Public Organization Design in the Post-Privatization Era," *Public Administration Review* 50 (March/April): 141–155.

Wisner, Graham G. (1987). "The Procurement Policies of the Kingdom of Saudi Arabia," *George Washington Journal of International Law and Economics* 21 (Fall): 115–125.

Witte, Oliver (1986). "California City Sells Bonds, Constructs Own Toll Bridge," *Roads and Bridges* (June).

Witte, Robert D. (1968). "Administrative Resolution of Government Breaches—A Problem," *Federal Bar Journal* 28 (Summer): 234–238.

Witzeman, Lou (1984a). "The Fire Department Goes Private," in R. Q. Armington and William D. Ellis, eds., *This Way up.* Chicago: Regnery Gateway: 65–92.

Witzeman, Lou (1984b). "What Do Private Sector Fire Protection Firms Have to Offer Local Governments?" *The International Fire Chief* 50 (February): 20–23.

Wolf, Maria T. (1989). "New Ventures on a Well-Traveled Road," *Perspective* 15 (1): 2–7, 12.

Wood, Robert Chapman (1986). "Wipe Out! One Tax Cut After Another Has Been Eaten up by the Tax No One Will Touch," *Reason* 18 (July): 37–39.

Woodside, William S. (1986). "The Future of Public-Private Partnerships," in Perry Davis, ed., *Public-Private Partnerships: Improving Urban Life.* New York: The Academy of Political Science: 150–154.

Woodson, Robert L. (1982). "Helping the Poor Help Themselves," *Policy Review* 21 (Summer): 73–86.

Woodson, Robert L. (1984). "Day Care," in R. Q. Armington and William D. Ellis, eds., *This Way up.* Chicago: Regnery Gateway: 149–163.

Wooldridge, Frank (1987). "Public Procurement in the European Community," *Journal of Business Law* (November): 505–513.

Woolley, Mary R. (1985). "Prisons for Profit: Policy Considerations for Government Officials," *Dickinson Law Review* 90 (Winter): 307–332.

Worthington, Margaret M. (1989). "Government and Industry: Changing Concepts in Cost Allowability," *Government Accountants Journal* 38 (Summer): 67–69.

Wright, Barbara (1988). "How To Beat Out Big-Name Competition," *Working Woman* (May): 55–57.

Wright, Don R. (1991). "The EC Single Market in 1991—Status Report," *Business America* 112 (February 25): 12–14.

Wylde, Kathryn (1986). "Partnerships for Housing," in Perry Davis, ed., *Public-Private Partnerships: Improving Urban Life.* New York: The Academy of Political Science: 111–121.

Wynne, George G., ed. (1983). *Cutback Management: A Trinational Perspective.* New Brunswick, N.J.: Council for International Urban Liaison.

Wynne, George G. (1986). "Privatization Initiatives Around the World," *Public Management* 68 (December): 19–22.

Yale Law Journal (1989a). "Joint Statement: Constitutional Scholars' Statement on Affirmative Action After City of Richmond v. J. A. Croson Co.," 98 (June): 1711–1716.

Yale Law Journal (1989b). "Scholars' Reply to Professor Fried," 99 (October): 163–168.

Yesner, Donna Lee (1983). "Control Data Corporation v. Baldrige: Restricting the Standing of Government Contractors to Challenge Administrative Procurement Actions," *Public Contract Law Journal* 13 (February): 346–368.

Young, Carlene (1977). "The Struggle of Black Entrepreneurs," *Executive* 4 (1): 30–32.

Young, David W. and Allen Brandt (1977). "Benefit-Cost Analysis in the Social Services: The Example of Adoption Reimbursement," *Social Service Review* 51 (June): 249–264.

Young, Peter (1986). *Privatization Around the Globe: Lessons for the Reagan Administration.* Houston: National Center for Policy Analysis (January).

Young, Peter (1987). "Privatization Around the World," in Steve H. Hanke, ed., *Prospects for Privatization.* New York: Proceedings of the Academy of Political Science 36 (3): 190–206.

Young, Peter and Stuart Butler (1987). *Privatization: Lessons From British Success Stories.* Washington, D.C.: Heritage Foundation.

Young, Rowland L. (1980). "Discrimination . . . Minority Grants," *ABA Journal* 66 (October): 1284.

Yuspeh, Alan R. (1989). "Stop Picking on Contractors," *Government Executive* 21 (May): 38–41.

Zahorjan, Joan (1981). "Equal Protection—Supreme Court Upholds Congressional Program Containing 10 Percent Set-Aside Provision for Minority Business Enterprises" (case note), *Suffolk University Law Review* 15 (April): 306–323.

Zalud, Bill and Kerry Lydon (1990). "Prison Business," *Security* 27 (March): 54–55.

Zanca, Jacqueline (1985). "Obscure Panel Gives Firm Unique Niche" (Committee for Purchase From the Blind and Other Severely Handicapped; Firm of Trilling & Kennedy), *Legal Times* 8 (September 9): 1.

Zedalis, Rex J. (1980). "Legal Effects of the Multilateral Trade Negotiations: Agricultural Commodities," *Denver Journal of International Law and Policy* 10 (Fall): 89–111.

Zee, Robin J. (1988). *Summary of Preferences In-State and for Cities Over 500,000 Population (as of August 1988).* Falls Church, Va.: National Institute of Governmental Purchasing.

Zemansky, Stanley D. (1978). "Survey of Competitive Procurement Practices," *The Public Purchaser*, Arlington, Va. (1st quarter).

Zemansky, Stanley D. (1979). "The Bottom Line—Public Procurement Management Cycle," *Governmental Purchasing* (September/October).

Zemansky, Stanley D. (1981a). "The Great Purchasing Mythstery," *Government Executive* 13 (July): 25–30.

Zemansky, Stanley D. (1981b). "Needed Reform in Federal Grant Procurement Management," *Government Executive* 13 (April): 30, 32, 34–35.

Zemansky, Stanley D. (1987). *Contracting Professional Services.* Falls Church, Va.: National Institute of Governmental Purchasing.

Zemansky, Stanley D. (1988). *Ethics and Quality Public Purchasing.* Falls Church, Va.: National Institute of Governmental Purchasing.

Zepke, Brent E. (1981). "Minority Business Enterprises in Public Works Projects," *Corporate Counsel Review* 4 (April): 16–20.

Zuckerman, Roger E. and Roger C. Spaeder (1986). "New Attention to Procurement Fraud," *The National Law Journal* 8 (March 17): 20.

Index